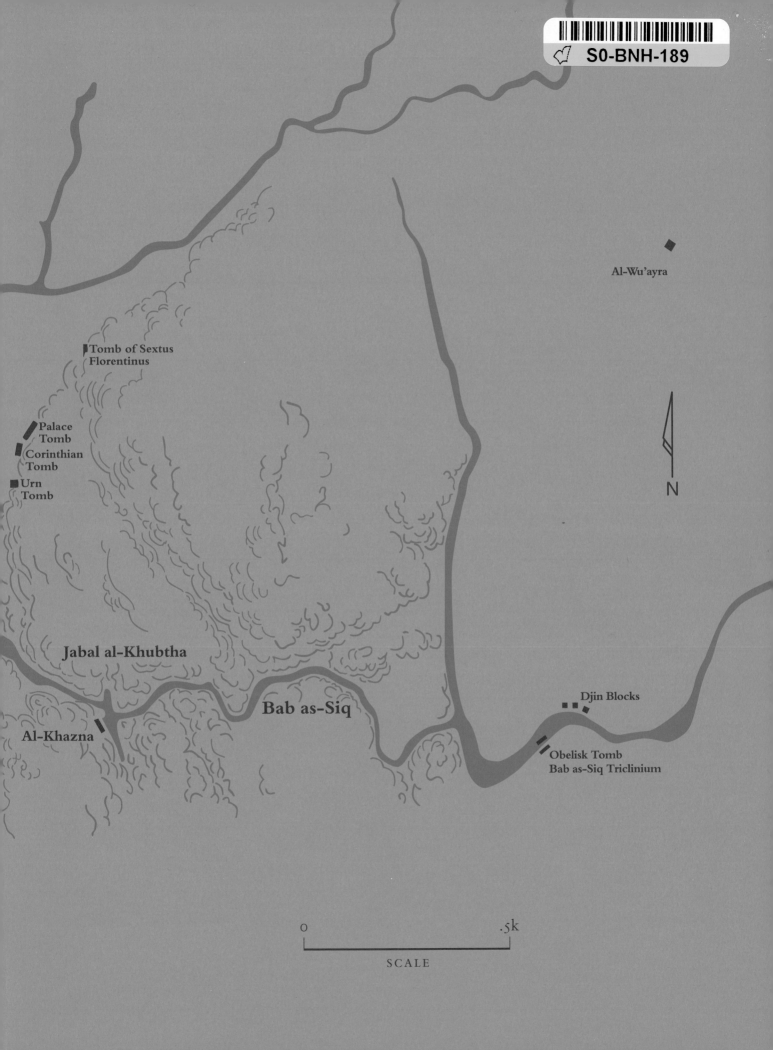

Al-Wu'ayra

N

Tomb of Sextus
Florentinus

Palace
Tomb
Corinthian
Tomb
Urn
Tomb

Jabal al-Khubtha

Djin Blocks

Bab as-Siq

Al-Khazna

Obelisk Tomb
Bab as-Siq Triclinium

O   .5k

SCALE

PETRA GREAT TEMPLE
VOLUME II

PETRA
GREAT TEMPLE

VOLUME II

Archaeological Contexts of the Remains and Excavations

Brown University Excavations in Jordan at the Petra Great Temple, 1993–2007

MARTHA SHARP JOUKOWSKY

Dedicated to my dearest friend and husband
Artemis W. Joukowsky

Library of Congress Cataloging in Publication Data
Petra Great Temple Volume II
by Martha Sharp Joukowsky
Includes bibliographical references and index.

LIBRARY OF CONGRESS CONTROL NUMBER 2007929618

ISBN 978-09797448-0-8

Published by the Brown University Petra Exploration Fund.

FRONT COVER: Collapse of Baroque Room Plaster.

FRONTISPIECE: Petra Great Temple at the end of the 2007 study season
with restored central stairs, to south.

BACK COVER: Elephant Capital.

TABLE OF CONTENTS

XI   List of Abbreviations

XV   List of Figures

XXVII   Foreword
        by Patricia and Pierre Bikai

XXIX   Preface
            Publication
            Introduction to Volume II
            Acknowledgments
            Sponsors

XLIX   Petra—Select Bibliography

LXV   Brown University
        Petra Great Temple—Site Bibliography

I   CHAPTER 1: History of Excavations, Stratigraphy and Chronology
            Surveying Strategy and Site Datum Points
            Elevations of Major Temple Precinct Components
            1993–2006 Excavation Summary
            Great Temple Databases 1993–2006
            Chronology
            Stratigraphy, Site Phasing and Dating of Archaeological Deposits

51   CHAPTER 2: The Petra Great Temple Propylaeum
            Introduction
            Propylaeum and Roman Street Measurements
            Propylaeum Wall Dimensions
            Stratigraphy and Phasing
            Excavation History
            Conclusions

87   CHAPTER 3: The Petra Great Temple Lower Temenos
            Lower Temenos Dimensions of Major Features
            Lower Temenos Wall Dimensions
            Stratigraphy and Phasing
            Excavation History
            Conclusions

135   CHAPTER 4: The Petra Great Temple Upper Temenos
          Upper Temenos Features
          Features to the West of the West Precinct Wall
          Stratigraphy and Phasing
          Excavation History
          Conclusions

215   CHAPTER 5: The Petra Great Temple(s)
          Introduction
          Great Temple(s) Features
          Excavation History
          Stratigraphy and Phasing
          Distyle in Antis Temple: Pronaos Excavations
          Tetrastyle in Antis Temple: Porch Excavations
          Theater and Stage Excavations
          Conclusions

279   CHAPTER 6: The Conservation, Consolidation, Preservation
      and Protection of the Petra Great Temple Precinct
          Introduction
          Financial Considerations
          Conservation Challenges
          The Petra Archaeological Park
          Artifacts on Tour
          Consolidation Efforts at the Petra Great Temple 1994–2006
          Conclusion

343   CHAPTER 7: Discussion and Conclusions
          Nabataea and Petra
          The Great Debate
          The Great Temple Precinct
          Sculpture
          Epigraphic Records
          Cult Objects
          Ceramics
          Great Debate Conclusions
          Roman and Byzantine Periods
          Last Days of the Great Temple
          Concluding Remarks

411   Glossary

427   A Précis of Selected Major Structures at Petra

432   Illustration Credits

433   Index

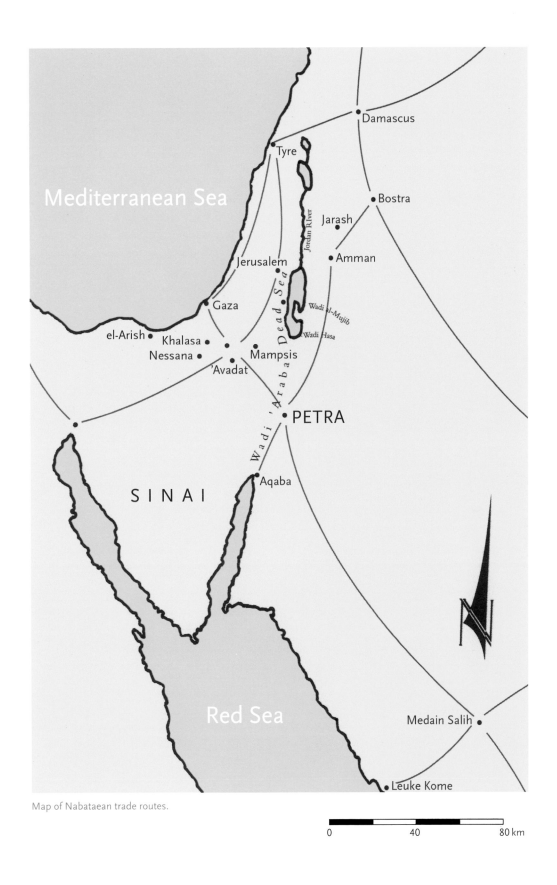

Mediterranean Sea

Damascus

Tyre

Bostra

Jarash

Jordan River

Amman

Jerusalem

Gaza

Wadi el-Mujib

Dead Sea

Wadi Hasa

el-Arish

Khalasa

Mampsis

Nessana

'Avadat

PETRA

Wadi 'Araba

SINAI

Aqaba

Red Sea

Medain Salih

Leuke Kome

Map of Nabataean trade routes.

0   40   80 km

LIST OF ABBREVIATIONS

1. BIBLIOGRAPHIC ABBREVIATIONS

Joukowsky 1998 or Vol. I.
Petra: The Great Temple, Vol. I—Brown University Excavations 1993–1997. With Contributions by Christian Augé, Deirdre G. Barrett, Joseph J. Basile, Jean Blackburn, Leigh-Ann Bedal, Donna J. D'Agostino, Sara G. Karz, Elizabeth E. Payne, Thomas R. Paradise, Erika L. Schluntz, Monica L. Sylvester, Stephen V. Tracy, Loa P. Traxler, Terry Tullis, Peter Warnock, and Paul C. Zimmerman, Brown University, Petra Exploration Fund.

Schmid (Phase)
Rolf A. Stucky, Yvonne Gerber, Bernhard Kolb and Stephan G. Schmid, "Swiss-Liechtenstein Excavations at Ez Zantur in Petra 1993, The Fifth Campaign," *ADAJ* XXXVIII, 1994, 281–286.

Stephan G. Schmid has created the widely used Nabataean pottery typology and sequence from the Ez Zantur ceramics. When reference is made to "Schmid (Phase)," it is for cross dating the P/GT pottery.

2. JOURNAL ABBREVIATIONS

AA	Archäologische Anzeiger
AAS	Annales archéologiques de Syrie
AASOR	Annual of the American Schools of Oriental Research
ACOR	American Center of Oriental Research, Amman
ACORN	ACOR Newsletter
ADAJ	Annual of the Department of Antiquities of Jordan
AfO	Archiv für Orientforschung, Graz
AI	Art International
AJA	American Journal of Archaeology
AN	American Center of Oriental Research Newsletter
ANRW	Aufstieg und Niedergang der römischen Welt
Antiquity	A Quarterly Review of Archaeology
Antk	Antike Kunst
Aram	International Conference(s). The Nabataeans. Oxford.
Archéologia	Archéologia (Paris)
Archaeology	Archaeology Magazine, Archaeological Institute of America
'Atiqot	'Atiqot, Journal of the Israel Department of Antiquities
BA	The Biblical Archaeologist
BAM	Brown Alumni Monthly
BAR	British Archaeological Reports
BARIS	British Archaeological Reports, International Series, Oxford

BASOR	Bulletin of the American Schools of Oriental Research	JRGZM	Jahrbuch des Römisch-Germanischen Zentralmuseums Mainz
Berytus	Berytus Archaeological Studies, Museum of Archaeology, American University of Beirut	JRS	The Journal of Roman Studies
BJ	Bonner Jahrbücher des Rheinischen Landesmuseums in Bonn im Land-schaftsverband Rheinland und des Vereins von Altertumsfreunden im Rheinlandes	LCL	Loeb Classical Library (Texts quoted with name of editor and translator[s])
		Levant	Journal of the British School of Archaeology in Jerusalem, London
BTS	Bible et Terre Sainte	LIMC	*Petra and the Caravan Cities.* Proceedings of the Symposium organized at Petra in September 1985 by the Department of Antiquities of Jordan and the Iconographic Lexicon of Classical Mythology with the financial support of UNESCO, Amman, Department of Antiquities
BUFB	Brown University Faculty Bulletin		
CAH	Cambridge Ancient History		
CIS II	Corpus Inscriptionum Semiticarum. Pars II. Tomus II. Fasc. I. Sectio Secunda. Inscriptiones Nabataeae. Paris.		
CQ	Church Quarterly	Man	A Monthly Record of Anthropological Science
CRAI	Comptes rendus de séances de l'Académie des inscriptions et belles lettres (Paris)	MASCA	Museum Applied Science Center for Archaeology, University Museum, University of Pennsylvania
DaM	Damaszener Mitteilungen	NC	The Numismatic Chronicle
Das Altertum	Das Altertum	NEA	Near Eastern Archaeology
DHA	Les dossiers d'archéologie	NM	Jahresmitteilungen der Naturhisto-rischen Gesellschaft
Hesperia	Hesperia, Journal of the American Schools of Classical Studies at Athens	PAPS	Proceedings of the American Philosophical Society
HI	L'histoire	PEFA	Palestine Exploration Fund Annual
HTR	Harvard Theological Review	PEQ	Palestine Exploration Quarterly
IEJ	Israel Exploration Journal, Jerusalem	Qadmoniot	Quarterly for the Antiquities of Eretz-Israel and Biblical Lands, Jerusalem
I.F.A.P.O.	Institute Français d'archéologie du Proche-Orient	QDAP	Quarterly of the Department of Antiquities in Palestine
ILN	Illustrated London News	Qedem	Monographs of the Institute of Archaeology of the Hebrew Uni-versity of Jerusalem
JA	Journal Asiatique		
JANES	Journal of Ancient Near Eastern Society, Columbia University	RB	Revue biblique
JEOL	Jaarbericht Vooraziatisch-Egyptisch Gezelschap "Ex Oriente Lux"	RR	Research Reports
		SHAJ	Studies in the History and Archaeology of Jordan
JNES	Journal of Near Eastern Studies, Chicago	SIMA	Studies in Mediterranean Archaeology
JQR	Jewish Quarterly Review	Syria	Revue d'Art Oriental et d'Archéologie, Paris
JRA	Journal of Roman Archaeology		
		ZDPV	Zeitschrift des Deutschen Palästina-Vereins

3. GREAT TEMPLE AND OTHER ABBREVIATIONS

The Great Temple database systems use different abbreviations for encoding the Catalog, Architectural Fragments, Coins, Lamps and Glass databases. The Grosso Modo database has specific fields for part, function, shape, liquid and paint color, motif, plastic decoration and culture. These abbreviations are available upon request.

AB	GM code for stucco abacus steps
AD	architectural decoration in encoding GM stucco moldings for function
A.D.	anno domini (year)
AF	GM code for stucco architectural fragment
Arch. Frag.	Architectural Fragment
asl	above sea level
-B-	in a catalog number indicating the object is bone
B.C.	before Christ
BCE	before the common (or Christian) era
BO	GM code for stucco boss
bsl	below sea level
-C-	in a catalog number indicating the object is a coin
c.	century(ies)
ca.	*circa*, about
CADD	Computer-aided design and drafting. CADD systems are CAD systems with additional drafting features.
Cat. No.	Catalog Number of object in site registry
CD	GM function code for stucco column decoration
CE	common (or Christian) era
cf.	*confer*, compare
cm	centimeter(s)
-CO-	stucco in a catalog number indicating the object is stucco
DFF	daily field form
DL	GM code for stucco dentil shape
DoA	Jordanian Department of Antiquities
DT	GM stucco dart/tongue shape
E	east
ed.	editor(s), edition, edited by
ED	GM code for egg/tongue stucco shape
EG	GM code for egg stucco shape
etc.	et cetera (and so forth)
-F-	in a catalog number indicating the object is faïence
F	GM code for flat stucco shape
FL	GM code for stucco floral shape
e.g.	*exempli gratia* (for example)
et al.	*et alii* (and others)
etc.	et cetera (and so forth)
Fig(s).	Figure(s)
-G-	in a catalog number indicating the object is glass
GM	Grosso Modo—database for multiple objects
GPR	ground penetrating radar
ibid.	*ibidem* (in the same place)
i.e.	*id est*, that is
INAA	instrumental neutron analysis
km	kilometer(s)
-L-	in a catalog number indicating the object is a lamp
LF	leaf when encoding Grosso Modo stucco shape
Loc.	Locus
LT	Lower Temenos (area)
-M-	in a catalog number indicating the object is metal
m	meter(s)
mm	millimeter(s)
msl	mean sea level
N	north
Nazzal's	name for dig house used before Burckhardt Center
No(s).	number(s)
OS	other string course when encoding GM stucco shape
-P-	in a catalog number indicating the object is pottery
P	Propylaea (area)
P/GT	Petra Great Temple

Pl(s).	Plate(s)
P/ST	Petra Southern Temple (used before 1995) and P/GT
RI	GM code for ribbed or fluted stucco shape
RQ	Residential Quarter
-S-	in a catalog number indicating the object is stone
S	south
Seq. No.	Excavation sequence in trench recovery
SF	Special Find (to go to the catalog)
-Sh-	in a catalog number indicating the object is shell
SH	GM code for shell
SP	Special Project (sondage or probe)
ST	GM code for stucco
T	Temple (area)
Tr.	Trench
Trans.	Translated by
UT	Upper Temenos (area)
-Veg-	in a catalog number indicating the object is vegetable matter
VI	GM code for stucco vine shape
VO	GM code for stucco volute
Vol.(s)	Volume(s)
W	west
WD	GM code for stucco wall decoration

LIST OF FIGURES

FRONTMATTER

Frontispiece: Petra Great Temple at the end of the 2007 study season with restored central stairs, to south.

IX   Map of Nabataean trade routes.

X   Fragment of sculpted acanthus capital.

PREFACE

Fig. 1.   Baroque Room ceiling, detail of the decorative cornice *in situ*.

Fig. 2.   Baroque Room central medallion reconstruction.

Fig. 3.   2003 Brown University Petra Great Temple Excavation Team.

Fig. 4.   2004 Brown University Petra Great Temple Excavation Core Team.

Fig. 5.   2005 Brown University Petra Great Temple Excavation Team.

Fig. 6.   2006 Brown University Petra Great Temple Excavation Team.

Fig. 7.   2006 Back to Earth—Team after photographing the site from the helicopter.

Fig. 8.   Flow Chart of Great Temple Databases 1993–2006.

Fig. 9.   Trenches excavated in the CAVE.

Fig. 10.   Eileen L. Vote using the CAVE to query artifact scatter.

Fig. 11.   Dakhilallah Qublan and Martha in the dig tent.

Fig. 12.   "Hogan" playing his *rababa* at tea time.

Fig. 13.   *Salaam* meaning "Peace" incised on the Temenos Gate.

CHAPTER 1: INTRODUCTION

Front: Map of the Region.

Fig. 1.1.   Map of the Petra city center.

Fig. 1.2.   Reconstruction of the Petra city center.

Fig. 1.3.   Aerial pre-excavation overview 1992.

Fig. 1.4.   The Petra Great Temple, to the south from the Temple of the Winged Lions.

Fig. 1.5.   Pre-excavation rubble and collapse of the Great Temple, 1993.

Fig. 1.6.   Aerial Great Temple, to south, 2006.

Fig. 1.7.   Petra Great Temple site plan, 2006.

Fig. 1.8.   Petra Great Temple site grid.

Fig. 1.9.   Petra Great Temple, Topographic Map.

Fig. 1.10.   Eleanor A. Power and Marshall C. Agnew surveying the West Entry Stairway.

Fig. 1.11.   Chart of Petra Great Temple, 1993–2006 Trenches excavated.

Fig. 1.12.   Aerial photograph of the Great Temple and its surround, 1992.

Fig. 1.13.   Great Temple, aerial, to the south, 2000.

Fig. 1.14.   Great Temple precinct, to the southwest, 2002.

Fig. 1.15.   Great Temple precinct, to the south, 2004.

Fig. 1.16.   Great Temple precinct, to the southeast, 2006.

Fig. 1.17.   Chronology of Nabataean Kings.

Fig. 1.18.   Summary chart of Great Temple Site Phasing.

Fig. 1.19.   Cup marks and early walls in the Upper Temenos.

Fig. 1.20.   Elephant-headed capital from the Lower Temenos.

Fig. 1.21.   Virtual Reality of the Grand Design, Site Phase IV.

Fig. 1.22.   The Petra Pool Garden Complex, to the south.

Fig. 1.23.   Great Temple, Phase V Theater inserted into the Phase IV Great Temple.

Fig. 1.24.   Great Temple, Theater from the rear, to the north.

Fig. 1.25.   Ballista balls in the Propylaeum West.

Fig. 1.26.   Aerial view of the Small Temple, to the south.

Fig. 1.27. Excavations of Petra Great Temple Trenches by Year and Area.

CHAPTER 2: PROPYLAEUM

Front: Aerial view of the Propylaeum to the southwest, 2006.

Fig. 2.1. Propylaeum plan.

Fig. 2.2. Propylaeum Portico Wall, and Central Stairs to the southeast, 2005.

Fig. 2.3. Propylaeum before excavation, 1993.

Fig. 2.4. Propylaeum, close-up of the street curbing partially restored, 2001.

Fig. 2.5. Propylaeum, Central Staircase, to south, 2002.

Fig. 2.6. Propylaeum, Central Staircase, to south, with the lower eight steps abutting the Portico Wall, 1993.

Fig. 2.7. Earlier Propylaeum Central Staircase, to west with Room 1 doorway, 2004.

Fig. 2.8. Propylaeum, view of the Portico Wall, to south, 2005.

Fig. 2.9. Propylaeum East, Rooms 1–3 from Room 4, to west, 2004.

Fig. 2.10. Propylaeum East, Rooms 1–3, to north, 2004.

Fig. 2.11. Propylaeum East, doorway of Room 1, to south, 2003.

Fig. 2.12. Propylaeum East, Room 1 doorway with iron pins in the threshold, 2003.

Fig. 2.13. Propylaeum East, Room 3 corridor, to north, 2004.

Fig. 2.14. Propylaeum East, Room 3 vault, 2004.

Fig. 2.15. Propylaeum West, North Gallery, to west, 2002.

Fig. 2.16. Propylaeum West, numbered ballista ball assemblage, 2005.

Fig. 2.17. Propylaeum West, weighing ballista balls, 2004.

Fig. 2.18. Propylaeum West, Room 1 entry with later stairs blocking the threshold, 2002.

Fig. 2.19. Propylaeum West, limestone *betyls* in the niche just after excavation, to east, 2001.

Fig. 2.20. Propylaeum West, detail of the front of the two limestone *betyls*, 2001.

Fig. 2.21. Propylaeum West, plan of *betyl* niche, 2001.

Fig. 2.22. Propylaeum West, South Gallery with the Central Stairway support wall, 1994.

Fig. 2.23. Propylaeum West, West Entry Stairway at the outset of the 2005 excavations.

Fig. 2.24. Propylaeum West, West Entry Stairway platform, 2002.

Fig. 2.25. Propylaeum West, South Gallery early Pre-Phase I deposits, 2005.

Fig. 2.26. Propylaeum West, North and South galleries with the *betyl* wall to the right, 2005.

Fig. 2.27. Chart of the Propylaeum Trenches excavated 1993–2006.

Fig. 2.28. Plan of trenches excavated in the Propylaeum 1993–2005.

Fig. 2.29. Propylaeum East, early morning excavations, 2003.

Fig. 2.30. Propylaeum East, excavation in progress to south, 2003.

Fig. 2.31. Propylaeum East, to south with completed excavations of Rooms 1 and 2 and doorway of Room 3, 2003.

Fig. 2.32. Sculpture of a male head.

Fig. 2.33. Propylaeum East, collapse of Doorway 1 to south with elephant head *in situ*, 2003.

Fig. 2.34. Propylaeum East, beginning excavation in Doorway 3 to south, 2003.

Fig. 2.35. Propylaeum East, Plan of Room 3, 2003.

Fig. 2.36. Propylaeum East, sandstone sculpture of a grape leaf cluster tied with a ribbon.

Fig. 2.37. Propylaeum East, helmet pilaster, 2003.

Fig. 2.38. Propylaeum East, Athena pilaster, 2003.

Fig. 2.39. Propylaeum West, showing the South Gallery with bench and arch collapse, 2002.

Fig. 2.40. Propylaeum West, to west, showing *in situ* south to north column collapse.

Fig. 2.41. Ballista Balls detail, 2005.

Fig. 2.42. Propylaeum West, moving an elephant-headed capital, 1997.

Fig. 2.43. Propylaeum West, moving an elephant-headed capital, 1998.

Fig. 2.44. Propylaeum West, drawing of the sandstone Horned Altar.

Fig. 2.45. Propylaeum West, Horned altar *in situ*, 2000.

Fig. 2.46. Propylaeum West, Early Nabataean Bowl, dating from ca. 50 to 25 BCE.

Fig. 2.47. Propylaeum West, West Entry Stairs, to north, 2004.

CHAPTER 3: LOWER TEMENOS

Front: Lower Temenos, aerial view, to south.

Fig. 3.1. Lower Temenos Plan.

Fig. 3.2. Lower Temenos, to southeast.

Fig. 3.3. Lower Temenos, West Entry Stairway, to north.

Fig. 3.4.   Lower Temenos excavation of the West Entry Stairway, to south, 2005.

Fig. 3.5.   Lower Temenos, West Entry Stairway cleared, to south, 2005.

Fig. 3.6.   Lower Temenos, West Entry Stairway Platform with the *nefesh* and *betyl in situ.*

Fig. 3.7.   Lower Temenos Plaza, to northwest as restored, 2001.

Fig. 3.8.   Lower Temenos elephant-headed capital, 2000.

Fig. 3.9.   Lower Temenos, drawing of elephant-headed capital from an engaged column.

Fig. 3.10.   Lower Temenos, East Triple Colonnade, to north, 2003.

Fig. 3.11.   Lower Temenos, West Cryptoporticus, to south, 2005.

Fig. 3.12.   Lower Temenos, West Cryptoporticus SP104 sondage, to east, 2005.

Fig. 3.13.   Lower Temenos, West Exedra, one of two freestanding columns.

Fig. 3.14.   Lower Temenos, Interior of the West Exedra showing niches.

Fig. 3.15.   Lower Temenos, bronze drain cover *in situ*, 1995.

Fig. 3.16.   Lower Temenos, hexagonal paver with bronze drain cover removed in antiquity.

Fig. 3.17.   Lower Temenos, cleaning the upper West Entry Stairway, to northeast.

Fig. 3.18.   Lower Temenos, column drums dividing the Bedouin field, 1997.

Fig. 3.19.   Lower Temenos, chart of trenches excavated 1993–2006.

Fig. 3.20.   Plan of Lower Temenos trenches excavated, 1993–2006.

Fig. 3.21.   Lower Temenos, Trench 17 sondage.

Fig. 3.22.   Lower Temenos, early exposure of the Hexagonal Pavement.

Fig. 3.23.   Lower Temenos, East Cryptoporticus showing *in situ* voussoirs.

Fig. 3.24.   Lower Temenos, elephant-headed capital.

Fig. 3.25.   Lower Temenos, restored elephant-headed capital.

Fig. 3.26.   Lower Temenos, limestone pilaster block of female holding a cornucopia.

Fig. 3.27.   Lower Temenos, pilaster of a woman *in situ.*

Fig. 3.28.   Lower Temenos, pilaster block of a female wearing an open weave *chiton.*

Fig. 3.29.   Lower Temenos, pilaster of a male wearing a *chiton.*

Fig. 3.30.   Lower Temenos, honorific wreath pilaster block.

Fig. 3.31.   Lower Temenos, drawing of the honorific wreath.

Fig. 3.32.   Lower Temenos, East Exedra, to south, 1994.

Fig. 3.33.   Lower Temenos, East Exedra stratigraphic profile.

Fig. 3.34.   Lower Temenos, collapsed entablature of the East Exedra, 2002.

Fig. 3.35.   Lower Temenos, restored East Exedra showing niches, podium and bench.

Fig. 3.36.   Lower Temenos lead pipe.

Fig. 3.37.   Lower Temenos, prepared passage for lead pipe.

Fig. 3.38.   Lower Temenos, newly cleared West Triple Colonnade to south, 2000.

Fig. 3.39.   Lower Temenos, twin galleries of the West Cryptoporticus, to south, 2000.

Fig. 3.40.   Lower Temenos, *voussoirs.*

Fig. 3.41.   Lower Temenos, West Cryptoporticus west, to south, 2001.

Fig. 3.42.   Lower Temenos, excavation of an elephant-headed capital.

Fig. 3.43.   Lower Temenos, West Cryptoporticus, 2005.

Fig. 3.44.   Lower Temenos, West Cryptoporticus iron arrowheads.

Fig. 3.45.   Lower Temenos, left cheek piece from a helmet after cleaning, 2004.

Fig. 3.46.   Lower Temenos, West Exedra before excavation, to southwest, 1993.

Fig. 3.47.   Lower Temenos, West Exedra during early excavation, to northeast, 1994.

Fig. 3.48.   Lower Temenos, West Exedra upper levels being drawn, 1995.

Fig. 3.49.   Lower Temenos, West Exedra and the Byzantine Platform, 1996.

Fig. 3.50.   Lower Temenos, excavation of the West Exedra ash layer, 1994.

Fig. 3.51.   Lower Temenos, Hexagonal Pavers, detail.

Fig. 3.52.   Lower Temenos 2006 overview of Hexagonal Pavement.

Fig. 3.53.   Lower Temenos, "domino" collapse of the East Colonnade column drums.

Fig. 3.54.   Lower Temenos, collapsed pavement showing the canalization, 1994.

Fig. 3.55.   Lower Temenos, canalization capstones, to northwest, 2005.

Fig. 3.56.   Lower Temenos, West Entry Stairway cleared, to the north, 2005.

Fig. 3.57.   Lower Temenos, West Entry Stairway Platform with the *nefesh betyl* removed.

Fig. 3.58.   Lower Temenos, *nefesh* detail.

Fig. 3.59. Lower Temenos, West Entry Stairway features, to west, 2006.

Fig. 3.60. Lower Temenos, West Entry painted wall fragment.

Fig. 3.61. Lower Temenos, East-West Retaining Wall during excavation, 2004.

Fig. 3.62. East-West Retaining Wall cleared, to southeast, 1997.

Fig. 3.63. Lower Temenos, East-West Retaining Wall as restored, 2005.

CHAPTER 4: UPPER TEMENOS

Front: Temple and Upper Temenos to southeast

Fig. 4.1. Plan of the Upper Temenos.

Fig. 4.2. Upper Temenos surround to the northwest, 2005.

Fig. 4.3. Upper Temenos East Staircase from the Lower to Upper Temenos.

Fig. 4.4. Upper Temenos, Central Stairway.

Fig. 4.5. Upper Temenos, consolidated East Perimeter Wall and upper Vault, to east.

Fig. 4.6. Upper Temenos, East Plaza Canalization outlet, to south.

Fig. 4.7. Upper Temenos, Great Cistern in the East Plaza.

Fig. 4.8. Upper Temenos, Great Cistern, west vault opening.

Fig. 4.9. Upper Temenos, East Plaza Great Cistern section.

Fig. 4.10. Sword Deity in the Upper Temenos South Passageway escarpment.

Fig. 4.11. Upper Temenos, Sword Deity in escarpment of the South Passageway.

Fig. 4.12. Upper Temenos, South Passageway, to east.

Fig. 4.13. Upper Temenos, Baroque Room Complex.

Fig. 4.14. Upper Temenos, Baroque Room Complex, plan.

Fig. 4.15. Upper Temenos, Baroque Room Complex, doorway.

Fig. 4.16. Upper Temenos, Baroque Room Complex, Settling Tank.

Fig. 4.17. Upper Temenos, West Precinct Wall below the West Walkway Wall, to east.

Fig. 4.18. Upper Temenos, aerial of East Plaza.

Fig. 4.19. Upper Temenos, West Plaza bedrock.

Fig. 4.20. Upper Temenos, quarry cuts in the West Plaza.

Fig. 4.21. Upper Temenos, section of the East-West Support Wall.

Fig. 4.22. Upper Temenos, West Plaza showing the West Precinct Wall.

Fig. 4.23. Upper Temenos, East-West Support Wall abutting the West Perimeter Wall.

Fig. 4.24. Upper Temenos, plan of the Residential Quarter.

Fig. 4.25. Upper Temenos, overview of the Residential Quarter, 2004, to south.

Fig. 4.26. Upper Temenos, Residential Quarter steps adjacent to the Settling Tank.

Fig. 4.27. Upper Temenos, Cistern-Reservoir with the Residential Quarter.

Fig. 4.28. Upper Temenos, limestone basin adjacent to the Cistern-Reservoir.

Fig. 4.29. Upper Temenos, aerial photograph of the Roman-Byzantine Baths 2006.

Fig. 4.30. Upper Temenos, Roman-Byzantine Baths 2006.

Fig. 4.31. Upper Temenos, Roman-Byzantine Baths, bathroom (toilet).

Fig. 4.32. Upper Temenos, Roman-Byzantine Baths, "Well Room."

Fig. 4.33. Upper Temenos, Temple Forecourt, to southeast.

Fig. 4.34. Upper Temenos, Chart of Trenches Excavated 1993–2006.

Fig. 4.35. Upper Temenos, East Staircase from the Lower Temenos to Upper Temenos.

Fig. 4.36. Upper Temenos, West Staircase from the Lower Temenos to Upper Temenos.

Fig. 4.37. Junction of the West Staircase and the Lower Temenos West Exedra, to south, 1997.

Fig. 4.38. Upper Temenos, east face of the West Stairway.

Fig. 4.39. Upper Temenos, collapsed east Porch columns, 1993.

Fig. 4.40. Upper Temenos, temple Forecourt, to south, 1993.

Fig. 4.41. Upper Temenos, partially excavated Forecourt and Pronaos, to east, 1995.

Fig. 4.42. Upper Temenos, Forecourt and west stylobate during excavation, to south, 1993.

Fig. 4.43. Upper Temenos, consolidation of the temple stylobate and capital elements.

Fig. 4.44. Upper Temenos, detail of temple Forecourt hexagonal pavement.

Fig. 4.45. Upper Temenos, subterranean canalization system, central artery.

Fig. 4.46. Upper Temenos, subterranean canalization system.

Fig. 4.47. Upper Temenos, Central Stairs bedding as first excavated in 1994, to south.

Fig. 4.48. Upper Temenos, Central Stairs, east wall after restoration, 2005.

Fig. 4.49. Upper Temenos, excavation of the "Cistern" to west, 1998.

Fig. 4.50. Upper Temenos, Plain Nabataean Blocked-out capital.

Fig. 4.51. Upper Temenos, East Perimeter Wall and Vault Collapse cleared.

Fig. 4.52. Upper Temenos, East Perimeter Wall being cleared, to east.

Fig. 4.53. Upper Temenos, East Perimeter Wall during excavation, to north.

Fig. 4.54. Upper Temenos, East Perimeter Wall and Vault.

Fig. 4.55. Upper Temenos, East Perimeter Wall and Vault.

Fig. 4.56. Upper Temenos, East Perimeter Wall and Vault.

Fig. 4.57. Upper Temenos, East Perimeter Wall, Room A north arch.

Fig. 4.58. Upper Temenos, East Perimeter Wall, Room A, Pilgrim Bottle.

Fig. 4.59. Upper Temenos, East Perimeter Wall, Room A, bedrock staircase.

Fig. 4.60. Upper Temenos, East Perimeter Wall, Room A east arch.

Fig. 4.61. Upper Temenos, East Perimeter Wall, Room B, to south, 2001.

Fig. 4.62. Upper Temenos, East Perimeter Wall, reservoir to the north of Room B, 2001.

Fig. 4.63. Upper Temenos, East Perimeter Wall, *Tabun* Room.

Fig. 4.64. Upper Temenos, East Perimeter Wall, *Tabun* Room to northeast, 2001.

Fig. 4.65. Upper Temenos, East Perimeter Wall, *Tabun* Room to east, 2001.

Fig. 4.66. Upper Temenos, East Perimeter Wall, *Tabun* Room with oven.

Fig. 4.67. Upper Temenos, east balk with *in situ* disarticulated human bones.

Fig. 4.68. Upper Temenos, East Perimeter Wall excavation, to southeast.

Fig. 4.69. Upper Temenos, East Plaza canalization, to north.

Fig. 4.70. Upper Temenos, East Plaza and South Perimeter Wall, to south, 2000.

Fig. 4.71. Upper Temenos, C. F. Cloke being lowered into the East Plaza Great Cistern.

Fig. 4.72. Upper Temenos, interior arch of the East Plaza Great Cistern.

Fig. 4.73. Upper Temenos, east sector of the South Perimeter Wall and escarpment.

Fig. 4.74. Upper Temenos, excavation and soil overburden in the South Passageway.

Fig. 4.75. Upper Temenos, cult niche in the Shrine Room.

Fig. 4.76. Upper Temenos, Baroque Room stucco collapse, to the south.

Fig. 4.77. Upper Temenos, Baroque Room during excavation, to southeast, 2002.

Fig. 4.78. Upper Temenos, Baroque Room cleaning of the stucco fall, 2002.

Fig. 4.79. Upper Temenos, Baroque Room painted plaster of a column and capital.

Fig. 4.80. Upper Temenos, Baroque Room, stucco column decorated in relief.

Fig. 4.81. Upper Temenos, Baroque Room, stucco grape cluster.

Fig. 4.82. Upper Temenos, Baroque Room, pomegranate in relief.

Fig. 4.83. Upper Temenos, Baroque Room, ceiling medallion *in situ*.

Fig. 4.84. Baroque Room Central Medallion.

Fig. 4.85. Upper Temenos, continued excavation of the west bedrock in the West Plaza.

Fig. 4.86. Upper Temenos, plan of the southwest bedrock.

Fig. 4.87. Upper Temenos, Residential Quarter.

Fig. 4.88. Upper Temenos, Residential Quarter looking through to Cave 2.

Fig. 4.89. Upper Temenos, Residential Quarter.

Fig. 4.90. Residential Quarter with the Great Temple in the background.

Fig. 4.91. Upper Temenos, Residential Quarter, basalt rotating grain mill.

Fig. 4.92. Upper Temenos, plan of the Cistern-Reservoir.

Fig. 4.93. Upper Temenos, limestone basin beside the Cistern-Reservoir.

Fig. 4.94. Upper Temenos, infant feeder in the shape of a hedgehog.

Fig. 4.95. Upper Temenos, head of a deity found in the West Precinct Wall.

Fig. 4.96. Upper Temenos, Roman-Byzantine Bath Plan.

Fig. 4.97. Upper Temenos, Roman-Byzantine Bath Platform to the east.

Fig. 4.98. *Caldarium* in Trench 126, to west showing hypocausts *in situ*.

Fig. 4.99. Lower level passageway between the *caldaria*.

Fig. 4.100. The Roman-Byzantine Bath, *Tepidarium/Laconicum*, to the west.

Fig. 4.101. The Roman-Byzantine Bath, view to the Vestibule-*Frigidarium*.

Fig. 4.102. Molded glass head vase from the "Well Room" water passage.

Fig. 4.103. The Roman-Byzantine Bath excavations in progress.

Fig. 4.104. Nabataean round lamp.

Fig. 4.105. Partial Greek inscription from the bath's "splash pool."

Fig. 4.106. Roman Inscription from the Colonnaded Court.

CHAPTER 5: TEMPLE

Front: Aerial View of the Temple Complex, to the north, 2006.

Fig. 5.1. Temple, plan of the Phase II *distyle in antis* Temple.

Fig. 5.2. Great Temple West, *distyle* column as restored, 1995.

Fig. 5.3. Temple, West Anta and collapsed west *distyle* column, to south, 2004.

Fig. 5.4. Temple, upper and lower capital elements as re-erected.

Fig. 5.5. Temple capital with lower and upper orders restored from different elements.

Fig. 5.6. Temple, southeast heart-shaped double engaged column.

Fig. 5.7. Temple, profile sketch of fluted plaster from column shaft.

Fig. 5.8. Temple, elevated Attic base of a column in the East Corridor.

Fig. 5.9. Temple, south doorway in the south wall.

Fig. 5.10. Temple, plan of the Phase IV *tetrastyle in antis* Great Temple.

Fig. 5.11. Temple, a severely weathered Porch column, to south, 1993.

Fig. 5.12. Temple, profiles of Attic column bases.

Fig. 5.13. Temple, temple stairs as originally defined in 1993, to south.

Fig. 5.14. Temple, flagstone pavement of the East Walkway.

Fig. 5.15. Temple, plan of the Phase V *tetrastyle in antis* Temple with the Theater.

Fig. 5.16. Temple, excavations of the Central Arch, to south, 1998.

Fig. 5.17. Temple, tilted construction of the Central Arch, 1998.

Fig. 5.18. Temple, Theater as excavated.

Fig. 5.19. Temple, Theater *diazoma* showing *in situ* ashlar paving as excavated, 1997.

Fig. 5.20. Temple, Theater *aditus maximus,* to west, 1997.

Fig. 5.21. Temple, plan of Phase VII *tetrastyle in antis* Temple with the doorways blocked.

Fig. 5.22. Temple, Site Phase VII blocking of the doorway in the South Corridor Wall.

Fig. 5.23. Chart of Temple trenches excavated, 1993–2006.

Fig. 5.24. Plan of Temple trenches excavated, 1993–2006.

Fig. 5.25. Temple, Attic base of the West Anta still clogged with fill and debris, 1994.

Fig. 5.26. Temple, Attic base of the west center Porch column, to west, 1996.

Fig. 5.27. Temple, original position of the West Porch Anta, to east, 1993.

Fig. 5.28. Temple, Pronaos sondage below the West Porch column, 2005, to north.

Fig. 5.29. Temple, Pronaos sondage showing the stratigraphy below the West Anta, 2005.

Fig. 5.30. Temple, Pronaos sondage showing the platform, to north, 2005.

Fig. 5.31. Temple, Pronaos sondage showing the "dimpled" platform.

Fig. 5.32. Temple, inner face of the East Corridor Wall after excavation.

Fig. 5.33. Temple, immense column collapse and overburden in the East Corridor.

Fig. 5.34. Temple, arched entry from the East Corridor.

Fig. 5.35. Temple, West Corridor Wall, east face, 1998.

Fig. 5.36. Temple, East Corridor excavations.

Fig. 5.37. Temple, East Corridor drawing of a divinity in a shrine.

Fig. 5.38. Photograph of a divinity in a shrine.

Fig. 5.39. Temple, layers of fluvial deposit and collapse in the East Corridor, 1996.

Fig. 5.40. Temple, West Corridor after excavation and consolidation, to south, 2000.

Fig. 5.41. Temple, West Anta wall showing the later staircase to the Theater stage.

Fig. 5.42. Temple, *in situ* plaster cassette on the South Corridor wall, 2000.

Fig. 5.43. Temple, West Corridor floor bedding, to south, 1998.

Fig. 5.44. Temple, immense overburden in the South Corridor area, to west, 2000.

Fig. 5.45. Temple, upper portion of columns in the South Corridor, to west, 2000.

Fig. 5.46. Temple, South Corridor North Wall, south face, 2002.

Fig. 5.47. Temple, doorway South Corridor into the Central Arch.

Fig. 5.48.   Temple, plaster snarling lion excavated in the South Corridor, 2000.

Fig. 5.49.   Temple, plaster pacific lion excavated in the South Corridor, 2000.

Fig. 5.50.   Temple, two plaster lions, a and b, facing one another.

Fig. 5.51.   Temple, roof tiles side and bottom.

Fig. 5.52.   Temple, Virtual Reality reconstruction of Phase V.

Fig. 5.53.   Temple, upper architecture of the South Corridor, 2000.

Fig. 5.54.   Temple, south face of the South Corridor Wall, 2001.

Fig. 5.55.   Temple, East Walkway and adjacent East Corridor Wall, 2001.

Fig. 5.56.   Temple, east face of the East Walkway Corridor Wall, 2001.

Fig. 5.57.   Temple, portable betyl.

Fig. 5.58.   Temple, beam holes cut along the east face of the East Corridor Wall.

Fig. 5.59.   Temple, East Walkway, Trench 73 plan, 2001.

Fig. 5.60.   Temple, West Walkway after the 1994 excavation, to the southeast.

Fig. 5.61.   Temple, West Walkway after the 1999 excavation, to the south.

Fig. 5.62.   Temple, West Walkway fragmented man's face.

Fig. 5.63.   Temple, West Walkway fragmented female face.

Fig. 5.64.   Temple, West Walkway reunited female face fragments.

Fig. 5.65.   Temple, west face of the West Corridor Wall.

Fig. 5.66.   Temple, West Walkway Wall built on rubble-ashlar fill.

Fig. 5.67.   Temple, mason's mark on the West Corridor Wall (outlined in black), 2005.

Fig. 5.68.   Temple, north doorway of the West Corridor Wall.

Fig. 5.69.   Temple, entrance to the East Vaulted Chamber before excavation, 1995.

Fig. 5.70.   Temple, rectangular layout of the East Vaulted Chamber.

Fig. 5.71.   Temple, narrowing of the East Vaulted Chamber doorway.

Fig. 5.72.   Temple, partial marble inscription.

Fig. 5.73.   Temple, Central Arch with overburden cleared.

Fig. 5.74.   Temple, east north-south interior staircase following excavation.

Fig. 5.75.   Temple, early excavation of the Theater, 1997.

Fig. 5.76.   Temple, Theater as restored, to west, 2000.

Fig. 5.77.   Temple, Theater orchestra floor before the SP200 sondage, 2005.

Fig. 5.78.   Temple, Theater orchestra showing the subterranean canalization system.

Fig. 5.79.   Temple, Theater orchestra with subterranean canalization system.

Fig. 5.80.   Temple, Theater orchestra SP200 sondage, detail of center pivot stone.

Fig. 5.81.   Temple, Theater with cavea seats marked for removal.

Fig. 5.82.   Temple, Theater seats removed for Trench 123 probe.

Fig. 5.83.   Temple, Theater Trench 123 probe, 2006.

CHAPTER 6: CONSERVATION, CONSOLIDATION, PRESERVATION AND PROTECTION OF THE P/GT

Front: Lifting the pilaster relief of a female for display in the East Exedra.

Fig. 6.1.   The Great Temple precinct at the close of the 1994 season.

Fig. 6.2.   Moving a column drum to the lapidary.

Fig. 6.3.   Moving an architectural fragment to the lapidary.

Fig. 6.4.   Cleaning between ashlars.

Fig. 6.5.   Deep sondage in the East Triple Colonnade.

Fig. 6.6.   Chiseling an ashlar for reconstruction.

Fig. 6.7.   A deteriorated in situ east Porch column.

Fig. 6.8.   Preparation for consolidation.

Fig. 6.9.   Typical scene of a doorway requiring consolidation.

Fig. 6.10.   On-site storage of smaller architectural fragments.

Fig. 6.11.   Sculpture Garden.

Fig. 6.12.   On-site lapidary for Lower Temenos column drums.

Fig. 6.13.   Replica of the nefesh on the West Entry Stairway Platform.

Fig. 6.14.   The Great Wall from above.

Fig. 6.15.   The Great Temple juniper tree.

Fig. 6.16.   Tools of the mason: the awl, the toothed chisel and the hammer.

Fig. 6.17.   A mason dressing an ashlar using the toothed chisel and hammer.

Fig. 6.18.   Extracting mortar samples from the Great Temple South Passageway Wall.

Fig. 6.19.   Conservation of the stucco elements of the West Corridor Wall.

Fig. 6.20.   Restored facsimiles of the double *betyls* in the West Propylaeum.

Fig. 6.21.   Restored walls of the East Propylaeum Rooms 1–3, to the west.

Fig. 6.22.   Wood support for the walls of the East Propylaeum Rooms 1–3, to the northeast.

Fig. 6.23.   Supporting the vault from collapse of the East Propylaeum Room 3.

Fig. 6.24.   Restored vault of East Propylaeum Room 3, to south.

Fig. 6.25.   Looking down on the roof of the restored vault of East Propylaeum Room 3.

Fig. 6.26.   Looking down on the roof of the restored vault of East Propylaeum Room 3.

Fig. 6.27.   A restored column of the Propylaeum with an elephant-headed capital.

Fig. 6.28.   Sweeping a West Entry Stairway upper platform.

Fig. 6.29.   Ongoing restoration in the West Cryptoporticus and the West Entry Stairway.

Fig. 6.30.   Restoration of the West Cryptoporticus west wall.

Fig. 6.31.   Restoration of the West Cryptoporticus and the top of the West Entry Stairway.

Fig. 6.32.   The Brown University Team posing as columns in the Lower Temenos East.

Fig. 6.33.   The East Triple Colonnade undergoing restoration.

Fig. 6.34.   The East Triple Colonnade undergoing restoration.

Fig. 6.35.   The East Triple Colonnade partial restoration.

Fig. 6.36.   The restored East Triple Colonnade.

Fig. 6.37.   Elephant-headed capital placed on top of the engaged column.

Fig. 6.38.   The Lower Temenos Triple Colonnades after restoration.

Fig. 6.39.   East Exedra restored, to the south.

Fig. 6.40.   East Stairway from the Lower to Upper Temenos as restored, to the south.

Fig. 6.41.   A typical problem of ashlars slumped out of position.

Fig. 6.42.   The West Stairway leading from the Lower Temenos to the Upper Temenos.

Fig. 6.43.   The West Stairway leading from the Lower Temenos to the Upper Temenos.

Fig. 6.44.   Lower Temenos, West Cryptoporticus, restoration of the arch.

Fig. 6.45.   Consolidation and restoration of the West Entry Stairway.

Fig. 6.46.   Area marked where collapse is imminent in West Cryptoporticus wall.

Fig. 6.47.   Bridge constructed from Turkish railroad ties.

Fig. 6.48.   Lower Temenos East-West Retaining Wall after restoration.

Fig. 6.49.   Lower Temenos to Upper Temenos Central Stairs as excavated.

Fig. 6.50.   Lower Temenos to Upper Temenos Central Stairs as excavated.

Fig. 6.51.   Lower Temenos East-West Retaining Wall after restoration.

Fig. 6.52.   Lower Temenos East-West Retaining Wall after restoration.

Fig. 6.53.   Upper Temenos East Plaza after restoration, to south.

Fig. 6.54.   Upper Temenos Residential Quarter with a gate placed at its entrance.

Fig. 6.55.   Upper Temenos East "Cistern" arches consolidated and the walls pointed, to east.

Fig. 6.56.   East Perimeter Wall, upper vault and entrance to Room A from the East Plaza.

Fig. 6.57.   East Perimeter Wall, upper vault and entrance to Room A from the East Plaza.

Fig. 6.58.   Upper Temenos West Plaza from the West Plaza to the South Passageway.

Fig. 6.59.   Upper Temenos Residential Quarter step removal.

Fig. 6.60.   Upper Temenos Great Temple Forecourt broken pavers *in situ*.

Fig. 6.61.   Upper Temenos Great Temple Forecourt, partially restored.

Fig. 6.62.   Upper Temenos Great Temple Forecourt, restored stairs.

Fig. 6.63.   Upper Temenos Roman-Byzantine Baths as excavated.

Fig. 6.64.   Upper Temenos Roman-Byzantine Baths during excavation.

Fig. 6.65.   Upper Temenos Roman-Byzantine Baths during excavation.

Fig. 6.66.   Upper Temenos Roman-Byzantine Baths, "Well" Room, curved facing blocks.

Fig. 6.67.   Great Temple southeast double-engaged column base as excavated.

Fig. 6.68.   Top of the Great Temple southeast double engaged (heart-shaped) column.

Fig. 6.69.   Great Temple southeast double engaged (heart-shaped) column, restored.

Fig. 6.70.   Moving the lower order of a Nabataean capital into place.

Fig. 6.71.   Great Temple West Corridor Arch jostled out of its original position.

Fig. 6.72.   Great Temple West Corridor Arch.

Fig. 6.73.   Great Temple West Corridor Arch with *anastylosis*.

Fig. 6.74.   Great Temple West Corridor Wall before pointing and *anastylosis*.

Fig. 6.75.   Great Temple West Corridor Wall in mid-conservation.

Fig. 6.76.   Great Temple West Corridor Wall fresco in a state of deterioration.

Fig. 6.77.   Great Temple West Corridor Wall and arch after consolidation.

Fig. 6.78.   Great Temple West Corridor during consolidation.

Fig. 6.79.   Great Temple Theater after consolidation.

Fig. 6.80.   Great Temple Theater *scalaria* after consolidation.

Fig. 6.81.   West (north-south) interior Theater Stairs restored.

Fig. 6.82.   West (north-south) Theater Stairs arched window.

Fig. 6.83.   West Chamber interior wall restored.

Fig. 6.84.   Central Arch interior restored.

Fig. 6.85.   Central Arch doorway from the South Corridor restored.

Fig. 6.86.   East rear east-west Theater Stairs restored.

Fig. 6.87.   West rear east-west Theater Stairs restored.

Fig. 6.88.   Restored portions of walls indicated by painted lines.

Fig. 6.89.   Tea Time!

CHAPTER 7: DISCUSSION AND CONCLUSIONS

Front: Evocative facial fragments from the Great Temple.

Fig. 7.1.   Great Temple with Pool Complex (left) and the Imperial Cult Building (right).

Fig. 7.2.   Nabataean bowl.

Fig. 7.3.   Nabataean bowl.

Fig. 7.4.   Nabataean coin.

Fig 7.5.   Nabataean silver coin.

Fig. 7.6.   Bronze Plaque with a partial Nabataean inscription.

Fig. 7.7.   Mason's mark on a limestone ashlar.

Fig. 7.8.   Mason's mark in the shape of a Nabataean "h."

Fig. 7.9.   Plaster painting of a face.

Fig. 7.10.   Watercolor drawings of stucco fragments.

Fig. 7.11.   Decorative swirls drawn with watercolor.

Fig. 7.12.   West Corridor fresco depicting the façade of a temple.

Fig. 7.13.   South Corridor fresco decoration.

Fig. 7.14.   Fresco wall decoration over the South Corridor Wall.

Fig. 7.15.   Remains of cable fluting found on a temple column drum.

Fig. 7.16.   Virtual Reality reconstruction of Great Temple precinct in Site Phase IV.

Fig. 7.17.   Virtual Reality reconstruction of the Great Temple in Site Phase V.

Fig. 7.18.   Virtual Reality reconstruction of the Great Temple precinct in Site Phase V.

Fig. 7.19a. Elephant half capital left head, right profile.

Fig. 7.19b. Half elephant-headed capital.

Fig. 7.19c. Elephant half capital right head.

Fig. 7.20a. Elephant-headed capital left profile.

Fig. 7.20b. Elephant-headed capital right profile.

Fig. 7.20c. Elephant-headed capital front and right profile.

Fig. 7.21.   Upper order of a Great Temple capital.

Fig. 7.22.   Pinecone boss set into an acanthus leaf.

Fig. 7.23.   Volute in the corner of the upper order of the Great Temple capitals.

Fig. 7.24.   A capital from the front of Al-Khazna.

Fig. 7.25.   Face of Tyche with her turreted crown.

Fig. 7.26.   Lively female figure emerging from a helix from the Propylaeum East.

Fig. 7.27a. Male athlete in motion.

Fig. 7.27b. Male athlete in motion.

Fig. 7.28.   Inscription fragments of King Aretas IV from the Petra Church.

Fig. 7.29.   Faint painted inscription of plaster found in the East "Cistern."

Fig. 7.29b. East "Cistern" Nabataean inscription.

Fig. 7.30.   Nabataean graffiti incised in the wall plaster from Wall K.

Fig. 7.31a. Painted potsherd.

Fig. 7.31b. Incised lamp base fragment.

Fig. 7.31c. Amphora handle stamped with a Rhodian Rose.

Fig. 7.31d.   Ostracon?

Fig. 7.31e.   Letters impressed into plaster/stucco in a vessel base.

Fig. 7.32.   PROVIN inscription.

Fig 7.33a.   Sandstone inscription fragment.

Fig 7.33b.   Partial marble inscription.

Fig. 7.33c.   Partial marble inscription with two cut characters.

Fig. 7.33d.   Partial marble inscription with incised characters on both flattened sides.

Fig.7.33e.   Partial marble inscription.

Fig. 7.34.   Stamped double-strand amphora handle with FELICI?A/S.

Fig. 7.35.   Lower Temenos platform with *nefesh* and *betyl in situ*.

Fig. 7.36.   Small limestone horned altar.

Fig. 7.37.   Mini limestone incense altar.

Fig. 7.38.   Nabataean goblet with stamped leaf impressions.

Fig. 7.39.   Pilgrim bottle with rouletted impressions.

Fig. 7.40.   Assorted painted fine Nabataean wares from Trench 94.

Fig. 7.41.   Assorted wares from Special Project 85.

Fig. 7.42.   Nabataean volute lamp, Upper Temenos Trench 94, Locus 18.

Fig. 7.43.   Nabataean round lamp.

Fig. 7.44a-b. Nabataean figurine fragment.

Fig. 7.45a.   Figurine head fragment.

Fig. 7.45b.   Figurine fragment.

Fig. 7.45c.   Nabataean figurine fragment.

Fig. 7.45d.   Figurine.

Fig. 7.45e.   Small plaque.

Fig. 7.46a.   Animal figurine.

Fig. 7.46b.   Horse figurine fragment.

Fig. 7.46c.   Ibex horn from a figurine.

Fig. 7.47a.   Bronze flower handle, top view.

Fig. 7.47b.   Bronze flower handle, side view.

Fig. 7.48.   Painted glass.

Fig. 7.49.   Petra Great Temple virtual reality of Site Phase VII.

Fig. 7.50.   Petra Garden-Pool Complex to the east of the Great Temple.

Fig. 7.51.   A homogeneous collection of Nabataean 3-d wares.

Fig. 7.52.   Painted Nabataean bowl with the figure of a bird.

Fig. 7.53.   Lamp, dating to the Islamic period from the Ridge Church.

Fig. 7.54.   Lower face fragment.

FOREWORD

When we first visited Petra in 1972, it had the magical quality of an orientalist painting: jumbles of columns and stone lay everywhere. It was picturesque, but the city and the people who built it were little understood as almost no excavation had taken place. In fact, Petra was almost unique in the constellation of great sites of the world in that more was known about the builders of the city from minor sites elsewhere than from their capital. This had given rise to such misinformation as the widespread belief that Petra was completely abandoned after the earthquake of 363 CE.

Large areas of the site still remain untouched, but in recent decades, there has been an explosion of knowledge about one of the great cultures of antiquity, that of the Nabataeans. Indeed, in the 1990s, and the early years of this decade, the central area of Petra was transformed by a number of projects. Some of these were conducted directly by the American Center of Oriental Research (ACOR). In our time overseeing ACOR, these included the Petra Church Project that uncovered spectacular mosaics and a cache of documents that revealed a great deal about Byzantine Petra. Nearby, two other Byzantine churches were excavated: the Blue Chapel and the Ridge Church. These showed that Petra was still an urban center in the Byzantine era. In the area of the churches two Nabataean tombs of the first century were excavated. Several of the shops along the main street, shops that were used in both the Roman and Byzantine eras, were cleared and restored, as was the staircase to the "Upper Market." During this same period,

ACOR sponsored the creation of a digital map of Petra's city center, a map with sub-centimeter accuracy; that map now serves as a tool for the Petra Park and shows exactly how much work has been accomplished in recent years.

Many other projects undertaken, such as the excavation of the Great Temple, were affiliated with and assisted by ACOR; indeed it was ACOR's aerial photography project that led to that excavation. In June of 1992, J. Wilson Myers and Eleanor E. Myers took spectacular aerial photos of Petra, including aerials of the Great Temple. On a visit to the U.S. in November of that year, we showed Martha Sharp Joukowsky those photos along with a video of the Great Temple area to see if she would be interested in working there. Having completed her previous project in Greece, she was interested, and she began planning for a project. When she arrived in Jordan several months later, she was stunned by the size of the monument; somehow the magnitude of the site had not been communicated by the photos or the video.

The Great Temple is enormous. The diameter of the columns alone, up to 1.5 m, puts it in the class of archaeological mega-monuments. How to even begin the project? But begin Martha did, in the summer of 1993. During 14 ten-week seasons, she and her team, a team that included Artie Joukowsky, peeled back layers of accumulated tumble and wind-blown sand to reveal a spectacular building and elements of Nabataean culture that were wholly unexpected. One example is the extraordinary art of the sculptors who created the elephant-headed capitals; originally there were over 500 elephant heads on those capitals and apparently no two were alike. The project added substantially to our awareness of the skill of the Nabataeans in challenging what is at base the hostile desert environment of Petra. In a place where less than 200 mm of rain fall each year, the Nabataeans used real creativity in devising ways to save and use as much of the water as possible; the Great Temple Project gave as much attention to the water-conservation infrastructure of the Great Temple as to its decorated superstructure.

One of the most significant parts of this project has been the involvement of students, many but not all from Brown University. Six of these students have gone on to write Ph.D. theses on the project, and even to lead their own archaeological projects at Petra, thereby continuing to expand our knowledge of the Nabataeans. Most notable are the excavations of the Small Temple, west of the Great Temple, and, to the east, the Garden-Pool Complex Project.

Beyond what she did for her students, Martha also tried very hard to give something to Jordan. Unfortunately, too many archaeologists excavate their site and then walk away without a thought as to what will happen to that site in the future. More than that, the results of many projects are either not published or are published in obscure journals seen only by specialists. The Joukowskys together made a commitment to the conservation of the site that continues today and will continue into the future. They have also spent a great deal of time and effort on public outreach in the form of making the site accessible to visitors and giving tours of the monument to a variety of groups. Martha has given so many public lectures that probably even she has lost count of the number; and she has published in a variety of venues, including websites, that are available not just to specialists but also to the public all over the world.

A project like the Great Temple is a living thing with many facets: scholarly, touristic, and most importantly, human. The connection that Martha made with her students, with the people of Petra, and with the wider community in Jordan, is a testament to her lifelong commitment to seeing that archaeology is not just about stones.

Pierre and Patricia Bikai
Aqaba
March 2007

PREFACE

I chose to excavate the Petra Great Temple in 1992 for several reasons. First I always wanted to excavate in the Nabataean capital—Petra— where so little was known about Nabataean freestanding architecture and the Nabataeans. I had visited the Petra[1] many times and was always fascinated by its remains. Second, because I had worked on prehistoric sites in the Middle East for several years, by contrast I wanted to deal with stone architecture and with a material culture I thought had been extensively studied and published so that I could "fit in" to what already was known from the archaeological record. Third, I knew well and enjoyed the Bedouin in the region, and more specifically in Petra, and I wanted to work with those I considered "family."

Contrary to my assumptions, in 1993 little was known about Central Petra except for a few excavations, and at that time no modern controlled surveys using GIS or GPS had been taken. In those "early days" of the 1990s there was limited excavation, a critical need for infor- mation, and incomplete publication of the data.[2] When I found there was this requisite lack I wanted to reconcile historical sources with the archaeological evidence.

In 1992 Pierre M. Bikai, Director of the American Center of Oriental Research in Amman, Jordan, for many years a colleague and close family friend, suggested that I take an interest in excavating the Petra Great Temple site. At the time, Pierre was excavating the Petra Church, and arranged to have Eleanor E. and J. Wilson Myers take aerial photographs of the site. Optimistically, I prepared a five-year prospectus for the Jordanian Department of Antiquities requesting permission to excavate the Great Temple. That same year the Depart-

ment of Antiquities extended an invitation to begin my research and to begin excavations in 1993. This publication, Volume II, is a summary of the 1993–2006 excavations, a study of the stratigraphy, the Petra Great Temple Site Phasing, and the measures we have taken for the extensive preservation of the Great Temple precinct.

Volume II incorporates all the material from our 14 years of excavations. Much more material and evidence became available since I wrote and edited our publication of Volume I in 1998. The interpretation of the evidence is my own, but I have received invaluable suggestions from my team and colleagues. In Chapter 2, we will examine the stratigraphy and excavations of the Propylaeum. Chapter 3 is devoted to the Lower Temenos. In Chapter 4 we consider the extensive excavations of the Upper Temenos, and Chapter 5 is devoted to the excavations of the temple area. Chapter 6 is a review of the consolidation and preservation methods we have undertaken, and Chapter 7 attempts to answer, as clearly as possible questions that are posed by the site itself. This volume closes with definitions and a brief verbal scan of the major monuments at Petra. This volume, Volume II should be considered a companion to Volume I, and Volume III will serve as a follow up to Volumes I and II.

Volume III will focus on specialist stud- ies including an analysis of the architecture of the temple and the theater, the sculpture, the iconography of the stucco decoration, and the vast hydraulic systems of the precinct, as well as the Roman-Byzantine Baths. It will also include coverage of the coins, pottery, the figurines and lamps, bone objects, metals, glass, archaeobo- tanical and faunal analysis, a shell study, and the results of the Great Temple databases.

In the beginning...

From the German surveys in the 1920s, the impressive column ridden precinct, at that time, had not been endowed with an Arabic identity, and was named the "Great Temple" by Bachmann in his 1921 publication. At the beginning of our excavations, so as not to confuse it with the Qasr al-Bint, I called it the "Southern Temple." In 1999 I returned it to its former name, the Great Temple, because that was how it was continually identified on the maps of the Petra central city.

Prior to excavations, the porch column collapse was the only feature visible above the ground. When I arrived at the site I thought I knew what to expect, but I was stunned by the formidable massive wreckage of tumbled architectural components and detritus. In truth, I had wondered if I could manage the project. My initial optimism waned. Keeping up my courage, I undertook a walkover survey, started a search for benchmarks, established datum control points and the site survey with a laser transit began.[3] Now, 14 years later, the excavations have revealed a series of two temples plus a theater-temple. The complete Petra Great Temple site, except an area between the West Walkway Wall and the West Precinct Wall has been excavated.

Assuming we were excavating a large temple, the site was subdivided into excavation areas dictated by the topography, labeled the Propylaeum, Lower Temenos, Upper Temenos and Temple. For 14 years excavations progressed in each of these areas.[4] A 10.00 m-by-10.00 m grid of squares was laid over the overall area to be excavated (Figure 1.8),[5] estimated to measure some 11,000 square meters.

Excavation results and information dissemination have changed in remarkable and unpredictable ways over the past 14 years. When we began our work, the very language of questions and answers that are fundamental to current professional archaeologists were non-existent. The Great Temple was not what we expected it to be, and our excavations have taken diverse research journeys along the way. Often we began with many a routine assump-

tion and ended up with unusual unforeseen conclusions. And in some cases we have made recensions to earlier published reports, such as our survey data. For example, we assumed the benchmarks we had been given in 1992–3 were accurate, however, all our data have now been changed to reflect true elevations. The information in 1992 was limited, but that situation for Petra and the Nabataeans has changed dramatically beginning in the early 1990s with noteworthy publications by many colleagues.[6]

Collaborative scholarship is part of our archaeological ethos in Petra. Although isolated in our separate projects, we share our ideas with others working in the field. All of us believe we are in a special place, and although we are excavating separate monuments, we are searching for cultural correspondences between our sites and others. Petra as one Nabataean cultural expression is what we are all trying to define and communicate. We are all on the search for the cultural and historic fabric of the Nabataeans. I am grateful to those other Nabataean researchers who over the years have shared their expertise with me.[7]

In this volume, I examine the archaeological evidence for the Great Temple in the Nabataean and Roman-Byzantine periods. It has taken four years to carry out the research for this excavation report. The agenda was demanding. There was a close examination of the over 100 trench notebooks plus the trench supervisors' final reports, site balk and wall drawings, and thousands of artifacts. Linking together the stratigraphy and chronology by trench, the cross analysis of trenches by area, the establishment of the Site Phases, and the division of each trench and locus into a Site Phase was a challenge. Often we were dealing with data that was totally unexpected, and the data itself raised puzzling and complex issues. We had to be content with the ambiguities provided by the evidence. Overall, I sought to know who the Nabataeans were, what they built and how they used the Great Temple. I learned an immense amount, and now after all these years I have some understanding of the Nabataean concept of a monumental precinct in their capital city. I have also gained a perspective on how Roman rule impacted the precinct and the city as a whole.

From our excavations and analysis we know more about Petra in the Nabataean period through its brilliantly constructed hydrological systems, its temple(s), Residential Quarter, and the Baroque Room Complex. Heretofore little supporting evidence has been available about the Nabataeans, and these features and buildings are a paramount expression of the culture of the royals, the elite and the local community itself. Can we see the Petra Great Temple as a reflection of a community with a self-governing polity? I think we can. Nonetheless the true character of its polity remains enigmatic because so little is known from the archaeological and epigraphic record. Luckily at the Great Temple we have captured a crucial period that defines Nabataean cultural identity in the city.

Then there is a shift from an independent Nabataea and Petra to a Roman province in 106 CE. We have a better understanding about the impact of Roman rule even before the Roman takeover with the recovery of the Great Temple Roman-Byzantine baths and the Imperial Cult Building. Clearly, this portrait of the Great Temple excavations allows us to see how one precinct in the Petra urban layout influenced the landscape. We are able to grasp some of the changes taking place from the first century BCE to the mid-second century CE. I hope that by making the Great Temple excavations part of the public record it will be more directly useful to those interested in the constructions and reconstructions of Petra's Nabataean and Roman period settings.

Of course, the measure of our success will be Volume III which will present more specific analyses. At present, however, I look forward to July 2007 in the field when we will be placing signs at the site to facilitate visitor understanding of the major features and chronology of the site, and making an assessment of the future demands for continued research and consolidation of the Petra Great Temple precinct as well.

My sincere hope is that the reader will glimpse something about the unique aesthetic principles of the Nabataeans through Volume II of the Great Temple excavations, and will feel rewarded for having done so.

Publication

In 1998, Volume I, which covers the first five years of excavation 1993–1997 with a CD-ROM was published (Joukowsky, 1998), and to date some 214 additional publications have become part of the public record, which can be found in the Petra Great Temple Site Bibliography. At this writing, Volume III, the comprehensive final excavation publication of these 14 years of excavations and specialist's reports, is underway. Annual reports can also be found in the *Annual of the Department of Antiquities of Jordan* and in the *American Journal of Archaeology*. Our Web page can be found on the World Wide Web at *<http://brown.edu/Departments/Anthropology/Petra/>* and our databases, phasing charts, drawings and trench reports can be accessed on *Open Context, <http://www.opencontext.org>*.

The excavation results presented here in Volume II are a prelude to Volume III, which will be devoted to the full scientific results of these excavations. Volume III will be divided into two main sections. The first section will deal with the temple architecture and how the temple was built—Nabataean construction techniques, water supply and hydraulic systems, the use of plaster decoration and stucco revetments, pilaster relief sculptures, elephant-headed capitals, Great Temple Nabataean capitals, *betyls* and other sculpture, theater in the temple, and the Roman-Byzantine Baths. The second section will focus on the material culture and include the Catalog of Objects, database methodology and results, a general ceramic typology of the pottery, both fine wares and plain wares, lamps, figurines, glass, numismatics, inscriptions, faunal and shell analyses as well as bone objects.

Introduction to Volume II

Volume II is devoted to the examination of each precinct area: Propylaeum, Lower Temenos, Upper Temenos and the temple proper. It presents the impressive quantity of our intensive field research from the beginning of our work at the site in 1993. Not only is there an abundance of new research since our preliminary report (Joukowsky 1998), but also the potential integration of each area's excavation showing insights well beyond what our 1998 results produced. Now, some years later, this study appears, and in the interim, as this volume demonstrates, the Great Temple continues to be a most productive and surprising site.

The detailed historical reconstruction of these excavations remains a tremendous challenge. Scholarly controversy with regard to issues such as the identity of the various precinct sectors may be problematic for some, but our findings are based on the systematic analysis of each sector to establish its sequence in the chronology, its relationship to other sectors of the site and development of the site as a whole.

The scope of this volume is to present a comprehensive overview focusing on a functional analysis of each area (Chapters 2–5). Each area opens with a general statement and then moves to the coverage of specific physical evidence—its major architectural features, their measurements, and their particularities. Again for each area, the stratigraphy and phasing are then presented, so that sequential architectural changes taking place within each part of the precinct can be appreciated and reflect the broad

focus for our understanding of its occupational history. The painstaking analysis and challenges presented by the diversity of the architecture has been undertaken by each of the experienced members of our team—the detailed treatment of which with each trench final report with their interpretation of the archaeological deposits is presented on our online web page.

Assuming the Great Temple's place in Petra's urban scheme, it is of particular interest that the rock-cut caves of the Upper Temenos Residential Quarter to its southwest complement the freestanding Great Temple architecture. This provides us with a view of domestic contexts also as an integral part of the Nabataean and Roman urban fabric. For this overall evaluation, we now turn to the presentation of the major architectural divisions beginning with the Propylaeum and moving south to the Lower Temenos, up to the Upper Temenos. Finally we define the temple(s) themselves.

In Chapter 6, site preservation is discussed. The consolidation, preservation and protection of the enormous Great Temple site have been

Fig. 1
Baroque Room Ceiling, detail of the decorative cornice *in situ*.

integral parts of our excavation research design from those early years, and various conservation measures are described that have been undertaken annually. Many of the recovered artifacts from the Great Temple have been selected by museums to be displayed abroad. To promote knowledge of Jordan's extraordinary cultural heritage, the Jordanian government transported a number of our sculptures, including elephant-headed capitals, on a well-publicized international museum tour, "Petra Rediscovered: Lost City of the Nabataeans." Exhibitions included the Natural History Museum in New York and other venues in America, plus the Museum of Canadian Civilizations in Ottawa, Canada. Independently, our celebrated Baroque Room ceiling (an *in situ* partial Baroque Room cornice is seen in Figure 1 and its hypothesized reconstruction is shown in Figure 2) and several other artifacts traveled to Berlin and Bonn, Germany, and other examples of our elephant-headed capitals were transported for display to Helsinki, Finland. These well-publicized expositions promoted a public recognition of Jordan's cultural heritage and the Great Temple for an unparalleled view of a Nabataean historic focus. It is hoped that international support will raise sufficient funds to construct a new Petra Museum so that when these objects return to Jordan they will be properly displayed and protected in a museum venue close to the site.

Chapter 7 concludes this volume with a discussion that I hope offers a broader view of some of the issues these excavations have raised, including "The Great Debate" that centers on whether the Great Temple is a sacred or secular monument, a temple or an administrative structure. The questions before us are, "Is it a temple?" "Can it be both sacred and secular?" Thereafter are some comments regarding the Roman-Byzantine Period, and the last days of the Great Temple precinct, and of course my perspective and understanding of the structure as an important element in the life and culture of the Nabataeans and of Petra in particular.

In conclusion, as this chapter has demonstrated, remains of the Nabataean Great Temple(s) attest to an extensive architectural record that Brown University archaeologists have unearthed. These excavations verify,

Doorway to the Eastern Annex

Doorway to the Northern Anteroom and the Western Walkway

Fig. 2
Baroque Room central medallion reconstruction.

unambiguously, the sacred and secular character of the site, while also reflecting Nabataean and Petraean architectural and sculptural traditions. Despite the significant change brought about by the Romans, it is possible to reconstruct the site's heterogeneous development in this period with the Roman Imperial Cult building and the Roman-Byzantine Baths. The evidence has helped us establish chronological parameters for the site, and our comprehensive program for preservation underscores the relevant contribution of the Great Temple excavations to the remarkable city of Petra. In conclusion, some of the main issues emerging from these excavations have been summarized. Until now the Nabataeans who constructed and used the Great Temple have been historically obscure, but fortunately we have found them again.

Acknowledgments

In my many years at Brown University I have been incredibly fortunate to work with some distinguished faculty members and students at the Center for Old World Archaeology and Art, now known as the Institute of Archaeology and the Ancient World. My Great Temple team was composed of my undergraduate and graduate students at Brown University, many of whom had worked with me for many years. Together we developed databases, undertook surveys, and were in a constant state of surprise by the unusual nature of our findings. My undergraduate and graduate student archaeologists have concentrated their efforts on this monumental complex, using it as an educational tool and training site to teach a new generation of archaeologists. Accuracy, thoroughness, and speed in fieldwork are essential, but even more these team members grew to care deeply about the site. We developed an esprit de corps and for all of us the field experience was extraordinarily rich and productive. Ranging in complexity from the removal of overburden and documentation to the stabilization and consolidation and partial restoration and preservation, the site stands as a testament to the legacy of the ancient Nabataeans. Brown University archaeologists have fully devoted their talents to its rebirth. Photographs of the 2003–2006 excavation teams are presented in Figures 3–6 and Figure 7 shows the 2006 team returned to Petra after taking aerial photographs in 2006.

Instituted by Douglas Pitney (1993), Loa P. Traxler (1994–1995), and Paul C. Zimmerman (1994, 1996, 1997), our survey strategy over the years has been implemented by Brian A. Brown (2000–2002, 2004), Christian F. Cloke (2001–2004), Marshall C. Agnew (2005–2006) and Eleanor A. Power (2005–2006). Our expert Brown University team has been indispensable in recording not only the on-going excavations but also all the artifacts recovered in our multiple site databases (Joukowsky 1998, 58–61, 237–343). Implementation and managing the site has also defined technological advancement for expanding and ensuring the continuity of information access and data preservation. Our databases now support the findings of approximately half million artifacts, and we have mounted internet-accessible databases on the worldwide web in *Open Context.*

Petra Great Temple Team Members 1993–2006

The unique masterpiece of the Great Temple has been brought to light by the collective vision of the following team members:[8] Marshall C. Agnew 2005–2006, Gyles T. Austin 1994, Deirdre G. Barrett 1995–2006, Joseph J. Basile 1995–1997, 1999, 2002, 2004, 2006, Pierre-Louis Bazin 2002, Heather Beckman 1994, Leigh-Ann Bedal 1994–1998, Francesca Bennett 1999–2006, Laurel D. Bestock 1996–1998, Josh Bell 1995, Geoffrey Bilder 1993–1995, Jean Blackburn 1995–1996, David Brill 1995, Adam M. Brin 2000–2006, Brian A. Brown 1996–1997, 2000–2002, 2004, Kimberly A. Butler 1996, Meredith Chesson 1993, Christian F. Cloke 2001–2004, Donna Jean D'Agostino 1997–2006, Emily Catherine Egan 2001–2004, Anne-Catherine Escher 2002, Patricia W. Farley 2000, John Forasté 1997, Rune Frederiksen 2005–2006, José I. Fusté 2001–2002, Juliette Gimon 1996, Samuel J. Ginsberg 1998, David Goldstein 1996, Zain Habboo 1995–1996, John Philip Hagen 2000–2002, Katrina M. Haile 1997–1998, Ann Harris 1995, Amanda Henry 2001–2002, Karen Jacobsen 1994, Artemis A. W. Joukowsky (1993–2006), Jane S. Joukowsky 2003–2006, Michael W. Joukowsky 2003–2006, Lamya Khalidi 1995, Arta Khakpour 2006, Tarek M. Khanachet 2004–2006, Benjamin H. Kleine 1997, Nina Köprülü 1993–2006, Sureya Köprülü 2006–2007, Steven Larson 2000, 2002, Emma Susan Libonati 1998, 2001–2006, Peter G. Lund 1993, Lauren Maddock 2006, Kathleen Mallak 1994–1995, Erin E. McCracken 2000, Hilary Mattison 1997, Elizabeth A. Najjar 1997–1998, Peter Nalle 1994, Margaret O'Hea 2006, Kathleen M. O'Meara 2006, Margaret G. Parker 1997, Madelaine Parr 1994, Peter J. Parr 1994, Elizabeth E. Payne 1993–1997, Megan A. Perry 2004, Douglas Pitney 1993–1994, Eleanor A. Power 2004–2006, Mary E. Prendergast 1998,

Fig. 3
2003 Brown University
Petra Great Temple
Excavation Team.

Fig. 4
2004 Brown University
Petra Great Temple
Excavation Core Team.
Back row from left to right:
Eleanor A. Power, Emily
Catherine Egan, Christian
F. Cloke, Sara Karz Reid,
Michael Zimmerman,
and Brian A. Brown.
Front row from left to
right: Tarek Khanachet,
Artemis W. Joukowsky,
Martha Sharp Joukowsky,
Dakhilallah Qublan,
Christopher A. Tuttle,
and Emma S. Libonati.
(Absent, Deirdre G. Barrett.)

Fig. 5
2005 Brown University
Petra Great Temple
Excavation Team.

Fig. 6
2006 Brown University
Petra Great Temple
Excavation Team.

Fig. 7
2006 Back to Earth—
Team after photographing
the site from the helicopter.
Back row from left to right:
Artemis W. Joukowsky,
Emma S. Libonati, Colonel
Ibrahim Yala, Chief of Jorda-
nian Air Force Operations
and Seventh Squadron
Commander, Anas Qaralleh,
First Lieutenant of the
7th Squadron. Front row
from left to right: Dakhilallah
Qublan, Eleanor A. Power,
Marshall C. Agnew,
Süreya M. Köprülü, and
Arta Khakpour.

Faisal Raad 1995, Sara Karz Reid 1998–2002,
2004, Alexandra R. Retzleff 1994, James M.
Roger 1998, John Rucker 1995, Shari L.
Saunders 2002–2005, Joshua J. Schwartz 1998,
Nadine Shubailat 1993, Erika L. Schluntz 1993–
1996, Lawrence Sisson 1995, Constantinos
Sistovaris 1997, Michael F. Slaughter 1994–
1997, Elizabeth A. Smolenski 1993, 2005–2007,
Thomas Smolenski 1997, 2005, Darryl B. Sneag
2001, Simon M. Sullivan 1997–1998, Karen B.
Stern 2000, Monica A. Sylvester 1995–1999,
2001, 2004, Randy Takian 1996, Laurent
Tholbecq 1995, David Thorpe 1993, Loa P.
Traxler 1994–1995, Christopher A. Tuttle
2004–2006, Pia Ward 1993, Peter Warnock
1994–1997, Andrew Willis 2002, Evan Wolf
1996, Michael S. Zimmerman 2004, Paul C.
Zimmerman 1994, 1996–1999, 2002.

This is an incredible group of people who
helped us play, laugh, and wrestle with the
details of excavation and the stratigraphy. For
me they continue to be a crucial repository of
knowledge. This team helped me discover,
create and disseminate the information presented
here. They rebuilt the Petra Great Temple for
the future. Because learning and training are
the scholarly force for the future, I am proud
that many of these team members have become
researchers in their own right.[9]

In the field each of these team members
recorded features and artifacts by trench and
locus. The databases shown in Figure 8 reflect
the meticulous counting and classification of all
cultural materials—ceramic fragments, bones,
metal, glass, vegetal matter in the Petra Great
Temple's Grosso Modo database, and they also
classified architectural fragments in the Architectural Fragment database. Deirdre G. Barrett
was our Catalog registrar and the mainstay of
the vast curatorial Great Temple challenge.
Coins were separately processed, as were lamps.
All the finds were processed on site. At the
conclusion of each season Deirdre G. Barrett
took the catalog of registered objects and turned
them over to the Jordanian Department of
Antiquities at the Petra Museum.

Furthermore, these team members played
an especially key role in the excavations, and
this volume is based on the excavation reports
of the whole team over the years. Weekly site
tours of the excavations culminated in trench
and special project reports that were submitted
as soon as the excavations were completed with
plans, section drawings, and suggested site phasing. At the end of each season the whole team
spent one to two days discussing the stratigraphy
and site phasing, and placing their respective
projects into the overall phasing for the site. The
summation of these reports, along with photographs and revised site plans, are presented on
our Great Temple web site, <*http://www.brown.
edu/Departments/Anthropology/Petra/*> instituted
in 1995 and maintained by Adam M. Brin.

While writing this report in 2006, because
our Great Temple Web site could not allocate
the requisite space we needed to share our data,
I elected to use *Open Context* to publish the
enormous compendium of materials we had
collected over the years. *Open Context* is an
open access publication system that has enabled
our Great Temple researchers to publish on
line their primary field data like trench reports
and databases, and media such as photographs,
site plans, stratigraphic drawings and our Great
Temple videos on the World Wide Web
(http://www.opencontext.org). All of the trench
and special project reports as well as our phasing
charts now are available at this site that provides
an easy to use, yet powerful, framework for
exploring, searching, and analyzing excavation

results, survey data, and the artifacts deposited in the Petra Museum collections. All the content is linked together as an integrated and cohesive resource and is freely available.[10] *Open Context* is unique in that it provides a framework for sharing archaeological research, free of burdensome copyright restrictions, while still protecting independent scholarly attribution. I would like to thank Sarah Whitcher Kansa and Eric Kansa for their interest in the Great Temple Project and for making *Open Context* available to us.

Additionally preliminary reports were published and became part of the public record at the end of each field season (see the Petra Great Temple Site Bibliography).

The Shape Project

The S.H.A.P.E. (Shape, Archaeology, Photogrammetry, Entropy) Lab was formed with a three-year, $1.25-million grant followed by a $2-million grant from the United States National Science Foundation to Brown's Center for Old World Archaeology and Art and the Departments of Anthropology, Engineering, Applied Mathematics and Computer Science. This was a significant interdisciplinary effort to develop technical applications for archaeological methodology, analysis and research in conjunction with computer science and mathematical vision.

As I was directing the ongoing excavations at the Petra Great Temple, I was one of this special collaborative project's principal investigators. The site has provided an excellent range of data for the project. Here I would like to thank my Brown University collaborators. The project's other principal investigators were David Cooper and Benjamin Kimia of the Department of Engineering; David Laidlaw, Department of Computer Science; and David Mumford, Department of Applied Mathematics. Key researchers also involved post-graduate specialists Eileen L. Vote and Frederic Leymarie, the latter a project leader in the Division of Engineering and specialist in computer vision problems. The team also included graduate

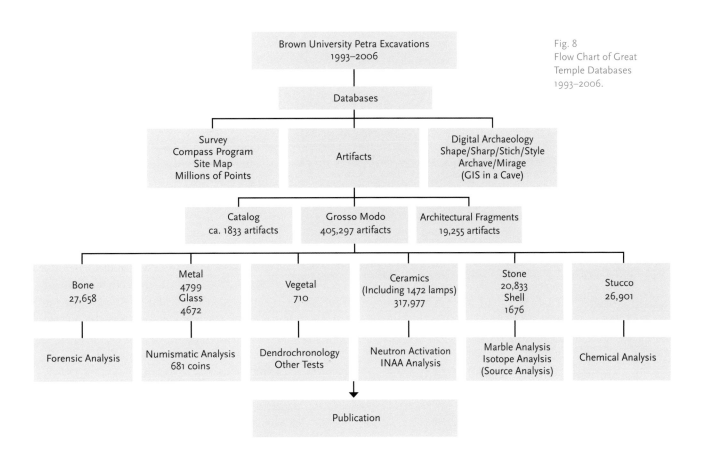

Fig. 8
Flow Chart of Great Temple Databases 1993–2006.

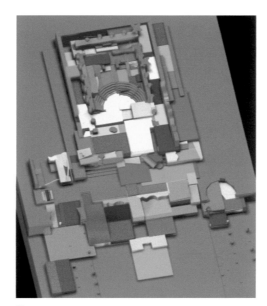

Fig. 9
Trenches excavated
in the CAVE.

Fig. 10
Eileen L. Vote using
the CAVE to query
artifact scatter.

students and undergraduates at Brown from affiliated departments.[11] During the past few years, the team has focused on two main research goals—developing a system for a 3-D GIS, and Automated Pottery Reconstruction.

An immediate contribution of the project has been the refinement of the first Virtual Reality 3-D GIS application for Archaeology research. The 3-D GIS system, called ARCHAVE, allows users to view and interact with different types of artifacts and architectural finds, *in situ,* in the context of a virtual room called a CAVE (Cave Automatic Virtual Environment). The CAVE is a nine-foot by nine-foot room with computationally referenced projections on three walls and the floor. Figure 9 shows an overview of the trenches to be explored on the CAVE floor. As can be seen in Figure 10, the user wears a headset and the system tracks movements within the space, then renders the scene to accommodate the user's location. In addition, a joystick is used that allows free navigation within the model. Within this virtual environment, the user has access to a life-size representation of the Great Temple site, its architecture, excavation trenches, trench loci and fifteen different types of artifacts represented in their find locations. The temple precinct covers approximately 7,560 square meters; therefore, the user has a large area to explore but with full mobility inside the environment.[12]

The project was designed to develop more descriptive and effective ways of using computers to model and make inferences about three-dimensional shapes and surfaces. The project's other major goals were to design more effective computer site models for unearthed artifacts and structures that would incorporate time, location, three-dimensional position and other data gleaned from object images. Using computers to construct three-dimensional models for reassembling artifacts including statues and columns and other structures from images, the aim was to build a database of those fragments, and to make use of computers to recognize or infer artisan or artistic style from fragments of larger pieces. This helped us as archaeologists determine what groups of ancient people produced the objects as well as to relate structures at one site to other sites.

Sponsors

Many people and organizations played critical roles by providing financial support. I have been fortunate to receive the assistance of Brown University from the inception of these excavations. I am particularly grateful to Brown University Presidents Howard R. Swearer, Vartan Gregorian, E. Gordon Gee, and Ruth J. Simmons, for without their encouragement these excavations would not have fulfilled their promise. Excavation subventions also were made possible by the Brown University Graduate School, Salomon Award and the Brown University Undergraduate Teaching and Research Awards (UTRA grants). We express our thanks to the Brown University faculty and administration for granting us these coveted awards.

Since 1998 the Luther I. Replogle Foundation has provided major financial assistance for the Great Temple excavations. This funding has been critical, and I am extremely grateful for this support. The Joukowsky Family Foundation has most generously underwritten the burdensome expenses of site consolidation, restoration, and preservation. We acknowledge with sincere appreciation Nina Köprülü, President, and Emily Kessler, Executive Director, for their interest and understanding.

We would like to acknowledge the generous assistance of the World Monuments Fund; the Samuel I. Kress Foundation; the American Express Company for Temple conservation; the Halmos Family Foundation; the Julie Chrystie Webster Award; the Manchester Growth Fund, Donald E. Besser, Chairman; Claire J. Henderson, with a matching grant from the CIGNA insurance company; Mr. and Mrs. Wuk Rai Cho; W. Chesley Worthington; Brown University Alumni Awards and Honoraria; and other donors for underwriting these excavations.

Shirley Gordon, Matilde Andrade and Kathy Grimaldi of the Brown University Anthropology Department helped me keep my financial and logistical records straight. I am most grateful to all of them.

In Amman

H.R.H. Prince Faisal, an honored Brown alumnus (class of 1985) and H.E. Prince Ra'ad Bin Zeid, a proud Brown University parent, provided invaluable support—human and material. The assistance of the Seventh Squadron of the Royal Jordanian Air Force has been irreplaceable in the preparation of a total photographic record with aerial photographs. I owe these fine gentlemen a tremendous debt. Further I am indebted to the pilots of the Seventh Squadron who have flown us safely above the site over the years.

The Jordanian Department of Antiquities

These 14 field campaigns would not have been possible without the generous assistance of the Jordanian Department of Antiquities of the Hashemite Kingdom. Most emphatically I record my gratitude to the committed Directors, Safwan Tell, Ghazi Bisheh, and Fawwaz al-Kraysheh, and to Suleiman Farajat, Director of the Petra National Park. All of them exemplify a commitment to archaeology and Petra —a commitment and loyalty that is rarely found. In addition we owe an enormous debt to Suleiman Farajat for his continued interest, logistical acumen and moral support over these many years.

The American Center of Oriental Research

In Amman, the American Center of Oriental Research (ACOR), Pierre M. Bikai, Director, (until 2006) has given limitless support to our project. Every now and again I would hear, "Lady, do you know where you are?" Pierre would be making a surprise visit to the site. And I am deeply grateful to my dearest friend, Dr. Patricia M. Bikai, who was always giving me helpful insights and wise counsel across the large stretches of Great Temple research and life in general. Our gratitude to both the Bikais is heartfelt.

In 2006, Barbara A. Porter assumed the director's position at ACOR. Barbara has continued the tradition of assisting us in every possible way, and we are grateful for her interest and support. All the members of the ACOR staff ably assisted us with logistical advice and negotiated formalities during the excavations. They were always quick to respond to whatever our needs have been. My thanks to Kathy Nimri, Nasreen Shaikh, Carmen Ayoubi, Kurt Zamora, and "our" own Chris Tuttle, Assistant Director of ACOR since 2006. All of them have been instrumental in providing our team with advice and help. Don Keller, Assistant Director of ACOR in Boston, has always been most helpful, for he provided the vital link between Boston and Amman.

In Petra—The Jordanian Department of Antiquities Representatives and the Petra Museum

I wish to thank the Jordanian Department of Antiquities representatives who have watched over us and facilitated our excavations in every possible way. Our representatives have been Mohammad Abd Aziz al-Marahaleh 1995–1998, 2006; Sami Al-Nawfleh 1999–2000, 2004; Hani Fallahat 2001–2002; Dia'eddin A. Tawabeh 2001; Samia Falahat 2005; and Suleiman Farajat 1993–1994, 1996, 2003, 2005–2006. The staff of the Petra Museum, in particular Mohammad Abdul Aziz al-Marahaleh and Samia Falahat, have been invaluable in their assistance in storing our artifacts and in locating them for further study and analysis. Qeis Twessi always made himself available to help us and rendered final drawings of some of the finds presented herein. To them all I express my sincere appreciation and thanks.

Specialist Studies

We have been fortunate to have had team experts in various disciplines: engineering, computer science art and architectural history, classics and classical epigraphy, remote sensing, ground penetrating radar, photography, and physical anthropology. A tremendous debt of gratitude is owed to the following specialists who have devoted their time and energies to the site research over the years. Talal Akasheh and Fawwaz Ishkat of the Hashemite University; Zaki Aslan 1996; Christian Augé, numismatics, 1994 – present; Ulrich Bellwald, fresco restorer, 1999, 2002; David L. Brill, photographer; Adam M. Brin, Petra web page; Donna D'Agostino, 1997–2006, database systems analyst; Boston University's Ricardo J. Elia, site preservation; Jacqueline Dentzer-Feydy, Zbigniew T. Fiema, Rune Frederiksen, theater consultant, 2005–2007; Traianos Gagnos, first readings of temple inscriptions; Yvonne Gerber, ceramic plain wares, 1995; Daniel Herbert 1999; Chrysanthos Kanellopoulos, Judith S. McKenzie 1997; architectural historians; Fatma Marii; Zeidoun Al-Muheisen; Megan A. Perry, physical anthropologist; Margaret O'Hea, glass expert; Thomas R. Paradise, and Rip Rapp, geologists; Stephan G. Schmid 1995, ceramic Nabataean fine wares, 1996; Stephan Simon of the GTZ (German Technical Research Institute); Stephen V. Tracy, epigraphist, 1999; Terry E. Tullis, seismic geologist; and Peter Warnock, botanical materials analysis. Andrew Willis and Pierre-Louis Bazin served as part of our United States National Science Foundation Grant (#BCS-9980091) staff devoted to archaeological applications of digital archaeology. Sarah Whitcher Kansa undertook the faunal analysis, and Naif Zaban was our artifact restorer.

This has been a collaborative effort by archaeologists working together.[13] Visitors to the site are often put to work as volunteers.[14] There have been too many to thank each individually, but they have brought great cheer and many thoughtful impressions to our work.

Particular Acknowledgments

I am indebted to Judith McKenzie for her help and our cogent discussions, and I am grateful for her encouragement to explore different explanations for the Great Temple. The site has posed a number of archaeological challenges that have presented demanding questions. Judith has always been one to critically assess many questions, aesthetically and archaeologically. I have also benefited from many discussions with Elizabeth ("Betsy") Gebhard who recommended that Rune Frederiksen explore the theater. Betsy is a rare and remarkable person, and I am grateful for her wise counsel and devotion to our work.

I have also immeasurably profited from discussions with Marshall C. Agnew who beyond surveying also kept all our information systems up and running. He helped us become a team machine with a myriad of moving parts. If only a few parts had been missing or broken, the team would have come to a halt. This never happened. I also express special gratitude to Eleanor A. Power who labored through my text and made several important corrections. Whatever syntactical errors remain are mine.

My Bedouins

As previously mentioned, our foreman, for the past 12 years of excavation is Dakhilallah Qublan who became my right and left hands during the excavation. I first met Dakhilallah in the 1960s when I visited Petra often and he was living with his family in one of the caves above the site. I refer to Dakhilallah Qublan as 'my brother.' Dakhilallah directed his attention to the challenges both of excavation and reconstruction. He always sought the most appropriate ways in which the expertise of trained personnel could be brought to bear on the numerous challenges that faced us. His was a long-term initiative that began in 1994 and has continued for 12 years. Dakhilallah not only brought a vigilant oversight of all excavations throughout the summer, but undertook all the restoration in the winter as well. Figure 11 is a typical scene of our discussion in the dig tent.

I thank Dakhilallah for his loyalty, care, excitement, devotion to the site and inspiration. Our whole team feels incredibly fortunate to have worked with Dakhilallah, a man of many talents and a brilliant understanding of structural engineering and the idiosyncrasies of the site. Every year Dakhilallah oversaw the site consolidation, conservation and preservation. Our guard, Abu Sha'ar, watched over the site every summer and comforted us with tea during the long days we were in the field.

We are ever grateful to the Al-Budul Bedouin villagers, primarily from Umm Sayhum and Amareen tribes, from Al-Bayda', and from the Liyatna tribe, and the villagers from Wadi Musa for their hard work in the recovery of the Great Temple. Figure 12 shows "Hogan," one of our favorite workmen, playing his *rababa* in celebration of a tea break. In starting the excavations a group of seven unusual boys became

Fig. 11
Dakhilallah Qublan and Martha in the dig tent.

known as the "Shadid team." They developed a reputation for being smart, strong, and willing to handle any complicated task. As the years wore on, the Shadids became older and were indispensable to our work because they set such a high standard for themselves and others. With family stories and time, they all married and continued to be crucial to the excavations. We are grateful to Suleiman Mohammad for leading this band of merry, strong, and stout men. And we are indebted to the people of the Petra region for their many hospitable acts throughout the years, a reflection of the Bedouins' amazing amount of generosity.

Volume II Special Recognition and Appreciation

Having retired from teaching at Brown University in 2004, I had the opportunity to focus on this report. I had written and edited the first five-year Volume I report, published in 1998, but much more material and evidence became available from the succeeding nine years of excavations. Here I incorporate some of the same information, minus some of the infelicities from Volume I, and present a more comprehensive phasing and some of the archaeological demands we faced over the years. It has been a challenge.

The production of this volume has been a collaborative effort. I owe a sincere debt of

Fig. 12
"Hogan" playing his *rababa* at tea time.

Fig. 13
Salaam meaning
"Peace" incised on the
Temenos Gate.

gratitude to Emily Catherine Egan for being instrumental in the collation of ideas for this report in 2003. Eleanor A. Power and Emily Catherine Egan gave the excavation and phasing charts the final shape that can be accessed in *Open Context*. Marshall C. Agnew designed the architectural site drawings, gave them their consistent appearance, and is now working on 3-D drawings of the site features.

In Providence I have relied completely on Jill Evans and David La Croix who have patiently and cheerfully helped me in every imaginary way; I couldn't have devoted my time to writing without them. Dr. Patricia Scola gave the preliminary draft a thorough reading and suggested that I include the glossary of terms and identify major monuments at Petra that are presented in the book. I benefited enormously from the peer review of this volume and appreciate the reviewer's informed opinions, scholarship, enthusiasm and interest. Again, Eleanor A. Power and Nan Sumner-Mack reviewed the final manuscript. My gratitude is to all of these wonderful people for their invaluable help. None of those mentioned above bear any responsibility for errors I may have made in this report.

The text and images that finally took form as a book did so under the careful direction of Joseph Gilbert of Gilbert Design. A special

thanks to book designers: Anne Boerner, Brendalee Peckham-Bell and Maureen Daniels for their patience and attention to detail.

My family have been enthusiastic archaeologists and have visited us every year to undertake arduous tasks and to bring joy into our lives. It is with great pleasure that I look back and reflect on three generations who have been actively engaged in the recovery of the Great Temple: Nina Joukowsky Köprülü has counted more architectural fragments than she ever wanted to, my superb son-in-law Murat, granddaughter Süreya (who became a member of the 2006–2007 teams), and grandson Artemis who celebrates his July birthday with us every year. Artemis W. Joukowsky III and his daughters Lydia, Alexandra and Natasha have cheered us on from the beginning. My astonishing Misha and his wife Jane have measured column drums, and their dear children, Elena Maria and Anthia Grace, have counted *opus sectile* fragments and swept until they could sweep no more! It is they who have had facsimiles of the elephant-headed capitals carved for me with Dakhilallah's astounding skill, so that they could be enjoyed in Providence. From the bottom of my heart, I love and thank them all for putting up with "Mommy Bow Wow," as I am known.

All of our site members played critical roles in the excavations, but finally and most emphatically I wish to acknowledge my dearest friend, my husband Artie, for his continued support of not only this endeavor, but of all those adventuresome journeys we have taken together for 50 years. Artie not only took remarkable photographs, but was always on hand to assist with every knotty situation, making sure I was ready for all eventualities. His photography truly depicts the site as it unfolds and provides the vital link between the site and our understanding of both its chronology and its stratigraphy.

I could never have found the Great Temple without Artie's understanding and patience. This volume is dedicated to him for his enduring patience, invaluable help, and love.

Figure 13 is *Salaam* in Arabic, meaning "Peace," which is a heartfelt wish from all of us who share in the blessings of Petra.

Notes

1.

Petra is located to the east of the Wadi 'Araba at 30°19'N, 35°25'E.

2.

As one of the most spectacular sites in the Middle East, and now celebrated as one of the "Wonders of the World," Petra has long attracted travelers and explorers. A brief history of research and excavations at Petra follows. Ulrich J. Seetzen visited Petra in 1806 but did not understand its significance. In 1812 the Swiss explorer, Johann Ludwig Burckhardt visited the site, and it is to Burckhardt that the credit for its rediscovery is given. The site was visited and documented by several Europeans, including Charles Irby, James Mangles and the artist William John Bankes, in 1818, and the Frenchman Léon de Laborde, in 1828. In 1839, the great British artist David Roberts produced his extraordinary lithographs of the site. British archaeologist Sir Austin Henry Layard, the excavator of Nimrud in Mesopotamia, visited Petra in 1840 and remarked on his disappointment with the ruins. In 1858, the renowned Edward Lear drew the ruins. Another intrepid British traveler, Charles Doughty, who visited Petra in the 1870s, published, *Travels in Arabia Deserta*, in which he referred to Petra as "an eyesore," with the exception of the Al-Khazna ("The Treasury") of which he said: "That most perfect of all monuments whose sculpted columns and cornices are pure lines of crystalline beauty without blemish, whereupon the golden sun looks from above, and Nature has painted that sand-rock ruddy with iron-rust."

In 1896, the Dominican fathers from the École Biblique at the Archéologique Française in Jerusalem published their explorations of Petra. In 1905, W. Libbey and F. E. Hoskins published a synthesis of Petra, presenting one of the earliest overviews in print. Further explorations began in earnest at the turn of the century, with the first scientific expedition being published in *Arabia Petraea* in 1907 by Alois Musil. The orientalist, R. E. Brünnow, and the classicist, A. von Domaszewski, who had surveyed the site in 1897–1898, published an ambitious three-volume mapping project in their *Die Provincia Arabia* (1904–1909). Sponsored by the German Evangelic Institute for Exploration of the Antiquities of the Holy Land in Jerusalem, G. Dalman explored the high places of worship and the necropolis before World War I. Orientalists, including R. Dussaud, A. Jaussen, R. Savingac and M. Dunand, explored evidence that related to Nabataean culture by researching cross cultural links with other sites. German interest in Petra continued with the German Society for Oriental Research sponsoring H. Kohl's exploration of the Qasr al-Bint. During World War I, W. Bachmann, C. Watzinger and T. Wiegand investigated the city structures under the Committee for the Preservation of Monuments of the German-Turkish Army.

In 1929, when Palestine was under the British Mandate, the Department of Antiquities of Palestine undertook the first archaeological excavations at Petra. They investigated the tombs, town dumps (on the Al-Katute ridge), some of the rock-cut houses and the city wall, under the direction of British researchers George Horsfield and Agnes C. Horsfield. Under the auspices of the American School of Oriental Research in Jerusalem, American scholars including William Foxwell Albright researched Petra in 1934. Meanwhile, beginning in 1933, Nelson Glueck surveyed Transjordan. The British School of Archaeology in Egypt sponsored excavations by Margaret Murray and J.C. Ellis, who continued the excavation of more rock-cut houses and tombs. This work was subsequently published by the British School of Archaeology in Egypt.

In the 1950s, modern scientific archaeological research brought British archaeologist Diana Kirkbride to Petra. From 1955–1956, she excavated the Colonnaded Street and a few of the shops bordering it. Peter J. Parr, under the auspices of the British School of Archaeology in Jerusalem, excavated the Temenos Gate and the Colonnaded Street, where he discovered walls of buildings dating from the third century BCE, and he found the first stratified Nabataean pottery sequence. Parr also excavated a domestic structure at Al-Katute, surveyed the town walls, drafted plans of the Baths and instituted damage control of the swollen waters of the Wadi Musa by the construction of revetment walls. Additionally, he instituted a photogrammetric plan of the city and studied the elevations of the tomb façades. In 1958, along with C. M. Bennett of the British School of Archaeology, Parr began an excavation of the city center, which remains the most informative and scientific to date. He later excavated the great Temenos of the Qasr al-Bint; he also excavated the podium and demonstrated that its placement was important evidence in its relationship to the Bench Inscription of Aretas IV found in the Temenos area. The Al-Khazna ("The Treasury"), which had suffered from earthquakes and erosion over the years, was excavated, studied, consolidated and partially restored in 1960 by G. R. H. Wright. In collaboration with Fawzi Zayadine of the Jordanian Department of Antiquities, he undertook the detailed architectural study of the Qasr al-Bint, and Wright also consolidated the Temenos Gate. Mohammad Murshed for the Jordanian Department of Antiquities excavated the entrance to the Baths-Palatial Complex. Also among these pioneers was the American Philip C. Hammond, Director of the American Expedition to Petra, who, under the sponsorship of the Princeton Theological Seminary and the Jordanian Department of Antiquities, excavated the Main Theater from 1962–1963, publishing his findings in 1965. Later in 1971, Hammond began the excavation of the Temple of the Winged Lions and adjoining buildings. These excavations continue today.

The University of Basel's Rolf Stucky has been actively engaged in the Swiss exploration of Petra for some time. Stucky has excavated the Ez Zantur residential structures located to the south overlooking the Great Temple. He has published his findings annually in the *Annual of the Department of Antiquities of Jordan* (ADAJ), and his final report, Petra-Ez Zantur I, covering 1988–1992 campaigns appeared in 1996. This work continues under the able direction of B. Kolb. The Jordanian archaeologist Fawzi Zayadine has excavated and written about several tombs of the Al-Khubtha triclinia in the Siq al-Barid in Al-Bayda' and pottery kilns in Wadi Musa. From 1973, Manfred Lindner of Nuremberg, with the Jordanian Department of Antiquities, has studied various aspects of the ancient city as well as the graves, roads, flora and geology of the nearby Nabataean Petra suburb of Wadi Sabra (as-Sabra), where he discovered extensive copper smelting activities and surveyed the small theater there. Lindner has also surveyed the Ad-Dayr ("The Monastery"). These surveys have since undergone many necessary revisions, the most recent of which was published by Judith S. McKenzie in 1990. McKenzie undertook extensive fieldwork by recording the rock-cut façades and their moldings, and she made a comprehensive survey of tomb plans.

In 1991, the American Center of Oriental Research (ACOR) in Amman undertook the excavations of the Petra Church, under the direction of Kenneth Russell. These excavations have continued under the direction of Pierre M. Bikai and Zbigniew T. Fiema, and a shelter was constructed in 1997 over the area to protect its precious mosaics. In 1992, ACOR began the excavations of the Petra Ridge Church, under the direction of Patricia M. Bikai, and these excavations continue to the present time with the assistance of Megan A. Perry. In 1996, the preliminary investigation of the Colonnaded Street was conducted by Chrysanthos Kanellopoulos, architectural historian, and Zbigniew T. Fiema, archaeologist on behalf of ACOR. In 1997, ACOR conducted the actual fieldwork of the Roman Street in the Petra project. The project, directed in the field by Zbigniew T. Fiema, concentrated on exposing several shops, the Monumental Stairway to the Upper Market and the sidewalk along the street. Following was the partial restoration of the uncovered structures, under the direction of Chrysanthos Kanellopoulos. Now joining these projects are the extensive Brown University, excavations of the Petra Great Temple, which were initiated in 1993 and continued under my direction until the present. It is hoped they will continue in the future. Research at the Small Temple has been undertaken by Sara Karz Reid and the Petra Pool Garden Project has been recovered by Leigh-Ann Bedal whose research continues. Both researchers were spawned by our Great Temple project and their results have been published. Annual publications of these excavations have appeared in various locations (see the Site Bibliography in the introductory material). And now there is a flurry of activity in Petra with Laurent Tholbecq's excavation of the Obodas Chapel, among other important projects taking place in front of the Khazna where earlier tombs have been discovered by Suleiman Farajat. Further a field in Beidha, Patricia M. Bikai leads an exciting exploration of the High Place at Beidha with Chrysanthos Kanellopoulos and Shari Saunders. This Nabataean structure which may be a shrine in the midst of a vineyard or an elegant banqueting villa has produced amazing capitals carved with deity heads (Medusa, Dionysos, Ampelos, Pan, etc.) as bosses.

3.
But I had no idea at that time just how much had to be done; I had no idea how powerfully the excavations would demand my patience, perseverance and determination.

4.
We also excavated a sondage in the west Upper Temenos to ascertain if there were cultural deposits below one

of the lapidaries before we stored large architectural fragments there.

5.
With the excavation of the West Entry Stairway, the grid was enlarged to 91 squares in 2006.

6.
I am most grateful to my colleagues all of whose work have kept Nabataean archaeology in the region alive. I have been privileged in using their work, including T. Akasheh, K. 'Amr, C. Augé, L.-A. Bedal, U. Bellwald, P. Bienkowski, Pierre and Patricia Bikai, J.-M. Dentzer, J. Dentzer-Feydy, S. Farajat, Z. Fiema, J. Frösen, P. Hammond, D. Johnson, C. Kanellopoulos, N. Khairy, B. Kolb, J. Oleson, P. J. Parr, M. Perry, R. Stucky, F. Larché, M. Lindner, J. McKenzie, I. Negev, L. Néhme, F. Villeneuvre, E. Netzer, T. Parker, S. Rababeh, S. Reid, E. L. Schluntz, S. Schmid, L. Tholbecq, R. Wenning, and F. Zayadine.

7.
Other archaeologists who have exchanged their ideas with me include, G. Rollefson, O. La Bianca, T. E. Levy, B. MacDonald, S. Thomas Parker, and J. Seigne.
    We are also grateful to he American Schools of Oriental Research Committee on Archaeological Policy (CAP Committee) for their annual visits to the site and the profitable exchange of ideas we have enjoyed with them. The Great Temple project has been given CAP approval since 1994.

8.
We pay for their travel to Jordan and for their accommodations and food. Each excavation season lasts ten weeks during June, July and August. Team members average about 10–12 persons, and on the 4th of July we play Bedouin softball in

Beidha. Excavation is carried out under shade cloths.
    As mentioned previously, from 1993–2006, every summer, we have worked for a ten-week season. The outbreak of hostilities and unrest in the Middle East in 2003 curtailed our team commitment, and only Shari L. Saunders was able to join us to help supervise the excavation of the Propylaeum East.

9.
In particular I would like to mention with pride the Brown University Petra Doctoral dissertations, Masters and Honors Theses under my supervision.

Schluntz, Erika L.
1999, "From Royal to Public Assembly Space: The Transformation of the "Great Temple" Complex at Petra." Ph.D. Brown University.

Vote, Eileen Louise
"A New Methodology for Archaeological Analysis: Using Visualization and Interaction to Explore Spatial Links in Excavation Data." Ph.D. Brown University.

Karz, Sara G.
1998, "The Change in Color of "Colorless" Glass at the Great Temple, Petra, Jordan." Brown University Department of Anthropology, M.A. Thesis.

Reid, Sara Karz
2004, "The Small Temple: A Roman Imperial Cult Building in Petra, Jordan," Ph.D., Brown University, Department of Anthropology.

Barrett, Deirdre Grace
1996, "How can the ceramic analysis of lamps reveal the fingerprint of Empire on the material culture of the Southern Temple, Petra, Jordan?" M.A. Thesis, Brown University, Department of Anthropology.

———. 2004, "The Ceramic Oil Lamp as an Indicator of Cultural Change Within Nabataean Society in Petra and its Environs Circa CE 106." Ph.D., Brown University, Department of Anthropology.

Bestock, Laurel D.
1999, Nabataean Pottery from the "Cistern:" Some Finds from the Brown University Excavations at the Petra Great Temple, ADAJ Vol. XLII: 241–248.

Cloke, Christian F.
Water in the Desert: The Water Systems of the Petra Great Temple. A Senior Honors Thesis 2003 Series, Brown University, Providence Rhode Island. Wayland Press.

Egan, Emily Catherine
"Putting the Pieces Together: An Analysis and interpretation of the stucco finds recovered from the South Corridor of the Petra Great Temple in Petra, Jordan during the 2001 excavation season." Brown University, Old World Archaeology and Art and Classics, Honors Thesis, 2002.

Payne, Elizabeth E.
"Nabataean Water Systems: An Evaluation of the System at the Southern Temple in Petra, Jordan and a Comparison of the Primary Examples Present throughout the Nabataean World." Brown University, Old World Archaeology and Art, Honors Thesis, 1995.

Mailé, Fabienne
"De la fouille à la modélisation animée 3-D de vestiges de archéologiques: reconstitution du cryptoportique ouest de Grand Temple de Pétra, Jordanie, Vols. I & II." Mémore de DEA, sous la direction de MM. Les Professeurs J.-D. Forest and J.-P. Thalmann avec la participation de Mme. M. Sharp Joukowsky, Université de Paris I—Panthéon-Sorbonne UFR 03, en partenariat avec Brown University, Providence, USA, Division of Engineering/Shape Lab-Lems.

Brin, Adam M.
"The Haffenreffer and Petra: Integrating Computers and Technology into Museums," Brown University, Department of Anthropology Honors Thesis, 1999.

Power, Eleanor A.
"The Roman-Byzantine Bath Complex at the Petra Great Temple in Jordan." Joukowsky Institute of Archaeology and the Ancient World at Brown Unviersity. Senior Honors Thesis, 2007.

10.
Those researchers who publish with Open Context retain the copyright of their material; this means all contributors are free to publish their material with other formats (including journals, books, and other Web sites). Each item in Open Context is licensed with an open, Creative Commons license, giving explicit permissions for users to freely use the material as long as they properly attribute the source. Creative commons licenses include machine-readable metadata that is captured by commercial search engines such as Yahoo and Google (See Kansa, E, 2005, A Community Approach to Data Integration: Authorship and Building Meaningful Links across Diverse Archaeological Data Sets, in Geosphere 1, 2, 97–109, and Kansa, E.C., J. Schultz, and A. Bissell, 2005, Protecting Traditional Knowledge and Expanding Access to Scientific Data, in the International Journal of Cultural Property 12, 3, 97–109.)
    This metadata facilitates discovery of openly licensed content, including Open Context resources. Such openness ensures that the Open Context content is of maximum value for

reuse in both instructional and research applications. Finally, to facilitate scholarly applications, citation information is automatically generated for each item in the database. The stable URLs to each item in *Open Context* facilitate citation and later retrieval. We believe this is a community approach to data integration, because it builds meaningful links across diverse archaeological data sets.

11.
I would like to thank Andries van Dam for his support of this project. Andy used our work in the CAVE as one of the flagship initiatives Brown University was taking in the realm of computer science.

12.
Upon entering the Great Temple virtual site, there is the option to view different layers of information. For example, if a user is not familiar with the site, he/she will probably want to view the terrain with the architecture only, to gain a frame of reference. As the user becomes familiar with the setting, additional layers can be added for a more complex investigation.

To begin to understand data derived from the archaeological excavation, the user can add, for example, a layer that shows the excavation trenches. With the trench layer added, the user will see a visual representation of the dig matrix that was imposed on the site by the archaeologists. The next layer that can be added is the locus formation within each trench. This information will help the user to understand how each trench was excavated and, when artifact data is added, artifact concentrations and special find information. Layers that will

be added at this point will have distinctive delineations that will allow for multiple types of data to be viewed together.

The user will be able to visually differentiate between the layers and data types by recognizing the different physical traits used. For example, a range of pottery concentrations will be shown by semi-transparent color definitions. Dark brown will indicate higher levels of pottery but the user will still be able to see features along with that locus. Additional features will be shown by other visual cues like texture and volume definition. For example, when the user asks to see bone find concentrations they can be shown by textural definition in particular trenches.

Not only does the system allow for simple queries like this but it is also capable of saving significant data defined by the user and a particularly sensitive amount of interactivity. For example, the user can do some preliminary queries and as he/she progresses, work with the system as if it were a physical entity. As relevant finds are located, the user can turn the architecture off, or make it transparent to see across the site. Also, loci and objects can be moved to other parts of the site for a more in-depth investigation. If a sculpture is found in an area of the site's lower precinct, the user can pick it up, call up a tablet that gives all relevant information on the piece and then move with the object to another location of the site for close comparison with other objects. In the foreseeable future, this feature might allow researchers to move "virtually" to other sites around Petra and outside of it for dynamic comparisons of relevant objects.

In summary, with the first implementation of the VR 3-D GIS, the kind of

queries that have been implemented involve requests for layers of information. That is, trench situation, locus situation per trench, pottery distribution across the trenches, special findings (coins, lamps, etc.) distribution, etc. Each query result will have individual physical traits (linear delineation, color, solid or transparent and texture) that can allow the user to distinguish between the various layers and ranges within each layer. Another part of the project's objective is to execute user studies that isolate what visual cues can be understood in the context of the VR environment and refining the system to allow for more advanced queries.

13.
And we celebrate the two marriages between team members and their families.

14.
Visitors (the list is incomplete) include: In 2001 we were honored to receive the visit of our dear friends Her Majesty Queen Noor Al-Hussein of Jordan, and HRH Prince Faisal Al-Hussein. Over the years we continued to receive a visits from His Highness Faisal Al-Hussein as well as volunteers Karen L. Asfour, Jad M. Asfour, and Harry Randolf Brubaker. ACOR Board members have also encouraged our work including Nancy Frederick, Harold Forshey, Widad Kuwar, Randolph B. Old, S. Thomas Parker, H. E. Senator Leila Abdul Hamid Sharaf, Judy Zimmerman, Henry Christensen III, and James Wiseman. Volunteers Betsy F. Alderman, David Barrett, Francesca Bennett, Seth Bright, Michael Cary, Will Carey, Donna D'Agostino, Constance Bumgarner Gee, Ali Jabbri, Elliot Jerud, Nina, Murat and Süreya Köprülü, Jane, Misha, Elena Maria

Joukowsky, Anthia Grace Joukowsky, Arnold Schaab, Forest Reid, Jane Taylor and Robert Zeolla, Thomas Smolenski, David Barrett, and Richard Ballou, We have also enjoyed visits from Elizabeth Gebhard and Matthew Dickie, Father Smith, Bepi Huidekoper, Elizabeth Williams and Joe Forte, Alexander Forte, The Hutchens Family, and Eleanor and Sid Guralnick, the Adlers, Tony and Chan Ittleson, Catherine and John Hanni, Francis and Patricia Scola, Joyce Johnson, Margaret O'Hea, Flo Perkins and Bill Agnew, and a myriad of others who have cheered us along in our work.

PETRA—
SELECT BIBLIOGRAPHY

The abbreviations used in this bibliography, for the most part, follow those used by the *American Journal of Archaeology*, 1991, 95, 4–16. Works cited are those considered to be most helpful. A comprehensive Petra bibliography can be found in L. Nehmé's *Provisional Bibliography on Petra and the Nabataeans* (1994) ERA 20 du CNRS, 3, rue Michelet 75006, Paris. A comprehensive bibliography can also be found in Judith S. McKenzie's *The Architecture of Petra*, 1990, 173–180, and a complete, yet dated, bibliography of Nabataean sites is given in A. Negev, 1983, *Tempel, Kirchen und Zisternen, Ausgrabungen in der Wüste Negev*, Stuttgart, 250–254, as well as in D. Homes-Fredericq and J. B. Hennessy, *Archaeology of Jordan*, Vol. I, 1986, Akkadica, Peeters, Leuven.

Ammianus, Marcellinus. 1963. English translation by J. C. Rolfe. LCL. Harvard Univ. Press, Cambridge, MA. 315.

'Amr, K. 1986. Instrumental Neutron Activation Analysis of Pottery and Clay from the Zurrabah Kiln Complex. *ADAJ* 30, 319–328.

———. 1987. The Pottery from Petra: A Neutron Activation Analysis Study. *BARIS* 324.

———. 1999. The Discovery of Two Additional Pottery Kilns at az-Zurrāba/Wādi Mūsā. *ADAJ* 175–194.

———. 1991. The Petra National Trust Site Projects: Preliminary Report on the 1991 Season at Zurrabah. *ADAJ* 35, 313–323.

Albright, W. F. 1935. The Excavation of the Conway High Place at Petra. *BASOR* 57, 18–26.

Anderson, B. 2003. Nabataean Crenelated Tombs and the Achaemenid Legacy. *ACORN* 15, 2, 7–8.

Arnaud, P. 1986. Naïskoi monoliths du Hauran. In *Hauran I: Recherches archéologiques sur la Syrie du sud à l'époque hellénistique et romaine*, Part 2. Edited by J-M. Dentzer. Geuthner, Paris.

Augé, C. 1990. Sur la figure de Tyché en Nabatène et dans la Province d'Arabie. In *Petra and the Caravan Cities: Proceedings of the Symposium Organized at Petra in September 1985*. Edited by F. Zayadine. Dept. of Antiquities, Amman, 131–146.

———. 1991. Les monnaies antiques de Pétra. *DHA* 163, 46–47.

Augé, C., and J. Dentzer. 2002. New Excavations in the Qasr Al-Bint Area at Petra. *ADAJ* 46, 309–13.

———. 1993. *Petra: Lost City of the Ancient World*. Edited by P. Cardinal. Abrams, New York.

Avi-Yonah, M. 1978. *Hellenism and the East, Contacts and Interrelations from Alexander to the Roman Conquest*. The Hebrew Univ., Jerusalem and Ann Arbor, MI.

———. 1984. *The Jews under Roman and Byzantine Rule: A Political History of Palestine from the Bar Kokhba War to the Arab Conquest*. Magnes Press, The Hebrew Univ., Jerusalem.

Avi-Yonah, M., and A. Negev. 1960. A City of the Negeb: Excavations in Nabataean, Roman and Byzantine Eboda. *ILN* 237, 944–947.

Avner, U. 2001. *The Nabataean Standing Stones and Their Interpretation. Aram* 12, 19–122.

Bachmann, W., C. Watzinger, and T. Wiegand. 1921. *Petra, Wissenschaftliche Veröffentlichungen des Deutsch-Türkischen Denkmalschutz-Kommandos*. Vereinigung Wissenschafftlicher Verleger, Berlin and Leipzig.

Ball, W. 2000. *Rome in the East: The Transformation of an Empire*. Routledge, New York.

Balty, J-C. 1980. Architecture et société à Pétra et Hégra. Chronologie et classes sociales; sculpteurs et commanditaires. In *Collection de l'Ecole Française de Rome*, Rome 66.

———. 1983. *Architecture et société de l'archaïsme grec à la fin de la République romaine*. Centre National de la Recherche Scientifique and Ecole de Rome. Paris and Rome, 303–324.

Note:
The Great Temple bibliography is listed separately after this general Petra bibliography.

Banning, E. B., and I. Köhler-Rollefson. 1986. Ethnoarchaeological Survey in the Beda Area, Southern Jordan. *ZDPV* 102, 152–170, pl. 15B–18.

Barjous, M. 1995. Petra and Wadi Al-Lahyana Map. 1:50,000. *NRA*, Amman.

Barrett, D. G. 2004. "The Ceramic Oil Lamp as an Indicator of Cultural Change Within Nabataean Society in Petra and its Environs Circa CE 106." Ph.D. diss., Department of Anthropology, Brown Univ.

Bartlett, J. 1990. From Edomites to Nabataeans: The Problem of Continuity. *Aram* 2, 25–34.

Bartlett, J. R. 1979. From Edomites to Nabataeans: A Study of Continuity. *PEQ* 111, 53–66.

Bedal, L.-A. 1999. A Paradeisos in Petra: New Light on the "Lower Market." *ADAJ* 43, 227–239.

———. 2001. A Pool Complex in Petra's City Center. *BASOR* 324, 23–41.

———. 2002. The Petra Garden Feasibility Study, 2001. *ADAJ* 46: 381–389.

———. 2003. *The Petra Pool Complex: A Hellenistic Paradeisos in the Nabataean Capital* (Results from the Petra Lower Market Survey and Excavations, 1998), Gorgias Press, Piscataway, NJ.

Bellwald, U. 2003. *The Petra Siq. Nabataean Hydrology Uncovered.* Petra National Trust, Amman.

Bennett, C-M. 1962. The Nabataeans in Petra. *Archaeology* 15, 233–243.

———. 1964. Umm el-Biyara-Pétra. Chronique archéologique. *RB* 71, 250–253.

———. 1965. Tombs of the Roman Period. In K. M. Kenyon, *Excavations at Jericho, Vol. II. BSA* 516–545.

———. 1966a Des fouilles à Umm el-Biyarah: les Edomites à Pétra. *BTS* 84, 6–16.

———. 1966b. Fouilles d'Umm el-Biyara. Rapport préliminaire. *RB* 73, 372–403, pl.14–25.

———. 1983. Petra. *AI* 26, 3–38.

Bennett, C-M. and P. J. Parr. 1962. Soundings from Umm el-Biyara, Petra. *Archaeology* 15, 277–279.

Besancon, A. 2000. *The Forbidden Image.* Univ. of Chicago Press, Chicago.

Bessac, J-Cl. and L. Nehmé. 2001. Un pic de creusement du grés d'époque Nabatéenne à Pétra. *Syria* 78, 83–88.

Bienkowski, P. 1990. Umm el-Biyara, Tawilan and Buseirah in Retrospect. *Levant* 22, 91–109.

———. 1990a. Edom and the Edomites. Review Article. *PEQ* 22, 139–142.

———. 1995. The Architecture of Edom. *SHAJ* 5, 135–143.

———. 2001. The Persian Period. In *Levantine Archaeology I. The Archaeology of Jordan*, Edited by B. MacDonald, R. Adams, and P. Bienkowski. Sheffield Academic Press, Sheffield. 347–366.

———. 2002. Busayra Excavations by C-M. Bennett 1971–1980. *British Academy Monographs in Archaeology* No. 13, Oxford Univ. Press, Oxford.

Bignasca, A., N. Desse-Berset, R. Fellmann Brogli, R. Glutz, S. Karg, D. Keller, B. Kolb, Ch. Kramar, M. Peter, S. G. Schmid, Ch. Schneider, R. A. Stucky, J. Studer, and I. Zanoni. *Petra Ez Zantur I: Ergebnisse der Schweizerisch-Liechtensteinischen Ausgrabungen 1988–1992*, by *Terra Archaeologica* 2. Von Zabern, Mainz.

Bikai, P. 2002. North Ridge Project. *ACORN*, Vol. 14, 1–4.

Bikai, P. M. and M.A. Perry. 2001. Petra North Ridge Tombs 1 and 2: Preliminary Report. *BASOR* 324, 59–78.

Bikai, P. M., C. Kanellopoulos, and S. L. Saunders. 2005a. Bayda Documentation Project. *ADAJ* 49, 339–344.

———. 2005b. The High Place at Beidha. *ACORN* 17.2, 1–3.

Blagg, T. 1990. Column Capitals with Elephant-Head Volutes at Petra. *Levant* 22, 131–137.

Blagg, T., and M. Lyttelton. 1990. Sculpture in Nabataean Petra, and the Question of Roman Influence. In *Architecture and Architectural Sculpture in the Roman Empire*. Edited by M. Henig. Oxford Univ., Committee for Archaeology 29, 91–107.

Boardman, J. et al. 1967. *The Art and Architecture of Ancient Greece.* Thames & Hudson, London.

———. 2000. *Persia and the West. An Archaeological Investigation of the Genesis of Achaemenid Art.* Thames and Hudson, London.

Bowersock, G.W. 1971. A Report on Arabia Provincia. *JRS* 61, 219–242.

———. 1975. Old and New in the History of Judaea. *JRS* 65, 180–195.

———. 1982. Review of A. Spijkerman, *The Coins of the Decapolis and Provincia Arabia*. *JRS* 72, 197–198.

———. 1983. *Roman Arabia.* Harvard Univ. Press, Cambridge, MA.

———. 1986. An Arabian Trinity. *HTR* 79:17–21, 465.

———. 1990a. The Cult and Representation of Dusares in Roman Arabia. In *LIMC*, Edited by F. Zayadine, 31–36.

———. 1990b. Edward Lear in Petra. *PAPS* 4, 309–320.

———. 1991. The Babatha Papyri, Masada and Rome, *JRA* 4, 336–344.

———. 2001. Note, p. 349. In *The Petra Church*, by Z. T. Fiema, C. Kanellopoulos, T. Waliszewski, and R. Schick, ACOR Publications 3, Amman.

———. 2003. The Nabataeans in Historical Context. In *Petra Rediscovered: Lost City of the Nabataeans*. Edited by G. Markoe. *Abrams*, New York. 19–25.

Bowsher, J. 1986. The Frontier Post of Medain Saleh. In *The Defense of the Roman and Byzantine East*. Edited by P. Freeman and D. Kennedy. *BAR* 297, 23–29.

Broneer, O. 1930. *Corinth, Results of Excavations conducted by the American School of Classical Studies at Athens. Terracotta Lamps*, Vol. IV, Part II, Harvard Univ. Press, published for the American School of Classical Studies at Athens, Cambridge, MA.

Browning, I. 1982. *Petra.* Chatto and Windus, London.

Broshi, M. 1992. Agriculture and Economy in Roman Palestine: Seven Notes on the Babatha Archive. *IEJ* 42, 230–240.

Brünnow, R. E., A. von Domaszewski and J. Enting et al. 1904. *Die Provincia Arabia.* (3 vols.). K. J. Trübner, Strasburg. (A detailed list of pre-1904 publications of visitors to Petra.) 481–510.

Burdon, D. J. 1959. *Handbook of the Geology of Jordan* (To Accompany and Explain the Three Sheets of the 1:250,000 Geological Map of Jordan East of the Rift by Albert Quennell.) Government of the Hashemite Kingdom of Jordan, Amman.

Burckhardt, J. 1822. *Travels in Syria and the Holy Land.* John Murray, London.

Cantineau, J. 1932a. *Le Nabatéen. I. Notions générales. écriture, grammaire.* Leroux, Paris.

———. 1932b. *Le Nabatéen. II. Choix de textes, lexique.* Leroux, Paris.

Casson, L. 1980. *Periplus Maris Erythraei*: Three Notes on the Text. *CQ* 30, 495–497.

———. 1989. English transl. and edited *Periplus Maris Erythraei.* Princeton Univ. Press, Princeton, NJ.

Charlesworth, M. P. 1974. *Trade-Routes and Commerce of the Roman Empire*, 2nd ed. Ares Publishers, Chicago.

Clermont-Ganneau, C. 1898a. La statue du dieu Obodas, roi de Nabatène. *Recueil d'archéologie orientale* 2. Paris.

———. 1898b. La statue du roi Rabel I à Pétra. *Recueil d'archéologie orientale* 2. Leroux, Paris.

Cohen R. 1982. New Light on the Date of the Petra-Gaza Road. *BA* 45/4, 240–247.

———. 1993. Negev: The Persian to Byzantine Periods. In *The New Encyclopedia of Archaeological Excavations in the Holy Land.* Israel Exploration Society, Jerusalem 3, 1133–1145.

Cohen, S. 1962. Nabataeans. *In The Interpreter's Dictionary of the Bible. An Illustrated Encyclopedia.* Edited by G. A. Buttrick. Abingdon Press, New York.

Comer, D. C. 1997. *Enhancing the Utility of SIR-C Radar Imagery in the Analysis and Monitoring of Archaeological Sites by Georeferencing with Larger Scale Imagery: A Test Project at Petra, Jordan.* National Park Service, Denver Service Center, RPG, Applied Archeology Center, Progress Report.

Conway, A. E. 1930. Exploring a City of Mystery. The First Excavations at Petra: Discoveries in the Remains of the "Built" City, and a New Explanation of the Rock-Cut "Sanctuaries." *ILN* 1 February, 160–161.

Conway, A., and G. Horsfield. 1930. Historical and Topographical Notes on Edom: With an Account of the First Excavations at Petra. *The Geographical Journal* 76, 369–390.

Corbeil, M-C. and K. Helwig. 1999. Analysis of Fresco Fragments from the Petra Great Temple. Analytical Research Laboratory (ARL) Report 3779, March 19, 1999. *Institut Canadien de Conservation*, Ottawa.

Cotton, H. M. 1993. The Guardianship of Jesus Son of Babatha: Roman and Local Law in the Province of Arabia. *JRS* 83, 94–108.

Coulton, J. 1976. *The Architectural Development of the Greek Stoa.* Clarendon Press, Oxford.

———. 1977. *Ancient Greek Architects at Work.* Oxbow Books, Oxford.

Dalley, S. and A. Goguel. 1997. The Sela' Sculpture: A New-Babylonian Rock Relief in Southern Jordan. *ADAJ* 41, 169–177.

Dalman, G. 1908. *Petra und Seine Felsheiligtümer*, J.C. Hinrichs, Leipzig.

———. 1911. The Khazneh at Petra. *PEF* 1911, 95–107.

———. 1912. *Neue Petra Forschungen und der heilige Felsen von Jerusalem.* Hinrichs, Leipsig.

Dentzer, J-M. 1979. À propos du temple dit de "Dusarès à Sî." *Syria* 56, 325–332.

———. 1984. Sondages près de l'Arc nabatéen à Bosrà. *Berytus* 32, 163–174.

———. 1985. Six campagnes de fouilles à Sî: Développement et culture indigène en Syrie méridionale. *DM* 2, 65–83.

————. 1986. Les sondages de l'Arc nabatéen et l'urbanisme de Bosrà. *CRAI*, 62–87.

————. 2003. The Nabataeans at Bosra and in Southern Syria. In In *Petra Rediscovered: Lost City of the Nabataeans*. Edited by G. Markoe. 109–11.

Dentzer, J-M., and J. Dentzer. 1981. Les fouilles de Sî et la phase hellénistique en Syrie du sud. *AAS* 32, 177–190.

Dentzer, J-M., P. Gentelle, and M. Gory. 1989. Petra: prospections. In *Contribution française a l'archéologie jordanienne*. Edited by F. Villeneuve, I.F.A.P.O, Amman.

Dentzer, J-M. et al. 1982a. Fouille de la porte monumentale à 'Iraq al-Amir la campagne de 1978. *ADAJ* 26, 301–321.

Dentzer, J-M. et al. 1982b. 'Iraq el Amir: Excavations at the Monumental Gateway. *SHAJ* 1, 201–207.

Dentzer-Feydy, J. 1985–1986. Décor architectural et développement du Hauran du Ier s. av. J-C. au VIIe s. ap. J.-C. In *Hauran I*. Edited by J-M. Dentzer. Paris, 261–310.

————. 1990. Khirbet Edh-Dharih: Architectural Decoration of the Temple. *Aram* 2, 161–81.

————. 1995. Remarques sur la métrologie et le projet architectural de quelques monuments d'époque hellénistique et romaine en Transjordanie. *SHAJ* 5, 161–173.

De Vries, B. 1982. *Umm el-Jimal. A Tour Guide.* Department of Antiquities, Amman.

————. 1992. Archaeology in Jordan. *AJA* 96, 503–542.

De Vries, B. and P. Bikai. 1993. Archaeology in Jordan. *AJA* 97, 457–520.

Dinsmoor, W. 1975. *The Architecture of Ancient Greece.* W. W. Norton, New York.

Dio Cassius. 1961–1984 *Dio's Roman History*, LXVIII LCL. English transl. E. Cary. Harvard Univ. Press, Cambridge, MA.

Dunand, M. 1934. *Mission archéologique au Djebel Druze. Le Musée de Soueïda: Inscriptions et monuments figurés. Bibliothèque archéologique et historique 20.* Geuthner, Paris.

Dussaud, R. 1904. Numismatique des rois de Nabatène. *JA* 3, 189–238.

————. 1955. *La penetration des Arabes en Syrie avant l'Islam.* Geuthner, Paris.

Eadie, J. W., and J. P. Oleson. 1986. The Water-Supply Systems of Nabataean and Roman Humayma. *BASOR* 262, 49–76.

Eddinger, T. 2004. A Nabataean/Roman Temple at Dhat Ras, Jordan. *NEA* 67, 1, 14–25.

Egan, E. C. 2002. Stucco Decoration from the South Corridor of the Petra Great Temple: Discussion and Interpretation. *ADAJ*, Jum'a Kareem Memorial Vol. 46, 347–361.

El-Khouri, L. S. 2002. *The Nabataean Terracotta Figurines.* BARIS 1034, Oxford.

Erickson-Gini, T. 2002. Nabataean or Roman? Reconsidering the Date of the Camp at Avdat in Light of Recent Excavations. Edited by P. Freeman et al. In *Limes III XVIII. Proceedings of the XVIIIth International Congress of Roman Frontier Studies held in Amman, Jordan. BARIS* 1084, 113–130. Oxford.

Farajat, S. 1991. The Nabataean Hydraulic System in the area of Humeima. *ADAJ* 35, 17–30 (Arabic Section).

————. 1991. *The Geological Map of Petra.* Natural Resources Authority, Amman.

————. 1994. The Role of the Nabataean Hydraulic System in the Protection of the Monuments at Petra. In *Siti e monumente della Giordania*, 25–32.

Farajat, S. and S. Al-Nawafleh. 2005. Report on the al-Khazna Courtyard Excavation at Petra (2003 Season). *ADAJ* 49, 373–393.

Fauth, W. 1975. Baitylia. In *Der Kleine Pauly*, Vol. I. Cols. 806–808, Artemis, Munich.

Fiema, Z. T. 1990. The Nabataean King-List Revised: Further Observations on the Second Nabataean Inscription from Tell Esh-Shuqafiya, Egypt. *ADAJ* 34, 239–248.

————. 1993. The Petra Project. *ACORN* 5, 1–3.

————. 1994. Une èglise byzantine à Pétra. *Archéologia* 302, 26–35.

————. 1998. The Roman Street of the Petra Project, 1997: A Preliminary Report. *ADAJ* 42, 395–425.

Fiema, Z.T., C. Kannellopoulos, T. Waliszwski and R. Schick. 2001. *The Petra Church.* Edited by P. M. Bikai. ACOR, Amman.

Fischer, M. 1988. Marble Imports and Local Stone in the Architectural Decoration of Roman Palestine: Marble Trade, Techniques and Artistical Taste. Edited by N. Herz and M. Waelkens, In *Classical Marble: Geochemistry, Technology, Trade.* NATO ASI Series 153, Kluwer, Dordrecht. 161–70.

Foerster, G. 1995. Masada V. *The Yageal Yadin Excavations 1963–1965. Final Report: Art and Architecture.* Edited by J. Aviram, G. Foerster and E. Netzer. The Hebrew Univ. of Jerusalem, Jerusalem.

Freeman, P. 1996. The Annexation of Arabia and imperial Grand Strategy. In *The Roman Army in the East*. Edited by D. L. Kennedy. *JRA* Supplement no 18, 91–118.

Freyberger, K. S. 1997. *Blattranken, Greifen und Elefanten in Petra: Antike Felsstadt zwischen arabischer Tradition und griechischer Norm.* Edited by T. Weber and R. Wenning. Von Zabern, Mainz.

Frösén, J., and Z. Fiema. 2002. *Petra: A City Forgotten and Rediscovered.* A volume associated with the exhibition organized by the Amos Anderson Art Museum in Helsinki, Finland. Helsinki Univ. Press, Helsinki.

Gerber, Y., and R. F. Brogli. 1995. The Late Roman Pottery from Ez Zantur, Petra. *SHAJ* V, 649–655.

Glueck, N. 1933–1934. Explorations in Eastern Palestine I. *AASOR* 14, 1–113.

———. 1934–1935. Explorations in Eastern Palestine II. *AASOR* 15, 1–202.

———. 1937b. The Nabataean Temple of Khirbet et-Tannûr. *BASOR* 67, 6–16.

———. 1937–1939 Explorations in Eastern Palestine III. *BASOR* 18–19, 1–288.

———. 1939. The Nabataean Temple of Qasr Rabbah. *AJA* 43, 381–387.

———. 1942. Nabataean Syria. *BASOR* 85, 3–8.

———. 1956. A Nabataean Painting. *BASOR* 141, 13–23.

———. 1959. *Rivers in the Desert: A History of the Negev.* Farrar, Straus and Cudahy, New York.

———. 1965. *Deities and Dolphins: The Story of the Nabataeans.* Farrar, Straus and Giroux, New York.

———. 1993. Tannur, Khirbet et-. In *The New Encyclopedia of Archaeological Excavations in the Holy Land.* Edited by E. Stern. Oxford Univ. Press. Vol. 4, 1441–1446.

Goodman, M. 1991. Babatha's Story. *JRS* 81, 169–175.

Graf, D. F. 1990. The Origin of the Nabataeans. *Aram* 2, 45–75.

———. 1992. Nabataeans. In *Anchor Bible Dictionary.* Edited by D. N. Freedman et al. Vol. 4, 970–973.

———. 1995. The Via Nova Traiana in Arabia Petraea. In The Roman and Byzantine Near East: Some Recent Archaeological Research. Edited by J. H. Humphrey. *JRA*, Supplementary Series. Ann Arbor, MI.

Graf, D., and S. Sidebotham. 2003. Nabataean Trade. In *Petra Rediscovered: Lost City of the Nabataeans.* Edited by G. Markoe, 65–75.

Graf, D. F., L-A. Bedal and S. G. Schmid. 2005. The Hellenistic Petra Project: Excavations in the Civic Center, Preliminary Report of the First Season, 2004. *ADAJ* 49, 417–441.

Greenfield, J. C. 1993. "Because He/She Did Not Know Letters": Remarks on a First Millennium C.E. Legal Expression. *JANES* 22, 39–43.

Greene, K. 1986. *The Archaeology of the Roman Economy.* Univ. of California Press, Berkeley, CA.

Gunneweg, J., I. Perlman, and F. Asaro. 1988. The Origin, Classification and Chronology of Nabataean Painted Fine Ware, *JRGZM* 35, No. 1–2, Mainz, 315–345.

Hadidi, A. 1980. Nabatäische Architektur in Petra. *BJ* 180, 231–236. (See also his 1982, 1985 and 1987 reports in *SHAJ*.)

Hammond, N. G. L. and H. H. Scullard. 1970. *The Oxford Classical Dictionary*, 2. Oxford Univ. Press, Oxford.

Hammond, P. C. 1960. Excavations at Petra in 1959. *BASOR* 159, 26–31.

———. 1965. *The Excavation of the Main Theater at Petra, 1961–1962.* Colt Archaeologica Institute Publications, Bernard Quaritch, London.

———. 1967. Desert Waterworks of the Ancient Nabataeans. *Natural History* 7, 36–43.

———. 1968. The Medallion and Block Relief at Petra. *BASOR* 192, 16–21.

———. 1973. The Nabataeans—Their History, Culture and Archaeology. *SIMA* 37.

———. 1975. Survey and Excavation at Petra, 1973–1974. *ADAJ* 20, 5–30.

———. 1977. The Capitals from the "Temple of the Winged Lions," Petra. *BASOR* 226, 47–51.

———. 1977–1978. Excavations at Petra 1975–1977. *ADAJ* 22, 81–101.

———. 1980. New Evidence for the 4th-Century A.D. Destruction at Petra. *BASOR* 238, 65–67.

———. 1996. *The Temple of the Winged Lions, Petra, Jordan, 1974–1990.* Petra Publishing, Norman, AR.

———. 1987. Three Workshops at Petra (Jordan). *PEQ* 129–41.

———. 1995. Nabataean Architectural Technology. *SHAJ* 5, 215–21.

———. 2000. Nabatean Metallurgy: Foundry and Fraud. *The Archaeology of Jordan and Beyond: Essays in Honor of James A. Sauer.* Edited by L. Stager et al. Eisenbrauns, Winona Lake, IN.

Hammond, P., and D. Johnson. 1994. American Expedition to Petra: The 1990–1993 Season. *ADAJ* 38, 333–345.

Hanson, J. 1959. *Roman Theater-Temples*. Princeton Univ. Press, Princeton, NJ.

Hayes, J. W. 1972. *Late Roman Pottery*. British School at Rome, London.

———. 1980. *A Supplement to Late Roman Pottery*. British School at Rome, London.

———. 1985. Sigillate orientali, Atlante delle forme ceramiche II. *Enciclopedia dell'arte antica*, 1ff.

———. 1997. *Handbook of Mediterranean Roman Pottery*. British Museum.

Healey, J. F. 1989. Were the Nabataeans Arabs? *Aram* 1, 38–44.

———. 2001. *The Religion of the Nabataeans: A Conspectus*. Brill, Leiden.

Healey, J. F. and A. R. al-Theeb. 1993. *The Nabataean Tomb Inscriptions of Mada'in Salih*. Journal of Semitic Studies Supplement, no. 1. Oxford Univ. Oxford.

Hendrix, R. E., P. R. Drey, and J. B. Storfjell. 1996. *Ancient Pottery of Transjordan: An Introduction Utilizing Published Whole Forms, Late Neolithic through Late Islamic*. Institute of Archaeology, Horn Archaeological Museum, Andrews Univ., MI.

Herz, N., and M. Waelkens, eds. 1988. *Classical Marble: Geochemistry, Technology, Trade*. NATO ASI Series 153, Kluwer, Dordrecht.

Horsfield, G., and A. Horsfield. 1938. Sela-Petra, The Rock of Edom and Nabatene I & II. *QDAP* 7, 1–60.

———. 1938–1939. Sela-Petra, The Rock of Edom and Nabatene III: The Excavations. *QDAP* 8, 87–116.

———. 1939–1942. Sela-Petra, The Rock of Edom and Nabatene IV: The Finds. *QDAP* 9, 105–204.

Ilan, T. 1992. Julia Crispina, Daughter of Berenicianus, A Herodian Princess in the Babatha Archive: A Case Study in Historical Identification. *JQR* 82, 3–4, 261–281.

———. 1993. Premarital Cohabitation in Ancient Judea: The Evidence of the Babatha Archive and the Mishnah (*Ketubbot* 1.4). *HTR* 86.3, 247–264.

Iliffe, J. H. 1934. Nabataean Pottery from the Negev: Its Distribution in Palestine. *QDAP* 3, 132–135.

———. 1938. Sigillata Wares in the Near East: A List of Potters' Stamps. *QDAP* 5, 4–53.

Isaac, B. 1992. The Babatha Archive: A Review Article. *IEJ* 42, 62–75.

Jaser, D. and Bargous, M. 1991. Petra Map. 1:5000. *National Resources Authority*, Amman.

———. 1992. *Geotechnical Studies and Geological Mapping of Ancient Petra City. National Resources Authority*, Amman.

Jaussen, A. J., and R. Savignac. 1909–1914. *Mission archéologique en Arabie*, Vols. 1 and 2. Geuthner, Paris.

Johnson, D. J. 1987. "Nabataean Trade: Intensification and Culture Change." Ph.D. diss., Univ. of Utah.

Johnson, D. J., J. Janetski, M. Chazan, S. Witcher and R. Meadow. 1999. Preliminary Report on Brigham Young Univ.'s First Season of Excavation and Survey at Wadi al-Mataha, Petra. *ADAJ* 43, 249–260.

Jones, M. W. 1989. Designing the Roman Corinthian Order. *JRA* 2, 35–69.

Jones, R. N. 2001. Nabataean Inscriptions. In *The Petra Church*, by Z. T. Fiema et al. Edited by Patricia M. Bikai. *ACOR* Publications 3, Amman, 346–349.

Josephus. 1965. *Jewish Antiquities*. Translated by L.H. Feldman, Heinemann, LCL. London.

———. 1969. *Jewish Wars*. Translated by G.A. Williamson, Harmondsworth, Penguin. London.

Joukowsky, M. S. 1980. *A Complete Manual of Field Archaeology*. Prentice-Hall, Englewood Cliffs, NJ.

———. 1998. *Petra: The Great Temple, Vol. I—Brown Univ. Excavations 1993–1997*. Brown Univ., Petra Exploration Fund, Providence, RI. (See the Great Temple Site Bibliography for a complete listing)

Kanellopoulos, C. 1993. *The Great Temple of Amman: The Architecture*. ACOR. Amman. (See also articles by P. Warnock and M. Pendleton in Appendix B.)

———. 1999. The Colonnaded Street and Shops in Petra. *AJA* 103, 507–509.

———. 2001. The Architecture of Shops and Colonnaded Street in Petra. *BASOR* 324, 9–22.

———. 2002. The Monumental Entrance to the Upper Market and the Trajanic Inscription at Petra, the Architectural Context. *ADAJ* 46, 295–308.

Kanellopoulos, C., and T. S. Akasheh. 2001. The Petra Map. *BASOR* 324, 5–7.

Katzoff, R. 1991. Papyrus Yadin 18 Again: A Rejoinder. *JQR* LXXXII.1–2, 171–176.

Kennedy, Sir A. B. W. 1925. Petra, Its History and Monuments. *Country Life*, London.

Khairy, N. I. 1975. "A Typological Study of the Unpainted Pottery from the Petra Excavations." Diss., Univ. College, London.

———. 1982. Fine Nabataean Ware with Impressed and Rouletted Decorations. *SHAJ* I, 275–283.

———. 1984. Preliminary Report of the 1981 Petra Excavations. *ADAJ* 28, 315–320.

———. 1987. The Painted Nabataean Pottery from the 1981 Petra Excavations. *Levant* 19, 167–181.

———. 1990. *The 1981 Petra Excavations*, I. Harrassowitz, Wiesbaden.

Kirkbride, D. 1960a. A Short Account of the Excavations at Petra in 1955–1956. *ADAJ* 4–5, 117–122.

———. 1960b. Le temple nabatéen de Ramm. Son évolution architecturale. *RB* 67, 65–92, pl. 3–9.

———. 1960c. The Excavation of a Neolithic Village at Seyl Aqlat, Beidha, near Petra. *PEQ* 92, 136–145, pl. 25–30.

———. 1961. Ten Thousand Years of Man's Activity Around Petra: Unknown and Little-known Sites Excavated or Explored. *ILN* 239, 448–451.

———. 1964. Seyl Aqlat, Beidha, près de Pétra. Chronique archéologique. *RB* 71, 246–250.

———. 1968. Beidha: Early Neolithic Village Life South of the Dead Sea. *Antiquity* 42, 263–274, pl. 37.

———. 1984. Beidha 1983: An Interim Report. *ADAJ* 28, 9–12, pl. 1.

———. 1985. The Environment of the Petra Region during the Pre-Pottery Neolithic. Edited by A. Hadidi, *SHAJ* II, 117–124.

Kloner, A. 2001–2002. Water Cisterns in Idumea, Judea and Nabatea in the Hellenistic and Early Roman Periods. *Aram*, 13–14, 461–85.

———. 2003a. Survey of Jerusalem. The Northwestern Sector Introduction and Indices. *Israel Antiquities Authority*, Jerusalem.

———. 2003b. Maresha Excavations: Final Report I. Subterranean Complexes 21, 44, 70. *The Israel Antiquities Authority* Reports, 17, Jerusalem.

Knauf, E. A. 1986. Die Herkunft der Nabatäer. In *Petra. Neue Ausgrabungen und Entdeckungen*. Edited by M. Lindner. Delp, Munich. 74–86.

———. 1989. Nabataean Origins. In *Arabian Studies in Honour of Mahmoud Ghul*. Edited by M. Ibrahim. Harrassowitz, Wiesbaden, 56–6.

Kolb, B. 1995. "Die spätantiken Wohnbauten von az-Zantur in Petra und der Wohnhausbau in Palästina vom 4.–6. Jh. N. Chr." Ph.D. diss., Univ. of Basel.

———. 1996. Die spätrömischen Bautennn In *Petra—Ez Zantur I: Ergebnisse der Schweizerisch-Liechtensteinischen Ausgrabungen 1988–1992*. Edited by A. Bignasca et. al., Von Zabern, Mainz, 47–89.

Kolb, B. *et al.* 1997. Swiss-Liechtenstein Excavations at az-Zantur in Petra 1996: The Seventh Season. *ADAJ* 41: 231–254.

Kolb, B., D. Keller and Y. Gerber. 1998. Swiss-Liechtenstein Excavations at az-Zantur/Petra, 1997. *ADAJ* 42, 259–277.

Kolb, B., D. Keller and Y. Gerber. 2000. Swiss-Liechtenstein Excavations at az-Zantur/Petra: The Tenth Campaign. *ADAJ* 44, 355–372.

Kolb, B., L. Gorgerat and M. Grawehr. 1999. Preliminary Report of the Swiss-Liechtenstein Excavations at ez-Zantur in Petra 1998. *ADAJ* 43, 261–278.

———. 2002. Swiss-Liechtenstein Excavations at az-Zantur/Petra: The Twelfth Season. *ADAJ* 46, 279–294.

———. 2003. Petra—From Tent to Mansion Living on the Terraces of Ez-Zantur. In *Petra Rediscovered: Lost City of the Nabataeans*. Edited by G. Markoe, 230–239.

Kolb, B. and R. A. Stucky. 1993. Preliminary Report of the Swiss-Liechtenstein Excavations at ez-Zantur in Petra 1992. The Fourth Campaign. *ADAJ* 37, 417–423, 425, pl. 1.

Kraeling, C. H. 1941. The Nabataean Sanctuary at Gerasa. *BASOR* 83, 7–14.

Kühlenthal, M., and H. Fisher. 2000. *Petra. The Restoration of the Rockcut Tomb Facade: German-Jordanian Project for the Establishment of a Conservation Center in Petra*. Karl M. Lipp, Munich.

Laborde, L. de. 1836. *Journey through Arabia Petraea to Mount Sinai and the Excavated City of Petra, the Edom and the Prophecies*. (Trans. of *Voyage de l'Arabie Pétrée*) Murray, London.

Lapp, N. L. 1979. The Hellenistic Pottery from the 1961 and 1962 Excavations at 'Iraq el-Emir. *ADAJ* 23, 5–15.

Lapp, P. W. 1961. *Palestinian Ceramic Chronology 200 B.C.–A.D. 70*. ASOR Publications of the Jerusalem School, *Archaeology*, Vol. III.

———. 1976. Iraq el-Emir. In *Encyclopedia of Archaeological Excavations in the Holy Land*, II. Edited by E. Stern and M. Avi-Yonah. Prentice-Hall, Englewood Cliffs NJ. 527–531.

Larché, F. and F. Zayadine. 2003. The Qasr al-Bint of Petra. In *Petra Rediscovered: Lost City of the Nabataeans*. Edited by G. Markoe. 199–213.

Lawlor, J. 1974. *The Nabataeans in Historical Perspective*. Baker Studies in Biblical Archaeology, Baker Book House, Grand Rapids, MI.

Lewis, N., Editor. 1989. *The Documents From the Bar Kokhba Period in the Cave of Letters: Greek Papyri. In Judean Desert Studies* 2. Israel Exploration Society, The Hebrew Univ., Shrine of the Book, Jerusalem.

Libbey, W., and F. E. Hoskins. 1905. *The Jordan Valley and Petra*. G. P. Putnam, New York and London.

Lindner, M., Editor. 1980. Deutsche Ausgrabungen in Petra. *BJ* 180, 125–136.

———. 1982a. Über die Wasserversorgung einer antiken Stadt. *Das Altertum* 28, 1, 27–39.

———. 1982b. An Archaeological Survey of the Theater Mount and Catchwater Regulation System at Sabra, South of Petra, 1980. *ADAJ* 26, 231–242.

———. 1982c. Eine Grabung in Sabra (Jordanien). *NM* 1982, 67–73.

———. 1984. Archäologische Erkundungen des Der-Plateaus oberhalb von Petra (Jordanien), 1982 und 1983. *AA* 1984, 597–625.

———. 1985. *Petra, Der Führer durch die antike Stat; Petra: The Guide Through the Antique City.* Grafische Werk Stätte Graf, Fürth.

———, Editor. 1986. *Petra Neue Ausgrabungen und Entdeckungen.* Delp, Munich.

———. 1988. Eine al-'Uzza-Isis-Stele und andere neu aufgefundene Zeugnisse der al-'Uzza-Verehrung in Petra (Jordanien). *Zeitschrift des Deutschen Palästina-Vereins* 104, 84–91.

———. 1989. Es-Sela: Eine antike Fliehburg 50 km nördlich von Petra. In *Petra und das Königreich der Nabatäer*, 5TH. ed. Naturhistorische Gesellschaft, Delp, Munich.

———. 1997. Cult and Passage: The Eagle Niche Area of Petra (Jordan). *Jahrbuch des Deutschen Evangelischen Instituts für Altertumswissenschaft des Heiligen Landes* 5, 98–115.

Lindner, M., and E. Gunsam. 2002. A Fortified Suburb of Ancient Petra: Shamm⁻asa. *ADAJ* 46, 225–42.

Lindner, M., and J. Zangenberg. 1993. The Re-discovered Baityl of the Goddess Atargatis in the Siyyag Gorge of Petra (Jordan) and Its Significance for Religious Life in Nabataea. *Zeitschrift des Deutschen Palästina-Vereins* 109, 141–151.

Ling, R. 1984. Hellenistic Civilization. In *CAH*, Vol. VII, Part II, *The Hellenistic World.* Edited by F. W. Walbank et al. Cambridge Univ. Press, Cambridge, 91–207.

———. 1998. *Roman Painting.* Cambridge Univ. Press, Cambridge.

Littmann, E. 1914. *Syria.* Publications of the Princeton Univ. Archaeological Expedition to Syria in 1904–5 and 1909. Vol. 4A, Brill, Leiden.

Lyttelton, M. B. 1974. Petra. In *Baroque Architecture in Classical Antiquity.* Cornell Univ. Press, Ithaca NY, 61–83.

———. 1990a. Aspects of the Iconography of the Sculptural Decoration of the Khasneh at Petra. In Edited by F. Zayadine, *LIMC*, Amman, 19–29.

———. 1990b. Sculpture in Nabataean Petra and the Question of Roman Influence. In *Architecture and Architectural Sculpture in the Roman Empire.* Edited by M. Henig, Oxford, Univ. Committee for Archaeology Monograph 29, 91–107.

———. 1990c. Sculpture from the Temenos of Qasr el-Bint at Petra. *Aram* 2, 267–286.

Lyttelton, M., and T. Blagg. Sculpture in Nabataean Petra, and the Question of Roman Influence. In *Architecture and Architectural Sculpture in the Roman Empire.* Edited by M. Henig. Oxford Univ., Committee for Archaeology. Monograph 29, 91–107.

MacDonald, B. 2000. *East of Jordan. Territories and Sites of the Hebrew Scriptures.* ACOR. Boston, MA.

MacDonald, W.L. 1982–1986. *The Architecture of the Roman Empire*, Vol. II. Yale Univ. Press, New Haven, CT.

G. Markoe, Editor. 2003. *Petra Rediscovered: Lost City of the Nabataeans.* Abrams, New York.

Mason, J., and K. 'Amr. 1990. A Study of Nabataean Pottery Manufacturing Techniques: An Experiment for Reconstructing the Production of Fine Bowls. *Aram* 2, 287–307.

Mattingly, G. L. 1990. Settlement on Jordan's Kerak Plateau from Iron IIC through the Early Roman Period. *Aram* 2, 309–335.

McKenzie, J. S. 1985. The Measurement of Inaccessible Mouldings by a Surveying Method: As Applied at Petra. *Levant* 17, 157–170.

———. 1987a. Corpus of the Principal Monuments at Petra. *RR* 19, 217–218.

———. 1987b. The Dating of the Principal Monuments at Petra and Khirbet Tannur. *PEQ* 120, 81–107.

———. 1987c. The Dating of the Principal Monuments at Petra: A New Approach. *SHAJ* 3, 295–305.

———. 1988. The Development of Nabataean Sculpture at Petra and Khirbet Tannur. *PEQ* 120, 81–107.

———. 1988. The Architecture of Petra. Oxford. British Academy Monographs in Archaeology 1.

———. 1988. The Beduin at Petra: The Historical Sources. *Levant* 23, 139–46.

———. 2001. Keys from Egypt and the East: Observations on Nabataean Culture in the Light of Recent Discoveries. *BASOR* 324, 97–111.

———. 2003a. Carvings in the Desert: The Sculpture of Petra and Khirbet et-Tannur. In *Petra Rediscovered: Lost City of the Nabataeans.* Edited by G. Markoe, 165–191.

———. 2003b. Glimpsing Alexandria from Archaeological Evidence. *JRA* 16, 35–63.

———. 2004a. Temples, Tombs, and other Recent Discoveries from the Rose Red City. *JRA* 17, 559–568.

McKenzie, J. (in preparation). *The Architecture of Alexandria and Egypt 300 BC–AD 700.*

McKenzie, J. et al. 2002. Reconstruction of the Nabataean Temple Complex at Khirbet et-Tannur. *PEQ* 134, 44–83.

McKenzie, J., and A. Phippen. 1983. Preliminary Report on the Measurement of Architectural Elements on the Façades at Petra. *ADAJ* 27, 209–212.

———. 1987. The Chronology of the Principal Monuments at Petra. *Levant* 19, 145–165.

Merklein, H., and R. Wenning. 1997. Die Götter in der Welt der Nabatäer. In *Petra: Antike Felsstadt zwischen arabischer Tradition und griechischer.* Edited by Norm. T. Weber and R. Wenning. Von Zabern, Mainz. 105–110.

Meshorer, Y. 1975. Nabataean Coins. *Qedem* 3, Jerusalem.

Mettinger, T. N. D. 1995. *No Graven Image? Israelite Aniconism in Its Ancient Near Eastern Context.* Coniectanea biblica. Old Testament Series 42. Almqvist and Wiksell International, Stockholm.

Meza, A. 1996. The Egyptian Statuette in Petra and the Isis Cult Connection. *ADAJ* 40, 167–77.

Mierse, W. E. 1999. *Temples and Towns in Roman Iberia: The Social and Architectural Dynamics of Sanctuary Designs from the Third Century B.C. to the Third Century A.D.* Univ. of California, Berkeley, CA.

Milik, J. T. 1959. Inscription nabatéenne de Turkmaniye à Pétra. IIIe partie. Notes d'épigraphie et de topographie palestiniennes. *RB* 66, 550–575, pl. 13–14.

———. 1976. Une inscription bilingue nabatéenne et grecque à Pétra. *ADAJ* 21, 143–152.

———. 1980. Quatre inscriptions nabatéennes. In *Petra, la cité rose du désert, Le Monde de la Bible.* Edited by J. Starcky. 14, 12–15.

———. 1982. Origines des Nabatéens. *SHAJ* I, 261–265.

Millar, F. 1993. *The Roman Near East, 31 BC–AD 337.* Harvard Univ. Press, Cambridge, MA.

Miller, J. I. 1969. *The Spice Trade of the Roman Empire 29 B.C. to A.D. 641.* Clarendon Press, Oxford.

Al-Muheisen, Z. 1986. "Techniques hydrauliques dans le sud de la Jordanie en particuliére l'époque nabatéene." diss. University of Paris.

Murray, M.A. 1939. *Petra, the Rock City of Edom.* Blackie, London.

Murray, M. A., and J. C. Ellis. 1940. *Street in Petra.* Egypt 62. British School of Archaeology in Egypt, Quaritch. London.

Musil, A. 1907. *Arabia Petraea*, Vol. 2. Topographischer Reise-bericht, Vienna.

Musti, D. 1984. Syria and the East in the Hellenistic World. *CAH*, Vol. VII, Part II, Edited by F. Walbank et al. Cambridge Univ. Press, Cambridge, 175–221.

Negev, A. 1966a. The Date of the Petra-Gaza Road. *PEQ* 98, 98–99.

———. 1966b. *Cities of the Desert*, trans. M. Roston. E. Lewin-Epstein, Tel-Aviv.

———. 1973. The Staircase-tower in Nabataean Architecture. *RB* 80, 374–383.

———. 1974. The Nabataean Potter's Workshop at Oboda. *Rei Cretarie Romanae Favtorum Acta Supplementa* 1. Habelt, Bonn.

———. 1976. The Early Beginnings of the Nabataean Realm. *PEQ* 108–109, 125–133.

———. 1977. The Nabataeans and Provincia Arabia. *ANRW* II 8, 520–684.

———. 1983. *Tempel, Kirchen und Zisternen, Ausgrabungen in der Wüste Negev der Nabatäer.* Calwerverlag, Stuttgart.

———. 1986a. The Late Hellenistic and Early Roman Pottery of Nabataean Oboda. *Qedem* 22.

———. 1986b. *Nabataean Archaeology Today.* Hagop Kevorkian Series on Near Eastern Art and Civilization. New York Univ. Press, New York.

———. 1988a. The Architecture of Mampsis. Final Report. Vol. I: The Middle and Late Nabataean Periods. *Qedem* 26. The Hebrew Univ. Press, Jerusalem.

———. 1988b. The Architecture of Mampsis, Final Report, Vol. II, The Late Roman and Byzantine Periods. *Qedem* 27, The Hebrew Univ. Press. Jerusalem.

———. 1990. Mampsis, The End of a Nabataean Town. *Aram* 2, 337–365.

———. 1993. Petra. In *The New Encyclopedia of Archaeological Excavations in the Holy Land.* Edited by E. Stern. 4, 1181–1193.

———. 1995. The Architecture of Oboda: Final Report. *Qedem* 36, Jerusalem: Institute of Archaeology, Hebrew Univ., Jerusalem.

———. 2003. The Negev and the Nabataeans. In *Petra Rediscovered: Lost City of the Nabataeans.* Edited by G. Markoe. 101–105.

Negev, A., and R. Sivan. 1977. The Pottery of the Nabataean Necropolis at Mampsis. *ReiCretActa* 17–18, 109–131.

Nehmé, L. 1994. "L'espace urbain de Pétra (Jordanie) de l'époque nabatéene à l'époque Byzantine à travers les sources archéologiques et épigraphiques," Vol. 1. Ph.D. diss., Université de Paris I.

———. 2000. The World of the Nabataeans 312 BC–106 AD. In *The Levant: History and Archaeology in the Eastern Mediterranean*. Edited by O. Binst. Könemann, France, 140–185.

———. 2003. The Petra Survey Project. In *Petra Rediscovered: Lost City of the Nabataeans*. Edited by G. Markoe. *Abrams*, New York. 144–163.

Nehmé, L., and F. Villeneuve. 1999. *Pétra. Métropole de l'Arabie antique*. Seuil (Paris) France.

Netzer, E. 1977. The Winter Palaces of the Judean Kings at Jericho at the End of the Second Temple Period. *BASOR* 228, 1–13.

———. 1981. Greater Herodium, *Qedem* 13. Institute of Archaeology, Hebrew Univ. of Jerusalem, Jerusalem.

———. 1992. Massive Structures: Processes in Construction and Deterioration. *The Architecture of Ancient Israel, from Pre-Historic to the Persian Periods*. Edited by R. Reich and A. Keminski. Israel Exploration Society, Jerusalem, 17–28.

———. 1996a. The Hasmonean Palaces in Palaestina, Basileia: Die Palaste der hellenistischen Könige: internationals Symposion in Berlin vom 16.12.1992 bis 20.12.1992. Edited by W. Hoepfner and G. Brands. Von Zabern, Mainz. 203–208.

———. 1996b. The Palaces Built by Herod. A Research Update. Edited by K. Fittschen and G. Foerster. *Judaea and the Greco-Roman World in the Time of Herod in the Light of Archaeological Evidence*. Vandenhoeck and Ruprecht, Göttingen.

———. 1999. Floating in the Desert: A Pleasure Palace in Jordan. *Archaeology Odyssey* 2, 1, 46–55.

———. 2001a. The Palaces of the Hasmoneans and Herod the Great. Yadin Ben-Zvi Press and the Israel Exploration Society, Jerusalem.

———. 2001b. Hasmonean and Herodian Palaces of Jericho. Vol. I. The Hebrew Univ., Jerusalem.

———. 2003. *Nabatäische Architektur*. Von Zabern, Mainz.

Nielsen, I. 1994. *Hellenistic Palaces: Tradition and Renewal*. Studies in Hellenistic Civilization, Vol. V. Aarhus Univ. Press, Denmark.

———. 1996. Oriental Models for Hellenistic Palaces, Basileia: Die Palaste der hellenistischen Könige: Internationals Symposion in Berlin vom 16.12.1992 bis 20.12.1992. Edited by W. Hoepfner and G. Brands. Von Zabern, Mainz. 209–212.

Oleson, J. P. 1986. The Humayma Hydraulic Survey: Preliminary Report of the 1986 Season. *ADAJ* 32, 157–169.

———. 1995. The Origins and Design of Nabataean Water-Supply Systems. Edited by K. 'Amr, F. Zayadine and M. Zaghloul. *SHAJ* V. Amman. 707–719.

Paradise, T. R. 1993. *Analysis of Weathering-Constrained Erosion of Sandstone in the Roman Theater of Petra*. National Science Foundation (#SES-9205055).

———. Regional Science Program in Washington D.C. and the United States Information Agency as administrated through the American Center of Oriental Research, ACOR, Amman.

———. 1994. Limestone Weathering Rate Analysis. C. Kanellopoulos 1993, 110–114.

Parker, S. T. 1987. *The Roman Frontier in Central Jordan: Interim Report on the Limes Arabicus Project, 1980–1985* (2 vols.). *BARIS* 340. Oxford.

———. 2006. *The Roman Frontier in Central Jordan, Final Report on the Limes Arabicus Project 1980–1989* (2 vols.). Dumbarton Oaks Research Library, Washington D.C.

Parlasca, I. 1986a. Die nabatäischen Kamelterrakotten — Ihre antiquarischen und religionsgeschichtlichen Aspekte. In *Petra. Neue Ausgrabungen und Entdeckungen*. Edited by M. Lindner. Munich. 200–213.

———. 1986b. Priester und Gott. Bemerkungen zu Terrakottafunden aus *Petra. In Petra. Neue Ausgrabungen und Entdeckungen*. Edited by M. Lindner. Munich. 192–199.

———. 1990. Seltene Typen nabatäischer Terrakotten. Östliche Motive in der späteren Provincia Arabia. In *Das antike Rom und der Osten. Festschrift für Klaus Parlasca zum 65. Geburtstag*. Edited by C. Börker and M. Donderer. Erlangen Universitätsbund, Erlangen-Nürnberg. 157–174.

Parr, P. J. 1957. Recent Discoveries at Petra. *PEQ* 89, 5–16.

———. 1960. Excavations at Petra 1958–1959. *PEQ* 92, 124–135.

———. 1962. Le Conway "High Place" à Pétra, une nouvelle interpretation. *RB* 69, 64–79.

———. 1963. The Capital of the Nabataeans. *Scientific American* 209, 94–103.

———. 1965a. The Beginnings of Hellenization at Petra. *8ieme Congrès International d'Archéologie Classique*. E. de Boccard, Paris. 527–533.

———. 1965b. Pétra. *RB* 72, 253–257.

———. 1965/6. The Date of the Qasr Bint Far'un at Petra. *Jaarbericht Ex Oriente Lux* 19, 550–557.

———. 1967. La date du barrage du Sîq à Pétra. *RB* 74, 45–49.

———. 1967–1968. Recent Discoveries in the Sanctuary of the Qasr Bint Far'un at Petra: Account of the Recent Excavations. *ADAJ* 12–13, 5–19.

———. 1968a. Découvertes récentes au sanctuaire du Qasr à Pétra: Compte rendu des dernières fouilles. *Syria* 45, 1–24.

———. 1968b. The Investigation of some "Inaccessible" Rock-Cut Chambers at Petra. *PEQ* 100, 5–15.

———. 1970. A Sequence of Pottery from Petra. In *Near Eastern Archaeology in the Twentieth Century: Essays in Honour of Nelson Glueck*. Edited by J. A. Sanders. Doubleday, NY. 348–381.

———. 1978. Pottery, People, and Politics. In *Archaeology in the Levant, Essays for Kathleen Kenyon*. Edited by P. R. S. Moorey and P. J. Parr. Aris and Phillips, Warminster, England, 202–209.

———. 1986a. Vierzig Jahre Ausgrabungen in Petra (1929 bis 1969). In *Petra. Neue Ausgrabungen und Endeckungen*. Edited by M. Lindner. Munich. 139–149.

———. 1986b. The Last Days at Petra. In *Proceedings of the Symposium on Bilad al-Sham during the Byzantine Period*. Edited by M. A. Bakhit and M. Asfour. Jordan Univ. Amman. 192–205.

———. 1990. Sixty Years of Excavation in Petra: A Critical Assessment. *Aram* 2, 1, and 2, 7–23.

———. 1996. The Architecture of Petra: Review Article. (J. S. McKenzie, 1990.) *PEQ* 128, 63–70.

———. 2003. The Origins and Emergence of the Nabataeans. In *Petra Rediscovered: Lost City of the Nabataeans*. Edited by G. Markoe. 27–35.

Parr, P. J., K. B. Atkinson, and E. Wickens. 1975. Photogrammetric Work at Petra, 1965–1968 An Interim Report. *ADAJ* 20, 31–45.

Patrich, J. 1990a. The Formation of Nabataean Art: Prohibition of a Graven Image Among the Nabataeans: The Evidence and its Significance. *Aram* 2, 185–196.

———. 1990b. The Formation of Nabataean Art: Prohibition of a Graven Image Among the Nabataeans. Magnes Press. Hebrew Univ., Jerusalem.

Periplus Maris Erythraei. 1989. Translated and edited by L. Casson. Princeton Univ. Press. Princeton, NJ.

Perry, M., and A. M. Al-Shiyab. 2005. A Late Roman Tomb Near Qasr ar-Rabba. *ADAJ* 49, 81–88.

Politt, J. 1986. *Art in the Hellenistic Age.* Cambridge Univ. Press, Cambridge.

Polotsky, H. 1962. The Greek Papyri from the Cave of Letters. *IEJ* 12, 259.

Rababeh, S. M. 2005. *How Petra was Built, An analysis of the construction techniques of the Nabataean freestanding buildings and rock-cut monuments in Petra. BARIS* 1460, Oxford.

Raschke, M. G. 1977. New Studies in Roman Commerce with the East. In *Aufstieg und Niedergang der Römischen Welt,* II. Edited by M. Temporini and W. Haase. 9.2, 604–1378. De Gruyter, Berlin and New York.

Reich, R. and A. Kempinski, Editors. 1992. *The Architecture of Ancient Israel.* Israel Exploration Society, Jerusalem.

Reid, S. K. 2002. Excavations at the Petra Small Temple 2000–2001. *ADAJ* 46, 363–379.

———. 2006. The Small Temple: A Roman Imperial Cult Building in Petra, Jordan. Gorgias Press, Piscataway, NJ.

Roche, M.-J. 1996. Remarques sur les Nabatéens en Méditerranée. *Semitica* 45, 73–99.

Roller, D. W. 1998. *The Building Program of Herod the Great.* Univ. of California, Berkeley, CA.

Rosenthal, R. and R. Sivan. 1978. Ancient Lamps in the Schloessinger Collection. *Qedem* 8, The Hebrew Univ., Jerusalem.

Rostovtzeff, M. 1957. *The Social and Economic History of the Roman Empire.* Oxford Univ. Press, Oxford.

Rotroff, S. I. 1982. Silver, Glass, and Clay: Evidence for the Dating of Hellenistic Luxury Tableware. *Hesperia* 51, 329–337.

Russell, K. W. 1980. The Earthquake of May 19, A.D. 363. *BASOR* 238, 47–64.

———. 1990. Ethnohistory of the Bedul Bedouin. *ADAJ* 37, 15–35.

Schluntz, E. L. 1998a. The Upper Temenos and the Great Temple. In *Petra Great Temple Vol. I.* Edited by M. S. Joukowsky, 209–224.

———. 1998b. The Architectural Sculpture of the Great Temple. In *Petra Great Temple Vol. I.* Edited by M. S. Joukowsky, 225–236.

———. 1999. "From Royal to Public Assembly Space: The Transformation of the "Great Temple" Complex at Petra, Jordan." Ph.D. diss., Brown Univ. Univ. Microfilms International.

Schmid, S. G. 1995a. Nabataean Fine Ware from Petra. Paper presented at the 5th International Conference on the History and Archaeology of Jordan, April 1992, Irbid (Jordan), *SHAJ* V, 637–647.

———. 1995b. "Die Feinkeramik der Nabatäer. Typologie, Chronologie und kulturhistorische Hintergründe." Diss., Univ. of Basel.

———. 1996a. Die Feinkeramik der Nabatäer im Spiegel ihrer kulturhistorischen Kontakte. In *Hellenistische und kaiserzeitliche Keramik des östlichen Mittelmeergebietes*. Arbeitskreis Frankfurt und die Antike, Archäologisches Institut der Johann Wolfgang Goethe-Universität, Kolloquium, Frankfurt 24–25 April 1995. 127–145.

———. 1996b. Die Feinkeramik, Petra, Ez Zantur. Von Zabern, Mainz. 151–218.

———. 1999.Un roi nabatéen à Délos? *ADAJ* 43, 279–98.

———. 1999. The Nabataeans: Travellers between Life Styles. *Levantine Archaeology I. The Archaeology of Jordan.* Edited by B. MacDonald, R. Adams, and P. Bienkowski. Sheffield Academic Press, Sheffield. 367–426.

———. 2002a. From Aretas to the Annexation, Petra and the Nabataeans. Edited by J. Frösén and Z. Fiema. In *Petra: A City Forgotten and Rediscovered.* A Volume associated with the Exhibition organized by the Amos Anderson Art Museum in Helsinki, Finland. Helsinki Univ. Press. 44–59.

———. 2002b. The International Wadi Farasa Project (IWFP) Preliminary Report on the 2001 Season. *ADAJ* 46, 257–277.

———. 2003 Nabataean Pottery. In *Petra Rediscovered: Lost City of the Nabataeans.* Edited by G. Markoe. Abrams, New York. 75–81.

Schmid, S., and B. Kolb. 2000. Petra. Ez Zantur II. Ergebnisse der schweizerisch-liechtensteinischen Ausgrabungen. Von Zabern, Mainz.

Schmid, S. et al. 2000. Petra ez-Zantur II. Von Zabern, Mainz.

Schmidt-Colinet, A. 1980. "Nabatäische Felsarchitektur. Bemerkungen zum gegenwärtingen Forschungsstand. *BJ* 180, 189–230.

———. 1983a. A Nabataean Family of Sculptors at Hegra. *Berytus* 31, 95–102.

———. 1983b. Dorisierende nabatäische Kapitelle. *DaM* 1, 307–312, pl. 66–67.

———. 1987. The Mason's Workshop of Hegra, its Relations to Petra, and the Tomb of Syllaios. *SHAJ* III, 143–150.

Schmitt-Korte, K. 1968 [1968–1969]. Beitrag zur nabatäischen Keramik. *AA* 83, 496–519.

———. 1971. A Contribution to the Study of Nabataean Pottery. *ADAJ* 16, 47–60.

———. 1989. Die bemalte nabatäische Keramik: Verbreitung, Typologie und Chronologie. In *Petra und das Königreich der Nabatäer. Lebensraum, Geschichte und Kultur eines arabischen Volkes der Antike.* Edited by M. Lindner. 5th ed., Delp, Munich, Nurberg, 228–232.

———. 1991. Die Nabatäer im Spiegel der Münzen. Edited by M. Lindner and J. P. Zeitler, In *Petra: Königin der Weihrauchstrasse,* 135–184.

Schmitt-Korte, K., and M. Cowell. 1989. Nabataean Coinage, Part I. The Silver Content Measured by X-Ray Fluorescence Analysis. *NC* 149, 33–58, pl. 11–17.

Sear, F. 1982. *Roman Architecture.* Batsford, London.

Seetzen, U. J. 1854–1859. *Reisen durch Syrien, Palästina, Phönicien, die Transjordan-Länder, Arabia Petraea und unter-Aegypten* (2 vols.). Heraus-gegeben und kommentiert von Pr. Dr. Fr. Kruse. Reimer, Berlin.

Segal, A. 1975. The Planning of the Cities Along the Via Trajana Nova in the Roman Period. The Hebrew Univ., Jerusalem.

———. 1983. *The Byzantine City of Shivta (Esbeita), Negev Desert, Israel. BARIS* 179, Oxford. 179.

———. 1995. *Theatres in Roman Palestine and Provincia Arabia.* Brill, Leiden.

———. 1995. From Function to Monument. Urban Landscapes of Roman Palestine Syria and Provincia Arabia. Oxbow Books, Oxford.

———. 2001. Hippos-Sussita: Fourth Season of Excavations, June–July 2003. Univ. of Haifa, Haifa.

Shaer, M., and Z. Aslan. 1997. Architectural Investigation on the Building Techniques of the Nabataeans with Reference to Tomb 825. *ADAJ* 41, 219–31.

———. 2000. Nabataean Building Techniques with Special References to the Architecture of Tomb 825 (Tomb of Fourteen Graves). Edited by M. Kühlenthal and H. Fisher, In *The Restoration of the Rockcut Tomb Façade: German-Jordanian Project for the Establishment of a Conservation Center in Petra,* Karl M. Lipp, Munich, 89–109.

Shiloh, Y. 1979. The Proto-Aeolic Capital and Israelite Ashlar Masonry, *Qedem* II. Hebrew Univ., Jerusalem.

Siculus, Diodorus. 1933–1967. Translated by C. H. Oldfather et al. *LCL Harvard Univ. Press, Cambridge, MA.*

Sidebotham, S. E. 1986. *Roman Economic Policy in the Erythra Thalassa 30 B.C.–A.D. 217.* E. J. Brill, Leiden.

Smith, C. 1956. *Tombs, Temples and Ancient Art.* Univ. of Oklahoma Press, Norman, OK.

Smith, R. R. R. 1988. *Hellenistic Royal Portraits.* Clarendon Press, Oxford.

Sourdel, D. 1952. *Les cultes du Hauran à l'époque romaine.* Bibliothèque archéologique et historique 53, Paul Geuthner, Paris.

Speidel, M. 1984. *Roman Army Studies* I, 229–273. Gieben, Amsterdam.

Starcky, J. 1955. The Nabataeans: A Historical Sketch. *BA* 18, 84–106.

———. 1965. Nouvelles stèles funéraires à Pétra. *ADAJ* 10, 43–49, pl. 21–22.

———. 1966. Pétra et la nabatène. *Dictionnaire de la Bible,* Supp. 7, 886–1017.

———. 1980. Pétra, la cité rose du desert. *Le Monde de la Bible*, 14, July, 9–11.

Starcky, J., and C. M. Bennett. 1967–1968. Recent Discoveries in the Sanctuary of the Qasr Bint Far'un at Petra. III. The Temenos Inscriptions. *ADAJ* 12–13, 30–50, pl. 22–26.

Starcky, J., and J. Strugnell. 1966. Pétra: deux nouvelles inscriptions nabatéennes. *RB* 73, 236–247, pl. 8–9.

Stewart, A. 2003. The Khazneh. In *Petra Rediscovered: Lost City of the Nabataeans*. Edited by G. Markoe. 193–198.

Strabo. 1968. *The Geography of Strabo*. Edited and translated by H. Jones. LCL, Harvard Univ. Press, Cambridge, MA.

Strugnell, J. 1959. The Nabataean Goddess Al-Kutba' and her Sanctuaries. *BASOR* 156, 26–36.

Stucky, R. A. et al. 1990. Preliminary Report 1988 Schweizer Ausgrabungen. In Ez-Zantur, Petra. Vorbericht der Kampagne 1988. *ADAJ* 34, 249–283.

———. 1991. Swiss-Liechtenstein Excavations at ez-Zantur in Petra 1989: The Second Campaign. *ADAJ* 35, 251–273.

———. 1992a. Preliminary Report 1991 Swiss-Liechtenstein Excavations at Ez-Zantur in Petra: The Third Campaign. *ADAJ* 36, 175–192.

———. 1992b. Das nabatäische Wohnhaus und das urbanistische System der Wohnquartiere in Petra. *Antk* 35, 129–140.

———. 1994. Swiss-Liechtenstein Excavations at Ez-Zantur in Petra 1993: The Fifth Campaign. *ADAJ* 38, 271–292.

———. 1995. The Nabataean House and the Urbanistic System of Habitation Quarters in Petra. *SHAJ* V, 193–198.

———. 1996. Die Nabatäische Bauten in Petra Ez Zantur I: Ergebnisse der Schweizerisch-Liechten-steinischen Ausgrabungen 1988–1992, by A. Bignasca, N. Desse-Berset, R. Fellmann Brogli, R. Glutz, S. Karg, D. Keller, B. Kolb, Ch. Kramar, M. Peter, S. G. Schmid, Ch. Schneider, R. A. Stucky, J. Studer, and I. Zanoni. *Terra Archaeologica* 2. Von Zabern, Mainz. 13–50.

Stucky, R. et al. 1995. Swiss-Liechtenstein Excavations at az-Zantur in Petra 1994: The Sixth Campaign. *ADAJ* 39, 297–316.

Tacitus. *Histories and Annals* (Ann.) Translated by C. H. Moore and J. Jackson. G. P. Putnam's sons, New York.

Taylor, J. 2001. Petra and the Lost Kingdom of the Nabataeans. I. B. Tauris, London.

Taylor, R. 2003. *Roman Builders. A Study in Architecture Process*. Cambridge Univ. Press, Cambridge.

Teixidor, J. 1973. The Nabataean presence at Palmyra. *JANES* 5, 405–409.

———. 1977. The Pagan God, Popular Religion in the Greco-Roman Near East, Princeton Univ. Press, Princeton, NJ.

———. 1991. Les inscriptions nabatéennes du Musée de Suweida. In *Le djebel al-'arab; Histoire et Patrimone au musée de Suweida. Guides archéologiques de l'Institut français d'archéologie du Proche-Orient*, no. 1. Edited by J.-M. Dentzer and J. Dentzer-Feydy. Editions Recherche sur les civilisations, Paris, 25–28.

Tholbecq, L. and C. Durand. 2005 A. Nabataean Rock-cut Sanctuary in Petra: Preliminary Report on Three Excavation Seasons at The Obodas Chapel. Jabal Numayr. *ADAJ* 49, 299–311.

Tracy, S. 1999. The Dedicatory Inscription to Trajan at the Metropolis of Petra. *JRA* Supplement 31, Edited by J. L. Humphrey, 51–58.

Vickers, M. 1994. Nabataea, India, Gaul and Carthage: Reflections on Hellenistic and Roman Gold Vessels and Red-Gloss Pottery. *AJA* 98, 231–248.

Villeneuve, F. 1979. Pétra et le royaume nabatéen. *HI* 11, 50–58.

———. 1986. Khirbet edh-Dharih (1985). In *Chronique archéologique. RB* 93, 247–252, pl. 5–6.

———. 1991. Tannour et Dharih sanctuaires de la Nabatène. *DHA* 163, 58–61.

Vitruvius. 1995. *The Ten Books on Architecture*. Edited and translated by D. Rowland. Cambridge Univ. Press, Cambridge.

Waelkens, M. 1992. Bronze Age Quarries and Quarrying Techniques in the Eastern Mediterranean and the Near East. In *Ancient Stones: Quarrying, Trade and Provenance*. Edited by M. Waelkens, N. Herz and L. Moens. Leuven Univ. Press, Leuven, 5–21.

Waelkens, M., P. DePape and L. Moens. 1988b. Quarries and the Marble Trade in Antiquity. Edited by N. Herz and M. Waelkens. In *Classical Marble: Geochemistry, Technology, Trade*, NATO ASI Series 153, Kluwer, The Netherlands, 29–31.

Waelkens, M. et al. 1990. *The Quarrying Techniques of the Greek World, Art Historical and Scientific Perspectives on Ancient Sculpture*. Edited by M. True and J. Podany. Getty Museum, CA, 47–73.

Ward-Perkins, J. B. 1981. *Roman Imperial Architecture*. Penguin, Harmondsworth, England, and New York.

———. 1992. *Marble in Antiquity*. Collected Papers of J. B. Ward-Perkins, Archaeological Monographs of the British School of Rome No. 6. Edited by H. Dodge and B. Ward-Perkins. British School at Rome, London.

———. 1994. *Studies in Roman and Early Christian Architecture*. Pinder, London.

Wasserstein, A. 1989. A Marriage Contract From the Province of Arabia Nova: Notes on Papyrus Yadin 18. *JQR* 80.1, 2, 93–130.

Weber, T., and R. Wenning, Editors. 1997. *Antike Felsstadt zwischen arabischer Tradition und griechischer Norm, Sonderheft/Antike Welt, Zaberns Bildbände zur Archäologie*. Von Zabern, Mainz.

Weippert, M. 1979. Nabatäisch-römische Keramik aus Hirbet Dor im südlichen Jordanien. *ZDPV* 95, 87–110.

Wenning, R. 1987. *Die Nabatäer—Denkmäler und Geschichte. Eine Bestandesaufnahme des archäologischen Befundes*. Novum Testamentum et Orbis Antiquus 3, Vendenhoeck und Ruprecht, Gottingen, Germany.

———. 1990. Das Nabatäerreich: seine archäologischen und historischen Hinterlassenschaften. In *Palästina in Griechisch Römischer Zeit*. Edited by H. Weippert and H. P. Kuhren. C. H. Beck, Munich. 367–415.

———. 1992. The Nabataeans in the Decapolis/Coele Syria. *Aram* 4.1–2, 79–99.

———. 1993. Eine neuerstellte Liste der nabäische Dynastie. Munstersche Beiträge zur Archaeologie, *BOREAS* Band 16, 25–38.

———. 2001. The Betyls of Petra. *BASOR* 324, 79–95.

———. 2003. The Rock-Cut Architecture of Petra. In *Petra Rediscovered: Lost City of the Nabataeans*. Edited by G. Markoe. 133–143.

Will, E. 1951. Le sanctuaire syrien de Délos. *Annales archéologiques de Syrie* I, 59–79.

Will, E. and F. Larché. 1991. *Iraq Al-Amir. Le château du Tobiad Hyrcan*. Paul Geuthner, Libraire Orientaliste, Paris.

Wilson-Jones, M. 2000. *Principles of Roman Architecture*. Yale Univ. Press, New Haven, CT.

Wright, G. R. H. 1961a. Structure of the Qasr Bint Far'un. A Preliminary Review. *PEQ* 93, 8–37.

———. 1961b. Petra—the Arched Gate, 1959–60. *PEQ* 93, 124–135.

———. 1962. The Khazne at Petra: A Review. *ADAJ* 6–7, 24–54.

———. 1966 Structure et date de l'arc monumental de Pétra. *RB* 73, 404–419.

———. 1967–1968. Recent Discoveries in the Sanctuary of the Qasr Bint Far'un at Petra: Some Aspects Concerning the Architecture and Sculpture, *ADAJ* 12–13, 20–29.

———. 1969. Strabo on Funerary Customs at Petra. *PEQ* 101, 113–16.

———. 1970. Petra—the Arched Gate 1959–1960: Some Additional Drawings. *PEQ* 112, 111–115.

———. 1973. The Date of the Khazne Fir'aun at Petra in the Light of an Iconographic Detail. *PEQ* 105, 83–90.

———. 1985. The Qasr Bint Fir'aun at Petra. A Detail Reconsidered. *DaM* 2, 321–325.

———. 1962. *How the Greeks Built Cities*. Macmillan, London.

Yadin, Y., Editor. 1963a. The Nabataean Kingdom, Provincia Arabia, Petra and En-Geddi in the Documents from Nahal Hever. *JEOL* 17, 227–241.

———. 1963b. The Finds From The Bar Kokhba Period In The Cave of Letters. Israel Exploration Society, The Hebrew Univ., Jerusalem.

———. 1971. *Bar Kokhba, the rediscovery of the legendary hero of the last Jewish revolt against Rome. Weidenfeld and Nicolson*, Jerusalem and London.

Yegül, F. 1992. *Baths and Bathing in Classical Antiquity*. Architectural History Foundation, New York. MIT Press, New York.

Yon, J. 2000. The Greco-Roman Era: BC 323–337 AD. In *The Levant: History and Archaeology in the Eastern Mediterranean*. Edited by O. Binst. Könemann, Cologne, 80–139.

Zayadine, F. 1973. Excavations at Petra 1973–74. *ADAJ* 19, 138–140.

———. 1974. Excavations at Petra (April 1973). *ADAJ* 18, 81–82.

———. 1979. Excavations at Petra (1976–1978). *ADAJ* 23, 185–197, pl.83–94.

———. 1980. Art et architecture des Nabatéens. *Le Monde de la Bible* 14,16–26.

———. 1981a. L'iconographie à'Al 'Uzza-Aphrodite. Edited by L. Kahil and C. Augé. In *Mythologie gréco-romaine. Mythologies périphériques. Etudes iconographiques*. Editions du Centre national de la recherché scientifique, (Colloques internnmationaux du CNRS, 593), Paris.

———. 1981b. Recent Excavations and Restoration at the Department of Antiquities 1979–80. *ADAJ* 25, 341–355.

———. 1982. Recent Excavations at Petra, 1979–1981. *ADAJ* 26, 365–393.

———. 1984. Al-Uzza Aphrodite. *LIMC* II, 1, Zurich and Munich.

———. 1985a. Recent Excavation and Restoration at Qasr el Bint of Petra. *ADAJ* 29, 239–249.

———. 1985b. Caravan Routes Between Egypt and Nabataea and the Voyage of the Sultan Baibars to Petra in 1276 AD. *SHAJ* 2, 159–174.

———. 1986a. Tempel, Gräber, Töpferöfen. In *Petra. Neue Ausgrabungen und Endeckungen.* Edited by M. Lindner. Delp, Munich. 214–272.

———. 1986b. Recent Excavations at the Qasr al-Bint of Petra. *AfO* 33, 177–180.

———. 1987. Decorative Stucco at Petra and other Hellenistic Sites. *SHAJ* 3, 131–142.

———. 1990. *Petra and the Caravan Cities.* Proceedings of the Symposium organized at Petra in September 1985 by the Department of Antiquities of Jordan and the Iconographic Lexicon of Classical Mythology (*LIMC*) with the financial support of UNESCO. Dept. of Antiquities, Amman.

———. 1990. The Pantheon of the Nabataean Inscriptions in Egypt and the Sinai. *Aram* 2, 151–174.

———. 1992. L'espace urbain du grand Pétra, les routes et les stations caravanieres. *ADAJ* 36, 217–241.

———. 2000. Notes on the Early History and the Kingdom of the Nabataeans. Edited by M. Kühlenthal and H. Fisher. In *Petra, The Restoration of the Rockcut Tomb Façade: German-Jordanian Project for the Establishment of a Conservation Center in Petra.* Karl M. Lipp, Munich, 52–67.

——— et al. 2003. *Le Qasr al-Bint de Pétra l'architecture, le décor, la chronolgie et les dieux.* Éditions Recherche sur les Civilisation, Paris.

———. 2005. Al-Khazna, The Treasure Re-visited, a Forgotten Document of Léon de Laborde. *ADAJ* 49, 395–402.

Zayadine, F., and P. Hottier. 1976. Relevé photogrammétrique à Pétra. *ADAJ* 21, 93–104.

Zayadine, F., and S. Farajat. 1991. The Petra National Trust Site Projects: Excavation and Clearance at Petra and Beida. *ADAJ* 35, 275–311.

Zayadine, F., F. Larché, and J. Dentzer Feydy. 2002. *Le Qasr al-Bint de Pétra: L'architecture, le décor, la chronologie et des dieux.* Association pour la diffusion de la pensee française. Ministère des Affairès étrangères, 6, rue Ferrus 75683, Paris cedex 14. Editions recherché sur les civilizations, Paris.

Zeitler, J. P. 1990a. Houses, Sherds and Bones: Aspects of Daily Life in Petra. In *The Near East in Antiquity. German Contributions to the Archaeology of Jordan, Palestine, Syria, Lebanon and Egypt,* Vol. I, 39–44.

———. 1990b. A Private Building from the First Century B.C. in Petra. In *First International Conference, The Nabataeans, Oxford 26–29 September 1989. Aram* 2, 385–420.

———. 1993a. Excavations and Surveys in Petra 1989–1990. Chronique Archéologique. *Syria* LXX, 257–259.

———. 1993b. Petra und die Wiehrauchstrasse. Exhibition Catalog for Zurich and Basel.

BROWN UNIVERSITY
THE PETRA GREAT TEMPLE—SITE BIBLIOGRAPHY

1993

1. Joukowsky, M. S. The Southern Temple at Petra. *ACORN* 5.2, 11.

2. Khuri, R. Results of First Year Dig. *Jordan Times*, 8 September.

3. ———. Results of First Year Dig. *Al Ra'i Daily Newspaper*, 8 September (In Arabic).

4. Zeitler, J. P. Excavations and Surveys in Petra 1989–90. In "Chronique Archéologique." *Syria* 70, 205–273.

1994

5. Joukowsky, M. S. 1993 Archaeological Excavations and Survey of the Southern Temple at Petra, Jordan. *ADAJ* XXXVIII, 293–322.

6. ———. Archaeological Survey of the Southern Temple at Petra, Jordan. *L'Orient Express* 2, 43–44.

7. ———. Petra Southern Temple, Archaeology of Jordan. Edited by G. L. Peterman, *AJA* 98, 543–544.

8. ———. Petra—The Brown University Excavations. *BUFB* VI, No. 3, 15–18.

9. Rodan, S. Bedouin Secrets. *The Jerusalem Post Magazine*, 29 July.

1995

10. Joukowsky, M. S. Le "Temple Sud" a` Pétra. *Le monde de la bible Archéologie et Histore*. No. 94, 43.

11. ———. Petra the Southern Temple. Archaeology of Jordan. Edited by P. M. Bikai and D. Koorings. *AJA* 99, 518–520.

12. ———. Archaeological Survey of the Southern Temple at Petra. *Syria* LXXII 1–2: 133–142.

13. ———. Petra Southern Temple, *ACORN*. Winter 7.2:7–8.

14. Joukowsky, M. S. and E. L. Schluntz. The Southern Temple at Petra: 1994 Excavations. *ADAJ* XXXIX 241–266.

15. Mamalaki, D. From the Field. *Haffenreffer Museum Newsletter*, Brown University Department of Anthropology.

16. Myers, J. W. and E. Myers. Low altitude aerial photography. *JRA* Supplement 14, 284–285, figures 5, 6, 7.

17. Negev, A. The Petra Southern Temple. *Qadmoniot* (in Hebrew) Jerusalem. Vol. XXVIII, No. 2,110.

1996

18. Barrett, D. G. "How Can the Ceramic Analysis of Lamps Reveal the Impact of Empire on the Southern Temple at Petra?" M.A. Thesis, Brown University, Department of Anthropology.

19. Blackburn, J. Ancient City in the Sands. *Views*. Rhode Island School of Design Alumni Magazine. Summer, Vol. 8, No. 3, 20–21.

20. Joukowsky, M. S. Petra, The Southern Temple. Archaeology in Jordan. Edited by P. M. Bikai and V. Egan. *AJA* 100, No. 3, 525–526.

21. ———. The Petra Southern Temple: Or What I do on my Summer "Vacations." *BUFB* VIII, 3, 30–35.

22. ———. The Petra Southern Temple: The Fourth Season, 1996. *AJA Abstracts*, 98th Annual Meeting 20, 6–7.

23. ———. Petra, The "Great" Southern Temple. *ACORN* Summer, Vol. 8.1, 6–7.

24. ———. 1995 Archaeological Excavations of the Southern Temple at Petra, Jordan. *ADAJ* Vol. XL, 177–206.

25. Khouri, R. Excavations unravel mysteries of Petra's Great Southern Temple. *Jordan Times*, Tuesday 23 April, 6–7.

26. ———. Fourth Season of Excavation Clarifies Important Architectural Aspects of Petra's Southern Temple. *Jordan Times,* 14 December, 7.

27. Schluntz, E. L. The Architectural Sculpture of the Southern Temple at Petra, Jordan. *AJA* Abstracts, 98th Annual Meeting. Vol. 20, 7.

28. Zimmerman, P. C. MiniCad 6—Another View. *CSA Newsletter: A Quarterly Newsletter for Architectural Historians and Archaeologists.* Vol. 9, 3, 9–11.

1997

29. Basile, J. J., A Head of the Goddess Tyche from Petra, Jordan. *ADAJ* Vol. XLI, 255–266.

30. Freyberger, K. S. and M. S. Joukowsky. Blattranken, Greifen und Elefanten: Sakrale Architektur in Petra und ihr Bauschmuck neuausgegrabene Peripteral-tempel. *Petra: Antike Felsstadt Zwischen Arabischer Tradition Und Griechischer*, Edited by N. T. Weber and R. Wenning, Verlagg Philipp Von Zabern. Mainz, 71–86.

31. Joukowsky, M. S. The Water Canalization System of the Petra Southern Temple. *SHAJ* Vol. VI, 303–311.

32. ———. The Southern Temple at Petra, *Encyclopedia of Near Eastern Archaeology.* Oxford University Press and *ASOR* Vol. 4, 306–307.

33. ———. The Petra Southern Temple: The Fourth Season, 1996. *AJA* 101, 339.

34. ———. Brown University Petra Great Temple Excavations. *BUFB* X, 1.29–32.

35. ———. Brown University Excavations at the 'Great' Temple of Petra. Jordan. *ASOR Abstracts* Vol. 47. 2, A–35.

36. ———. Petra: Great Temple. *ACORN* Vol. 9, 1.7.

37. ———. The Great Temple at Petra. *Edited by* P. M. Bikai, V. Egan. *AJA* 101, 3, 520–521.

38. ———. 1997 Brown University Excavations at the "Great" Southern Temple of Petra. *AJA* Abstracts, 99th Annual Meeting, Vol. 21, 100.

39. ———. 1996 Brown University Archaeological Excavations of the "Great" Southern Temple at Petra, Jordan. *ADAJ* Vol. XLI, 195–218.

40. Schluntz, E. L. The Architectural Sculpture of the Southern Temple at Petra, Jordan. *AJA* 101, 339.

41. Twair, P. M. Temple at Petra Challenges Veteran American Archaeologist. In *The Washington Report on Middle East Affairs Monthly*, March Vol. 55, 98.

1998

42. Barrett, D. G. The Lamps, *Petra: The Great Temple, Vol. I—Brown University Excavations 1993–1997.* Edited by M. S. Joukowsky. 275–286.

43. ———. Other Small Finds, *Petra: The Great Temple, Vol. I—Brown University Excavations 1993–1997.* Edited by M. S. Joukowsky 287–315.

44. ———. The Coins, *Petra: The Great Temple, Vol. I—Brown University Excavations 1993–1997.* Edited by M. S. Joukowsky. 317–324.

45. Basile, J. J. The Lower Temenos, *Petra: The Great Temple, Vol. I—Brown University Excavations 1993–1997,* Edited by M. S. Joukowsky. 188–208.

46. Bedal, L.-A. Neutron Activation Analysis of Pottery. *Petra: The Great Temple, Vol. I—Brown. University Excavations 1993–1997.* Edited by M. S. Joukowsky. 345–367.

47. Boucher, N. Mystery in Stone and Sand. *BAM* 98:3, 30–37.

48. Joukowsky, M. S. Re-Discovering Elephants at Petra! *Ancient Egyptian and Mediterranean Studies: In Memory of William A. Ward,* Edited by Leonard H. Lesko, Brown University, Department of Egyptology, 133–148.

49. ———. Brown University Excavations in Jordan at the Petra Great Temple, 1988. *Occident and Orient*, Newsletter of the German Protestant Institut of Archaeology in Amman, 10–11.

50. ———. Petra: Brown University Excavations of the Great (?) Temple. *ACORN,* Summer 1998 Vol. 48, No. 2: A–21.

51. ———. The Great Temple at Petra. *AJA,* July, Vol. 102 No. 3, 593–596.

52. ———. The Petra Great Temple Project, 1993–1995: A Three-Year Assessment. In *HESED VE-EMET, Studies in Honor of Ernest S. Frerichs. Edited by* J. Magness and S. Gitin, Brown University Judaic Studies Scholars Press, No. 320: 291–312.

53. ———. Brown University 1997 Excavations at the Petra Great Temple. *ADAJ* XLII, 293–318.

54. ———. *Petra: The Great Temple, Vol. I—Brown University Excavations 1993–1997.* With Contributions by Christian Augé, Deirdre G. Barrett, Joseph J. Basile, Jean Blackburn, Leigh-Ann Bedal, Donna J. D'Agostino, Sara G. Karz, Elizabeth E. Payne, Thomas R. Paradise, Erika L. Schluntz, Monica L. Sylvester, Stephen V. Tracy, Loa P. Traxler, Terry Tullis, Peter Warnock, and Paul C. Zimmerman. Edited by M. S. Joukowsky. Brown University, Petra Exploration Fund.

55. ———. Introduction, *Petra: The Great Temple, Vol. I—Brown University Excavations 1993–1997.* 1–46.

56. ———. History of the Brown University Excavations, *Petra: The Great Temple, Vol. I—Brown University Excavations 1993–1997.* 47–148.

57. ———. Preface, *Petra: The Great Temple, Vol. I—Brown University Excavations 1993–1997.* xli–xlvi.

58. Joukowsky, M. S. and D. J. D'Agostino. Artifact Studies and Databases. *Petra: The Great Temple, Vol. I—Brown University Excavations 1993–1997.* Edited by M. S. Joukowsky. 236–274.

59. Karz, S. G. *"The Change in Color of "Colorless" Glass at the Great Temple, Petra, Jordan."* Brown University Department of Anthropology, M.A. Thesis.

60. ———. The Roman and Byzantine Glass, *Petra: The Great Temple, Vol. I—Brown University Excavations 1993–1997.* Edited by M. S. Joukowsky. 325–343.

61. Paradise, T. R. Environmental Setting and Stone Weathering. *Petra: The Great Temple, Vol. I —Brown University Excavations 1993–1997.* Edited by M. S. Joukowsky. 150–166.

62. Payne, E. E. Evidence for the Nabataean Subterranean Canalization System. *Petra: The Great Temple, Vol. I—Brown University Excavations 1993–199.* Edited by M. S. Joukowsky. 170–178.

63. Schluntz, E. L. The Upper Temenos and the Great Temple, *Petra: The Great Temple, Vol. I—Brown University Excavations 1993–1997.* Edited by M. S. Joukowsky. 209–224.

64. ———. The Architectural Sculpture of the Great Temple, *Petra: The Great Temple, Vol. I —Brown University Excavations 1993–1997.* Edited by M. S. Joukowsky. 225–234.

65. Tracy, S. V. The dedicatory inscription to Trajan at the 'metropolis' of Petra. *JRA Supplementary Series* No. 31, The Roman and Byzantine Near East, Some Recent Archaeological Research. Edited by J. H. Humphrey, Vol. 2, 51–58.

66. ———. An Imperial Inscription, *Petra: The Great Temple, Vol. I—Brown University Excavations 1993–1997.* Edited by M. S. Joukowsky. 339–375.

67. ———. Inscribed Finds, *Petra: The Great Temple, Vol. I—Brown University Excavations 1993–1997.* Edited by M. S. Joukowsky. 376–379.

68. Tullis, T. E. and C. Worthington. Ground Penetrating Radar Study of the Petra Great Temple. *Petra: The Great Temple, Vol. I—Brown University Excavations 1993–1997.* Edited by M. S. Joukowsky. 179–186.

69. Warnock, P. Palynological Analysis from the Great Temple. *Petra: The Great Temple, Vol. I— Brown University Excavations 1993–1997.* Edited by M. S. Joukowsky. 167–168.

1999

70. Basile, J. J. Preliminary Report of the Notes on the Head of the Goddess Tyche from Petra, Jordan. *ADAJ* XLII, 223–226.

71. Bestock, L. D. Nabataean Pottery from the "Cistern:" Some Finds from the Brown University Excavations at the Petra Great Temple. *ADAJ* XLII, 241–248.

72. Corbeil, M-C. and K. Helwig. *Analysis of Fresco Fragments from the Petra Great Temple.* Analytical Research Laboratory Report 3779, 19 March, Institut Canadien de Conservation Ottawa.

73. Khuri, R. Petra Great Temple Excavations Reveal Massive, Elaborate Nabataean Complex. *Jordan Times* 6 December, 7.

74. Joukowsky, M. S. Petra: Brown University Excavations of the Great Temple: Questions about Functional Analysis. Seventh International Congress on the History and Archaeology of Jordan. Jordan by the Millennia, *SHAJ* VII.

75. ———. Petra. The Great Temple. Edited by Virginia Egan and Patricia M. Bikai. *AJA* 103, No. 3, 504–506.

76. ———. The Petra Great Temple—Brown University Excavations. In *The First Conference on Nabataean Research and Studies.* Conference Abstract. German Protestant Institute, Amman, 9–10.

77. ———. The Water Canalization System of the Petra Great Temple. *Men of Dikes and Canals: The Archaeology of Water in the Middle East, Conference Abstracts.* Petra, Wadi Musa, 15.

78. ———. Petra, Great Temple. *Brown University Center for Old World Archaeology and Art, Report of the Director,* 1988–1999, R. Ross Holloway, 2–4.

79. ———. Petra: Great Temple. *ACORN* Summer 1999, Vol. 11. No.1, 9–10.

80. ———. The 1998 Brown University Excavations at the Great Temple, Petra. *ADAJ* Vol. XLIII, 195–222.

81. Nehmé, Leila and François Villeneuve. *Pétra: Métropole de l'Arabie Antique.* Editions du Seuil, 27, 81–86.

82. Schluntz, E. L. *"From Royal to Public Assembly Space: The Transformation of the "Great Temple" Complex at Petra."* Ph.D. diss., Brown University, Center for Old World Archaeology and Art.

83. Taylor, Jane. *The so-called "Great Temple," Petra. In Petra and the Lost Kingdom of the Nabataeans.* Aurum Press, London, 59–60.

2000

84. Acevedo, D. and E. L. Vote. ARCHAVE, Andries van Dam et. al. Immersive VR for Scientific Visualization: A Progress Report. *IEEE Computer Graphics and Applications*, IEEE Computer Society, November/December, 20.6.

85. Basile, Joseph J. When People Lived at Petra. *Archaeology Odyssey*, July/August, Vol. 3, 4, 14–31.

86. Bedal, L-A. Paradise Found: Petra's Urban Oasis. *Expedition*, 42, 2, 23–36.

87. Hadingham, E. Secrets of a Desert Metropolis: The hidden Wonders of Petra's Ancient Engineers. *Scientific American Discovering Archaeology* September/October 2, No. 4, 70–77. See especially, An Amazing Temple, 74–77.

88. Khuri, R. Volume on Great Temple at Petra Targets Specialists, General Readers Alike. *Jordan Times*, 21 February 7.

89. Joukowsky, M. S. Brown University 1999 Excavations at the Petra Great Temple. *Contexts: The Newsletter of the Friends of the Haffenreffer Museum of Anthropology, Brown University* Winter 2000, Vol. 28, No.1, 4–5.

90. ———. *Petra Great Temple Excavations Volume I, Brown University Excavations 1993–1997*, Edited by M. S. Joukowsky, CD-ROM, designed by Adam Brin. *Petra: The Great Temple, Vol. I—Brown University Excavations 1993–1997. Petra Exploration Fund, Providence.*

91. ———. Exploring the Great Temple at Petra: The Brown University Excavations 1993–1995. *The Archaeology of Jordan and Beyond: Essays in Honor of James A. Sauer.* Edited by L. E. Stager, J. A. Greene and M. D. Coogan. Eisenbrans/Semitic Museum, Winona Lake, IN: 221–234.

92. ———. Brown University 1999 Excavations at the Petra Great Temple. *ADAJ*, Vol. XLIV, 313–334.

93. ———. The Center's Research Continues in Old and New Directions. Prof. Martha Joukowsky has kindly provided the following report of work at Petra in 2000, Edited by R. R. Holloway, *Brown University Center for Old World Archaeology and Art, Report of the Director* 1999–2000, 2–4.

94. ———. Petra. The Great Temple. Edited by V. Egan, P. M. Bikai, and K. Zamora. *AJA*, 104.3, 582.

95. ———. Petra 2000: Brown University Excavations of the Great Temple. *ASOR Annual Meeting Abstracts*, 15–18 November, 5.

96. ———. Petra: Great Temple, *ACORN*, Summer 2000 12. 1, 3–4.

97. Leymarie, F. F., D. B. Cooper, M. S. Joukowsky, B. B. Kimia, D. H. Laidlaw, D. Mumford, E. L. Vote. The SHAPE Lab: New Technology and Software for Archaeologists. *Computer Applications in Archaeology, CAA 2000: 28th Annual International Conference*, Ljubljana, Slovenia, 18–21 April 2000, Archaeopress, publishers of *BAR*.

98. Romey, K. M. Fourth in the Field, Celebrating Home Abroad. *Archaeology*, 12–13 July/August, 53, 4.

99. Vote, E. L., D. Acevedo, D. Laidlaw, and M. S. Joukowsky. ARCHAVE: A Virtual Environment for Archaeological Research. *Computer Applications in Archaeology, CAA 2000, 28th Annual International Conference.* Ljubljana, Slovenia, 18–21 April 2000.

100. ———. ARCHAVE: A Three-Dimensional GIS for a CAVE Environment (As Applied to Petra's Great Temple Project). *ASOR Annual Meeting Abstracts*, 15–18 November, 4.

101. van Dam, A., A. S. Forsberg, D. H. Laidlaw, J. J. LaViola, Jr., and R. M. Simpson. Archave, Daniel Acevedo Feliz and Eileen L. Vote. Sidebar in article, Immersive VR for Scientific Visualization: A Progress Report. *IEEE Computer Graphics and Applications.* November/December.

102. Vote, E. L, D. Acevedo, M. S. Joukowsky, and D. Laidlaw. Virtual Reality and Scientific Visualization in Archaeological Research. *Virtual Archaeology between Scientific Research and Territorial Marketing*, Arezzo (Italy), 24–25 November 2000.

103. Vote, E. L., and M. S. Joukowsky. Using Desktop Photogrammetry to Document Archaeological Remains: The Great Temple at Petra, Jordan. *Proceedings of Computer Applications in Archaeology, 27th annual international conference.* Held in Dublin Castle April 1999. Archaeopress BAR. Dublin, Ireland.

104. Zimmerman, P. Mapping Petra. *Expedition*, 42, 2, 37–41.

2001

105. Acevedo, D. "Scientific Archaeology vs. The Discovery Channel." M.A. Thesis, Brown University.

106. Acevedo, D. D. Laidlaw, and M. S. Joukowsky. ARCHAVE: A Virtual Environment for Archaeological Research, *CAA 2000 Proceedings Computing Archaeology for Understanding the Past.* Edited by Z. Stancic and T. Veljanovski. *BARIS* 931, Archaeopress, Oxford, England. 313–316.

107. Acevedo, D., E. L. Vote, D. H. Laidlaw, and M. S. Joukowsky. Archaeological Data Visualization in VR: Analysis of Lamp Finds at the Great Temple of Petra, a Case Study. *Visualization* 2001 *Proceedings*, October. (Winner, Best Case Study.)

108. Cloke, C. Chris. Cloke gets Petra-fied. *The College Hill Independent*, 13.3, 1–11.

109. Joukowsky, M. S. 2000 Brown University Excavations at the Great Temple of Petra, Jordan. *AIA 102nd Annual Meeting Abstracts* 24, 57.

110. ———. 2000 Brown University Excavations at the Great Temple of Petra, Jordan. In *102nd Meeting of the Archaeological Institute of America. AJA* 105.2, 273.

111. ———. Petra: Brown University Excavations of the Great Temple: Questions About Functional Analysis. *SHAJ*, VII, 447–455.

112. ———. Petra. The Great Temple. In "The Archaeology of Jordan." Edited by S. H. Savage, K. Zamora, and D. R. Keller. *AJA* July, 105.3, 451–453.

113. ———. Petra, The Great Temple, In *Archaeological Encyclopedia of the Holy Land*. Edited by A. Negev and S. Gibson, 384–388.

114. ———. Guest Editor, *BASOR* November 2001, No. 324.

115. ———. Nabataean Petra. *BASOR* 324, 1–4.

116. ———. A Day of Excavation at Petra: An Archaeological Experience. *Cultural Horizons, Volume I, A Festschrift In Honor of Talat S. Halman*. Edited by J. L. Warner. Yapi Kredi Yayinlari, Syracuse University Press, 240–246.

117. ———. Prof. Martha Sharp Joukowsky was on Sabbatical Leave During the Second Semester of the Year and Has Kindly Offered the Following Account of Her Research This Year. Edited by R. R. Holloway, *Brown University Center for Old World Archaeology and Art, Report of the Director* 2000–2001, 2–3.

118. ———. Petra: Great Temple Excavations. *ACORN* 13.1, 5–6.

119. ———. Brown University Excavations in Jordan at the Petra Great Temple, 2002. *BUFB*, October, 40–43.

120. ———. Brown University Excavations of the Great Temple of Petra, Jordan, ASOR *2001 Annual Meeting Abstracts*, November 14–17, 2.

121. ———. Brown University 2000 Excavations at the Petra Great Temple. *ADAJ*, 45, 325–342.

122. ———. Petra: Brown University Excavations of the Great Temple, Questions about Functional Analysis. *SHAJ* Vol. VII, 447–455.

123. ———. Joukowsky, M. S. and J. J. Basile, More Pieces in the Petra Great Temple Puzzle. *BASOR*, 324, 23–41.

124. Leymarie, F., D. Cooper, M. S. Joukowsky, B. Kimia, D. Laidlaw, D. Mumford and E. Vote, The SHAPE Lab: New Technology and Software for Archaeologists. Edited by Z. Stancic and T. Veljanovski. *The CAA* 2000 *Proceedings, Computing Archaeology for Understanding the Past*—CAA 2000, *BARIS* 931, Oxford, England, 79–90.

125. Reid, S. K. The 2001 Season at the Petra Small Temple. *ASOR* 2001 *Annual Meeting Abstracts*, 14–17 November 2001, 34–35.

126. Taylor, J. *Petra and the Lost Kingdom of the Nabataeans*. I. B. Tauris & Co. Ltd. London and New York, 106–111.

127. Vote, E. L. "A New Methodology for Archaeological Analysis: Using Visualization and Interaction to Explore Spatial Links in Excavation Data." Ph.D. diss., Brown University.

128. ———. New Archaeology Analysis Tools. *BUFB*, October 2001, 44–45.

2002

129. Basile, J. J. Recently Discovered Relief Sculptures from the Great Temple at Petra, Jordan. *ADAJ* 46, 331–346.

130. ———. *Dig Magazine*. Petra Rocks! Tales from the Ancient Rock City, in issue devoted to Petra with contributions by members of the Brown University Petra Great Temple excavation team: Deirdre G. Barrett, Brian A. Brown, Christian F. Cloke, Emily Catherine Egan, Artemis A. W. Joukowsky, Martha S. Joukowsky, Sara Karz Reid, Edited by M. S. Joukowsky. 5.5 (September/October).

131. ———. Two Visual Languages at Petra: Aniconic and Representational Sculpture of the Great Temple. *NEA* 65.4, 255–259.

132. Bodel, J., and S. K. Reid. A Dedicatory Inscription to the Emperor Trajan from the Small Temple at Petra, Jordan. *NEA* Vol. 65, No. 4, 249–250.

133. Egan, E. C. Stucco Decoration from the South Corridor of the Petra Great Temple: Discussion and Interpretation. *ADAJ* 46, 347–361.

134. ———. "Putting the Pieces Together: An Analysis and interpretation of the stucco finds recovered from the South Corridor of the Petra Great Temple in Petra, Jordan during the 2001 excavation season." Senior Honors Thesis, Brown University Center for Old World Archaeology and Art and Department of Classics.

135. Gilles, D. "Une nouvelle methode d'analyse archéologique: l'analyse du Petit Temple de Pétra assistée par une technique de visualisation en 3-D." Mémoire de D.E.A. Sous la direction de M. Le Professeur J. D. Forest, 2001–2002.

136. Gillespie, K. Petra's Great Temple rises again 2,000 years later. *Jordan Times*, 25 August 2002.

137. Joukowsky, M. S. The Petra Great Temple Elephant-Headed Capitals as a Cultural Artifact. *AIA 103rd Annual Meeting Abstracts*, Philadelphia, PA, 3–6 January 2002, 106–107.

138. ———. Petra. Great Temple, In Archaeology in Jordan, 2001 Season. Edited by S. H. Savage, K. Zamora and D. R. Keller. *AJA* 106 435–458, see 451–452.

139. ———. Technologies in Use at the Brown University Excavations of the Petra Great Temple. In *The Hashemite University, Zarqa, Jordan, for International Conference on Science and Technology in Archaeology and Conservation, Under the Patronage of Her Majesty Queen Rania Al Abdullah of Jordan, with the Sponsorship of UNESCO, Abstracts*, 38.

140. ———. Petra: Great Temple, *ACORN* Vol. 14 No. 1, 10–11.

141. ———. The Brown University 2002 Petra Great Temple Excavations Offer More Surprises. *ADAJ* Vol. 46, 315–330.

142. ———. The Petra Great Temple: A Nabataean Architectural Miracle. *NEA* Vol. 65, No. 4, 235–248.

143. ———. From the Guest Editor. *NEA* Vol. 65, No. 4, 23:i.

144. Khalifeh, I. *Ad-Dustour Daily Newspaper, Amman* (in Arabic) July 20, 2002, 5.

145. Lubell, S. Virtually Rebuilt, A Ruin Yields Secrets. *New York Times*, 2 May 2002.

146. Mailé, F. "De la fouille à la modélisation animée 3-D de vestiges de archéologiques: reconstitution du cryptoportique ouest de Grand Temple de Pétra, Jordanie Vols. I & II." Mémore de DEA, sous la direction de MM. Les Professeurs J-D. Forest and J-P. Thalmann avec la participation de Mme. M. S. Joukowsky, Université de Paris I—Panthéon-Sorbonne UFR 03, en partenariat avec Brown University, Providence, USA, Division of Engineering/Shape Lab—LEMS.

147. Reid, S. K. Excavations at the Petra Small Temple 2000–2001. *ADAJ* 46, 363–379.

148. Ronay, V. The Soul of Petra: Bedouin Residents of a Hidden City; Patterns The World. June 2002, 188–199. "The Petra Great Temple," 196–197.

149. Savvidou, M. Petra—The Magical City in Jordan, "ΠΕΤΡΑ—Της Μαριας Σαββιδου." ΑΝΕΞΓΗΤΟ (*Anexigiton*). November 2002, 171, Ευρω 44, 118–123 (in Greek).

150. Seigne, J. Compte rendu of M. Sharp Joukowsky, *Petra: The Great Temple, Vol. I—Brown University Excavations 1993–1997*. Edited by M. S. Joukowsky. (1998) Petra Exploraton Fund, Providence RI, In ΤΟΠΟΙ 10/2 507–516.

151. Shanks, H. The State of the Profession: Few Bright Lights at Annual Meeting. *Archaeology Odyssey*, May/June 2002, Vol. 5, 3, 4.

152. Vote, E. L., D. A. Feliz, D. H. Laidlaw, and M. S. Joukowsky. Discovering Petra: Archaeological Analysis in VR. *IEEE Computer Graphics and Applications*. Issue devoted to Art History and Archaeology (September/October), 38–49.

2003

153. Basile, J. J. The Relief Sculpture Program from the Great Temple at Petra, Jordan. The Near East in the Hellenistic and Roman Periods. *AIA, 104th Annual Meeting Abstracts*. Philadelphia, PA, 3–6 January 2003, 61.

154. Borg, L. At Brown, a virtual temple takes shape. *The Providence Journal.* 15 April 2003, G 4.

155. Cloke, C. F. *Water in the Desert: The Water Systems of the Petra Great Temple*. 2003 Series Publications, Brown University. Wayland Press, Providence, Rhode Island.

156. Curtis, M. J. Scientists and artists partner to create virtual Petra: Digital technology electronically preserved the deteriorating temple and its artifacts. In *Liberal Arts: An Arts and Humanities Supplement to the George Street Journal*. 28 Feb 2003, 1–3.

157. Glouberman, N. SHAPE, Higher Learning Technology Serving Education. *http://www.teachmag. com/higher_learning.asp*, 17–18.

158. Henry, A. Out of School: Unearthing the History of Petra with Brown University. *The Lawrentian*, Spring 2003, 18 No. 306–700 Vol. 67, No. 2, 14–15.

159. Higher Learning: Technology Serving Education. *SHAPE, Higher Learning—Projects*. (May/June), 18–19.

160. Joukowsky, M. S. The Unconventional Nabataeans: Reflections from the Petra Great Temple, in Colloquium: Cultural Relations in the Greco-Roman Near East. *AIA, 104th Annual Meeting Abstracts*. Philadelphia, PA, 3–6 January 2003, 119.

161. ———. Ten Years of Excavation at the Petra Great Temple: A Retrospective. *ACORN* 14–2, (Winter), 1–2.

162. ———. Petra. Great Temple. In "Archaeology in Jordan, 2002 Season," Edited by S. H. Savage, K. Zamora, and D. R. Keller, *AJA* 107, 466–468.

163. ———. Portal to Petra. *Natural History* 112.9, 40–43.

164. ———. Ten Years of Excavation at the Petra Great Temple: Another Retrospective. In *O Qui Complexus et Gaudia Quanta Fuerunt. Essays Presented to Michael C.J. Putnam by His Brown Colleagues on the Occasion of His 70th Birthday*. Brown University, Prov. RI.

165. ———. The Great Temple, Petra Rediscovered: Lost City of the Nabataeans, Edited by G. Markoe. Abrams, Inc. New York, Chapter 18, 214–222.

166. ———. A Decade of Brown University Excavations at the Petra Great Temple. *ASOR Annual Meeting Abstracts*, (19–22 November) 16–17.

167. ———. Excavations at the Petra Great Temple: The Eleventh Campaign. *ACORN* (Winter 2003) Vol. 15–2, 6.

168. ———. More Treasure and Nabataean Traditions at the Petra Great Temple: The Brown University 10th Campaign. 2002. *ADAJ* 47, 389–406.

169. Mayercik, V. Virtual Archaeology—Can you Dig It? *The Catalyst* 10.1, 20–21.

170. Nelson, L. Documentary on Petra Debuts at Brown after two years spent in the making, "Academic Watch." *The Brown Daily Herald*, Vol. CXXXVIII, 52, 16 April 2003, 6, 9.

171. Netzer, E. *Die Tempel der Nabatäer: Der Grosse (Süd-) Tempel in Nabatäische Architektur: Inbesondere Gräber und Tempel*. Verlag Philipp von Zabern, Mainz. 72–81.

172. Reid, S. K. Excavations at the Small Temple of Petra, Jordan, The Near East in the Hellenistic and Roman Periods. In *AIA 104th Annual Meeting Abstracts*, Philadelphia, PA, 3–6 January, 2003. 61.

173. ———. Excavations at the Small Temple of Petra." *ASOR Annual Meeting Abstracts*, November 17, 19–22.

174. Rossner, T. Hats Off! In "Old Time Almanack." *Eastside Marketplace* (27 July – 2 August), 8.

175. Villeneuvre, E. La chamber baroque. In *Le Monde de la Bible*, No. 150.9, 51.

2004

176. Barrett, D. G. "The Ceramic Oil Lamp as an Indicator of Cultural Change Within Nabataean Society in Petra and its Environs Circa CE 106." Ph.D. diss., Department of Anthropology, Brown University.

177. Curtis, M. J. Joukowsky's work on exhibit at American Museum of Natural History. *George Street Journal Special Edition* (March 2004) 8.

178. DeKeukelarere, L. Piecing the Past: An Algorithm Quickly Fits Together Potsherds. *Scientific American*, September, 30.

179. Egan, Emily Catherine. Petra's Wealth. *Archaeology*, (March/April) 57, 2, 60.

180. Joukowsky, M. S. The Petra Great Temple's Water Strategy. *The Ninth International Conference on the History and Archaeology of Jordan, "Cultural Interaction Through the Ages."* Ministry of Tourism and Antiquities, Department of Antiquities and Al-Hussein Bin Talal University, 23–27 May 2004. Petra, Under the Patronage of His Majesty King Abdullah II of Jordan. *Abstracts*, 25.

181. ———. Petra. The Great Temple. In Archaeology in Jordan, 2003 Season. Edited by S. H. Savage, K. A. Zamora, and D. R. Keller, *AJA* 108.3, 441–443.

182. ———. The 2004 Brown University Excavations at the Petra Great Temple. *ASOR 2004 Annual Meeting Abstracts*, San Antonio, Texas, 44.

183. ———. Brown University 2003 Excavations at the Petra Great Temple: The Eleventh Field Campaign. *ADAJ* 48, 155–170.

184. ———. 2004e. The Water Installations of the Petra Great Temple. In *Men of Dikes and Canals: The Archaeology of Water in the Middle East*. International Symposium held at Petra, Wadi Musa (H. K. of Jordan) 15–20 June 1999. Edited by H-D. Bienert and J. Häser. Deutsches Archäologisches Institut Orient-Abteilung, Orient-Archäologie, Band 13, Marie Leindorf GmbH, Rahde/Westf, 123–141.

185. ———. Crawford, Gregory A. Review: *Petra and the Nabataeans: A Bibliography*. ATLA Bibliography Series, Vol. 49. The Scarecrow Press Lanham, MD. 2003. Pp. xxii + 275. *JAOS*, 124.2, 407.

186. ———. Review: *Petra Ez Zantur II: Ergebnisse der Schweizerisch-Liechtensteinischen Ausgrabungen*. By Stephan G. Schmid and Bernhard Kolb. Pt. 1: *Die Feinkeramik der Nabatäer*; Pt. 2: *Die spätantiken Wohnbauten*. Terra Archaeologica, Vol. 4, Mainz: Verlag Philipp von Zabern, 2000. Pp. xvii + 311, plates, plans. *JAOS* 124.2, 350–351.

187. Kansa, S. Food and Religion in the Petra Region: A Zooarchaeological Study of Two Nabataean Temples. In *ASOR Abstracts*, 2004 Annual Meeting, San Antonio, Texas, 35.

188. Reid, S. K. "The Small Temple: A Roman Imperial Cult Building in Petra, Jordan." Department of Anthropology, Ph.D. diss. Department of Anthropology, Brown University.

2005

189. Abou-Assaly, E. K. Conférence du professeur Martha Sharp Joukowsly au Musée de l'AUB: Le Grand Temple de Pétra: récente découverte archéologique. *La Revue du Liban et de l'Orient Arabe*, 14–21 May, 54.

190. Dergham, O. Martha Sharp Joukowsky gives a lecture at the AUB [The American University of Beirut]: The discovery of the PETRA GREAT TEMPLE: The city of history is a never-ending series of surprises. *An-Nahar*, (Lebanese Newspaper), 5 May 2005, 21 (in Arabic).

191. Ho, T. Archaeology team's excavation of Petra Great Temple heading into its final year. *The Brown Daily Herald* CXL 101, 2 November 5, 6.

192. Jacobson, M. Melanie Jacobson takes us on a backstage tour of the Great Temple excavation conducted by the Brown University archaeological team. *The Jordan Times* 30, 9051, (11 August 2005) *The Jordan Times Weekender*, 4–5.

193. Joukowsky, M. S. Excavating a Priceless Heritage: Scientific and Other Applications Used by the Brown University Explorations of the Petra Great Temple. In *Terra Marique: Studies in Art History and Marine Archaeology in Honor of Anna Marguerite McCann on the Receipt of the Gold Medal of the Archaeological Institute of America*. Edited by John Pollini. Oxbow, Ch. 4, 40–55, pl. 2–4.

194. ———. Petra Great Temple, *ACORN* (Summer 2005) 17–1, 4–5.

195. ———. Lecture sheds light on different uses of Great Temple of Petra: Functions include place of worship, fortress and market place. *The Daily Star*, 6 May. Beirut Lebanon, No. 11, 688, 12.

196. ———. Brown University Archaeological Research at the Petra Great Temple 2004. *ADAJ* 49, 147–165.

197. Saidi, L. Recent Discoveries at the Petra Great Temple. In *American University of Beirut Archaeological Museum NEWSLETTER*, Published by the Society of Friends, Vol. XXI, 2, 10–15.

198. Seeley, N. Picking Up the Pieces. With photographs by S. Zureikot. In *JO Magazine*. (July) 46–51.

2006

199. Joukowsky, M. S. Petra: The Great Temple. In Archaeology in Jordan, 2005 Season, Edited by S. H. Savage and D. R. Keller. *AJA* 110, 478–481.

200. ———. Brown University's 2005–2006 Excavations at the Petra Great Temple. *ASOR 2006 Annual Meeting Abstracts*, Washington DC, 58–59.

201. ———. The Petra Great Temple: A Final Chapter. *ACORN* 18–1, 1–2.

202. ———. Challenges in the Field: The Brown University 2005 Petra Great Temple Excavations. *ADAJ* Vol. 50, 351–372.

203. Levintova, H. Joukowsky to stop work on Jordanian dig after 14 years, *The Brown Daily Herald*. Tuesday September 19, 2006.

204. Macaulay-Lewis, E. R. Planting pots at Petra: a preliminary study of *ollae perforatae* at the Petra Garden-Pool Complex and at the 'Great Temple.' *Levant* No. 38, 159–160.

205. Praeger, M. In a land of kings, these relics are awesome, like their setting. *Boston Sunday Globe*, 19 March 2006. M1, M12.

206. Reid, S. K. *The Small Temple: A Roman Imperial Cult Building in Petra, Jordan.* Gorgias Dissertations, Near Eastern Studies: GD 20, NES 7. Piscataway, NJ.

207. Shao, W. "Animating Autonomous Pedestrians." Ph.D. diss., Department of Computer Science, Courant Institute of Mathematical Sciences, New York University.

2007

208. Lawler, A. Reconstructing Petra. *Smithsonian Magazine*, Vol. 38, No. 3, June, 42–49.

209. Joukowsky, M. S. Surprises at the Great Temple from 1993 to 2006. In *Crossing Jordan: North American Contributions to the Archaeology of Jordan*. T. E. Levy, P. M. M. Daviau, R. W. Younker and M. Shaer, Eds., Equinox Publishing Ltd., London and CT, 385–392.

210. ———. More Surprises at the Petra Great Temple. *10th International Conference on the History and Archaeology of Jordan Abstracts*, Washington DC, 38.

211. ———. Petra: The Great Temple. In Archaeology in Jordan, 2006 Season, Edited by S. H. Savage and D. R. Keller, *AJA* 111, 542–544.

212. Joukowsky, M. S. and Christian F. Cloke. The Petra Great Temple's Water Strategy, *SHAJ*, Vol. IX, 431–437.

213. Power, Eleanor A. "The Roman–Byzantine Bath Complex at the Petra Great Temple in Jordan." Honors Thesis at the Joukowsky Institute for Archaeology and the Ancient World at Brown University.

RESEARCH IN PROGRESS

214. Shaer, M. and S. Simon The Plasters, Renders and Mortars of the Petra Great Temple. In *The 6th International Symposium on the Conservation of Monuments in the Mediterranean Basin* (in press).

215. Tuttle, Christopher A. *"Life in Miniature: Figurines as Indicators for the Socio-Religious Culture of Petra and the Nabataean Kingdom."* Ph.D. diss. Institute for Archaeology and the Ancient World Brown University.

216. Acevedo, Daniel, Eileen Vote, David H. Laidlaw, and Martha S. Joukowsky. ARCHAVE: A Virtual Environment for Archaeological Research. Work in Progress report, *IEEE Visualization* 2000, Salt Lake City, Utah, October 2000. (pdf/ps/html).

217. Cooper, D. B., A. Willis, Stuart Andrews, J. Baker, Y. Cao, D. Han, K. Kang, W. Kong, F. F. Leymarie, X. Orriols, E. L. Vote, M. S. Joukowsky, B. B. Kimia, D. H. Laidlaw, D. Mumford, S. Velipasalar. Assembling Virtual Pots from 3-D Measurements of Their Fragments. In *VAST* 2001.

218. Joukowsky, Martha Sharp. Excavation and Consolidation of Archaeological Structures: An Example from the Great Temple at Petra, Jordan. In Guardians of Monuments and Museums, New York University, Graduate School of Arts and Science Museum Studies Program, Edited by Flora E. Kaplan.

219. Vote, Eileen. 2002. A Virtual-Reality Application for Post-Excavation Archaeological Analysis. In *IEEE Computer Graphics and Applications, special issue on Art History and Archaeology* (September).

WEB PAGES

2005–2007. (Web pages and for digital videos and 3D images) <The Joukowsky Institute Workplace>The Petra Great Temple Database Project or *http://proteus. brown.edu/PGTdata/Home* or *http://proteus.brown.edu.*

2007. *Open Context, <http://www.opencontext.org>.* 1993–2006 Petra Great Temple site plans of trenches excavated, catalog, coin catalog, architectural fragment, and Gross Modo databases, phasing charts of every trench and locus, site plans, aerial photographs of the site by year, 1998–2006 *ADAJ* reports, and architectural and artifact drawings.

1995. Southern Temple Excavations at Petra, Jordan, Brown University. <*petra@stg.brown.edu*>

1996. "Petra" on *ASOR Digs* 96. The American Schools of Oriental Research, Committee on Archaeological Policy: Reports of Affiliated Projects. <*http://www.cobb.msstate.edu/asordigs.html*>

1997, 1999–2004 updated, "The Petra Great Temple." *http://www.brown.edu/Departments/ Anthropology/Petra/*

2003. *http://www.lems.brown.edu/shape/#news.* 2003 May/June issue of Higher Learning. *Higher Learning* pp.18–19 <*http://www.teachmag.com/higher-learning. html*> Published by *TEACH* Magazine, 258 Wallace Ave. Ste 206, Toronto, Ontario, M6P 3M9, Canada.

Bazin, P. L., and A. Henry. *2003 Wall Drawer: A Simple Solution to Traditional Drawing and Photographic Recording of Archaeological Features. http://www.lwms. brown.edu basin/Research/WallDrawer.html*

MEDIA AND VIDEO

2003. *Petra Great Temple,* A 54-minute film of the Brown University Excavations. Amedia Production by Michael Udris and David Udris ©Martha Sharp Joukowsky. 124 Washington St. Providence, RI 02903 (401 523 4222, *www.udris.com.* Cost $35.)

"Petra and the Nabataeans, Trade, Intercultural Contacts and Associations, Influence of Hellenism, Crossroads of Occidental and Oriental Worlds, The Great Temple, City Planning, Hydrological Engineering." Open Curriculum, *Mariners of Greece International Education Program,* Video Roundtable with schools in Amman Jordan, Athens Greece, Copenhagen, Denmark and New York City, USA. George Newman, ed. Technology Applications Research LLC. (May). Can be accessed at *www.oneplaneteducation.com>* Webcast Segment II.

"ARCHAVE: A Virtual Environment for Archaeological Research." June 14, 2000. Brown University Department of Computer Science. D. Acevado, E. Vote, D. Laidlaw, and M. S. Joukowskyy.

TELEVISION, RADIO, & OTHER

2006. National Canadian Radio. Interview for "Petra" at the *Canadian National Museum of Civilization,* Ottawa, 29 September 2006.

2001. *Inaugural Faculty Program for President Ruth J. Simmons.* "Simulation and Visualization in the Petra Project," with David Laidlaw, Computer Science, Martha Sharp Joukowsky, Old World Art and Archaeology and Department of Anthropology, with Eileen Vote and Daniel Acevedo, Computer Science.

1997. Mannis, Avi. "Coins of the 'Great' Southern Temple, Petra," *The Digital Archive Project* (CD ROM) for Honors Thesis at Brown University's Center for Old World Archaeology and Art.

1996. *Search, Archaeology 101.* North Carolina State University. Short appearance as Brown University's Director, Petra 'Great' Temple Excavations.

1995. *Ancient Mysteries. Arts and Entertainment* (Arts and Entertainment Network Series) documentary film produced by Bram Rose et al., "Petra." 52 minutes, color program, narrated by Kathleen Turner.

1995–1994. *Archaeology* series, "Petra, City in the Sand." *Learning Channel,* New Dominion Films, color, narrated by John Rhys Davies. (Re-aired SEVERAL times to the present.)

1995. Video Lecture on Petra "Great" Southern Temple. *St. Louis Society of the Archaeological Institute of America.* Martha Sharp Joukowsky, 17 October 1995.

CHAPTER ONE

1

History of Excavations,
Stratigraphy and Chronology

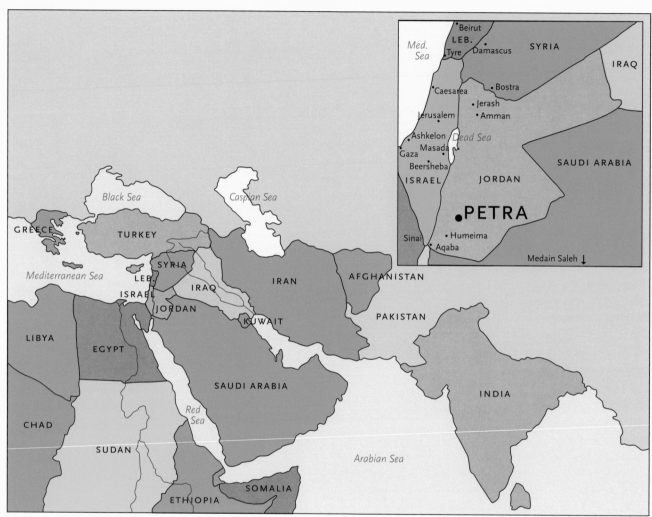

Map of the Region.

CHAPTER ONE:

History of Excavations, Stratigraphy and Chronology

The orientalist R.E. Brünnow, and the classicist, A. von Domaszewski, surveyed Petra at the end of the nineteenth century, in 1897–1898, and published an ambitious three-volume mapping project in their *Die Provincia Arabia* (1904–1909). During World War I, W. Bachmann, C. Watzinger and T. Wiegand investigated the city structures under the auspices of the Committee for the Preservation of Monuments of the German-Turkish Army. It was Walter Bachmann who in the nineteen twenties is credited with the identifications of various sites in the central city and designated the names for both the Great Temple and the Small Temple, names that identify the sites today—both of which Brown University archaeologists have excavated. The Central Petra city plan is shown in Figure 1.1, and Figure 1.2 depicts the structural reconstruction of the city center with both structures identified.

The genesis of the Petra Great Temple excavations can be traced to 1992. Under the sponsorship of Brown University, extensive excavations were launched in 1993. We instituted tactical and strategic research designs, and used survey programs developed by the Museum of Applied Science at the University of Pennsylvania for a site grid, topographic map, and for recording the step-by-step excavation process with a GIS interface. Since 1993, 14 successive field campaigns have been conducted annually between 1993 and 2006 in various sectors of the precinct. We are fortunate to have the same basic data collection systems in use from the inception of the excavations until the present.

Brown University's excavations uncovered the vast temple complex and adjoining areas spread over 11,524 m², among one of the most spectacular architectural wonders of Petra.

Founded over two millennia ago the Great Temple site was abandoned until its rediscovery by Brown University archaeologists in 1992. Excavations of its complex construction history commenced under my direction in 1993 and restoration will continue into the future. Figure 1.3 is an aerial overview of the Petra Great Temple before our excavations began in 1993. Figure 1.4 shows the devastation and collapse of the Great Temple precinct and Figure 1.5 shows the massive wreckage of the building with which we were confronted. Figure 1.6 shows the site at the close of the 2006 excavations and Figure 1.7 is a plan of the site with the major components identified.

The Great Temple represents one of the major archaeological and architectural components of metropolitan Petra. It is the largest free-standing building yet excavated in the city. Located to the south of the Roman Street and southeast of the Temenos Gate, this precinct is comprised of a Propylaeum, a Lower Temenos, and monumental east and west stairways and center stairway which in turn lead to the Upper Temenos—the sacred enclosure for the Temple proper. In general, the temple precinct is oriented northeast-by-southwest. Typical of Nabataean temples, there is a lack of uniform alignment that underscores the Nabataean penchant for orientation according to the terrain; they did not adhere to the principle that the direction of prayer had to be fixed. The area designated for construction had to be manipulated and the necessity of placing the entrance on the street allowed Nabataean architects to satisfy the desire to maintain an integral connection between the precincts, the major thoroughfare of the central city and the Wadi Musa beyond.

In Volume I (Joukowsky 1998, 51), we outlined our survey procedures before the excavation began. Now that we have an integrated site plan of the central city produced by the Hashemite University and the American Center of Oriental Research, we are on much firmer ground of knowing where the Great Temple is situated and the interrelationships between the Great Temple and other structures both on the Great Temple site itself and to the city of Petra as a whole.

Surveying Strategy and Site Datum Points

For 14 years Petra Great Temple annual site plans were supplemented with aerial photographs, each of which have been previously published in our annual reports. In 1992 and 1993, before our excavations began, J. Wilson

Myers and Eleanor E. Myers conducted an aerial photographic balloon survey of the site. With each successive season, we have continued to document the area extensively with low altitude aerial photographic and photogrammetric coverage. In 1997, the United States National Park Service carried out a Test Project at Petra. This project established coordinates for the site with a global positioning system (GPS). Because the Great Temple was visible, these studies began the processing of radar-generated and related imagery. Additionally, geo-referencing was begun. The net result of such map research, as well as our own aerial photography, laser EDM (electronic distance measurement) surveys and the use of CADD (computer-aided design and drafting) programming, has produced one of the most detailed and accurate site-specific Petra maps for the archaeological record.

Fig 1.1
Map of the Petra city center.
A: Temple of Dushara (Qasr al-Bint)
B: Small Temple
C: Temenos Gate
D: South Tower
E: Baths-Palatial Complex
F: North Tower
G: Lower Temenos of the Great Temple Complex
H: Great Temple and its Upper Temenos
J: Bridges across the Wadi Musa
K: Colonnaded Street and Shops
L: Pool and Garden Complex ("Lower Market")
M: Middle "Market"
N: "Upper Market" ("Agora")
P: "Trajanic Arch"
Q: South Nymphaeum
R: North Nymphaeum
S: "Byzantine Tower"
T: "Royal Palace"
U: Temple of the Winged Lions or Temple of Al-'Uzza (Gymnasium)
V: Area A (Household)
W: Petra Church
X: Blue Chapel
Y: North Ridge Church against the so-called "Inner" City/ Defense Wall
Z: "Inner" City Wall and courtyard building

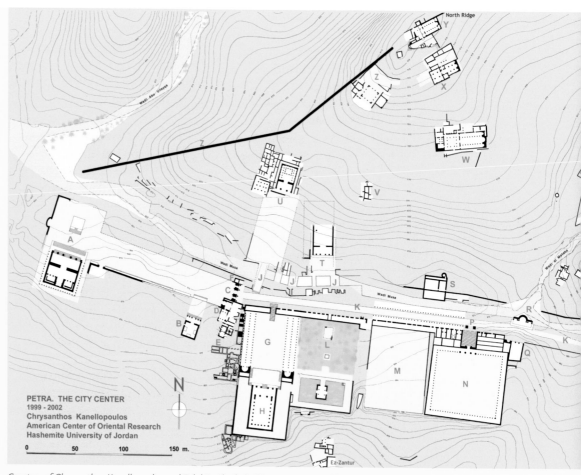

PETRA. THE CITY CENTER
1999 - 2002
Chrysanthos Kanellopoulos
American Center of Oriental Research
Hashemite University of Jordan

0   50   100   150 m.

Courtesy of Chrysanthos Kanellopoulos and Talal S. Akasheh. The map presented here is created by the Hashemite University of Jordan and the American Center of Oriental Research. It covers 650-by-500 m and extends from the Wadi Mataha and the Nymphaeum in the east and al-Habis to the west. This project was conducted with the assistance of the Higher Council for Science and Technology, Jordan, under the direction of Professor Talal Akasheh; Junior Volunteer Overseas Program; Japanese International Cooperation Agency and the United States Agency for International Development (USAID). This plan is an update with the Roman-Byzantine Bath Complex and the Residential Quarter superimposed on the original plan.

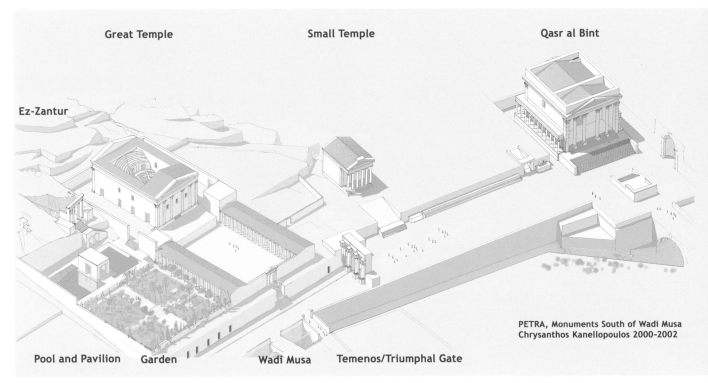

Great Temple   **Small Temple**   **Qasr al Bint**

Ez-Zantur

PETRA, Monuments South of Wadi Musa
Chrysanthos Kanellopoulos 2000-2002

Pool and Pavilion   Garden   Wadi Musa   Temenos/Triumphal Gate

Fig. 1.2
Reconstruction of the
Petra city center, a bird's
eye view of the slope south
of the Wadi Musa.
1999, © Chrysanthos
Kanellopoulos, ACOR and
Hashemite University. This
specific map is created by
C. Kanellopoulos, funded
by the American Center
of Oriental Research and
based on the points and
contours of the Hashemite
University Survey. This
reconstruction depicts
(from left to right) the Pool
and the Garden Complex,
the Great Temple Complex,
the Temenos Gate and the
Small Temple and Qasr
al-Bint and its Temenos as
they would have looked at
the end of the CE second
century. The Qasr al-Bint
appears with a pitched
roof and roof tiles, following the latest conclusions
by Larché (1984), instead
of a flat roof, which was
the favored solution of
other reconstructions.
The open-air Great Temple
is represented so that its
theater can be seen.

Our general approach to survey is to automate and integrate the collection of field data. We use a series of programs to chart and document the site, and the systems we deploy have proven so successful that they have been used as the model for other archaeological field operations. We utilize software packages that include a CADD program (MiniCad 6) and the COMPASS/ForeSight, SiteMap, and Vector-Works programs, a survey data acquisition and plotting package developed at the University of Pennsylvania Museum. These software packages combined with our use of a Topcon laser transit ensure the continuity of all our data files. Our system, therefore, is a combination of computer hardware (Apple laptop computers) and software that allows input, editing, storage, retrieval and display of spatially referenced data.

In 1993, once preliminary research and general site assessments were completed, one of the first and most critical tasks to be performed before excavation was the charting of master site plans and establishment of Control Points. Utilizing the Topcon laser transit to establish elevations and distances, a topographic survey was initiated (Joukowsky 1998, Figure 2.4). Control Points had to be selected and tied into the known benchmarks on the Al-Katute ridge. On top of the east wall of the precinct, we established the Site Datum Point known as CP 103 with an elevation of 915.04 m; a second point was located to the south of the West Exedra wall, CP 104, with an elevation of 903.90 m, and a third point, CP 10, was located at the top of the Stairs of the Propylaeum at an elevation of 898.29 m.

A comprehensive grid system of nominally 10 m squares aligned north–south also served as a control for the excavations. Illustrated in Figure 1.8, this grid superimposed on the 2006 data allowed us the flexibility to record architectural surface finds that were not associated with any specific trench or Special Project. The topography of the site is shown in Figure 1.9 where it should be noted there is a considerable elevation falling off on the west.

These data also appear in tabular database files to which other digital data, such as scanned images, may be added. These files can be viewed

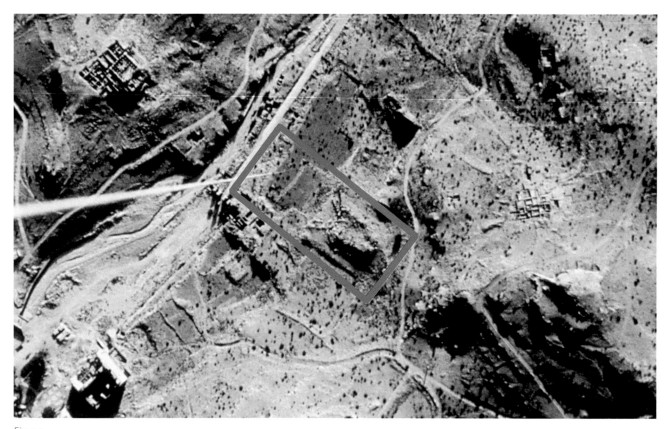

Fig. 1.3
Aerial pre-excavation
overview 1992.

as displays or printouts according to the field researcher's needs. Thus, these programs provide a means for accessing data sets from a variety of sources. Additionally, their capability renders them an excellent tool for the storage, retrieval and interpretation of archaeological information. These surveys are the backbone of the Great Temple excavation, for they have produced cumulative multidisciplinary data necessary for our research and long-term management of the site.

Data currently combined in this project include architectural plans, datum and sub-datum points, topographic features, walls and strati-graphic drawings, and trench maps with loci. The location of each trench and locus allows us the flexibility to determine if the architecture is associated or not. For example, daily field data processing produces maps of each trench's characteristics, which then are documented the following day in the field, and significant features

are recorded, measured, drawn and photographed. Copies of all of these maps have been turned over to the Department of Antiquities in Petra, to the Hashemite University, and to the American Center of Oriental Research for their use as reference tools.

In 1996, our voluminous multiple-year survey data files were converted to a new system —a most time-consuming undertaking that involved the conversion of the COMPASS data files and the updating of the data collection program. The new program, known as ForeSight, developed by our surveyor, Paul C. Zimmerman, is more versatile, speeds up results, and is easier to manipulate. This program has continued in use through the 2006 excavation season.

During the 1998 season we had the oppor-tunity to collaborate with the surveyors of the Petra Mapping Project (PMP), a joint project of the American Center of Oriental Research and the Hashemite University. In the course of their survey, our control points, CP 103 and CP 104, were shot in along with the Al-Katute

Fig. 1.4
The Petra Great Temple to
the south from the Temple
of the Winged Lions, 1993,
pre-excavation.

Fig. 1.5
Pre-excavation rubble
and collapse of the
Great Temple, 1993,
before excavations began.

datum. Since the PMP survey is keyed in to sub-centimeter GPS coordinates, these data allowed us to correlate our site plans with UTM (Universal Transverse Mercator) coordinates (WGS84 datum)—and, therefore, the entire site of Petra and indeed the world. The transformations were completed, and inspection of the data, after Volume I had gone to press, showed that our control points had to be adjusted; 19.556 m had to be added to all the datum and sub datum points we had used, and we had to make a 2-degree rotation adjustment to CP 103. Our internal measurements of feature dimensions remained constant, however, and each of our elevations in all the files, including trench reports,

had to be changed to reflect the correct readings. Thankfully, now the results are accurate.

Each of these datum points was clearly marked with cemented stakes and has served our surveying needs since the inception of the excavations. Thus, all elevations listed in this report are referenced to these datum points. Figure 1.10 shows the survey of the West Entry Stairway in progress.

Measurements for the four major sectors of the Precinct are given in their respective chapters. Below are the site datum points and the elevations for major features, followed by the measurements for the precinct and its major features.

Fig. 1.6
Aerial Great Temple, to south, 2006.

Petra Great Temple
Brown University Excavations

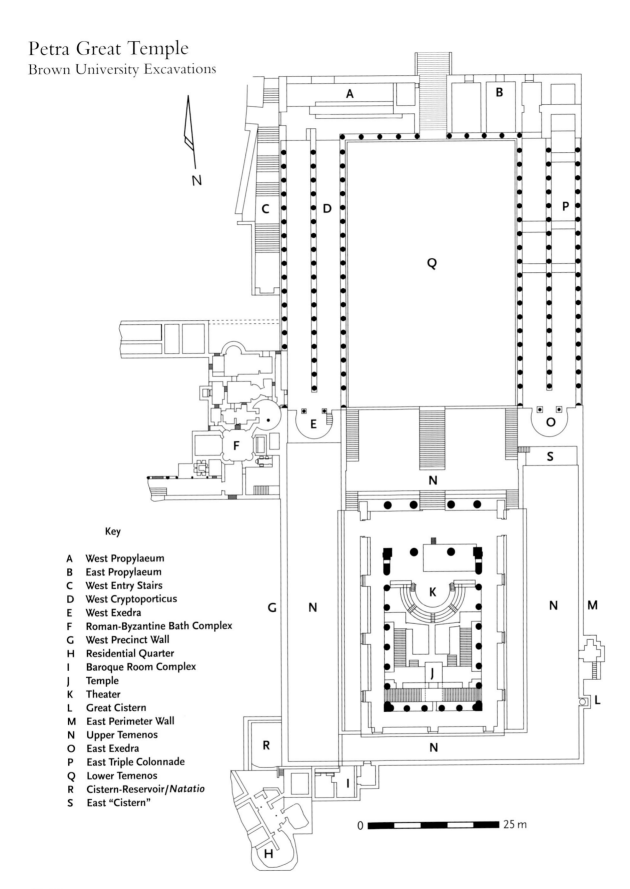

N

Key

A   West Propylaeum
B   East Propylaeum
C   West Entry Stairs
D   West Cryptoporticus
E   West Exedra
F   Roman-Byzantine Bath Complex
G   West Precinct Wall
H   Residential Quarter
I   Baroque Room Complex
J   Temple
K   Theater
L   Great Cistern
M   East Perimeter Wall
N   Upper Temenos
O   East Exedra
P   East Triple Colonnade
Q   Lower Temenos
R   Cistern-Reservoir/*Natatio*
S   East "Cistern"

0   25 m

Fig. 1.7
Petra Great Temple site plan, 2006.

Petra Great Temple
Brown University Excavations
Site Grid

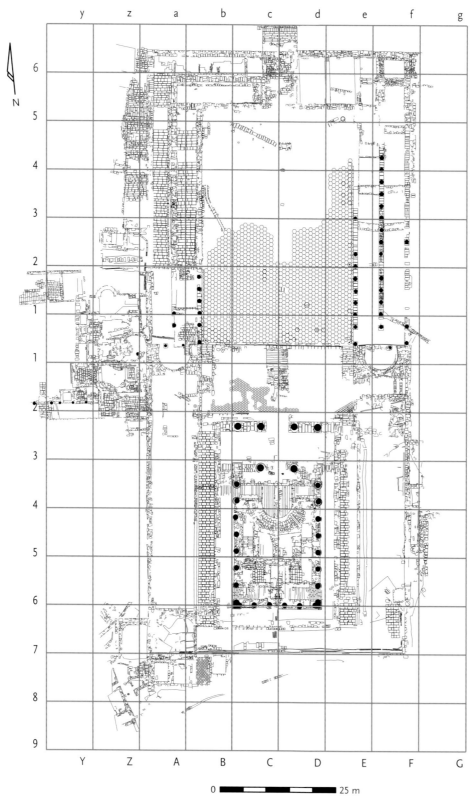

Fig. 1.8
Petra Great Temple site grid with north-south site orientation.

0 ⬛⬛⬛⬛⬛⬛ 25 m

Petra Great Temple
Brown University Excavations
2007 Site Plan

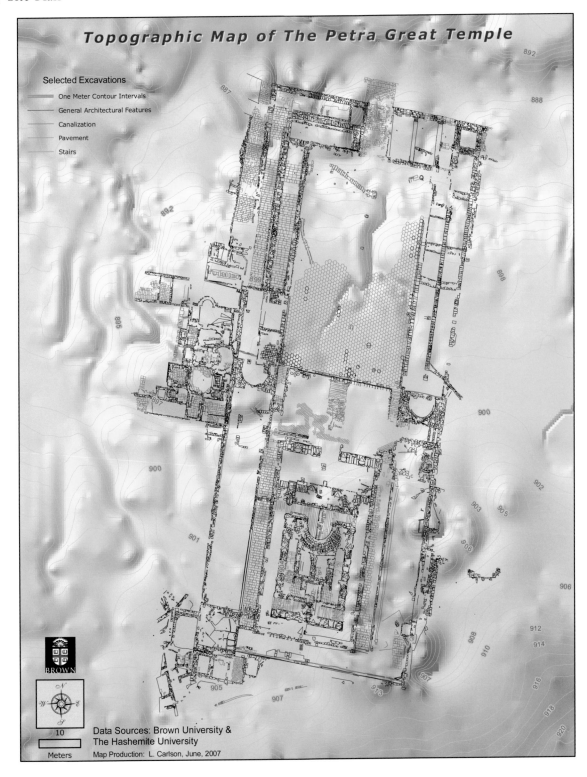

Fig. 1.9
Petra Great Temple Topographic Map, Lynn Carlson,
Geographic Information System Analyst, Brown University.

Elevations of Major Temple Precinct Components in Meters asl

Site Datum Points

Al-Katute—930.79 m

CP 103—915.04 m

CP 104—903.90 m

CP 10—898.29 m

1993–2006 Excavation Summary

Specific excavation procedures, research design and methodology are outlined in Volume I (Joukowsky 1998, 52–58). Plans and photographs of our yearly progress to 1997 as well as line drawings of the stratigraphy, and walls are presented in the CD-Rom that accompanied that volume. Figure 1.11 is a chart outlining the Trenches excavated by Year from 1993 to 2006, and at the conclusion of this chapter is a detailed listing of Trenches by Year and Area with their measurements and excavator(s) (Figure 1.27).

A summary of the annual excavations now can be outlined. Figure 1.12 is a reminder of the appearance of the site before the excavations began. In the earliest season we cleared the temple façade. Thereafter from 1994 to 1996 site recovery centered on the excavations in all areas of the precinct, and in 1995 GPR (ground penetrating radar) was used to define

Fig. 1.10
Eleanor A. Power and Marshall C. Agnew surveying the West Entry Stairway.

the subterranean canalization system. In 1997 the theater was recovered and excavations continued there in 1998. From 1999 to 2000 work resumed in all sectors and in 2001 the Great Cistern was unearthed. Figure 1.13 shows the progress of the excavations after the 2000 field season. Excavation also took place at the Small Temple, a Roman Imperial Cult Building located to the west of the temple precinct. During the 2002 season the Great Cistern excavation continued, but the most significant discovery was the Baroque Room Complex with the remains of its magnificent gilded plaster ceiling. Figure 1.14 depicts the site at the close of the 2002 season. The 2003 campaign concentrated on the definition of the East Propylaeum and the three rooms there which lie perpendicular to the principal artery of the central city, the Roman Street. In 2004 several sondages (Special Project test trenches) were undertaken in various areas, but excavation concentrated in the West Cryptoporticus with the additional recovery of a West Propylaeum ballista ball assemblage. Figure 1.15, taken at the close of the 2004 season, shows the clearance of the West Cryptoporticus. Again in 2005 several significant sondages were excavated to test the stratigraphy in the Great Temple Pronaos and the Theater orchestra. The West Entry Stairway was excavated, and the Roman-Byzantine Bath Complex commenced in earnest. In 2006 the excavation focus again was the Roman-Byzantine Baths. Shown in Figure 1.16 is the complete exposure of the West Entry Stairway with the Roman-Byzantine Baths beyond. A most important undertaking in 2006 was the removal of two rows of Theater seats and the excavation of a sondage below them.

In toto within four Areas[1] we have excavated 124 trenches and 70 Special Projects.[2] Essentially the archaeological investigations of the Great Temple structure and the majority of the precinct has been completed, but analysis of the remains, most particularly the architecture, will continue for some time to come. Additional major reference elevations and distance measurements are given below, but detailed measurements of each architectural feature are given in each excavation area in their respective chapter.

PROPYLAEUM	TEMPLE	LOWER TEMENOS	UPPER TEMENOS
Trench 50 (SP53)	Trench 9 (SP7, 52)	Trench 5 Part I	Trench 1
Trench 51	Trenches 8, 10, 11	Trench 5 Part II	Trench 2 Part I
Trench 69	Trench 12 (SP14)	Trench 6 Part I	Trench 2 Part II
Trench 70	Trench 15 Part I (SP8)	Trench 6 Part II (SP45, 46)	Trench 3
Trench 80	Trench 15 Part II	Trench 13	Trench 4
Trench 81	Trench 19	Trenches 14, 20 (SP22, 24, 29)	Trench 7
Trench 82	Trench 22 Part I	Trench 16 Part I	Trench 18
Trench 86	Trench 22 Part II	Trench 16 Part II	Trench 18A
Trench 87	Trench 23	Trench 17 Part I (SP25)	Trench 32
Trench 88	Trench 24	Trench 17 Part II	Trench 38
Trench 93	Trench 26, 27 Part I, 35 Part I	Trench 21 (SP31, 32, 33)	Trench 41
Trench 95	Trench 27 Part II	Trench 25	Trench 44
Trench 96	Trench 29	Trench 28	Trench 46
Trench 99	Trench 34 Part I (SP42, 43)	Trench 30	Trench 49
Trench 100	Trench 34 Part II	Trench 31 (SP41)	Trench 53
Special Project P	Trench 35 Part II	Trench 33	Trench 54
Special Project 70	Trench 40	Trench 36	Trench 67
Special Project 87	Trench 45	Trench 37	Trench 68 (SP61)
Special Project 88	Trench 47	Trench 39	Trench 72
Special Project 95	Trench 48	Trench 42 (SP48, 49)	Trench 75
Special Project 114	Trench 55	Trench 43	Trench 7
Special Project 118	Trench 55A	Trench 52	Trench 77 Part I
Special Project 125	Trench 56	Trench 60	Trench 77 Part II
Special Project 150	Trench 57	Trench 61	Trench 83 (SP83)
	Trench 58	Trench 66	Trench 84 (SP91)
	Trench 59	Trench 71	Trench 89
	Trench 62	Trench 79	Trench 90
	Trench 63	Trench 97	Trench 91
	Trench 64	Trench 98	Trench 94
	Trench 65 Part I	Trench 98B	Trench 101
	Trench 65 Part II	Trenches 102–103	Trench 105-106
	Trench 73	Trench 104	Trench 120
	Trench 85	Trench 121	Trench 125
	Trench 92	Trench 122	Special Project 4 Part I
	Trench 123	Trench 126	Special Project 4 Part II
	Special Project A	Trench 127	Special Project 4 Part III
	Special Project 1	Special Project 20	Special Project 21
	Special Project 2	Special Project 26	Special Project 30
	Special Project 3	Special Project 27	Special Project 35
	Special Project 9	Special Project 28	Special Project 44
	Special Project 10	Special Project 36	Special Project 60
	Special Project 11	Special Project 37	Special Project 84
	Special Project 12	Special Project 38 Part I	Special Project 85
	Special Project 13	Special Project 38 Part II	Special Project 89
	Special Project 15	Special Project 39 Part I	Special Project 94
	Special Project 16	Special Project 39 Part II	Special Project 96
	Special Project 23	Special Project 47	Special Project 108
	Special Project 34	Special Project 51	Special Project 110
	Special Project 40	Special Project 54	Special Project 111
	Special Project 50	Special Project 56	Special Project 120
	Special Project 71	Special Project 57	Special Project 121
	Special Project 72 (Tr 77 Part III)	Special Project 73	Special Project 123
	Special Project 93	Special Project 92	
	Special Project 107	Special Project 104	
	Special Project 109	Special Project 105	Special Project 21 (the baths)
	Special Project 200	Special Project 124	

Trenches by Area
1993–2006

Color Key:

- 1993
- 1994
- 1995
- 1996
- 1997
- 1998
- 1999
- 2000
- 2001
- 2002
- 2003
- 2004
- 2005
- 2006

Fig. 1.11
Chart of Petra Great Temple 1993–2006 Trenches excavated.

Fig. 1.12
Aerial photograph of the Great Temple and its surround, 1992
(Courtesy of J. Wilson Myers and Eleanor Emlen Myers).

Great Temple Sidewalk and Curbing: 5.25 m
north-south × 56.68 m east-west (—297.57 m²)

Propylaeum Measurements

Propylaeum: (external) 12.41 m north-south
× 56.68 m east-west

Propylaeum: (internal) 9.81 m north-south
× 53.98 m east-west

Lower Temenos Measurements

*From the Propylaeum Retaining Wall to the Lower
Temenos Retaining Wall:* 49.00 m north-south
× 56.00 m east-west

Upper Temenos Measurements

South Passageway: (external) 5.80 m north-south
× 27.20 m east-west × 5.44 m depth; (internal)
2.90 m north-south × 24.70 m east-west

South Perimeter Wall: 1.10 m north-south
× 55.46 m east-west × 7.11 m depth

BAROQUE ROOM COMPLEX

From the Anteroom to the Settling Tank: 5.77 m
north-south × 17.26 m east-west

RESIDENTIAL QUARTER

*From the Settling Tank in the east to west (excavated
extent):* 15.48 m north-south × 9.22 m east-west

EAST UPPER TEMENOS

East Perimeter Wall: 36.69 m north-south
× 1.33 m east-west × 6.40 m depth

East Plaza: 45.37 m north-south × 9.53 m to
14.00 m east-west

UPPER TEMENOS WEST

West Plaza: 49.33 m north-south × 10.20 m
east-west

Cistern-Reservoir: 7.00 m north-south × 5.40 m
east-west; Total area 37.80 m²

Roman-Byzantine Baths: 32.00 m north-south
× 28.40 m east-west

Temple Measurements

Distyle Temple: 30.07 m north-south × 18.36 m east-west

Tetrastyle Temple: 42.50 m north-south × 27.10 to 35.50 m east-west. *Tetrastyle* Temple —The largest freestanding structure in Petra

Porch stylobate: 2.20 m north-south × 28.00 m east-west

From the East Walkway to the West Walkway: 35.50 m

Great Temple Precinct Features
Dimensions in meters

Note: All measurements are external and include wall thicknesses unless otherwise noted.
When a depth is irregular e.g., steps, it is averaged.

GREAT TEMPLE PRECINCT
From Portico wall in the Propylaeum to the preserved south Precinct Wall: 135.00 m north-south × 56.00 m east-west:
   Total Temple Area: 7560 m² (¾ hectare)

Added Precinct Excavated Features

Sidewalk and Curbing: 5.25 m north-south × 56.68 m east-west—297.57 m²

Roman-Byzantine Baths: 32.00 m north-south × 28.40 m east-west; Total area 908.80 m²

West Entry Stairs: 37.20 m north-south × 4.60 m east-west; Total area 171.12 m²

Cistern-Reservoir: 7.00 m north-south × 5.40 m east-west; Total area 37.80 m²

Cistern-Reservoir/Natatio area excavated: 11.86 m north-south × 10.67 m east-west; Total area 126.50 m²

Baroque Room Complex: 6.12 m north-south × 18.29 m east-west; Total area 111.87 m²

Residential Quarter: 15.48 m north-south × 9.22 m east-west; Total area 142.73 m²

East Perimeter Wall: 36.69 m north-south × 4.00 m east-west; Total area 146.94 m²

   Additional Precinct Features and Measurements Total: 1,817 m²

   Total Great Temple Features Excavated (excluding the Small Temple): 9,377 m²

Fig. 1.13
Great Temple aerial, to the south, 2000.

Fig. 1.14
Great Temple precinct,
to the southwest, 2002.

Fig. 1.15
Great Temple precinct to
the south, 2004.

Just to the west of the Great Temple precinct is the Small Temple, which we also excavated. This has been published by Sara Karz Reid (2006).

Small Temple Precinct 76.00 m north-south × 31.00 m east-west; Total area 2356 m²

Small Temple (internal) 14.62 × 14.62: Total area 213.744 m²

Small Temple and Portico: Total area 338 m²

Total Great Temple Features Excavated (including the Small Temple) 9,417 m²

Brown University Excavations 1993–2006 Total Excavated Area, 11,524 m²

Noteworthy is the breadth of architectural remains recovered from these excavations. Perhaps most striking is the enormity of the area excavated. Beyond that it is obvious that these building complexes brought dramatic changes to the cultural landscape of Petra. They reveal the dramatic impact on and growth of the central city with the creation of the Great and Small Temples strategically placed along the principal street of the city.

Fig. 1.16
Great Temple precinct to
the southeast, 2006.

Great Temple Databases 1993–2006

Our Brown University team has recorded not only the on-going excavations but also all the artifacts recovered in our multiple site databases (Joukowsky 1998, 58–61, 237–343). Implementation and managing the site has also resulted in technological advancement for expanding and ensuring the continuity of information access and data preservation. Our databases now support the findings of approximately a half million artifacts, and the development of an internet-accessible database. In our Great Temple databases,[3] 405,291 fragments have been registered in the Grosso Modo database. Our architectural fragment database now numbers 19,255 registered architectural fragments, coins number 681, and the catalog of small finds numbers 1,833 artifacts. Ongoing are specialist analyses of 4,672 glass fragments, 27,658 bones, 1,472 lamps, and 317,977 ceramic fragments, a sample of which has been examined with Neutron Activation INAA analysis (Bedal, 1998; Barrett, 2004). In keeping with the stratigraphy, each of these registered artifacts in our databases has been assigned to a site phase. Additionally we have performed chemical analysis on a specimen number of our 26,901 stucco plaster fragments (Corbeil and Helwig, 1999). These indicate the Nabataeans used true fresco, meaning that no binding medium was detected between the pigments and the plaster base, but that pigments were placed directly onto the wet support. The painted decorative schemes used for the Great Temple corridor walls have been published by Emily Catherine Egan (2002). Additionally we have traced the quarry origins of our marble through isotopic analysis (Karz 2006, 113–147, 202).

Moreover we have developed the CAVE (Cave Automatic Virtual Environment), the first virtual reality three-dimensional (3-D) GIS application for ongoing field archaeological research (Vote, 2001). The 3-D GIS system, called "ARCHAVE," allows users to view and interact with different types of artifacts and architectural finds, *in situ*, in the context of a virtual room, the CAVE.

Chronology[4]

We will not dwell on the particulars of Early Petraean/Nabataean history and rule here, because it would be a repetition of Volume I. (Joukowsky 15–31). As a point of reference, Figure 1.17 presents the names and dates of the Nabataean rulers. Here we refer to the Nabataean period to cover the earliest reference to the Nabataeans in 312 BCE by the classical writer, Diodorus Siculus, until the Roman annexation in 106 CE. Dating of the accession to the Nabataean throne is fairly well established. However, there are some unresolved inconsistencies in the Nabataean King list (McKenzie 1990,15) with little known figures like Aretas I, Rabbel I and Aretas II, so the chronology cannot be considered absolute. The Nabataean reign exists for approximately 264 years. The Roman period follows the annexation in 106 CE and extends to the Byzantine period, or to 325 CE. The earthquake of 551 CE in the Late Byzantine period is all but the final devastation of the site, for thereafter only localized activities take place.

Aretas I	ca. 168 BCE
Rabbel I	Uncertain
Aretas II	120/90–96 BCE
Obodas I	96–85 BCE
Aretas III Philhellenos	85–62 BCE
Obodas II	62/61–59 BCE
Malichus I	59/58–30 BCE
Obodas III	30–9/8 BCE
Aretas IV, Lover of His People	9/8 BCE–40 CE
Malichus II	40–70 CE
Rabbel II	70–106 CE

Fig. 1.17
Chronology of
Nabataean Kings.

A Note about Radiocarbon Dating and Dendrochronology

Because the majority of our strata are disturbed, we avoided attempts to radiocarbon our deposits. We were concerned that soil contaminants might skew the picture and there is the possibility that both later and earlier deposits might have infiltrated a specific locus. Although samples have been collected, they have not been analyzed for ^{14}C, because the results rarely give a range of less than 100 years.

Most of the wood at the Great Temple has disintegrated. One juniper beam discovered in the West Corridor was sent to The Malcolm and Carolyn Weiner Laboratory for Aegean and Near Eastern Dendrochronology. No conclusive evidence was provided because the sample was reported to be "stressed juniper." (We have retained samples for further examination and analysis.)

Stratigraphy, Site Phasing and Dating of Archaeological Deposits

As a *terminus post quem* snapshot of the phased remains, we have divided them into 15 main periods, beginning with a Pre-Great Temple Phase I in the mid first century BCE, Phase II a *distyle* temple first century BCE, Phase IV The Great *tetrastyle* Temple—the Grand Design first century BCE, Phase V the Theater CE first century, Phase VI when we think a possible Roman attack took place in 106 CE, and Phases IX–XI are the major collapses and periods of abandonment after the 363 CE and 551 CE earthquakes, after which the site, again, was all but abandoned. During the approximate 1500–year period of final occupational/abandonment, the Great Temple site and its precinct withstood numerous earthquakes and vandalism, falling into decay amidst its desert environment. As we are unable to construct a monolithic chronological scheme, below is our reasoning behind the placement of our site phases. The phasing charts that place every locus of each site trench and Special Project into one of these 15 Great Temple Site Phases is too extensive to reproduce here, thus we have elected to publish it on the web at *Open Context, <http://www.opencontext.org>*.

It must be mentioned that the stratigraphy of the site has been problematic due to the erosion and post abandonment debris that has impacted the site that was sometimes as great as 12.00 m in depth. Many of our deposits are disturbed, and display secondary use or include intrusive materials. However, we have established "absolute dates" from the relative dating of the sequence of the Ez Zantur typology so that there is more or less a reliable synchronism for our absolute chronology.

In general we have a paucity of textural evidence, so what are the benchmarks that can be securely dated? As for the Nabataean period, we have the Ez Zantur ceramic horizons with beginning and ending dates, so we are able to cross-reference the internal local dates for the deposits.[5] Therefore we can be confident of the Nabataean period chronology established at Ez Zantur, the formal Roman takeover in 106 CE, and the earthquakes of 363 and 551 CE. It must be remembered, however, that the continuing construction and destruction of the Petra Great Temple renders a complex stratigraphy and at some points partial rebuilding activities or the ubiquitous earthquakes and tremors blur the issue.

Great Temple Closed Contexts

Our dating rests on a few internal chronological benchmarks, which serve as fixed points in the stratigraphy. Deposits are dated by the combined use of the ceramic evidence, the architectural and sculptural remains, numismatic evidence and lamp analyses. For example, in the 2001 Propylaeum Trench 86, the pottery can be dated to the first century BCE or earlier. In the Lower Temenos West Cryptoporticus (2005 SP104, Locus 24) the ceramics are dated from 125 to 50 BCE, and additional ceramics also have been identified to belong to 100–50 BCE (Schmid Phase 1), but the majority of sherds possibly can be assigned to 50–0 BCE (Schmid Phase 2a). A mid-second-century date for the homogeneous fill between the walls of the Lower Temenos (1995–1996 Trench 17) is securely dated by the pottery. This intentional infilling of the East Cryptoporticus to create a flat surface for the East Triple Colonnade also serves as a chronological linchpin.[6] The Lower Temenos Retaining Wall excavated in 1997 in Trench 18A has provided a late-first-century BCE date for the building up of the Temple Forecourt. The pottery from the Upper Temenos Residential Quarter (2002 Trench 94) and Room A of the East Perimeter Wall (2001 Trench 84) includes an extraordinary corpus of distinctive Nabataean wares, which can be dated to Nabataean Site Phase IV, and the Tabun Cave Room above the Great Cistern (2001 SP84) has also been assigned a late-first-century BCE date. The Great Cistern (2001 SP85) is assigned to the first century CE, and Site Phase IV, and the East "Cistern" (1997 Trench 41, 1998 Trench 53) also shares its deposits with Site Phase IV, dating between the first century BCE and the first century CE. As for the Temple Pronaos sondage (2005 SP107), the majority of predominant diagnostics date from 150 to 100 BCE. Those in Locus 1 date from 50 BCE to 0 BCE/CE, and the general chronology for this deposit is assigned to the first century BCE, and from 50 to 25 BCE. It could be said that in general the dates for this deposit are close to the mid first century BCE.

The key stratum, Great Temple Site Phase IV, reveals a flurry of activity, but it is clear that there are deposits earlier than those assigned to Site Phase IV, specifically to Site Phase II, confirming that the Nabataeans constructed monumental structures before the last quarter of the first century BCE. These early deposits may complicate the overall chronology for the site and we may have erred by assigning these loci later dates. When the artifact record is carefully scrutinized in the future we should be able to clarify these assignments for the earliest site deposits.

Through Pre-Site Phase I to Site Phase IV

Before the stratigraphy is investigated in Chapters 2–5, it will be necessary to examine the different phases identified within the Petra Great Temple deposits. The reconstruction of the Great Temple chronology is a difficult issue. Even with disturbances in the depositional sequence, our dates we believe to be reasonable and broadly accurate. As was mentioned previously, our internal chronology and stratigraphic reconstruction can be found in the phasing charts in *Open Context*. The Brown University archaeological team has supported this stratigraphic and chronological reconstruction, although future stratigraphic evidence and refinements may emerge.

Based on site deposition, the general sequence of some 15 phases (Pre-Site Phase I and Site Phases I–XIV) is now evident for the Great Temple construction, collapse and abandonment. Although these sequences (progressing from earliest to latest) indicate the following stages of construction, future excavations may modify these ideas. Building periods are sometimes separated from artifact periods moving the latter to *later* phases, depending upon the context in which the materials are found. Therefore, even if an elephant head we ascribe to the Propylaeum colonnade was constructed in Site Phase IV, it is placed in Site Phase IX where it was found mixed in with other elements of the 363 CE collapse.[7] The data, therefore, do not permit more than a general dating. The Great Temple chronology can be thought of as floating due to the fact that there is a lack of absolutely dated phases. But it does provide a general framework into which we have placed the architecture and artifacts in our databases.

A summary chart of the Site Phasing is shown in Figure 1.18.

Nabataean Great Temple Pre-Site Phase I, ca. first century BCE and before, is allocated to activities taking place in all parts of the precinct before the temple preparation and construction. This pushes back this phase approximately 50 to 100 years earlier than we previously assumed. Architectural fragments can be connected with archaeological deposits of the earliest excavated occupation of the site, evidence for which we have throughout the site. Both the walls in the West Propylaeum South Gallery (2001 Trench 86) and in Room 2 of the Propylaeum East (2005 Special Project 150) have an orientation that is in variance with the rest of the temple Propylaeum complex, for their orientation is

PHASE	DATE	MAJOR CONSTRUCTION/DESTRUCTION
Pre-Site Phase I	ca. Pre-1st c. BCE	Odd walls and cup marks in bedrock
Site Phase I	ca. Early 1st c. BCE	Bedrock Preparation and Canalization
Site Phase II	ca. Mid 1st c. BCE	*Distyle in Antis* temple: Portico Wall, Lowest Steps of Central Staircase
Site Phase III	ca. Mid-to-Late 1st c. BCE–1st c. CE	Minor Damage
Site Phase IV	ca. 1st c. BCE–1st c. CE	Grand Design (Expansion), *Tetrastyle in Antis Temple*, Full Propylaeum, West Entry Stairway, *Nefesh*, Lower Temenos Triple Colonnades, Exedrae, Cryptoporticoes, Upper Temenos Great Cistern, East Perimeter Wall, Residential Quarter, Baroque Room
Site Phase V	ca. 1st c. CE	Nabataean Redesign and Repair, Theater Added to Great Temple, *Betyl*s in Propylaeum
Site Phase VI	106 CE and 113/114, Earthquake	Roman Takeover, Damage to Propylaeum West, Repairs to Lower Temenos, Baroque Room Collapse, Temple Doorways and Corridors Narrowed, Bath Complex Constructed
Site Phase VII	ca. Mid 2nd c. CE	Propylaeum Repair, Wall K Razed in East and Rebuilt in West, West Room 1 Constructed, Roman Street Paved, East Propylaeum Rooms 1–3 Constructed, East Exedra Repair, Lower Temenos East-West Cross Walls in East Colonnade, Benches, Temple Doorways Narrowed and Walled-In, Theater Stage Constructed
Site Phase VIII	ca. Late 2nd c. CE	Damage, Abandonment, Collapse, Dumping
Site Phase IX	363 CE, Earthquake	Collapse of Propylaeum and Lower Temenos West Triple Colonnade, West Cryptoporticus Collapse, Upper Temenos Added Features
Site Phase X	ca. 4th and 5th c. CE	Abandonment, Fluvial Deposit Accumulates, Lower Temenos Reconstruction of Colonnades with Reused Ashlars, Domestic Secondary Reuse in All Temple Areas
Site Phase XI	Post 551 CE, Earthquake	Further Collapse, East Triple Colonnade Collapse, West Entry Stairs Collapse, Temple East Porch Column Collapse, Baths Out of Use
Site Phase XII	Late Byzantine 551–640 CE	Abandonment and Robbing
Site Phase XIII	Islamic Period	Series of Major Collapses
Site Phase XIV	Modern Period	Farming of the Lower Temenos by Bedouin, Dumping, Construction of Bedouin Walls, Brown University Excavations

Fig. 1.18
Summary chart of Great Temple Site Phasing.

northeast-southwest. In a preliminary assessment of their construction, they may be part of the same earlier structure. These walls are of a different character than the early Propylaeum walls. In the Lower Temenos the soundings below the West Cryptoporticus floors (2005 Special Projects 104–105) show evidence of earlier activities as well. In the Upper Temenos west the makeshift walls under the Cistern-Reservoir and the circular, grouped cup marks chiseled into the bedrock shown in Figure 1.19 reasonably can be placed earlier in Pre-Site Phase I. The archaeological evidence of the Pre-Site Phase I activities also have been found in the Temple Pronaos west (2005 Special Project 107) with a stuccoed platform. These localized features appear to predate other buildings on the site. Pre-Site Phase I is difficult to understand, however, because there is no certain link between any of the walls assigned to this phase, and the evidence is localized. It is not clear if this was a humble settlement, but there are a few signs of monumental building activity. What is abundantly clear is that prior to the preparation of the site for the temple(s) there is earlier site use.

This is confirmed by one of the most interesting Pre-Site Phase I deposits at the Great Temple with more direct implications both for dating and for our understanding of the architectural and temporal sequence at the Great Temple site. Specifically this is the 2006

Trench 123 probe under the Theater seating. The definitive conclusion is that there is earlier architecture under the temple prior to the construction of the *distyle* structure. The implications of this are that there may have been a major structure on the temple site before the Great Temple Site Phase II *distyle* temple is erected. Unquestionably the *distyle* temple is important, but as with the earliest structure we have excavated to date, the direct implications for a Pre–Site Phase I construction can no longer be avoided. Regrettably the architecture from Trench 123 is so rudimentary it is difficult to conclude definitively that any monumental structure was erected there during the earlier occupation of the site. This excavation will be treated more fully in Chapter 5.

Although Pre–Site Phase I finds have been separated by area and locus, they have not been studied in detail, so it is difficult to find parallels from other sites in the region or to find homogeneity within them. Indeed extensive study is required to analyze the seemingly diverse traditions they represent. In the Great Temple Pronaos (2005 Special Project 107) Hellenistic ceramics are identified as part of the fill. Other finds include Hellenistic glaze wares, a few stamped Rhodian type jar handles, dating to the ca. second century BCE, but it must be kept in mind that the site was literally razed by the construction of the subterranean canalization systems and the early temple. At this point, there is no way for us to determine these chronological stages or to identify a Pre–Site Phase I architectural plan, but it must have played a key role in the early development of the site. The accumulation dates and possibly a refinement of the ceramic chronology along with dendrochronology will help us clarify the picture.

There may be continuity of settlement, of which we are not sure. Were these people Proto-Nabataeans? Nabataeans? It is difficult to say.

Site Phase I is assigned to the preparation of the precinct for the construction of the early *distyle in antis* temple. This approximate 50-year span for the preparation and building may be questioned, but it is reasoned that Nabataean masons had to spend some time in chiseling away enormous amounts (some 12 m) of bedrock to place the early temple (30.07 m north-south × 18.36 m east-west) onto a finely prepared stable surface. The quarrying of

Fig. 1.19
Cup marks and early walls in the Upper Temenos adjacent to the Cistern-Reservoir/*Natatio*.

bedrock, particularly on the east, west, and south for the terrace, as well as the import of fill for areas requiring leveling and support, was essential for the creation of a monumental terrace and a colossal temple situated some 30 m in height above the central artery of the city. For this time, in the first century BCE, this is planned to be the most impressive and extensive building in central Petra. A West Precinct Wall and an additional East-West Support wall are constructed to build up the west of the precinct where the bedrock had fallen away. (The quarrying cuts of the West Plaza bedrock belong to this phase.) A substantial subterranean canalization system underlying the entire complex also had to be constructed.

Thereafter in Site Phase II, placed in the mid-first century BCE, is the first and earliest major Nabataean construction phase. It includes the years when the Propylaeum east-west Portico Wall, which delimits the precinct from the major thoroughfare that later becomes the *via sacra*, the Roman Street, is built. In the temple sector of the precinct a monumental *distyle in antis* temple is erected (Joukowsky 1998: 147 note 4). A central stairway accesses the structure embellished with colorfully stuccoed columns, two at the front, eight to the sides, and six in the rear. Colorfully frescoed side corridors that serve as the structure's perimeter enclose the temple.[8] This appears to have been a relatively short-lived phase.

In Site Phase III, after the *distyle* temple has been in use for an indeterminate period, there is a catastrophe of some sort, perhaps an earthquake or tremors, evident by a series of collapses. Site Phase III marks this period of minor damage[9] to the *distyle* building.[10] We place its date in the mid-first-century BCE.

In Site Phase IV the Nabataeans undertake a monumental rebuilding renewal that includes the whole precinct.[11] Site Phase IV is assigned to the last quarter of the first century BCE and the beginning of the first century CE. Known as "The *Grand Design,*" a major decision is taken to rebuild not only the partially destroyed temple, but to elegantly embellish the entire precinct.

This phase sees the completion of the full Propylaeum with two additional east-west walls behind the Portico Wall, "Wall K" (Paar 1970) and the Propylaeum Retaining Wall, the southernmost wall that separates the Propylaeum from the Lower Temenos. The Portico Wall is breeched at this time for the construction of the Propylaeum West Entry Stairway that is shared with the Baths-Palatial Complex to the west. This is the phase in which we place the West Stairway platform and the cultic installations of the *nefesh* and *betyl.*

In the Propylaeum and the Lower Temenos this phase also includes the construction of cryptoportici under the triple colonnades and the installation of 145 remarkable limestone Asian elephant-headed capitals to embellish the roofed triple colonnades. Figure 1.20 shows the recovery of one of these extraordinary capitals just after it had been removed from its excavation provenience.

These Lower Temenos triple colonnades lead into semi-circular buttressed exedrae adorned with smaller elephant-headed capitals at their entrances. Flanked in the east, west and north by the colonnades and twin exedrae is the sweep of the great Lower Temenos plaza with its white limestone Hexagonal Pavement positioned above the Site Phase I extensive subterranean canalization system.

In the Upper Temenos southwest, the Baroque Room Complex including the Anteroom, Shrine Room, the elegant Baroque Room and a Settling Tank are constructed.[12] (In the Baroque Room, to our astonishment, we find the massive wreckage of delicately designed painted and gilded plaster collapse (Figures 4.76–4.84). To the west of the Baroque Room Complex is the 11-room domestic Residential Quarter where masses of figuratively painted and plain Nabataean ceramics and masses of animal bones are unearthed.

Additional measures include the building of the Upper Temenos walls and arches of the East Cistern, and the precinct's East Perimeter Wall and its plaza are also completed. Beyond the temple proper, a sword deity relief is carved into the bedrock wall of the Upper Temenos above an underground cistern holding 390,000 liters of water. Other monumental structural changes take place as well, coinciding with the building up of the temple Forecourt with fill and its embellishment with small white hexagonal flagstones.

Fig. 1.20
Elephant-headed capital
from the Lower Temenos
awaiting fragments to be
found for restoration.

The focal point of the complex, the then freestanding *distyle* temple, has been expanded into an even more spectacular *tetrastyle in antis* structure with a new stylobate, and an extended porch bordered by east and west antae decorated with pilaster reliefs and exterior walkways. As seen today, this refurbished Grand Design Great Temple measures 35 m east-west, and 42 m in length.

A stairway approaches a broad deep pronaos (entry), which in turn leads into the Site Phase II side corridors, which are reused in Site Phase IV. Exterior paved walkways now frame the new temple, where sculpted facial fragments and fine deeply carved architectural elements including pilasters are found. Approximately 15 m in height, the porch columns plus the triangular pediment and entablature hypothetically place the structure's height to a minimum of 19 m.

On the basis of the floral decoration stylistics, especially seen on the limestone capitals and elements of the entablature, the Petra Great Temple Phase IV iconography appears to be similar to that of the Al-Khazna.[13] This evidence also suggests that the Great Temple,

the Baroque Room Complex and the adjacent Residential Quarter to the southwest are originally constructed sometime in the last quarter of the first century BCE[14] by the Nabataeans who combined their native traditions with the classical spirit, during the reign of Malichus I (62–30 BCE), or Obodas II (30–9 BCE).

As we mentioned previously, this expanded Great Temple is the largest freestanding building yet excavated in Petra; its 7560 m² precinct consists of a Propylaeum, Lower Temenos, and Upper Temenos, the sacred enclosure for the temple proper.

Petra Pool Complex

On a terrace at the same elevation as the Lower Temenos to the Great Temple east and adjacent to the Great Temple is the Petra Pool Complex (Figure 1.22), excavated and published in 2003 by our former team member Leigh-Ann Bedal. It is an integral part of the Great Temple complex, composed of a large ornamental pool with a rectangular pavilion on an island accessed by a bridge. The pavilion is richly decorated with colored plaster and marble. As suggested by scholar researchers (Bowersock 2003, 24; Taylor 2001, 111), this pool paradise may have served for the ancient Middle Eastern water festival known as the Maioumas when water games were held (Segal 1995, 23). Originally identified as the "Lower Market" by Bachmann, the architectural remains document the monumental character of this Pool Complex. Now of certain function, its placement beside the Great Temple attests to its importance and to the grandeur of the precinct as a whole. Bedal (2003, 68) attributes the earliest phase of the Pool Complex to our Phase IV time frame; thus its construction was a major component of the Great Temple's Grand Design.

Leigh-Ann Bedal's (*ibid.*183) account reflects on its significance:

> "The presence of a large formal garden—a virtual oasis—in Petra would have delivered a powerful statement to merchants and foreign delegates entering the city after a long journey through the harsh desert environment.

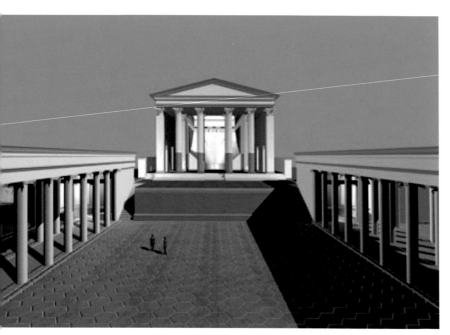

Fig. 1.21
Virtual Reality of the Grand Design, Site Phase IV.

Site Phases V and VI

Site Phase V of the first century CE[15] is a time of Nabataean redesign and repair. Many exciting changes occur in the Propylaeum West—most notably the installation of the double *betyls* (Joukowsky: 2002, 317–318, Figs. 4–5), which will be further discussed in Chapters 3 and 7. In the Upper Temenos, the East "Cistern" is used for storage and most probably as a marble workshop; the ceramics from the lowest level date before 100 CE. In the East Perimeter Wall there is evidence of a reuse of Room A including replacement of the hearth. In the Residential Quarter there is expansion to the southeast and southwest, including new walls and a plaster and sandstone floor in Room 4.

The Great Temple Theater

Also in Site Phase V, major changes take place within the Great Temple. Intercolumnar walls are built between the columns; four internal monumental stairways are constructed, as well as east and west interior chambers and an extraordinary Central Arch. The character of the traditional temple building is dramatically changed, because all of these internal structures provide support for a 620-seat theater (Figure 1.23) inserted into the center of the building. Figure 1.24 clearly shows the theater seating with a focus to the north. The directional orientation of the Great Temple with this latest innovative theater structure has been turned 180 degrees!

These major changes include a formidable remodeling of the temple interior to bear the weight and the angled incline for the theater seats. The theater is supported by the contemporary additions of casemate intercolumnar walls, a monumental Central Arch, and vaulted chambers. Also constructed are four vast interior stairways, two with landings and small steps for entrance into the Theater rear. New limestone floor pavements also are put in place.[16]

It would appear that at this time there is a shift to more secular concerns and the temple is used for more public ritual. At this point there may be an emerging secularized civic identity and consciousness that defined the Petraean community in political as well as religious terms. This renovation we place sometime in the first or early second centuries CE near the end of

Fig. 1.22
The Petra Pool Garden
Complex, to the south, 2005.

the reign of Aretas IV, ca. 40–44 CE, or to the rule of Malichus II (40–44–70 CE), or possibly later to the reign of Rabbel II (70–106 CE).[17] Analysis, debate, and conflicting interpretations concerning the theater largely have centered on its functional and cultural character and on the interpretation of the Great Temple as either a secular or ritual entity. (Further discussion can be found in Chapter 7, "The Great Debate.") Shown in Figure 1.21 is a virtual reality representation of the precinct.

The Early Roman-Byzantine Baths

The Nabataean-Roman transition, Great Temple Site Phase VI, serves as an excellent example of the fact that Nabataean activities are not static but change in dynamic and unexpected ways. In 2005–2006 another prominent complex that provides evidence for discussion is the discovery of a modest bath system with

Fig. 1.23
Great Temple Phase V Theater
inserted into the Phase IV Great
Temple, to the southeast.

Fig. 1.24
Great Temple Theater from
the rear, to the north.

well-preserved features. It is located in to the
west of the West Exedra. Dates for these baths
are determined by a combination of ceramic
evidence, glass artifacts and inscriptions placing
the complex construction circa 70 CE or in Site
Phase VI, sometime around the Roman Annexation to their destruction in 551 CE.

The material culture and architecture suggest
that the bath installations—*caldaria, tepidarium* or
laconicum, praefurnium, cold plunges, service
corridor, and the features present in the formal
rooms were constructed at the same time in Site
Phase VI. This is a small, compact bathing facility,
a *balneum,* covering 32 m north-south × 28.40 m
east-west or 908.80 m² as excavated. Its plan is
presented in Chapter 4 and an aerial photograph
appears there as well.

Dated to the late second century, Nabataean-
Roman Site Phase VI also coincides with the
ca. 106 CE Roman annexation—witnessing
collapse in the Propylaeum along with the
collapse of the south cryptoporticus of both
the Propylaeum West and Propylaeum East.
In the Lower Temenos repairs are made to the
Hexagonal Pavement and the East Exedra
walls, and the subterranean canalization system

shows signs of reconstruction due to silt and
soil accumulation. Some of this soil build up
contains first century CE ceramics.

In the Upper Temenos is the probable
cataclysmic collapse of the Baroque Room, and
damage occurs in both the Anteroom and Shrine
Room. Shortly thereafter there is the abandonment of the Shrine Room and the modification
with reconstruction of the Anteroom's east
wall. This phase may also be the terminal use of
the Residential Quarter, which has an unusual
degree of preservation and, except for fill, little
post-depositional disturbance.[18]

In the temple proper, the East, West
and South Corridor doorways are narrowed,
restricting access to the sanctuary's interior.
Further collapse is indicated by damage to the
east and west walls of the East Interior Staircase.
It is reasonably clear that the major structure
remained standing. With the annexation of
Nabataea by the Romans, new architectural
concepts are introduced, which will be discussed
in Chapter 7.

(Sometime before our Site Phase VI, in 64–63 BCE, before the Roman annexation, the Roman general, Pompey, subjugated the Nabataeans. Nabataea was regarded as a client state of Rome, taxed by the Romans and serving as a buffer territory against desert tribes. In 25–24 BCE, Aelius Gallus led an unsuccessful expedition from Nabataea to conquer Arabia Felix—the land of frankincense and myrrh, the kingdom to the south in present-day Yemen. The Roman propaganda of the day reported this expedition as a success.)

The Roman Period, Site Phases VII through IX

The Nabataean period comes to a formal close with the Roman annexation in 106 CE. From Ammianus (14.8.13), we know that on behalf of Trajan, A. Cornelius Palma, the governor of Syria, subdued part of Arabia including Petra, subjecting it to Roman rule; this is one reference we have to the annexation of the Nabataean kingdom and its incorporation into the Roman province of Arabia. Rome absorbed Nabataea, and Nabataea completely succumbed to Roman hegemony. Dio Cassius (LXVIII, 14, 5) tells of Trajan's victory over the Dacians and offers a statement about the Roman annexation of Nabataea by writing, "About this same time, Palma, the governor of Syria, subdued the part of Arabia around Petra and made it subject to the Romans." It has never been clear, however, from archaeological or historical sources if Cornelius Palma led a military expedition to Petra. The lack of a recorded aggression suggests that Palma oversaw a peaceful takeover, and Roman coins minted a few years after the annexation inscribed with "*Arabia adquisita*," not "*Arabia capta*," indicate a pacific annexation.

The picture might not have been as peaceful as the Roman sources report. In addition to localized destruction at the Great Temple (*supra*), we were astonished to uncover 423 ballista balls averaging 12–18 cm in diameter, 162 arrowheads, and two bronze helmet cheek pieces, several javelin points, a scabbard tip, buckles, rings, possible harnesses, as well as nails, spikes and knobs, pins, tacks, fragments of a bracelet and a toggle pin, plus four crescent-shaped pendants. The large ballista repository (Figure 1.25) of the West Propylaeum is assigned

to Site Phase VI dating to ca. 106 CE, the Late Nabataean period, when there are a number of collapses probably due to Roman aggression. Subsequent researchers will continue to debate this issue, but it is clear that in broad cultural terms, the Nabataean period at this time came to a close. Thus Petra's apogee was from the first century BCE to the CE second century. Its material culture reached its zenith in the second half of the first century BCE, before the Romans established control. What is clear is that the Petra Great Temple does not come to a catastrophic end with the Roman intervention. Additionally it is during this phase that we date the earliest construction of the Roman-Byzantine Baths.

Site Phase VII, (mid-second century CE),[19] is a period of repair and reconfiguration in the Propylaeum with the building of the upper treads of the Central Staircase to provide direct access from the Roman Street to the Lower Temenos. The Roman Street is also paved at this time,[20] and Wall K is rebuilt in the west, but razed in the Propylaeum East. Also in the Propylaeum West, benches are installed against Wall K in Room 1, and the east Portico Wall is reconfigured with the insertion of the three north-south doorways of Rooms 1–3; their thresholds securely fitted with iron bars. The Lower Temenos East Cryptoporticus has cross walls built between the stylobate walls of the East Colonnade, and between the cross walls an intentional fill is deposited supporting their structural integrity. There is also continued repair of the East and West Exedrae. A lead pipe is laid across the base of the Lower Temenos Retaining Wall extending east-west across the precinct between the two exedrae.

In the Upper Temenos, it would appear that the Roman-Byzantine Baths continue to operate in this phase, the Cistern-Reservoir walls are rebuilt, and there are modifications in East Perimeter Room A. In the casemate room section of the East Perimeter Wall, the floor of Room A is built up with purple sandstone bedding and a low blocking wall is installed across the doorway to retain the fill. Tethering holes are cut beside a trough set into the room's east arch, transforming Room A into a possible

Fig. 1.25
Ballista balls in the
Propylaeum West.

animal shelter and blocking the entrance to the east Pool Complex garden area. A bench is constructed along the South Corridor Wall facing the South Passageway, and drains of the Great Temple Forecourt are repaired with ceramic pipes for aboveground canalization. As far as the temple is concerned, there are visible repairs, as well as the robbing of structural elements seen in the removal of the Pronaos floor pavements and the blocking of the East, West and South Corridor doorways restricting access to the temple; there is also the installation of the east and west walls at the south end of the East and West Walkways, and benches are set up in the West Walkway. Phase VII in the temple also sees the reuse of large ashlars and worked architectural fragments with the building of the theater *pulpitum* or stage, which is a later addition to the theater.

It is later in this phase that the Great Temple may have been recycled into a defensive facility, for each of the corridor doorways is blocked and walls are built between the porch columns. This suggests there may have been an impending disaster of some sort; either an additional earthquake or some sort of conflict was anticipated.

Closely following is Site Phase VIII, predating the late second and third centuries CE. During this time there is another period of damage, abandonment, collapse and reuse. In the Propylaeum there is the collapse of the north colonnade, and floor pavements in the east and west are lifted and some architectural elements are robbed out.

The Lower Temenos also shows the abandonment and robbing of some stylobate elements of the East and West Triple Colonnades, and a layer of fill accumulates above the Hexagonal Pavement. In the Upper Temenos there is the removal and collapse of some of the arches spanning the East "Cistern." This is the time of the possible placement of an infant jar burial in the East Perimeter Wall Room B. As for the Great Temple, there is also robbing of the floor pavements including those in the corridors, the Residential Quarter, the East and West Vaulted Chambers, and at the thresholds of the East and West Interior Staircases. There is also evidence of localized conflagrations.

Site Phase IX[21] is dated to the major 363 CE earthquake—a cataclysmic event bringing about the cave-in of the Propylaeum and the Lower Temenos cryptoportici with their arches tumbling onto the floors. Another feature that should be mentioned is the partial disintegration of the Propylaeum Retaining Wall. In the Lower Temenos the collapse of the West Colonnade is clearly indicated by repeated rows of deep indentions in the Hexagonal Pavement (Figure 3.53) and the shattering of the hexagonal flagstones. The Lower Temenos is enveloped by the accumulation of architectural fragments mixed with fill, and sedimentation extends over the West Precinct Wall. Some damage is also seen in the south of the East Triple Colonnade. In the Upper Temenos, there is the major collapse of large features—the West Precinct Wall and the Cistern-Reservoir—and fluvial and wash-down deposits accumulate—the lower levels of which were found to contain scanty remains of two human bodies that were caught by a sudden disaster. In the Shrine Room, abandonment occurs followed by collapse from structural weakness, followed by the accumulation of debris. The West Walkway wall is destroyed, as is the Residential Quarter and the Cistern-Reservoir, after which more sediment accumulates. The Roman-Byzantine Baths continue to be used, although in a very restricted manner thanks to partial collapse. The temple west Porch columns plummet onto the temple Forecourt pulverizing the hexagonal pavement there, and other temple elements crash and fall into the west Upper Temenos and the Lower Temenos. In the temple, at some point in this phase predating the cataclysm, the floors are raided and debris covers the lower risers of the interior staircases, allowing for the removal of the upper treads. Subsequent silting of the areas occurs, and the west intercolumnar wall buckles under the pressure of falling debris.

The Small Temple

Just to the west of the Great Temple precinct and just below the Great Temple Roman-Byzantine Baths, the Romans construct a Roman Imperial Cult building, known as the "Small Temple," shown in Figure 1.26. Under the Brown University 2000 to 2002 Jordanian Excavation Permit from the Department of Antiquities, our team supervisor, Sara Karz Reid, excavated the so-called "Small Temple." Reid (2006) has published these results.

In building the Small Temple the Romans reconfigured and reshaped the south side of the terrain between the Petra Great Temple and the Qasr al-Bint. Because the Small Temple shares the same alignment with the Qasr al-Bint

Fig. 1.26
Aerial view of the Small Temple to the south.

Temenos Bench, the Qasr al-Bint itself, the Temple of the Winged Lions and the Temenos Gate, it is surely associated with these structures.

Constructed on a high podium, this imperial cult building is of a Roman prostyle design with six columns across its façade. This freestanding building consists of two levels— a lower courtyard to the north and the main building on the south, which is raised on a platform with a portico and square main hall. The building is accessed by a stairway on the west. The interior is decorated with platforms and basins (Reid 2006, Fig. 46) and decorated with more than 614 fragmentary Roman inscriptions, dedicated to post annexation Roman emperors. The most important inscription has been dated to the Emperor Trajan (Reid 2006, 123–124) from 106 to 114 CE, and refers (*ibid.*) to his victory over the Dacians. A second inscription (*ibid.* 131) may refer to the Emperor Marcus Aurelius Antoninus, better known as Elagabalus, who ruled from 218–222 CE, or to his successor Severus Alexander (222–235 CE). A third inscription refers to Emperor Severus Alexander who elevated Petra to the status of a *colonia*, and has been dated by Reid and Bodel (2002) to 222 CE. These inscriptions indicate that the Small Temple remained in use at least through the third century CE.

The Byzantine Period, Great Temple Site Phases X–XI

THE ROMAN-BYZANTINE BATHS

During Site Phase IX the Roman-Byzantine Baths reflect frequent modifications that include the filling in of vaults, the additions of flooring and the renovation of some of the rooms and walls. Reflected in the archaeological record is change, and these changes occurred as a result of the additional modifications or needs of the weakened architecture itself, or because of earth tremors and the devastating earthquake of 19 May 363 CE. This earthquake and its tremors so disrupt life in Petra that the bath site never fully recovers and some of the rooms are never fully rebuilt.

In Site Phase X there is little activity in the Propylaeum, and all signs indicate an abandonment of the precinct represented by the collection of a fluvial deposit dated to ca. 4th–5th centuries CE. As a period of Byzantine reuse the Lower Temenos deposits indicate secondary destruction levels and the rebuilding of intercolumnar walls using temple pilaster reliefs as building components. There are industrial activities taking place as well, including lime manufacture in the south East Triple Colonnade and exedrae. Using fallen architectural elements including column drums, a platform is constructed in front of the West Exedra with steps leading down into the apse. There are continued industrial reuses of several areas, in some cases leaving significant quantities of burned ash residue particularly in the West Exedra. During this period in the Upper Temenos the East Plaza floors are stripped, haphazard masonry walls are constructed, drainpipes are installed clumsily, and scattered shabby walls are built. Multiple drainage systems are set into place, and the westernmost precinct wall is rebuilt along with its aboveground canalization system. As was mentioned previously, the sequence of the Great Temple Roman-Byzantine Baths is of five consecutive stages. Building begins in Site Phase VI and the baths are in use until the 19 July 363 CE earthquake of Site Phase IX. After the Site Phase IX earthquake there is a striking change in the character of the baths. Some rooms are no longer used, doorways are narrowed or closed off completely, and there is a dramatic contrast between the late Nabataean working bath and the features that are then re-used. Later in Site Phase X a kiln may have been constructed over the remains of the southernmost *caldarium*.

In the temple there is the robbing of various elements including the upper treads of the interior staircases and the east and west landings. There is, however, some attempt to rebuild the East and West Walkways. Scattered domestic secondary uses are found in the temple Theater stage, Vaulted Chambers, the Great Cistern, Central Arch, and East Corridor.

In Site Phase XI there is further collapse that possibly postdates the fifth century CE and possibly may be the result of the earthquake of 9 July 551 CE. In the Propylaeum major collapses continue, and in the Lower Temenos there is continued accumulation of fill and the West Entry Stairs go out of use. The East Triple Colonnade collapses along with the East Exedra's entablature. The Upper Temenos also is subject to further collapse, with the accumulation of fill after disuse of the canalization system, and areas of localized burning. Modifications take place in the Roman-Byzantine Baths and a final collapse occurs after which the bath site is finally abandoned. To fix a precise date for the termination for the baths' last use is tricky, although it is unlikely that the complex functioned beyond the mid sixth century and the site's final abandonment. In conclusion, the Great Temple Roman-Byzantine Baths were in use for some 400 or more years, from ca. 70 to 551 CE; however, the period of active use is gauged from 70 to 363 CE, a period of less than 300 years. By the early sixth century CE when Petra experienced a general slump, the bath complex was abandoned. The temple East Porch columns collapse, and fluvial deposits continue to accumulate. The earthquakes, along with the earthquake of 551 CE, certainly contributed an economic decline of the community, and finally put an end to the Roman-Byzantine Baths and the Great Temple precinct as well. This is the terminal phase of site occupation.

The Late Great Temple Site Phases XII–XIV

Site Phase XII is a time of abandonment and robbing. Another fluvial deposit then accumulates. In Site Phase XIII, again, there are a series of major collapses, and Site Phase XIV encompasses the modern era when the Lower Temenos is used for Bedouin farming marked by the division of the area into two fields by overturned column drums (Figure 3.18). The Bedouin also construct various makeshift walls in the Upper and Lower Temenoi.

In the Upper Temenos temple Forecourt, fill is found including pieces of plastic tent stakes and an Israeli bullet casing. Nazzal's dump is dug between the collapsed Porch columns. There is the German survey of the temple stylobate and Forecourt, resulting in the reverse stratigraphy of these deposits. By this time the temple precinct is deeply buried under successive collapses and topsoil. When we arrive in 1993, the only visible components are the collapse of the East Porch columns, and the faint outline of temple walls.

The depositional history of the Great Temple as we have seen here and further examine in the chapters to come, is complex. But Brown University archaeologists are in basic agreement that the stratigraphic sequence presented here is as secure as the stratigraphic correlations permit.

———

Included in the original trench reports on the *Open Context* website are detailed descriptions of the loci and stages of each trench, an explanation of the excavator's reasoning behind the assignments for site phases, and their interpretation. In an effort to determine the overall site phasing of the Petra Great Temple, we have phased each trench and each locus within it. (This phasing is reproduced on *Open Context* website.) It may not always correlate exactly with the original trench reports, as new discoveries have resulted in new interpretations for many parts of the site.

Excavations of
Petra Great Temple
Trenches by
Year and Area

(Figure 1.27)

Petra Great Temple Trenches Excavated in 1993

AREA	TRENCH	MEASUREMENT (M) (N-S × E-W)	EXCAVATOR(S)
Propylaeum	No work done here		
Lower Temenos	No work done here		
Upper Temenos			
Temple Forecourt	1	9 × 9	Schluntz
Temple Forecourt Stylobate West	2 (Part I)	6 × 10	Smolenski, Thorpe
Temple Forecourt Stylobate West	3	4.5 × 5	M. Joukowsky
Temple Forecourt Stylobate East	4	4 × 10	Shubailat
Canalization System	SP4 (Part I)	1 × 1.5	Schluntz
Temple			
Porch Columns	SPA	2 × 28	Payne

Petra Great Temple Trenches Excavated in 1994

AREA	TRENCH	MEASUREMENT (M) (N-S × E-W)	EXCAVATOR(S)
Propylaeum			
Central Staircase	SPP	20 × 6	M. Joukowsky
Lapidary West			
West of Temple	7	2 × 3	Retzleff
Lower Temenos			
West Exedra	5 (Part I)	7 × 10	Beckman, Retzleff, Schluntz
South Center of the Hexagonal Pavement	6 (Part I)	9 × 4	Payne
Center of the Hexagonal Pavement	13	10 × 10	M. Joukowsky
Upper Temenos			
Temple Forecourt Stylobate West	2 (Part II)	6 × 10	Schluntz
Canalization System	SP4 (Part II)	4 × 2	Payne
Temple			
Interior Anta West	12 SP14	10 × 10	Parr M. Joukowsky
Theater Southeast	9, SP7	7.5 × 10	Bedal
Theater Southeast	15 Part I, SP8	6 × 5	Austin
West Walkway	8, 10, 11	18.5 × 7	Slaughter, A. Joukowsky
West Walkway	SP1 SP2 SP3	No measurements	M. Joukowsky
Temple East	SP9	No measurements	M. Joukowsky
Temple East	SP11	No measurements	M. Joukowsky
Temple East	SP12	No measurements	M. Joukowsky
East Pronaos column	SP10	No measurements	M. Joukowsky
Temple West	SP13	No measurements	M. Joukowsky
Temple West	SP16	No measurements	M. Joukowsky
Temple South	SP15	No measurements	Jacobsen

Petra Great Temple Trenches Excavated in 1995

AREA	TRENCH	MEASUREMENT (M) (N-S × E-W)	EXCAVATOR(S)
Propylaeum	No work done here		
Lower Temenos			
Eastern part of the West Exedra	5 Part II	9 × 4, 2m probe	Basile, Rucker
Eastern part of the West Exedra	21, SP26/SP31	4 × 7	Rucker, Basile, Khalidi
Western part of the West Exedra	16 Part I	7 × 10	Basile, Rucker
Bedouin wall north of the West Exedra	SP37	none taken	M. Joukowsky
West Perimeter Wall of the Lower Temenos	SP39 Part I	~2.75 × 0.24 or 0.17	M. Joukowsky
Subterranean canalization system	SP20	1.5 × 2.5	Payne, Barrett
Subterranean canalization system	SP36	0.43 × 0.41	M. Joukowsky
East Colonnade	14 SP22 SP24 SP29 20	8.2 × 11 4 × 2 7 × 2.2 2 × 2 9 × 4.3	Sisson, Bell Sisson, Bell Sisson, Bell Sisson, Bell Habboo, Sisson, Bell
East Colonnade	17 Part I, SP25	10 × 14, 1.6 × 2.5	Payne
East Colonnade east	SP38 Part I	none taken	M. Joukowsky
Upper Temenos			
Central Stairs	SP4 (Part III)	9.75 × 2.8	Payne, Slaughter, Barrett
Northeast Temple Forecourt	SP30	4.6 × 7.2 × 8.2	Tholbecq
Temple			
East Walkway	19	5.2 × 3.4	Tholbecq, Habboo
Northwest central Pronaos	23	10 × 6.5, 3 × 3.6	Schluntz
Southwest Pronaos	SP23	3.1 × 3.6	Harris
Theater Southeast Staircase	15 (Part II)	7.35 × 2.23	Harris, Khalidi
Theater Southeast Staircase	22 (Part I)	7.5 × 10	Bedal

Petra Great Temple Trenches Excavated in 1996

AREA	TRENCH	MEASUREMENT (M) (N-S × E-W)	EXCAVATOR(S)
Propylaeum	No work done here		
Lower Temenos			
West Exedra West	16	1.2 × 1.95	Brown, Takian
West Exedra West	31, SP41	7.5 × 9.72 1.65 × 1.65	Butler, Goldstein
East Colonnade	17 (Part II)	10 × 14	Payne
East Colonnade	28	13 × 2.8	Bestock, Gimon
East Colonnade	25	26.67 × 2.37	Slaughter, Butler, Goldstein
East Colonnade	30	19 × 4	M. Joukowsky
East Colonnade	36	11 × 4	Bestock, Gimon
East Colonnade east	SP38 (Part II)	3 × 3	Goldstein, Butler
East Colonnade	SP39 (Part II)	19 × 4.1 × 1.9	M. Joukowsky
East Colonnade	33	4.7 × 6	Warnock
East Exedra	37	19 × 15	M. Joukowsky
Southwest part of the Hexagonal Pavement	39	4 × 4	Brown
Upper Temenos			
Western Temple Forecourt	32	17.65 (N) × 3.6 (E) 15.36 (S) × 16.45 (W)	Brown
East Archway	38	7.5 × 4	M. Joukowsky
Temple			
West Stairway and E-W Retaining Wall	18	17.5 (S) × 16 (N) 14.5 (E) × 10 (W)	Basile
Northeast central Pronaos	24	9.8 × 9.95	Bestock
Northwest Corridor	29	8.25 × 3.36	Slaughter
Theater West N-S Stairway and Vaulted Room	22 (Part II)	7.5 × 10	Bedal
Theater South	26 27 35 (Part I)	5.5 × 4.5 4.75 × 3.5 3.75 × 3.5	Payne
Southeast Corridor	34 (Part I) SP42 SP43	14 × 5 2 × 1.5	A. Joukowsky A. Joukowsky G. and C. Hisert
Suleiman Corner Column	SP40	5 × 2.6	M. Joukowsky

AREA	TRENCH	MEASUREMENT (M) (N-S × E-W)	EXCAVATOR(S)
Propylaeum			
West of Central Staircase	50, SP53	4.55 × 4.75	Haile, Parker
Lower Temenos			
Center West Hexagonal Pavement	42, SP48, SP49	18 × 14	Haile, Parker
South Center of the Hexagonal Pavement	6 (Part II)SP45, SP46	8 × 3	Basile, Najjar, Sylvester; Payne
Center	43 cut	4 × 9.7 1.45 × 2.3	Basile, Najjar Sylvester
West Colonnade	SP47	No measurements	Haile, M. Joukowsky
East Colonnade (space for reerection of columns)	SP51	No measurements	Haile, Parker
East Colonnade	SP54	1 × 0.60	British excavation team
Upper Temenos			
East Archway	41	4.5 × 9.5	Bestock, Mattison, Sistovaris
Temenos East	44	10.1 × 8.85 (W) 9.75 (E)	Bestock, Mattison, Sistovaris
Forecourt West (Western Bath Complex dump)	SP44	No measurements	Brown
Retaining Wall between West and Central Stairs	18A	7.35 (N) × 7.5 (S) 14.5 (E-W)	Basile, Najjar, Sylvester
Center East Retaining Wall	46	7 (N) × 8 (S) 14.5 (E-W)	Basile, Najjar, Sylvester
East Stairway	49 14.5 (W)	6 × 17.7 (E)	Basile, Najjar, Sylvester
Temple			
Northeast Pronaos	48	2 × 10	Slaughter
West Corridor	45	7.5 × 3	Payne, M. Joukowsky
Theatron west	47	9.8 × 6	Bedal
Stage west	40	6 × 9.8	Slaughter
Theater South	27 (Part II)	4.75 × 3.5	Payne
Southeast wall of temple	34 (Part II)	5 × 4	Brown, M. Joukowsky
Base of the East Rear Stairway	35 (Part II)	2.47 × 4.38	Brown, Parker

Petra Great Temple Trenches Excavated in 1998

AREA	TRENCH	MEASUREMENT (M) (N-S × E-W)	EXCAVATOR(S)
Propylaeum			
West/Arched Passage	51	3.76 × 7	Haile, Roger
Lower Temenos			
East Exedra	52	15.3 × 18	Basile, Sylvester, Karz
East Colonnade dirt removal	SP56	3.3 × 2.6	Ginsberg
East Colonnade dirt removal	SP57	2 × 1.6	Ginsberg
Upper Temenos			
East "Cistern"	53	3.15 × 11.05	Bestock, Sullivan, Schwartz
Temple			
East Vaulted Room	55	7.5 × 4.8	Brown
West Corridor	56	8.5 × 3	A. Joukowsky, M. Joukowsky
West Corridor	59	11.18 × 3.4	A. Joukowsky, M. Joukowsky
Central Arch	57	6.96 × 3.32	Libonati, Prendergast, Sullivan
East Corridor	58	11 × 3	Schwartz, Haile

Petra Great Temple Trenches Excavated in 1999

AREA	TRENCH	MEASUREMENT (M) (N-S × E-W)	EXCAVATOR(S)
Propylaeum	No work done here		
Lower Temenos			
East center Hexagonal Pavement	60	25.3 × 11.3	Karz
West Hexagonal Pavement	66	13.5 × 9	M. Joukowsky, Karz
East Colonnade center	61	6 × 13.7	Karz
Upper Temenos			
East Upper Temenos	54	10.2 × 5.05	Karz
Sondage in the Upper Temenos West Landing	SP60	2 × 1.50	M. Joukowsky
East Wall of the Upper Temenos (North)	67	9.90 × 3.50	A. Joukowsky, M. Joukowsky
East Perimeter Wall	68	15.90 × 5.20	A. Joukowsky, M. Joukowsky, Qublan
Temple			
East Vaulted Chamber	55A	7.5 × 4.8	Brown
Theater	62	11 × 12.50	Basile, Sylvester
East Corridor	65 Part I 65 Part II	14 × 3.5	Brown M. Joukowsky
West Walkway	63	22.70 × 3.74	A. Joukowsky
East Walkway	64	6.80 × 3.80	M. Joukowsky, Sylvester, Karz

Petra Great Temple Trenches Excavated in 2000

AREA	TRENCH	MEASUREMENT (M) (N-S × E-W)	EXCAVATOR(S)
Propylaeum			
Propylaeum West	69	5.90 x 4.50	Larsen, Brown
Propylaeum West	70	8.30 x 11.80	Larsen
Propylaeum West	SP70	4.17 x 12.25	Larsen
Lower Temenos			
West Colonnade	71	22.50 x 19.80	M. Joukowsky
East Colonnade	SP73	26 x 3.5	Karz
Upper Temenos			
Upper Temenos East, Balk	75	9.00 × 0.96	J. Farley, P. Farley, McCracken
East and South Perimeter Wall	77 (Part I) 77 (Part II)	18.40 × 5.20	McCracken, A. Joukowsky
East Bedrock	72	6.00 × 6.40	M. Joukowsky
West of West Walkway	76	3.00 × 11.00	P. Farley, J. Farley
Temple			
East Walkway	73 SP71	21.00 × 3.60, 1.30 × 1.5	Stern, Brin
South Corridor	SP72 (77 Part III)	4.50 × 21.80	M. Joukowsky

Petra Great Temple Trenches Excavated in 2001

AREA	TRENCH	MEASUREMENT (M) (N-S × E-W)	EXCAVATOR(S)
Propylaeum			
Propylaeum West	80	7.00 × 12.00	Sneag, Egan, Brown
Propylaeum West	86	4.20 × 2.00	Brown
Propylaeum East	82	6.00 × 12.00	Basile
Lower Temenos			
West Cryptoporticus	79	13.50 × 12.50	M. Joukowsky
Upper Temenos			
Passageway	83, SP83	6.45 × 31.20	Libonati, Egan
East Perimeter Wall interior Rooms A and B	84, SP91	10.53 × 6.46	Fusté
East Fluvial Deposit	SP84	4.58 × 3.20	Cloke
Cistern	SP85	2.50 × 1.50	Cloke
Temple			
South Corridor	85	2.73 × 17.27	Egan, Libonati

Petra Great Temple Trenches Excavated in 2002

AREA	TRENCH	MEASUREMENT (M) (N-S × E-W)	EXCAVATOR(S)
Colonnaded Street & Sidewalk			
West of Propylaeum Staircase	SP88	6.10 × 34.30	M. Joukowsky
Propylaeum			
Propylaeum West	87	4.39/5.30 × 19.41	Henry, M. Joukowsky
Propylaeum West Entry Stairs	88	10.10 × 3.80/2.80	M. Joukowsky
Propylaeum West South Gallery	81	11.70 × 6.70	M. Joukowsky
Propylaeum East	93	15.45 × 13.00	M. Joukowsky
Lower Temenos			
South of the Propylaeum Central Staircase	SP92	2.00 × 3.00	Brown
Upper Temenos			
East Perimeter Wall	91	2.74 × 0.80	Fusté
Cistern	90	36.00 × 13.00	Cloke
Shrine Room and Baroque Room	89/94 Part I	6.65 × 9.28	Libonati, Fusté
Residential Quarter	89/94 Part II	16.00 × 10.00	Libonati, Fusté
Temple			
Stage	92	4.00 × 6.18	Fusté
South Corridor	SP93	2.00 × 2.50	Cloke

Petra Great Temple Trenches Excavated in 2003

AREA	TRENCH	MEASUREMENT (M) (N-S × E-W)	EXCAVATOR(S)
Propylaeum East			
Propylaeum East Rooms 1 and 2	95	10.50 × 23.50	M. Joukowsky, Saunders
Propylaeum East Room 1	SP95	2.00 × 2.40	M. Joukowsky, Saunders
Propylaeum East Room 3	96	6.50 × 4.00	M. Joukowsky, Saunders
Lower Temenos	No work done here		
Upper Temenos	No work done here		
Temple	No work done here		

Petra Great Temple Trenches Excavated in 2004

AREA	TRENCH	MEASUREMENT (M) (N-S × E-W)	EXCAVATOR(S)
Propylaeum			
West	SP87	1.96 × 7.66	Reid
Northeastern corner of the Propylaeum	99	5.5 × 8.0	Basile
Propylaeum East, Room 3	100	17.34 × 3.80 to 4.30	M. Joukowsky
Propylaeum Staircase	SP125	6.35 × 1.20	Zimmerman, Reid
Lower Temenos			
West Cryptoporticus East	97	25.77 × 6.10	Tuttle
West Cryptoporticus West	98		Khanachet, Power
Central Staircase	SP124	5.90 × 4.56	Libonati, Egan
Upper Temenos			
Baroque Room North Door	SP89	0.30 × 1.30	Egan
Corridor between Settling Tank and Res Quarter	SP94	4.9 × 1.66	Khanachet
Southwest Bedrock Plateau	SP96	8.85 × 15.38	Egan, Libonati
Settling Tank	101	5.25 × 4.82	Libonati, Khanachet
Sondage in South Passageway	SP121	1.50 × 1.50	Zimmerman
Sondage in Shrine Room	SP123	0.86 × 0.60	Libonati, Egan
Temple			
Central Arch Water Systems	SP120	2.26 × 3.60	Libonati, Egan

Petra Great Temple Trenches Excavated in 2005

AREA	TRENCH	MEASUREMENT (M) (N-S × E-W)	EXCAVATOR(S)
Propylaeum			
Propylaeum Staircase	SP114	0.86 × 0.36	Khanachet
Propylaeum West South Gallery	SP118	2.35 × 3.00	Tuttle
Propylaeum East Room 2	SP150	2.30 × 2.30	Tuttle
Lower Temenos			
West Cryptoporticus West	98B	17.21 × 4.40	Khanachet
West Entry Stairway	102–103	30.75 × 4.55	M. Joukowsky
Hexagonal Pavement northwest sondage	104	8.00 × 10.00	Khanachet
West Cryptoporticus West, Sondage	SP104	4.00 × 4.30	Tuttle
West Cryptoporticus East, below pavement	SP105	1.50 × 4.20	Tuttle
Upper Temenos			
Roman-Byzantine Bath Complex southeast	105–106	18.00 × 12.00	Power, Agnew
West Bedrock Plaza and Temple E-W Support Wall	SP108	12.40 × 9.20	Libonati
West Precinct Wall and Cistern-Reservoir	SP110	62.00 × 2.50	M. Joukowsky
Residential Quarter steps	SP111	4.90 × 1.66	Khanachet
Temple			
Pronaos East sondage	SP107	6.40 × 3.55	Libonati
West Walkway	SP109	2.00 × 3.06	Khanachet
Orchestra Floor sondage	SP200	6.96 × 1.96	Libonati

Petra Great Temple Trenches Excavated in 2006

AREA	TRENCH	MEASUREMENT (M) (N-S × E-W)	EXCAVATOR(S)
Propylaeum	No work done here		
Lower Temenos			
Roman-Byzantine Bath Complex northwest	121	9.00 × 16.00	Khakpour
West Entry Stairway south	122	7.90 × 9.00	M. Joukowsky, Khakpour
Roman-Byzantine Bath Complex northeast	126	4.55 × 13.00	Tuttle
Roman-Byzantine Bath Complex central	127	10.11 × 14.00	M. Joukowsky
Upper Temenos			
Roman-Byzantine Bath Complex southwest	120	13.50 × 17.00	Power, Khakpour, Agnew
"Well Room" sondage	125	1.93 × 2.52	Libonati
Temple			
Theater seats sondage	123	1.30 × 2.80	Libonati

Notes

1.

There are four main building Areas for the site, identified as follows: P—Propylaeum, LT—Lower Temenos, UT—Upper Temenos, and T—Temple.

2.

In the Propylaeum are 15 trenches, in the Lower Temenos 36, in the Upper Temenos are 34 and 37 that have been excavated in the Temple. Special Projects number 70. Many Special Projects developed into trenches.

3.

These figures do not include the databases developed at the Small Temple.

4.

For Middle East chronology, we follow Walter Rast's (1992) overall chronology.

Early Hellenistic 332–198 BCE; Late Hellenistic 198–63 BCE; Early Roman 63 BCE–135 CE, Nabataea annexed by Rome 106 CE; Middle Roman 135–250 CE; Late Roman 250–360 CE; Early Byzantine 360–491 CE; Late Byzantine 491–640 CE; Islamic Umayyad Dynasty 661–750 CE; Abbasid Dynasty 750–1258 CE.

5.

We cannot be confident these apply to the entire Nabataean region, because regionally the ceramic repertoire may have moved beyond Petra at a gradual rate.

6.

Sherds of *Terra Sigillata* (TSA) imports are found (there are no complete vessels) which do not help us with our dating because they could have come from an earlier deposit and/or originated in the fill for a later deposit.

7.

Thus objects are not phased with the architecture, but with the fill in which they are associated. All objects have been recorded, and complete or semi-complete pottery forms have been cataloged, and phased with their locus.

8.

In the Propylaeum the Portico Wall is constructed as well as the lowest eight steps of the Propylaeum Central Stairs leading from the then sand and gravel path to a landing, which may have been the site of an early altar. From the Lower Temenos to the Upper Temenos the Central Staircase is built. In the Upper Temenos there is continued construction of the canalization system under the temple Forecourt and the Central Stairs leading down from the temple to the area of the not as yet paved Lower Temenos, and the East "Cistern" is constructed. The *distyle in antis* temple is erected with east and west interior antae and two freestanding columns in front, eight columns on the sides and six in the rear. There is the plastering of the columns and placement of a slab over the temple flooring beneath the columns' raised Attic bases.

9.

This could possibly be attributed to the earthquake of 312 BCE.

10.

There is minor damage perhaps due to an earthquake to the Propylaeum East (Trench 95). In the Lower Temenos the damage is not well defined, but perhaps this is when there was the reconstruction of the Central Stairs from the Lower to Upper Temenoi. And in the Upper Temenos, the damage also is not well defined. But in the early temple are some small repairs and the presumed collapse of some elements that are reconstructed in Site Phase IV.

11.

This idea is suggested in Joukowsky 1998:147, note 45.

12.

In the Upper Temenos there is the construction of the subterranean canalization system including the East Plaza Great Cistern, which also undergoes repair during this phase. Also constructed is the southeast canalization system, coeval with the East and South Perimeter walls of the temple precinct; and in the east and south the plazas are leveled and paved. Room A (with its arches) with hearth and Room B are constructed in the East Perimeter Wall, and a staircase is chiseled out of bedrock between Room A and the Tabun Cave Room. The adjacent East Reservoir is also built. Also there is the construction of the Anteroom, Shrine and Baroque Rooms and the Residential Quarter rooms are built in the Upper Temenos southwest. In the Residential Quarter there is the cutting of the original caves and construction of the early architectural arrangement, as well as the reinforcement of the caves and their expansion in front of Cave 2 with remodeling of the major construction elements. The Great Temple Forecourt is constructed, and there is the repaving of the Forecourt with the small hexagonal flagstones.

13.

The temple undergoes expansion into a *tetrastyle in antis* form with the Porch extension, and the East and West Porch Antae are erected. The stylobate and leveling fill are installed, after which the Pronaos floor is laid. At this time, the East, West and South Corridor walls as well as the East and West Walkway Walls are built. A well-cut limestone pavement is installed on all the floors that may have been the extension of the original flooring installed in Site Phase II.

14.

J. McKenzie's (1990) chronological assessments assign the structures including the Qasr al-Bint, Al-Khazna, the Temple of the Winged Lions and the Baths to this time period.

15.

In the Near East this spans the Early Roman Period 63 BCE–135 CE.

16.

A second story constructed at the rear of the temple, and renovated limestone pavements are laid on all new floor areas.

17.

Pompey, the architect of Rome's expansion, arrived in Syria at the end of 64 BCE and annexed the Seleucid kingdom and reorganized it as a new province of Syria. But Nabataea remained an independent kingdom until 106 CE.

18.

This deposit is a time capsule, a frozen moment in time. Private lives are illuminated because artifacts are left *in situ*.

19.

This spans the Middle Roman Period in the Middle East from ca. 135–250 CE and the Late Roman Period 250–360 CE.

20.

The Street is set at an oblique angle in front of the temple, but the bottom of the Central Staircase pavement compensates for the fact it is not perpendicular to the Central Stairs. Rather than using wheeled vehicles, they used pack animals—the camel and the donkey (as they do today).

21.

This is the Early Byzantine Period in the Near East, 360–491 CE.

CHAPTER TWO

The Petra Great Temple

Propylaeum

Aerial view of the Propylaeum, to the southwest, 2006.

The Petra Great Temple Propylaeum

Introduction

The northernmost introductory component to the monumental Petra Great Temple complex, the Propylaeum, is situated just south of the street, 6.90 m east of the Qasr al-Bint Temenos Gate at its westernmost edge. Figure 2.1 is the Propylaeum plan. Its full dimensions measure approximately 55.00 m east-west × 12.50 m north-south. Extending across the front of the temple precinct, the Propylaeum is divided into two equal sections, one in the east and one in the west, by the Propylaeum Central Staircase ascending from the Roman Street below. In the south, the architecture of the Propylaeum is braced against the Propylaeum Retaining Wall, into which the *voussoirs* of a vaulted cryptoporticus are set. In the north, positioned parallel to the street, the Portico Wall fronts the entire edifice (Figure 2.2), separating the internal rooms of the Propylaeum from the sidewalk and street below. Figure 2.3 shows the Propylaeum before excavation in 1993. Measurements of the major features of the Propylaeum are presented below.

Propylaeum and Roman Street Measurements

Elevations asl

COLONNADED STREET

Crown directly north of the Propylaeum—890.33 m

South gutter directly north of the Propylaeum—890.15 m

PROPYLAEUM

Curbing—890.66 m

Lowest Step—890.75 m

Upper Step—897.25 m

Dimensions

Note: All measurements are external and include wall thicknesses unless otherwise noted.
When a depth is irregular e.g., steps, it is averaged.

Propylaeum: (external) 12.41 m north-south × 56.68 m east-west

Propylaeum: (internal) 9.81 m north-south × 53.98 m east-west

PROPYLAEUM EAST

From Room 4 east wall to Propylaeum Central Staircase: north-south 22.41 m

Room 1: (internal) 10.20 m north-south × 6.40 m east-west × 4.80 m depth

Room 2: 10.00 m north-south × 6.70 m east-west × 5.00 m depth

Room 3: (corridor) 19.00 m north-south × 4.20 m east-west × 4.80 m depth

Room 4: (internal) 3.74 m north-south × 5.40 m east-west × 4.00 m depth

PROPYLAEUM CENTRAL STAIRCASE

Propylaeum Central Staircase: (partially restored) 17.00 m length north-south × 7.40 m east-west

Earlier Propylaeum Staircase (excavated): 6.35 m north-south × 1.20 m east-west

Propylaeum

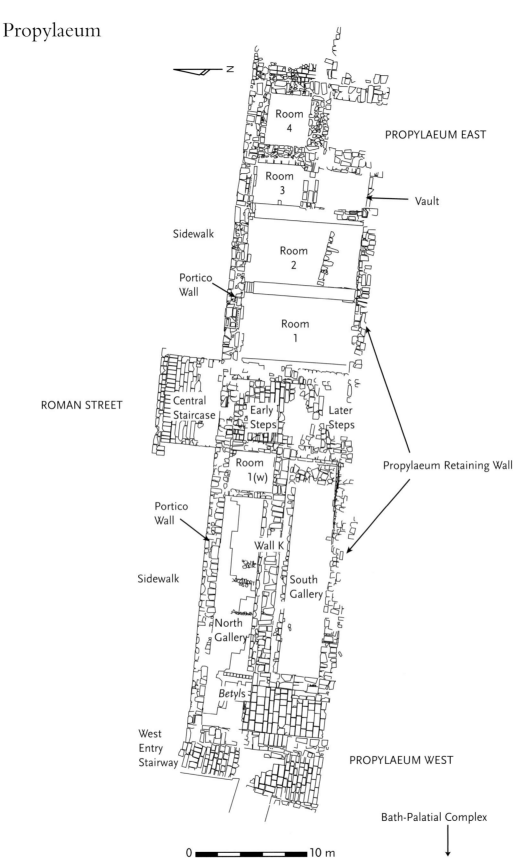

N

Room
4

PROPYLAEUM EAST

Room
3

Vault

Sidewalk

Room
2

Portico
Wall

Room
1

ROMAN STREET

Central
Staircase

Early
Steps

Later
Steps

Propylaeum Retaining Wall

Room
1(w)

Portico
Wall

Wall K

Sidewalk

South
Gallery

North
Gallery

Betyls

West
Entry
Stairway

PROPYLAEUM WEST

Bath-Palatial Complex

0   10 m

Fig 2.1
Propylaeum plan.

PROPYLAEUM WEST

From West Stairs to Propylaeum Central Staircase: 25.05 m east-west

Wall K bench on south: 0.76 m north-south × 17.19 m east-west × 0.50 m depth

West Entry into the West Propylaeum: 2.29 north-south × 1.47 m east-west × 0.07 m depth

West Entry into South Gallery on W of Wall K: 2.38 m north-south × 1.20 m east-west × 0.14 m depth

NORTH GALLERY

Room 1: (external) 6.52 m north-south × 4.75 m east-west × 2.60 m depth; (internal) 3.93 m north-south × 3.39 m east-west

North Gallery: (external) 6.46 m north-south × 21.52 m × 1.30 m depth; (internal) 3.45 m north-south × 19.60 m east-west

Bench along north face of Wall K: 0.77 m north-south × 14.59 m east-west × 0.43 m depth

Ceramic Pavement: 3.40 m north-south × 19.55 m east-west × 0.10 m depth

SOUTH GALLERY

South Gallery: (external) 6.78 m north-south × 20.56 m east-west; (internal) 4.36 m north-south × 18.13 m east-west

Voussoirs inter-axial distance: 0.53 m

WEST PROPYLAEUM WEST

West Entry Stairs: 37.20 m north-south × 4.80 m east-west

West Entry Doorway: 2.42 m north-south × 1.50 m east-west × 2.18 m depth

West Entry Threshold: 2.18 m north-south × 0.30 m east-west × 0.12 m depth

Betyl Wall: 39.19 m north-south × 1.50 m east-west × 2.72 m depth

Betyl Wall Bench: 36.39 m north-south × 0.72 m east-west × 0.77 m depth

Limestone Pavement in betyl entry: 6.50 m north-south × 3.94 m east-west

Fig. 2.2
Propylaeum Portico Wall, and Central Staircase, to the southeast, 2005.

Propylaeum Wall Dimensions
(Thickness and height, as excavated and restored)

Portico Wall: 1.30 m north-south × 25.05 m east-west × 2.44 m depth

Wall K: 1.20 m north-south × 19.74 m east-west × 1.42 m depth

Propylaeum Retaining Wall: 1.45 m north-south × 35.12 m east-west × 6.70 m depth

West Wall: 11.62 m north-south × 1.47 m east-west × 3.00 m depth

PROPYLAEUM WEST

West Room 1 Wall: (North) 1.34 m; (South) 1.10 m, (East) 0.90 m; (West) 0.90 m

PROPYLAEUM EAST

Room 1: (North) 1.13 m; (South) 1.10 m; (East) 1.03 m; (West) × 1.09 m depth

Room 2: (North) 1.24 m; (South) 1.10 m; (East) 1.26 m; (West) × 1.03 m depth

Room 3: (North) 1.37 m; (South) 1.10 m; (East) 1.53 m; (West) × 1.26 m depth

Room 4: (North) 1.70 m; (South) 1.10 m; (East) 1.20 m; (West) × 1.53 m depth

West Entry Wall: 1.30 m thickness × 4.35 m height

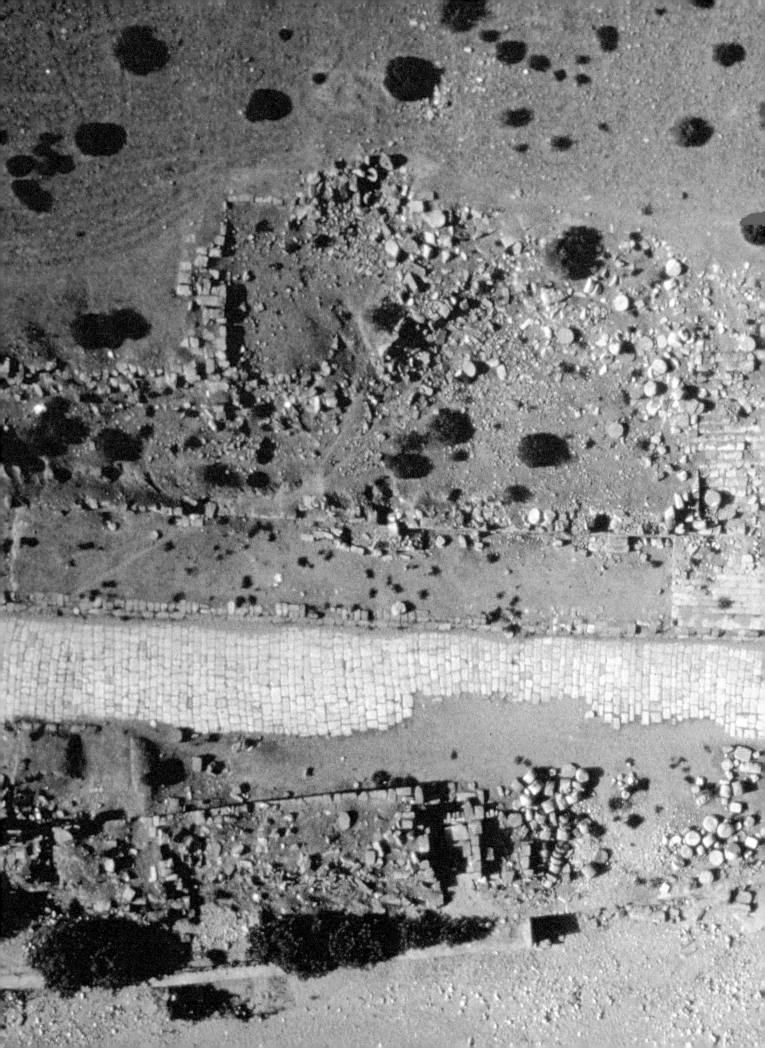

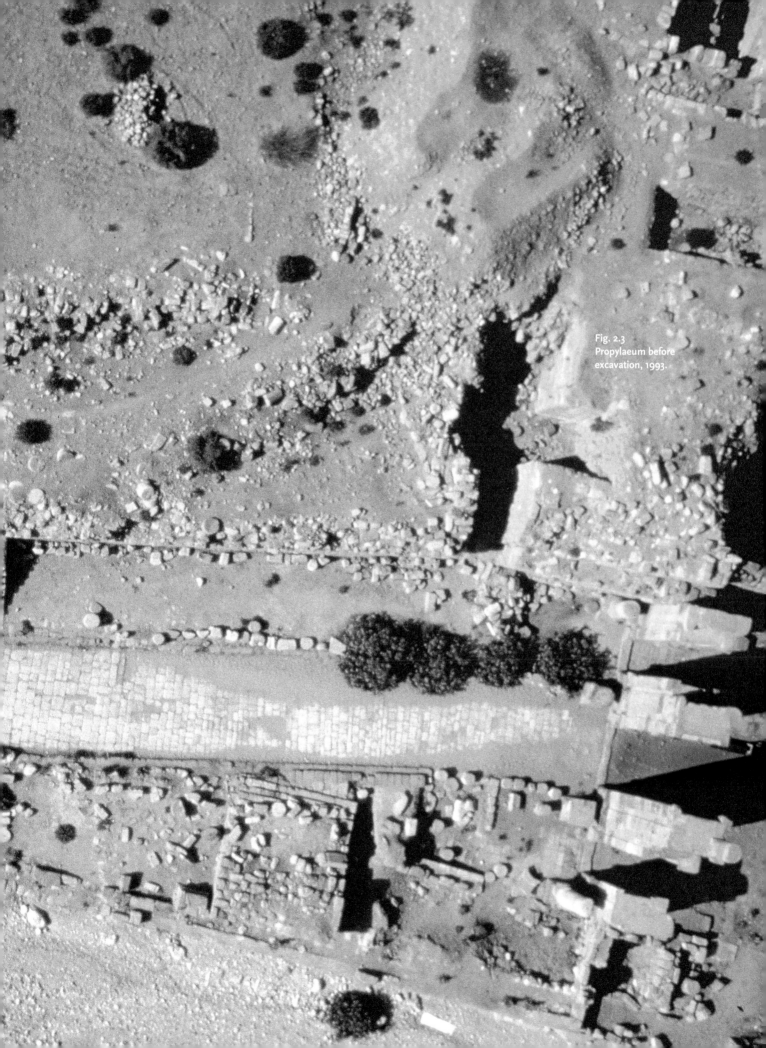

Fig. 2.3
Propylaeum before
excavation, 1993.

Sidewalk and Street

The main thoroughfare of central Petra, identified by some as a ritual street, serves as the principal access to the central city and lies perpendicular to the north-south axis of the Great Temple precinct. Initially a sand or gravel path, the Roman Street is refashioned between 9 BCE and 76 CE (Parr 1960:124–35) and embellished with large limestone flagstones to a total width of 6.00 m in front of the temple. The curbing along both sides of the street in front of the Great Temple is composed of an inner row of stretchers averaging 0.38 m in height surmounted by an outer row of headers approximately 0.75 m in height. The curbing (Figure 2.4) is put into place after the flagstones are laid. Dimensions for the sidewalk and curbing are 5.25 m north-south × 56.68 m east-west, for a total of 297.57 m^2. Directly north of the Propylaeum staircase, the current elevation of the crown of the street averages 890.33 m and the south gutter rests at 890.15 m.

Fig. 2.4
Propylaeum, close-up of the street curbing partially restored, 2001.

Propylaeum Central Staircase and the Portico Wall

Perpendicular to the street, the Propylaeum Central Staircase (Figure 2.5) is positioned between the east and west sections of the Propylaeum, connecting the south edge of the street with the elevated temple's Lower Temenos. At the lowest step a small limestone pavement averaging 0.80 m in north-south length connects the Central Staircase with the curbing of the street. The uneven alignment of these two features suggests that the bottom courses of the staircase are built before the street is paved, necessitating the use of irregularly cut limestone slabs to bridge the gap from the stairs to the curb. South of the street curbstones, eight original steps lead up to a mid-staircase landing that cuts into and abuts the north face of the Portico Wall. Figure 2.6 pictures the lower eight steps of the Propylaeum Central Staircase cleared in 1993. Above the landing are 34 severely eroded steps added during the early second century CE, completing the ascent from the street to the temple Lower Temenos. In total, the Propylaeum Central Staircase measures approximately 17.00 m north-south × 7.40 m east-west, and its base rests at an elevation of 890.75 m. To the south, the staircase tapers to an east-west width of 5.40 m at its top, its uppermost tread resting at an elevation of 897.25 m. Between the Portico Wall and Wall K[1] the presence of eight earlier steps under the Central Staircase connect West Propylaeum Room 1 to Wall K shown in Figure 2.7. The fact that architectural fragments from the main collapse of the Great Temple were found beneath the Central Staircase suggests that they were built after the earthquake of 363 CE. (This staircase was restored in 2007.)

Extending to either side of the Central Staircase is the Portico Wall,[2] the northernmost wall of the temple complex, averaging 1.72 m in north-south thickness. Figure 2.8 gives a 2005 wide-angle view of the Portico Wall. In the west, the wall is preserved to a height between 5.00 and 6.00 m and is composed of three extant rows of sandstone ashlars each measuring approximately 0.95 m in length × 0.70 m in width × 0.53 m in depth. A number of rebuilding episodes are represented within the Portico

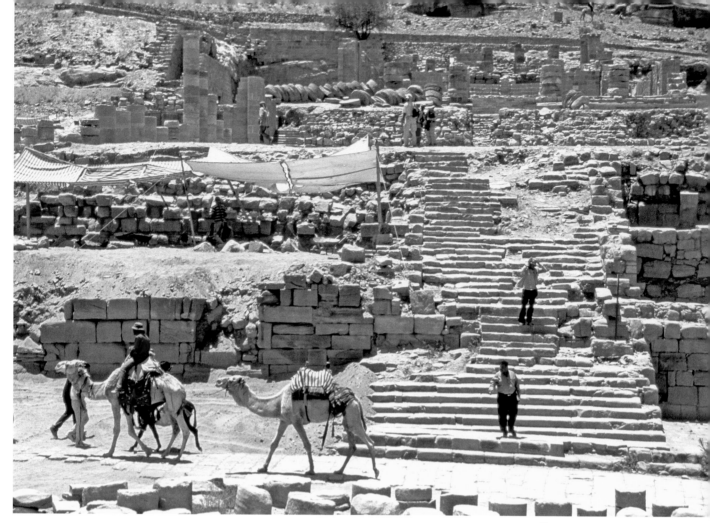

Fig. 2.5
Propylaeum Central
Staircase, to south, 2002.

Wall's construction characterized by visible changes in the style of masonry and modifications to its functionality. While the original height of the Portico Wall is unknown,[3] its foundations are assumed to be below the level of the Roman Street, which its construction predates.

Propylaeum East

East of the Central Staircase, the Portico Wall to the north and the Propylaeum Retaining Wall to the south contain the area of the Propylaeum East. Measuring approximately 12.50 m north-south × 25.00[4] m east-west the Propylaeum East is subdivided into a series of two rectangular north-south rooms, a corridor and Rooms 4 and 5 to the east. With the exception of Room 4 each room is accessible by a doorway perpendicular to the street. Figure 2.10 is a view of Rooms 1, 2, and 3.[5] Two north-south dividing walls separating the three interior rooms

Fig. 2.6
Propylaeum Central Staircase, to south, with the lower eight steps abutting the Portico Wall, 1993.

Fig. 2.7
Earlier Propylaeum Central Staircase, to west, with
Room 1 doorway, 2004.

comprise the main architectural features in the
east. Built from well-dressed, well-preserved,
sandstone ashlars wet-laid with mud mortar, the
dividing walls are preserved at best to a height
of 2.80 m. In this unusual construction, each
doorway of the three rooms is appointed with a
raised threshold with ten closely fitted vertical
iron bars, of which vestiges still remain *in situ*.
Fig. 2.11 pictures the raised doorway of Room 1
and Figure 2.12 shows the remains of the iron
bars fitted across Room 1's threshold. (Rectilinear limestone threshold blocks and door jambs
remain *in situ*.) Rooms 1 and 2 (in the west
and center) are isolated chambers, accessible
only from the street. Conversely, the Room 3
corridor is composed of three chambers
(Chambers 1–3) separated by interior buttresses.
Corridor Room 3, narrower than Rooms 1

Fig. 2.8
Propylaeum, view of the Portico Wall, to south, 2005.

Fig. 2.9
Propylaeum East,
Rooms 1–3 from Room 4,
to west, 2004.

Fig. 2.10
Propylaeum East, Rooms 1–3, to north, 2004.

Fig. 2.11
Propylaeum East, doorway of Room 1, to south, 2003.

Fig. 2.12
Propylaeum East, Room 1
doorway with iron pins in
the threshold, 2003.

Fig. 2.13
Propylaeum East, Room 3 corridor, to north, 2004.

Fig. 2.14
Propylaeum East, Room 3 vault, 2004.

Fig. 2.15
Propylaeum West, North Gallery, to west, 2002.

and 2, joins in the south with the west gallery of the Lower Temenos East Cryptoporticus. Incompletely excavated, the Room 3 corridor contains an *in situ* vault set 5.20 m above the floor. On the floor just below this vault a large deposit of burned incense was found as if some undetermined ceremony had taken place. Figure 2.13 is a view of the corridor of Room 3 to the north with its buttressed walls. Figure 2.14 is a view under the vault, supported by wood, awaiting 2005 consolidation. Moving from west to east, the internal measurements of Room 1 are 9.70 m north-south × 5.05 m east-west. Room 2 measurements are 9.68 m north-south × 5.05 m east-west and Room 3 is an excavated 17.34 m north-south × 3.44-4.13 m east-west. To the east are two more rooms, Rooms 4 and 5, bordering the Propylaeum East. Whereas Room 4 is inaccessible from the Roman Road, Room 5 opens onto the road and has a hexagonally paved passageway that serves the Garden-Pool complex to the east of the Great Temple.

Propylaeum West

West of the Central Staircase, the Propylaeum West, also measuring approximately 12.50 m north-south × 25.00 m east-west, is divided into two long parallel east-west galleries, which also lie parallel to the street. Positioned between the galleries, the east-west dividing wall of the Propylaeum West, "Wall K" (Parr 1970), is situated 3.00 m south of the Portico Wall and 4.20 m north of the Propylaeum Retaining Wall. At the front of the complex, between the Portico Wall and Wall K is the Propylaeum West north gallery. Figure 2.15 shows the east-west expanse of the Propylaeum West north gallery. In length, this gallery extends 25.00 m east-west from the west wall of the precinct to the west face of the Central Staircase. At its west edge it extends approximately 11.00 m south, creating an "L-shape" and connecting with the south gallery of the West Cryptoporticus. Near the center of the gallery the elevation of the *in situ* ceramic tile flooring averages 892.74 m. Associated with this flooring is an extraordinary deposit of 423 ballista balls, 162 arrowheads, and two helmet cheek pieces. Clearly some sort of offensive action was anticipated or had taken place.[6] Figure 2.16 shows the ballista ball assemblage against the Portico Wall in the north gallery of the West Propylaeum where they were recovered. Figure 2.17 illustrates how each ballista was being weighed.

At the north gallery's east edge is a small room roughly 9.00 m² in size, Propylaeum West Room 1, separated from the north gallery west by a 3.00 m north-south crosswall built between the Portico Wall and Wall K. The *in situ* east threshold and doorway of Propylaeum West Room 1 lead from the earlier staircase and serve as the sole point of access to the room's interior. Figure 2.18 is a photograph of the doorway to Propylaeum West Room 1 and Figure 2.7 shows the Room 1 entry from the earlier Central Staircase.

At the southwest end of the north gallery's L-shaped extension is a large niche measuring 0.97 m in width and 0.69 m in depth cut into the west face of the Propylaeum West central north-south wall, an extension of the central stylobate wall of the Lower Temenos West Cryptoporticus. In this niche rest exquisitely carved twin aniconic white limestone *betyls* averaging 0.50 m in height and 0.21 m in width adhered to the base and rear wall of the niche

Fig. 2.16
Propylaeum West, numbered ballista ball assemblage, 2005.

Fig. 2.17
Propylaeum West, weighing ballista balls, 2004.

Fig. 2.18
Propylaeum West, Room 1 entry from above, (Note the later stairs blocking the threshold.) 2002.

Fig. 2.19
Propylaeum West
limestone *betyls* in the
niche just after excavation,
to east, 2001

by a thin layer of plaster. Figure 2.19 shows the *in situ betyls* just after their discovery in 2001, and Figure 2.20 provides line drawings of the *betyl* front views. Positioned directly beneath the niche is a bench constructed from medium-sized sandstone ashlars and packed earth resting on the floor of the north gallery at a base elevation of 892.51 m, shown in the plan in Figure 2.21.

Parallel to the north gallery, the south gallery of the Propylaeum West, a vaulted cryptoporticus, measures 4.50 m in interior north–south width. Figure 2.22 shows the south gallery during excavation in 1994 and displays the later-constructed support wall for the Central Staircase. It is separated from the north gallery by Wall K and is bordered in the south by the Propylaeum Retaining Wall. In total, the south gallery delimits an area approximately 19.00 m east-west and connects with the east gallery of the Lower Temenos West Cryptoporticus at its western edge. The elevation of the gallery floor rests at 892.65 m. Unlike the Propylaeum East, access to this area from the street is indirect, by way of the West Entry Stairway located along the west edge of the temple precinct. Figure 2.23 shows the West Entry Stairway at the outset of the 2005 excavations.[7] From the street

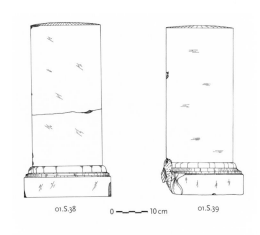

Fig. 2.20
Propylaeum West, detail of the front of the two limestone *betyls*, 2001. Cat. No. 01-S-38, Seq. No. 80432A+B Trench 80, Locus 35 (north *betyl*); Height 50.9 cm, width 21.0 cm, thickness 9.80 cm. Flat base. Broken, but since repaired. Cat. No. 01-S-39, Seq. No. 80433 (south *betyl*); height 50 cm, width 21 cm, thickness 9.9 cm. Fine rounded base, decorated in classical style with pedestal; intact.

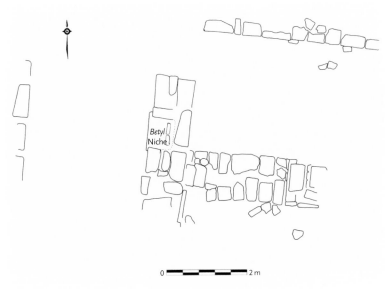

Fig. 2.21
Propylaeum West, plan of *betyl* niche, Trench 80, 2001.

sidewalk, a small entryway measuring 1.40 m north-south × 2.48 m east-west abuts seven steps averaging between 2.80 and 3.80 m in width. These steps in turn connect to a landing that opens directly into the Great Temple Propylaeum to the east and the adjacent first century CE Baths-Palatial Complex[8] to the west (McKenzie 1990, #408, p.138). Figure 2.24 shows the West Entry Stairway adjoining the Propylaeum West Entrance. In total, the lower steps comprise an area 2.40 m in north-south distance, and the adjacent landing measures 3.50 m north-south × 3.66 m east-west. The extent of these steps further south and their juncture with upper flights of stairs is determined in the 2005 Lower Temenos excavations. The excavated north-south length of the lower Propylaeum West Entry Stairway and its associated landing in the Propylaeum West measures 10.10 m.

Fig. 2.22
Propylaeum West, South Gallery, to east, 1994.
(Note the support wall of the Central Staircase.)

Fig. 2.23
Propylaeum West,
West Entry Stairway
at the outset of the
2005 excavations.

Fig. 2.24
Propylaeum West, West
Entry Stairway platform
adjoining the Propylaeum,
to east, 2002.

Fig. 2.25
Propylaeum West, South
Gallery early Pre-Phase I
deposits, 2005.

Stratigraphy and Phasing

The stratigraphy of the Great Temple Propylaeum is best defined within the context of the site phasing for the area. From the excavated data, 15 stages of development are visible within the Propylaeum architecture. Assigned to Pre-Site Phase I are the earliest deposits and architectural features that underlie the current structure of the Propylaeum as well as the 2005 investigations of the cross wall in Room 2 East Propylaeum. (Figure 2.25 pictures these excavations.) Results from a preliminary test trench in the south gallery of the Propylaeum West and a sondage in the northwest corner of the Propylaeum East indicate that these features predate the construction of the temple in the first century BCE and may be part of a larger terrace adjacent to, and aligned with, the flow of the Wadi Musa on which the original street path of sand and gravel is laid.

Soon after this initial terracing period, the Nabataean primary construction of the Great Temple complex begins during Site Phase II, evidenced in the north by the erection of the Portico Wall separating the temple precinct from the path of the gravel street. One of the temple's earliest architectural features, the Portico Wall's masonry reveals multiple stages of construction. Based on its current position, it is likely that in its original configuration during Site Phase II, it continues in a straight line west of the precinct. At the center of this wall is a later abutment of eight original steps leading up from the gravel path to a small platform, which may have been the site of an early altar.

In Site Phase III, a period of minor collapse occurs prompting the reorganization and expansion of the Great Temple complex in Site Phase IV, "the Grand Design," dating between the first century BCE and the first century CE. In this phase, the Portico Wall is breached to permit the construction of the West Entry Stairway, to provide access to the Temenos West Baths in the west and the Propylaeum West in the east. Coeval with this period of redesign is the construction of the Propylaeum Retaining

Wall and Wall K in both the Propylaea East and West.[9] A vaulted cryptoporticus is built between the Propylaeum Retaining Wall and Wall K and between Wall K and the Portico Wall. The west wall of Propylaeum West Room 1 is also built.

Shortly after this expansion, during a period of Nabataean redesign in the first century CE in Site Phase V, the north-south stylobate wall in the Propylaeum West south gallery is extended northward, and the previously mentioned double limestone *betyl*s are installed into an elevated niche, thus defining the sacred character of this part of the precinct during this period. Figure 2.26 shows the sweep of the Propylaeum West with the Site Phase IV–V structures. In Site Phase VI ca. 106 CE, a period of minor collapse results in repairs of the south gallery cryptoportici, Wall K, and the Portico Wall, which are damaged possibly as the result of an offensive ballista attack, perhaps by Roman general Cornelius Palma.

During the Roman acquisition of the site in the mid-second century CE, the Portico Wall is breached a second time to construct the south continuation of the Propylaeum Central Staircase connecting the newly paved Roman Street to the Hexagonal Pavement of the temple Lower Temenos in Site Phase VII. To complete this addition, the foundations and treads of 34 steps are built over the earlier platform (and over the threshold to Propylaeum West Room 1) adjoining the original eight steps constructed in Site Phase IV. Also during this time is the addition of benches built against the north and south faces of Wall K and beneath the *betyl* niche in the Propylaeum West. In the Propylaeum East, Wall K is dismantled and the area is reorganized into three north-south rooms accessed by three new doorways cut into the east Portico Wall, each perhaps originally accessible but later blocked by 10 vertical iron bars mortared into their thresholds.

In Site Phase IX, the earthquake of 363 CE compromises the structural integrity of the Propylaeum, leading to the collapse of the south gallery cryptoporticus in the Propylaeum West. The temple north colonnade falls from south to north across the Propylaeum and damage is sustained on the Propylaeum Retaining Wall. Inter-

Fig. 2.26
Propylaeum West, North
and South galleries, to
east, with the *betyl* wall to
the right, 2005.

mittent collapse and accumulation of fill continue throughout the Propylaeum East and West from Site Phases X–XIII or X to XIII, punctuated by periods of robbing and abandonment.

Excavation History

Overall, excavations of the Great Temple Propylaeum East and West are conducted in 1994, 1997 and 1998, resuming again from 2000 to 2005 (See Figure 2.27, Chart of the Propylaeum Excavations 1993–2005). Figure 2.28 provides the plan of the Propylaeum trenches excavated from 1993 to 2005. In total, the architectural fragments recovered from the Propylaeum number 3956 including 460 column drums, 1953 ashlars, 244 elephant head fragments, a number of complete capitals found only in the Propylaeum East, and 274 cornice fragments, amounting to 28 percent of the total architectural fragments recorded in the overall site database.

Sidewalk And Roman Street Excavations

Moving through the Propylaeum from north to south and east to west, excavations in Special Project 88 in 2002 preliminarily investigate a portion of the street and sidewalk between the northwest corner of the Propylaeum Central Staircase and the Temenos Gate. In the area between the street and the sidewalk the street curbing is delineated, comprised of an inner row of headers and outer course of stretchers oriented perpendicular to the street and presumably set in place after the street is paved. North of the curbing, the simultaneous investigation of a portion of the street reveals four stages of construction. The first two stages are evidenced by the laying of foundations over the sand and gravel street of the first century BCE followed by the positioning of a finely cut limestone pavement (of which only portions are preserved) in the second century CE. Subsequently, prior to the initial major collapse of the Petra Great Temple as a result of the 363 CE earthquake, the sidewalk pavement is robbed out allowing for the accumulation of debris and soil on top of the exposed foundation blocks in the site's later periods.

Propylaeum Central Staircase Excavations

Moving into the central area of the Propylaeum, excavations in 1994 and 2005 witness the cleaning and delineation of the Propylaeum Central Staircase. The newly cleaned Central Staircase can be seen in a photograph taken in 2003 (Figure 2.31) with the Propylaeum East Rooms 1–3. As part of Special Project P in 1994, surface weeds and debris are removed from the heavily eroded steps revealing a number of distinct stages of architectural construction. Close examination of the northern part of the staircase leads to the discovery of an early landing constructed at the top of the original eight steps abutting the Portico Wall. From the surrounding deposit, it appears that this landing withstood multiple burnings evidenced by discolored ashlars and an accumulation of fine black ash. Visible on the west face of the lowest of the eight steps between the abutting step wall and the Portico Wall, this localized ash deposit may indicate the presence of an early altar. In an ash-filled pocket under one of the platform ashlars a cache of first century CE Nabataean painted wares is recovered, and several fragments of sculptural reliefs are found resting against the north face of the Portico Wall. Among these are limestone blocks finely embellished with relief carvings of male and female heads and the upper torso of a draped figure. In 2004 an earlier Propylaeum staircase extending from the Portico Wall to Wall K abutting the entry to Room 1 is verified (Figure 2.7). In 2005 a probe at the bottom of these stairs in Special Project 114 confirms that at the entry to Room 1, the ballista assemblage is not under the stairs, so the ballista balls used as rubble fill and leveling for the flooring of the Propylaeum West do not continue under the pavers of the landing for the earlier steps. If the terracotta tiling under the pavers of the landing is understood to be the same as those tiles found in the two west rooms of the Propylaeum, then the ballista balls must predate both sets of Central Staircases of the Propylaeum. If that is the case, then two possibilities emerge: if the current date for the ballista balls is correct, then both the early and

TRENCH	YEAR	DESCRIPTION	MEASUREMENT(M) (N-S × E-W)	EXCAVATOR(S)
Sidewalk and Roman Street				
Special Project 88	2002	Sidewalk and Roman Street north of the Propylaeum Central Staircase	6.10 × 34.30	M. Joukowsky
Propylaeum Central Staircase				
Special Project P	1994	Cleaning of the Propylaeum Central Staircase	20.00 × 6.00	M. Joukowsky
Special Project 125	2004	Propylaeum Central Staircases	6.35 × 1.20	Zimmerman, Reid
Special Project 114	2005	Propylaeum Central Staircases	0.86 × 0.36	Khanachet
Propylaeum East				
Trench 82	2001	Upper levels of the Propylaeum East, Room 3	6.00 × 12.00	Basile
Trench 93	2002	Upper levels in the Propylaeum East	15.45 × 13.00	M. Joukowsky
Trench 95	2003	Propylaeum East Rooms 1 and 2	10.50 × 23.50	M. Joukowsky, Saunders
Trench 96	2003	Propylaeum East Room 3	6.50 × 4.00	M. Joukowsky, Saunders
Special Project 95	2003	Sub-floor deposits in Propylaeum East Room 1	2.00 × 2.40	M. Joukowsky, Saunders
Trench 99	2004	Northeastern corner of the Propylaeum	5.50 × 8.00	Basile
Trench 100	2004	Propylaeum East, Room 3	17.34 × 3.80 to 4.30	M. Joukowsky
Special Project 150	2005	Propylaeum East Room 2	2.30 × 2.30	Tuttle
Propylaeum West				
Trench 50 (SP53)	1997	Upper levels of the north gallery west of the Propylaeum Central Staircase	4.55 × 4.75	Haile, Parker, M. Joukowsky
Trench 51	1998	Upper levels of the north and south galleries west of the Propylaeum Central Staircase	3.76 × 7.00	Haile, Roger
Trench 69	2000	Propylaeum West south gallery cryptoporticus	5.90 × 4.50	Larsen, Brown
Trench 70	2000	Intersection of the Propylaeum West south gallery and the LT west cryptoporticus	8.30 × 11.80	Larsen
Special Project 70	2000	East part of the Propylaeum West south gallery	4.17 × 12.25	Larsen
Trench 80	2001	Continuation of Trench 70 in the Propylaeum West south gallery to the west of SP70.	7.00 × 12.00	Sneag, Egan, Brown
Trench 86	2001	Test trench of the lower levels of the Propylaeum West south gallery	4.20 × 2.00	Brown
Trench 81	2002	Propylaeum West south gallery	11.70 × 6.70	M. Joukowsky
Trench 87	2002	Propylaeum West north gallery, east and Propylaeum West Room 1	4.39/5.30 × 19.41	Henry, M. Joukowsky
Trench 88	2002	Propylaeum West Entry Staircase	10.10 × 3.80/2.80	M. Joukowsky
Special Project 87	2004	Propylaeum West	1.96 × 7.66	Reid
Special Project 118	2005	Propylaeum West south gallery	2.35 × 3.00	Tuttle

Fig. 2.27
Chart of the Propylaeum Trenches excavated 1993–2006.

Propylaeum Trenches

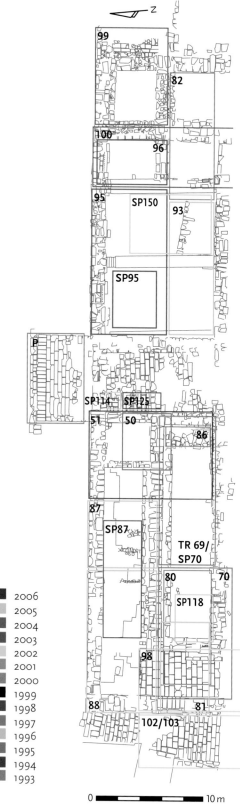

2006
2005
2004
2003
2002
2001
2000
1999
1998
1997
1996
1995
1994
1993

0   10 m

Fig. 2.28
Plan of trenches excavated in the Propylaeum 1993–2005.

later stairs must be dated to the Roman period; alternatively, the ballista balls could be earlier and the earlier stairways could be dated from the Nabataean period. A careful analysis of the remains will have to be made to shed more light on the dating of this area of the Propylaeum.

Propylaeum East Excavations

East of the Central Staircase, excavation of the Propylaeum East is undertaken during the 2001–2004 seasons. In 2001, a preliminary investigation in Trench 82 in the easternmost part of the Propylaeum East commences, continuing westward in Trench 93 in 2002. These initial excavations, intending to determine the plan and integrity of the area as well as to define the stratigraphy where the Propylaeum East abuts the Central Staircase in the west, expose the dense rubble matrix of the Lower Temenos terrace supported by the Propylaeum Retaining Wall. Upper layers of collapse are also removed from the Propylaeum East in preparation for the full excavation of the area in the following season. Figure 2.29 pictures the early morning of excavations in the Propylaeum East and Figure 2.30 shows these excavations in progress before the rooms are defined. Architectural remains of particular interest found in the fill include a number of limestone hexagonal pavers fallen from the Lower Temenos plaza and a decorative life-size male head with open lips finely sculpted in white limestone shown in Figure 2.32. The dense overburden of this area (like that in the west) also contains a high concentration of column drums and capital fragments, clearly indicating the original placement of the temple's north colonnade above Wall K and the Propylaeum Retaining Wall, fronting the Great Temple precinct both in the Propylaeum East and West. Figure 2.33 shows an *in situ* collapsed elephant-headed capital found in the doorway of Room 1.

In 2003–2004, the discovery of *voussoirs* set into the north face of the Propylaeum Retaining Wall in Trenches 95 and 96 sheds additional light on the original construction of the Propylaeum East in Site Phase IV. Originally designed to mirror the architectural arrangement of the Propylaeum West, the Propylaeum East

Fig. 2.29
Propylaeum East, early morning excavations, 2003.

Fig. 2.30
Propylaeum East excavation in progress, to south, 2003.

Fig. 2.31
Propylaeum East, to south, with completed excavations of
Rooms 1 and 2 and doorway of Room 3, 2003.

Fig. 2.32
Sculpture of a male head.
Seq. No. 93095. Propy-
laeum, Trench 93 Locus 1,
2002. Length 18 cm, width
18 cm, thickness 27 cm.
1/2 of lower male face with
evocative chin and hair
tendril just above the ear-
mouth, nose damaged.

Fig. 2.33
Propylaeum East, collapse
of Doorway 1, to south, with
elephant head *in situ*, 2003.

undergoes major architectural modifications following the Roman annexation of Petra in 106 CE resulting in the dismantling of Wall K and the reorganization of the area into two rectangular rooms, a corridor and an enclosed room oriented north-south. Moving from west to east, Propylaeum East Rooms 1 and 2, of roughly the same size and shape, are of unknown function. Separated from each other and from the surrounding architecture, these rooms may serve as shop fronts, later evolving into confined spaces (marked by the addition of iron bars across their doorways) where state funds or exotica such as wild animals are kept. Until also closed by bars, Room 3, positioned further to the east, serves as a vaulted corridor between the Propylaeum East and the Lower Temenos East Crypto-porticus. Figure 2.34 represents the Room 3 doorway excavation in progress, and Figure 2.35 is a plan of the three Chambers.

Discovered within the fill of this area are 15 relief sculptures, which are among the most striking examples of architectural finds recovered from the temple precinct. This collection includes a grape leaf cluster tied with a ribbon (Figure 2.36) and two pilaster reliefs—one of a helmet with a cheek piece (Figure 2.37) and another of Athena with her weapons and a battered Medusa relief on her chest (Figure 2.38).

Fig. 2.34
Propylaeum East, beginning excavation in Doorway 3, to south, 2003.

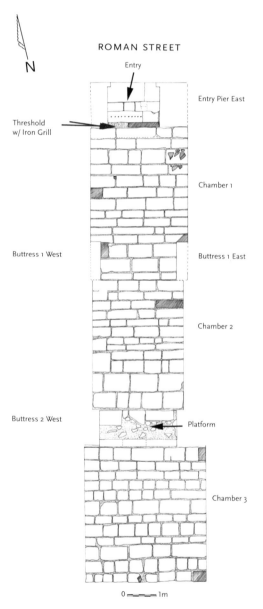

Fig. 2.35
Propylaeum East, Trench 100 Plan of Room 3, 2003. (Hatching indicates *in situ* pavers)

In 2005 the excavation of Special Project 150 revealed an assemblage of architectural features at a shallow depth below the floor level in the East Propylaeum Room 2. The complexity of these features is such that at present they are not completely understood.

The earliest stage encompasses all of the early wall constructions found in the sounding, although it is not at all certain that these three architectural features are contemporary, or even interrelated. Massive wall stones may be part of Wall K; however, not enough of this feature has been exposed to determine this fact with certainty.

Propylaeum West Excavations

Moving west, the counterpart to the Propylaeum East, the Propylaeum West, is excavated over the course of five seasons in 1997, 1998, 2000, 2001 and 2002, and a ballista ball sondage is undertaken in 2004. During the early investigation of this area in Trenches 50 and 51 and Special Project 53, the upper courses of Wall K and of the Propylaeum Retaining Wall are revealed. A number of *voussoirs* are found packed into the fill of the support wall for the southern section of the Propylaeum Central Staircase indicating the late construction of this feature following the restructuring of the original Propylaeum East south gallery cryptoporticus in Site Phase VII. Excavations in Trench 51 also confirm that the Portico Wall (built first), and Wall K and the Propylaeum Retaining Wall (built second) are the original northern terrace walls of the temple precinct, the latter two undergoing structural modification and heightening during Site Phase IV to hold the *voussoirs* of the south gallery's vaulted cryptoporticus.

At the western edge of the north gallery of the Propylaeum West, Trench 87 (excavated in 2002) fully exposes a small room, Propylaeum West Room 1, located between the Portico Wall and Wall K and adjacent to the Central Staircase.[10] Figure 2.39 is of the south gallery of the Propylaeum West during the 2002 excavation. First, a massive overburden of soil and architectural elements is removed down to the level of the preserved ceramic flooring previously uncovered in the north gallery west. Once cleared, the discovery of a threshold in the east wall of Room 1 raises questions about access to

Figure 2.36
Propylaeum East, sandstone sculpture of a grape leaf cluster tied with a fillet (ribbon) 2003. Propylaeum, Trench 95 Locus 10. Length 41 cm, width 12 cm, thickness 19 cm.

Fig. 2.37
Propylaeum East, helmet pilaster, 2003, Seq. No. 96014. Trench 96, Locus 1. Length 65 cm, width 42 cm, thickness 28.5 cm. Helmet with ear-flap decorated with engraved scroll and plume (?); accompanied by quiver? The earflap with two holes is 13 cm in length, helmet is 29.5 cm in length, plume (?) is 7 cm long. Partial but weathered *cyma reversa* on left face; on the upper right is a gouge approximately 8 cm in length.

Fig. 2.38
Propylaeum East, Athena pilaster, 2003. Seq. No. 95977. Trench 95, Locus 11, 2003. Height 36 cm, width 30 cm, thickness 18 cm. Athena, part of a limestone pilaster. Remains of *cyma reversa* on top with evidence of it having been broken away on left side. Herringbone (fish scale) pattern distinguishes breastplate. Vestiges of Medusa pendant visible, hanging from snake "necklace." Twisted hair plait draped on left shoulder. Two large arrow points well-preserved behind figure's left shoulder. Round hole carved in base at back—perhaps for attaching to another block or to a wall. Two holes at neck location perhaps used for attaching head. Site Phase IX.

Fig. 2.39
Propylaeum West to
west showing the South
Gallery with bench and
arch collapse, 2002.

the area. If the south extension of the Propy-laeum Central Staircase, which currently overlies the threshold, is constructed after the west cryptoporticus system is installed (as we posited earlier, placing the two events in Site Phases VII and IV respectively), then the east doorway to Room 1 is from an earlier period, perhaps originally accessed via a separate staircase. Under this arrangement, the pottery found in Room 1 gives a *terminus post quem* for the construction of the full Central Staircase. The east wall of Propylaeum West Room 1 could be constructed at the same time as the upper treads of the staircase, significantly narrowing the east-west dimension of the room, but not entirely restricting access. This would explain why the west wall of Room 1 (cur-rently assigned to Site Phase IV) overlies the ceramic floor of the north gallery, indicating

that it is built after the floor is laid. It might also explain why the stair treads directly east of the doorway are missing, since there is a platform here as part of the staircase's original construc-tion by which access to the area was granted.

Further west, the column drums found in the main part of Trench 87 offer significant evidence for the collapse pattern of the north colonnade resting on top of the Propylaeum East. The *in situ* column collapse onto the north gallery is pictured in Figure 2.40. From the excavated data, those columns found in the fill appear to have tumbled from south to north, collapsing from their places on top of the Propylaeum Retaining Wall and Wall K. Other evidence also supports a south to north fall pat-tern, including heavier damage to the floor tiles in the north part of the north gallery as well as a clear northward slump of the ashlars in Wall K. The diameter of the column drums that fall next to each other is greater on the southern drums

Fig. 2.40
Propylaeum West, to west, showing *in situ* south to north column collapse in the North Gallery, 2003.

(0.83 m) than on those in the north (0.81 m) indicating the presence of entasis in the columns of the northern colonnade.

Also evident from the overlying debris is that prior to the collapse of the arches covering the south gallery cryptoporticus in the Propylaeum West, the area is relatively undisturbed. First, there is surprisingly little damage to the floor underneath the arch stones, implying that the arches may not have tumbled from a great height above the floor. Second, in several places the collapsed *voussoirs* and arch stones are positioned on the floor directly beneath their *in situ* positions, arguing for the collapse of the area prior to the accumulation of fill. This noted lack of accumulated earth between the fallen stones and the floor indicates that the arch collapse, and not the collection of debris, may have prompted the initial abandonment of the south gallery.

In 2005 Special Project 118 is undertaken to clarify the nature of the access into the West Cryptoporticus East, which was not evident following the excavations of Trench 97 in 2004 or Trench 69 Special Project 70 in 2000. The excavation of SP 118 succeeded in clarifying the nature of the access from the Propylaeum into the West Cryptoporticus East. The current awkward height difference between the West Propylaeum East floor level and that of the West Propylaeum south gallery would have been ameliorated in antiquity by a set of stairs. Unfortunately, due to the extent of the damage to the stair bedding, the exact dimensions of these stairs can no longer be determined. It is also not possible to know with certainty the nature of the material used in the construction of the stairs. The total absence of any holes or other features in the stone platform/stair bedding suggests, however, that the stairs would have been built with layers of stone slabs rather than with wood. Furthermore, the evidence from the collapsed architectural elements found in the sounding indicates that the stairs themselves were no longer extant at the time of the destruction event(s), which could suggest that the West Cryptoporticus East had already ceased to have a primary function before the collapse occurred.

The artifact repertoire for the north gallery of the Propylaeum West is also intriguing, particularly due to the presence of 417 ballista balls (averaging 0.12 to 0.16 m in diameter) discovered predominantly in the fill just above the ceramic floor level and lodged in the gray mortar underlying the floor tiles. A detailed photo of the ballista balls is pictured in Fig. 2.41. We cannot ascertain if these projectiles are part of a bombardment and the balls crashed through the tiles to become embedded in the mortar. But with the presence of so many ballista balls, we cannot help but speculate that the Propylaeum either is intentionally bombarded from across the Wadi Musa from the north, and that some form of skirmish did indeed take place, or that a ballista armory is prepared by the Nabataeans in preparation for an attack. From Ammianus (14.8.13), we know that Cornelius Palma, then governor of Syria, subdues part of Arabia (including Petra), subjecting it to Roman rule. This is the sole epigraphic reference we have for the annexation

Fig. 2.41
Ballista balls detail, 2005. Propylaeum Trench 87 Locus 7. The average diameter for these balls is 12 to 16 cm.

Fig. 2.42
Propylaeum West,
moving an elephant-
headed capital, 1997.

of the Nabataean kingdom and its incorporation into the Roman province of Arabia. It has never been clear from the archaeological or historical sources, however, if Cornelius Palma led a military expedition to Petra. The lack of recorded aggression suggests that Palma oversaw a peaceful takeover, corroborated by Roman coins minted after the annexation inscribed "Arabia adquista," not "Arabia capta." (See Volume III for further discussion of these events and the ballistas.)

In related work in the south gallery, excavations in 2000 and 2001 further define the decorative program and architectural phasing of the Propylaeum West. In 2000, two complete elephant-headed capitals are found underlying collapsed columns in Trench 70, providing corroborating evidence for the continuation of the elephant motif in the north colonnade. Fig. 2.42 shows the removal of the complete

elephant-headed capital in Trench 80 in 1997. Fig. 2.43 shows the delicate procedure of moving the capital. Other remarkable finds include a limestone horned altar with a beveled lower edge, carved-out sections for the "horns" in relief at its four corners and a depressed bowl-shaped central cavity. Figure 2.44 is a drawing of the horned altar, and the altar is shown *in situ* in Figure 2.45.

In 2001, a test trench, Trench 86, located at the eastern end of the Propylaeum West, uncovers evidence of early construction in the area of the Propylaeum West prior to the building of the Great Temple. Here, an oddly aligned pavement constructed of large, hewn sandstone ashlars south of Wall K is found

Fig 2.43
Propylaeum West, moving an elephant-headed capital, 1998.

Fig. 2.44
Propylaeum West, drawing of the sandstone Horned Altar. Seq. No. 70195. Propylaeum Trench 70 Locus 1. Height 33 cm, width 52–63 cm, thickness 33 cm. This Nabataean Horned altar has a carved out depression in the center (top). Bottom edge is beveled. May have been unfinished.

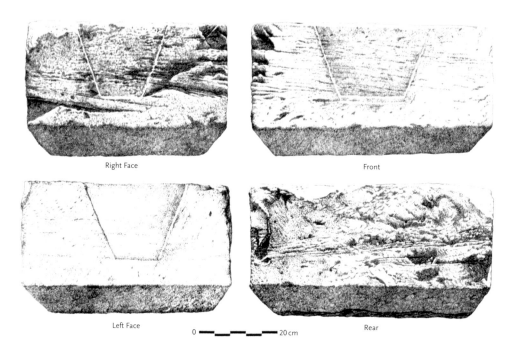

Right Face

Front

Left Face

0 ▬▬ _ ▬ _ ▬ 20 cm

Rear

Fig. 2.45
Propylaeum West, Horned altar *in situ*, 2000.

underlying the floor bedding of the south gallery. Further submerged is a layer of floor bedding into which the foundations of Wall K are sunk. In a later phase, ten courses of the Propylaeum Retaining Wall are built on top of these early constructions. From a sealed context in the floor bedding associated with the retaining wall's foundation deposit a nearly complete Nabataean bowl dating to the time of this construction is recovered. Figure 2.46 is a drawing of this early bowl with the unpainted areas suggesting an early date for its manufacture. A close parallel found in Stephan Schmidt's (2000 Abb.81) Phase 2a, dates from ca. 50 to 25 BCE to the last quarter of the first century CE. We can posit, therefore, that this floor existed before the building of Wall K; the bowl providing a convenient *terminus ante quem* for the construction of the Lower Temenos platform, the oddly aligned stone pavement, the lowest floor and Wall K, and a *terminus post quem* for the construction of all other architectural features in the area.

Further 2001 excavations in the west Propylaeum West in Trench 80 reveal a third complete elephant-headed capital (engaged) and the pair of carved limestone *betyl*s, sacred aniconic representations of Nabataean deities, in remarkably pristine condition. Excavations in front of and below the niche continue in 2002, exposing a bench (Figure 6.20) and the floor level of the south gallery, clarifying its direct association with the West Stairs (Trenches 81 and 88). Figure 2.47 shows the clearing of the West Entry Stairway and its entrance into the West Propylaeum. Excavations in the south confirm the use of the west door as a principal point of access to the Propylaeum, accented by a clear view of the double *betyl*s. The prominent placement of the *betyl*s suggests that the Propylaeum West may serve as a ritual entry, intimately connected with the sanctity of the precinct and emphasized by the presence of the adjoining bench resting below on a finely cut pavement of rectangular flagstones. Figure 6.15 displays the *betyl* wall and bench after the completed excavation of the area.

Conclusions

During the excavation of the Great Temple Propylaeum a great deal is revealed concerning its structural history. With nearly 4000 architectural fragments registered in the database, we are able to address the evolution of the Propylaeum's architecture, tracing it through a series of construction and destruction phases until its ultimate collapse. Judging from the material remains, we are able to infer that the original structural layout of the Propylaeum is integrally planned as the natural northern extension of the East and West Lower Temenos Cryptoportici and Colonnades, alike in plan and decoration. Later, following a series of minor collapses (either the result of natural causes or an offensive attack) the upper treads of the central staircase of the Propylaeum are built and extended southward. At this time, the reconfiguration of the Propylaeum East into a series of three north-south chambers takes place while the north and south galleries of the Propylaeum West remain virtually unchanged. This series of major structural alterations visible in the lifespan of the Propylaeum punctuates its complex character, the various incarnations of this monumental façade reflecting the ever-changing form of the overall precinct.

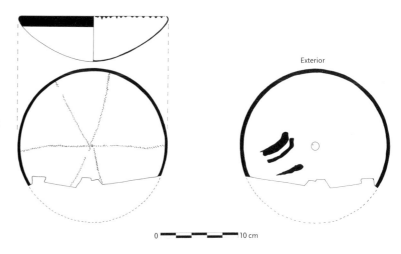

Fig. 2.46
Propylaeum West, Early Nabataean Bowl, dating from ca. 50 to 25 BCE to the last quarter of the first century CE.

Fig. 2.47
Propylaeum West, West
Entry Stairs to north, 2004.

Notes

1.
Wall K was so named by P.J. Parr, and we have elected to use it to identify the middle wall of the Propylaeum West. Wall K was razed in the East Proplaeum, probably due to its collapse.

2.
The Portico Wall holds a unique position at the Petra Great Temple. No other construction can so symbolically and physically delimit the precinct, segregating the sacred Great Temple precinct from the mundane sphere of the Roman Street. Positioned across the entire north, it spans the east-west perimeter to the north as well as continuing across contiguous areas to the east—the Garden Pool Complex—and to the west to the West Baths-Palatial Complex and the Temenos Gate of the Qasr al-Bint. The Portico Wall is also responsive to the changing needs of the people. Throughout all site phases it is used to reflect the changing and particular need of the Great Temple's environment. It is a dynamic physical space, first constructed by the early Nabataeans, which is then breeched and redefined by later Nabataeans (the West Entry Stairway) and later on, in the east, by the Romans, to create Rooms 1 and 2, perpendicular to the wall.

3.
But we suggest it is as high as the Lower Temenos Retaining Wall.

4.
This east-west measurement represents the full length of the Propylaeum East.

5.
The depth of deposit is approximately 7.00 m below the level of the Lower Temenos.

6.
The Great Temple Propylaeum was purposefully built on the Roman Street. Here Petra's population could find refuge in case of impending attack.

7.
This West Entry Stairway is discussed in Chapter 3, Lower Temenos. Excavated in 2005, most of its excavation took place in the Lower Temenos.

8.
The Baths-Palatial Complex (not to be confused with the Great Temple Roman-Byzantine Baths of the Upper Temenos) were previously excavated by the Jordanian Department of Antiquities years ago. Were these baths constructed at the same time as the Petra Great Temple? No, we believe they were later. Is their layout part of a single architectural program? If it is, the architects realized they had to change the orientation of these baths either to conform to the Roman Street or to re-orient the West Entry Stairway into a building pattern that had already been laid out. Of course the buildings may have been constructed simultaneously, and the orientation of the two complexes had to be justified. What appears clear is that the West Entry Stairs and the lower courses of their construction were oriented to the Great Temple. This would suggest that the west wall would have been constructed at a slightly later time than the entry walls below the entry platform. The continuation of this wall to the south above the entry platform seems to be later because the ashlars are smaller in dimension. This might be a difficult assertion to accept; it is such a monumentally high wall that this idea can only be accepted as conjecture at this point.

It is only to the south of the main Platform-Landing which serves as both the entry into the West Cryptoporticus as well as to the as yet unexcavated stairs to the Baths-Palatial Complex to the west that there is a change in orientation. Would those who were using this stairway even take note of the change in orientation? It is difficult to say.

In appearance the west wall has had its north-south orientation compromised in antiquity and it leans to the west, pulling away from the staircase. But it is also here that the Nabataean builders may have had a problem with orientation and the blending of the Great Temple precinct with the Baths-Palatial Complex. As can be seen from the aerial photograph shown in the beginning of this chapter, the axis of the two sectors is appreciably different, and yet this stairway served both areas; its west wall might have been intentionally compromised and oriented more to the west to serve both precincts. This evidence suggests that the city plan may have been modified with the construction of the Baths-Palatial Complex, but this is conjecture.

9.
As found during excavation, Wall K is currently in place in the west and is certainly part of the original Phase IV configuration of the east, although it has been razed in the east.

10.
This "Room 1" is not to be confused with Room 1 of the Propylaeum East.

The Petra Great Temple
Lower Temenos

Lower Temenos, aerial view, to south, 2006.

CHAPTER THREE

The Petra Great Temple Lower Temenos

The formal introduction to the Petra Great
Temple proper, the monumental expanse of the
Lower Temenos, is integral to our understanding of what the Nabataeans sought to achieve in
the construction of the precinct. Situated to the
immediate south of the Propylaeum and elevated
8.50 m above the level of the street, the broad
expanse of the Lower Temenos extends 49.00 m
north-south × 56.00 m east-west and rests at an
average elevation of 898.70 m.[1] The plan of the
Lower Temenos is presented in Figure 3.1 and
an overview to the southeast is illustrated in
Figure 3.2.

   Dimensions of major features of the Lower
Temenos are presented below.

Lower Temenos Dimensions of Major Features

Elevations asl

Hexagonal Pavement—898.67 ± 0.12 m

Easternmost Colonnade—898.63 ± 0.16 m
(pavers and stylobate slope downward slightly)

Sondage SP25 depth—891.97 m

WEST EXEDRA

Height (maximum)—903.52 m

Porch Column Stylobate—899.35 m

Byzantine Platform—900.25 m

WEST STAIRWAY

Lowest step-curb—899.14 m

Restored upper step—903.94 m

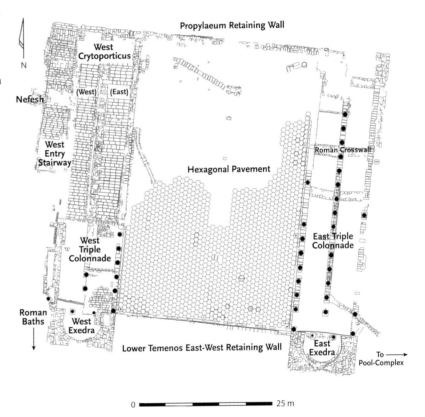

Fig. 3.1
Lower Temenos Plan

Fig. 3.2
Lower Temenos, to southeast.

EAST EXEDRA

Height (maximum)—905.16 m

Porch Column stylobate—899.15 m

EAST STAIRWAY

Lowest step-curb—899.14 m

Excavated upper step—902.58 m

Dimensions

*Note: All measurements are external and include
wall thicknesses unless otherwise noted. When a depth
is irregular e.g., steps, it is averaged.*

*From the Propylaeum Retaining Wall to the
Lower Temenos Retaining Wall:* 49.00 m north-
south × 56.00 m east-west

East Exedra to the West Exedra: 32.70 m east-west

*Inter-axial distance between Triple Colonnade
columns:* 1.80 m

Hexagonal Pavement: 49.00 m north-south ×
31.00 m east-west

EAST LOWER TEMENOS

East Triple Colonnade: From the East Exedra to
the Propylaeum Retaining Wall: 54.00 m north-
south × 11.80 m east-west

East Exedra: 5.40 m north-south × 6.80 m east-
west × 4.80 m depth

WEST LOWER TEMENOS

West Triple Colonnade: (external) from the West
Exedra to the Propylaeum Retaining Wall 50.19 m
north-south × 11.96 m east-west width

West Exedra: 5.30 m north-south × 6.50 m east-
west × 4.80 m depth

West Cryptoporticus: (external) 38.89 m north-
south × 12.08 m east-west × 5.18 m depth;
(internal) 38.89 m north-south × 9.50 m
east-west

West Cryptoporticus East: from Cryptoporticus
Retaining Wall 36.89 m north-south × 4.30 m
east-west × 4.39 m depth

West Cryptoporticus West: 39.03 m north-south × 4.30 m east-west × 5.18 m depth

West Cryptoporticus Bench West: 39.16 m north-south × 0.74 m east-west × 0.66 m depth

West Cryptoporticus Bench South: 0.68 m north-south × 3.63 m east-west × 0.53 m depth

West Entry Stairway: 37.15 m north-south × 4.60 m east-west, Total area 171.12 m²

Lower Temenos Wall Dimensions
(Thickness and height, as excavated and restored)

East Exedra: (south) 4.68 m height, (east) 3.21 m height; (west) 3.22 m height

West Exedra: (south) 4.33 m height, (east) 3.31 m height; (west) 3.17 m height

Retaining Wall: 1.01 m north-south × 28.00 m east-west × 2.76 m height

Byzantine Platform: 8.13 m north-south × 5.45 m east-west × 1.40 m height

Cryptoporticus East (east): 1.18 m thickness × 4.60 m height

Cryptoporticus West (west): 1.46 m thickness × 3.40 m height

Cryptoporticus Center vault wall: 1.88 m thickness × 5.33 m height

West Entry Stairway[2]

Located at the extreme west of the Lower Temenos in the 2005 excavations of Trenches 102–103 and Trench 122 of 2006, this grand stairway is a continuation of the West Stairway excavated in Trench 88, 2002. The 2004 recovery of the West Entry Stairway extending to the West Propylaeum platform (Figure 3.3) made it obvious that these steps might continue up to the Upper Temenos. To demonstrate this concept, the 2005 excavations, including the removal of mountains of rubble (Figure 3.4), enable us to interrogate the data. The final dimensions of the 2006 trenches are 37.20 m north-south × 4.60 m in width.

This West Entry Stairway follows the slope of the Great Temple precinct that "falls away" at a dramatic angle from the Lower Temenos to the Roman Street. Beginning at an 891.87 m elevation and closing at 899.49 m, the 2005 excavations of the West Entry Stairway exca-

Fig. 3.3
Lower Temenos, West Entry Stairway, to north.

Fig. 3.4
Lower Temenos excavation of the West Entry Stairway, to south, 2005.

Fig. 3.5
Lower Temenos West
Entry Stairway cleared,
to south, 2005.

vated a total depth of 7.62 m. Combined with the earlier excavations of the West Entry Stairway where the north block rests at 889.96 m in elevation, there is a difference of 9.53 m, suggesting that this stairway is one of the most impressive sets of stairs so far found associated with free-standing buildings in Petra. Indeed, as can be seen in Figure 3.5, the structure provides a fascinating insight into the Nabataean understanding of structural engineering.

The stairway is composed of five stair flights that are interrupted by four platform landings set at irregular intervals. The largest landing accesses the West Cryptoporticus and an additional series of steps lead down to the Roman Street,[3] creating a monumental entry passage measuring 37–40 m in north-south length. An additional three steps and uppermost platform existed at the top of the stairway, but there is scant evidence for these features due to collapse. (In 2007 the steps were restored.)

These Nabataean steps create a direct north to south ascent from the Roman Street to either the Baths-Palatial Complex[4] or access to the Roman-Byzantine Baths.

The excavation of the steps uncovered over 900 ashlars, little pottery, some bone, glass, and metal. In addition, a bronze lance head, four coins as well as the remarkable *nefesh*,[5] shown with an associated *betyl* in Figure 3.6.[6] Since this area has been subject to considerable erosion over the millennia, the artifact repertoire does not originate from sealed deposits, so little dating can be ascribed to the artifact record. The *nefesh* installation, however, appears to be coeval with the construction of the West Stairway.

As previously noted, the staircase follows the slope of the Great Temple precinct. It appears that wadi fill was brought in to build up the natural fill to support the stairs. The inner faces of the walls are constructed of plain dressed

Fig. 3.6
Lower Temenos West Entry Stairway Platform with the *nefesh* and *betyl in situ*, 2005, to west. (For *nefesh* and *betyl* descriptions, see Figures 3.57 and 3.58.)

Fig. 3.7
Lower Temenos Triple
Colonnade and hexagonally
paved plaza, to northwest,
as restored, 2001.

sandstone ashlar masonry averaging courses of 0.40 m in height with lime mortar between the ashlars in both the vertical and horizontal joins. With the exception of a repair portion of the east wall, all the wall and step surfaces were plastered and some of the wall surfaces were decorated with finely executed lively floral designs with red leaves over a yellow background and pastel colors in striped patterns with blues, yellows, greens and light reds. For the most part, however, the painted frescos have been pushed off the walls and fell in antiquity. Integrated elements have not been recovered to give an idea of the overall original decoration.

East and West Triple Colonnades and Cryptoportici

Flanking the Lower Temenos plaza to the east and west are triple colonnades displayed in Figure 3.7, containing a total of 120 columns (60 on each side, and 20 in each row) extending north-south. Each column is crowned by an exquisitely carved, limestone Asian elephant-headed capital. One of the nearly complete elephant-headed capitals found in 2000 is presented in Figure 3.8, followed by a drawing of the same capital shown in Figure 3.9. Extending the full north-south length of the plaza, each colonnade rests on a substantial stylobate constructed from hewn alternating sandstone and white limestone ashlars (averaging 0.52 × 0.96 × 0.10 m in height). The columns of the triple colonnades, displaying a visible *entasis*, are constructed of stacked sandstone drums measuring 0.76 to 0.84 m in diameter and spaced at regular north-south inter-axial intervals of 2.50 m. The walkways between the colonnades extend some 4.40 m, and the total width of the triple colonnades in both the east and west measures approximately 12.50 m. Judging from the presence of ceramic roof tiles in the excavated fill of this area it can be reasoned that the colonnades are roofed. Rising to a projected height of at least 7.60 m (calculated from the collapse shown in Figure 3.53) and coated with a protective bright red and yellow painted plaster below a white plaster with cable fluting, the columns of the colonnades provide a spectacular and imposing border for the Lower Temenos central plaza. Figure 3.10 shows the partially restored East Triple Colonnade to the north.

Fig. 3.8
Lower Temenos elephant-headed capital, 2000.

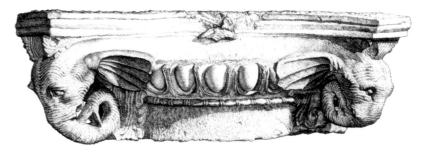

0 — — — — 10 cm

Fig. 3.9
Lower Temenos drawing of elephant-headed capital from an engaged column.

Concealed beneath each of the colonnades are twin, vaulted Cryptoportici (Figure 3.11). Set into the walls of the cryptoportici are *voussoirs*, which support a series of vaults spanning approximately 4.30 m east-west. The vaults extend from the front of the fifth column to the north of the West Exedra to the temple north colonnade, which serves as its terminus. Judging from the *in situ voussoirs*, the approximate height of the vaulted galleries is 6.00 m and the elevation of the floor of the West Cryptoporticus rests at 893.84 m. The interior measurements of the galleries of the West Cryptoporticus are 32.80 m north-south in length × 4.30 m in east-west width. In antiquity, the beaten earth sub-floors of the twin cryptoportici are covered with sharply cut rectangular limestone flagstones set into a mortar bedding discovered *in situ* in both the east and west galleries of the West Cryptoporticus. Entry into these Cryptoportici is from the north.

Centered between the east-west vaults of the West Cryptoportici pavement, a deep sounding, shown during its excavation in Figure 3.12, revealed a series of very thin strata, followed by two human activity strata separated by a natural deposit. The dimensions of the central sondage were approximately 1.30 m north-south × 1.30 m east-west × 3 m in depth. The deepest deposits in the central sondage were identified as having resulted from a series of sterile floodwater deposits, devoid of material culture.

East and West Exedrae

In the north, each of the triple colonnades connects to the precinct's north colonnade, the superstructure on top of the south galleries of the Propylaeum East and West. In the south, the termination of the colonnades is marked by buttressed exedrae. Executed in the classical style, each exedra measures approximately 6.50 m in interior width and 5.50 m in depth, fronted by two columns constructed from sandstone drums measuring 0.60 m in diameter. The columns rest on Attic bases and stand 1.20 m out from the slightly incurving opening of the apse, which measures 6.80 m in total width. Figure 3.13 is one of the two freestanding columns at the mouth of the West Exedra. In antiquity,

ornate Ionic style elephant-headed limestone capitals crowned these freestanding columns. Flanking the exedrae are two engaged columns mounted onto the facades also embellished with elephant-headed capitals. In the interior of both exedrae are five niches, each measuring 1.15 m in width and 0.55 m in depth, set into the curved walls of each sandstone apse. Figure 3.14 pictures the interior of the West Exedra (during excavation) showing its interior niches.

Hexagonal Pavement and Canalization

Situated between the east and west colonnades and exedrae is the sweep of the vast paved plaza measuring approximately 49.00 m in north-south length and foreshortened by the East and West Triple Colonnades to 30.00 m in east-west width. This open space is laid with large sandstone hexagonal pavers. In the east and west, a curb of red and yellow sandstone 0.37 m wide edges the length of the plaza, separating the flanking colonnades from the central pavement. A low level of curb stones north of the Lower Temenos Retaining Wall marks the southern extent of the pavement and contains a cut for a narrow lead pipe (installed during the Roman annexation of the area) extending the full width of the plaza.

Concealed beneath the Hexagonal Pavement is a complex network of canalization channels descending from the Upper Temenos beneath the treads of the East and Central Stairs and stretching across the Lower Temenos to the east and west. Along the perimeter of the Hexagonal Pavement, the path of the canalization is marked by ten equidistant bronze drain fittings set into the centers of ten hexagonal paving stones. The hexagonal bronze drain cover is illustrated in Figure 3.15 and a hexagonal paver with the bronze cover removed is shown in Figure 3.16.

Stratigraphy and Phasing

Following the completed excavation of the Lower Temenos, fifteen stages of activity are visible in the stratigraphy. The deposits below the East Gallery of the West Cryptoporticus belong to Pre-Site Phase I. The earliest construction takes place in the first century BCE

Fig. 3.10
Lower Temenos East
Triple Colonnade, partially
restored, to north, 2003.

Fig. 3.11
Lower Temenos
West Cryptoporticus,
to south, 2005.

during Site Phase I with the buildup of the plaza terrace for the installation of the subterranean canalization systems that feed the precinct. In Site Phase II, as part of the Great Temple complex's *distyle in antis* form, the area of the Lower Temenos bridges the great expanse between the temple proper and the lower eight treads of the Propylaeum Central Staircase serving as the formal approach from the street during the early phase of its construction.

Later, in Site Phase IV between the first century BCE and the first century CE, the vision of the "Grand Design" leads to the full construction and buildup of the present level of the Lower Temenos complete with the installation of the West Entry Stairway, the Hexagonal Pavement, East and West Triple Colonnades, Cryptoportici and Exedrae, and additional subterranean channels and drains. This massive effort of reorganization also witnesses construction of the Lower Temenos Retaining Wall (blocking the Upper Temenos main Central Stairway) and the lateral East and West Staircases ascending from the Lower to Upper Temenoi. Additionally, an east-west crosswall is built in the West Cryptoporticus approximately 20.00 m north of the West Exedra, blocking entry to the southern part of the cryptoporticus at the time of its original construction. In the latter half of the first century CE the structure of the Lower Temenos undergoes minor repairs in Site Phases V and VI including the rebuilding of parts of the Hexagonal Pavement and the walls of the East Exedra. At this time the northwest subterranean channel becomes clogged with first century CE pottery.

Fig. 3.12
Lower Temenos, West Cryptoporticus SP104 sondage, to east, 2005.

Fig. 3.13
Lower Temenos West Exedra, one of two freestanding columns to southwest. Originally these were topped with smaller elephant-headed capitals.

Fig. 3.14
Lower Temenos, Interior of the West Exedra showing
niches during the 1995 excavations, to southwest.

Fig. 3.15
Lower Temenos bronze drain cover *in situ*, 1995.

Fig. 3.16
Lower Temenos hexagonal paver with bronze drain cover
removed in antiquity.

During Roman occupation of the site some time after 106 CE, the Lower Temenos first undergoes serious renovations and repairs in Site Phase VII. As previously mentioned, a sandstone channel with lead pipeline is installed across the width of the Lower Temenos from the East Exedra to the West Exedra along the base of the Lower Temenos Retaining Wall. It is inferred from the collapse stratigraphy that the East Exedra is damaged at this time and that the East Cryptoporticus collapses. To stabilize the subterranean areas, east-west crosswalls are built between the north-south walls of the crypto-portici and fill is deposited, effectively restricting access to this area of the complex. In the West Cryptoporticus, where collapse at this time is not evident, the support walls are appointed with low benches. Simultaneously, the Propylaeum Central Staircase is increased in height and length, redefining the main entrance to the Lower Temenos from the street.

Preceded by a period of abandonment in Site Phase VIII during which elements of the colonnade stylobates are robbed out, the 363 CE earthquake is directly responsible for the initial major collapse of elements of the Lower Temenos architecture in Site Phase IX. The columns of the West Colonnade become dislodged and tumble directly onto the Hexagonal Pavement below, leaving well-defined impressions where the individual drums impact the surface (Figure 3.53). This early upset also results in the accumulation of soil in the West Cryptoporticus and over the East Perimeter Wall, which by this time has become riddled with architectural debris including fragments of elephant-headed capitals.

Between the fourth and fifth centuries CE in Site Phase X, Byzantine use of the precinct results in the construction of new masonry elements as well as a number of industrial installations. Intercolumnar walls are built between the columns of the East Triple Colonnade and a large stepped platform, measuring roughly 5.30 m in north-south length × 4.50 m in east-west width and resting at an elevation of 900.24 m, is immediately installed north of the

Fig. 3.17
Lower Temenos, cleaning the upper West Entry Stairway, to northeast (with the West Cryptoporticus in the background).

West Exedra. At this time slag deposits indicate the use of the exedrae for lime manufacture and there is also evidence for the reconstruction of the Roman-Byzantine Bath Complex west of the West Exedra.[7]

In the years following these installations the site undergoes further collapse with the collection of debris, possibly the result of the earthquake of 512 CE. In Site Phase XI the destruction of the Lower Temenos architecture continues, including the probable collapse of the East Colonnade, falling onto an accumulated layer of earthen fill. In Site Phase XII, periods of robbing and abandonment continue during which time many of the hexagonal paving stones in the northern part of the Lower Temenos plaza (where the accumulation of overfill is noticeably less) are robbed out. This is also the time when the West Entry Stairway collapses and is covered over with fill (Figure 3.17). Disturbance to the Lower Temenos continues into Site Phase XIII with additional collapses and culminates in Site Phase XIV with the use of the central, north and west portions of the Hexagonal Pavement for Bedouin farming. Figure 3.18 shows the columns dividing the Bedouin fields in the Lower Temenos as they were found before our excavations began.

Excavation History

Figure 3.19 is a chart of Lower Temenos Trenches excavated, and the plan on Figure 3.20 shows the positions of these trenches.

Excavations of the Great Temple Lower Temenos are conducted yearly from 1994 to 2006, bringing to light 4614 recorded architectural fragments including 337 column drums, 2427 ashlars, and 457 elephant head fragments as well as several complete capitals and 236 cornice fragments, amounting to 23 percent of the total architectural fragments recorded in the site database.

In the following excavation discussions we will begin on the Lower Temenos East and move to the Lower Temenos West and the West Entry Stairway. Finally, excavations in the hexagonally paved plaza and the subterranean system will be presented.

East Triple Colonnade Excavations

Along the Lower Temenos east perimeter, extensive excavations begin with the exploration of the East Triple Colonnade north in 1995 and 1996. Intending to clarify the stratigraphy of the area, excavations in Trenches 25 and 28 and in Special Project 38 in 1996 uncover the East Perimeter Wall (situated alongside the easternmost row of the East Colonnade), which separates the architecture and canalization systems of the Lower Temenos from the Garden Pool complex to the east. To the north and west, the Trenches 30 and 33 excavations clear the stylobates of the inner and middle colonnades, returning a number of fallen drums to their original positions. During excavation the upper courses of two Roman period east-west crosswalls are uncovered between the north-south walls of the East Cryptoporticus; the one in Trench 25 serves as the east continuation of a crosswall discovered during the previous

Fig. 3.18
Lower Temenos column drums dividing the Bedouin field, 1997.

TRENCH	YEAR	DESCRIPTION	MEASUREMENT(M) (N-S × E-W)	EXCAVATOR(S)
East Triple Colonnade and East Cryptoporticus				
Trenches 14 and 20 (SP22, 24, 29 combined)	1995	Central Area between the inner and middle stylobates of the East Triple Colonnade	TR 14=8.20 × 11.00 TR 20=9.00 × 4.30 (SP22=4.00 × 2.00, SP24=7.00 × 2.20, SP29=2.00 × 2.00)	Sisson, Bell
Trench 17 Part I (SP25)	1995	East Triple Colonnade and sondage north of Trenches 14 and 20	10.00 × 14.00, 1.60 × 2.50	Payne
Special Project 27	1995	Column #3 to the south of SP24	No measurements taken	M. Joukowsky
Special Project 28	1995	The second column in the East Colonnade	No measurements taken	M. Joukowsky
Special Project 38 Part I	1995	Sondage in the East Colonnade east	No measurements taken	M. Joukowsky
Trench 17 Part II	1996	Continuation of the 1995 excavations in Trench 17	10.00 × 14.00	Payne
Trench 25	1996	East Perimeter Wall of the Lower Temenos and adjacent area of the East Triple Colonnade	26.67 × 2.37	Slaughter, Butler, Goldstein
Trench 28	1996	East Triple Colonnade south of Trench 25	13.00 × 2.80	Bestock, Gimon
Trench 30	1996	East Triple Colonnade west of Trench 25	19.00 × 4.00	M. Joukowsky
Trench 33	1996	East Triple Colonnade north and west of Trenches 25 and 30	4.70 × 6.00	Warnock
Trench 36	1996	East Triple Colonnade west of Trench 28	11.00 × 4.00	Bestock, Gimon
Special Project 38 Part II	1996	Continuation of SP38	3.00 × 3.00	Goldstein, Butler
Special Project 39 Part II	1996	Brief investigation of the southern part of the East Triple Colonnade, just north of the East Exedra	19.00 × 4.10 × 1.90	M. Joukowsky
Special Project 45	1997	Recovery of the southernmost column in the central row of the East Triple Colonnade, north of the East Exedra	No measurements taken	Payne
Special Project 46	1997	Recovery of the second column from the south in the central row of the East Triple Colonnade, north of the East Exedra	No measurements taken	Payne
Special Project 51	1997	East Triple Colonnade (space for re-erection of columns)	No measurements taken	Haile, Parker
Special Project 54	1997	Excavation by visiting British team of an *in situ* decorated pilaster, built into the intercolumnar wall between the columns of the East Triple Colonnade	1.00 × 0.60	British excavation team
Special Project 56	1998	Sondage in the East Triple Colonnade to remove an island of earth created during the excavation of SP54	1.80 × 2.60	Ginsberg
Special Project 57	1998	Sondage in the East Triple Colonnade to remove a "tongue" of earth adjacent to Trench 14	2.00 × 1.60	Ginsberg
Trench 61	1999	East Triple Colonnade, center	6.00 × 13.70	Karz
Special Project 73	2000	Intercolumnar wall in the center row of the East Triple Colonnade	26.00 × 3.50	Karz
East Exedra				
Trench 37	1996	East Exedra	19.00 × 15.00	M. Joukowsky
Trench 52	1998	East Exedra	15.30 × 18.00	Basile, Sylvester, Karz

Fig. 3.19
Lower Temenos, Chart of Trenches Excavated 1993–2006. (continued on page 104)

1995 season in Trench 17 and Special Project 25. Figure 3.21 pictures the Trench 17 sondage showing the walls of the East Cryptoporticus and (to the right) one of the Roman period cross walls.

During the investigation of the surface in these two areas, the Hexagonal Pavement and a few elegantly carved drains are exposed, as well as a large number of roof tiles indicating that the colonnade is originally covered. Figure 3.22 shows the early exposure of the Hexagonal Pavement alongside the East Colonnade. In Trench 17 in 1996, a deep sondage to the west of the East Triple Colonnade's east stylobate uncovers the base of the central Roman east-west crosswall at a depth of nearly 6.00 m. Despite concentrated efforts, the base of the east stylobate wall and the floor level of the East Cryptoporticus remain undiscovered, potentially resting at the level of the Roman Road.

Further investigation in Trenches 14 and 20 and Special Projects 22, 24 and 29 reveal the masonry of both the inner and middle stylobates, including a number of arch springers associated with the East Cryptoporticus. Figure 3.23 of the East Cryptoporticus portrays the *in situ voussoirs*. Closer to the surface, canalization pipes and plaster fragments are found as well as evidence of modern agricultural activity and a partially burned lime deposit that may represent a localized industrial activity. Evidence of a limekiln found nearby in Trench 36 is also linked to a later period of likely Byzantine use, and suggests that this area may have become a collection and disposal point for decorative limestone elements to be reduced to lime.

Moving further south, excavations in 1998 reveal additional evidence of extensive rebuilding, reuse and redesign of the East Triple Colonnade particularly noticeable in the secondary

Lower Temenos Trenches

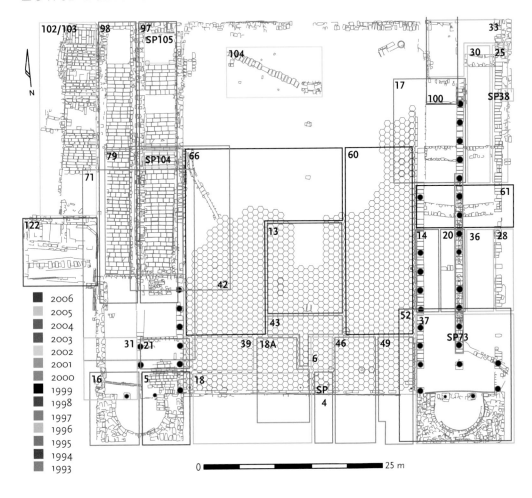

Fig. 3.20
Plan of trenches excavated in the Lower Temenos, 1993–2006.

TRENCH	YEAR	DESCRIPTION	MEASUREMENT(M) (N-S × E-W)	EXCAVATOR(S)
West Triple Colonnade and West Cryptoporticus				
Special Project 37	1995	Cleaning of a Bedouin wall north of the West Exedra	No measurements taken	M. Joukowsky
Special Project 39 Part I	1995	Search for the west perimeter wall of the Lower Temenos	No measurements taken	M. Joukowsky
Trench 31 (SP41)	1996	West Triple Colonnade and West Bath, southwest of the West Exedra	7.50 × 9.72, 1.65 × 1.65	Butler, Goldstein
Special Project 47	1997	Recovery of a portion of the west stylobate of the West Triple Colonnade	No measurements taken	Haile, M. Joukowsky
Trench 71	2000	West Triple Colonnade and Cryptoporticus, north of the West Exedra	22.50 × 19.80	M. Joukowsky
Trench 79	2001	Central area of the West Cryptoporticus	13.50 × 12.50	M. Joukowsky
Trench 97	2004	West Cryptoporticus east	25.77 × 6.10	Tuttle
Trench 98	2004	West Cryptoporticus west	32.00 × 4.20	Khanachet, Power
Trench 98 B	2005	West Cryptoporticus west	17.21 × 4.04	Khanachet
Special Project 104	2005	West Cryptoporticus east, sondage	4.00 × 4.30	Tuttle
Special Project 105	2005	West Cryptoporticus east, below pavement	1.50 × 4.20	Tuttle
West Exedra				
Trench 5 Part I	1994	East part of the West Exedra	7.00 × 10.00	Beckman, Retzleff, Schluntz
Trench 5 Part II	1995	East part of the West Exedra	9.00 × 4.00, 2.00m probe	Basile, Rucker
Trench 16 Part I	1995	West part of the West Exedra	7.00 × 10.00	Basile, Rucker
Trench 21 (SP31, SP32, SP33)	1995	East part of the West Exedra	4.00 × 7.00	Rucker, Basile, Khalidi
Special Project 26	1995	East part of the West Exedra	2.00 × 2.00	Khalidi
Trench 16 Part II	1996	Hunt for the foundations of the Byzantine canal and of the northwest wall of the West Exedra, found in 1995	1.20 × 1.95	Brown, Takian
Hexagonal Pavement and Subterranean Canalization Systems				
Trench 6 Part I	1994	South center of the Hexagonal Pavement, north of the Central Stairs	9.00 × 4.00	Payne
Trench 13	1994	Center of the Hexagonal Pavement	10.00 × 10.00	M. Joukowsky
Special Project 36	1995	Cleaning of a sink hole associated with the main subterranean canalization artery	No measurements taken	M. Joukowsky
Special Project 20	1995	Subterranean canalization system, collapse in Trench 13	1.50 × 2.50	Payne, Barrett
Trench 39	1996	Southwest section of the Hexagaonal Pavement	4.00 × 4.00	Brown
Trench 6 Part II	1997	South center of the Hexagonal Pavement, north of the Central Stairs	8.00 × 3.00	Basile, Najjar, Sylvester
Trench 42 (SP48, SP49)	1997	West center of the Hexagonal Pavement and the adjacent part of the West Triple Colonnade	18.00 × 14.00	Haile, Parker, Brown
Trench 43	1997	Hexagonal Pavement between Trenches 6 and 13	4.00 × 9.70 1.45 × 2.30	Basile, Najjar, Sylvester
Trench 60	1999	East center of the Hexagonal Pavement	25.30 × 11.30	Karz
Trench 66	1999	Hexagonal Pavement west	13.50 × 9.00	M. Joukowsky, Karz

Fig. 3.19 (continued from page 102)

employment of stylobate elements and the construction of poorly executed intercolumnar walls from battered architectural remains. Trenches 60 and 61 (opened in 1999) define the southern limit of the ten intercolumnar walls constructed between adjacent columns of the middle colonnade—all of which are dismantled in the same year as part of Special Project 73.[8] As excavations again approach the stylobate level, the tops of two additional east-west crosswalls are discovered, the first extending between the west and middle stylobates and the second between the middle and east stylobates repeating the construction style uncovered previously to the north in Trenches 25 and 17.

Despite an overall dearth of small finds, excavations in the East Triple Colonnade reveal a few intriguing elements of sculptural decoration. In 1996, the clearing of the middle stylobate in Special Project 39 produces a large number of elephant head fragments broken

Fig. 3.21
Lower Temenos, Trench 17 sondage showing the walls of the East Cryptoporticus and a Roman period cross wall to right, 1996.

Fig. 3.22
Lower Temenos, early exposure of the Hexagonal Pavement alongside the East Triple Colonnade, to north, 1995.

TRENCH	YEAR	DESCRIPTION	MEASUREMENT(M) (N-S × E-W)	EXCAVATOR(S)
Hexagonal Pavement and Subterranean Canalization Systems (continued)				
Special Project 92	2002	Sondage directly south of the Propylaeum Central Staircase	2.00 × 3.00	Brown
Special Project 124	2004	Central Stairs	5.90 × 4.56	Libonati, Egan
Trench 104	2005	Hexagonal Pavement northwest sondage	8.00 × 10.00	Khanachet
West Stairway				
Trench 102–103	2005	West Entry Stairway	30.75 × 4.55	M. Joukowsky
Trench 122	2006	West Entry Stairway south	7.90 × 9.00	M. Joukowsky, Khakpour
Roman-Byzantine Bath Complex				
Trench 121	2006	Bath Complex northwest	9.00 × 16.00	Khakpour
Trench 126	2006	Bath Complex northeast	4.55 × 13.00	Tuttle
Trench 127	2006	Bath Complex central	10.11 × 14.00	M. Joukowsky

Fig. 3.19 (continued from page 104)

from the ornate capitals that once decorated the columns of the Lower Temenos colonnades. Figure 3.24 is a photograph of one of the elephant capital fragments, and Figure 3.25 shows a restored capital on top of one of the East Triple Colonnade columns. Additionally, integrated into the fabric of the later intercolumnar wall and an adjacent oblique wall, extraordinary carved pilaster reliefs from the original temple façade are discovered. These elements, fallen from the temple during one of the earlier periods of collapse, are presumably found by later construction workers, who then utilize them as recycled building components. In a particularly remarkable state of preservation is a pilaster sculpture discovered as part of the later intercolumnar wall between the columns of the east colonnade featuring a female figure measuring 0.52 m in height, 0.84 m in width and 0.38 m in thickness wearing a *chiton* and holding a cornucopia in her left hand. Visible in Figure 3.26, her hair, curled in ringlets and falling over her left shoulder, is representative of a popular carving style found in Petra with comparable examples seen in two limestone masks found in the temple West Walkway in 1994 (Joukowsky 1998, Figures 5.55, 5.56).

Several relief-sculpted pilaster torsos are also recovered lying upside down in a gray mortar deposit extending throughout the trench. In Lower Temenos Special Project 54 in the middle colonnade, a second female torso shown *in situ* during excavation is pictured in Figure 3.27. Bordered by a partial *cyma reversa* molding and depicting an open-weave chiton carved in the "wet drapery" style, this panel is built into the intercolumnar wall abutting the fifth column from the north. Measuring 0.53 m in width and 0.38 m in height, this Amazonian or Aphrodite-type figure has her right, battered breast exposed and wears a chiton with a braided border and delicately rendered button fastenings extending down her left arm. Figure 3.28 is an image of this sculpture. Additionally, built into the southeast oblique intercolumnar rubble wall is the sculpture of yet another pilaster relief of a male figure with his right chest exposed and a chiton draped over his left shoulder. Figure 3.29 shows this figure's *in situ* position in the later intercolumnar wall. Including the *cyma reversa* molding, this figure measures 0.50 m in height and 0.85 m in width. Additionally, reused and installed as part of the south intercolumnar wall's west face is an exquisite low relief of an ornamental wreath embellished with a ribbon

Fig. 3.23
Lower Temenos, East Cryptoporticus showing *in situ voussoirs*, 1995.

Fig. 3.24
Lower Temenos elephant-headed capital.

Fig. 3.25
Lower Temenos, restored elephant-headed capital on top one of the columns in the East Triple Colonnade, to southeast, 2000.

Fig. 3.26
Lower Temenos Trench 52, Locus 2. Cat. No. 98-S-44, Seq. No. 52310. Limestone pilaster block of a female (perhaps a Fortuna or Tyche figure) holding a cornucopia. Height 52 cm, width 84 cm, thickness 38 cm. Relief sculpture of the bust of a female wearing a *chiton* over the left shoulder, and holding a cornucopia in her left hand. Deep chisel marks define the folds in her clothing. Corkscrew or finger curls fall in front and over both shoulders. The head has been removed in a later period leaving a deep rectangular cut. (The residue of plaster for affixing the head can be seen in the cut.)

Fig. 3.27
Lower Temenos, pilaster of a woman *in situ* as part of a late wall construction, 1997–1998. (See description, Figure 3.28).

Fig. 3.28
Lower Temenos 1997–1998.
Left side of a limestone
pilaster block of a female
figure (a maenad or
Aphrodite type) wearing
an open weave chiton,
wet drapery style. Architectural Fragment No. 2003-1,
Seq. No. 95345. Lower
Temenos, Surface. Height
41 cm, width 53 cm, thickness 21 cm. *Cyma reversa*
molding on sides of block,
11 cm in width. Right breast
is fractured. Left shoulder
is covered by a diaphanous
chiton with a herringbone
braid around neck and
buttoned open loops on
the left shoulder and upper
arm. Vestiges of two corkscrew curls on left shoulder.
In antiquity this block was
refashioned for reuse in the
East Triple Colonnade wall.

Fig. 3.29
Lower Temenos Trench 52,
Locus 29, 1998. Limestone
pilaster of a male figure
wearing a *chiton* draped
over his left shoulder
extending diagonally to
the right, and right full
shoulder and nude bust
exposed. Height 50 cm,
width 85 cm, thickness
40 cm. *Cyma reversa* molding on the right. Block
has been cut down and
the head cut as a separate
piece (found filled in with
a small rock). This panel
was built face up into a
late oblique wall.

tied at the top measuring 0.82 m in length, 0.52 m in width and 0.24 m in thickness; a photo is shown in Figure 3.30 and a drawing is shown in Figure 3.31.[9] Overall, the recovered reliefs reflect common carving techniques and similar styles of execution. Among other shared features, most of the figures are headless. While it is possible that iconoclasts destroyed the heads, we reason rather that these torsos were likely fitted with separately sculpted heads (perhaps crafted by a special school of sculptors), sunk into the principal form, and then mortared in place before finishing touches were applied to the block and it was mounted onto the temple façade. Joseph J. Basile further discusses the details of these panels in Volume III.

East Exedra Excavations

Serving as the southernmost features of the Lower Temenos, the grand East and West Exedrae mark the termination of the East and West Triple Colonnades at the base of the elevated Upper Temenos. Figure 3.32 shows the East Exedra terminating the East Triple Colonnade. Exploration of the East Exedra begins in 1996 with Trench 37 in order to confirm the symmetrical arrangement of the Lower Temenos east with the previously excavated west and to reveal the conjunction of the East Exedra and the East Triple Colonnade. Judging from the stratigraphy, numerous layers of soil and architectural debris are deposited on top of the exedra during later periods, punctuated by the deposition of a thick gray mortar throughout the area indicating its possible reuse as a limekiln. A photograph taken during the 1998 excavations, Figure 3.33, shows the East Exedra stratigraphy. Additionally, at the base of these deposits fragments of an arched entablature are recovered, Figure 3.34, indicating that the upper portion of the East Exedra is originally in the shape of a half-dome—the only solid evidence of any entablature recovered in the Great Temple complex.

The continued excavation of the East Exedra commences in 1998 with Trench 52 revealing the exedra interior in further detail, its walls constructed from fine, diagonally dressed ashlars and curved stones fronting the rear of the structure. The interior is embellished with four

buttresses set between five niches each measuring approximately 2.00 m in width. Below the central niche is a red sandstone and limestone podium measuring 1.63 m in width, 0.34 m in depth and 1.65 m in excavated height curved to conform to the north face of the south wall, perhaps serving as a placement for statuary. Figure 3.35 pictures the restored East Exedra showing the niches, podium and bench elements. Unlike its counterpart in the west, the East Exedra is also appointed with interior benches, likely added after its original construction. At the mouth of the apse of the East Exedra stand twin columns with elephant-headed capitals (now lost). To either side, engaged columns define the exedra's east and west flanks, also embellished with elephant-headed capital decoration. During the Roman acquisition of the area, a lead pipe (Figure 3.36) is inserted through the bases of the engaged columns of the East Exedra, directing water across the Lower Temenos plaza to the West Exedra, a total of 32.70 m. Figure 3.37 portrays the built-on channel for the lead pipe stretching across the Lower Temenos from the East Exedra to the West Exedra.

West Triple Colonnade and West Cryptoporticus Excavations

Situated along the Lower Temenos western perimeter, the counterparts of the East Triple Colonnade, the West Triple Colonnade and underlying West Cryptoporticus, are excavated during the course of several seasons—1996, 1997, 2000, 2004 and 2005. Notable small finds from this area include 38 elephant head fragments, a loom weight with Greek lettering, a Roman belt buckle, a cache of Nabataean pottery and numerous plaster fragments indicating the ornate embellishment of these features in antiquity.

In 1997 and 2000, excavations progress northward, following the architectural lines of the colonnade. Trench 42 and Special Project 49 in 1997, both located in the central part of the West Triple Colonnade, do not uncover any *in situ* evidence of the north continuation of the inner colonnade and stylobate. Figure 3.38 is a 2000 photograph of the newly cleared West Triple Colonnade. The discovery of 15 column drums, numerous arch stones and a wealth of elephant head fragments in the surrounding overburden, however, confirm its previous existence. Evidence of a secondary deposit marked by a thick layer of ash surrounding the west wall of the West Cryptoporticus is also found during continued excavations at the level of the stylobate, indicating the area's reuse perhaps as part of a limekiln or furnace for the first-century CE Roman-Byzantine Baths west of the precinct.

Exploring the deposits beneath the level of the colonnades, Trench 71 in 2000 reveals the upper levels of the Lower Temenos West Cryptoporticus. Forming the subterranean support structure for the colonnade above, the West Cryptoporticus is laid out as two parallel north-south galleries, mirroring the arrangement in the east. Figure 3.39 shows the twin galleries of the West Cryptoporticus. The west wall of the cryptoporticus is constructed from sandstone ashlars averaging 0.50 to 0.55 m in length by 0.21 to 0.32 m in width set with white mortar. Well-dressed arch springers and *voussoirs* extend from the east and west parent walls connecting with centrally placed piers housing arch springers on both sides. Figure 3.40 pictures the *voussoirs* springing eastward from the central pier of the West Cryptoporticus. Found in the collapse of Trench 71 are several large rectangular limestone slabs (1.10 m in length by 0.18 m in thickness), which originally cover the cryptoporticus arches. Other artifacts of note include seven partial inscriptions, a worn but complete elephant-headed capital, plus a smaller, battered elephant-headed capital likely from one of the engaged columns of the West Exedra.

The east and west galleries of the West Cryptoporticus are further explored in Trench 79 during the 2001 season revealing a beautifully preserved swath of limestone flooring 4.77 m below the level of the colonnade above. Excavations also bring to light later benches built up against the east wall of the cryptoporticus and against the north face of an east-west crosswall spanning the east gallery. Figure 3.41 shows the

Fig. 3.30
Lower Temenos, honorific wreath pilaster block. Architectural Fragment and Seq. No. 52410. Lower Temenos Trench 52, Locus 1. Length 82 cm, width 52 cm, thickness 24 cm. Limestone relief carving of a wreath with a (fillet) ribbon tied around the top. Panel was reused as an intercolumnar wall piece, installed upside down.

0 ▬▬▬▬▬▬ 20 cm

Fig. 3.31
Lower Temenos, drawing of the wreath.
(See description in Figure 3.30)

Fig. 3.32
Lower Temenos, East
Exedra, to south, 1994.

Fig. 3.33
Lower Temenos East
Exedra stratigraphic profile,
to southwest, 1998.

Fig. 3.34
Lower Temenos,
collapsed entablature of
the East Exedra, 2002.

Fig. 3.35
Lower Temenos, restored
East Exedra showing
niches, podium and bench
elements, 1998–1999.

Fig. 3.36
Lower Temenos, lead pipe
found in the Lower Temenos
in front of the East-West
Retaining Wall, 1996.

Fig. 3.37
Lower Temenos, prepared
passage for the lead pipe
extending across the Lower
Temenos, to the west, 1997.

Fig. 3.38
Lower Temenos newly cleared West Triple Colonnade, to south, 2000.

east Gallery of the West Cryptoporticus with the early discovery of the benches. Trenches 97 and 98 of 2004 and Trench 98B in the 2005 season completely uncover the parallel galleries of the West Cryptoporticus, seen in Figures 3.39–3.43, with 1732 architectural fragments, including four well-preserved elephant-headed capitals in Trench 97. These excavations also uncover metal martial artifacts including 105 arrowheads (Figure 3.44), a helmet cheek piece (Figure 3.45), and javelin points—all of which may be associated with the ballista deposit found just to the north in the Propylaeum West (*supra*). Several coins, examples of decorated glassware, worked bone and ivory artifacts as well as many lamp fragments and two complete lamps are also recovered.

During the 2004 season we wrestle with an important question: What lay below the pavement of the West Cryptoporticus galleries? In 2005 we decide to remove a section of flagstone pavement and extend a sondage below the east gallery floor known as Special Project 104. Thirteen stages in the stratigraphy were identified, beginning with a Pre-Site Phase I pottery assemblage dating to between 125 BCE and 50 BCE. Several occupation strata with intervals of sedimentation strata were identified. Bedrock was not reached. The Cryptoporticus galleries are built directly on top of earlier remains; however the pavement must have been built after 50 BCE. But how long after? That remains a question.

The Special Project 104 sounding revealed a complex sequence of natural and human events. The stratigraphy indicated that prior to Site Phase IV the Lower Temenos precinct hosted at least one earlier period of architectural development. It also revealed that the course of the wadi was likely to have been further to the south prior to the construction of the artificial terracing for the precinct, and possibly even before the main roadway. In addition, the presence of two early human activity strata also raises the intriguing possibility of tent habitation sites in the area dating from the elusive period of Nabataean history before the development of permanent stone buildings.

Fig. 3.39
Lower Temenos, twin
galleries of the West Cryptoporticus, to south, 2000.

Fig. 3.40
Lower Temenos, *voussoirs*
springing eastward from
the central pier of the
West Cryptoporticus, 2000,
before the excavation of
the West Cryptoporticus
is completed.

The nature and sequence of the vaults and the transverse walls between them were constructed at the same time as the lower courses in the Middle Pier Wall and the East Boundary/East Stylobate Wall. Regrettably, the sounding did not provide any conclusions regarding the function of the vaults and the walls between them. No definitive earlier floor was discovered. Inside the east vault, there were no indications that the interior surfaces were ever finished. Both the absence of these latter features and the general characteristics of the walls suggest that the vaults serve a purely utilitarian function as passageways used during the construction of the Lower Temenos area of the precinct. Once this function is accomplished, the vaults and the corridor-like features between them are blocked, and the West Cryptoporticus east gallery floor is installed. However, Special Project 104 did not provide a definitive date for the original installation of the floor pavers. The fortunate recovery of several coins immediately beneath the pavers may only provide the chronology for the posited period of repair discussed above.

West Cryptoporticus Special Project 105

To better understand the stratigraphy of the West Cryptoporticus, an additional sondage is excavated in 2005; Special Project 105 is placed in the east gallery of the West Cryptoporticus. Here terracing is found underlying the

Fig. 3.41
Lower Temenos, West Cryptoporticus west, to south, partially cleared to the floor, 2001.

Fig. 3.42
Lower Temenos, excavation of an elephant-headed capital in the West Cryptoporticus, Trench 97, 2004.

Fig. 3.44
Lower Temenos West Cryptoporticus iron arrowheads.
Typical example: Cat. No. 05-M-13, Seq. No. SP105004,
tri-tanged arrowhead with shaft. Lower Temenos Special
Project 105, Locus 1. Length 4.29 cm, width 1.08 cm,
thickness 0.26 cm. Weight 2.6 grams.

Fig. 3.43
Lower Temenos, West Cryptoporticus west, to north, 2005.

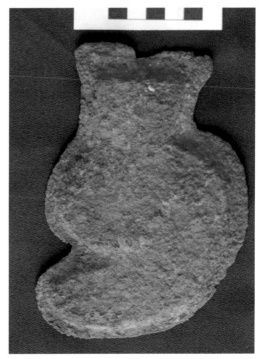

Fig. 3.45
Lower Temenos, left cheek piece from a helmet after
cleaning, 2004. Cat. No. 04-M-32, Seq. No. SP87090.
Propylaeum Special Project 87, Locus 9. Length 15.30 cm,
width 10.90 cm, thickness 0.26 cm. Weight 139.5 grams.
Corroded.

Fig. 3.46
Lower Temenos, West
Exedra before excavation,
to southwest, 1993.

preparatory construction for the gallery. It is
now possible to identify at least four stages in
the construction sequence of the West Cryptoporticus East; these are summarized as under
terracing, preparatory constructions, wall
constructions, and floor leveling.

Concentrating on the phasing of the area,
the excavations disclose much about the area's
later uses and ultimate collapse. The lowest
layers of Special Projects 104 and 105, associated
with Pre-Site Phase I through Site Phase II,
attest to various earliest strata of natural sedimentation, possible periodic habitation and
pre-construction preparation. Above this is the
Site Phase IV Grand Design when the West
Cryptoporticus is constructed with the insertion
of vaults. In Site Phase V, the vaults are blocked
when the floors of the Cryptoportici are laid,
and repairs take place in the center cryptoporticus wall that supports the vaults extending to

the east and west. In the Roman period of Site
Phase VII, there is an early collapse and the
addition of new ashlars in the center wall, and
benches are constructed along the south and
east walls. With the 363 CE earthquake there is
major collapse and destruction. Due to numerous column drums and elephant-headed capital
elements, it is posited that the overall collapse
of the West Cryptoporticus is triggered by the
collapse of the West Triple Colonnade, and
sedimentation, fill and an ash layer collect over
the collapsed architecture. While the similar
construction of the side-by-side galleries suggests
that initially they serve the same function, the
remarkably distinct smaller finds recovered in
the collapse debris of each indicate the changing
use of the areas over time. The soil of the west

gallery is compact and ashy, containing numerous plaster fragments, glass sherds, sections of flue pipes, bone and pottery as well as discarded industrial construction materials often carrying a thick mortar on their exterior surfaces. In the east gallery, there is neither the same amount of ash, nor the particularly heavy concentration of flue pipe fragments, likely used to conduct hot air to an unknown location. As yet, the noticeable difference in the deposits of these two areas is not fully understood, but may be attributable to the construction of the Roman-Byzantine Baths west of the Great Temple site in Site Phase VI.

(The Roman-Byzantine Bath Complex straddles the division between the Lower Temenos and the Upper Temenos. The discussion of this complex will be presented in Chapter 4, Upper Temenos.)

West Exedra Excavations

At the south end of the West Triple Colonnade, the complete excavation of the less stable West Exedra is undertaken in 1994 and 1995 in Trenches 5, 16 and 21 and in Special Projects 26 and 31. Figure 3.46 is a 1993 photo of the West Exedra before excavation, and Figure 3.47 pictures the early excavations in 1994. The mirror image of its counterpart in the east,[10] the West Exedra is constructed from well-hewn sandstone ashlars and is fronted by two freestanding columns supporting elephant-headed capitals. In its interior are five cut niches of equal size intended for the exhibition of statuary. Figure 3.48 represents its upper levels being drawn in 1995. While lacking a central podium and low bench (both seen in the East Exedra), the West Exedra prominently exhibits evidence of the Lower Temenos' reuse in later periods. In 1995, Trench 21 and Special Project 26 examine the secondary construction of a large Byzantine platform just north of the exedra, built between the southernmost columns of the east gallery of the West Triple Colonnade. Figure 3.49 pictures the West Exedra and the Byzantine platform. Here, excavations delineate a rough east-west wall north of the platform and the intentional fill, burgeoning with collapsed architectural elements. On this fill the remains of a limestone floor pavement are uncovered.

Tertiary periods of reuse in the area are defined during the excavation of Trenches 5 (1994 and 1995) and 16 (1995), which uncover the remains of a limekiln built over fill layers from an intermediary period of disuse or abandonment. Debris and sediment associated with the activity of the kiln mark a fourth period of accumulation, underlying a thick ash deposit concentrated in the curve of the West Exedra perhaps blown in from squatter fires of the modern period. Figure 3.50 shows the ash deposit found before the limestone pavement on top of the platform was unearthed.

Hexagonal Pavement Excavations

Centrally positioned between the architecture of the Lower Temenos east and west, the sweeping expanse of the Hexagonal Pavement is the single largest element of the temple complex. Spanning 49.00 m north-south by 30.00 m east-west the plaza is laid with large limestone hexagonal paving tiles, about half of which remain *in situ*, concentrated in the

Fig. 3.47
Lower Temenos, West Exedra during early excavation, to northeast, 1994.

south and east. Figure 3.51 pictures some of the extant pavement. Laid on a thick layer of bedding exposed during the excavation of Trench 14 in 1997 just north of the Lower to Upper Temenoi Central Staircase, the hexagonal pavers show evidence of later repairs. A number of circular pavers are present in the southwest corner of the pavement. Conspicuously shaped among the adjacent hexagonal tiles, the rounded examples indicate an apparent lack of concern for continuity in their manufacture suggesting that they are the result of a later repair either of the pavement itself or of the underlying canalization system. Also a sign of reuse in the plaza area, the noted absence of paving tiles in the north and west is attributable to modern Bedouin farming. In viewing the Lower Temenos from the air (see Figure 3.52), it should be noted that in the center of the robbed out plaza there is a striking rectangular area devoid of pavement. This may be the site of a Site Phase IV altar, which, if present, would be in direct alignment with the north-south axis of the precinct and be easily approachable via the Propylaeum Central Staircase.[11] In addition to indicating wear to the plaza itself, the battered surfaces of many of the *in situ* pavers in the Hexagonal Pavement also point to episodic destruction and repair of its associated

Fig. 3.48
Lower Temenos, West Exedra
upper levels being drawn
by Jean Blackburn, 1995.

Fig. 3.49
Lower Temenos, West Exedra
and the Byzantine Platform,
to north, 1996.

Fig. 3.50
Lower Temenos, excavation of the West Exedra ash layer, 1994.

features. In the east, the collapse of the East
Triple Colonnade is clearly indicated by a
distinct sequence of shattered and broken pavers
at regular intervals lying perpendicular to the
westernmost row of the colonnade. Figure 3.53
displays the "domino" collapse of the East
Colonnade drums onto the Hexagonal Pavement. Excavated as part of Trenches 60 and 61
in 1999, nine visible lines of column collapse
appear on the damaged pavement.[12] In some
examples, significant depressions where battered
elephant-headed capital fragments are uncovered further establish the original location of the
elephant-headed capitals crowning the columns
of the triple colonnades in the Lower Temenos.
Conversely, excavations in the west (Trench 66
in 1999) reveal an intact pavement surface without the lines of collapse featured prominently in
the east. It can be inferred, therefore, that the
collapse of the West Triple Colonnade occurs at

Fig. 3.51
Lower Temenos hexagonal pavers, detail.

Fig. 3.52
Lower Temenos 2006
overview of the Hexagonal
Pavement showing
the rectangular cut in
the pavement.

a later time than that of the East Triple Colonnade, after a layer of fill is deposited to cushion the columns' fall.

Subterranean Canalization Excavations

Hidden beneath the plaza pavement or below fill, the network of subterranean canalization also offers valuable information about the construction and destruction of the precinct. First discovered in 1994, the canalization is plotted in 1995 by Ground Penetrating Radar[13] as a series of secondary channels branching to the east and west from a central north-south artery. A major construction measuring between 0.60 to 0.70 m in width and 1.70 to 1.90 m in depth, the central artery is located beneath the treads of the temple Central Stairs during the excavation of the stairs in Special Project 4 and in Special Project 124 (*infra*), and in subsequent excavations to the north under an area of pavement collapse in Trench 13. Figure 3.54 shows the collapsed pavement revealing the canalization beneath; the canalization is just large enough for a person to turn around in. In 1997, Trench 42 investigates a branch of the canalization just east of the West Triple Colonnade. Here, a wealth of coins and elephant head fragments are found as well as a cache of pottery caught in a turn in the canal's path dating the disuse of this section of canalization to the first century CE.

In 2002, an additional test trench, Special Project 92, is opened in the lower area of the plaza, approximately 5.00 m south of the top of the Propylaeum Central Staircase. Here, excavations reveal a major intersection of the subterranean canalization system. Covered with hydraulic plaster, a north-south channel is identified as the south continuation of the central north-south artery uncovered in 1994. This 2002 examination of the canalization also confirms the 1995 GPR finding that the central artery extends as far north as 3.00 m south of the top of the Propylaeum Central Staircase, and, based on a comparison with its other major

intersections, that this full extent is constructed in Site Phase I. Because the two east-west channels bond with the north-south channel, they too are coeval, and in all probability they connect with the canalization of the Propylaeum East and the central artery of the temple.

Expecting to find a deep feature revealed by the 1995 GPR, in 2005 Trench 104, an extension of the canalization system is uncovered. It mystifies us because it does not appear to be functional. Pictured in Figure 3.55, it may serve as an overflow for the central subterranean system.

For a complete discussion of the subterranean canalization of the Petra Great Temple, please, see Christian F. Cloke's contribution in Volume III.

West Entry Stairway

Returning to the West Entry Stairway, features are discovered in the 2005 excavations. Although each flight of steps and platforms is different in dimensions, the platforms serve (Figure 3.56) to stabilize the steps by providing a secure foundation between flights. The surviving platforms are composed of well-laid plain white flagstone pavements with tightly fitted blocks set with mortar. In view of the survival of these features and their preservation, it is worth noting that the ancient Nabataean stonemasons had a developed technology in their design. We are aware of just how precise the Nabataean design of these features is.

Underlying debris collapse and fill off to the west between the two uppermost flights of extant stairs and the west wall is a terraced platform landing measuring 4.97 m north-south × 4.35 m east-west. The platform elevations are 896.4811 m in the north and 896.533 m in the west, and it is bordered to its east with smoothed blocks measuring 0.25 m to 0.32 m in size. Behind this platform to the west is a small corridor leading to the Baths-Palatial Complex. Resting on this platform, supported by a collapse of ashlars, is found a *nefesh* accompanied by a *betyl* and positioned behind an ash-discolored deposit. Figure 3.57 exhibits the platform with the *nefesh* and its accompanying *betyl*.

Fig. 3.53
Lower Temenos "domino"
collapse of the East Colonnade column drums onto
the Hexagonal Pavement
(note the horizontal depressions), to north 1999.

Fig. 3.54
Lower Temenos collapsed
pavement showing the canalization underneath, 1994.

Fig. 3.55
Lower Temenos
canalization capstones,
to northwest, 2005.

Fig. 3.56
Lower Temenos West
Entry Stairway cleared,
to the north, 2005.

This *nefesh* is an incised white limestone/ sandstone block with an incised obelisk carved above a squared cut *betyl* block, which is removable.[14] When the *betyl* was removed, it was found that the block had been completely carved through, and the *betyl* had been placed in a "window" of the block. A detail of the stele can be seen in Figure 3.58. The block itself measures 0.78 m in height × 0.57 m in width. The carved obelisk is 0.19 m in height × 0.14 m in width and the small *nefesh betyl* measures 0.14 m wide × 0.13 m in height. The elevation of the *nefesh* is at 896.50 m and its closing elevation is at 896.01 m. It rests at a 0.78 m depth below the doorway threshold for the corridor leading into the Baths-Palatial Complex to their immediate west and the Great Temple Roman-Byzantine Baths to their south.

In 2006 Trench 122 at 899.0 m elevation the uppermost platform of the West Entry Stairway is revealed, positing there were three steps missing from the stair upper flight. (These have been reconstructed in 2007.) The overall length of the Site Phase IV stairway is 37.2 m north-south × 4.60 m east-west, and its total area

Fig. 3.57
Lower Temenos, West Entry
Stairway Platform *nefesh*
(with the *nefesh betyl*
removed). Standing at
an angle to the left of the
nefesh is a separate plain
limestone *betyl*, Architectural Fragment and Seq.
No. 102928, measuring
40 cm in height, 24 cm in
width and 20 cm in thickness. It has a flanged base,
and its front surface is
damaged near the top.

covered 171.12 m². To the west and perpendicular to the stairway is a major three-course east-west Nabataean terrace wall, probably constructed earlier than Site Phase IV against which the West Entry Stairway rests. Uncovered at the top of the stairs, a threshold emerges with door drop lock notches and a shattered limestone slab landing. A Nabataean north-south canalization with intact lead pipes encased in a limestone carved channel extends under the threshold and upper platform. The route of the pipe can be followed leading south from the West Exedra area, parallel to the West Cryptoporticus galleries to extend under the platform and the upper flight of steps. It then takes a downward slope to the north, under the threshold and platform of the West Entry Stairway, under and across the uppermost stair platform to a notch, and from there it disappears into the Baths-Palatial Complex. To the southeast of the stairway are the remains of a doorway leading to the east, which originally would have accessed the West Propylaeum West Triple Colonnade.

Also recovered just to the south of the upper platform is a Site Phase II subterranean slab-covered east-west Nabataean canalization system at 898.83 m elevation. This major artery of the Great Temple canalization system is covered by 18 capstones, and its depth is approximately 0.20 m. The evidence suggests it carried wastewater from the Great Temple Roman-Byzantine Baths to a conduit over the West Cryptoporticus, ultimately to empty into the central outlet of the subterranean canalization under the Hexagonal Pavement of the Lower Temenos. Figure 3.59 illustrates these features. Found in the fill are red, yellow and green marbleized wall plaster fragments and a few coins. The image of an elegantly designed West Entry wall plaster fragment appears in Figure 3.60.

Several superimposed east-west walls in the south of the trench can be assigned to the Great Temple Roman-Byzantine Bath Complex, discussed in Chapter 4. The southernmost east wall extends directly west to the Roman-Byzantine Baths and appears to correspond with the north wall fronting the bath platform.

Fig. 3.58
Lower Temenos, *nefesh* detail. Lower Temenos Trench 102–103, Locus 13. Opening elevation: 896.53 m. Closing elevation: 896.01 m. This limestone *nefesh* measures 0.57 m in height × 0.79 m in width. The carved obelisk is 0.19 m in height × 0.14 m in width and the *betyl* measures 0.14 m wide × 0.13 m in height. (The *betyl* block in the *nefesh* moved when touched, so the earth was removed. Upon examination it could be seen that the *betyl* originally had been affixed into the square with white mortar, part of which we removed for sampling.)

Canalization
System

Threshold

Upper Platform
West Entry Stairway

Canalization with lead pipe

West Cryptoporticus

Fig. 3.59
Lower Temenos, West Entry
Stairway features, to west, 2006.

Fig. 3.60
Lower Temenos, West Entry
painted wall fragment.

10 cm

Now we have more physical evidence for an important west access to the Petra Great Temple—contemporary with its Grand Design in Site Phase IV. The date of its final use we ascribe to be in Site Phases XII–XIII or to post-date the 512 CE earthquake, after which the West Entry Stairway is covered with a massive fill of collapse. Thus the West Entry Stairway is in use for approximately 500 years. Constructed in Site Phase IV, these stairs (Figure 3.5) are well built from the bottom to the top—from the entrance on the Roman Road they follow the natural slope of the site and are perched on the steep slope today overlooking the Lower Temenos. This is one of the finest and most impressive examples of a Nabataean stairway. We speculate that the top of the stairs is destroyed by natural causes. It is clear that the connecting walls provide the link between the Great Temple and the Baths-Palatial Complex.

This stairway is clearly a product of desired access, bypassing the Lower Temenos and providing direct access from the Roman Road to the Great Temple Upper Temenos.[15]

Fig. 3.61
East-West Retaining Wall unearthed in Trench 6 Part II during excavation, to southeast, 1997.

Conclusions

Apart from the West Entry Stairway, the construction of the Lower Temenos on a leveled terrace with the site water supply extending beneath it, the striking presence of the East and West Triple Colonnades with their opulent elephant-headed capitals, the buttressed East and West Exedrae, the massive Lower Temenos Retaining Wall (shown in Figures 3.61–3.63), and the immense Hexagonal Pavement, which unites all of these components together, constitute an extraordinary expression of power. The construction of an architectural feat of this magnitude could only have been planned at a time when the development of the site was at its zenith, necessitating the need for ordered and centrally planned congregational space. This exhibition of formal planning with ties to the city cult certainly involved the effort of a large number of people and required a thriving political economy, through which the remarkable quality of Nabataean workmanship is demonstrated.

Fig. 3.62
East-West Retaining Wall, cleared, to southeast, 1997.

Fig. 3.63
Lower Temenos, East-West
Retaining Wall as restored,
to south, 2005.

Notes

1

These measurements do not include the West Entry Stairway.

2

Technically these stairs are located in the Lower Temenos, but they are a continuation of the steps that originate in the Propylaeum West at the level of the Roman Street.

3

The question also has to be posed as to whether the upper steps were constructed at the same time as the lowest flight of entry steps from the Roman Road. Because they are laid in a different architectural style, it appears that the lowest flight of steps also was re-laid sometime in antiquity.

4

See Note 8 of the Propylaeum discussion.

5

A *nefesh* is a sacred Nabataean commemorative monument. It was carved to consecrate a person or a family, and to be the receptacle of the soul. Often there is no burial associated with it, as in the case at the Great Temple. It serves as a witness to a Nabataean shared belief. It also symbolizes the Nabataean attachment to the aniconic representation of their god in association with an honorific memorial.

6

To avoid confusion, the *nefesh* has a *betyl* inserted within the block. An independent *betyl* is associated with the *nefesh* and its *betyl*.

7

Utilizing the West Exedra walls for its support, this bath complex will be discussed with its major features in Chapter 4 devoted to the Upper Temenos.

8

In 1999 the decision is made to remove these later walls to better define the East Triple Colonnade as part of the building program of Site Phase IV.

9

This triumphal wreath is re-published by Basile 2002a, 256.

10

The East Exedra was merely speculation at the time the West Exedra was being excavated.

11

This potential altar location was suggested by Emily Catherine Egan.

12

A conscious decision is taken to leave these collapse lines *in situ*.

13

For a complete discussion of the results of the Ground Penetrating Radar investigation of the canalization systems see Joukowsky 1998: *Petra Great Temple Vol. I: Brown University Excavations 1993 through 1997*, 171–185.

14

For safekeeping the *nefesh* was removed from the site, and a carved reproduction has been placed in its original position.

15

The stairs are integral to the precinct, although clearly outside the Lower Temenos. They existed independently or interdependently between the Great Temple and Upper Temenos and the Baths-Palatial Complex by providing access to the baths as well as the Great Temple. The Petra Great Temple has regained one of its most important and yet puzzling entries with this monumental stairway.

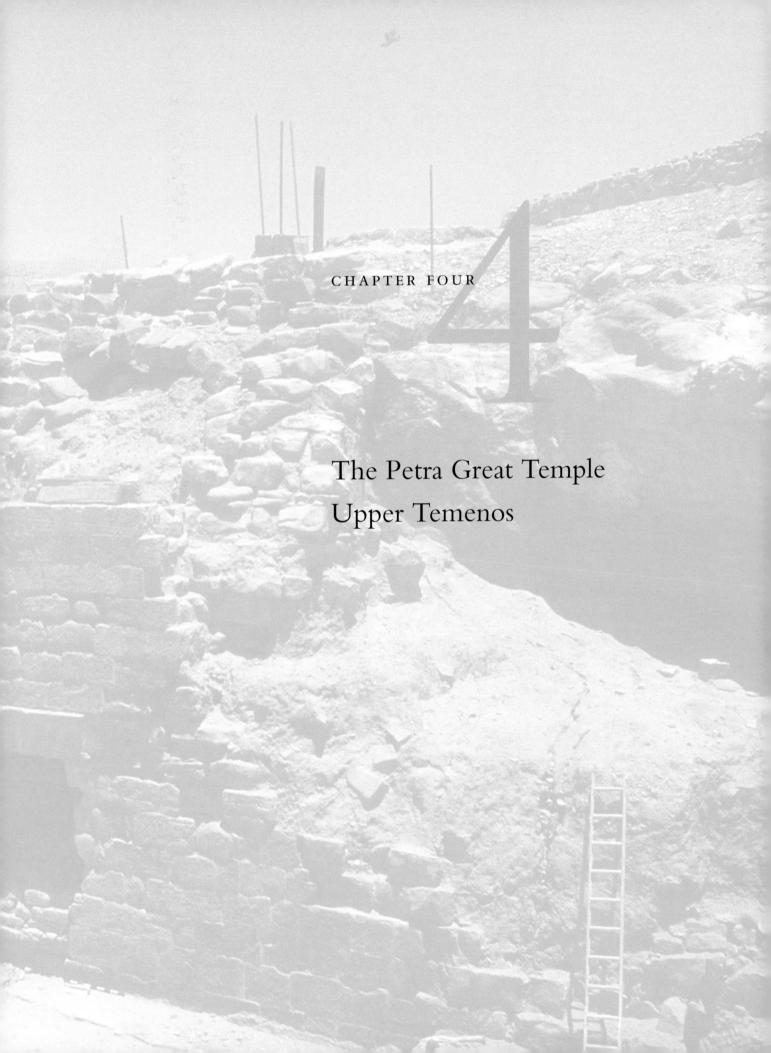

CHAPTER FOUR

4

The Petra Great Temple
Upper Temenos

Upper Temenos Features
1. East Plaza
2. East Perimeter Wall
3. South Escarpment and South Perimeter Wall
4. Great Cistern
5. Baroque Room Complex
6. Residential Quarter
7. Cistern-Reservoir
8. Sculpture Garden
9. Roman-Byzantine Baths
10. Temple Forecourt

CHAPTER FOUR

The Petra Great Temple Upper Temenos

Situated on an elevated bedrock platform, the impressive Petra Great Temple Upper Temenos comprises a rectilinear area at the rear of the precinct surrounding the temple proper. The plan is shown in Figure 4.1. Overburdened by an immense 12.00 m depth of deposit, this area is among the most difficult on the site to excavate, complicated by an extraordinary range of architectural features. In the north, the Upper Temenos is approached by two staircases in the east and west, each of which rises 6.00 m in height to connect the upper and lower terraces of the temple precinct. The earlier Central Stairs is part of the original access to the temple. Enclosed by massive perimeter walls to its east and south, the Upper Temenos contains a lavishly paved Forecourt, east and south broad paved plazas and passageways, above and below ground plastered cisterns, a series of vaulted rooms in the east, and the Baroque Room Complex. Further to the west lie an extensive Residential Quarter and the Cistern-Reservoir, and to the west the Roman-Byzantine Baths. Figure 4.2 is an aerial view of the Upper Temenos, taken facing the northwest. Major dimensions of the Upper Temenos features are given below.

Upper Temenos Features

Elevations and Dimensions

TEMPLE FORECOURT—904.02 m

Central Staircase—5.80 m north-south × 4.56 m east-west

CANALIZATION SYSTEM

Temple Forecourt, capstone upper elevation —903.85 m

Floor elevation—901.60 m

Dimensions

Note: All measurements are external and include wall thicknesses unless otherwise noted. When a depth is irregular, e.g., steps, it is averaged.

UPPER TEMENOS SOUTH

South Passageway: (external) 5.80 m north-south × 27.20 m east-west × 5.44 m depth; (internal) 2.90 m north-south × 24.70 m east-west

BAROQUE ROOM COMPLEX

From the Anteroom to the Settling Tank: 5.77 m north-south × 17.26 m east-west

Anteroom: (external) 3.90 m north-south × 4.90 m east-west × 2.19 m depth; (internal) 2.70 m north-south × 5.54 m east-west

Shrine Room: (external) 4.67 m north-south × 6.78 m east-west × 3.10 m depth; (internal) 3.79 m north-south × 5.70 m east-west

Shrine Niche: 0.74 m height × 0.53 m width × 0.33 m depth

Baroque Room: (external) 5.85 m north-south × 5.27 m east-west; (internal) 4.55 m north-south × 3.54 m east-west

Baroque Room East Door: 1.05 m north-south × 0.51 m east-west × 1.60 m depth

Baroque Room North Door: 0.44 m north-south × 1.02 m east-west × 0.70 m depth

Baroque Room Corridor: 1.32 m north-south × 9.77 m east-west × 2.49 m depth

Settling Tank: (external) 5.39 m north-south × 5.34 m east-west × 1.46 m depth; (internal) 3.86 m north-south × 3.00 m east-west

Upper Temenos

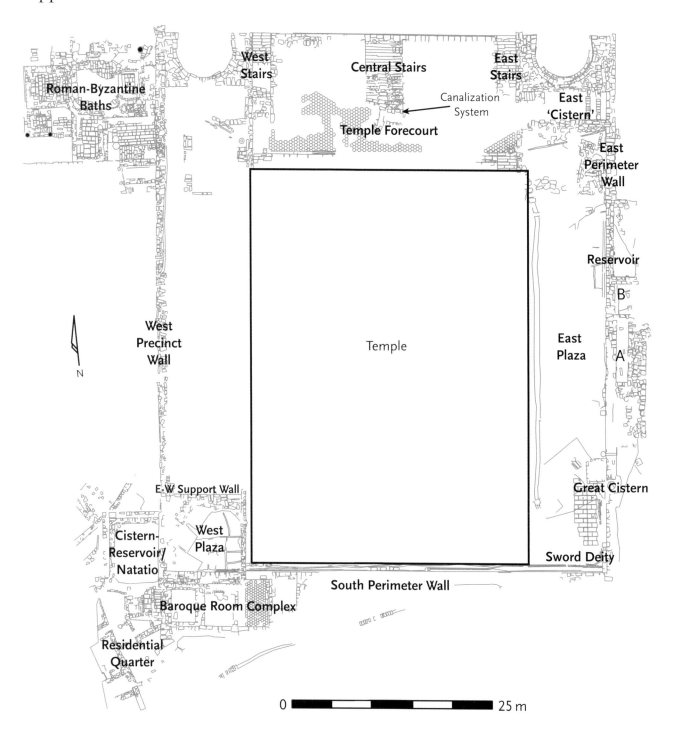

West Stairs

Central Stairs

East Stairs

Roman-Byzantine Baths

East 'Cistern'

Canalization System

Temple Forecourt

East Perimeter Wall

Reservoir

B

West Precinct Wall

Temple

East Plaza

A

Great Cistern

E-W Support Wall

Sword Deity

Cistern-Reservoir/ Natatio

West Plaza

N

South Perimeter Wall

Baroque Room Complex

Residential Quarter

0   25 m

Fig. 4.1
Plan of the Upper Temenos.

Fig. 4.2
Upper Temenos surround
to the northwest, 2005.

RESIDENTIAL QUARTER

From the Settling Tank in the east to west (excavated extent) north–south 15.48 m × 9.22 m east–west

Steps between the Settling Tank and Residential Quarter Room 3: (external) north–south 2.91 m × 1.18 m east–west; (internal) 2.91 m north–south × 0.77 m east–west × 1.01 m depth

Cave 1: 4.60 m north–south × 3.46 m east–west × 2.40 m depth

   Room 9: 4.60 m north–south × 3.46 m east–west × 2.40 m depth

Cave 2: (with Rooms 10 and 11) 6.50 m north–south × 6.65 m east–west × 3.54 m depth

   Room 7: (external) 5.94 m north–south × 3.42 m east–west × 2.24 m depth; (internal) 4.82 m north–south × 2.59 m east–west

Room 8: (external) 3.18 m north–south × 3.95 m east–west × 3.40 m depth; (internal) 1.94 m north–south × 3.37 m east–west

Room 10: (external) 4.94 m north–south × 4.16 m east–west × 3.80 m depth; (internal) 4.14 m north–south × 3.68 m east–west

Room 2 Corridor: (external) 7.79 m north–south × 3.47 m east–west × 3.57 m depth; (internal) 6.85 m north–south × 2.08 m east–west

Room 11: (external) 6.17 m north–south × 2.96 m east–west × 3.54 m depth; (internal) 5.71 m north–south × 2.40 m east–west

Other Rooms:

   Room 1: (external) 2.91 m north–south × 3.59 m east–west × 2.17 m depth; (internal) 1.95 m north–south × 2.53 m east–west

Room 3: (external) 2.94 m north–south × 3.05 m east–west × 2.39 m depth; (internal) 1.92 m north–south × 2.57 m east–west

Room 4: (external) 1.82 m north–south × 2.15 m east–west × 0.86 m depth; (internal) 1.20 m north–south × 1.80 m east–west

Room 5: (external) 1.96 m north–south × 7.12 m east–west × 1.57 m depth; (internal) 1.40 m north–south × 6.10 m east–west

Room 6: (external) 6.10 m north–south × 3.37 m east–west × 1.19 m depth; (internal) 4.27 m north–south × 2.49 m east–west

Upper Cave: 3.24 m north–south × 5.14 m east–west × 2.32 m depth

EAST UPPER TEMENOS

East Plaza: 45.37 m north–south × 9.53 m to 14.00 m east–west

East Reservoir to the south escarpment: 45.37 m north–south

Reservoir: 8.30 m north–south × 2.80 m east–west × 1.30 m depth

From the East "Cistern" behind the East Exedra to the south escarpment: 58.81 m north–south

East "Cistern" Arch Upper Elevation—905.23 m

Lowest excavated elevation (quarry)—898.76 m

Lowest plaster floor—900.62 m

Great Cistern: 8.50 m north–south × 7.80 m east–west × 5.17 to 5.88 m depth, 37.64 m cubed; 86,562 gallons of water or 327,640 liters. Depth of shaft 1.64 m, diameter of shaft 1.41 m.

EAST PERIMETER WALL

Room A: (external) 8.69 m north–south × 3.15 m east–west × 4.35 m depth; (internal) 7.75 m north–south × 1.53 m east–west

Room B: (external) 4.77 m north–south × 2.45 m east–west × 1.83 m depth

Tabun ("Oven," in Arabic) Cave Room: 6.19 m north–south × 2.34 m east–west × 1.20 m depth

Stairway between Room A and Tabun Room: 3.17 m north–south × 0.77 m east–west × 1.80 m depth

WEST UPPER TEMENOS

West Plaza: 49.33 m north–south × 10.20 m east–west

Cistern-Reservoir 7.00 m north–south × 5.40 m east–west

ROMAN–BYZANTINE BATH COMPLEX

32.00 m north–south × 28.40 m east–west, 908.80 m²

Dimensions for specific rooms in the Roman-Byzantine Bath Complex can be found in the endnotes.[1]

Upper Temenos Wall Dimensions
(Thickness and preserved height)

South Precinct Wall: 1.50 m thickness × 3.00 m height

East Perimeter Wall: 1.34 m thickness × 6.40 m height

South Perimeter Wall: 1.10 m north–south × 55.46 m east–west × 7.11 m depth

East Perimeter Wall: 36.69 m north–south × 1.33 m east–west × (with Arch) 11 m depth

East Perimeter Wall Arch: (external): 5.50 m north–south × 4.88 m east–west × 7.83 m depth; (internal) 4.05 m north–south × 3.32 m east–west

This Upper Temenos discussion will begin with the Central and East and West Staircases that ascend from the Lower to the Upper Temenos to the Great Temple Forecourt.[2] We will then move to the East Perimeter Wall, followed by the East Plaza with the Great Cistern. Thereafter we will describe the South Passageway and then shift further west for the evidence from the Baroque Room Complex, the West Plaza—its bedrock installations, the East-West Support Wall and the West Temple Sondage between the West Walkway Wall and the West Precinct Wall. Beyond the West Precinct Wall, progressing in a south to north line, we move on to to a description of the southwest Residential Quarter and the Cistern-Reservoir. Having encircled the Upper Temenos, we conclude this section with the Roman-Byzantine Bath Complex.

East, West and Central Staircases, and Lower Temenos Retaining Wall

EAST AND WEST STAIRCASES

Approaching the Upper Temenos from the Lower Temenos are three staircases—the Central, East and West Staircases, shown in the overview from the Lower Temenos in Figure 3.60. The East Staircase can be seen in Figure 4.3. Cut into the Great Temple Forecourt both the East and West Staircases extend for some 9.00 m north-south and are comprised of 30 limestone treads some 2.70 m wide and 0.35 m deep and flanked on either side by north-south sandstone retaining walls. Extending between these lateral staircases is the massive Lower Temenos Retaining Wall (Figures 3.62 and 3.63), which serves as both the south boundary of the Lower Temenos Hexagonal Pavement and as the northern support for the elevated terrace of the Great Temple Forecourt. Constructed to a length of 38.00 m between the two exedrae, the north face of the retaining wall measures 1.03 m in height and is constructed from substantial sandstone ashlars surmounted by a finished reverse cornice. South of the retaining wall, a thick rubble layer elevates the Forecourt above the level of the Lower Temenos.

CENTRAL STAIRCASE

Beneath the Forecourt deposits are the remains of the Central Staircase with 22 stairs remaining. A fine, white stucco step bedding suggests that originally they are clad in either marble or limestone. Most likely they serve as the original approach to the temple and go out of use with the construction of the Lower Temenos Retaining Wall. The top treads of the Central Stairs are initially recovered in our early campaigns of 1993–1995 but are fully exposed in 2004 in Special Project 124. They measure 5.90 m north-south-by 4.56 to 4.70 m east-west; they are 3.98 m in depth, and by design are blocked off and covered over in Site Phase IV when the Lower Temenos Retaining Wall is constructed. Figure 4.4 shows the exposed bedding of the Central Stairs.

Fig. 4.3
Upper Temenos, East Staircase from the Lower to Upper Temenos.

Fig. 4.4
Upper Temenos, Central Stairs.

Fig. 4.5
Upper Temenos, consolidated East Perimeter Wall and upper Vault, to east.

Temple Forecourt

Positioned directly north of the Great Temple and partially bordered by the East and West Exedrae is the northernmost component of the Upper Temenos, the temple Forecourt shown to the southeast in Figure 4.33. Measuring approximately 15.00 m north-south by 27.50 m east-west, the Forecourt rests at an elevation of 904.02 m, nearly 6.00 m above the level of the Lower Temenos pavement. The floor of the Forecourt is paved with small limestone hexagonal pavers measuring 0.36 m from end to end—a small-scale replica of the Hexagonal Pavement below.

East Perimeter Wall and Internal Rooms

Marking the eastern extent of the temple Upper Temenos is the massive East Perimeter Wall measuring approximately 56.10 m in length by 10.00 to 12.00 m in height by 9.53 m in width, crowned by a freestanding vaulted arch, which can be seen in Figure 4.5. Sturdily constructed, this casemate wall stands sixteen courses in height (with the arch above amounting to an additional nine preserved courses), built like a veneer to cover the face of the bedrock surround. The interior face of the wall, built against the bedrock, is comprised of large irregularly hewn sandstone ashlars bonded together with wet mud-lime mortar. To the west of the interior wall stands the exterior wall, constructed from well-dressed ashlars bearing traces of plaster. Within its casemate construction, the East

Perimeter Wall contains a number of interior chambers accessed from the once lavishly paved East Plaza. At an approximate distance of 18.00 m from the south end of the plaza is a doorway 3.39 m in height by 1.30 m in width adorned with a beautifully preserved lintel leading into a small room, Room A, measuring roughly 2.50 m². Standing the full preserved height of the east wall, Room A is embellished with two finely crafted niches 3.40 m in height surmounted by arches (Figure 4.57). Sometime after the first century BCE, once the niches cease to serve their primary function, later installations of an oven and raised trough are added.

To the immediate south of Room A is the *Tabun* Cave Room, cut into the bedrock escarpment 2.85 m above the opening of the East Plaza Great Cistern. This room, originally connected to Room A via a small bedrock cut staircase, houses a chiseled bedrock basin and the remains of a small oven. Measuring 6.00 m north-south by 5.60 east-west, this hollowed out chamber demonstrates several phases of use, serving initially as an access point to Room A and the Great Cistern and later as a residential or squatter enclosure. North of Room A is a third enclosed room, Room B. A long, narrow, rectilinear room also contained within the casemate of the East Perimeter Wall, Room B contains two arched niches cut into its east and west walls, a raised floor and a low retaining wall at its northern end. A small reservoir is located north of Room B, bonded to the retention wall of the chamber.

East "Cistern," Reservoir and the East Plaza Great Cistern

Throughout its north-south expanse, the East Plaza is equipped with several canalization features and systems. North and east of the preserved extent of the East Perimeter Wall are the two main cisterns of the precinct, the East "Cistern"[3] at the north end of the East Plaza and the immense East Plaza Great Cistern carved into the bedrock beneath the plaza floor. Presumed to be an earlier construction likely associated with the *distyle in antis* temple building of Site Phase II, the plastered East "Cistern" measures 4.50 m in north-south width by 9.50 m in east-west length and is surmounted by seven north-south arches, the upper elevation of which is 905.23 m. Once the cistern ceases to function, the room is used for the storage and perhaps the manufacture of worked and un-worked marble. Its ultimate use as a dump or manufacturing area is indicated by the large quantity of decorative stucco fragments, first century CE Nabataean fine wares and marble fragments discovered in the upper levels of fill.

In Site Phase IV, major additions are made to the temple's water systems, coeval with the construction of the East and South Perimeter Walls. In the southeast corner of the precinct, channels are cut into the parent bedrock, sealed with hydraulic plaster and set under the pavers that abut and circumvent the perimeter walls. Beneath the plaza floor, additional channels are found; some are cut directly into the bedrock and others are constructed at a later date from reused limestone ashlars or ceramic pipes. All are lined or affixed with hydraulic plaster. One such conduit can be seen in Figure 4.6.

Cut into the bedrock beneath the East Plaza is the main water catchment of the Petra Great Temple complex, the immense East Plaza Great Cistern, the east opening of which can be seen in Figure 4.7 and the west opening in

Fig. 4.6
Upper Temenos, East Plaza
Canalization outlet, to south.

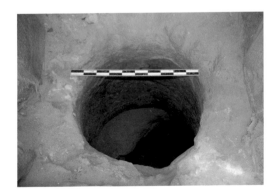

Fig. 4.7
Upper Temenos, Great Cistern east access in the East Plaza with bedrock carved step on the interior.

Fig. 4.8
Upper Temenos Great
Cistern, west vault opening.

Figure 4.8. Supported by bedrock, a masonry
pillar and twin east-west arches (as can be seen
in the section drawing of Figure 4.9), the Great
Cistern is accessed by two bedrock-cut shafts,
one in the southeast and one in the southwest.
The depth of the cistern measures 5.17 m, and
its full interior capacity is estimated at 327.64 m³
(filled to the ceiling, although not overflowing
into either shaft) holding approximately 86,562
gallons or 327,640 liters of water.[4] Christian F.
Cloke covers the details of these structures in
Volume III in a discussion of the Great Temple
water systems.

The South Perimeter Wall and Passageway

Bonded to the southeastern corner of the East
Perimeter Wall and extending westward from
the southern edge of the grand East Plaza is the
south boundary of the Great Temple precinct,
the South Perimeter Wall. Like its counterpart
in the east, the South Perimeter Wall is constructed against the bedrock escarpment from
double rows of sandstone ashlars, bearing traces
of plaster on their exterior surfaces. Unfortunately, all but two of the lowest courses and
three or four of the upper courses of the wall
have buckled, exposing the bedrock beneath.

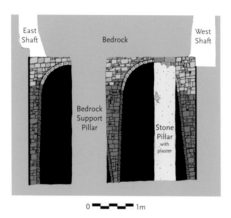

Fig. 4.9
Upper Temenos, East
Plaza Great Cistern section
showing bedrock, masonry
pillars, arched wall, entry
and exit shafts and other
features.

Fig. 4.10
Upper Temenos, South
Passageway escarpment,
Sword Deity carved into
the South Perimeter Bedrock
Wall. Upper Temenos
Trench 77, Locus 96. Opening elevation: 908.62 m.
Closing elevation: 907.71 m.
Size: 0.91 m in height by
0.28 m in width. This figure
has the shape of a dagger
or sword figure standing
on or in a stone altar,
which looks like an anvil.
The stone altar may have
been horned.

Fig. 4.11
Upper Temenos, Sword
Deity in escarpment of the
South Passageway.

Also visible is the schematic cult figure of a sword deity carved in relief just under a natural fissure in the bedrock escarpment. Figure 4.10 shows its position in the escarpment and Figure 4.11 is a line drawing of this feature. The figure measures 0.65 m in height. The short arms (or dagger hilt) extend approximately 0.19 m from the body, and the altar stone stands 0.27 m in height by 0.28 m in width at its base. Placed at a high, inaccessible point on the southeastern cliff face at the rear of the complex, this deity may have been chiseled by Nabataean stonemasons as an act of contrition to the deity, Dushara (Dalman 1908: 244–245), for the defacement of the living rock. Alternatively, as the relief is located just below a natural fissure in the cliff (which may have served as a water channel) it may have been carved in praise of water, honoring this scarce commodity as would befit a deity.

At the foot of the South Perimeter Wall is a second paved plaza, the South Passageway shown in Figure 4.12. Measuring approximately 5.00 m in north-south width by 40.00 m in east-west length, this passage joins with the pavement of the East Plaza, the few *in situ* rectilinear flagstones in the south bearing the same orientation and style of construction as the East Plaza examples. Following the line of the South Perimeter Wall westward, the preserved span of the wall terminates in the southwest corner, opening into a series of four rectilinear rooms, known as the Baroque Room Complex. Beyond this, lying outside the formal temple precinct to the west, is the irregularly shaped Residential Area, the Cistern-Reservoir and the Roman-Byzantine Baths.

The Baroque Room Complex—
Anteroom, Shrine Room and Baroque Room

The three fully excavated series of interconnected rooms represent ornately decorated chambers possibly reserved for a religious function. Figure 4.13 is a view of the Anteroom and the Shrine Room, and Figure 4.14 is a plan of the complex. Behind the west wall is the opening from the Shrine Room into the Baroque Room. The most fully preserved of these rooms, the Shrine Room, measures 6.78 m in north-south length by 4.67 m in east-west width and is constructed from well-hewn, diagonally dressed ashlars preserved to a height

Fig. 4.12
Upper Temenos South Passageway, to east.

Fig. 4.13
Upper Temenos, Baroque Room Complex. Anteroom to the left, Shrine Room with niche, and behind the Shrine Room sidewall, a doorway into the Baroque Room, to south.

Baroque Room Complex

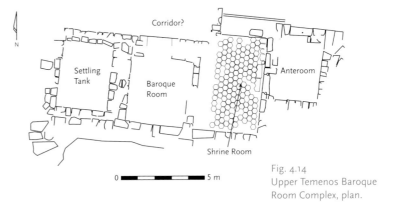

Fig. 4.14
Upper Temenos Baroque Room Complex, plan.

Fig. 4.15
Upper Temenos, Baroque
Room Complex, doorway
between the Shrine Room
and the Baroque Room,
to west.

Fig. 4.16
Upper Temenos, Baroque
Room Complex, Settling
Tank adjacent to the
Baroque Room.

of 3.22 m in the east and 4.00 m in the south. The once ornate decoration of the Shrine Room is revealed by the discovery of numerous brightly painted fresco fragments and a finely laid limestone hexagonal pavement. Set into the south wall of the shrine 1.32 m above the floor level is a cult niche with a preserved height of 1.02 m and a recessed platform providing a prepared surface for a sacred object, most likely a statue or a *betyl*.

Leading into the Shrine Room from the east is an anteroom measuring 3.44 m north-south by 3.20 m east-west. Evidencing its late construction, the east wall of the Anteroom is composed of seven courses of scavenged building material, among which are a number of large blocks with marginal drafts and smaller fragments used as snecking stones for leveling the wall blocks. The walls and thresholds of the Anteroom display evidence of redesign, eventually being closed off from the Shrine Room by tightly laid courses of dressed limestone blocks

of arguably Nabataean construction. In the west, the Shrine Room is accessed via the sumptuously plastered Baroque Room. The doorway from the Baroque Room to the Shrine Room is shown in Figure 4.15 looking into the Baroque Room from the east. Measuring 5.85 m north-south by 5.27 m east-west, the Baroque Room held the massive wreckage of incredible and extensive stucco decoration, the most remarkable elements of which include a large molded ceiling medallion and wall fragments displaying delicate vegetal and architectural designs, brightly-painted panels and gilding.

An interesting feature is the so-called Shrine Room North Corridor. Located to the north of the north doorway of the Baroque Room (*supra*), the north corridor appears to be the northeast continuation of the adjacent Shrine Room. The small, cut-to-fit hexagonal pavement of the corridor is identical to that of the Shrine Room, even down to the use of bonded half-hexagons as edging. In its location, the corridor provides an alternative point of access between the Shrine Room and the Baroque Room, allowing for a circular traffic pattern in this most sacred area of the precinct. Patrons, presumably a privileged few, based on the small size and spectacular decoration of these interior rooms, likely would have used the North Corridor as either a point of indirect exit or entry to the Baroque Room, circling either towards or away from the Baroque Room's east doorway.[5] Based on this architectural arrangement, traffic flow within this complex also may have proceeded as follows: from the South Passageway west, visitors also may have entered the Anteroom, moving west into the Shrine Room and then into the Baroque Room either directly through the door between the two (set into the Shrine Room's west wall) or by way of the north corridor. Most likely one door (either in the north or in the east) to the Baroque Room would have been designated as the entrance and the other as the exit in order to minimize the disruption of the ceremonial flow. The lack of direct access from both the Shrine Room and the Baroque Room to the temple plazas reinforces the sacred character of these areas—screened from public view by the South Perimeter Wall.

Fig. 4.17
Upper Temenos, West Precinct Wall
below the West Walkway Wall.

To the west and associated with the
Baroque Room Complex is an adjacent southwest Settling Tank excavated in 2004 and
shown in Figure 4.16. Measuring 1.46 m in
depth, 5.39 m north-south by 5.34 m east-west,
its walls are coated with a thick hydraulic plaster, and it is probably used for the collection of
water from run-off from the hillside above and
for the collection of rainwater. An exposed edge
of a lead pipe in the Baroque Room Complex
likely connects to this water system, and we
question its relevance.

Further to the north of the Baroque Room
Complex, excavations recovered elements of
the West Plaza which is bordered on its west by
the West Precinct Wall (Figure 4.17), 61.80 m
in north-south length by 2.40 m in east-west
width. As can be seen in Figure 4.18, in the
south between the West Walkway Wall and the
West Precinct Wall investigations found the
West Plaza (Figure 4.19) to be partially sited

Fig. 4.18
Upper Temenos, aerial of East Plaza with bedrock adjacent
to the East-West Retaining Wall, and to bottom left, Settling Tank.

Fig. 4.19
Upper Temenos, West Plaza
bedrock looking towards the
West Perimeter Wall, to east.

PETRA GT
SP 96
LOCI
19 VII 2004

Fig. 4.20
Upper Temenos, quarry cuts in the West Plaza.

SP108 East-West Support Wall

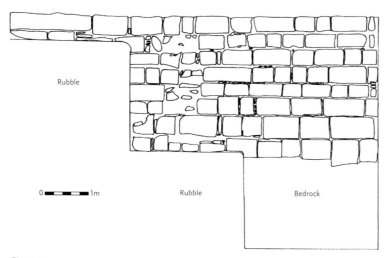

Rubble

0 ▬▬▬ 1m   Rubble   Bedrock

Fig. 4.21
Upper Temenos, section of the East-West Support Wall.

on a bedrock plateau, 49.33 m north-south by
10.20 m east-west. (The West Plaza itself measures 49.33 m north-south × 10.20 m east-west).
To the north and west of the plateau, the bedrock drops away. Chiseled into the bedrock and
aligned north-south were three caves pre-dating
the building of the temple precinct.[6] Although
there were no artifacts of note, these caves were
used for habitation; postholes and niches had
been carved into their walls. Associated with
the caves are a series of quarrying cuts, set 1.10
m apart, shown in Figure 4.20. These cuts offer
valuable insight into the early temple construction and argue strongly that the stone used to
build the temple originated from local as well
as more distant sources. The massive rock fill
blocking the three caves were part of the same
platform built by the Nabataeans to compensate
for the bedrock loss in the west of the precinct
prior to the construction of the earliest temple.

East-West Support Wall

With the fall off of the bedrock an East-West
Support Wall is found extending beneath the
temple corridor and walkway walls to the east
face of the West Precinct Wall. During the
excavations of 2005 Special Project 108, it
becomes clear that the West Plaza architecture
is much more extensive than we expect. Set
on bedrock, the East-West Support Wall opens at
a 904.85 m elevation and closes at an elevation
of 901.55 m; it is 12.00 m in length by 2.00 m
in width, and 5.10 m in height. This wall
is composed of five to eight ashlar courses,
constructed on bedrock with the lowest two
courses potentially from an earlier building
phase. The East-West Support Wall, which in
itself is a monumental construction, is designed
and constructed with the express purpose of
providing an artificial platform for the temples.
The wall section is shown in Figure 4.21, and
photographs in Figure 4.22 and Figure 4.23
illustrate its distinctive elements.

Features to the West of the West Precinct Wall

Whereas the East and South Perimeter Walls
delimit the precinct in those directions, on the
west the West Precinct Wall bounds it. To the
west, beyond the West Precinct Wall, additional

Fig. 4.22
Upper Temenos, West Plaza showing the West Precinct Wall, bedrock,
and on lower left the East-West Support Wall, to southeast.

Fig. 4.23
Upper Temenos, East-West
Support Wall abutting
the West Perimeter Wall,
to south.

Residential Quarter

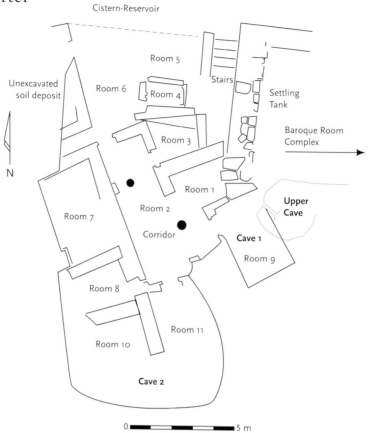

Cistern-Reservoir

Room 5

Stairs

Unexcavated soil deposit

Room 6

Room 4

Settling Tank

Baroque Room Complex

N

Room 3

Room 1

Upper Cave

Room 7

Room 2

Corridor

Cave 1

Room 9

Room 8

Room 11

Room 10

Cave 2

0 ▬▬▬ 5 m

Fig. 4.24
Upper Temenos, plan of the Residential Quarter.

Fig. 4.25
Upper Temenos, overview of the Residential Quarter, to south, 2004.

building took place. Because they are not backed by bedrock, the standing remains tend to be less well preserved and have suffered greater collapse. This is seen particularly from the West Precinct Wall, which over time has undergone frequent re-buildings. Apart from the features found inside the West Precinct Wall, evidence from distinctive architectural elements outside the precinct is fundamental to our understanding of how the precinct was used. For excavation purposes, these features are included in our designation for the Upper Temenos, although they lie beyond the traditional boundaries for the area. They do, however, share at least one wall with features in the precinct proper.

The three complexes to be discussed are the Residential Quarter, the Cistern-Reservoir, and the Roman-Byzantine Baths, all of which share walls with other west Upper Temenos architectural components.

Residential Quarter

Adjacent to the Baroque Room Complex is the extensive Residential Quarter, situated south and west of the West Precinct Wall shown in plan in Figure 4.24 and in overview in Figure 4.25. Just to the west of the Settling Tank, steps measuring 4.90 m north-south by 1.66 m in width, Figure 4.26, lead up into an east entry of the Residential Quarter.[7] Here, a series of two caves and eleven rooms are discovered, deep within Petra's city center. Cave 1, the smaller east cave, measures 3.00 m in north-south length by 4.00 m in east-west width, and its uneven floor rests at an elevation of 907.22 m. Cave 2 with Rooms 10 and 11 is the larger west cave measuring 6.25 m in length by 5.40 m in width with a floor elevation of 908.13 m and a standing height of 3.85 m from floor to ceiling. Situated above Caves 1 and 2 is the "Small Upper Cave" 2.90 m in north-south length by 2.50 m in east-west width with a height of 3.05 m. Contained within Caves 1 and 2 are Rooms 1 through 11. Rooms 1 through 8 progress counter-clockwise through the complex, moving from Room 1 directly in front of Cave 1, to Room 2 in the central corridor, to Rooms 3 through 8 in front of Cave 2. Room 9 consists of the Cave 1 interior, and Rooms 10 and 11 are located inside the subdivided Cave 2.

Fig. 4.26
Upper Temenos, Residential Quarter steps adjacent to the Settling Tank, to south.

Fig. 4.27
Upper Temenos, Cistern-Reservoir with Residential Quarter
behind, to the south.

Cistern-Reservoir

A stand alone, monumental cistern-reservoir measuring 37.8 m² by an average 1.96 m in depth is located at the foot of the Residential Quarter to the north (Figure 4.27). Recovered by the South and West Precinct Walls, its holding capacity is 19,548 gallons of water. Associated with it is a monumental limestone basin 0.82 m in height shown in Figure 4.28. With the exception of water storage, this feature's function is unknown.

Roman-Byzantine Bath Complex

Previous probes of a bath complex had been undertaken in 1996 at which time it was hypothesized the scanty recovered features were associated with a bathing establishment. No further excavations had taken place; however, the area was heavily trafficked by mechanical equipment between 1999 and 2004 for the removal of overburden and architectural fragments from the Propylaeum and Lower Temenos West Cryptoporticus.

The 2005–2006 excavations ascertain that these remains are baths. We discover a platform in the north, and moving north to south, a "splash pool" (cold water washing room), at least two *caldaria* (hot rooms), and a *tepidarium* or a *laconicum*. Below the floor level a partially sunk service corridor extends along the rear of the caldaria and isolates the baths from the Great Temple West Exedra. To the south of the heated rooms is an apsidal marble-clad vestibule-*frigidarium* (with a cold plunge), an ornamental pool, an elegant "well room" with semi-circular cavities for drawing water, a possible *apodyterium* (changing room), bathroom (toilet for six persons), a small cistern, and a columned colonnade fronting on a probable *palaestra*-gymnasium. This is a small, compact bathing facility, a *balneum*, covering 908.80 m² as excavated; its plan is presented below in Figure 4.96. An aerial photograph appears in Figure 4.29 and a labeled view to the northwest in Figure 4.30. The interior of the tastefully appointed toilet is shown in Figure 4.31, and the "well room" is shown in Figure 4.32. As can be seen in the plan, the complex of 22 rectangular and square rooms

Fig. 4.28
Upper Temenos, limestone basin adjacent to the Cistern-Reservoir. SP110, *Locus 30*. Opening elevation: 903.114 m, Closing elevation: 902.29 m, 1.15 m in diameter by 0.55 m in interior depth, 0.82 m exterior depth. Preserved height: 0.82 m. This outsized limestone basin is masterfully hewn from an enormous block of limestone. Its exterior is well dressed with chisel marks. Unfortunately its rim is broken but it could still serve as a gigantic water receptacle. It may have been manufactured earlier and reused. However, it was found associated with the Cistern-Reservoir.

Fig. 4.29
Upper Temenos, aerial photograph of the Roman-Byzantine Baths at the close of the 2006 season.

Fig. 4.30
Upper Temenos, Roman-Byzantine Baths, to the
northwest at the close of the 2006 season.

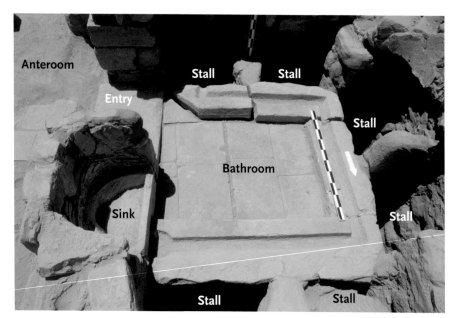

Fig. 4.31
Upper Temenos, Roman-Byzantine Baths, bathroom,
to the south.

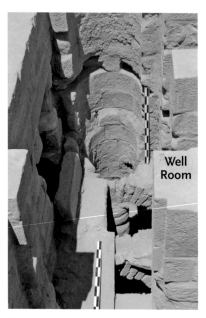

Fig. 4.32
Upper Temenos, Roman-Byzantine Baths,
"Well Room," to the west.

appears to follow the Pompeian type of bath plan (Yegül 1992, 66ff) with a simple row of windowed parallel rectangular rooms overlooking the palaestra to the west.

Stratigraphy and Phasing

As with the adjoining areas of the precinct, the stratigraphy of the Petra Great Temple Upper Temenos is best understood through the chronological development of the area, for which 15 phases of activity have been identified. Beginning sometime before the area is reserved for a major structure, in Pre-Site Phase I (pre-first century BCE) natural caves and bedrock are manipulated for habitation. This is clearly evident on the West Plaza bedrock platform, the Residential Quarter caves, and on the bedrock north and west of the Cistern-Reservoir which can be seen in Figure 4.27. Therefore, by Site Phase I, the bedrock terrace of the Upper Temenos is carved out from the living rock, and where the bedrock falls away it is leveled with a hard-packed coarse yellow fill in the west and north. As the bedrock is quarried, early subterranean canalization channels are cut into the central and northern areas of the terrace including those associated with the East "Cistern." Significant evidence of quarrying also is found in the West Plaza between the West Walkway Wall and the West Precinct Wall. Also at this time the substantial East-West Support Wall is put in place to ensure the stability of the temple where the bedrock is lacking. At the rear of the precinct, the Sword Deity is carved into the south bedrock escarpment. Following this period of preparation, the original *distyle in antis* precinct is erected during Site Phase II (also in the first century BCE), resting on the newly leveled Upper Temenos terrace. The East "Cistern" is built and additional subterranean canalization channels are cut, including the main artery beneath the temple Forecourt, which descends below the treads of the newly built Central Staircase. Sometime thereafter the Cistern-Reservoir is erected in the west.

Toward the end of the first century BCE and moving into the CE first century, the grand reorganization of the Great Temple into a *tetrastyle in antis* structure following a period of minor collapse leads to a series of massive construction efforts in the Upper Temenos. At this time, during Site Phase IV, additional subterranean canalization channels are cut including those in the southeast corner of the Upper Temenos, extending alongside the base of the South and East Perimeter Walls. The cavernous Great Cistern is also built immediately east of the temple proper beneath the extensive East Plaza along with an associated major north-south canalization artery. The towering East and South Perimeter Walls, the associated interior Rooms A, B and the *Tabun* Cave Room are also put in place and a smooth pavement of hexagonal limestone flagstones is laid in the East Plaza and along the South Passageway. In the north, the Lower Temenos Retaining Wall and east and west lateral staircases are built, accessing the newly paved temple Forecourt. In Site Phase IV, the East "Cistern" presumably goes out of use (perhaps converted into a marble workshop); the main water supply for the complex now provided solely by the East Plaza Great Cistern. In the southwest corner of the complex, the Anteroom, Shrine Room and Baroque Room are built, as is the Residential Quarter, which undergoes early periods of construction and reinforcement in this phase. On the west the Cistern-Reservoir floor is reconstructed.

Later in the first century CE during Site Phase V, the East "Cistern" is used for storage and possibly continues to serve as a marble workshop, with the ceramics at the lowest levels of deposit dating to before 100 CE. In Room A the hearth goes out of use and is replaced, and new walls and flooring are installed in Room 4 of the Residential Quarter.

A period of collapse in Site Phase VI results in the destruction of the Baroque Room and the partial collapse of the Shrine and Anteroom, dating roughly between 95 and 105 CE, determined by the pottery contained within the fill debris. During this period, in Site Phase VI, to the northwest, the Roman-Byzantine Baths are constructed.

In Site Phase VII, post 106 CE, late above ground canalization is crudely cut into the bedrock of the South Passageway and East Plaza and covered by loose floor tiles. A bench is added along the base of the south face of the temple South Corridor Wall. In Room A, new floor bedding and a low blocking wall are installed and tethering holes are cut beside the trough, indicating the area's convenient reuse as an animal shelter. There is a reconfiguration of the Roman-Byzantine Bath Complex and an above ground pipe is inserted in the West Precinct Wall to carry water into the complex from the Cistern-Reservoir. A new drain is added in the temple Forecourt, appointed with ceramic pipes for additional aboveground canalization.

In the mid fourth century CE, a brief period of abandonment occurs in Site Phase VIII, during which five of the seven arches covering the East "Cistern" collapse. In Site Phase IX the earthquake of 363 CE contributes to the primary collapse of the major features of the Upper Temenos including the upper courses of the South and East Perimeter Walls. Prominent in the stratigraphy of this major devestation are

a number of deep fluvial layers and reverse-stratigraphy deposits indicating the northward thrust of the earthquake, a breach in the South Perimeter Wall allowing large amounts of sediment and debris to wash down into the Upper Temenos from the rear escarpment. In the west, the West Walkway Wall is destroyed, as is the Residential Quarter; both are buried beneath a deep accumulation of fill and fluvial material. In the subsequent period of abandonment during Site Phase X between the fourth and fifth centuries CE the newly built west wall of the precinct is appointed with canalization. In the west, new, shabbily constructed drainage systems are installed in connection with the West Precinct Wall. Additional collapses and periods of abandonment lead to robbing in the Upper Temenos during the later Byzantine and Islamic periods in Site Phases XI through XIII, followed by the deposition of modern debris in Site Phase XIV.

As far as the Roman-Byzantine Baths are concerned, as mentioned previously, building begins in Site Phase VI and the baths are in use until the 19 July 363 CE earthquake of Site Phase X. After the earthquake there is a striking change in the character of the baths. Some rooms are no longer used, doorways are narrowed or closed off completely, and there is a dramatic contrast between the late Nabataean working bath and the features that are then reused. Later in Site Phase X it is probable that a kiln may have been constructed over the remains of the southernmost *caldarium*. Modifications take place and a final collapse occurs with the Site Phase XI earthquake dated to 9 July 551 CE after which the site is finally abandoned. To fix a precise date for the termination for the baths' last use is tricky, although it is unlikely that the complex functioned beyond the mid sixth century and the site's final abandonment. In conclusion, the Great Temple Roman-Byzantine Baths were in use for some 400 or more years, from ca. 70 CE at the earliest to 551 CE. However, the period of active use is gauged to be from ca. 70 to 363 CE, a period of less than 300 years. By the early sixth century CE when Petra experienced a general slump, the bath complex was abandoned.

Fig. 4.33
Upper Temenos, temple Forecourt, to southeast.

TRENCH	YEAR	DESCRIPTION	MEASUREMENT(M) (N-S × E-W)	EXCAVATOR(S)
Temple Forecourt Central Stairs and Subterranean Canalization Systems				
Trench 1	1993	Temple Forecourt center, stair bedding and podium	9.00 × 9.00	Schluntz
Trench 2 Part I	1993	Temple Forecourt, podium and west stylobate	6.00 × 10.00	Smolenski, Thorpe
Trench 3	1993	Temple stylobate and West Forecourt	4.50 × 5.00	M. Joukowsky
Trench 4	1993	Temple Forecourt and stylobate, Upper Temenos east	4.00 × 10.00	Shubailat
Special Project 4 Part I	1993	Subterranean canalization system	1.00 × 1.50	Schluntz
Trench 2 Part II	1994	Temple Forecourt and west podium	6.00 × 10.00	Schluntz
Special Project 4 Part II	1994	Subterranean canalization system beneath the Central Staircase	4.00 × 2.00	Payne
Special Project 4 Part III	1995	Subterranean canalization system beneath the Central Staircase	9.75 × x2.8	Payne, Slaughter, Barrett
Special Project 124	2004	Central Stairs	5.90 × 4.56	Egan, Libonati
Special Project 30	1995	Temple northeast podium at the intersection of the East Staircase and the small hexagonal pavement of the Forecourt	4.60 × 7.20 × 8.20	Tholbecq
Special Project 35	1995	Extension of SP4 to the east	No measurements taken	Slaughter
Trench 18	1996	West Staircase and Lower Temenos Retaining Wall	17.50 (S) × 16.00 (N),	Basile
Trench 32	1996	Western half of the temple Forecourt	17.65 (N) × 3.60 (E), 15.36 (S) × 16.45 (W)	Brown
Trench 18A	1997	Lower Temenos Retaining Wall between the West and Central Staircases	7.35 (N) × 7.50 (S) 14.50 (E-W)	Basile, Najjar, Sylvester
Trench 46	1997	Lower Temenos Retaining Wall between the Central and East Staircase	7.00 (N) × 8.00 (S) 14.50 (E-W)	Basile, Najjar, Sylvester
Trench 49	1997	East Staircase	6.00 × 17.70 (E) 14.50 (W)	Basile, Najjar, Sylvester
Special Project 60	1999	Temple Forecourt sondage north of the West Walkway	2.00 × 1.50	M. Joukowsky
East "Cistern"				
Trench 38	1996	East arch of the East "Cistern", south of the East Exedra	7.50 × 4.00	M. Joukowsky
Trench 41	1997	Upper strata of the East "Cistern", south of the East Exedra	4.50 × 9.50	Bestock, Mattison, Sistovaris
Trench 53	1998	Lower strata of the East "Cistern", south of the East Exedra	3.15 × 11.05	Bestock, Sullivan, Schwartz
East Perimeter Wall and Reservoir				
Trench 67	1999	East Perimeter Wall, Reservoir and associated canalization of the Upper Temenos	9.90 × 3.50	A. Joukowsky, M. Joukowsky
East Perimeter Wall				
Trench 68 (SP61)	1999	East Perimeter Wall south of Trench 67	15.90 × 5.20	A. Joukowsky, M. Joukowsky, Qublan
Trench 84 (SP91)	2001	East Perimeter Wall interior Rooms A and B	10.53 × 6.46	Fusté
Trench 91	2002	East Perimeter Wall	2.74 × 0.80	Fusté

Fig. 4.34
Upper Temenos, Chart of Trenches Excavated 1993–2006. (continued on page 160.)

TRENCH	YEAR	DESCRIPTION	MEASUREMENT(M) (N-S × E-W)	EXCAVATOR(S)
East Plaza				
Trench 44	1997	East Plaza, south of the East "Cistern"	10.10 × 8.85 (W) 9.75 (E)	Bestock, Mattison, Sistovaris
Trench 54	1999	East Plaza northwest of the East "Cistern"	10.20 × 5.05	Karz
Trench 72	2000	Continued excavation of the bedrock shelf south of Trench 54	6.00 × 6.40	M. Joukowsky
Trench 75	2000	Removal of the balk between Trenches 54 and 67	9.00 × 0.96	J. Farley, P. Farley, McCracken
Trench 77 Parts I and II	2000	Southeast areas of the East Perimeter Wall, the South Perimeter Wall and the south canalization systems	18.40 × 5.20	McCracken, A. Joukowsky
East Plaza Great Cistern				
Special Project 84	2001	*Tabun* Cave Room and early investigation of the EPGC	4.58 × 3.20	Cloke
Special Project 85	2001	East Plaza Great Cistern Part I	2.50 × 1.50	Cloke
Trench 90	2002	East Plaza Great Cistern Part II and the East Artery, platform and associated canalization	36.00 × 13.00	Cloke
South Passageway				
Trench 83 (SP83)	2001	South Passageway and preliminary excavation of the Anteroom and Shrine Room	6.45 × 31.20	Libonati, Egan
Trench 89	2002	Shrine Room and Baroque Room	6.65 × 9.28	Libonati, Fusté
Special Project 89	2004	Baroque Room North Door	0.30 × 1.30	Egan
Trench 101	2004	Settling Tank	5.25 × 4.82	Libonati, Khanachet
Special Project 121	2004	Sondage in South Passageway	1.50 × 1.50	Zimmerman
Special Project 123	2004	Sondage in Shrine Room	0.86 × 0.60	Libonati, Egan
Residential Quarter				
Trench 94	2002	Residential Quarter	16.00 × 10.00	Libonati, Fusté
Special Project 96	2004	Southwest Bedrock Plateau	No measurements taken	Egan, Libonati
Special Project 94	2004	Corridor between Settling Tank and Residential Quarter	4.90 × 1.66	Khanachet
Special Project 111	2005	Removal of Residential Quarter steps	4.90 × 1.66	Khanachet
West Upper Temenos				
Special Project 21	1995	Examination of the Baths-Palatial Complex	No measurements taken	Clapp
Special Project 44	1997	South of the West Exedra (West Bath dump)	No measurements taken	Brown
Trench 76	2000	Area west of West Walkway	3.00 × 11.00	P. Farley, J. Farley
Special Project 108	2005	West Bedrock Plaza and Temple East-West Support Wall	12.40 × 9.20	Libonati
Special Project 110	2005	West Precinct Wall and Cistern-Reservoir	62.00 × 2.50	M. Joukowsky
Roman-Byzantine Bath Complex				
Trench 105–106	2005	Bath Complex southeast	18.00 × 12.00	Power, Agnew
Trench 120	2006	Bath Complex southwest	13.50 × 17.00	Power, Khakpour, Agnew
Trench 125	2006	"Well Room"	1.93 × 2.52	Libonati
Lapidary				
Trench 7	1994	Lapidary West	2.00 × 3.00	Retzleff

Fig. 4.34
Upper Temenos, Chart of Trenches Excavated 1993–2006. (continued from page 159.)

Excavation History

In total, excavations of the Great Temple Upper Temenos are conducted yearly from 1993 to 2006. Over these years 4098 recorded architectural fragments are unearthed and recorded, including 231 column drums, 1476 ashlars, 38 elephant head fragments, 12 bosses, 878 capital fragments and 263 cornice fragments amounting to approximately 21 percent of the total fragments recorded in the site database.

In the following section we describe the progression of excavations taking place in each of the areas discussed above.

East, West and Central Staircases, Lower Temenos Retaining Wall and Temple Forecourt

Extending the full east-west width of the Lower Temenos plaza between the two flanking exedrae, the massive Lower Temenos Retaining Wall separates the broad plaza of the Lower Temenos from the elevated temple Forecourt to the south. Figures 3.61–63 show the Lower Temenos Retaining Wall. First uncovered in 1996, early excavations at the center of the retaining wall in Trenches 18 and 18A expose a complex series of substructures predating the wall's construction. The foremost of these discoveries is the Lower to Upper Temenoi Central Stairs measuring 4.56 m in width, × 5.90 the early and original approach to the two-columned *distyle in antis* temple structure. Excavation of the Central Stairs as part of Special Project 4 in 1995 and Special Project 124 in 2004 indicates that during the construction of the four-columned *tetrastyle in antis* temple this staircase is overfilled to create the foundation for the substantial temple Forecourt. The Lower Temenos Retaining Wall is then constructed to brace this fill from the north, and two lateral staircases are installed adjacent to the East and West Exedrae to access the elevated Upper Temenos and the Great Temple proper.

Excavated in 1997, Trenches 43 and 49 expose the masonry of these east-west lateral staircases, confirming the full symmetry of the Lower Temenos area during Site Phase IV. Figure 4.35 shows the East Staircase during excavation in 1997 (Figure 4.3 illustrates its excavated completion), and Figure 4.36 and

Fig. 4.35
Upper Temenos, East Staircase from the Lower to Upper Temenos during excavation, 1997.

Fig. 4.36
Upper Temenos, West Staircase from the Lower to Upper Temenoi after excavation, to south, 1998.

Fig. 4.37
Junction of the West Stair-
case and the Lower Temenos
West Exedra, to south, 1997.

0 —–—–— 1 m

Fig. 4.38
Upper Temenos, east face
of the West Stairway from
the Lower to Upper Temenoi.

Figures 4.37 and 4.38 depict the excavated West Staircase after excavation. Rising 6.00 m over the course of 30 treads, these twin staircases are supported on either side by north-south retaining walls formed by the east and west boundaries of the Forecourt buildup and by the exterior walls of the exedrae, indicating the contemporary construction of these features. The junction of the West Staircase and the West Exedra can be seen in Figure 4.37.[8]

Temple Forecourt Excavations

Further north, situated directly south of the Lower Temenos Retaining Wall, the monumental Forecourt of the Great Temple is among the earliest features of the Great Temple to be exposed with the painstaking hand and rabotage clearing of its southeast edge in Trenches 4 and 19 in 1994 and 1995. Figure 4.40 shows the Forecourt surrounded by sandbags in its early excavation. Delicately removing a significant overburden of debris, excavations delineate the prominent "domino" collapse patterns of the east Porch columns, left *in situ*, and further clarify the temple Porch stylobate. The column collapse of the east Forecourt can be seen in Figure 4.39, and the partially excavated Forecourt and the Great Temple proper to the east is shown in Figure 4.41. In Trench 4, the

Fig. 4.39
Upper Temenos, collapsed
east Porch columns, 1993.

Fig. 4.40
Upper Temenos, Temple
Forecourt, to south, 1993.

Fig. 4.41
Upper Temenos, partially
excavated Forecourt and
Pronaos, to east, 1995.

preserved east extent of the Porch stylobate is defined, revealing a number of masons' marks on the upper surface of the stylobate ashlars.[9] In Figure 4.42 can be seen the Forecourt, the Pronaos steps and the stylobate during excavation.

In the southwest area of the Forecourt, excavations in Trench 4 reveal a deeper deposit with a larger concentration of architectural fragments, the majority of which are capital elements including carved volutes and vegetal material (pomegranates, poppies, grapes, pine-cones and vines) that overlie the Porch stylobate and its adjoining east staircase. Figures 4.42 and 4.43 show collapsed capital fragments including exquisitely carved volutes and vegetal material. In the central area of the Forecourt, Trenches 1 and 3, intended to isolate and confirm the north limit of the Porch stylobate, expose the battered surface of a small section of hexagonal pavement (Figure 4.44). Near the center of the pavement, a patchy area of disturbed soil level is removed revealing an *in situ* finely carved ashlar block

with two masons' marks (Figure 7.7) deliberately put in place to block the entrance to a network of subterranean canalization channels stretching to the north, south, east and west. The walls of the four channels are constructed from regularly sized sandstone ashlars measuring between 0.50 and 0.60 m in length and between 0.35 and 0.40 m in width. Overall, the corners at the channels' junction are better constructed than the walls that extend away from them. The walls occasionally show signs of chinking, but no plasterwork or masons' marks are visible.

The larger system, extending north-south, is determined to belong to the precinct's central artery, drawing water from the temple, across the Forecourt and down to the Lower Temenos passing beneath the treads of the Central Stairs. During the 1994 season and continuing in 1995, investigation of the central artery in Special Project 4 further reveals its construction; the full 11.28 m north-south extent of the feature across the Forecourt can be seen in Figure 4.45.

Fig. 4.42
Upper Temenos, Forecourt and west stylobate during excavation, to south, 1993.

Fig. 4.43
Upper Temenos, consolidation of the temple stylobate and collapsed capital elements, to south, 1993.

Fig. 4.44
Upper Temenos, detail of temple Forecourt hexagonal pavement.

Fig. 4.45
Upper Temenos, subterranean canalization system, central artery under the Forecourt; the early recovery of the Central Stairs to the right center to north.

Fig. 4.46
Upper Temenos, subter-
ranean canalization
system, detail of the
main artery, to north.

Fig. 4.47
Upper Temenos,
Central Stairs bedding
as first excavated
in 1994, to south.

Cracked capstones are removed, and the main
tunnel, sloping at a 45-degree angle downward
from south to north, is explored with the help
of Mining Engineer Consultant, P. Nalle,
revealing a dense accumulation of overfill as well
as a fine level of silt containing lamp fragments
and a collection of Nabataean and Roman
pottery dating to the use periods of the system.
Figure 4.46 illustrates the main tunnel to the
north. The 1995 and 2004 excavations focus
on the delineation of the Central Staircase, the
upper steps of which are uncovered in 1994.
The partially exposed stair bedding, completely
covered with mortar, retains 22 original treads
made from small, friable sandstone slabs, also
with a coating of mortar, which overlie the path
of the canalization central artery. Figure 4.47
shows the bedding of the Central Staircase
before it was completely excavated in 1994, and
Figure 4.4 illustrates the East-West Retaining
Wall and the Central Staircase taken from the
Lower Temenos in 2004. On the east side of the
Central Staircase are the remains of a contemporary Nabataean ashlar wall, preserved to four
courses in height and retaining traces of the
same mortar present on the staircase. The east
face of this wall after the 2004–2005 restoration,
is shown in Figure 4.48.

Continued excavation of the temple Forecourt commences during the following three
seasons of excavation in Trench 19 in 1995, in
Trenches 32 and 18 in 1996 and in Trenches
18A and 46 in 1997, clearing the center and
north edge of the Forecourt. More of the small
hexagonal pavement is exposed beneath a deep
deposit of overburden. The fill removed from
these areas of the Forecourt is found to contain
a variety of architectural elements including
large numbers of carved limestone capital
fragments probably collapsed from the Porch
columns and Antae.

East "Cistern" Excavations

Located immediately south of the East Exedra, an unusual feature dubbed the East "Cistern" is partially excavated in Trench 41 in 1997, and is completed in Trench 53 in 1998. Figure 4.49 is of the 1998 excavations in progress. Bounded by three bonded walls in the west, north and south, and one abutting wall in the east, the East "Cistern" interior is coated with a patchy layer of light chalky plaster more closely resembling decorative rather than hydraulic plaster. Whether or not this surface treatment would have provided an effective watertight seal is uncertain. Other complicating evidence includes the noted absence of pipes or channels by which water would enter and exit the cistern. A small seven-step service staircase discovered adjacent to the East Staircase in the northwest corner of the room would have allowed for water to be collected by hand, but its means of deposition remains to be identified.

In the upper layers of fill, large quantities of colorfully yellow, red and green painted

Fig. 4.49
Upper Temenos, excavation of the "Cistern," to west, 1998.

and molded stucco fragments are recovered. It has been suggested that perhaps this room is embellished with stucco decoration; however, the lack of any *in situ* fragments argues instead for the use of the room as a dump in Sites Phase V or VI. On and above the floor level, excavations reveal a rich deposit containing fragments of Nabataean and Greek inscriptions, coins, bronze decorative elements, glass and an astonishing amount of pottery, much of it complete. Punctuated by anomalous architectural elements including a fragment of a Nabataean Type 1 blocked out capital (McKenzie 1990:

190, h–I; Figure 4.50) uncharacteristic of those found in the Great Temple precinct,[10] the finds roughly date to the second century CE at which time Roman remodeling may have resulted in the disuse of this temple area. Resting on the floor of the cistern, a substantial quantity of partially worked white marble slabs and ashlars are found in close association with several long flat iron objects. While too corroded to easily identify, these objects may have been chisels and saws used to work the marble, suggesting an early reuse of this area as a marble workshop prior to its later function as a dump.

Fig. 4.50
Upper Temenos, plain Nabataean blocked-out capital found in the East "Cistern," 1998.

Fig. 4.51
Upper Temenos, East Perimeter Wall and Vault collapse cleared, to the northeast.

Fig. 4.52
Upper Temenos,
East Perimeter Wall
being cleared, to east.

East Perimeter Wall (Figure 4.5),
Reservoir, Room A and Room B Excavations

Just north of the East Perimeter Wall, excavation in Trench 67 in 1999 determines the character of the deposit east of the East "Cistern" and west of the *Paradesios* (Garden Pool Complex east of the Great Temple precinct). Here, a complex network of canalization pipes and channels and low wall foundations comprising a feature known as the East Reservoir are revealed. Bounded in the east by a casemate wall constructed from parallel ashlars and rubble fill, this reservoir is coated in hydraulic cement and appointed with clay pipes set into the east wall's base. A puzzling system of artificial platforms and terracing walls also discovered beneath the fill in the areas immediately surrounding the reservoir reveals additional canalization installations that may represent later manipulation of the water supply held there, but no physical connection between the two areas is currently present.

Moving south along the Upper Temenos eastern perimeter, excavations of the East Perimeter Wall commence in 1999 with the opening of Trenches 54 and 68. Figure 4.51 is of the East Perimeter Wall and East Vault after partial excavation and prior to restoration.

Immediately south of the East "Cistern," Trench 54 further investigates the canalization identified in the west of the same trench in 1997 and defines the connection between this area and the East "Cistern," especially the construction of an arch springer wall at the north boundary of the trench. Excavations begin with the removal of a clay pipe in the north, which revealed the rubble fill behind the East "Cistern" arch springer wall containing a deep deposit of gravel. Continued excavations of the gravel deposit do not reveal its founding level, but it is posited to rest on the bedrock shelf underlying the entire plaza.

Continuing south along the temple's east perimeter, Trench 68 reveals a large section of the bedrock sub floor underlying the elegantly paved surface of the East Plaza bounded by the monumental East Perimeter Wall. Preserved to a height of 14 courses, the exterior wall of the East Perimeter Wall is uncovered from beneath a debris deposit over 10.00 m deep at its highest point. Figure 4.52 shows the soil removal from the East Perimeter Wall. During excavation, the south part of the wall is found to be in a superior state of preservation compared to that

of the north, protected from corrosive elements by a noticeably deeper deposit. While clearing the upper courses of the East Perimeter Wall, the casemate character of the wall is revealed. Figure 4.53 and Figure 4.54 portray the wall during excavation. Bonded to each other, and to a partially collapsed vault surmounting the structure, both the interior and exterior façade walls date to the same period of construction, Site Phase IV. Figures 4.55 and 4.56 represent the complexities of the East Vault excavations.

Coeval with the construction of the East Perimeter casemate wall is the installation of a series of internal rooms. Initially discovered during the exposure of the exterior perimeter wall in 1999 is an immaculately preserved door-way with a stepped lintel (which can be seen in Figures 4.51 and 4.52), a design not present in any other architectural elements of the Great Temple. In Trench 84 in 2001, further investi-gation of the doorway's interior reveals a small square room, Room A, with two high arched niches and well-preserved ceiling beams con-structed from tightly laid blocks of variegated sandstone. Figure 4.57 pictures the north arch in Room A after consolidation. Based on the stratigraphy and ceramics of this room, the earli-est features of this room include a small rock-cut basin in the floor and a bedrock staircase (discovered in Trench 91 in 2002) connecting Room A to the *Tabun* Cave Room to the south. Figure 4.58 serves as a fine example of a Nabataean pilgrim bottle found in the deposit and Figure 4.59 illustrates the bedrock staircase

Fig. 4.55
Upper Temenos, East Perimeter Wall and Vault during 1998 excavation, to east.

Fig. 4.56
Upper Temenos, East Perimeter Wall and Vault during 2001 excavation, to east.

Fig. 4.57
Upper Temenos, East Perimeter Wall, Room A north arch after consolidation.

Fig. 4.58
Upper Temenos, East Perimeter Wall, Room A, Pilgrim Bottle. (See the description for this vessel in the caption of Fig. 7.45.)

Fig. 4.59
Upper Temenos,
East Perimeter Wall,
Room A, bedrock
staircase and rock-cut
basin, to south, 2002.

Fig. 4.60
Upper Temenos,
East Perimeter Wall,
Room A east arch.
Note that a trough has
been built into the arch
to east.

and rock-cut basin in Room A. At a later stage (possibly Site Phase VII) once the two niches cease to serve their primary function sometime in the first century BCE, the deteriorated stucco is removed from the walls and a plastered water basin (Figure 4.60) is set into the east arch's niche. A hearth surrounded by rocks is also installed inside of the north arch niche, leaving soot-marks on the arch as well as on the bedrock floor and the fill directly above. At this point, Room A functions as a kitchen, identified by a large number of Nabataean cooking pots found in the fill. After enough dirt mixed with ash accumulates, the hearth falls out of use and an oven (*tabun*, in Arabic) is dug into the floor in the room's southwest corner.

In yet a later stage (presumably Site Phase VII), the doorway to Room A, accessed from the East Plaza, is partially blocked directly above the threshold. Also at this time, a thickly packed plaster floor covered with purple sandstone pavers is laid on top of the occupational debris. The oven (now fallen into disuse) is converted into a storage area for Nabataean pottery including finely rouletted cups, red slipped jugs with twisted handles and the Nabataean pilgrim bottle shown in Figure 4.58. Over the oven, a stone shelf is constructed from reused floor pavers and the water basin in the east niche is reused as a trough (Figure 4.60). Three tethering holes are bored into the ashlars to either side of the trough, designating the use of this area as an animal shelter.

North of Room A, Room B, also situated in the casemate construction of the East Perimeter Wall, is excavated in 2001 as an extension of Trench 84. A long, narrow rectilinear north-south chamber, Figure 4.61, it is located just to the south of the water reservoir, Figure 4.62, discovered during the 1999 season. In Room B's interior, two small niches are installed on both the east and west walls, and to the north a low retention wall is constructed to hold back the fill of the room's raised floor bedding. On top of the bedding, presumably in a later period, an infant jar burial is placed.[11] Above the jar burial is a thick deposit of debris, accumulated from the collapse of the East Perimeter Wall.

South of Room A, excavations in Special Project 84 in the east bedrock escarpment above the opening of the East Plaza Great Cistern

Fig. 4.61
Upper Temenos,
East Perimeter Wall,
Room B, to south, 2001.
In the foreground is
the reservoir.

Fig. 4.62
Upper Temenos, East
Perimeter Wall, reservoir to
the north of Room B, 2001.

reveal a rock-cut domestic installation known as the *Tabun* Cave Room. In Figure 4.63 the excavation of the *Tabun* Cave Room is taking place in 2001, Figure 4.64 is an image of the room following the removal of detritus, and Figure 4.65 pictures the cleaned cave room itself. Here, in addition to a rock-cut plastered basin and small oven (Figure 4.66), considerable Nabataean ceramics are found constituting a homogeneous assemblage. Likely built to service the Great Cistern below, the *Tabun* Cave Room sits directly above a series of crudely constructed rock installations into which small water channels are cut, most likely associated with a later period of the East Plaza Great Cistern's use.

During the excavation of the upper levels of fill in Trench 77 in 2000, a natural cavity in the east bedrock (which is later determined to be the upper part of the *Tabun* Cave Room) reveals the additional remains of two partial, disarticulated, primary human burials shown in the fill covering the east bedrock escarpment (Figure 4.67). Examined by physical anthropologist Megan A. Perry, these remains are found to be those of a male child and an adult. The child is found lying on his right side, the skull oriented toward the southwest and the face pointing due west. A number of bones are recovered, including those from the skull, leg and arm, as well as fingers and teeth. No burial containers are present. Overall, the bones are in a very poor state of preservation due to their exposure to water and other corrosive environmental elements, and, as a result, the cranium collapsed during excavation. Judging from the deep fluvial deposit of sand surrounding these remains, we posit that these human beings may have been caught in a flood following the collapse of the East Perimeter Wall.

Fig. 4.63
Upper Temenos, East Perimeter Wall, excavation of the *Tabun* Cave Room, to northeast, 2001.

Fig. 4.64
Upper Temenos, East Perimeter Wall, excavation of the *Tabun* Cave Room, to northeast, 2001.

Fig. 4.65
Upper Temenos, East Perimeter Wall, *Tabun* Cave Room, to east, 2001.

Fig. 4.66
Upper Temenos, East Perimeter Wall, *Tabun* Cave Room with oven *in situ*, to northeast, 2001.

Fig. 4.67
Upper Temenos, east balk with *in situ* disarticulated human bones, 2000.

East Plaza and Canalization Excavations

Moving from north to south, excavation of the East Plaza commences in 1997 with the opening of Trench 44 between the temple East Walkway and the northwest extent of the East Perimeter Wall. Here, a wide range of architectural features including several ceramic pipelines, a stone channel bedding and Byzantine walls provides many surprises and raises numerous questions about this portion of the precinct. To explain the noticeable lack of uniform flooring remains, it is posited that this area may have originally been stepped or multi-tiered.

In 2000, excavations move south to clear the east surround of the Great Temple, opening Trenches 72, 74, 75 and 77. Figure 4.68 displays the early excavation of the East Perimeter Wall and Figure 4.69 reveals the canalization and the cleared East Plaza after excavation. Collectively, these trenches encompass the full East Plaza revealing a myriad of canalization systems cut

into and beneath the paved floor surface. One of the largest and most remarkable excavations undertaken at this time is Trench 77 Part I, opened in the central area of the East Plaza, which witnesses the complete exposure of the bedrock sub floor and of the few rectangular flagstone pavers that remain *in situ*. Once covering the entire surface of the plaza, the pavers are found to extend underneath the temple East Walkway Wall (see discussion of Trench 73, *infra*) and into the temple East Corridor proper. Stratigraphically, this discovery suggests that the walkway wall is a secondary construction—that the entire area to the temple's east originally functions as one extensive, open plaza. Just to the west of the East Walkway Wall the additional discovery of a series of squared-off postholes cut into sections of the plaza pavement are found to be in direct alignment with similar cuts made

Fig. 4.68
Upper Temenos, East
Perimeter Wall excavation,
to southeast.

Fig. 4.69
Upper Temenos,
East Plaza canalization,
to north.

in the east face of the East Corridor Wall. This discovery sheds further light on the early architectural arrangement of this area, which was likely covered with an anchored canopy.

Alongside the south extent of the East Perimeter Wall, Trench 77 Part II is opened to determine the relationship between this wall and the South Perimeter Wall and to gain a better understanding of the canalization systems at the rear of the complex. Originally concentrating on the removal of fill in the south of the East Plaza, once the South Perimeter Wall is discovered, excavations alter their course to follow the natural bedrock outcrop stretching an additional 22.00 m west. Figure 4.70 shows the bedrock escarpment and the South Perimeter Wall. Here, during an intensive survey of the slope to the south of the South Perimeter Wall, an aboveground canalization system is uncov-

ered, channeling water across the rear of the complex to the Great Cistern in the east.

Centrally situated beneath the pavement of the East Plaza and fed by this complex series of cut channels is the massive subterranean East Plaza Great Cistern (Figs. 4.7–4.9). The discovery of this astonishing feature in 2001 in Special Project 85 (Figure 4.71) and its subsequent excavation in the same year and in Trench 90 in 2002 give a more accurate idea of the water storage capabilities of this massive structure. In the interior are found the remains of a wall containing two masonry arches spanning the south, a centrally located substantial support column carved out of bedrock and a masonry pillar to the west, all of which are sealed with hydraulic plaster. Figure 4.72 pictures the cistern interior and the wall section is shown *supra* in

Fig. 4.70
Upper Temenos, East
Plaza and South Perimeter
Wall, to south, 2000.

Fig. 4.71
Upper Temenos, Christian F. Cloke being lowered into the East Plaza Great Cistern.

Fig. 4.72
Upper Temenos, interior arch of the East Plaza Great Cistern.

Figure 4.9. Constructed at this same time is the southeast canalization of the Upper Temenos East Plaza, which feeds the Great Cistern through an opening in its southwest ceiling. These two large systems provide a significant influx of water, furnishing the temple with an abundant supply even in dry seasons.

South Passageway Excavations

Stretching across the rear of the temple, directly west of the East Plaza is the substantial South Passageway. During the 2001 season, excavations in Trench 83 concentrate on the delineation of this area and the complete exposure of the remains of the precinct's South Perimeter Wall. Figure 4.73 presents the excavated depth of the east sector of the South Perimeter Wall.[12] As the overburden is cleared away, deep stratigraphic layers are revealed. Within the overburden deposit, levels of architectural debris alternate with fluvial wash originating from the settlements south and east of the temple, often resulting in a complex, reverse-stratigraphic deposit. As excavations progress, the towering 10.00 m high south bedrock escarpment and several collapsed architectural features are revealed—telling evidence of a cataclysmic collapse attributed to the 363 CE earthquake and subsequent tremors, in which seismic events force the collapse of masonry elements and roof tiles from the temple South Corridor against the South Perimeter Wall. Figure 4.74 shows the tumbled architecture and soil overburden in the South Passageway at the start of excavation. Once fully covering the south escarpment at the temple's rear, only small sections of the South Perimeter Wall's original structure now remain *in situ*, rising two or three courses in height. In the east central section of Trench 83, six courses remain intact but dramatically slump into the passageway toward the northwest at a precipitous angle of approximately 30 degrees. This remaining section of the rear façade evidences the earthquake's powerful force and the pressure of the weight of the terraces retaining walls to the south.

On the floor of the South Passageway, portions of the original limestone pavement are recovered in fairly good condition, stretching north-south at its widest point for 1.73 m. In the

Fig. 4.73
Upper Temenos, east
sector of the South
Perimeter Wall
and the escarpment,
to southwest.

Fig. 4.74
Upper Temenos, excavation and soil overburden in the South Passageway to the southwest.

Fig. 4.75
Upper Temenos, cult niche in the Shrine Room.

east and west, the majority of the paving stones are missing, most likely robbed out during the period of abandonment in Site Phase VIII prior to the major collapse of the area. At the rear of the South Passageway is a slab-covered water channel system, measuring approximately 45.00 m in length by 0.30 m in width by 0.73 m in depth and lined with hydraulic cement, which abuts the South and Southeast Perimeter Walls. Later, additional channels are cut into the south pavement and bedrock in order to provide a supplementary water flow. Such later construction indicates that the pre-existing water systems eventually become inadequate and additional surface canalization is necessary to channel water away from the west.

In 2004 in Special Project 121 two small sondages are opened in the center of the South Passageway between and adjacent to the South Corridor Wall. Excavated to bedrock, this sondage determines that the channels end abruptly and that they do not link with any other water systems. These channels are placed in Site Phase II when they are cut into the bedrock, and to Site Phase IV when they are covered with fill for the laying of the paved floor of the South Passageway.

Baroque Room Complex Excavations

During the removal of fallen ashlars from the southwest terraces of the South Passageway in 2001, are uncovered the remains of an Anteroom and Shrine brilliantly embellished with frescoed walls, a hexagonal pavement and an empty cult niche (Figure 4.75) are uncovered. Initially explored as part of Trench 83 in 2001 and later re-examined in 2002 and 2004, the Shrine Room sheds new light on the cultic character of the rear of the temple complex. So-named for the niche which could hold a statue or *betyl* carved into its south wall, the Shrine Room partially retains the outline of its original plan with preserved wall heights between five and ten ashlar courses in its east and south. In the north, the foundations and threshold of a façade wall are present. The floor of the Shrine Room, a finely laid limestone hexagonal pavement, is custom cut after the surrounding walls are constructed and reveals localized burning in the northwest corner and

plaster collapse in the west. In Special Project 123, 2004, six hexagonal floor tiles from the hexagonal pavement in the southwest corner of the Shrine Room floor are removed to find dateable material located below them. Here are two ceramic fragments that securely date the *terminus post quem* of the floor to the first century CE. It also confirms that the Shrine Room floor is founded on bedrock for greater architectural stability. The significance of this room is its well-executed architecture and ornately decorated plaster comprised of multi-colored fragments as well as molded dentils, volutes, plain columns, and columns with vine relief decoration. Preserved to a 2.09 m height in the southeast corner of the room is a brilliantly painted *in situ* plaster panel with a purple border surrounding a red interior field.

Excavated also as part of Trench 83 is an Anteroom accessing the Shrine Room from the east. In 2001, excavations reveal the north-south rectangular plan of the Anteroom's walls, built against the bedrock escarpment in the east and south. In the west, careful investigation of the shared wall between the Anteroom and Shrine Room reveals finely carved limestone blocking ashlars across the doorway between the two rooms. The high quality of the material used and the delicate carving style of these stones indicate that this threshold is intentionally and meticulously filled in, possibly the result of structural reorganization in the area or as a measure to contain collapse debris in one of the two rooms.

A year later, excavations continuing westward in Trench 89 reveal two additional rooms west of the Shrine Room: the Baroque Room and the Southwest Settling Tank. Originally intending only to reveal the west wall and extent of the Shrine Room, excavations in 2002 undergo a drastic change in strategy following the astonishing discovery of the Baroque Room with its intriguing plaster collapse and spectacular decorative program. Figure 4.76 and Figure 4.77 portray the Baroque Room excavations. First discovered along the base of the west wall, the remains of the stucco fall are soon exposed

Fig. 4.76
Upper Temenos, Baroque
Room, stucco collapse, to
south.

Fig. 4.77
Upper Temenos, Baroque
Room during excavation,
to southeast, 2002.

across the full extent of the trench through delicate cleaning using trowels, bulb syringes, dental tools and soft brushes, Figure 4.78.[13] Overall, the stratigraphy indicates that the wall plaster falls before the collapse of the ceiling plaster, both of which are found face up in the fill. Fortunately, only two ashlars fall with the plaster, and, fortuitously, a cushion of accumulated soil no doubt assists in preserving the delicate fragments. Additionally, the collapse events of the Baroque Room propitiously render it inhospitable to future plunder and occupation, protecting its great cache of decorative stucco from subsequent domestic and industrial reuse seen in the outlying rooms of the East Plaza.

Judging from those fragments recovered during excavation, the Baroque Room walls are covered with flat painted stucco as well as three-dimensional elements with naturalistic designs. The intact plaster on the west wall indicates that the room is designed with dark-colored plain panels in midnight blue, intended perhaps to draw the eye upwards to the spectacular ceiling features decorated with bright colors and rich detail. Not only do the remains

Fig. 4.78
Upper Temenos, Baroque
Room, cleaning of the
stucco fall, 2002.

Fig. 4.79
Upper Temenos, Baroque Room painted plaster depicting a column and its capital.

Fig. 4.80
Upper Temenos, Baroque Room, stucco column decorated in relief with a vine and leaf pattern.

Fig. 4.81
Upper Temenos, Baroque Room, stucco grape cluster.

imitate architectural and natural subjects carved in the round but also some are flat-painted to resemble trompe d'oeil designs. Figure 4.79 is the photograph of painted plaster depicting the capital of a column. Three-dimensional fragments include decorative red painted stucco columns with swirling vine and leaf patterns and a few stucco grape clusters and leaves. A stucco column modeled in relief with a vine and leaf pattern is shown in Figure 4.80 and a grape cluster is shown in Figure 4.81. Most striking of all is a pomegranate carved in high relief embellishing the center of a large ceiling medallion. Figure 4.82 and Figure 4.83 are record photographs of the ceiling medallion as it was recovered. A reconstruction of the ceiling can be seen in Figure 1.28, and Figure 4.84 depicts the reconstruction of the central medallion. Surrounded by the rigidity of formalized designs seen elsewhere in the temple precinct, these pieces demonstrate freedom in artistry and execution, exhibiting an uncanny sense of play and spontaneity. Based on the discovery of Nabataean coins and pottery within and around the plaster collapse, the decorative canon of the Baroque Room can be assigned roughly to the Second Style of Pompeian Wall painting (dating between the first century BCE and the first century CE). For further information on these decorative elements, see Emily Catherine Egan's discussion in Volume III.

Fig. 4.82
Upper Temenos, Baroque Room, open
pomegranate in relief in the center from
the ceiling medallion.

Fig. 4.83
Upper Temenos, Baroque Room,
ceiling medallion *in situ*.

Fig. 4.84
Baroque Room Ceiling,
Central Medallion.

The lavish decoration of the Shrine and Baroque Rooms not only raises questions concerning the unusual artists who decorated their walls, but also the function of the rooms and the activities and intentions of the people who used them. Unlike the storage chambers under the Theater, there is no clear indication of the Shrine and Baroque Rooms' use as domestic, industrial or cultic spaces. The small size and isolated plan of both rooms, however, does suggest that only an elite and limited number of people must have enjoyed their opulence, heightening their prominence within the precinct. Clearly, the wealth of information gleaned during the excavation of the Shrine and Baroque Rooms provides an invaluable resource for the continued examination of decorative styles found in Nabataean contexts, and more specifically in considering rooms with likely semi-private functions that are associated with massive religious or civic structures.

Additionally, the rooms' complex architecture and stratigraphy offer further insight into the episodic collapses and periods of reuse at the rear of the temple complex. While largely intact to the south and east, the walls to the north and west of the Anteroom and Shrine Room are largely robbed out. For this reason, it is difficult to know how and when access to these two rooms is constructed. In contrast, the doorway between the two rooms is well preserved (Figure 4.13). In this doorway stands a low blocking wall 0.48 m in height built from finely carved limestone stones. This minimal obstruction argues that the relatively low height of this wall, and the nearly complete absence of the north wall (robbed almost entirely down to the level of its threshold), are probably attributable to the reuse of the area following a period of early collapse. At this time salvageable ashlars are removed and re-employed elsewhere, perhaps in the blocking of the nearby South Corridor doorways following the addition of the Theater in Site Phase V. Under this arrangement, these two rooms go out of use sometime soon after 106 CE.

A complete excavation of these walls reveals that the west wall of the Baroque Room abuts (rather than bonds) with the room's north wall, suggesting that the west wall is a later feature. At this time the ceiling and walls of the Baroque Room are embellished with brilliant plaster decoration and the west wall is thickened to a substantial 1.20 m in order to withstand the water pressure from the adjacent Settling Tank. The major cataclysmic event of 363 CE then puts the Settling Tank out of commission, allows for the accumulation of fill and debris, and ultimately results in the collapse of the Baroque Room's walls and decoration. As the south façade wall of the Baroque Room is founded on and against the abutting the bedrock, its added stability saves it from the fate of the adjacent Anteroom and Shrine Room, which undergo more serious earthquake shock, crumbling their plaster.

The adjacent Baroque Room displays a different pattern of collapse and reuse. Unlike the Anteroom and Shrine Room, the Baroque Room retains two full courses of its north façade wall, extending 3.67 m east-west and punctuated by a doorway, investigated in Special Project 89, 2004, 1.15 m wide opening directly into the South Passageway. While it is unclear if and how this outer doorway functioned, it is firmly identified as an original point of entry from the north. However, the west wall of the Baroque Room, clearly a secondary construction, indicates the changing use of the area. In the 2004 excavations, above the threshold and floor bedding is found a great quantity of collapsed molded decorative plaster similar to the plaster debris discovered in the Baroque Room collapse in 2002. One important discovery is a Nabataean coin found in the threshold's west posthole. Abundantly clear is that the perceived break in the north wall of the Baroque Room is a door that accessed not the West Plaza, as would be expected, but a small hexagonally paved east-west corridor, which also appears to continue on to the Shrine Room to the east.

The construction of the hexagonally paved corridor can be dated to the Grand Design construction of the Great Temple in Site Phase IV. And the Late Nabataean redesign of the precinct in Site Phase V dating to the first century CE was the time in which we place the Baroque Room collapse. Presumably after that time this area was filled with debris. In Site Phase VII, secondary construction is evidenced by the addition of a ceramic piping in a channel, after which there is abandonment, and a period of robbing ensues in Site Phase VIII. With the 363 CE earthquake there is major collapse and destruction, and in Site Phase X dated to the Byzantine period, there is the construction of the late West Walkway Wall and two low walls in the South Passageway. Site Phase XI with further collapse and the accumulation of debris follows.

Southwest Settling Tank Excavations

The Southwest Settling Tank discovered to the west of the Baroque Room is purposefully left unexcavated in 2002 to enable the full recovery of the plaster and the cleaning of the Baroque Room—a lengthy and delicate operation. But in 2004 this excavation in Trench 101 is undertaken (Figure 4.16, *supra*). The settling tank's external dimensions are north-south 5.39 m × east-west 5.34 m × 1.14 m depth. It is comprised of six to seven courses of diagonally dressed Nabataean ashlars stabilized with chinking stones, coated with hydraulic plaster.

Of primary importance is this hydraulic construction's relationship to the southwest rooms of the Upper Temenos (i.e., Anteroom, Shrine and Baroque Rooms) to the east and the Residential Quarter to the west. The excavation is of further importance in determining the relationship to other water installations identified in 2001 in the South Passageway of the Upper Temenos. An exposed edge of a lead pipe on the south face of these southwest rooms likely connects to the primary and secondary water systems that extend parallel to the south façade wall. The settling tank was constructed as an add-on in Site Phase V after the construction of the South Retaining Wall in the Grand Design of Site Phase IV, and it ceased to function in Site Phase IX when it was filled in with overburden and collapse.

West Precinct Wall, West Plaza Bedrock Installations and the East-West Support Wall

Located to the southwest of the temple proper and serving as its border to the west is the West Precinct Wall. Located to the east of the wall lies the West Plaza with its bedrock installations and the East-West Support Wall. Excavations continued to the east inside the West Precinct Wall in the West Plaza in 2005 as well as other investigations to the west outside the wall.

Backing and supporting the collapse of the West Precinct Wall's east face is the unexcavated overburden between the West Walkway Wall's west face and the West Precinct Wall's east face. As is noted *infra*, Trench 76 of 2000 and Special Project 108 are the only evidence we have for the understanding of this *terra incognita*. We do know the West Walkway Wall shows successive rebuilding, and its collapse before its final rebuilding that we see today was left *in situ*. Although leveled, clearly more questions remain about this large unexcavated area extending some north-south 40.00 m × east-west 11.00–12.00 m.

West Precinct Wall

The original purpose of the excavations of the West Precinct Wall in 2005, Special Project 110, is to clarify the use and construction technique of the West Precinct Wall by exposing the upper portion of the wall along its full length. Trench 105–106 is originally meant to be a sondage exposing the full height of the West Precinct Wall, but the discovery of the Roman-Byzantine Baths (discussed below) redirects its focus.

The length of the West Precinct Wall was cleared in trench Special Project 110 in 2005. Looking from west to east at the exposed ground level the West Precinct Wall is, at most, three courses in height, and most of these are slumped out of position with only the deteriorating rubble interior in view. Three north-south ashlars are channeled as if to hold a canalization conduit for pipes, likely meant for the Roman-Byzantine Baths. Perhaps the Baths, *infra*, required additional sources of water? The wall extends nearly 62.00 m in total length from north to south. With the excavations of the southwest temple precinct we estimate its original depth at 899.75 m elevation or 3.28 m

Fig. 4.85
Upper Temenos, continued
excavation of the west
bedrock in the West Plaza,
to south, 2004.

in preserved height. Although they do not bond, the East-West Support Wall and the West Precinct Wall are built at the same time, because both walls rest on an intentionally carved lip of bedrock that provides added support to both.

West Plaza Bedrock Installations

Trenches Special Project 96, excavated in 2004 and Special Project 108 excavated in 2005 are located in the southwest corner of the Great Temple precinct. The purpose of these trenches is to expose the south part of the temple late West Walkway Wall. Removal of the deposit of mixed collapse and intentional debris uncovers lower level architectural features including the bottom courses of the late north wall of the Baroque Room, the paved floor of the pro-

posed north corridor of the Baroque Room (*supra*), the foundation courses of the temple South Perimeter Wall and associated canalization features. The lower levels contain delicate stucco fragments, a large quantity of Nabataean pottery similar to those recovered during the excavation of the nearby Residential Quarter, and significant quantities of bone, glass, metal and stucco fragments, plus a carved limestone capital volute. Special finds include two complete Nabataean vessels, a ridged drinking cup and an unguentarium, Nabataean oil lamps, the base of a figurine, and a fragment of ridged faience.

As can be seen in Figure 4.85 and the plan shown in Figure 4.86, the excavations of Special Project 96 and Special Project 108 brought to light a number of new architectural features in the southwest corner of the Great Temple precinct, and with them a number of new theories

SP96 Southwest Bedrock

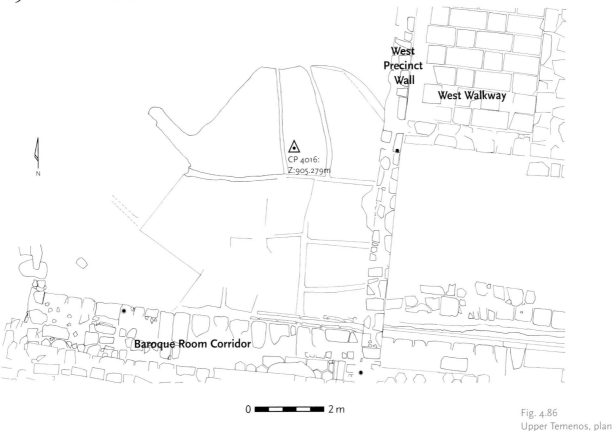

West
Precinct
Wall

West Walkway

CP 4016:
Z:905.279m

Baroque Room Corridor

0 ▰▱▰▱ 2 m

Fig. 4.86
Upper Temenos, plan
of the southwest bedrock.

concerning the construction and use of this area. The most striking features are the quarrying cuts, prominently positioned in the central area of the trench on an elevated bedrock plateau. As yet unseen at the Great Temple, quarrying cuts such as these offer valuable insight into the early construction of the temple and argue strongly that the stone used to build the temple originated from both local and more distant sources. The cuts are made in a rough grid pattern, each set approximately 1.10 m apart. In antiquity, each cut would have been filled with wet wood that would expand, splitting large blocks of raw sandstone loose from the bedrock. For contemporary construction parallels, one can see a similar style of grid quarrying nearby in Beidha and on the bedrock outcrop east of the pediment of ed-Deir.

Immediately west of the quarrying cuts are a second group of intriguing features: three bedrock caves. Aligned north to south, the three caves hug the edge of the bedrock plateau, each opening to the west. In Special Project 108 these caves are excavated. Like the caves in the Residential Quarter, located to the immediate west, these three caves show evidence of human manipulation. In the floor of the south cave are two square cuts, one near the cave's entrance and another smaller in the rear north corner, presumably used to anchor posts to support either a doorway or a ceiling. In the central cave, the north bedrock partition wall is chiseled into a doorjamb. In the north cave, only partially excavated, a carved ledge is visible, presumably to support a roof structure. This evidence of chisel working, combined with large quantities of ceramic and bone material, sheds light on the early use of the southwest area of the precinct prior to the Great Temple's construction. Once plans for the temple are set and quarrying begins, the caves are shaved down and the remaining cavities of the south and central caves are filled with large unhewn stones. The north cave, however, is carefully filled with stacked hewn sandstone ashlars.

A third interesting feature exposed during the excavation of Special Project 96 is the so-called Shrine and Baroque Room North Corridor discussed above.

The East-West Support Wall

During the excavations of Special Project 108 it becomes clear that the West Plaza architecture is much more extensive than had been believed, and in fact the evidence of the East-West Support Wall is unexpected. The East-West Support Wall is found at an opening elevation of 904.849 m and closed at an elevation of 901.549 m. It is 12.00 m in length by 2.00 m in width, and 5.10 m in height. It is composed of five to eight courses built from ashlars, but the lowest two courses are potentially from a different, earlier building phase. The foundations are set on bedrock, and the walls are built of two parallel casemate walls with the center filled with rubble. The 2005 excavations provide additional insight into the temple building program. Through the exposure of the juncture between the West Precinct Wall and the East-West Support Wall, it becomes clear that both walls are originally constructed at the same time in Site Phase I and therefore are intrinsically linked.

The East-West Upper Temenos Support Wall, which in itself is a monumental construction, is designed and constructed with the express purpose of providing a solid foundation for the temple platform.

The West Upper Temenos Sondage

Parallel to the East Plaza, excavations in the Upper Temenos west in 2000 open a sondage, Trench 76, just west of the West Walkway Wall. Oriented east-west, this rectilinear test trench measures 3.00 m in width by 11.00 m in length

and is excavated to an approximate depth of 1.78 m. The goal for the excavation of this area is threefold: to locate, further expose and delineate the West Precinct Wall; to locate and expose a western colonnade, if one should exist; and to remove sequential horizontal layers of the trench in 0.25 m increments until sterile soil is reached. With a projected depth of deposit in the range of 7.00 to 8.00 m, work commences with the rediscovery of evidence of canalization in the form of a plaster-enclosed pipe extending along a section of the far western wall. As excavations progress, a large quantity of boulders and ashlars uncovered as well as heavy overburden from the collapse of the temple West Walkway Wall, completely congesting the area between it and the West Precinct Wall. When it becomes obvious that the collapsed wall debris will continue up to the western border of Trench 76, the decision is made to close the trench.

While architectural debris dominates the area, numerous Special Finds are also recorded here, among which are two complete Nabataean ceramic vessels: a small bowl dating to 100 CE (Schmid 2000 Abb. 97, Phase 3a–c Group 8 Abb. 57 or 58) and a juglet (Schmid 2000 Phase 2a, Abb. 288) dating between 50 BCE and 20 CE. Lamps encompass the Nabataean, Roman and Byzantine periods, large amounts of stucco, and several finely carved temple architectural fragments indicate that at some point in the Roman/Byzantine period, this area witnesses a catastrophic wall collapse and is subsequently used as a dump. Phasing the southwest features, including the West Precinct Wall, the East-West Support Wall, the West Plaza Bedrock Installations, and the West Upper Temenos Sondage is now clearer because we have excavated to their founding levels. Pre Site Phase I is when the North Cave is chiseled out. In Site Phase I the bedrock lip that supports the East-West Support Wall and the West Precinct Wall is prepared, the East-West Support Wall and the West Precinct Wall are constructed, and the North Cave is purposefully filled in with construction fill.

Site Phases IV–V find human activities in the area, and in Site Phase VI there is sedimentation. Site Phase VII is possibly the phase during which the ceramic pipe was inserted into the West Precinct Wall. Site Phase IX is represented by major destruction and intentional fill. In Site Phase X the West Walkway Wall is reconstructed, and in Site Phase XI there is the accumulation of wash and debris.

We now turn to the features lying to the west beyond the West Perimeter Wall, including, the Residential Quarter, the Cistern-Reservoir and the Roman-Byzantine Baths. Moving from south to north, we will consider these features in that order.

Residential Quarter Excavations

From the west sectors of the site (the plan appears in Figure 4.24) that might not at first glance appear to be integral to the site development, we discover a wealth of information, including the Residential Quarter, the Cistern-Reservoir and the Roman-Byzantine Baths. With the 2000–2005 excavations of the west sector there is a recovery that few would have dared to predict.

What accounts for the delay in our excavation of this sector of the precinct? One reason is that since the inception of the excavations we had to concentrate on the east sector of the precinct, so that backfill could be removed to the west. The structure of the precinct is such that there is no outlet to the east, and the west, although vulnerable to the ravages of excavation, had to serve for the staging of soil removal.

In 2002, in order to protect and not impede the excavations of the Baroque Room's spectacular plaster fall, Trench 89 is extended an additional 12.00 m to the west into an area we identify as Trench 94, the Residential Quarter. A 2004 photograph is shown in Figure 4.25, and photograph Figure 4.87 displays the excavations at the close of the season. Situated outside and beyond the line of the West Perimeter Wall, preliminary excavations in this area successfully uncover a series of caves and masonry rooms serving as households within the urban core of Petra. Figure 4.88 is a look through the Residential Quarter to Cave 2, and Figure 4.89 is the view of the Residential Quarter from the caves above it. Constructed over the course of at least six distinct stages of development, the character of this complex changes from simple domestic dwellings to a more complicated schema of apartments. As revealed during

Fig. 4.87
Upper Temenos, Residential Quarter looking into Cave 2 2002, to northwest.

Fig. 4.88
Upper Temenos, Residential
Quarter looking through to
Cave 2, to south.

excavation, the earliest construction stage for the Residential Quarter is similar to the temple preparation phase, consisting of the cutting and leveling of the bedrock. For the temple, the bedrock is dramatically scaled back in order to create the massive platform for the structure. The bedrock cutting for the Residential Quarter, however, is less invasive. Those who build and live here make use of what nature provides rather than undertaking significant changes. In structure, Cave 1 is intentionally cut in a cubic configuration, whereas Cave 2 is a natural bedrock cavity necessitating only minimal manipulation visible in a cut floor, small niche and beam slots for a ceiling structure. The small Upper Cave is also a natural geologic cavity, modified only by a basin and channel cut into the floor for water catchment. Figure 4.90 shows the temple in the background from the Residential Quarter caves. Room 3, near the mouth of the complex contains additional cuts for water channels, but the bedrock itself is otherwise minimally manipulated. Outside of Room 8 in Cave 2, the bedrock suddenly falls away, necessitating the buildup of the floor in this room to create a level surface. Compared

with the considerable amount of labor put into the construction of the temple, the Residential Quarter's minimalist construction may be due to lack of interest, simpler needs or limited economic and/or human resources.

Following the preparation of the Residential Quarter's bedrock is the construction of the cave façades enclosing them for habitation. A modern parallel for this can be commonly found in the façades built by the Bedouin onto caves and tombs in order to convert them into living quarters. To provide a surface against which architectural elements could be constructed, the façades of Caves 1 and 2 are carved, and, in a later stage, reinforced to buttress new features. At this later time, Caves 1 and 2 are joined making them part of a larger domestic complex or apartment, and a long north-south wall abutting the Cave 2 façade is constructed. The combination of these two caves and the addition of Rooms 1, 2 and 3 convert this area into a single unit, with Room 2 serving as the central north-south corridor connecting the rooms with an entrance in the north. Here, a rotating grain mill (Figure 4.91) is discovered *in situ*, standing as if ready for this year's wheat harvest. Outside of this enclosure are three chambers, Rooms 4, 5 and 6, all of which are later additions. Room 6 appears to be a vestibule, providing access to both the east and west domestic spaces and covered by a single roof supported by arches surmounting two columns. While the overall function of Room 6 is yet to be determined, it is arguably a key transitional area, providing access from the west Upper Temenos. It is also possible that there may be more domestic architecture on a lower terrace obscured by debris.

Also revealed during the excavation of Trench 94 is the eastern portion of a separate house/apartment to the west, consisting of Rooms 7 and 8. Unfortunately, the excavators are unable to uncover the entirety of this struc-ture due to time constraints. We do know, however, that Rooms 7 and 8 are partitioned with interior walls, doors and windows, and that a meter of bedding is laid to raise the floor. One observation regarding the quality of construction visible in all of these architectural features is that the masonry is least elaborate in the earliest construction phases. Later, the Residential Quarter ashlars are well cut and expertly dressed and the area is appointed with arches and columns.

In 2004 seven steps connected by walls and architecture to both the Residential Quarter and the Settling Tank are recovered in Special Project 94 indicating a west entrance to the Residential Quarter (Figure 4.26) In 2005 Special Project 111 involves the removal of these steps to test the stratigraphy, and they are found to be built on layers of rubble and soil fill with layers of wadi mud directly underneath. Phasing

Fig. 4.90
Upper Temenos, Residential Quarter with the Great Temple in the background.

places the construction of the steps to Site Phase IV, the Grand Design.

Perhaps the greatest difficulty encountered in the excavation of the Residential Quarter is the appearance of multiple water channels—in the Small Upper Cave as well as in Cave 1 and Rooms 1, 2, 3, 4 and 6. The major water installations in the east (noted earlier) may or may not be related to these channels, particularly in the case of those found in Room 6, which do not show any clear relationship to nearby systems. It seems plausible that such channels are installed at different times. Nevertheless, because they could not be fully excavated, it is impossible to determine their phasing. Presumably, they connect to the adjacent southwest Settling Tank, or to the canalization of the South Passageway to the north. In Room 4 of the cave complex, yet another puzzling water installation is a limestone-paved sluice gate lined with hydraulic cement that must have served for water collection. It is currently unclear, however, how it might operate, but it must bear some relationship to the Cistern-Reservoir found just below the Residential Quarter façade (*infra*).

Overall, the existence of these cave households reveals the unique urban planning employed at the rear of the temple complex, characterized by the use of compacted, concentrated structures and an organic building plan, possibly representing part of a larger domestic zone extending south to the Swiss-excavated Nabataean villas of Ez-Zantur. Judging from the remains, the exact date of these structures is unknown. Containing upwards of 32,349 recorded pottery fragments,[14] among which are a number of complete Nabataean vessels, it is possible that the area is in use before the Great Temple is even constructed. Pottery and numismatics from the temple and its surroundings are contemporaneous with the lowest sealed contexts of Rooms 3 and 7, indicating that the Residential Quarter was inhabited while the temple was in use. And, as with the Great Temple, these residential units are most probably destroyed or compromised during the 363 CE earthquake of Site Phase IX as is seen in the collapse of the rooms to the east and the dramatic south to north deposition of debris.

Fig. 4.91
Upper Temenos, Residential Quarter, basalt rotating grain mill. Seq. No. 94209, Upper Temenos Trench 94, Locus 74. Height 32 cm, diameter 40 cm.

The unforeseen and novel discovery of Nabataean dwellings in such close proximity to the Great Temple offers insight into the diverse character of architectural forms in Nabataean Petra. Indeed, this discovery and the evidence of the newly excavated villas next to the Qasr al-Bint and at Ez Zantur (Bignasca et al. 1996, and Kolb and Keller 2001) on the hillside above the Great Temple indicate that the urban environment is densely populated, and due to space constraints houses are pressed close to these precincts. As more civic and religious structures are excavated, it seems likely that more domestic spaces will be recovered in close association.

Now we turn first to the Cistern-Reservoir and then to the Roman-Byzantine Baths.

The Cistern-Reservoir[15]

In 2005 the area of the West Precinct Wall is further examined in the south of Special Project 110. This special project involves the discovery and excavation of the Cistern-Reservoir of the Roman-Byzantine Bath Complex (Figure 4.92) extending to the west adjacent to the Residential Quarter.

The monumental Cistern-Reservoir measures 38.8 square meters by an average of

SP110 Cistern-Reservoir Plan

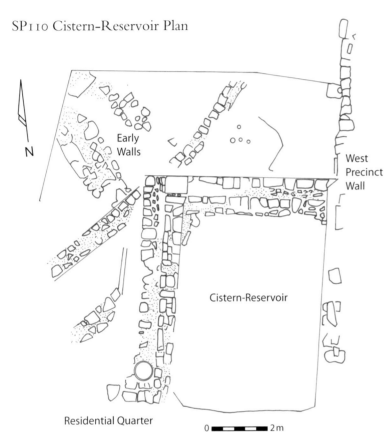

Early Walls

N

West Precinct Wall

Cistern-Reservoir

Residential Quarter

0 ▬▬▬ 2 m

Fig. 4.92
Upper Temenos plan of the Cistern-Reservoir

1.96 m in depth, which would have held approximately 19,571.97 gallons of water. On the north and west are walls that were repaired in antiquity. Resting beside the west wall is a monumental stone basin (Figure 4.93). With the discovery of the Roman-Byzantine Bath Complex to its north, we hypothesize that this feature may have served as the *natatio* or swimming pool for the baths. Future excavators will want to discover more about this feature's functional analysis and confirm if this is a probability.[16]

Perhaps as important is the discovery of a series of pre-Cistern-Reservoir walls that indicate how the area is manipulated and used by earlier builders. In its pre-Cistern-Reservoir days, the organization of carved out features and built walls are signs that it serves as a pre-Nabataean or early Nabataean residential area. The material culture is edifying, for the most part because of the recovery of quantities of bones, ceramics and coins. Exceptionally appealing is ceramic infant feeder/lamp filler in the shape of a hedgehog (Figure 4.94) recovered from the earliest deposits. Also noteworthy is a stray find, the sculpted head of a male deity, (Figure 4.95), found among the blocks of the West Precinct Wall.[17]

The Roman-Byzantine Bath Complex[18]

The Roman-Byzantine Baths undergo extensive excavations in 2005 and 2006. All of the 2005–2006 trenches are located just to the west of the West Precinct Wall and the West Exedra, and the excavated bath area covers some 32 m north-south × 28.40 m east-west, or 908.80 m². The bath plan is reproduced in Figure 4.96, and here in Figure 4.97 is shown the north Platform, possibly a main entry for the baths. (The dimensions for each architectural component are listed in Note 1 at the beginning of this chapter.)

The 2005 Trench 105–106 recovers the "Well Room," the small Court, the marble clad Vestibule-*Frigidarium* and the Settling Tank. In 2006 four trenches are excavated exposing other features of the complex, including the Platform in Trench 121, the apsed *caldarium* in Trench 126, and in Trench 127 a second *caldarium*, the *praefurnium*, a "Splash Pool," the *tepidarium* or *laconicum*, and a Service Passage. Trench 120 architecture includes the small Cistern, Bath-

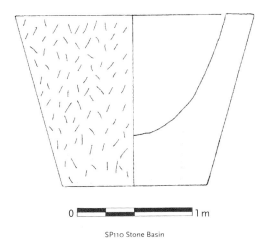

Fig. 4.93
Upper Temenos limestone basin beside the Cistern-Reservoir

0 [scale bar] 1 m

SP110 Stone Basin

Fig. 4.94
Upper Temenos, infant feeder in the shape of a hedgehog found in the Cistern-Reservoir, 2005. Cat. No. 05-DL-60, Seq. No. SP110376 Special Project 110 Locus 46. Of 2/5YR6/6 light red ware. Length 7.08 cm, width 2.88 cm, thickness 0.46 cm, width of perforation in snout 0.04 cm. Small molded zoomorphic vessel. It has a small filling hole on its upper surface and it has a perforated snout. Possibly lamp, lamp filler or infant feeding vessel, showing no signs of use.

Fig. 4.95
Upper Temenos, head of a deity found in the West Precinct Wall. Cat. No. 05-S-8. Seq. No. SP110195. SP110 Locus 16. L. 14.83 cm, Width 13.98 cm, Thickness 6.07 cm. Small sculptured relief in the Hellenistic style with curling hair, moustache and beard, with the eyes gazing heavenward. Nose worn away and head broken at neck either accidentally or intentionally. The back of the head is flattened which would seem to indicate the placement of the figure against a wall or on flat surface.

Petra Great Temple
Roman–Byzantine Bath Complex

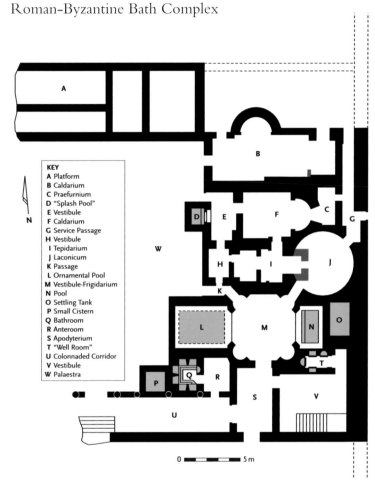

KEY

A Platform
B Caldarium
C Praefurnium
D "Splash Pool"
E Vestibule
F Caldarium
G Service Passage
H Vestibule
I Tepidarium
J Laconicum
K Passage
L Ornamental Pool
M Vestibule-Frigidarium
N Pool
O Settling Tank
P Small Cistern
Q Bathroom
R Anteroom
S Apodyterium
T "Well Room"
U Colonnaded Corridor
V Vestibule
W Palaestra

0 ▬▬ 5 m

Fig. 4.96
Upper Temenos,
Roman-Byzantine Bath Plan.

room (toilet), a hypothesized *Apodyterium*, and the Colonnaded Corridor. Trench 125 is devoted to a more complete examination of the "Well Room" and its subterranean features.

Trench 121 measures 9.00 m north-south × 13.00 m east-west and uncovers the Platform (A on the plan). Found here is the north wall of the bath complex and within a rectangular paved plaza composed of white sandstone flagstones bisected by a foundation wall, indicating there is a subdivision of activity. Logically this Platform serves as the one of the entries into the baths. Shown in Figure 4.97, at the east end of this Platform are the remains of *opus sectile* floor and revetment slabs indicating that there is at least one as yet undiscovered hot room here—either a *caldarium* or *tepidarium*.

Adjacent to Trench 121 is a *caldarium* (shown as B on the plan), in Trench 126, measuring 4.55 m north-south × 13.00 m east-west. Here is a hypocaust chamber with a suspended floor superimposed on two vaults constructed at the same level as the hypocausts. These features along with both round and square hypocaust piers are illustrated in Figure 4.98.[19] Adjacent to Trench 126 is Trench 127, with a lower level

Fig. 4.97
Upper Temenos, Roman-Byzantine Bath Platform to the east.

Caldarium with hypocausts

Fig. 4.98
Caldarium in Trench 126 to west showing hypocausts *in situ.*

passage between the north *caldarium* and the
Trench 127 *caldarium* shown in Figure 4.99.
Trench 127 measures 9.00 m north-south ×
16.00 m east-west and is comprised of two
parallel east-west long rectangular rooms (D-J
on the plan). These are identified as a *caldarium*,
a possible *praefurnium*, the main heating source
for the baths, plus a *tepidarium* or a large
once domed *laconicum* shown in Figure 4.100.
Access from the *tepidarium* and *laconicum* takes
the bather-client into the elegant Vestibule-
Frigidarium excavated in 2005 and shown in
Figure 4.101.

Trench 125 measures 1.93 m north-south ×
2.52 m east-west and it is conclusively identified
as a "Well Room" (T on the plan and shown in
Figure 4.32). As can be seen in Figure 4.32 there
are two hemispherical niches plus two rectangular niches used for drawing water and an intricate
substructure of arches and columns supporting
the room floor. A subterranean water conduit

Fig. 4.99
Lower level passageway
from the *caldarium* to the
praefurnium.

Fig. 4.100
The Roman-Byzantine Bath
tepidarium to the west.

system is recovered leading from the east and exiting to the west. Its tunneled conduit is followed by the excavators at a 2.00 m depth, underground, for a 9.00 m stretch[20] who find it clogged with debris, but suggest it drains just to the north of the Colonnaded Corridor.[21] Among other important small finds found in this conduit is an exquisite delicate Roman head vase illustrated in Figure 4.102.

Excavation in progress is shown in Figure 4.103 in Trench 120 measuring 13.5 m north-south × 17.00 m east-west. This is the formal, elegant area of the bath complex (L to V on the plan). Besides the Vestibule-*Frigidarium* excavated in 2005, the 2006 field season exposes several rooms including a Colonnaded Corridor along the south of the complex (U on the plan), an Anteroom leading into a Bathroom (toilet) shown in Figure 4.31 (R and Q on the plan), adjacent to a Settling Tank (P on the plan) covered with hydraulic plaster. The focal point of this area is the central Ornamental Pool (L on the plan) that possibly serves as an elegant fountain, adjacent to the marble clad Vestibule-*Frigidarium* (M on the plan).

INTERNAL FLOW PATTERN

From the Roman Road, the bath complex entrance can be accessed in the north from the West Entry Staircase, which, theoretically, is linked to the Platform. As yet unknown is how the complex is accessed from the west since that region of the baths is largely unexplored. There is, however, an efficient logic in the arrangement of the rooms that indicates a flow pattern for their usage. It is assumed that most visitors could also enter the complex from the Colonnaded Corridor and progress either to the Bathroom or to change their clothes in the hypothesized *Apodyterium*. From there the bather could move into the Vestibule-*Frigidarium* or perhaps relax beside the Ornamental Pool. From the Vestibule also there is passage either into the *laconicum* to the east, or through the Passageway (K on the plan) into the Vestibules (H and E) to gain entry into the *caldaria*. The bather might elect to take a dip in the "Splash Pool" (D on the plan) where there is one option for cooling off or return instead to the

Fig. 4.101
The Roman-Byzantine Bath View to the Vestibule-*Frigidarium* to east.

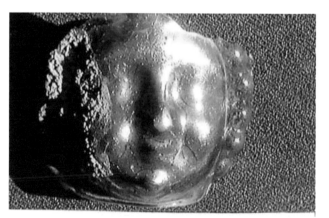

Fig. 4.102
Molded glass head vase from the "Well Room" water passage, (Cat. No. 06-GL-1); Small head vase in green iridescent glass, framed by clear molded glass "hair" in the form of bubbles, which is only present on the left hand side of the molded face. The hair was originally green, but has since flaked off. The face is that of a young child or putto. The remainder of the vase is missing, Length 3.83 cm, Width 3.56 cm, Thickness 0.06 cm, Weight 7.6 grams. This head vase compares nicely with Cat. No. 94-G-4 (Joukowsky 1998:334 Fig. 6.129, Seq. No. 5114) found in the 1994 West Exedra Trench 5 Locus 37 excavations.

Fig. 4.103
The Roman-Byzantine Bath excavations in progress, showing the Ornamental Pool to the left, with the Vestibule-*Frigidarium* behind, the Anteroom with the "Well Room" behind and the Colonnaded Corridor to the right.

Fig. 4.104
Nabataean round lamp found in a closed context under the Ornamental Pool Room. Cat. No. 06-L-5 is a locally made round lamp with ovolos impressed on the shoulder rim with a raised un-perforated handle, slightly concave base, a sooty rounded spout, and a depressed discus with small central filling hole. Length 8.22 cm, Diameter 6.36 cm, Height 3.29 cm. This lamp is dated to the last third of the CE first century and offers us a *terminus post quem* for the building of the baths.

0   5 cm

06-L-5

Fig. 4.105
Partial Greek inscription from the "Splash Pool." The most complete panel of two joining fragments, Cat. No. 06-S-13, is the largest (the left edge is finished, Length 0.228 m, Width 0.168 m, Thickness 0.0237 m

Vestibule-*Frigidarium* for a plunge in the pool there. Thereafter refreshments are served in the small Court (V on the plan) beside the hypothesized *Apodyterium* (S on the plan), which adjoins the "Well Room" (T on the plan). Steps then are retraced to the *Apodyterium* to exit through the Colonnaded Corridor (U on the plan), or there is the choice to return to the Palaestra for discussions or for more physical activity. An alternative plan might be is to stroll some 40 meters south to enjoy the *natatio* or swimming pool (hypothesized) identified *supra* as the Cistern-Reservoir.

ARTIFACTS FROM THE
ROMAN-BYZANTINE BATHS

Artifacts from the 2005–2006 excavations of the baths are prolific. Besides the obvious importance of the architectural features revealed, artifacts include 2,273 architectural fragments, the majority of which are ashlars found in the collapse layers of the trench, but also there are significant amounts of marble *opus sectile* tile and revetment fragments, indicating that all the public rooms are marble clad. There are a number of interesting artifacts recovered and cataloged finds number 159, including nine faïence beads, some 23 glass beads, and added to these are 112 coins.[22]

Two important lamp fragments (Cat. Nos. 06-L-4 and 06-L-5) are found buried in the earliest deposits under the Ornamental Pool Passageway. Cat. No. 06-L-4 is a Nabataean volute lamp type B with two rosettes of four circles and one rosette with nine petals at the rear of the rim, dated by D. G. Barrett (2004:98) from the beginning of the first century CE through the reign of Malichus II (40–70 CE), and a round Nabataean lamp, Cat. No. 06-L-5, can be seen in Figure 4.104. These two lamps are found in a closed context and offer us a *terminus post quem* for the building of the baths.

Most special of the 2006 finds are ten marble Greek inscribed fragments recovered from the "splash pool."[23] The most complete panel, Cat. No. 06-S-13, is the largest and is illustrated in Figure 4.105). However, of extreme importance is the intact, footed sandstone *stele* illustrated in Figure 4.106, which is unearthed in the Colonnaded Corridor in secondary reuse blocking the water passage from the "Well

Room."[24] A provisional assessment of this inscription by Traianos Gagos of the University of Michigan suggests that the name inscribed on the *stele* is one Marcus Aelius Aurelius Theon Serenus who also appears in two inscriptions from Bostra as the governor of the province of Arabia from 253 to 259 CE. Further interpretation will help us understand more about this individual and whether he governed the province from Petra or Bostra. This places this inscription's date to the mid-third century CE, and its reuse as a block in the water channel to sometime later.

DATING THE BATHS

Of primary importance is establishing a chronology for the construction and destruction events that shaped the baths. The earliest event is the construction of the West Precinct Wall, which took place as a key component of the site preparation in Site Phase I (first century BCE). This massive wall is, we conclude, the exterior boundary of the Temple precinct, defining the extent of the inner temple precinct. The following stage of construction, shortly thereafter, is the erection of a major Nabataean east-west wall against which the Colonnaded Corridor is built. It is illustrated in Figure 4.103. This wall, which clearly abuts the West Precinct Wall, is sizeable and of a well-built construction extending across the entire excavated precinct, and we posit it continues further to the west. Perhaps this wall is a precinct terrace wall that can be assigned to Site Phase IV of the Great Temple phasing, as part of the Nabataean Grand Design, suggesting that the scope of the Grand Design extended beyond the confines of the temple precinct and possibly linked to other structures and complexes further to the west.

The material culture and architecture suggest that the bath installations—*caldaria*, *tepidarium*, *laconicum*, "splash pool," and the features present in the formal rooms are constructed at the same time as a unit. Reflected in the archaeological record are alterations, and these changes occur either as a result of the additional requirements for the weakened architecture itself, or as a result of the earth tremors and the devastating notorious earthquake that takes place on 19 May 363 CE. It is then that frequent modifications take place with the filling in of vaults, the additions

Fig. 4.106
Roman Inscription from the Colonnaded Court. Intact sandstone inscription, Cat. No. 06-S-18 (Seq. No. 120A050), Height 0.63 m, Width 0.31.5 m, Thickness 0.18 m) was unearthed in the Colonnaded Corridor in secondary reuse as an architectural element to block the water passage. This inscribed honorific is composed of a complete footed *stele* with well-dressed surfaces. The surface is inscribed on both the upper and lower surface (foot).

of flooring and the renovation of some of the walls. This earthquake and its tremors so disrupt the cultural life in Petra and, in particular, the bath architecture that the site never fully recovers, and it appears that some of the bath rooms are never fully rebuilt. The earthquakes most certainly contribute to the devastation of a more impoverished community, and finally put an end to the Great Temple precinct as well.

In conclusion, the sequence of the Great Temple Baths is of several consecutive stages. It is in the Petra Great Temple Site Phase VI the baths are constructed,[25] probably soon after the annexation in 106 CE but possibly as early as ca. 70 CE, and are in use until the 19 July 363 CE, the earthquake of Site Phase X. After this earthquake there is a striking change in the character of the baths. Some rooms are no longer used, doorways are narrowed or closed off completely, and there is a dramatic difference between the late Nabataean working bath and the features that remain in use.[26] The final disaster and collapse takes place with the Site Phase XI earthquake dated to 9 July 551 CE when the site is completely and finally destroyed. It is difficult to fix a precise date for the termination for the baths' last use, although it is unlikely that they are in use much beyond the mid sixth century CE and the site's final abandonment. By the early sixth century CE when Petra experiences a general slump, the bath complex is completely abandoned, for the sterility of the upper bath deposits without signs of habitation or use suggests abandonment and a subsequent desertion of the bath site. To summarize, the Great Temple bath system is in use for some 400 or more years, from ca. 70 to 551 CE, and the period of active use is gauged from ca. 70 to 363 CE, a period of less than 300 years.

Baths reflect public traditions and the everyday lifestyles of the time, and the Great Temple baths suggest that during the later Nabataean and early Roman period there was a well-organized society with a firm economic structure. The building of the Roman-Byzantine Baths at the Great Temple is a large-scale venture for the Petraeans whom we imagine hold their own concept of a planned city and the heart of the city with the Great Temple as its monumental cult and administrative center. A large sector of the local community must have appreciated these extraordinary baths and now they should be viewed as a part of the architectural programmatic layout of the city.

Before the Great Temple is destroyed the site prospers with the advent of the baths, (which for our team of archaeologists becomes an unexpected reality). The baths are configured as an up-to-date facility that propagandize their city as a significant urban center. The concept of the Great Temple baths represents a Petraean political, social and economic development borrowed from a pre-existing Hellenistic-

Roman urban tradition. (The Herodian Baths at Jericho, *inter alia*, provide a worthy example.) The Petraeans co-opt the bath prototype, and select the Great Temple's massive West Perimeter Wall as a location for such a complex. The Roman-Byzantine Baths against the West Precinct Wall do not disrupt the architectural or artistic appearance of the Great Temple. Their placement completely separates them from the temple area, and the ritual focal point of the temple is unchanged. The building of the Roman-Byzantine Baths at the Great Temple is a large-scale venture for a well-planned bath system suggesting a great degree of continuity from the late Nabataean to the early Roman period.

Conclusions

The challenges and idiosyncratic remains found during the excavation of the Upper Temenos grant our team exposure to a compelling array of archaeological features. The uncovering of the East Perimeter Wall, its Rooms A and B and East Plaza, the East Plaza Great Cistern, the Sword Deity carved into the South Perimeter Wall and the associated South Passageway emphasizes the remarkable quality of Nabataean workmanship and artistry in the architecture of their capital city. At the southwest corner of the precinct, the Baroque Room Complex with its Anteroom, Shrine Room, Baroque Room and Settling Tank attest to one of the most fascinating and powerful ornamental developments in the history of Nabataean art. In contrast to the Great Temple, the character of this area is private with intricately embellished rooms to be enjoyed by a select few.

The extensive Residential Quarter attests to the unusual allocation of domestic space within the fabric of Petra's city center. Judging from the proximity of these dwellings to the temple proper, these are likely the residences of the families who service the Great Temple, who employ shrewd planning to tap the water resources to the south and west of the precinct. We can hypothesize that initially artisans and technicians who are employed for building and or creative functions like the master craftsmen who created the extraordinary Baroque Room decoration occupy this quarter. Later, perhaps, families who provided on-going services for

Great Temple activities occupy the Residential Quarter. If the 32,000 fragments of pottery recovered from this area is any indication, these rooms are inhabited for a lengthy period of time. A vibrant site, the Petra Great Temple complex no doubt requires residents to work and live nearby.

The Brown University excavations have made progress in associating events and the archaeological evidence at the Great Temple. The blueprint of a small bath plan, a *balneum*, seems to have been conceived and developed in the initial phases before the annexation of Petra by Rome. The Nabataeans who resided in Petra, the nucleus of what would be subsumed by Rome, constructed these modest baths as a large-scale venture that represent their city as a significant urban center. This bath expansion, resting up against the west boundary of the Petra Great Temple, is a Hellenistic and most particularly a pervasive Roman tradition (grand baths cannot be disassociated from the Romans). The indigenous Petraeans borrow the Roman bath prototype, and adopt it, and the Great Temple is selected as the site for the public baths. In its initial phase, the concept of the Great Temple baths is closely related to baths of the time, representing a Petraean political, social and economic development borrowed from a Roman urban tradition. Now the terminus of the Nabataean rule and the beginning of the Roman period at Petra cannot be seen in isolation, for it is but one aspect of a larger historic picture that recovers some definition at the Petra Great Temple site and for the Nabataeans themselves.

Overall, the architectural remains of the Upper Temenos remain provocative, the unique function and plan of each area finding its own place in the complex design of the tantalizing site.

Notes

1.
In the following Figure 4.96 Key for the Roman-Byzantine Bath Complex, internal dimensions for specific rooms are given. Specific dimensions for features can be found in the trench reports which are on the World Wide Web at <http://www.opencontext.org>.

A Platform 5.45 m north-south × 14.25 m east-west

B *Caldarium* 5.22 m NW wall 5.00 m NE wall × 11.70 north wall, 11.45 m south wall

C *Praefurnium* 3.26 m north-south × 1.60 m east-west

D "Splash Pool" 1.40 m north-south × 1.20 m east-west

E Vestibule 4.06 m north-south × 2.15 m east-west

F *Caldarium* 2.82 and 3.98 m north-south × 6.15 m east-west

G Service Passage 13.20 m north-south × 1.30 m/1.80 m east-west

H Vestibule 1.98 m north-south × 1.20 m east-west

I *Tepidarium* 1.55 m and 3.55 m north-south × 4.20 m east-west

J *Laconicum* diameter 5.17 m

K Passage 0.84 m × 2.74 m and 2.80 m east-west

L Ornamental Pool 3.50 m north-south × 5.08 m east-west

M Vestibule-*Frigidarium* 5.70 m north-south × 5.80 m east-west

N Pool 2.25 m north-south × 1.47 m east-west

O Settling Tank 0.80 m north-south × 1.50 m east-west

P Small Cistern 1.75 m north-south × 1.75 m east-west

Q Bathroom (toilet) 2.76 m north-south × 2.78 m east-west

R Anteroom 2.48 m north-south × 2.98 m east-west

S *Apodyterium* 5.54 m north-south × 3.25 m east-west

T "Well Room" 1.84 m north-south × 3.12 m east-west

U Colonnaded Corridor 3.05 m north-south × ca. 13.70 m east-west

V Court 7.15 m north-south × 6.01 m east-west

2.
The Forecourt contains both the Central Stairs and the subterranean canalization system.

3.
Due to conflicting evidence, the function of this room remains uncertain. While its vaulted construction and plastered surface show parallels with cisterns such as that at al-Humayma, its comparatively poor construction and the marked absence of connecting canalization suggest the possibility of an additional or alternative use.

4.
This water probably comes from the 'Ain Brak, and some of it may originate in the 'Ain Musa.

5.
The function of this feature as a corridor, however, remains uncertain. Currently, the south and east portions of the hexagonal paving are obscured by the late north wall of the Baroque Room and late temple West Walkway Wall respectively. Further complicating the picture is the noted absence of hexagonal paving to the west of the small step, which marks the boundary between the North Cor-

ridor and the Shrine Room proper. Located in what should be the northwest corner of the Shrine Room, the irregular sandstone paving in this area was initially thought to be a type of sub floor bedding. A brief sondage beneath the hexagonal pavement in the southwest corner of the Shrine Room (*supra*), however, revealed that the pavers rest directly on packed soil and are held together by white plaster. There is no stone sub floor. As such, the possibility remains that the perceived corridor is a unique feature, stylistically but not functionally related to the adjacent Shrine Room.

6.
The opening elevation for these caves varies from 905.12 m for the North Cave to 905.30 m for the South Cave. The North Cave measures 1.46 m north-south × 1.65 m east-west; the Central Cave measures 2.28 m north-south × 1.95 m east-west, and the largest, the South Cave, measures 2.60 m north-south × 4.35 m east-west. Surely these caves predate the quarrying and leveling of the West Plaza bedrock.

7.
These steps are removed, analyzed and replaced in 2005 to determine the dating for their construction.

8.
An alternative possibility argues that the Lower Temenos Central Staircase, completely excavated in 2004 (originally constructed during Site Phase II), remains in use for some time in conjunction with the lateral staircases until it is overfilled by the buildup for the temple Forecourt and fronted by the Lower Temenos Retaining Wall at a later date in Site Phase IV.

9.
Masons' marks can be seen in Figures 7.7 and 7.8, p. 357.

10.
J. McKenzie (1990, 116–117) states: "The Type 1 Nabataean capitals are the blocked out form of the Type 1 floral capitals… although examples of this occur in Alexandria it is the custom of their use as the finished capital which is characteristically Nabataean.…"

11.
This burial is removed en bloc with its jar, and in 2004 the remains are analyzed by Megan A. Perry, physical anthropologist, and published by Perry and Joukowsky, "A Roman Period Infant Jar Burial from Petra," in *ADAJ*, 2005.

12.
In the early days of excavation we took our tea breaks under the juniper tree pictured here. The overburden of fill was at the same level as the tree.

13.
During excavation, our conservator, Ulrich Bellwald, assisted by Anne-Catherine Escher, removes the plaster on wooden trays and relocates it to the protective safety of a storage room where restoration is completed. After their removal, José I. Fusté completes excavation underneath the collapse to find the vestiges of a crude plaster floor. Probably the original floor for this elegant room is robbed out before the cataclysmic collapse of the ceiling takes place. The decorative panels have been on tour at the Altes Museum in Berlin, and upon their return to Jordan they are turned over to the Petra Museum.

14.
This represents nearly 12 percent of all the pottery recovered from the Petra Great Temple site.

15.
It might be questioned why the excavator has connected the terms "cistern" and "reservoir" for this feature —"Cistern-Reservoir." According to Bellwald 2003:137 in The Petra Siq: Nabataean Hydrology Uncovered, a "cistern is a closed storage for runoff water, not spring water," and a reservoir is a "closed (i.e. covered) tank for storing drinking water from a spring." In actual fact we are not sure if our feature is one or the other or can be defined as either of these structures. As a matter of fact it may be a detention storage control basin for storm water run off. Unfortunately we just do not know enough about the inlets to the Cistern-Reservoir, and at this point in our investigations we have little idea of how the collected water is dispersed. And with the recent recovery of the baths we hypothesize it may be a *natatio* or swimming pool.

16.
This is a complicated area to excavate. Firstly, we had no expectations of what we would find below an otherwise solid block of fill approximately 3.58 m in depth. Secondly, once it becomes apparent it is a cistern or reservoir (or a *natatio*), we want to discover more about the processes that bring about its being situated where it is and to undertake a functional analysis of how it works and appears. But these too become complicated not only by the bedrock formation, but also because of the walls and scattered patches of what we term "platforms." Why did these pre-Nabataean builders leave such scant remains? How was this area used before it was "organized" into a Cistern-Reservoir (or *natatio*) unit?

Now that the Cistern-Reservoir is cleaned there are more questions that require answers. A most compelling question is why this Cistern-Reservoir is needed and installed. How is it roofed? Is there a flat roof or are the ashlars seen on the west shelf of the structure foundations for an arched structure? Does it collapse bringing down those arches that span east-west? And there are hydro-logical questions: How does water enter the Cistern-Reservoir? How is the water dispersed? Does it travel along and over the West Precinct Wall? There are no openings in the cistern itself evident from the excavated evidence, so we have to speculate. What is its rela-tionship to the Residential Quarter? We assume that it is in use at the same time; however access to the Residential Quarter would have been difficult given the placement of the cis-tern. Existing evidence so far offers no answers to these questions.

The Great Cistern in the East Plaza excavated in Special Project 85 in 2001 measures 389.84 cubic meters or held 102,984.83 gallons of water, whereas this Cistern-Resevoir mea-sures 19.548 cubic meters and holds only 5,164.04 gallons. In comparison, the Great Cistern is a much larger installation. Why were two such entities totaling 108,148.87 gallons of water required for the Great Temple and its environs? The best answer may be that it serves quite another purpose, as a *natatio*.

17.
Upon completion of excava-tions, the following phases are identified. Discussed from earliest to latest, the stages of development within Special Project 110 are assigned as follows: Pre-Site Phase I is the manipulation of the bedrock. The cutting away of bedrock, we assume, predates the subsequent building of the temple. The shelf of bedrock appears to continue at a relatively high elevation in the south, and on the east, where it begins to drop off, it is cut away for the construction of the Cistern-Reservoir (or *nata-tio*). Chisel marks on the east and south walls attest to this premeditated plan. In Site Phase I are the con-struction and use of early installations, as well as the building of the West Pre-cinct Wall. In Site Phases III and IV the early Cistern-Reservoir is built. In Site Phase VI, there is collapse and fire damage to Cistern-Reservoir walls, which are repaired in Site Phase VIII. In Site Phase IX the Cistern-Reservoir collapses and is then abandoned, and in Site Phase X are signs of continued abandonment, but the water systems may be repaired and partially still in use. Site Phases XI-XIII show no signs of use, but in Site Phase XIV there is the construction of a Bedouin Wall over the Nabataean wall.

18.
Eleanor A. Power is compiling research on the baths for the Vol. III Great Temple publication.

19.
Here is also found a partial Latin inscription, an iron horse harness, a silver brace-let and a carnelian bead.

20.
The finds from this conduit and the "Well" include 14 coins, beads of amber and faïence, quantities of glass, a bone pin, a complete Byzantine lamp, plus a Nabataean juglet and various vessels that serve for draw-ing water.

21.
The interior of the tunnel is blocked by debris, but it is assumed to exit into the Colonnaded Corridor where it probably drains into the subterranean canal-ization system.

22.
Other notable finds are complete lamps, reused triglyphs, a head of Helios and painted wave patterned decoration.

23.
Most important of the 2005 special finds are two marble Greek inscriptions both dating to the second and third centuries CE. The first, Cat. No. 05-S-7, is a two-line inscription of five letters in the first line, and the second line of two words and 12 letters car-ries the Homeric word "prudent" on it (Tryanos) and may have been written in hexameter. The second inscription Cat. No. 05-S-11, of one line and four let-ters is not as yet translated, but may be part of the same "A style" of writing. An epigrapher must study both more closely. Both of these inscriptions are published in the 2006 *ADAJ*, Vol. 50.

24.
A number of structural reconfigurations of the bath water systems resulted from earthquake action.

25.
There is much more continuity from the Late Nabataean period into the Roman period than previously thought. These changes at Petra have not been fully analyzed; no paradigm fully comprehends the overall shift from the Nabataean period to the Roman period.

26.
It is difficult to know what areas continue to provide bathing or other activi-ties, but a kiln may have been constructed over the remains of the southern-most *caldarium* at this time.

CHAPTER FIVE

5

The Petra Great Temple(s)

Aerial view of the
Temple Complex to
the north, 2006.

CHAPTER FIVE

The Petra Great Temple(s)

Introduction

The focal point of the vast Petra Great Temple precinct, the temple proper, is prominently positioned on an elevated terrace to the immediate south of the sweeping Lower Temenos. Enclosed to the east, west and south by the Upper Temenos, the temple today is approached by two small staircases connecting the hexagonal pavement of the temple Forecourt to the temple Pronaos in the east and west.

To synthesize the available evidence, this chapter focuses on three re-buildings or reincarnations of the temple area, and we have elected to entitle it, "The Petra Great Temple(s)." The interpretation of these unusual remains infers that there are three structures constructed onto or added to the earliest original building. The first temple is a modest Site Phase II *distyle* configuration, built within the first century BCE. This original structure is transformed by the addition of a colossal *tetrastyle* monumental *pronaos* (porch) and flanking walkways in Site Phase IV, the last quarter of the first century BCE. This is the second temple built as a part of a "Grand Design" when the whole precinct is expanded. The third and final form is a temple with a theater inserted into the center of the building at ground level within the Site Phase IV construction. This Site Phase V theater-in-temple, dated to the first century CE, shares all the architectural features of the first and second temples. It is striking that the interrelationships between these three structures is centered on and bounded within a single design. The motives for these changes are difficult to interpret, but serve as a confirmation of the site's unique history over a relatively brief span of time.

Expertly constructed from hewn sandstone and limestone blocks, the massive Great Temple is a composite structure, exhibiting elements of both its original and restructured designs. Originally conceived as a *distyle in antis* building with peripteral columns, flanking antae with East, West and South Corridors and accessed by a Central Stairway, the temple proper is later expanded to include a broad Porch (*tetrastyle in antis*) and perimeter East and West Walkways. A third major renovation witnesses the addition of a central Theater supported from beneath by a complex series of intercolumnar walls, a monumental Central Arch, internal staircases, platforms and twin interior vaulted chambers. The temple and its architectural features and the dimensions of features are presented below.

Great Temple(s) Features—
Dimensions in meters

Elevations asl

TEMPLE

Stylobate 905.63 ± 0.05 m

Pronaos 905.35 ± 0.04 m

Preserved height of West Anta—2.60 m

Preserved height in south—8.50 m

Restored porch columns average—907.96 ± 0.10 m

West Anta (inner) elevation—909.15 m

East Anta (inner) elevation—907.75 m

West Walkway 905.54 ± 0.01 m

WEST CORRIDOR—905.47 ± 0.06 m
West Corridor maximum height—909.02 m

EAST CORRIDOR—905.53 m

East Corridor maximum height—910.07 m

THEATRON

Orchestra 905.53 ± 0.02 m

Lowest diazoma 907.11 ± 0.02 m

Lowest seating 907.50 ± 0.01 m

Uppermost excavated seating—908.59 m

Projected last seat (approximate)—914.67 m

Lowest step—905.97 m

Restored uppermost step—910.49 m

Upper platform (rear)—910.49 m

EAST STAIRWAY (NORTH-SOUTH)

Floor at the bottom of the stairs—905.61 m

Lowest step—905.98 m

Restored uppermost step—910.52 m

Upper Platform (in rear)—910.53 m

WEST STAIRWAY (NORTH-SOUTH)

Floor at the bottom of the stairs—905.63 m

Lowest step—905.97 m

Restored uppermost step—910.49 m

Upper Platform—910.49 m

CENTRAL ARCH

Top of Keystone—910.51 m

Heart-shaped east rear column (Suleiman Column) restored height—912.49 m

Dimensions

Note: All measurements are external and include wall thicknesses unless otherwise noted. When a depth is irregular e.g., steps, it is averaged.

Distyle Temple: 30.07 m north-south × 18.36 m east-west

Tetrastyle Temple: 42.50 m north-south × 27.10-to-35.50 m east-west. *Tetrastyle* Temple—The largest freestanding structure in Petra

Porch stylobate: 2.20 m north-south × 28.00 m east-west

From the East Walkway to the West Walkway: 35.50 m

Porch inter-axial distance between the East Anta and East Porch Column: 4.40 m

East porch columns inter-axial distance: 5.03 m

Central Porch Columns inter-axial distance: 7.06 m

West Porch Columns inter-axial distance: 5.03 m

PRONAOS

Pronaos: width from the stylobate south edge to the front of the Anta East and Anta West: 6.50 m north-south × 24.70 m east-west

Side columns inter-axial distance east and west: 3.51 m

Rear columns inter-axial distance: 3.27 m

TEMPLE SOUTH

South Corridor: (external) 5.80 m north-south × 27.10 m east-west × 6.90 m depth; (internal) 3.10 m north-south × 24.70 m east-west

Rear East-West Stairs East: 2.40 m north-south × 8.50 m east-west × 5.12 m depth

Rear East-West Stairs West: 2.40 m north-south × 8.60 m east-west × 5.12 m depth

South Doorways (average) 2.06 m width × 6.90 m height × 1.18 m depth

TEMPLE EAST

East Corridor: (external) 33.90 m north-south × 6.12 m east-west × 6.12 m depth; (internal) 5.89 m north-south × 3.12 m east-west

East Walkway: 41.55 m north-south × 3.67 m east-west × 0.20 m depth

East Chamber: (external) 7.16 m north-south × 4.37 m east-west × 5.10 m depth; (internal) 5.30 m north-south × 3.00 m east-west

North-South Stairs East: north-south 6.60 m north-south × 2.27 m east-west × 4.80 m depth

East Corridor Doorways: (average) 2.05 m width × 1.29 m depth × 4.37 m height

TEMPLE WEST

West Corridor: length from the front of the West Anta to the rear: 12.00 m north-south × 3.00 m east-west × 2.21 m depth

West Walkway: from the front of the West Anta 33.30 m north-south × 3.67 to 3.70 m east-west × 0.81 m depth

West Corridor Doorways: (average) 2.05 m width × 2.21 m height × 1.35 m depth

West Chamber: (external) 6.88 m north-south × 4.66 m east-west × 4.78 m depth; (internal) 5.52 m north-south × 3.03 m east-west

North South Stairs West: north-south 6.82 m × 2.23 m east-west × 4.76 m depth

TEMPLE CENTER

Central Arch: (external) 9.81 m north-south × 5.77 m east-west × 5.58 m depth; (internal) 6.89 m north-south × 3.21 m east-west

East Steps (rear of theatron): 2.50 m north-south × 0.90 m east-west × 1.54 m depth

West Steps (rear of theatron): 2.50 m north-south × 0.90 m east-west × 1.54 m depth

THEATRON

Orchestra floor diameter: 6.43 m

Proposed diameter of outermost seats according to Paul Zimmerman's reconstruction 33.2 m × 2.96 m depth

Estimated seating capacity (0.5 m per person) 565; (0.45 m per person) 620

Central Staircase (*scalarion*) Steps 0.90 m height × 0.26 m depth

East Staircase 2.80 m length × 0.60 m width

Steps 0.19 m height × 0.26 m depth

Theater Seats: 0.40 m height × 0.58 m depth

Temple Wall Dimensions
Thickness and heights

West Interior Anta: 5.97 m north-south × 1.57 m east-west × 3.86 m height

East Interior Anta: 6.00 m north-south × east-west 1.57 m × 2.30 m height

South Corridor Wall: 1.18 m thickness × 5.36 m height

East Corridor Wall: 1.29 m thickness × 5.51 m height

East Walkway Wall: 0.66 m thickness × 0.60 m height

East Chamber Wall: 1.92 m thickness × 2.80 m height

East and West Shared Wall between East and West Chambers: 1.21 m thickness × 3.20 m height

West Corridor Wall: 1.35 m thickness × 3.90 m height

West Walkway Wall: 0.67 m thickness × 1.32 m height

West Chamber Wall: 1.27 m thickness × 3.20 m height

Central Arch: Arch 0.40 m thickness × 5.90 m height

East Steps (rear of Theatron): 1.70 m thickness × 1.40 m height

West Steps (rear of Theatron): 1.70 m thickness × 0.80 m height

If the Great Temple is 19.00 m in height as we suppose it is, the temple would have stood some 34.00 m above the Colonnaded Street.

Temple Phase II

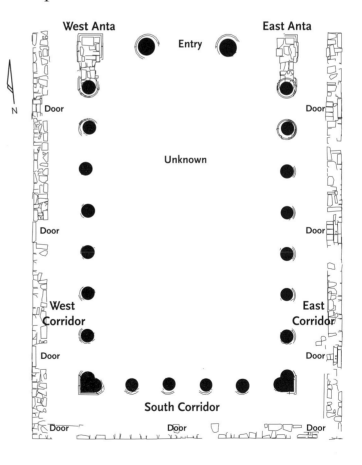

Fig. 5.1
Temple, plan of the Phase II *distyle in antis* Temple.

Fig. 5.2
Great Temple West, *distyle*
column as restored, 1995.

Fig. 5.3
Temple, West Anta and
collapsed west *distyle*
column, to south, 2004.

Excavation History

Distyle in Antis Temple

The remains of its earliest structural incarnation, the *distyle in antis* colonnades of the Great
Temple, measure 30.00 m in north–south
length × 19.50 m in east–west width. The plan
is found on Figure 5.1. Founded directly on the
prepared bedrock surface, two sandstone columns stand in front of the edifice in the north,
flanked by two massive interior antae resting
at an average elevation of 908.45 m. Figure 5.2
shows the west distyle column as restored, and
Figure 5.3 pictures the West Anta as it appeared
before it was cleared of debris and column collapse. Along the sides of the temple in the east
and west are eight columns, each crowned by
an intricately carved limestone Corinthian-style
capital of Nabataean type, shown in the photo
in Figure 5.4 and by drawing in Figure 5.5. In
the south, six columns extend across the temple
rear, two of which (shared with the sides) in the
southeast and southwest corners prominently
display a heart-shaped shaft of double-engaged
design. Figure 5.6 presents the upper courses of
the slumped southeast double-engaged column
during excavation. Along the east, west and
south sides of the temple, the diameter of the
diagonally dressed column drums averages
1.20 m and that of the Pronaos columns and
rear double-engaged columns is approximately
1.50 m. The inter-axial distance between the
columns measures 3.27 m at the temple south
and 3.51 m in the east and west.

Traces of pigment still clinging to the
sandstone, *in situ,* illustrate that the lower third
of the shafts of the *distyle* temple's peripteral
columns are veneered with smooth plaster,
brightly painted in alternating hues of red and
yellow. In contrast, the upper two thirds of each
column are embellished by white plaster
molded in a cable design.[1] The profile of cable
fluted plaster can seen in Figure 5.7. and Figure
7.15. At the front of the temple, the twin
Pronaos columns are plastered in a similar
fashion, the lower portions of both painted red.
In the temple's interior, and presumably extending for an unknown distance beyond the
colonnades and antae in all directions, is the earliest floor of the temple precinct. Possible remnants of this original pavement (indicated by *in
situ* limestone flagstones in the north part of the

West Corridor) are expertly laid, cut to fit snugly beneath the slightly elevated Attic bases of the temple columns and antae as can be seen in Figure 5.8. The cella or main room of the temple presumably extends the full interior length and width of the colonnades. No traces of this large room remain, as it is covered over by later construction.

Along the temple east, west and south, towering walls are added alongside the colonnades marking the outer boundaries of the internal East, West and South Corridors. Encasing the temple structure, each of these corridor walls, rising to a projected 15.00 m height, is constructed from diagonally dressed sandstone headers (averaging 0.36 m × 0.33 m)

Fig. 5.4
Temple, upper and lower capital elements as re-erected (not restored).

Fig. 5.5
Temple capital with lower and upper orders restored from different elements. A typical Great Temple capital lower order (34/192, Trench 34, Locus 12, 3-VIII-96), measures 1.17 m in diameter, 0.77 m in width and 0.52 m thickness. The upper order (58086, Trench 58, Locus 5, 4-VIII-98) is 0.57 m in height, 0.82 m in width and 0.78 m in thickness. The pinecone boss (58103, Trench 58, Locus 5, 5-VIII-98) is 0.45 m in length, 0.20 in width, and 0.78 m in thickness.

Fig. 5.6
Temple, southeast heart-shaped double-engaged column slumped out of position probably due to earthquake action in antiquity.

and stretchers (averaging 1.38 m × 0.45 m). Most of the courses and rows are well laid with Nabataean mortar and are founded directly on the prepared bedrock. As they stand today, each of the three walls is divided into four north-south (or in the case of the rear wall, east-west) sections. Between the sections of the corridor walls are four broad doorways fitted with finely cut limestone thresholds averaging 2.10 m in length, providing direct access to the corridor interiors. Figure 5.9 is of the doorway leading into the south doorway in the East Corridor. Displaying an irregular construction, the rugged interior faces of the corridor walls are concealed in antiquity by thick layers of decorative plaster,[2] a quantity of which still remains *in situ* in the south and west. (Figures 5.42, 7.12–7.14) Plaster

decoration also covers the exterior surfaces of the walls, keyed into the striated diagonal tooling of the ashlar masonry.

Tetrastyle in Antis Temple

The plan of the Grand Design *tetrastyle* temple can be seen in Figure 5.10.

In the north, serving as the grand façade of the temple's expanded *tetrastyle* design, stand the weathered remains of four massive Porch columns averaging 1.50 m in diameter. Figure 5.11 illustrates the severely eroded condition of one of the Porch columns as it was recovered in 1993. These columns, erected between two massive outer antae and covered with red and yellow painted plaster, are positioned 6.30 m north of the original *distyle* columns and antae, and extend across the full east-west

0 ▬▬▬▬ 5 cm

Fig. 5.7
Temple, Trench 17 profile sketch of fluted plaster from column shaft.

Fig. 5.8
Temple, elevated Attic base of a column in the East Corridor snugly fit between two later Site Phase V intercolumnar walls, 1999.

Fig. 5.9
Temple, south doorway in the south wall looking into the East Corridor, to the north, 2000.

width of the temple with an inter-axial distance between 5.03 and 7.06 m. Comparative profiles of column bases are displayed in Figure 5.12. Between the center two columns, a staircase provides access from the temple Forecourt to the Pronaos, a miniature model of the *distyle* temple's grand Central Stairs, now gone out of use. Figure 5.13 shows the partially collapsed stairs between the Porch columns as they were first defined in 1993.

Flanking the East and West Corridors are paved East and West Walkways. Measuring approximately 3.70 m in width, each of the walkways is bounded by a low outer wall some 0.60 m wide. Coeval with the construction of the outer corridor walls, the East and West Walkways serve as primary points of access from the temple plazas. Directly aligned with the lateral east and west staircases of the Lower and Upper Temene, the East and West Walkways directed pedestrian traffic alongside the precinct, feeding directly into the four doorways of the East and West Corridors. Additionally, cut postholes discovered at regular 3.50 m intervals in the East Walkway (Figure 5.14) and high in the east face of the East Corridor Wall (Figures 5.58) suggest that this outer area is covered at one time, perhaps by tethered awnings, providing welcome shade for visitors entering the temple from the east.

Theater and Attending Support Structure

Following the *tetrastyle* expansion of the Great Temple edifice, the structure undergoes a third major structural revision during which a large semi-circular theater is installed into the central cavity of the building. This Site Phase V building plan can be seen in Figure 5.15. The construction of the Theater and its massive substructure results in a complete reorganization of space within the temple walls. Strengthening the existing architecture, newly built intercolumnar walls between the columns of the *distyle* colonnades provide a firm substructure on which new architectural elements are founded. In the temple south, staircases are built along the sides and two across the rear, and platforms are built to support and access the Theater from the rear of the complex. To the temple east and west, interior north-south staircases are elevated approximately 5.00 m above the temple floor to

Temple Phase IV

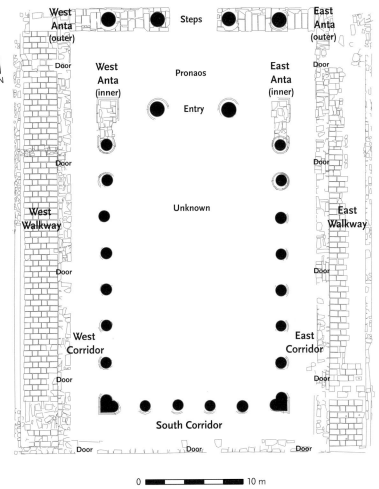

Fig. 5.10
Temple, plan of the Phase IV *tetrastyle in antis* Great Temple.

Fig. 5.11
Temple, a severely
weathered Porch column,
to south, 1993.

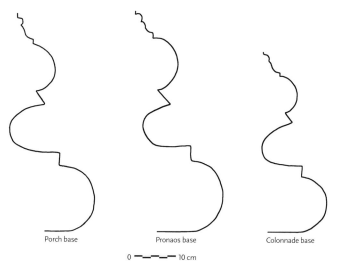

Porch base   Pronaos base   Colonnade base

0 ▬ ▬ ▬ 10 cm

Fig. 5.12
Temple, profiles of Attic column bases.

Fig. 5.13
Temple, temple stairs as originally
defined in 1993, to south.

Fig. 5.14
Temple, flagstone pavement of the
East Walkway, to south.

the second level of the precinct. Mirror images of each other, the East and West Internal Staircases measure approximately 2.40 m in width by 7.00 m in length and are each constructed from 21 finely laid stair treads. Built into the interior and exterior (intercolumnar) walls flanking the staircases are arched windows, Figure 5.35, providing light and an outward view of the temple East and West Corridors and an inward view of the East and West Vaulted Chambers.

At the top of each staircase is a paved landing 2.70 m in length by 2.26 m in width from which the four remaining treads of an upper pair of staircases begin the south to north ascent to the presumed upper tiers of Theater seating at the temple rear. Situated between these two landings, a large adjoining platform covers the Central Arch, extending south to abut the east-west intercolumnar wall at the temple rear. Here, flanking southeast and southwest staircases provide alternate access to the Theater *cavea*, accommodating pedestrian traffic flow from the temple South Corridor.

Underlying this extensive array of staircases and platforms, three interior chambers are present. The largest of these, located at the rear of the temple beneath the central platform, is the main support for the Theater substructure, the Central Arch. Figure 5.16 illustrates the fully-excavated Central Arch. Cut into the bedrock, the arch chamber floor (measuring 8.52 m north-south × 3.32 m east-west) contains a large four-channel canalization system with an additional smaller series of subsidiary shallow bedrock-cut channels aligned roughly parallel to one another. Directly above the canalization system is a hard-packed clay floor installed over smaller cut channels. Although the north and south portions of the arch are collapsed, much of the substructure remains, consisting of roughly hewn sandstone ashlars measuring on average 0.35 m × 0.55 m, set in rows of eight. Its 16 courses are set parallel to the bedrock floor in the southern half of the arch and tilt upward in the north at an angle of 60 degrees. Figure 5.17 pictures the slanted construction of the walls of the Central Arch. To the south, the temple south intercolumnar wall forms the rear wall of the Central Arch chamber. Here, a small doorway measuring 0.67 m in width by 2.04 m in height is constructed, becoming the sole entrance to the arch interior.

Temple Phase V

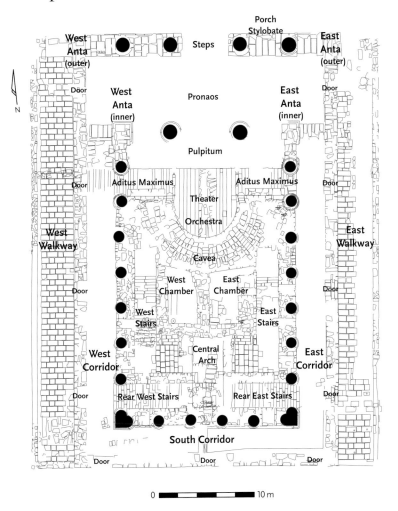

Fig. 5.15
Temple, plan of the Phase V *tetrastyle in antis* Temple with the Theater addition.

Fig. 5.16
Temple, excavations
of the Central Arch, to
south, 1998.

To the north of the Central Arch are two side-by-side self-contained vaulted chambers. In the east and west, the chambers are each accessed by a doorway directly opposite the central doors in the east and west intercolumnar walls and perpendicular to the bases of the East and West Interior Staircases. The layout of the chambers is identical, the floor of each measuring approximately 5.50 m north-south × 3.00 m east-west. The walls of the chambers are constructed from hewn sandstone ashlars roofed by a vaulted ceiling. Inserted into the outer wall of each chamber, and facing onto the East and West Interior Staircases, is a single vaulted window, serving as the sole source of light for each of these enclosed rooms.

Surmounting the interior of the temple is the elegant central Theater. Truly the most extraordinary and enigmatic component of the Petra Great Temple visible today, the Theater is constructed from finely carved sandstone ashlars arranged in a semicircular plan. Figure 5.18 pictures the fully excavated Theater in 1997. At the top of the preserved *cavea*, broken edges of

Fig. 5.17
Temple, tilted construction
of the Central Arch, 1998.

Fig. 5.18
Temple, Theater
as fully excavated, 1997.

Fig. 5.19 (left)
Temple, Theater *diazoma* showing *in situ* ashlar paving as excavated, 1997.

Fig. 5.20 (right)
Temple, Theater *aditus maximus*, to west, 1997.

the upper *in situ* risers indicate the Theater's original projection upward and toward the rear of the temple, housing at one time an estimated capacity of approximately 620 persons. Of interest is that with the Theater, the orientation of the building would have been turned 180 degrees to the north.

At the base of the Theater, extending the full length of the first level of the *cavea* seating is a walkway (diazoma) paved with sandstone flagstones. Figure 5.19 is an image of the Theater diazoma showing broken paving slabs. Above the walkway, each of the five remaining tiers of seating is approximately 0.40 m high and 0.58 m deep. Overall, the Theater seating is arranged into four *cunei* (wedge-shaped sections) divided by three *scalaria* (staircases). Deep channels cut in the sandstone seats at irregular intervals are likely to have been inlaid with wooden armrests, serving as dividers for single and double seating. Below the *cavea* to the north is the floor of the orchestra, paved with decorative white, red and purple sandstone rectilinear pavers that abut the *cavea's* northern face. Figure 5.20 displays the west *aditus maximus* and partial orchestra as excavated in 1997. Facing the orchestra are the remains of a stage/*pulpitum* (added at a later date), four courses high and approached by two staircases on the platform's west side. Immediately south and perpendicular to the stage are found limestone thresholds on

either side of the stage, each with two deep square grooves and close by a number of metal fragments were excavated. This combination of finds strongly indicates that doors or gates originally separate the walkways of the *aditus maximus* (parodoi) from the inner orchestra, thus defining the orchestra space more clearly.

Stratigraphy and Phasing

During the excavation of the Great Temple proper, fifteen phases of activity are identified linking the architectural growth and collapse of this structure with that of its surrounding features. Pre-Site Phase I is represented by the construction of the early temple platform as well as the structures discovered in the Theatron *cavea* excavation. Beginning in the first century BCE, in Site Phase I, the bedrock floor beneath the temple and its east and west surroundings is cut away, and where the bedrock is absent a hard yellow fill packed with pebbles is brought in to level the area. In line with the north-south axis of the main temple building, the central artery of the subterranean canalization is also cut into the bedrock at this time, as well as a series of channels in the temple south beneath the present South Corridor and below the Theater. In Site Phase II, also in the first century BCE, the major architectural elements of the *distyle in antis* temple are constructed, including the construction of what may be a side altar in the northeast, building up of the temple platform on the west, the stylobate and twin Pronaos columns, the East and West Antae and the Corinthian-Nabataean[3] style peripteral columns forming the sides of the temple in the east, west and south. Surrounding these elements, a finely cut limestone pavement is laid, extending beneath the raised Attic bases of the columns and antae.

Site Phase III, a period of minor collapse, prompts the vast restructuring of the Great Temple's design in Site Phase IV,[4] expanding the structure into a *tetrastyle in antis* form. Occurring sometime between the first century BCE and the first century CE, in this phase the *distyle* temple is modified in the north to include an expanded Porch punctuated by four massive columns and fronted by the newly leveled Forecourt paved with small hexagonal pavers. At the temple rear, towering East, West and South Corridor Walls enclose the original peripteral columns of the temple, redirecting access to the inner temple through three doorways cut into each of the corridor walls. Further east and west, newly constructed East and West Walkway Walls mark the full lateral extent of the temple structure.

Further redesign in the first century CE in Site Phase V witnesses the insertion of the Theater and its substructure into the central cavity of the temple. Supporting the Theater *cavea* from the sides, intercolumnar walls are built between the columns of the peripteral colonnades. Underneath the Theater, the Central Arch and twin East and West Vaulted Chambers form a network of interior walls and vaults on which the *cavea* rests, accessed by a series of interconnected staircases and associated landings. Soon after the Theater's installation, a second period of minor collapse ensues, dating to the Late Nabataean period. The date is pre-106 CE Site Phase VI evidenced by damage sustained to the walls of the East and West Staircases and the West Anta. During this phase it is likely that the Great Temple withstands an attack by the Romans, perhaps led by the general, Cornelius Palma. As an act of defense, the doorways of the East, West and South Corridor Walls are narrowed or blocked, significantly limiting access to the temple proper from the surrounding plazas.

Temple Phase VII

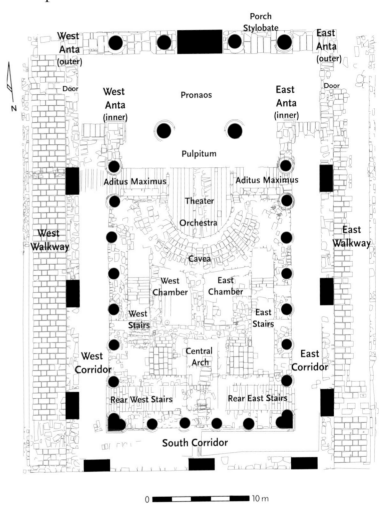

Fig. 5.21
Temple, plan of the Phase VII *tetrastyle in antis* Temple with the doorways blocked. (Blackened areas in the wall indicate blocked doorways.)

Fig. 5.22
Temple, Site Phase VII
blocking of the doorway in
the South Corridor Wall.

In Site Phase VIII, many of the temple's floor-ing elements are robbed out. Presumably fallen into disuse, lower level features of the structure are quarried for deployment elsewhere, includ-ing the floor pavements of the East and West Vaulted Chambers, the East, West and South Corridors and the stone landings at the bases of the East and West Interior Staircases, of which almost no traces remain. As evidence of indus-trial reuse, rows of stones are deposited on the floors of the Theater and inside the vaulted chambers, most likely waiting to be re-carved and re-installed outside the walls of the precinct. Looking at the stratigraphy, the robbing of these elements can be assigned to a long period of abandonment throughout the site marked by the accumulation of a homogeneous layer of clean chocolate brown soil. In the temple, the deposi-tion of this soil is most heavily concentrated on top of the robbed-out east and west landings and the pavement of the Theater orchestra.

Immediately following the initial abandon-ment of the temple, major destruction occurs in Site Phase IX probably as a result of the massive 363 CE earthquake. Exhibiting a conspicuous south to north fall pattern, a great number of architectural elements within the temple collapse at this time, burying the lower levels of the sanctuary beneath a barrage of soil, architectural debris and primary fluvial deposits. Among the first elements to fall are the West Porch columns, landing directly on top of the pavement of the temple Forecourt. In the east, architectural debris accumulates around and under the east colon-nade, and in the west, the west intercolumnar wall begins to buckle. In Site Phase X, the temple proper experiences a final period of structural modification. Between the fourth and fifth centuries CE, Byzantine occupation of the site results in the robbing out of the upper (exposed) treads of the East and West Rear and Interior Staircases and the pavements of the east and west landings. Various areas of the complex also evidence additional occupational reuse including the east South Corridor where patches of ash and fragments of plaster inscribed with Greek graffito are found in the collapse deposit.

These changes to the building are clearly reflected on the Great Temple Site Phase VII plan shown in Figure 5.21. The Phase VII blocking of the doorway in the South Corridor Wall can be seen in Figure 5.22. Subsequent restructuring occurs with the deliberate removal of the Pronaos floor pavers to allow for the construction of the stage/*pulpitum* north of the Theater orchestra. Around the temple perim-eter, low walls are built to the south of the East and West Walkways, separating the areas in the east and west from the rear of the complex.

In Site Phase VII, blocking walls are added at the south ends of the temple East and West Walkways, and benches are appointed in the West Walkway interior. Also at this time the walls of the East Interior Staircase are rebuilt.

In Site Phase XI, the temple structure endures further post- fifth-century CE damage, identified by the collapse of the East Porch columns and the continued deposition of fluvial deposits throughout the precinct. This final period of major collapse is followed by an additional period of robbing and abandonment (in Site Phase XII) and a minor period of collapse (in Site Phase XIII) ultimately leading to the nearly complete submersion of the architectural remains of the temple structure beneath a dense cover of accumulated soil and debris.

Overall, excavations of the temple proper were conducted yearly from 1994 to 2002 and 2004–2005. In total, the architectural fragments recovered from the temple number 4877, including 410 column drums, 846 ashlars, 8 elephant head fragments and 577 cornice fragments, amounting to 44 percent of the total architectural fragments recorded in the overall site database.[5]

Figure 5.23 is a chart of the trenches excavated in the temple from 1993 to 2006. Figure 5.24 presents a plan showing the position of the various temple trenches.

Distyle in Antis Temple: Pronaos Excavations

Roughly moving across the *distyle* temple from north to south, the twin columns and interior antae are cleared over four consecutive seasons, from 1994 through 1997, in Trenches 12, 23, 24 and 48. In the Pronaos east, Trenches 24 and 48 define the east and north limits of the Pronaos and examine the relationship of its architectural elements to those features in the west. The removal of large masonry elements and fill in Trench 24 exposes the finely carved Attic bases of the east column of the *distyle* façade and the interior East Anta. More severely weathered than the west *distyle* column, the deteriorating east column is partially restored by the addition of three new drums. In Trench 48, excavations move further east, fully revealing the interior East Anta. From the fill, three distinct construction phases are identified in the northeast, including the erection of the *distyle* and *tetrastyle* temple buildings followed by a tertiary period of reconstruction, probably after a minor collapse, at which time the northeast doorway between the East Corridor Wall and the East Porch Anta

is narrowed. The final abandonment of the east Pronaos occurs sometime after this reconstruction, following prominent periods of Hellenistic and Byzantine presence at the site indicated by the discovery of an amphora handle stamped with the Rhodian rose and Byzantine lamp fragments found in the fill.

Moving westward, Trenches 12 and 23 clarify the northwest corner of the temple structure. The removal of large amounts of debris and collapse from this area reveals two major architectural elements from the *distyle* building, including a buildup of hard-packed yellow fill determined to be the bedding of the Pronaos floor and the northwest corner of the interior West Anta with a finely carved limestone base. The Attic base of the West Anta is shown in Figure 5.25. Contributing to the phasing of the temple, close investigation of the base of the interior West Anta reveals an underlying layer of clean sand rather than the usual hard-packed fill, distinguishing this feature's foundation from that of the West Porch Anta to the north. From this discovery, we posit that this element is constructed during an earlier building phase, corroborating the later full delineation between the *distyle* and *tetrastyle* temple constructions.

Tetrastyle in Antis Temple: Porch Excavations

Coeval with the expansion of the temple into a *tetrastyle in antis* edifice is the construction of a number of monumental architectural features, the furthest north of which is the broad temple Pronaos. Situated directly south of the four massive Porch columns and two flanking antae that front the temple façade, the Pronaos is excavated largely in tandem with the adjacent *distyle* columns and antae. In the east in Trench 24 in 1996, the removal of fill reveals the remarkable Attic bases of the two east Porch columns. One of the Porch columns has its Attic base carved away for the insertion of a structure between the columns. This is visible in Figure 5.26. At the base of the trench, the floor bedding for the Pronaos is exposed, composed of irregularly placed sandstone blocks ranging greatly in size and color and bonded with mud

TRENCH	YEAR	DESCRIPTION	MEASUREMENT(M) (N-S × E-W)	EXCAVATOR(S)
Porch/Pronaos				
Special Project A	1993	No excavation undertaken. Measurements of the collapsed debris on top of the temple Porch columns	2.00 × 28.00	Payne
Trench 12 (SP14)	1994	Northwest Pronaos and Interior West Anta	10.00 × 10.00	Parr, M. Joukowsky
Special Project 10	1994	East Pronaos column	No measurements taken	M. Joukowsky
Trench 23 (SP23)	1995	Northwest central Pronaos	10.00 × 6.50, 3.00 × 3.60	Schluntz, Harris
Special Project 34	1995	East Anta	No measurements taken	Qublan
Trench 24	1996	Northeast central Pronaos	9.80 × 9.95	Bestock
Trench 48	1997	Northeast Pronaos	2.00 × 10.00	Slaughter
Special Project 107	2005	Pronaos East Sondage	6.40 × 3.55	Libonati
Temple East				
Special Project 9	1994	Search for the third and fourth columns from the south in the temple east colonnade	No measurements taken	M. Joukowsky
Special Project 11	1994	Search for the sixth column from the south in the temple east colonnade	No measurements taken	M. Joukowsky
Special Project 12	1994	Search for the fifth column from the south in the temple east colonnade	No measurements taken	M. Joukowsky
Trench 15 Part I (SP8)	1994	East Interior Staircase and landing	6.00 × 5.00	Austin
Trench 15 Part II	1995	East Interior Staircase and landing	7.35 × 2.23	Harris, Khalidi
Trench 19	1995	East Staircase, north of the East Walkway between the temple Forecourt and Porch	5.20 × 3.40	Tholbecq, Habboo
Trench 34 Part I (SP42 and 43)	1996	Further excavation of Locus 6 of Trench 34 in the East Corridor south	14.00 × 5.00	A. Joukowsky
Trench 34 Part II	1997	Continued clarification of the southeast wall of the temple	5.00 × 4.00	Brown, M. Joukowsky
Special Project 50	1997	Moving 4 column drums from East Porch column to central East Porch column	No measurements taken	M. Joukowsky
Trench 55	1998	Upper levels of the East Vaulted Chamber	7.50 × 4.80	Brown
Trench 58	1998	East Corridor including the third, fourth and fifth columns from the south in the east colonnade	11.00 × 3.00	Schwartz, Haile
Trench 55A	1999	East Vaulted Chamber	7.50 × 4.80	Brown
Trench 64	1999	Extension of the East Walkway at the point where it abuts the temple Pronaos in the east	6.80 × 3.80	M. Joukowsky, Sylvester, Karz
Trench 65 Part I	1999	East Corridor center and south	14.00 × 3.50	Brown
Trench 65 Part II	1999	East Corridor center and south	21.00 × 3.15	M. Joukowsky
Special Project 71	2000	Sondage along the East Walkway cutting into Trench 72 in the east and Trench 73 in the west	1.30 × 1.50	Brin
Trench 73	2000	Area between the East Corridor Wall and the east colonnade	21.00 × 3.60	Stern

Fig. 5.23
Chart of Temple trenches excavated, 1993–2006.

TRENCH	YEAR	DESCRIPTION	MEASUREMENT(M) (N-S × E-W)	EXCAVATOR(S)
Temple West				
Trench 9 (SP7, SP52)	1994	West Interior Staircase and landing	7.50 × 10.00	Bedal
Special Project 1	1994	West Walkway drain sondage	Absorbed into Tr. 8, 10, 11	M. Joukowsky
Special Project 2	1994	West Walkway sondage	Absorbed into Tr. 8, 10, 11	M. Joukowsky
Special Project 3	1994	Brief exploration of the West Walkway Wall	Absorbed into Tr. 8, 10, 11	M. Joukowsky
Trenches 8, 10, 11	1994	West Walkway	18.50 × 7.00	Slaughter, A. Joukowsky
Special Project 13	1994	Removal of fallen column drums in the temple west in preparation for the excavation of Trench 12	No measurements taken	M. Joukowsky
Special Project 16	1994	Search for the northernmost column of the west colonnade	No measurements taken	M. Joukowsky
Trench 22 Part I	1995	West Vaulted Chamber and West Interior Staircase	7.50 × 10.00	Bedal
Trench 22 Part II	1996	West Vaulted Chamber and West Interior Staircase	7.50 × 10.00	Bedal
Trench 29	1996	West Corridor north	8.25 × 3.36	Slaughter
Trench 45	1997	West Corridor, west of the Theater	7.50 × 3.00	Payne, M. Joukowsky
Trench 56	1998	West Corridor center	8.50 × 3.00	A. Joukowsky, M. Joukowsky
Trench 59	1998	West Corridor and western part of the South Corridor	11.18 × 3.4	A. Joukowsky, M. Joukowsky
Trench 63	1999	West Walkway	22.70 × 3.74	A. Joukowsky
Special Project 109	2005	West Walkway	2.00 × 3.06	Khanachet
Temple South				
Special Project 15	1994	Investigation of a localized plaster deposit in grid square D5	No measurements taken	Jacobsen
Trench 26	1996	Cental Arch and the Rear East Staircase	5.50 × 4.50	Payne
Trench 27	1996	Cental Arch and the Rear East Staircase	4.75 × 3.50	Payne
Trench 35 Part I	1996	Cental Arch and the Rear East Staircase	3.75 × 3.50	Payne
Special Project 40	1996	Southeast double-engaged column	5.00 × 2.60	M. Joukowsky
Trench 27 Part II	1997	Cental Arch and the Rear East Staircase	4.75 × 3.50	Payne
Trench 35 Part II	1997	Base of the Rear East Staircase	2.47 × 4.38	Brown, Parker
Trench 57	1998	Central Arch	6.96 × 3.32	Libonati, Prendergast, Sullivan
Trench 77 Part III (SP72)	2000	Upper levels of the temple South Corridor	4.50 × 21.80	M. Joukowsky
Trench 85	2001	South Corridor	2.73 × 17.27	Egan, Libonati
Special Project 93	2002	Sondage into the foundation platform and subterranean features in the southwest of the South Corridor	2.00 × 2.50	Cloke
Special Project 120	2004	Central Arch Water Systems	2.26 × 3.60	Libonati, Egan
Theater and Stage				
Trench 40	1997	Stage west	6.00 × 9.80	Slaughter
Trench 47	1997	Theater west	9.80 × 6.00	Bedal
Trench 62	1999	Theater, stage and East Corridor north	11.00 × 12.50	Basile, Sylvester
Trench 92	2002	Pronaos/Stage platform west sondage	4.00 × 6.18	Fusté
Special Project 200	2005	Orchestra Floor Sondage	6.96 × 1.96	Libonati
Trench 123	2006	Theater seats sondage	1.30 × 2.80	Libonati

Temple Trenches

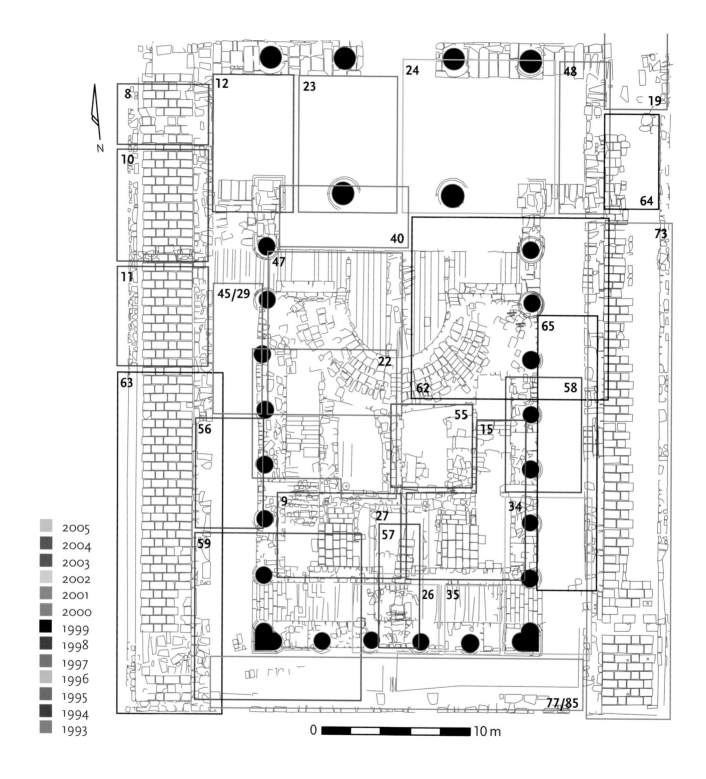

■	2005
■	2004
■	2003
■	2002
■	2001
■	2000
■	1999
■	1998
■	1997
■	1996
■	1995
■	1994
■	1993

0 ▮▮▮▮▮ 10 m

Fig. 5.24
Plan of Temple trenches excavated, 1993–2006.

Fig. 5.25
Temple, Attic base of the
West Anta still clogged
with fill and debris, 1994.

Fig. 5.26
Temple, Attic base of the
west center Porch column,
to west, 1996.

Fig. 5.27
Temple, original position of the West Porch Anta, to east, 1993.

mortar. Uncovered in the west, a small roughly circular assemblage of un-worked blocks measuring approximately 1.00 m in diameter is posited to be a type of "manhole" providing access to the subterranean canalization beneath the Pronaos floor.

In the temple west, excavations in Trenches 12 and 23 in 1994 and 1995 reveal the original position of the west Porch stylobate and the fragmentary remains of the West Porch Anta as can be seen in Figure 5.27. In the temple front, excavators undertake the partial re-erection of the two West Porch columns (the second from the west having been entirely knocked out during a destruction event) from excavated drums. As in the east, the Pronaos floor bedding is exposed, composed of uneven sandstone blocks, patches of mortar and hard-packed mud.

In 2005 Special Project 107, a sondage in the East Pronaos proves that at least a portion of the Pronaos and *tetrastyle in antis* is a later addition to the original *distyle in antis* Temple. Shown in Figure 5.28, it is located at the east end of the Pronaos. Based on the uncovered construction technique of the foundation walls for both the *distyle in antis* and the East Corridor Wall, it can be concluded that the *tetrastyle in antis* is a later addition to the original façade. Figure 5.29 shows the sondage set against the East Anta and East Corridor Walls. Additionally, the construction technique and soil fill of the platform of the Pronaos differs markedly from the buildup immediately adjacent to the *distyle in antis* construction. This sondage also provides a definitive terminus for the construction of this section of the temple proper by reaching bedrock. Additionally, two very important structures are unearthed: an early stuccoed platform/wall construction and a presumed early east–west canalization system. Figure 5.30 illustrates the stuccoed platform set between the walls of the Pronaos.

The water system is located directly below the *distyle in antis* foundation wall and may be part of an installation built to capitalize on a seepage spring from the bedrock. The stuccoed platform/wall is located north of the water system at an oblique angle to the *distyle in antis* foundation wall. Its exposed section makes it difficult to determine both its function and its

Fig. 5.28
Temple Pronaos sondage
below the West Porch
column, to north, 2005.

overall size since only one side is exposed. The south face of the articulated platform is two-tiered or ledged. It is covered by thick gray white stucco decorated with dimpled finger impressions for an unknown decorative purpose, which can be seen in Figure 5.31. In association with this platform are a layer of Hellenistic and Early Nabataean ceramics and a significant quantity of animal bone.

It is observed that the subterranean canalization follows a fairly linear route slightly east of the center axis of the building itself, except in the Pronaos where it is directed westward before swinging eastward again to flow underneath the Central Staircase between the Upper

Fig. 5.29
Temple Pronaos sondage showing the stratigraphy below the West Anta, 2005.

and Lower Temene. This pattern is disrupted in the Pronaos area of the temple by the westward bend, which leads to some architectural questions. Is it necessary to avoid the central area of the Pronaos in order to skirt a pre-existing architectural feature, or perhaps is this section of the canalization rebuilt when the *tetrastyle in antis* is constructed? Based on the results recovered in Special Project 107, early east-west water installations exist in the area of the Pronaos that possibly contribute to a westward jog or suggest that there may be a lower earlier water system in place. Its main linear canalization route is directly under the Lower Temenos.

The site phasing for these features is dependent on whether the early platform wall is associated with the Great Temple or with a structure from the site's previous use.

East Corridor Excavations

East and west of the *distyle* façade stand the three towering East, West and South Corridor Walls. Constructed from tightly laid sandstone ashlars, the corridor walls expand the perimeter dimensions of the *distyle* temple building by enclosing three new paved corridors in the east, west and south (as we already described above). The inner face of the East Corridor Wall as it was excavated in 1999 reveals its partially plastered surface in Figure 5.32. Presumably roofed (judging from the hundreds of ceramic tiles recovered from adjacent collapse deposits), each of these walls and their adjoining corridors were examined from 1997 to 2002 in a series of trenches laid out end to end alongside the temple colonnades.

Beginning in the east, excavations in 1998 and 1999 fully expose the temple East Corridor. In 1998, Trench 58 (the continuation of excavations in the same trench begun in 1996) is opened in the north in order to remove fallen columns and capitals congesting the corridor and to expose its walls. Figure 5.33 typifies the immense column collapse and overburden in the East Corridor during excavation. Along the west border a number of architectural features are exposed including the two arched windows and an arched doorway built into the east intercolumnar wall forming one side of the East Interior Staircase. The arched entry from the

Fig. 5.30
Temple Pronaos sondage
showing the platform, to
north, 2005.

Fig. 5.31
Temple Pronaos sondage showing
the "dimpled" platform.

Fig. 5.32
Temple, inner face of
the East Corridor Wall
after excavation.

Fig. 5.33
Temple, immense column
collapse and overburden
in the East Corridor.

East Corridor to the bottom of the east interior north-south staircase can be viewed in Figure 5.34 and the drawing of this wall can be seen in Figure 5.35. In the corridor fill, a number of elegantly carved floral capitals are unearthed as well as two extraordinary pinecone bosses. Other registered finds include numerous red, white and yellow fragments of wall and column plaster in addition to a pile of roof tiles and quarried architectural elements that suggest the use of this area as a storage facility.

In 1999, the excavation of Trench 65 continues the removal of the dense architectural debris in East Corridor to permit unimpeded access to the East Vaulted Chamber and the staircase in the southeast from the north. Figure 5.36 pictures the final excavations in the East Corridor, allowing for full access to the east rear staircase and the East Vaulted Chamber. The preservation of *in situ* decorative stucco panels on the west face of the East Corridor Wall becomes a high priority. With a striking similarity to the design and placement of elements recovered in the opposing West Corridor, the East Corridor stucco further confirms the north-south axial symmetry of the temple building and its decoration.

During the excavation of late collapse debris (dated to Site Phase XI) in the East Corridor north, a number of ornate finds are recovered including a fragment of marble sculpture, a bone needle, a cosmetic spoon, leg fragments of two molded figurines, a complete lamp dating to the first century CE and several coins, one of which is Nabataean. Of particular interest is a crude limestone carving of a male figure in a shrine with two columns. The figure wears a *chiton* over one shoulder while the other shoulder and the breast are bare. Shown in Figures 5.37 and 5.38, the piece measures 9.50 cm in length by 8.70 cm in width and 5.10 cm in thickness and may represent a male divinity.[6]

Deposited in a contemporary fluvial deposit, larger architectural elements found in the north East Corridor collapse include doorjambs, a seat from the Theater, decorative vegetal elements and one half of an upper higher order capital. The upper layers of fluvial and collapse deposits covering the East Corridor can be visualized in Figure 5.39. Close examination of the east

Fig. 5.34
Temple, arched entry from
the East Corridor.

temple colonnade reveals the presence of two
mason's marks on the third column from the
north, sixth drum from the base. One mark
appears to be an "x" and the other, a Nabataean
"g." In the collapse of the East Corridor Wall's
northernmost doorway is another complete
drum with two mason's marks, one, a Nabataean
"t" and the other, a Nabataean "h." Mixed in
among the architectural remains are more delicate
stucco cornices and panel fragments from the
decoration of the East Corridor Wall, as well as
pockets of collapsed plaster column fluting.
Two large preserved juniper beams (the larger
measuring 1.60 m in length) are also recovered.
Offering strong evidence for the prominent use
of wooden elements in the temple's construction, samples from the two beams as well as
additional wood remains are collected and sent
to Cornell University's Malcolm and Carolyn
Wiener Laboratory for Aegean and Near
Eastern Dendrochronology for analysis, which
determines they are "stressed juniper."

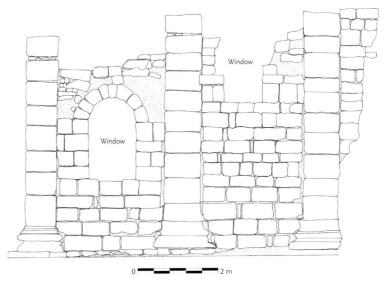

Fig. 5.35
Temple, West Corridor Wall,
east face, 1998.

Fig. 5.36
Temple, East Corridor
excavations.

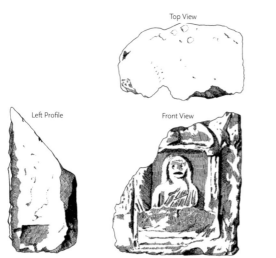

Fig. 5.37
Temple, East Corridor
Trench 65 drawing of a
divinity in a shrine.

Fig. 5.38
Photograph of a divinity
in a shrine.

Despite inherent limitations in dating fill deposits, the broad range of finds collected in Trench 65 suggests that the East Corridor functions as an enclosed area once the temple falls out of use. The ceramics date this occurrence to the fourth century CE, placing the associated underlying deposits within a range of four centuries, if not more. Contained within these deposits is an overwhelming amount of animal bone (to be reported in Volume III.) Several explanations exist to explain this concentration of finds—the first and perhaps preferred being that the debris is of random origin, deposited over a period of a time by desert nomads. A second possible interpretation is that the architecture of the East Corridor serves as an enclosure in its later phases for the keeping of camels and other animals for domestic or agricultural purposes. Third, the detritus may represent imported fill, possibly washed down from the south escarpment, which would negate its designation as an actual use level within the temple stratigraphy.

West Corridor Excavations

The mirror image of the East Corridor is the temple West Corridor, structurally identical to its eastern counterpart. Figure 5.40 shows the West Corridor after excavation and consolidation in 2000. Between 1996 and 1998 four excavation efforts are undertaken in this area: Trenches 29 and 45 in the north and Trenches 56 and 59 in the south. In 1996, excavation begins in Trench 29 in order to delineate the architectural features of the corridor north, just west of the Theater orchestra. In addition to large masonry elements and roof tiles, the fill of Trench 29 produces numerous fragments of decorative wall plaster. Multiple plastering events are visible in the assortment of collapsed fragments, brightly painted in solid Pompeian red and polychromatic yellow, red and blue-green hues. In the center of the trench, many fragments painted with blue and black floral motifs and with a brown-banded design are recovered as well as molded elements including bands of egg and tongue and dentils from plaster cornices (similar to the Baroque Room Ceiling, Figure 4.82).

Also included as part of the excavation of Trench 29 are the full recovery of the interior West Anta and the exposure of the bases of the three northernmost columns of the west temple colonnade. Canalization capstones are uncovered on the floor of the West Corridor north, as are the remains of a possible late statue platform. In the space between the interior West Anta and the northernmost west column, a small staircase is revealed, which likely provides access to the Theater stage. The West Anta wall showing the later staircase to the Theater stage is shown in Figure 5.41.

Continuing work in the north, in 1997 Trench 45 is opened to the immediate south of Trench 29. While defining the architecture of the central West Corridor, excavation here unearths a number of finds similar to those found in the north. A great cache of painted plaster fragments are found, many of which are discovered *in situ* adhered to the east face of the West Corridor Wall. (Figure 5.42 pictures an *in situ* plaster cassette on the south face of the South Corridor Wall, similar to the West Corridor) The roughly hewn sandstone ashlar construction of the West Corridor Wall is purposeful, allowing plaster elements to be keyed in, and brightly painted in hues of green, red, yellow and white. Mixed in among the collapsed fragments are elements with geometric designs as well as molded egg and tongue and vegetal reliefs. One limestone capital fragment is discovered in the debris with delicate *in situ* gold leaf still adhering to its surface.

At the south end of the West Corridor, adjacent excavations in Trenches 56 and 59 expose the flooring in the temple west. While no pavers remain *in situ* in the West Corridor south, impressions in the floor bedding indicate the earlier presence of lavish limestone flagstones. The West Corridor floor bedding can be seen in Figure 5.43; the exposed corridor bedding is greatly damaged by earthquake collapse leaving an irregular and uneven surface. At the corridor south, in Trench 59, the lower eight drums of the double-engaged, heart-shaped southwest corner column are recovered in excellent condition, standing plumb to a 4.75 m height. As there is a 0.15 m earth accumulation between the upper drums, the two upper

Fig. 5.39
Temple, upper layers of fluvial deposit and collapse in the East Corridor, 1996.

Fig. 5.40
Temple, West Corridor
after excavation and con-
solidation, to south, 2000.

Fig. 5.41
Temple, West Anta wall
showing the later stair-
case to the Theater stage,
to north.

courses are removed for their consolidation and re-erection. During the removal of these drums, *in situ* bonding plaster is found in fine condition along with considerable amounts of wood, straw reeds, and the remains of metal fittings.

With the removal of the upper courses of this double-engaged column, elements of its Nabataean construction are revealed. Prior to the placement of each hewn drum, it is cushioned with reeds and plaster and leveled. For reinforcement, vertically placed iron bars are affixed to the drum, serving as clamps to secure the joins between four or five column components. Once in place, more plaster is poured into the joins, and yet another plaster coat containing a straw binder mixed with ground and crushed potsherds is applied. After the drums are bonded and the capital is in place, the exterior column surface is generously coated with stucco so that any construction irregularities are masked from view.

South Corridor Excavations

Connecting the East and West Corridors across the rear of the temple building is the temple South Corridor, excavated during the 2000 and 2001 seasons. Beginning in 2000, excavations in Special Project 72 (part of Trench 77) are devoted to the removal of the upper levels of overburden surrounding the corridor wall. Though ostensibly suffering less earthquake damage than other elements of the temple proper due to the forcible projection of large masonry elements toward the north, the upper layers of the South Corridor debris are congested with a tumble of enormous ashlars as can be seen in Figure 5.44. To the south, the upper courses of the South Corridor Wall are uncovered revealing the upper parts of three rectilinear doorways (east, central and west), which are blocked in antiquity along with the doorways of the East and West Corridors.

The following year, the excavation of Trench 85, spanning nearly the full east-west and north-south dimensions of the South Corridor, removes the collapse and fill deposits down to the floor level. In the north and south, the boundary walls of the South Corridor are revealed. Enclosed by the South Corridor Wall to the south, the corridor is bounded in the north by the temple south colonnade and its

Fig. 5.42
Temple, *in situ* plaster cassette on the South Corridor wall, 2000.

Fig. 5.43
Temple, West Corridor floor bedding, to south, 1998.

Fig. 5.44
Temple, immense
overburden in the South
Corridor area, to west, 2000.

connected intercolumnar wall system. Figure 5.45 is a close-up image of the upper portion of the columns and intercolumnar wall system in the South Corridor. Figure 5.46 illustrates the south face of the South Corridor Wall. Between the six rear columns, the intercolumnar wall (2.39 m in width) now stands to an average 6.43 m in height, with some 24 courses of diagonally chiseled ashlars set between the columns. Built into the central section of the intercolumnar wall is a narrow doorway, the sole point of access to the Great Temple Central Arch. Figure 5.47 shows the doorway from the South Corridor into the Central Arch.

Discovered *in situ* on the north face of the South Corridor Wall, east and west of the central doorway, are the well-preserved remains of ornately painted and molded stucco decorations. The excellent preservation of this plaster can be largely attributed to the accumulation of fluvial deposits against the temple South Corridor Wall, protecting the plaster from falling architectural debris at the time of the Great Temple's collapse. Most surprising here is the discovery of two massive sculpted lion heads recovered from the collapse near the base of the central

Fig. 5.45
Temple, upper portion of columns in the South Corridor, to west, 2000.

Fig. 5.46
Temple, South Corridor North Wall, south face, 2002.

Door

0 ▬▬▬▬▬ 5 m

Fig. 5.47
Temple, doorway
South Corridor into
the Central Arch in
a state of collapse.

doorway. One lion, thought to be male, faces westward and appears to be snarling (Figure 5.48). The second lion (Figure 5.49), the female of the pair, faces eastward with an observably more pacific expression. Both lions have open mouths with exposed teeth, and a tongue originally painted red is visible on the lower jaw of the eastward facing example Figure 5.50. Due to their location within the fill and their size, it is thought that the two lions flanked the upper part of the central doorway. Further detailed analyses of this decoration is undertaken by Emily Catherine Egan[7] who reports on the excavation and design of these walls, their sculptures and the attendant wall paintings in Volume III.

In addition to its architectural and decorative discoveries, the South Corridor excavations renew discussion of a number of architectural problems noted within the temple. Outstanding issues include the question of corridor roofing. It may be presumed that the temple corridors are roofed; however, the precise form of the

roofing is as yet unknown. One of the roof tiles found in the collapse is depicted on Figure 5.51. As shown in the three-dimensional reconstructions generated of the site by the ARCAVE project,[8] we posit that the tile roof is constructed on a slant, higher in the interior and lower on the exterior as shown in Figure 5.52. Although arch springers are present in the temple collapse, no springers remain *in situ* built into the extant walls. The upper architecture of the South Corridor Wall can be seen in Figure 5.53. Hence it is not altogether clear if the Great Temple contains an upper, vaulted ceiling that extends above the extant walling, or if the roof rests just above the height of the column capitals. The south face of the South Corridor Wall can be seen in Figure 5.54.

East Walkway Excavations

To either side of the East and West Corridors, extending the breadth of the Great Temple's lateral flanks, are the East and West Walkways. Directly aligned with the east and west staircases leading up from the Hexagonal Pavement of the Lower Temenos, the East and West Walkways serve as the outermost access points to the temple interior. Starting in the east, Special Project 30 in 1995 is opened to investigate the northeast corner of the temple podium, revealing a north-south wall constructed of sandstone ashlars parallel to the east side of the Pronaos. Between this wall and the east edge of the Pronaos, a small staircase constructed of seven limestone stair treads leading up from the temple Forecourt is uncovered. At the base of the stairs, beneath the Forecourt hexagonal pavement and an overburden of numerous architectural fragments, a major north-south subterranean canalization artery is discovered, containing a fill of mixed Nabataean and Roman pottery.

Moving south, the full expanse of the East Walkway is revealed during the 2000 season with the excavation of Trench 73. Extending from the south end of Trench 64 (located to the north and excavated in 1999) to the South Corridor Wall of the temple, Trench 73 excavations uncover and delineate the east face of the East Corridor Wall (the trench's west boundary) and the adjoining pavement. Figure 5.55 pictures the East Walkway and the adjacent East

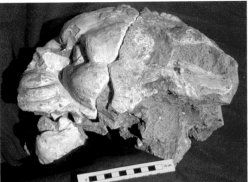

Fig. 5.48
Temple, plaster snarling
lion excavated in the South
Corridor, 2000.

Fig. 5.49
Temple, plaster pacific lion
excavated in the South
Corridor, 2000.

Fig. 5.50
Temple, two plaster lions,
facing one another.

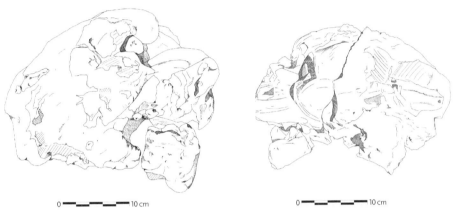

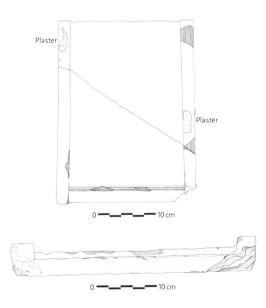

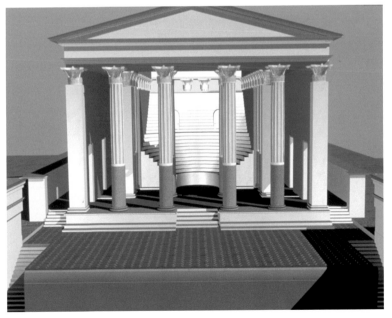

Fig. 5.51
Temple, roof tiles side (bottom) and bottom (top).

Fig. 5.52
Temple, virtual reality
reconstruction of Phase V.

Fig. 5.53
Temple, upper architecture
of the South Corridor, 2000.

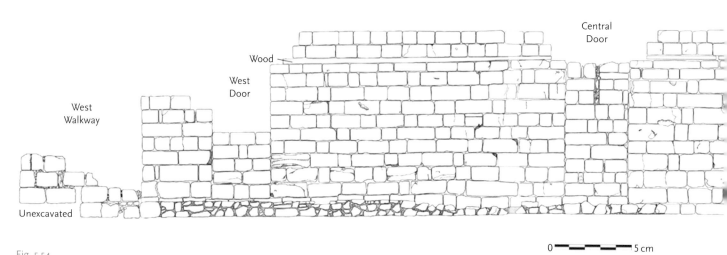

West
Walkway

Unexcavated

West
Door

Wood

Central
Door

0 ▬ ▬ ▬ 5 cm

Fig. 5.54
Temple, south face of the
South Corridor Wall, 2001.

Corridor Wall, and Figure 5.56 illustrates the East Face of the East Corridor Wall facing the East Walkway. In this effort, the three doorways of the East Corridor Wall and a quantity of *in situ* plaster are revealed. Also during excavation numerous artifacts are recovered from the primary and secondary collapses of the adjacent Upper Temenos, including a portable *betyl* drawn in Figure 5.57. Through the exposure of artifacts and architecture, it is established that the original construction of the East Walkway closely parallels that of the West Walkway. However, visible episodes of architectural rebuilding in both the east and west indicate the disparate use of the two areas in later periods.

Focusing on the excavation of the East Corridor Wall, it appears that all associated architectural elements are simultaneously built. In its earliest building phase, the corridor wall comprises a casemate construction of two abutting walls measuring 1.30 m in width. Layers of mud mortar, stones and rubble are applied between the abutting walls to bond them, each side depending on the other for support. Facing the exterior East Walkway, the east wall is composed of large finely dressed ashlars, while the west wall (facing the interior East Corridor) is constructed from roughly hewn blocks and chinking stones (Figure 5.32). The rough inner surface and tooled outer surface of the East

Fig. 5.55
Temple, East Walkway and adjacent East Corridor Wall, 2001. (Note post-holes.)

Corridor Wall and the recovery of numerous stucco architectural fragments in the fill indicate that both sides of the wall were originally plastered.

Simultaneously with the construction of the corridor wall is the installation of its three doorways. They share similar construction, with the interior sides of each doorway bearing evenly carved doorjambs and postholes for doors. The east sides of the doorways have identical widths of 1.80 m. The limestone thresholds of these doorways also show identical tripartite construction. In the central and south doorways, the middle register of the threshold contains two holes for drop locks. The ashlars surrounding these rectilinear doorways are evenly and deliberately spaced for the insertion of the doors.

Adjacent to the East Corridor Wall, the pavement of the East Walkway also appears to be a contemporaneous installation. Unfortunately, the original parameters and design of the East Walkway remain elusive. The existing walkway is paved with limestone slabs and measures 3.60 m east-west × 21.00 m north-south. Little more than one half remains extant.[9] The relative dating of the East Walkway and the East Walkway Wall is also difficult to determine, as evidence for the relationship between the two

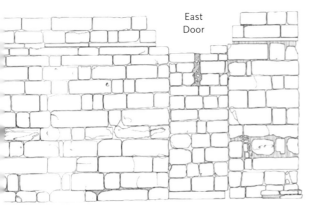

East Door

remains inconsistent. In the north, the pavers of the walkway abut, but they do not undercut the existing portions of the wall. In the south, later walls are built on top of the pavers obscuring their relationship to the walkway wall. In total, two distinct stages of construction are discernable. Potentially, the earliest version of the East Walkway Wall may be narrower and parallel only one section of the East Corridor Wall. In this case, the pavers originally create a larger, uninterrupted East Plaza, which extends the full distance between the East Corridor and East Perimeter Walls. Later, a number of these pavers may be removed and the earliest version of the East Walkway Wall is built in the north. Under this arrangement, the earliest wall construction postdates the paving of the walkway. Extant architecture, however, provides no evidence for this, leaving open a number of phasing possibilities.[10]

Despite contested dates of origin for the various architectural features, certain modifications to the wall's construction appear to be coeval. The walkway pavement, the east face of the East Corridor Wall and the thresholds of the doorways all appear to be altered simultaneously, perhaps coinciding with a change in the area's use. One such alteration is the cutting of socket holes in the flagstone pavement alongside the East Corridor Wall. These roughly cut postholes are positioned at regular intervals in the south walkway pavement, either at the intersection of two pavers or in the middle of an individual paver.[11] Corresponding beam holes are also extant in the eighth course of the south sections (the north sections have not been preserved) of the East Corridor Wall. Figure 5.58 portrays these beam holes in the East Corridor wall, measuring some 0.20 m × 0.15 m and aligned on an east-west axis with the placement of the holes in the floor shown above in Figure 5.14 (p. 224). Figure 5.59 is the plan of the East Walkway. Some of these holes have broken, crumbled edges while others, alongside the south and central doorways, are incised more deeply and evenly. Each hole in the East Corridor Wall corresponds to two evenly placed holes in the walkway flagstone pavement. These two holes are also placed at an even distance from one another, oriented along a north-south axis. These correspondences between the beam holes in the wall and those in the floor may indicate the presence of a canopy covering this area.

At the temple rear, some evidence for the continuation of these postholes further east also exists on the floor of the adjacent East Plaza. The placement of the double postholes both in the East Walkway and in the East Plaza may indicate the concurrent use of these two areas, which perhaps share a large covered waiting area adjoining the south door of the East Corridor Wall. The exact reason for the construction of the postholes remains speculation, but their presence provides strong evidence for contemporary traffic flow between the Upper Temenos and the temple southeast.

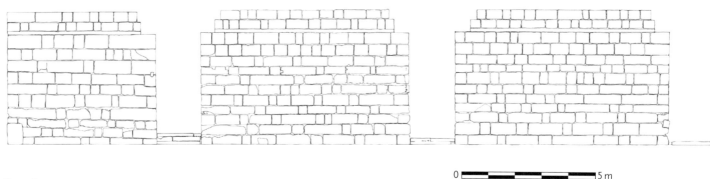

Fig. 5.56
Temple, east face of the East Walkway Corridor Wall, 2001.

0 ▬▬▬▬ 5 m

In the East Walkway, evidence of abandonment and destruction in the excavated stratigraphy further separates the north from the south. After a period of general abandonment, soil deposits with charcoal inclusions found exclusively in the north part of the walkway indicate that the walkway south, seemingly unaffected by destruction at this time, enjoys a prolonged period of use. During a later stage of activity the East Corridor south doorway is blocked, and the adjacent area of the walkway undergoes extensive burning (possibly of the light wooden construction in the south) resulting in a massive deposit of tiles mixed with ash. While the distinct construction patterns within the separate areas of the East Walkway are largely inconsistent, overall it is clear that the periods of rebuilding in the East Corridor Wall, the East Walkway and the East Walkway Wall occur in rapid succession. The entire East Walkway area, including the visible stages of reuse of the East Walkway Wall, falls out of use prior to the initial collapse of the Upper Temenos. Major activity in the temple proper also appears to terminate before the major collapse caused by the earthquake in 363 CE.

Fig. 5.57
Temple, Trench 73 portable *betyl*.

Left   Front

Top   Bottom

0 ▬▬▬▬ 10 cm

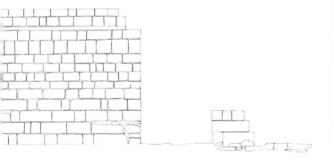

Fig. 5.58
Temple, beam holes cut along the east face of the East Corridor Wall.

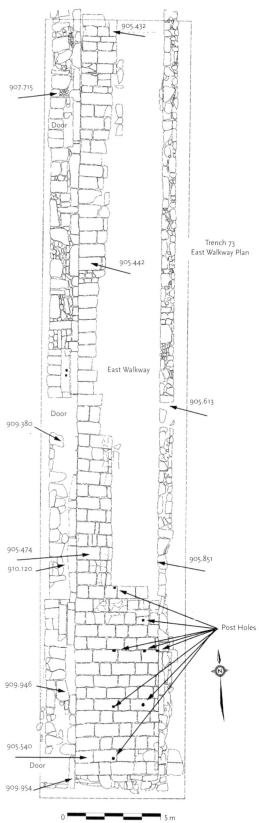

905.432

907.715

Door

Trench 73
East Walkway Plan

905.442

East Walkway

Door

909.380

905.613

905.474
910.120

905.851

Post Holes

N

909.946

905.540

Door

909.954

0   5 m

Fig. 5.59
Temple, East Walkway,
Trench 73 plan, 2001.

West Walkway Excavations

In 1994, excavation of the Great Temple West
Walkway begins with Special Projects 1, 2 and
3. Designed as soundings to clarify individual
areas of the temple northwest, these initial
sondages are expanded and renamed as Trenches
8, 10 and 11 in order to fully explore the
walkway's architecture. Figure 5.60 shows the
1994 overburden in the West Walkway after its
preliminary excavation. Delineating the bordering walls to either side of the walkway north
and identifying two major points of access to
the temple interior, excavations bring to light
the remains of a largely *in situ* flagstone limestone pavement. A number of intriguing small
finds are also recovered including fragments of
limestone sculptures, and perhaps including a
theatrical mask, Figure 5.64, discovered in the
topsoil of Trench 8. Several fragments of
painted plaster also are recovered in the Trench
10 fill, foreshadowing the impending discovery
of greater quantities of such decoration *in situ*
on the interior face of the adjacent West
Corridor Wall. A low east-west crosswall at the
north of the walkway is also discovered,
regulating access to the temple through the
doorways in the corridor wall. Figure 5.61
shows a later low east-west cross wall at the
south of the West Walkway.

Recovered from these early excavations of
the West Walkway is the sculpture of remarkable limestone heads (Figures 5.62–5.64) clearly
demonstrating the virtuosity of the Nabataean
sculptor. Figure 5.62, the partial face of a male,
shown *in situ,* is particularly evocative, and the
detail of its sculpting shows outstanding skill in
execution. Of quite a different, rougher style is
the half facial fragment of a female with its open
mouth and corkscrew curls shown *in situ* in
Figure 5.63. During the excavations of the following year the other side of her weathered face is
unearthed. The two halves can be seen together
in Figure 5.64. From their find spots it might be
reasoned that they originally are part of a decorative embellishment of the temple exterior.

In 2000, excavations of the walkway
resume, exposing the full north-south extent of
its features in Trench 63. Here, the east face of
the West Walkway Wall is revealed, along with
more of the walkway pavement and a late east-

Fig. 5.60
Temple, West Walkway
after the 1994 excavation,
to the southeast.

Fig. 5.61
Temple, West Walkway
after the 1999 excavation,
to the south.

Fig. 5.62
Temple, West Walkway
fragmented man's face.

Fig. 5.63
Temple, West Walkway
fragmented female face.

Fig. 5.64
Temple, West Walkway reunited
female face fragments.

west crosswall at the south end of the trench, separating the walkway from the adjacent South Passageway at the temple's rear. Uncovered as well is the west face of the West Corridor Wall with each of its four doorways excellently preserved. The west face of the West Corridor Wall and the adjacent West Walkway can be seen in Figure 5.65. In the doorway areas, delicate frescoes are found *in situ*, wrapped around the doorway and threshold blocks from the corridor wall's eastern face.

A West Walkway sondage, Special Project 109, is excavated in 2005. Figure 5.66 depicts the West Walkway Wall abutting the East-West Support Wall and the temple platform with rubble fill beside it. The previous excavations prove that the bedrock on which the temple is built slopes off steeply to the south and immediately to the west of the West Walkway. A platform is then purposefully built up with monumental ashlar and rubble fill above the bedrock, as part of a total temple building plan. During the course of the Special Project 109 excavation, a gap is noticed beneath one of the ashlars, which is thought to be canalization. Upon removal, the gap is found to be a vertical shaft down into the fill created by the space left between layers of monumental ashlars when the platform is constructed. This probe reveals, therefore, that the West Walkway, and indeed the west portion of the temenos platform, is built up by enormous rough-cut ashlars, resting directly on bedrock. Moreover, it is shown that the West Walkway Wall is built on a soil foundation, approximately 0.40 m west of the original platform edge. The East-West Support Wall (see the Upper Temenos discussion) is bonded directly with the platform construction and rubble-ashlar fill, probably to support the monumental platform construction.

Following excavation, interpretation of the Trench 63 deposits identifies a number of developmental stages. Looking first at the area's earliest architectural features, the Nabataean construction of the West Corridor Wall is confirmed by the presence of an extraordinary number of mason's marks in the corridor wall, featuring the repetition of a deeply carved "s"

Fig. 5.65
Temple, west face of the West
Corridor Wall, to northeast.

Fig. 5.66
Temple, West Walkway Wall
built on rubble-ashlar fill.

Fig. 5.67
Temple, mason's mark
on the West Corridor Wall
(outlined in black), 2005.

Fig. 5.68
Temple, north doorway of the
West Corridor Wall.

or Nabataean "t." Figure 5.67 pictures one of these marks on the West Corridor Wall. The contemporary installation of the adjacent West Walkway is argued by the presence of doorjambs and threshold blocks built into the West Corridor Wall doorways, providing access between the corridor and walkway areas. The north doorway in the West Corridor Wall shown in Figure 5.68 serves as an example for the doorjamb behind the remains of a later blocking wall. It is assumed that the earliest doorways of Site Phase IV are appointed with wooden doors that can be closed and locked from the inside of each of the East, West and South Corridors. The evidence for locking mechanisms is seen just behind the doorjamb blocks where large cavities are cut into the ashlars to support the insertion of a beam. In the second doorway there are two cuts on the upper surface of the threshold block, serving as guides for a support rod.

With the installation of the Theater, the wooden doors of the West Corridor Wall are removed and the doorways are blocked or narrowed, redirecting access to the main temple building to the north. Later still, following the partial collapse of the temple in the fourth century CE, a Byzantine east-west wall is constructed at the rear of the West Walkway and a makeshift bench is built just before the second doorway. To solve a massive flooding problem in the West Walkway, a blockage wall or dam is erected so that water flow can be regulated.

Theater and Associated Substructures: East and West Vaulted Chambers Excavations

Sustaining the staircases and upper levels of the Theater substructure are the core support elements of the Site Phase V temple infrastructure—the East and West Vaulted Chambers and the Central Arch. Fully excavated in Trenches 55 in 1998 and 55A in 1999, the small rectangular East Vaulted Chamber is cleared in order to find evidence of the room's function, to prove or disprove the proposed extent of the Theater seating, and to determine reasons for the narrowed doorway in the eastern wall, which is markedly smaller than its counterpart in the West Vaulted Chamber. Figure 5.69 displays the entrance to the East Vaulted Chamber

blocked with collapse before excavation in 1995. Cleared from beneath a thick deposit of masonry debris, the main architectural features of the room include its four walls, one of which, the north wall, is angled and serves as a support for the Theater *cavea*. The chamber's single window, installed into the east wall, is also delineated. The rectangular layout of the East Vaulted Chamber is shown in Figure 5.70.

Evidenced by a conspicuous area of articulated arch fall in the north of the trench, the vaulted character of the east chamber ceiling is revealed. A number of carved Theater seats are also recovered, arguing strongly for the projection of the Theater as far south as the vaulted chambers and Central Arch south, with vaulted ceilings providing ample structural support. In the southeast and southwest corners of the room, the foundations of the Vaulted Chamber are explored, revealing a segment of the temple's main canalization artery extending along the chamber's west side. This segment seems to connect the artery discovered under the Central Arch with the site's main canalization junction under the temple Forecourt. More importantly, at least two of the chamber walls are partially founded upon the walls and capstones of this canalization. The southwest corner of the south wall rests on a capstone of the canal, and the west wall is founded on several layers of small, tightly packed stones, which in turn rest on the canalization's west wall. This discovery indicates that the canalization and East Vaulted Chamber are built in subsequent stages, the walls, capstones and first layers of hydraulic cement being installed directly into the platform on which the chamber walls are then founded.

Resting on top of the exposed sandstone floor bedding of the East Vaulted Chamber are two primary deposits discovered beneath a thick layer of collapsed roof tiles. Possibly indicative of the room's later reuse as a storage area for construction material, the tile layer provides a relative *terminus ante quem* for the period of abandonment during which the chamber's pavement is removed. Containing a noticeable lack of large masonry collapse, this deposit likely corresponds with the industrial reuse of other areas throughout the precinct. Two thin soil layers sealed beneath the tiles offer additional

Fig. 5.70
Temple, rectangular layout of
the East Vaulted Chamber.

information about the abandonment of the area, each containing the remains of a broken pot. Coeval with the reuse of the East Vaulted Chamber is the narrowing of the chamber doorway as can be seen in Figure 5.71. The addition is composed of sandstone ashlars and doorjamb elements measuring between 0.37 m and 0.40 m in width. The bottom block of this single course add-on is tilted approximately 45 degrees from the alignment of the original construction. As the addition to the doorway rests a few centimeters above the sandstone bedding, the narrowing can be best explained as a repair following minor damage to the doorway, which is installed once the chamber's original floor pavement is removed.

In the west, excavations in Trench 22 in 1996 at the base of the West Interior Staircase expose the arched entrance to the West Vaulted Chamber. Accessible, like the East Vaulted Chamber, only by this doorway and an arched window carved into the outer chamber wall, the clearing of this room reveals three ashlar walls preserved to a height of 3.80 m (11 courses) in the south. The east and west walls slope downward from north to south and are originally roofed by a sloping vaulted ceiling of which a few courses are preserved in the room's northeast corner. The result of one of the temple's earlier abandonment periods, the finished pavement of the chamber, overlying a subfloor of variegated sandstone, is almost entirely robbed out. In the southeast corner of the room, a small intact area of paved surface is found, covered by a homogeneous layer of clean chocolate brown earth defined as abandonment fill found in considerable quantities (0.34 m to 0.83 m in depth) above the adjacent undisturbed floors of the west landing and over the lower treads of the West Interior Staircase. As this fill is not present on the sandstone bedding of the chamber floor, it is presumed that the missing floor pavement is robbed out after this layer is deposited. In its place is approximately 0.05 m of accumulated earth in which numerous small finds are discovered including a brain coral and five fragments of a Trajanic inscription dating to the second century CE (Figure 5.72. See Joukowsky 1998,

p. 370 ff.). Densely packed roof tile fragments strewn across the entire extent of the room are also found in this layer, pointing at the potential use of the West Vaulted Chamber, like its counterpart in the east, for roof tile storage in a later period.

Central Arch Excavations

South of the East and West Vaulted Chambers and providing the primary support for the upper stories of the theater *cavea* at the rear of the Great Temple's construction is the massive Central Arch. A complex excavation requiring extensive consolidation, repeated attempts in Trenches 26 and 27 in 1996, and renewed efforts in 1997 remove the initial overburden from the arch, successfully exposing the intact south face of its north wall. Figure 5.73 shows the north portion of the Central Arch in 1997. In 1998, following repeated stabilization attempts, the Central Arch is fully exposed in Trench 57 (Figure 5.16). Preserved to a height of nearly 3.00 m from ceiling to floor, the Central Arch room contains a number of canalization features. Extending the full north-south length of the arch are a line of capstones characteristic of those found in the temple Pronaos and Forecourt in earlier years, shown in Figure 5.18. Longer than they are wide, these capstones average 0.50 m in length by 0.35 m in width by 0.19 m in thickness and rest on chinking stones set above the bedrock-cut canalization wall as leveling. Several capstones are removed in order to expose the interior of the canalization and to collect samples. Within the canalization a dark brown (Munsell 7.5YR 3/4) fine silty deposit is found, increasing in depth as the channel descends from south to north. In this deposit is found a Nabataean cup dating to Phase 3a–c (Schmid: 2000 Abb. 97), approximately the year 100 CE. The canalization walls are mortared with thick, water-resistant, very dark gray (Munsell 5Y 3/1), hydraulic cement with inclusions of small rocks and potsherds.

In the areas where the capstones are removed, sondages determine the character of the canalization. Initially, it is postulated that the channels are cut into the bedrock in a strictly north-south direction, traveling beneath the north wall and presumably heading into the

Fig. 5.71
Temple, narrowing of the East Vaulted Chamber doorway.

Fig. 5.72
Temple, partial marble inscription.

central area of the temple. Discovered beneath one of the capstones is an east-west intersection, forming a T-shaped junction. The east branch continues to the east wall and the west branch extends 0.30 m under the west wall, once again confirming that the canalization predates the temple intercolumnar walls and the walls of the Central Arch room. In 2004 Special Project 120 further investigates its canalization system. The central canalization system is proved definitively to terminate in the Central Arch and to connect neither to the Eastern Plaza Cistern nor to the water systems in the Upper Temenos South Passageway. This would suggest that as far as possible the shallow bedrock cut canalization system (referred to as "channelization" by our team) originated in the South Passageway of the Upper Temenos. In the future this system should be followed to the north through the temple to determine its use in the West Vaulted Chamber and beyond. The Site Phasing for the bedrock preparation for the water systems places the installation of the central canalization under the Central Arch in Pre-site Phase I sometime in ca. the mid-first century BCE. This is before the Grand Design of the Great Temple in the late first century BCE-first century CE, and the Site Phase V Late Nabataean 106 CE redesign that includes the construction of the Central Arch, the Intercolumnar Corridor, and the Theater Walls. The lead pipes are inserted in Site Phase V. Thus, it is assumed that this canalization functioned until the 363 CE earthquake of Site Phase IX.

In the Site Phase VII debris above the arch room floor, 160 bronze coins are recovered, tentatively dating to the fourth-fifth centuries CE. This cache is recovered from a 0.80 × 0.80 m square deposit of soil. Comprised of a compact, artifact-rich layer of moist, clay-like greasy soil that is patchy in areas, this deposit also contains bones, burnt residue, charcoal, limestone chips, plaster chips, shells and some sand along with fragments of glass, tesserae and metal nails. The 101 architectural fragments found in this debris include cornices, acanthus leaves and other decorated fragments of pomegranate/poppies, corner volutes, pinecones, flower petals including hibiscus, and *cauliculi*.

The pottery from this area varies in date, and large storage vessels are predominant, although jars, jugs, cooking pots and Nabataean fine wares are also present. In the fill, a complete Roman lamp in excellent condition is unearthed, paralleling a late third century CE lamp (Rosenthal and Sivan 1978:96). This lamp has a depressed discus, a perforated handle and a rounded spout. Made from pink clay, a Munsell red 2.5YR 6/6, it is decorated with splashes of red slip on its upper half. Based on the analysis of this piece and other materials, the closing date for the Central Arch deposit is as late as the fifth century CE.

East and West Interior Staircases and Associated Landings Excavations

Built over the top and up against the underlying rooms of the Central Arch cavity are a complex series of staircases, platforms and landings providing support and access to the central Theater *cavea*. Beginning in 1994, two trenches are opened to either side of the Central Arch in order to clear a massive overburden of architectural collapse and debris. In the east, excavations in Trench 15 reveal the top few treads of the East Interior Staircase positioned between the outer wall of the East Vaulted Chamber and the temple east intercolumnar wall. Figure 5.74 pictures the east interior staircase following excavation in 1995. At the top of the staircase, a large landing is revealed, appointed with windows on its west and south sides. A doorway to the west adjoins this landing to a (now collapsed) platform that overlies the Central Arch. At the landing's north end three steps of a south to north staircase are uncovered, presumably leading to the upper tiers of Theater seating.

During the full exposure of the east north-south staircase in 1995, the suspected vaulted character of its ceiling (similar to that discovered in the East and West Vaulted Chambers) is confirmed by a large number of voussoirs discovered in the dense collapse. Nine bronze coins, predominantly dating to the Late Roman period, are also found in the fill, providing a *terminus post quem* for the destruction of this area of the site. At the foot of the staircase, the debris is cleared to reveal an arched doorway

Fig. 5.73
Temple, Central Arch
with overburden cleared,
to south, 1997.

leading west into the East Vaulted Chamber and an open doorway leading east into the adjacent East Corridor.

In Trench 9 to the west, an architectural arrangement mirroring that seen in the east is uncovered. In between the outer wall of the West Vaulted Chamber and the temple west intercolumnar wall, the southern portion of the West Interior Staircase is discovered leading up to a large landing with windows installed on its east and south sides. A doorway to the east connects this landing to the platform originally built directly over the Central Arch. To the north, four steps of a second north-south staircase are found *in situ*, the complement of the east approach to the upper levels of the Theater seating. Moving to the southwest, during the 1995 and 1996 seasons the West Interior Staircase is fully delineated in Trench 22 (an extension of Trench 9) exposing a series of pristine windows and doors cut into the west intercolumnar and vaulted chamber walls paralleling the arrangement found in the east. Typically Nabataean in construction, both walls are constructed from neatly dressed ashlars exhibiting fine diagonal tooling, tilted at forty-five degrees, used for keying stucco, of which only traces now remain.

East and West Rear Staircases and Associated Landings Excavations

South of the Central Arch, a second platform, exposed during the excavation of Trench 26 in 1996, accesses the east and west landings from the temple rear. Approached by two lateral east-west staircases leading up from the East and West Corridors, this platform serves to further manage the flow of pedestrian traffic to and from the Theater. Joined to the platform's east face is the East Rear Staircase, excavated in 1997 in Trenches 34 and 35. Concealed beneath a large overburden of collapsed plaster and ashlars, the packed earth and plaster bedding for the staircase is revealed, overlain by three limestone risers still *in situ* at its base. Incorporating Special Projects 40, 42 and 43 (which delineate the upper shaft of the southeast double-engaged column and expose the window between the East Corridor and the east landing), Trench 34 completes the clearing of debris at the base

Fig. 5.74
Temple, east north-south interior staircase following excavation, to south.

of the staircase, removing a large number of ashlars, roof tiles and assorted stucco fragments. Here, excavations reveal the junction between the East Rear Staircase and the East Corridor, uncovering the lower drums and carved limestone Attic bases of the two southernmost columns of the temple east colonnade.

In 1998, the West Rear Staircase is fully excavated in Trench 59. The total dimensions of this staircase measure 2.42 m in width by 9.50 m in length. Although the upper stair treads (like those in the east) are robbed out, the bottom seven courses are found intact and *in situ*. A large number of architectural fragments are unearthed in the collapse resting on these stairs, including several quarter fragments of upper order capitals. This may be an indication that the earthquake tremors in this part of the structure shook these walls to collapse first to the west and then to the east, surrounding the east fall with a cushion of earth.

In terms of phasing, excavations of the Theater substructure clarify the building sequence at the rear of the temple. Attributed to a single building event in Site Phase V, the east, west and south intercolumnar wall systems are added. In between these new perimeter walls, the crosswalls of the East and West Vaulted Chambers and the Central Arch are built, followed by the foundations and stair treads of the East and West Interior and Rear Staircases, which abut the intercolumnar and chamber walls on both sides. Coeval with this construction, the connecting landings and platforms are paved. Windows and doorways are then built into the East and West Vaulted Chamber walls and into the south and outer walls of the east and west landings, also contemporary with the laying of the staircases, which are noticeably constructed to accommodate the positioning of these features.

Theater and Stage Excavations

An unexpected discovery at the end of the 1996 season excavation of Trench 22 is an unusual semi-circular wall. Initially thought to be the rounded rear wall of the west half of the temple interior, this feature is revealed to be part of a tier of seating of a small Theater set into the center of the temple proper. Dur-

ing the excavations of Trench 47 in 1997, the unusual architectural character of this element prompts a detailed investigation of its structure and association with the rest of the temple. Figure 5.75 shows the early excavation of the Theater in 1997. Comprised of five *in situ* tiers of seating and once holding a projected capacity of more than 600 spectators, the Theater orchestra is decoratively embellished with polychrome sandstone pavers and elegantly carved single and double seats. Figure 5.76 is a view of the Theater seating. North of the Theater seats is the orchestra floor on the other side of which stand the remains of a stage/*pulpitum* four courses high and accessed by two staircases on the platform's west side—one cut through the West Anta wall and the other leading up from the orchestra shown in Figure. 5.79. During the continued clearing of Trench 62 debris in 1999 and a localized investigation of the west part of the stage in Trench 92 in 2002, a more detailed analysis of the architectural forms of the full Theater installation is undertaken. While little

Fig. 5.75
Temple, early excavation of the Theater, 1997.

Fig. 5.76
Temple, Theater as
restored, 2000, to west.

material is found to aid with absolute dating, a number of significant discoveries are made. The complete exposure of the extant *cavea* and stage confirms the north-south axis of these installations and the prominent presence of classical influences in their design and construction. Also, theories regarding the relative phasing of the construction of the Theater and its associated features are verified. First, the discovery of a low curb wall (preserved only to one course) in Trench 62 south of the stage curb and north of the original retaining wall of the *cavea* identifies two distinct construction phases. Built on top of the *aditus maximus* pavement, this low wall is most likely a later installation, narrowing access to the *aditus maximus* during the building of the stage north of the *cavea* in Site Phase VII. The limestone gate sills in the Theater interior, which separate the floor of the orchestra from that of the *aditus maximus*, also appear to be a secondary construction, extending underneath the south wall of the stage but abutting the stage's foundations. Additionally, the complete removal of the west part of the stage reveals raw floor bedding underlying the stage, exposed when the pavers of this area are robbed out, further arguing for the later construction of the stage feature.

Evidence in the masonry of the stage also points to its late construction. More haphazardly built than the other features of the Theater, the south wall of the stage is built from a hodge-podge of small, un-worked sandstone blocks, and larger, diagonally dressed sandstone blocks, as well as limestone ashlars and decorated architectural fragments, including bushy acanthus capital pieces. Some of the limestone elements are clearly reused, quarried perhaps from the temple's original entablature that may have undergone a period of collapse predating the stage's installation.

By assigning the stage to a later period of construction, the question of the form and function of the earlier Site Phase V Theater is raised. While no direct evidence is recovered, noted architectural parallels at other sites sug-

gest the possible use of the early Theater as a "sacred theater,"[12] utilizing the landscape and surrounding architecture as a backdrop for the open orchestral space. As noted by the Theater's excavator, Joseph J. Basile, in his final excavation report of the east Theatron (1999 Trench 62, 32), important comparanda for the Great Temple Theater exist

> …largely in the Hellenistic-Roman Near East, and some of the most important occur in Syria and Jordan, in the Nabataean sphere of influence. Attached to the Nabataean temple at Sahr, for instance, [is] a small theatron with a high orchestra wall, but lacking a fully developed pulpitum. The Nabataean theater at Wadi Sabra, also, is of unique design and lacks a traditional stage building. At Jerash, the so-called "Festival Theater" at Birketein [is] designed so that the attention of the seated spectator [is] drawn not so much to the small stage as to the sacred pool beyond. At Dura Europas, the Temple of Artemis Nannaia consists of a small square building enclosing a horseshoe-shaped seating area, without a Pulpitum.

Resting on the orchestra floor, a stockpile of ashlars, arch stones and doorjambs shed light on the later reuse of the Theater as a storage area. Lying obliquely from northwest to southeast, the stones rest on top of a compact layer of chocolate brown soil characteristic of the temple's first abandonment, dating before most of its reuse phases, but after the robbing of the floor pavements of the East Corridor and east landing. Deposited in neat rows, these stones, like those found in the East and West Vaulted Chambers, are probably placed here during a period of industrial reuse, waiting to be reworked and repositioned elsewhere.

In 2005 a sondage, Special Project 200, is excavated below the Theater orchestra floor. Figure 5.77 shows the orchestra floor before the sondage is inserted. The goal of Special Project 200 is to further examine the construction technique of the Theater and to recover datable material remains. Figure 5.78 shows the same area with the sondage to the south against the *cavea* wall, and Figure 5.79 is of the sondage to the north against the *pulpitum* wall. Special Project 200's main significance comes from the uncovering of the central pivot stone used for

laying out the semicircular design of the *cavea*,
an unusual feature to find *in situ*. Figure 5.80 is
a detail of this pivot stone. The stone, which
looks like an un-fluted column drum, is located
in the middle of the orchestra exactly in the
center of the circles that constitute the seating
of the *cavea*, and is therefore likely to have been
used as a reference point for the layout of the
theater. It was covered entirely by the paving
and would therefore not have played any role in
the finished building; it was just left to support
the orchestra floor alongside the rest of the
fill. The find is highly interesting for our insight
in practical theater construction and design,
since whereas it is clear from a theoretical point
of view that architects and masons would
have used such reference points, they are rarely
identified among the hundreds of ruins of
Greek and Roman theaters.

   Just as puzzling is the discovery of the
subterranean canalization system extending
below the orchestra floor. There is a discrep-
ancy between the orchestra wall and height of
the canalization central artery capstones. In
comparison in the East Vaulted Chamber
(Trench 55A 1999), the top of the capstones is
at 905.34 m and in the orchestra itself in the
north the top level of the capstones is 905.15 m,
but the orchestra floor itself is at 905.53 m
suggesting a build up and leveling during the
construction of the theater area.

   The exploration of the central canalization
system in the Theater is based not on excavation, but on measurements and general observation. The central canalization artery accumulated
a tremendous amount of sediment, requiring
repairs for flushing it out in antiquity. The
deposition is higher, or perhaps the canal is
deeper in the Pronaos area of the Temple. The
reexamination of the Central Arch room portion
of the system in Special Project 120 in 2004
proves that there is no south inlet for the central
artery but the central artery is constructed with
the first architectural site phase of the complex
as a whole. This has been further confirmed by
examinations of the artery in the Theater area.

Fig. 5.77
Temple, Theater orchestra
floor before the SP200
sondage, 2005.

Fig. 5.78
Temple, Theater
orchestra showing
the subterranean
canalization system,
to south, 2005.

Gate   Gate

Fig. 5.79
Temple, Theater orchestra
with subterranean canali-
zation system, to north.

With few exceptions the capstones of the central artery are cracked in the middle. Whether this results from earthquake damage or is prior to the abandonment of the temple is difficult to say, but clearly the structural integrity of the system is not flawless and might have brought about the abandonment and general rebuilding of the water systems in the Great Temple precinct. There are arteries from the west and east by the Central Stairs which are the viable water carrying systems in the first phase of canalization construction, whereas the central artery may have been a builder's mistake or an overflow valve for the entire water system.

Of particular note for the construction of the canalization is its progressive narrowing in the area underneath the *pulpitum* and the *distyle in antis* foundation wall. The west wall of the canalization consistently slopes westward, while the east wall narrows at roughly 2.00 m intervals and also banks gently to the west. The result is a gradual narrowing of the canalization: the width at the north of the orchestra is 0.76 m while at the blockage in the Pronaos it is 0.56 m. The most significant narrowing is at 3.80 m from the canalization opening in the Theatron where the *distyle in antis* foundation wall intercepts the canalization. From an examination of the construction technique, the *distyle in antis* foundation wall is built together with the central canalization and is probably a contributing factor to its westward direction.

In 2006 in the Great Temple Trench 123 is excavated in the Theater seating, and this excavation elucidates the earliest stratigraphy of the site. The west side of the Theater is selected primarily because limited restoration is undertaken there, and the bedrock escarpment of the temple's founding is higher in the east than in the west; thus it is reasoned that a west probe would yield substantially more evidence.

The methodology involves the marking, measuring and photographing of the two rows of seating of the lowest bank of seats on the *cavea* west side between the central and central west Theater staircases. Figure 5.76 shows the Theatron after restoration and Figure 5.81 illustrates the seats marked in preparation for removal. The two rows of seats are skillfully removed (Figure 5.82) and the ashlars are

measured and are placed in an assigned area for future restoration. Trench 123 is a small opening measuring 1.30 m north-south × 2.80 m east-west; it is excavated to a 5.80 m depth from the *diazoma* pavement.

Six stages are assigned to the excavated remains, three of which are assigned to Pre-Site Phase I. The earliest, Stage 1, is characterized by north and south large dry laid ashlar foundations, with an opening elevation of 901.72 m and a closing elevation of 901.36 m, providing perhaps a platform for a structure. Stage 2 is composed of fill, a sandy deposit and leveling

Fig. 5.80
Temple, Theater orchestra SP200 sondage, detail of center pivot stone.

Fig. 5.81
Temple, Theater with
cavea seats marked
for removal.

Fig. 5.82
Temple, Theater seats
removed for Trench 123
probe.

soil. Stage 3 is the construction of a 12-course tightly laid fieldstone wall with a boulder substructure. This wall, with an opening elevation of 904.90 m and a closing elevation of 903.04 m is comprised of slabs. One painted Nabataean ceramic found in this deposit belongs to early Site Phase II or to 50 BCE. Stage 4 is assigned to Great Temple Site Phase I and is characterized by intentional sedimentation and fill added to serve as the foundation level of the *distyle* platform. Stage 5 belongs to Site Phase II and is represented by a plaster floor surface at 905.33 m for the *distyle* temple. Stage 6 belongs to Site Phase V and is the leveling fill for the Theater seating. Figure 5.83 illustrates the sondage.

Exposing a series of early architectural walls, fills and surfaces of dissimilar construction from any not yet recovered monumental buildings at the Great Temple or in Petra, this probe concludes there are earlier structures in the temple interior *prior* to the construction of the *distyle in antis* structure. Not only is the dry laid fieldstone wall at an orientation different than any other architecture in the temple, it is not associated with the *distyle in antis* temple. It is significantly lower in elevation (904.90 m) than the depth, 905.35 m, of the *distyle in antis* foundation wall. Therefore the fieldstone wall at its closing presumably is built prior to the leveling out of the Upper Temenos for the construction of the *distyle* temple structure. Furthermore, this wall neither shares any architectural characteristics with early Nabataean construction as uncovered by Peter J. Parr's sondage (1970, Figure 1 Trench III) nor can it be cross referenced to any other first-century published ashlar Nabataean masonry. We definitively conclude that there are finely constructed earlier structures on the site of the Great Temple. Further, the probes both in the Temple and in the Upper Temenos demonstrate an active and materially rich community using the site prior to the construction of the *distyle* temple in Petra Great Temple Site Phase II.

Rune Frederiksen will analyze the Theater-In-The-Temple in Great Temple Volume III.

Conclusions

Enriched by trade, the Nabataeans employed local and foreign architects to build a great number of sumptuous buildings across Petra's landscape. One of the most prominent of these structures, the Petra Great Temple, illustrates the originality and eclecticism of the Nabataean craftsmen who constructed and embellished this monumental edifice. Over the course of their dynamic growth and change, the many structural incarnations of the temple help to trace the changing tastes and needs of its Nabataean clientele. In the earliest building phase, Site Phase II, the *distyle* temple with its corridor roughly corresponds to the formation of the Nabataean polity. Sometime toward the end of the first century BCE a profound change takes place, resulting in the expansion of the temple building into a *tetrastyle* form with the addition of lateral walkways and an immense Pronaos and Forecourt. Likely prompted by a minor earthquake tremor or other destructive natural phenomenon, this augmentation of the temple building enhances its visual and functional prominence corresponding, perhaps, to a change in the pattern of government. A second significant shift occurs with the installation of the central Theater, supported from beneath by an intricate maze of interior chambers, staircases and landings. Though an arguably Nabataean addition, the Theater also indicates growing foreign presence in Petra, further marked by the subsequent addition of the stage.

Although scholars agree that the Petra Great Temple is one of the most important monuments of the Nabataean capital, its function and purpose remain a topic of controversy.[13] Buried beneath a dense overburden of debris amassed over multiple periods of abandonment and collapse, the true character of the temple is difficult to determine. Based on excavations and analysis, we believe that while the Great Temple is predominantly a religious structure, it also serves in a political capacity. The distinction between the two functions, however, is a matter of interpretation of the presented archaeological and architectural evidence and will be treated more fully in Volume III.

Fig. 5.83
Temple, Theater Trench 123
probe, 2006.

Notes

1.

Smooth red or yellow plaster extends to a point 3.16 m above the base, and above this is cable fluting.

2.

Some of the cassettes on the walls are decorated with a plaster mimicking fancy variegated types of stone.

3.

McKenzie: 1990: 190 Diagram 4, f.

4.

The diagnostic pottery from SP107, a sondage in the Great Temple Pronaos, confirms the dating of this Site Phase to the first century BCE.

5.

During the earthquake of 363 CE many of the temple elements were flung far and wide, collapsing into other areas of the Great Temple complex as well as likely into perimeter areas in the east and west.

6.

Dr. Robert Wenning (personal communication) states," It reminds me of the bust of a male deity...(Zayadine, *ADAJ* 25, 1981, pl.103.1) Also see (Hammond *BASOR* 192, 1968). "[These] reliefs can represent Dushara, but there is so far no way to prove this suggestion."

7.

For further discussion also see Egan's published study in *ADAJ* Vol. 46 in 2001, pp. 347–361.

8.

See page 19 for discussion of this project.

9.

The 2.00 m east-west × 18.00 m north-south pavement of the walkway floor, from the northeastern corner, is robbed out or removed. At one time, these flagstone pavers, we presume, cover the entire walkway area. The present state of preservation, however, cannot verify this possibility.

10.

Careful excavation of soil deposits on the extant wall indicate that one portion of this wall belongs to a pre-destruction phase of building. During the cleaning of the top of the wall, a hard, brown clay layer with pellet-like charcoal inclusions adheres to the top course. This section of wall is 4.70 m in length × 0.60 m in width. The section is only one course high, and is comprised of smoothly dressed sandstone and limestone blocks. The average size of these blocks measures approximately 0.50 m in width × 0.28 m in height. This layer suggests that this wall is built (and destroyed) before the abandonment and destruction layers are deposited.

11.

Some of the pavement encircling the postholes appears to have broken away during their carving. Presumably, if they are originally planned for the area, they should have been carefully carved before the tiles are placed in the floor.

12.

The idea of the "sacred theater" is referenced in Arthur Segal's *Theatres in Roman Palestine and Provincia Arabia* (1995) and is cited by the excavator (Basile 1999, 26, unpublished Final Report Trench 62 excavations), as a place "where sacred pageants, ceremonial banquets and

rituals that required mass audiences are held. The major requirements of such theatres are that they have no stage building (or a small or 'underdeveloped stage') and that they have an unobstructed view to a landscape of sacred feature."

13.

There are those who view it strictly as an administrative center. Our view is that particularly in Site Phases II–VII it serves as a temple with administrative functions. See Chapter 7 for the discussion of "The Great Debate."

CHAPTER SIX

The Conservation,
Consolidation, Preservation
and Protection of the
Petra Great Temple Precinct

Lifting the pilaster relief of a female (see Fig. 3.26) for display in the East Exedra.

CHAPTER SIX

The Conservation, Consolidation, Preservation and Protection of the Petra Great Temple Precinct

Introduction

In Petra we live with the environmental uncertainties of flash floods, earthquakes and erosive action. To us, conservation is essential for the care and protection of the Great Temple site, although we are sure that these natural disasters will continue to threaten the site and cause widespread damage. It is too soon for us to have any feeling of security about either our short-term or long-term Great Temple site conservation efforts or for the future of Petra as a whole. A battle we wage at every stage of our fourteen-year excavation process has us pitted against "Mother Nature."[1] Figure 6.1 is a view of the Petra Great Temple site at the close of the 1994 excavations.

The Great Temple site demanded the same sorts of resources used by the Nabataeans and Nabataean masons, and this has involved a myriad of different challenges. In short, our requirements are the same as they were in Nabataean times. We are just beginning to explicate Nabataean culture by addressing the most basic aspects of the physical manifestation of the Great Temple and its precinct and by isolating the architectural, chronological and spatial characteristics of this structure in relation to its seismic environment.

Often archaeologists leave behind a denuded wasteland, as excavation has brought destruction to many sites while simultaneously destroying the vegetation. In our attempts to excavate the Great Temple, we have tried to control the damage and minimize the effect of the excavations on the environment. The success and final result requires planning and vision during the execution of an excavation. It is often subject to, and the question of, attitudes,

values and financial resources all working in concert. We have attempted to look beyond the immediate survival of the Great Temple precinct for its well being and its future use as an archaeological resource, and, ultimately to preserve and restore the Petra Great Temple as a national monument.

Conservation and restoration reflect multiple values that can be stated briefly as the scientific interest and value of the remains, their aesthetic value for art historians and tourists, the unique archaeological features and information they provide, and recognition of the technological acumen of the Nabataeans. Maintaining the function of the Petra Great Temple environment helps to perpetuate the precinct in its environment. Our aim is to restore and consolidate a stable structure in as stable an environment as possible.

Inherently a destructive science, archaeological excavation raises the issue of on-site efforts of consolidation and restoration. In the act of rescuing architecture and material culture from a dense cover of debris and accumulation, the elements of a site are exposed anew to the threats of human contact and environmental decay. Fortunately the Great Temple site was untouched by modern development. (Figures 6.2 and 6.3 depict the energies involved with the moving of architectural elements.) From the beginning of our work, the fundamental philosophy of the Petra Great Temple excavations has been to treat the site as a fragile and nonrenewable resource requiring protection. Constructed primarily from friable sandstone and degraded limestone, the temple complex is a prime target for material exfoliation as a result of wind and water erosion and the deposition

of insoluble salts. This assumption of potential for structural deterioration makes efforts of consolidation and restoration an ongoing priority. To combat these natural threats a number of measures are taken to reinforce the physical structure of the site with vigorous support from Ghazi Bisheh and Fawwaz al-Kraysheh, Directors of the Department of Antiquities of the Hashemite Kingdom of Jordan, and from Suleiman Farajat, Director of the Petra National Park. Attempting to undertake conservation efforts during excavation and following the completion of each season, annual consolidation plans are proposed to the Jordanian Department of Antiquities where site-specific measures are proposed and discussed, and problems are addressed. In most cases, solutions are found.

This management requires a high degree of international cooperation with the Jordanian Department of Antiquities and a willingness to agree to some forms of control. As far as the site is concerned, conservation-oriented recommendations are annually exchanged with the Jordanian Department of Antiquities and the American Center of Oriental Research (ACOR). ACOR monitors the status of many aspects involved with our consolidation-conservation strategies. All of our proposals are carefully considered before a decision is made to conserve a particular wall, column, or other feature.

In a continued effort to uphold the principles proposed by the International Council on Monuments and Sites, the International Committee on Archaeological Heritage Management (the World Heritage Convention in 1972), the 1966 Venice Charter, the Hague Convention and the tenets of the 1956, 1970 and 1985 UNESCO Conventions, we choose to adhere to field treatments that prevent any harm to the site and are reversible. To this end, it is important to note that architectural restoration at the Petra Great Temple has not been undertaken in a true sense. With elements frequently lack-

Fig. 6.2
Moving a column drum to the lapidary.

Fig. 6.3
Moving an architectural fragment to the lapidary.

Fig. 6.1
The Great Temple precinct
at the close of the 1994
season, to south.

Fig. 6.4
Cleaning between ashlars.

ing a clear basis for their reconstruction based on archaeological context, the measures we are taking are geared solely toward the immediate, though impermanent, preservation of the structural integrity of the precinct. When intact, original stones are reconstituted into temple masonry. In almost all cases original building materials are used. When fragmentary or robbed out, original constructions are replaced by new stone fills quarried from the Petra bedrock. Our conservation-preservation team has been on site since the inception of our project in 1993.

This labor-intensive detailed work of consolidation and restoration (Figure 6.4) is performed under the expert direction of site foreman Dakhilallah Qublan with the assistance of some 20 local workmen and the aid of skilled specialists or technicians including architect May Shaer and conservator Ulrich Bellwald, and under the watchful eye of Pierre M. Bikai and Barbara A. Porter, Directors of the American Center for Oriental Research. All of the

aforementioned people have helped us identify issues, know about available resources and select the materials or technical experts and skilled individuals to perform the work. This group helps to guide our major decisions.

At the outset of the 1994 excavations, we organized a long-term plan for our site preservation. These measures often were impacted by short-term year-by-year excavation progress that served as immediate temporary expedients to strengthen elements that required specific stabilization.

The conservation of the Petra Great Temple also includes the preservation of those *in situ* elements that were essentially undisturbed by excavation but required structural protection because of natural processes of deterioration such as spalling ashlars and loose mortars. We attempt to carry out restoration so that the structural integrity of the architecture is sustained.

Financial Considerations

From the beginning, it was made clear that the Department of Antiquities would not be able to financially support the conservation measures. This meant that our project had to incorporate conservation plans concurrent with the excavation. As there are no governmental agencies that can care adequately for Petra, the site is at risk. We formed a scientific advisory committee to help us rule on the appropriateness of any proposed consolidation and restoration. We knew that careful planning had to be undertaken if we were to modify the landscape naturally or artificially. In the early years with deep trenches exposed, we had to set these fragile areas off limits and protect visitors and animals from falling into them. We also had to carefully plan the means of human access to the site. Figure 6.5 pictures Trench 17 below the Lower Temenos Triple Colonnade excavated to a depth of 6.00 m, which was barricaded to safeguard and protect the curious public.

Yearly conservation efforts were made financially possible by two awards from The World Monuments Fund, a grant from the Samuel H. Kress Foundation through an American Express Award from World Monuments Watch (1996 and 1998, respectively), a program of the World Monuments Fund, and the generous support of the Joukowsky Family Foundation. From 2000, the Joukowsky Family Foundation has provided subventions for annual conservation expenses. These funds are generously matched several times over by special subventions through donations to the Petra Excavation Fund constituted at Brown University.

Although the importance of consolidation and conservation may seem obvious, most excavation budgets are so tight that to be concerned with anything more than excavation is difficult. Since our annual budget is not guaranteed, we have to select our projects carefully, and planning for site conservation has always been in doubt when excavation costs alone have been a cause for concern. Such activities—excavation, conservation, consolidation, preservation and publication—are always planned along with our Brown University annual budgets, although when finances are tight there

Fig. 6.5
Deep sondage in the East Triple Colonnade with *voussoirs* appearing to the right.

have been moments of conflict and financial readjustments between these areas. Each year we have to outline and refine what we are realistically capable of conserving over the period of years we will be working at the Great Temple.

Once the annual excavations ended it was found that there was time to consolidate those individual areas that required repair. Each year we proposed a long-term plan and prioritized which projects required immediate attention. Once the short-term annual goals had been met, the longer-term goals of a working plan could be resolved by deciding on what the priorities were for consolidation, mapping out and photographing the areas. Decisions were made as to what materials would be needed, such as scaffolding, mortar components, stones that needed to be cut and dressed (Figure 6.6), and finally the placement or implementation of each project.

Conservation Challenges

In 1993, although the precinct had largely been abandoned, we found the Great Temple site had been exploited by locals for building and farming; there was serious deterioration of many of the architectural elements while others were severely eroded. This is clearly depicted by the erosive state of the Porch Column shown in Figure 6.7. The Great Temple site had suffered from neglect, as is common in Petra. Individuals who had over many years used the area for farming had plundered the Lower Temenos. Elephantheaded capitals when found on the surface had been carried away as souvenirs—and one still serves as a doorstop in a local Bedouin house!

Conservation is essential to the Great Temple site, which depends upon the proper "consolidation" of each of the elements with the ultimate purpose of maintaining the elements that are imperiled and require care and protection. It also involves the controlled use and systematic protection of local natural resources. The ultimate goal is to preserve and protect the site for the future.

Preventative preservation of the site is undertaken through the construction of flood channels to divert heavy winter rains away from the complex, the backfilling of trenches to limit exposure of weak structural elements

Fig. 6.6
Chiseling an ashlar for reconstruction.

Fig. 6.7
A deteriorated *in situ* east Porch column.

to air and water seepage, and the wrapping of delicate areas with a plastic mesh covered with zinc sheeting secured by sandbags. Figure 6.8 illustrates the cleaning of wall surfaces before restoration takes place, and Figure 6.9 shows a doorjamb about to split and collapse due to its exposure to the elements—salts, air and water. It is probably jostled out of position by the impact of a seismic event. Protective fencing is also placed around the site perimeter[2] and open excavation areas are partitioned in order to insure the safety of both the visitors to the site and the site itself.

A planned comprehensive management plan for the protection, conservation and interpretation of the Petra Great Temple was initiated in 1994. Primary necessities included two factors: the ecosystem of the site itself to prevent further strain on the site due to erosion from both soil and water, as well as the careful management of consolidation and restoration of its archaeological components. In order for the archaeological remains to remain stable and consolidation measures to be preserved, the recurring processes of soil and water erosion that had been a serious problem had to be limited.

We planned our archaeological investigations as a long-term commitment to the Great Temple, to Petra, and to Jordan. With the continued excavation of the site, the research design, including the needs of its architectural elements, required expansion. It became essential to organize and direct conservation efforts over an increased area. Progress for the protection of a site must involve, first, a rational planning for the public use and access to the site. The long-term benefits have been considerable not only for the aesthetic value of the archaeological remains but also for the public understanding of its architectural statement. Unfortunately as excavations progress, the extent of new discoveries cannot be anticipated.

Fig. 6.8
Preparation for consolidation.

Fig. 6.9
Typical scene of a doorway requiring consolidation.

Excavation

Excavation is invasive; it has made the site vulnerable and our challenge has been to assure its preservation in the most effective ways possible. In 1993 we initiated training in excavation, and we have trained more than 90 students in excavation methodology, including surveying and conservation. From this group of students, many have gone on to graduate studies and are now qualified and respected archaeologists in their own right. Over the years these researchers have devoted at least ten weeks a year to excavating, preparing measured drawings, site mapping, writing final reports and interpreting the site. The tasks range in complexity from the careful removal of debris and documentation to interpretation. But of all these important aspects, they are also required to recommend and prioritize the specifics of conservation and consolidation of the areas they have been involved in excavating. These recommendations have been integral to our planning as they are then reprioritized for the consolidation program.

Working painstakingly beside us are local Jordanian workmen who willingly help us to reverse existing damage that is discovered during the excavation process. They have become skilled in moving architectural fragments with the attendant dangers of imminent collapse. They fill vulnerable cracks in the walls with broken bits and chunks of stone to keep the wall ashlars from collapse. Such restorative work imitates the methods used by the Nabataeans who used chinking extensively in the original construction of the precinct. They also sweep the site, cut back the weed growth, pick up detritus, and monitor the site's well being throughout the year. This adds immeasurably to the effort for ongoing site maintenance.

Although excavation can reveal a site, it can be poorly related to the consequences that take place as the site is excavated, and these consequences may produce side effects that are not anticipated, thereby disrupting the overall excavation research plan. A multitude of varying examples of such situations were encountered, among which was when in 2004 the Propylaeum Room 3 arch was unearthed in a state of collapse or when the Lower Temenos West Cryptoporticus walls required support.

The Upper Temenos Baroque Room and the Residential Quarter were recovered in 2002 with considerable time-consuming restorative needs. During the same year the Great Cistern was discovered, which required additional, different conservation measures. Our excavation plans had to be flexible and innovative to meet the challenges the excavation posed. In each instance we had to reorganize our excavation research. When we discovered the temple West Corridor west wall, the arched passage entrance seriously buckled and in a state of imminent collapse, we immediately concluded that its restoration was demanded. In each instance, the research design needed to be completely adjusted, so that recovery would be in keeping with the overall site integrity. To the non-archaeologist these aspects of excavation may seem to be the exception to the rule, but it is striking that during every excavation season at the Great Temple, such exceptions have become commonplace. Similar to the step-by-step process by which areas are selected to excavate, our selected preservation projects have to be the most appropriate and meaningful, and priorities have to be identified. In spite of these considerations, the results are that we have had remarkable breakthroughs that speak for themselves.

During excavation, each trench supervisor records all stones that are trench coded, number referenced and marked with that reference number. This number is carried both to our site database and to the lapidary where the stones are stored by type. We use a minimum of mechanical equipment to remove the debris from the site and to lift heavy objects. Rollers (metal pipes) are used dexterously to bring large stones into position for removal. The stones are then wrapped in a steel reinforced strap and are lifted by the bulldozer bucket prongs to be moved to their disposal area. If the object is decorated, it might be swaddled in a blanket or wrapped in foam before lifting. The steel reinforced straps serve to cradle the fragments to be lifted and placed into their specifically prepared storage areas. (See photograph opposite p. 281 in which the pilaster block of Fortuna is shown being hoisted in this fashion.)[3] This system has proved invaluable for protecting finely sculpted capitals—for example spectacular elephant-headed capitals, one of the crowning discoveries of the Great Temple protect—and pilaster blocks as well as the more mundane ashlars. Debris from the site is trucked to a place that has been reserved by the authorities for our spoil heap.

During restoration the workers use wooden scaffolding for platforms along with a simple block and tackle to lift heavy architectural fragments such as column drums, capitals, vault slabs, ashlars and lintels. This process can be seen in Figures 6.70 and 6.73.

The Lapidaries—Storage for Architectural Elements

The objectives in our varied stone object storage areas—"lapidaries"—are to keep architectural elements in a favorable and separate microenvironment until they can be used for restoration. Every architectural element excavated has been numbered, measured and recorded in our site database. Included in this database are ashlars, thousands of wall blocks that originally served as the defining building blocks of the structure. There are also arch ashlars, voussoirs and arch slabs used to embellish the walls, as well as doorjambs and threshold blocks and flagstones used for pavements. Other elements include many hundreds of column drums and associated column decoration such as Attic bases, capitals and capital elements. During excavation architectural fragments have overwhelmed us, and from the first we established lapidaries for these elements divided by type. By sorting the architectural fragments according to their physical characteristics, we felt we could better manage their storage. We realize as well that some of the most serious conservation problems are associated not with the way such elements have been excavated, but with the methods by which they are stored. We make every effort to protect these storage areas.

We have six main areas for architectural storage. Small decorative elements including pinecones, hibiscus flowers, poppies, vines and the like have been placed in boxes and stored underground at the site in especially prepared trenches that are the result of previous excavation, basically returning them to their microenvironment. Figure 6.10 pictures the architectural fragment storage area in the Lower Temenos.[4] In a fenced off area to the west of the temple is

Fig. 6.10
On-site storage of smaller architectural fragments.

Fig. 6.11
Sculpture Garden.

our so-called "sculpture garden" (Figure 6.11), which is reserved for larger elements such as pilaster blocks, volutes from capitals, bosses, nearly complete capitals, and large domestic implements such as grinders and millstones. In the West Lapidary is the storage of column drums (Figure 6.12), and on the West roadway *voussoirs* and arch blocks are stored along with arch slabs. Another area is reserved only for ashlars that have promise of reuse, and finally there is an area designed for broken and fragmented pieces that have little structural or decorative integrity, but that may be used for snecking stone support for other architectural elements. Elephant capital-associated fragments and the complete massive elephant-headed capitals that we have recovered have been restored, drawn,

photographed and cataloged in our artifact registry. Some have been turned over to the Petra Museum for safekeeping.[5] The few that have been bruised have been retrofitted to the tops of columns in the Propylaeum and Lower Temenos. We have had limestone facsimiles made of the *betyl*s (Figure 6.20) found in the West Propylaeum and have reinstalled them, and the originals also have been turned over to the Petra Museum. In the West Entry Stairs we commissioned the carving of a fine replica of the *nefesh* (Figure 6.13; see also Figures 3.57–3.58), which replaced the original found on the platform in the West Entry Stairway. The original has been deposited with the Petra Museum for display.

A Concern about Water

The Nabataeans developed their city plan with great skill, creating agricultural landscapes that reflected such skills in the management of water resources. They equipped themselves with the ability to modify what available water resources they had.[6] As Petra became a growing metropolis there must have been an increasing demand for water, both for domestic and agricultural purposes.

Now Jordan witnesses unusually severe water shortages, and there has been a serious lowering of the water table. The seasonality of water flow in Petra is acute. As expert water conservationists report, the subsurface aquifers today have all but run dry. There have been extreme changes in the landscape and in Petra, within the memory of a single generation, accompanied by changes in the abundance of wildlife. The continued survival of wild nature is limited. Although Petra has become a National Park, there is a real need for its continued protection.

As water is a scarce, exhaustible resource, we know that the total water supply is underground. The rates at which available reserves are being depleted exceed the rate at which new resources can be formed. The Nabataean rock-cut channels and supplementary built up subterranean water channels had to be consolidated so the water run off would protect the site as it did in the Nabataean period.

Fig. 6.14
The Great Wall from above.

The Great Wall

Knowing that the site is finite, we also know that it must be protected in ways that provide for stability, and through measures, possibly, we can help to reverse the process of its deterioration, at least temporarily. But of course the hope is that the measures taken will have long-term benefits. Like most of Petra, the Great Temple is extremely vulnerable to flash floods. The most effective way of ensuring the least impact from flash floods and rains was to build a terrace wall along the south flank of the site to deflect the water and ensure that the soils of the Ez Zantur ridge would have a barrier preventing their falling on the site. This offset inset wall has increased the protection of the site to ensure its architectural preservation.

The Great Wall is a freestanding structure safeguarding the Great Temple precinct. Located on the south flank of the precinct, it follows the bedrock surround. It is comprised of excavated stones bound together with mortar. In a direct line it measures 104 m in length by 1.50 m in width, but it is constructed with offsets and insets to conform to the topography. The overall constructed length, including the offsets and insets, totals 110.63 m. A retaining wall of sandstone ashlars protects the planting of aloe and cacti with perennials that are planted along its top as a shelter bed to hold the soil in place and to support the wall. Thus, the wall holds soil in place and provides a guarantee of water flow away from the site. It helps to place as little strain on the temple precinct as possible.

The Great Temple precinct has one glorious tree on the site, an elegant antique juniper, which is shown in Figure 6.15. During the excavation of the South Passageway and southeast temple Corridor Walls, we found the roots had spread to the north for about 5.00 m and had grown between the wall ashlars of the temple's South Corridor Wall, weakening the joins between them. A close study indicated some roots had to be cut and this was done in 2000. We, of course, were concerned that we would seriously disrupt the tree's growth, but it seems to have maintained its balance with the environment and continues to thrive, deserted, but still beautiful.

Other Walls

With restoration we have set forth a few standards for our work. Walls partially recover their original heights only when these heights are known. Not only are the ashlars in the wall pointed, but also the upper wall courses are reinforced with wood beams when we have known them to exist. The tops or exterior uppermost course of the walls are covered with a protective layer of waterproof cement.

Fig. 6.15
The Great Temple juniper tree.

Recycling

One of our plans was to recycle sandstone ashlars and column drums, as well as the limestone elements used in the Great Temple. Recycling involves the reprocessing of architectural elements. Although the grains of many blocks are dissolved from leaching, and the surfaces have become etched and friable, each is studied, and if sufficient structural integrity is present they are reclaimed and re-cut. Figure 6.16 shows the tools—the wedge, the toothed chisel and the hammer—masons use to cut and dress stones, and Figure 6.17 pictures an ashlar being dressed at a 45-degree angle as the Nabataean would have scored the stone (to provide a bedding for plaster).

From the impact of the elements, sandstone blocks are often cracked by natural action and decompose, thusly reverting to sand. It is quite common to see them flaked or pitted, incrusted with salts or other erosive elements responsible for their disintegration. Before a strong block can be used for reconstruction, it has to be determined if its physical structure remains suited to its continued reuse for restoration. Recyclable blocks with structural integrity have often been used, so we gather together and set aside the excavated materials in our ashlar lapidaries for re-processing, and reclaim these Nabataean materials.

Mortar

During the conservation process, several studies have been made of consolidates for the restoration of both standing structures and decorative detailing, leading to the successful identification of solutions for structural fragility and other material sensitivities. Effective measures had to be undertaken to analyze Nabataean mortars. Figure 6.18 shows samples being extracted between the ashlars in the South Corridor Wall for chemical testing. Directed by Helge H. Fischer, the Conservation and Restoration Center (CARCIP) in Petra, funded by German Technical Assistance (GTZ), has trained Jordanian experts. Working on tomb Br. Monument 825 (the Tomb of the Eleven Graves), they have chemically analyzed the Nabataean mortar used for grouting architectural elements and

Fig. 6.16
Tools of the mason:
the awl, the toothed chisel
and the hammer.

Fig. 6.17
A mason dressing an
ashlar using the toothed
chisel and hammer.

Fig. 6.18
Extracting mortar samples from between the blocks of the Great Temple South Passageway Wall to analyze their chemical composition so that similar mortars are used in restoration.

have undertaken multiple analyses of mortars at Petra. As clean sand is an essential ingredient for the mixture, a search was made of the Petra area to find the best and purest sand. It was found nearby in Wadi Farasa. As transportation from Wadi Farasa is difficult, restoration team members excavate the sand and load it onto donkeys to transport it to the site where it is sifted. The mortar mixture, of lime (calcium carbonates), clay, and clean sifted sand, is water resistant and is compatible with the architectural elements. The elements are crushed and ground to a fine powder, blended to the desired proportions and mixed with water. White cement is used to set and harden the mixture. The hydration of the calcium silicates takes place when the water evaporates. As far as extant mortars between blocks are concerned, we remove only that increment that needs to be replaced.

Stonemasons

In the early years of our work, professionally qualified master stonemasons needed to be located for the restoration of the Great Temple. Such masons were hired and brought from Amman to help us duplicate the dressing of the original stone. Within a few years, these master sculptors had trained a number of local Bedouin workmen, as they have been trained to understand the techniques of the ancient Nabataeans in consolidation. This involves an understanding of the techniques not only of the Nabataean stonemason, but the strategies of the actual conservation and consolidation of the stone. For the past ten years it is local stonemasons who have restored the Great Temple.

Stucco Decoration

One of the most difficult and yet fascinating battles we have had to wage is with the weathered and collapsed Great Temple plaster. In 1998 we requested a chemical analysis of the Great Temple plasters and stuccos by the Canadian Conservation Institute. Additionally in 2000 conservator May Shaer of the Jordanian Department of Antiquities conducted an independent analysis of the plasters. Both studies were subsequently published, and the results became important for understanding of the Nabataean plasterer's art.[7]

As plaster covered most of the visible surfaces of the temple—stairways, columns, and walls, as well as the Baroque Room ceiling—facilitation of the work had to be undertaken by a skilled plaster restorer. Much of the plaster fall in the temple excavations was found in pieces mixed with the fill. In the Baroque Room the thick richly embellished plastered ceiling fell with reed impressions from the roofing (Figures 4.76–4.83). Figure 6.19 shows the West Corridor restoration of the plaster behind the scaffolding.[8]

The Petra Archaeological Park

The archaeological park encompasses the site in which the region, environment and site monuments can be preserved. The director of the Park, appointed by the Department of Antiquities, is Suleiman Farajat who over the years oversees and coordinates our efforts. Although Farajat is an empowered governmental authority, there are very limited funds to support the park financially, and regulations tend to be ineffective. The Petra National Park and local Bedouin restorers are devoted to the site and its comprehensive preservation and restoration plan. The Bedouin of Petra have turned Petra as a whole into a mono-economy based on eco-tourism. Many of them have become engaged in tourism, and they appreciate the value of the site and its restoration and preservation.

Artifacts on Tour

To promote knowledge of Jordan's extraordinary cultural heritage, the Jordanian government transported a number of pieces of sculpture, including elephant-headed capitals, on tour to museums in America and Canada. Independently, the stucco Baroque Room ceiling and several other artifacts traveled to Berlin and Bonn, Germany, and other of our elephant-headed capitals were transported to Helsinki, Finland, for display. These well-publicized expositions promoted a public recognition of Jordan's cultural heritage and an unparalleled view of a Nabataean historic focus. It is hoped that international support will raise funds to address the inadequacy of the Petra Museum so that when these objects return they will be properly displayed in a new Petra Museum venue close to the site.

Fig. 6.19
Conservation of the stucco elements of the West Corridor Wall.

Consolidation Efforts at the Petra Great Temple 1994–2006[9]

Keeping in mind the strategy outlined above, the following record will present a summary of conservation efforts undertaken at the Petra Great Temple in annual field campaigns from 1994 to 2006. Each part of the precinct will be presented separately, as a summary—the Propylaeum, Lower Temenos, Upper Temenos and the Great Temple—so that the overall efforts in each area might be better understood.

Propylaeum

Beginning in 1994, consolidation efforts in the Petra Great Temple Propylaeum focused on the *anastylosis* (reconstruction stone by stone) of the lower curbing and steps of the Propylaeum Central Staircase. In 1996, the stair foundations were partially consolidated with mud mortar and small fieldstones, and the steps were reconstructed using freshly cut ashlar blocks. In 2007 the steps were completely restored. During the 1998 and 2001 seasons, reconstruction efforts moved to the Propylaeum East and West where a number of collapsed arch springers were consolidated and reset into the cryptoporticus walls. In 2000 and 2001, the Brown University team installed two complete elephant-headed capitals recovered in the Propylaeum West at the entrance of the Petra Museum.[11] Also in 2001, the double *betyls*, discovered in a niche in the Propylaeum West, were turned over to the Petra Museum for safekeeping and replacement stone copies were carved to indicate their *in situ* excavated position. Figure 6.20 portrays the restored *betyls*, bench and wall. In the following 2002 season, the walls of the newly exposed north cryptoporticus of the Propylaeum West were consolidated.

From 2003 through 2005 restoration concentrated on the Propylaeum East. The first project involved the restoration of the interior partition walls between Rooms 1, 2, and 3 to a height of 3.20 m. An overview of these walls can be seen in Figure 6.21. Pointing between the out-of-position ashlars also consolidated the Portico Wall and the doorways of these rooms. The 2004 excavation of the Chamber 3 vault posed a significant challenge for restoration,

Fig. 6.20
Restored facsimiles of the double *betyls* in the original position in the West Propylaeum above the bench below.

Fig. 6.21
Restored walls of the East Propylaeum Rooms 1–3, to the west.

undertaken during the fall of 2004 and winter of 2005. As can be seen in Figures 6.22 and 6.23, the large vaulted space when excavated was in danger of collapse and needed to be supported with wooden scaffolding. Figure 6.24 shows the vault as it looks today, Figure 6.25 details the north end of the vault with its projecting *voussoirs* indicating that the restoration of the vault, although stabilized, is incomplete and appears unfinished. In antiquity this vault did continue, probably to the north buttress, (but we refrained from its over restoration). Figure 6.26 is an image of the restored flat roof above the vault as it appears today.

After the 2003 excavation season we re-erected four columns on the level of the Lower Temenos—two adjacent to the Propylaeum Central Stairs and another two at the end of the Propylaeum Retaining Wall, respectively. When elephant capitals were recovered during the 2004 excavation, they were mounted atop the four to five stacked column drums at a height of 2.40 m to 2.50 m. Figure 6.27 shows one of these columns with five drums restored with its elephant-headed capital. Of course, in antiquity these columns stood much higher, to a height of more than seven meters, but we opted in this case to indicate the placement of the columns and the idea of their positions and not to restore them to their original height.

In 2004–2005, the West Entry Stairway had been recovered. Figure 6.28 shows the brushing of these stairs. In 2005 it was apparent that the east entry to the stairway had to be consolidated and restored, and three or four steps from the Roman Street and Sidewalk had to be placed to access the entry doorway, using the entry width as a guide. Additionally the ashlar entry blocks had to be cleaned out and pointed, particularly those that were in jeopardy of collapse.

The entry to the Great Temple precinct gives rise to our concern about visitor access. In 2006 some thought was given to the Central Stairway, which required fill to be imported to level a depression in the west side of the stairs. We also decided to extend the Roman treads to the west, leaving the Nabataean Stairs open, so the flight of earlier stairs could be appreciated by the visitor. Because it is difficult to ascend the West Entry Stairway from the Roman Road Sidewalk, three new stairs were placed across the opening for ease in access to the stairway threshold.

In the West Cryptoporticus, the difficult job of *anastylosis* of the West Cryptoporticus West gallery wall called for immediate attention, for its relationship to the walls on its east and west was tenuous. There was fear not only of its collapse, but also of the danger of its ashlars falling 5.00 m onto the West Cryptoporticus pavement and hurting someone in the process. Figures 6.29–6.31 illustrate this complicated restoration procedure.

In 2005 Special Project 104 had been undertaken in the East Corridor of the West Cryptoporticus, and a number of flagstones had been removed. This area had to be refilled and the original pavement put back in place.

Fig. 6.22
Wood support for the walls of the East Propylaeum Rooms 1–3, to the northeast.

Fig. 6.23
Supporting the vault from collapse of the East Propylaeum Room 3.

Fig. 6.24
Restored vault of East
Propylaeum Room 3, to south.

Fig. 6.25
Looking down on the roof of the restored vault
of East Propylaeum Room 3.

Fig. 6.26
Looking down on the roof of the restored vault
of East Propylaeum Room 3, to north.

Fig. 6.27
A restored column of
the Propylaeum with an
elephant-headed capital.

Fig. 6.28
Sweeping a West Entry
Stairway upper platform.

Fig. 6.29
Ongoing restoration in the
West Cryptoporticus and
the West Entry Stairway.

Fig. 6.30
Restoration of the West
Cryptoporticus west wall,
to the west.

Fig. 6.31
Restoration of the West
Cryptoporticus and the top
of the West Entry Stairway,
to north.

Lower Temenos

Conservation efforts in the Petra Great Temple Lower Temenos east began in 1994 with the replacement of a number of weathered column drums in the East Colonnade. Figure 6.32 shows the 1996 Brown team standing in place of the columns in the East Triple Colonnade and Figures 6.33 and 6.34 illustrate the same colonnade to the north during restoration in 2000. In 1998, work continued with the restoration of six columns of the colonnade to a maximum height of 6.80 m. In 2000, additional columns were re-erected as can be seen in Figure 6.35. A carved elephant-headed capital was placed atop the highest of the six columns to give visi-

tors a better understanding of the position and appearance of these features within the complex (Figure 6.36). This effect was later mirrored during the 2001 season with the placement of an elephant-headed capital atop a consolidated column of the West Colonnade north of the West Exedra (Figure 6.37). In 2002, additional columns of both the East and West Colonnades were re-erected as shown in Figure 6.38.

In 1996, efforts moved to the central plaza of the Lower Temenos where a number of hexagonal paving tiles were removed to allow for the refilling and leveling of the fill between the subterranean canalization capstones and the pavement above. The insertion of new fill material was a delicate procedure calling for

Fig. 6.32
The 1996 Brown University Team posing as columns in the Lower Temenos East Triple Colonnade before restoration.

a preliminary investigation of the pavement substructure to determine the optimal type and weight of the new fill prior to installation. In the southeast, conservation efforts included the repair of the East Exedra shown in Figure 6.39, following structural damage incurred during the winter downpours of 1996. In the same year, collapsed elements of the East Staircase adjacent to the East Exedra shown in Figure 6.40 were restored, and the canalization below the staircase was accessed and consolidated. Stabilization of the East Exedra continued into the 1998 and 2001 seasons with the removal and replacement of deteriorating blocks weakening the integrity of the overall structure. In 2002, additional eroded blocks in the East Exedra walls were replaced and were rebuilt to the height of the West Exedra walls.

In the southwest, comparable degradation was visible in the gaps along the eastern portion of the West Exedra walls. Figure 6.41 typifies

the dislodged weathered ashlars, which were filled with mud mortar and small stone wedges in 1996. In the same year crumbling drums and an east buttress of the columns in the West Exedra entry were removed, treated with mud mortar fills, and replaced. North of the West Exedra, a drainage channel was covered with sand and backfilled. East of the West Exedra, the east and west walls of the West Staircase were pointed, and missing ashlars were replaced with newly carved stone blocks. Figure 6.42 shows these stairs before restoration, and Figure 6.43 is a view of the steps after their consolidation and restoration. The foundation of the staircase was treated with fills of mud mortar and small fieldstones prior to the restoration of the steps, using both original and newly cut ashlars.

During several years, the West Cryptoporticus had come to light (Figures. 3.39–3.43). All the walls of the structure required consolidation—the east and west walls of the twin galleries as well as the central buttress wall. Vaults were constructed between the central wall and

Fig. 6.33 and Fig. 6.34
The East Triple Colonnade
undergoing restoration.

the east and west walls so that this originally subterranean structure could be better understood. In 2002, two of the dramatic end vaults were rebuilt in the West Cryptoporticus. One of these restored twin vaults can be seen in Figure 6.44.[10]

The West Stairway east wall and West Cryptoporticus west wall were in danger of collapsing into the adjacent West Cryptoporticus. The West Entry Stairway shares its east wall with the west wall of the west gallery of the West Cryptoporticus, as can be seen in Figure 6.45. There were signs that this wall had partially eroded in antiquity and the erosion was perhaps one of the reasons behind the collapse of the West Cryptoporticus East Gallery. While excavating, we found that a portion of the east wall had fallen into the east gallery in antiquity, and with excavation it was further compromised. In a ruined state, this wall section needed to be completely dismantled, reconstructed, and pointed. The area conserved in 2006–2007 is illustrated in Figure 6.46.

For the safety of pedestrians using the West Entry Stairway, conservation had to be undertaken as soon as the excavations were completed. This was an enormous responsibility demanding that the integrity of both the remaining elements of the this stairway and the West Cryptoporticus walls be respected. An interrelated project was to create a sand platform over the portion where the stairway ended, to protect the deposits, and then to construct a wooden platform with a banister railing support to prevent those using the stairs from falling 5.00 m into the West Cryptoporticus.

A shoddy set of elevated planks linking the Upper Temenos to the Lower Temenos West Triple Colonnade had been used for years to move from one part of the precinct to the other. This elevated "bridge" was a precarious passage until it was solidly rebuilt in 2005–2006 (Figure 6.47).

Fig. 6.35
The East Triple Colonnade, to north, partial restoration, 2006.

In 2006 the top of the West Entry Stairway and its platform were excavated. It was found that two to three steps were missing, and excavated ashlars steps have been placed at the top of the West Entry Stairs. Now there is a direct entrée from the Roman Street to the top of the stairway. Additionally, one of the questions we asked is how the visitor could access the Roman-Byzantine Baths from the stairway. From the top of the West Entry stairway we created a pathway to the west so that tourists can gain entry without difficulty onto the Platform of the Roman-Byzantine Bath Complex.

At the extreme south of the temple Lower Temenos, the foundations of the Central Stairs cut into the Lower Temenos East-West Retaining Wall, (Figures 3.61 and 3.62) were consolidated using mud mortar and large pebbles. The Central Stairs bedding course was consolidated in 2004, and in 2006–2007 several of the limestone steps were replaced, leaving the remaining bedding open, so that visitors can experience the originally excavated stairs and compare them with those repaired. The north curbing of the Lower Temenos East-West Retaining Wall underwent preliminary consolidation in 1997. In 2004 the Lower Temenos Retaining Wall required additional consolidation due to the fact that the fill behind the wall was in a state of collapse. Therefore, in 2004–2005 four courses of blocks were added to the top of the wall on both the east and the west (Figure 6.48) leaving the earlier stair bedding exposed (Figure 6.49). A view from the Central Stairs to the north is seen in Figure 6.50. The new blocks are smaller than the original wall ashlars, so it is evident to the visitor that this part of the wall is restored. A view skimming the beautifully restored reversed cornice of the Lower Temenos Retaining Wall from the West Stairway Wall to the east is shown in Figure 6.51, and from East Stairway to the west in Figure 6.52.

Fig. 6.36
The restored East Triple Colonnade.

Fig. 6.37
Elephant-headed capital
placed on top of the
engaged column of the
West Exedra.

Fig. 6.38
The Lower Temenos Triple Colonnades after restoration,
as they appear at present.

Fig. 6.39
East Exedra restored,
to the south.

Fig. 6.40
East Stairway from the
Lower to Upper Temenos
as restored, to the south.

Fig. 6.41
A typical problem of ashlars
slumped out of position.

Fig. 6.42
The West Stairway leading from the Lower Temenos
to the Upper Temenos before restoration, to south.

Fig. 6.43
The West Stairway leading from the Lower Temenos
to the Upper Temenos after restoration.

Fig. 6.44
Lower Temenos
West Cryptoporticus,
restoration of the arch.

Fig. 6.45
Consolidation and restoration of the West Entry Stairway.

Fig. 6.46
Area marked where collapse is imminent in the West Cryptoporticus wall.

Fig. 6.47
Bridge constructed from Turkish railroad ties.

Fig. 6.48
Lower Temenos East-West Retaining Wall after restoration, to south.

Fig. 6.49
Lower Temenos to Upper Temenos Central Stairs as excavated with only the bedding left *in situ*.

Fig. 6.50
Lower Temenos to Upper
Temenos Central Stairs
as excavated with the
sidewalls restored, to
north. The opening for
the subterranean canali-
zation system is shown.

Fig. 6.52
Lower Temenos East-West
Retaining Wall after restoration,
showing the east reverse cornice
with the original corner wall
reverse cornice block of the wall,
to west.

Fig. 6.51
Lower Temenos East-
West Retaining Wall after
restoration, showing
the west reverse cornice
of the wall, to east.

Fig. 6.53
Upper Temenos East Plaza after restoration, to south.

Upper Temenos

Following the 1998 excavation season, the walls of the East "Cistern" shown in Figure 6.55 were reinforced and its arches were re-pointed after their initial consolidation in 1997. In 2001, the south extension of the East Perimeter Wall was pointed and the East Vault was dismantled, consolidated and returned to its original position as can be seen in Figures 6.56–6.57, (which also have been illustrated *supra* in Chapter 4). As a comparison, also see Figures 4.54–4.56 for the recovery of this feature. Figure 6.53 pictures the East Perimeter Wall and its southeast corner. The walls and niches of East Perimeter Wall Room A were stabilized and a double wall 2.00 m in height was erected around the perimeter, extending east above the East Plaza Great Cistern. In 2006, it became apparent that Room A was being physically abused by tourists. A grill was installed across that doorway to restrict entry. The mouth of the cistern was fitted with a cover to prevent winter rains from collecting beneath the complex. During the 2002 season the southeast ashlars of the South Passageway were consolidated and the site terrace wall, the Great Wall, mentioned earlier (Figure 6.14) was constructed in the precinct southwest to deflect water away from the Shrine and Baroque Rooms and the Residential Quarter. That portion of the Great Wall offering protection to the Residential Quarter features can be seen in Figure 6.54.

At the onset of the 2004 excavations, it became clear that visitors (tourists) were abusing both the Baroque Room Complex and the Residential Quarter. In order to curtail such degradation, we installed a gate barring access to these out-of-the-way areas, which can be seen in Figure 6.54. During the 2004 season, in the excavation of the southwest ramp, we uncovered the West Walkway Wall, which prevented tourist access from the temple South Passageway to the West Plaza of the temple precinct. As can be seen in Figure 6.58, wooden stairs using recycled Turkish railroad ties were constructed —ten steps east of the wall and 12 steps west of the wall, providing safe access across the wall from one area to the other. This accomplished two purposes; the wall was preserved and safe passage was assured.

In 2005 we had re-excavated the Residential Quarter Steps (Figure 4.26) by removing them to find dateable material below (Figure 6.59). These steps had to be reinstalled in their original positions and pointed, a project undertaken in 2005. A part of the temple's expansion into a *tetrastyle in antis* structure, the temple Forecourt foundations were consolidated in 1994 using re-cut hexagonal pavers mud mortar and small fieldstones. The condition of the small hexagonal forecourt pavers had been sorely compromised by the falling porch columns, as can be seen in Figure 6.60. The damaged Forecourt hexagonal pavement was also covered with a protective layer of clean sand prior to its consolidation a number

Fig. 6.54
Upper Temenos Residential Quarter with a gate placed at its entrance.

Fig. 6.55
Upper Temenos East "Cistern"
arches consolidated and
the walls pointed, to east.

Fig. 6.56
East Perimeter Wall, detail, upper vault and entrance to Room A from the East Plaza, restored, to east.

Fig. 6.57
East Perimeter Wall upper vault and entrance to Room A from the East Plaza, restored, to east.

of years later in 1999 and 2000 when damaged tiles were reconstructed using re-cut ancient blocks from the site. A portion of this Forecourt pavement was restored in 2002 as can be seen in Figure 6.61. And in 2005–2006 we elected to complete a major portion of the pavement by mixing original hexagonal pavers with newly cut pavers, leaving the subterranean canalization system open to view. This restoration continued in 2006 so that the west side of the Forecourt would be completely restored and preserved.

The Central Stairs of the temple itself (Figure 6.62) was also constructed at the temple entrance to facilitate current access to the structure and to punctuate the Site Phase IV Grand Design's original point of entry. In 1998, the steps leading to the West Walkway from the Upper Temenos Forecourt, many of which were broken, slumped out of position or robbed out, were stabilized, and in 2005 the earlier steps were lengthened to the width of the entry.

In 1995, exposed crumbling sections of the canalization system underlying the east Forecourt were reinforced using mud and lime mortars while a number of ceramic drainage pipes were covered with clean sand and back-filled. In 2006–2007 we placed a see-though grill over the Central Water Passage System and replaced a 1.30 m × 0.80 m of the canalization's missing cover slabs.

With the discovery of the Roman-Byzantine Baths in 2005 (Figures 4.29–4.32 and 4.95–4.100), a major restoration and consolidation project had to be initiated. First

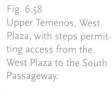

Fig. 6.58
Upper Temenos, West Plaza, with steps permitting access from the West Plaza to the South Passageway.

Fig. 6.59
Upper Temenos, Residential Quarter step removal in preparation for stratigraphic analysis and in preparation for consolidation, to west.

Fig. 6.60
Upper Temenos, Great Temple Forecourt, broken pavers *in situ*.

Fig. 6.61
Upper Temenos, Great Temple Forecourt, partially restored.

Fig. 6.62
Upper Temenos Great Temple Forecourt restored
stairs to Great Temple Porch entrance.

Fig. 6.63
Upper Temenos Roman-Byzantine Baths as excavated, showing ashlars
slumped out of position in the West Precinct Wall and eroded steps.

Fig. 6.64
Upper Temenos Roman-
Byzantine Baths during
excavation, showing
part of the heating
unit collapsed into the
apsidal vestibule.

the West Precinct Wall had to be stabilized and pointed. Figure 6.63 graphically demonstrates the ashlar slump in the Precinct Wall. All the bath walls needed pointing, and fallen elements like the lintel, shown in Figure 6.64, had to be removed from their *in situ* collapse positions. The north, south and east walls had to be reconstructed to the same heights as the north wall and door. The frigidarium entry had many decorative stones that had fallen out of position. Although many of the original *opus sectile* elements had been recovered during the excavation, we were unsure of where they belonged. As a result white plaster was used to build the walls up to one level for the stabilization of *in situ* elements. The pipe extending around the base of the "Well Room" (Figure 6.65) had to be cleaned, fully exposed and supported with mortar, so its position would be evident to the public. The most important project, however, was directed to the "Well" itself. During the excavation curved beautifully fashioned apsidal limestone walls had fallen away from their parent walls. These can be seen waiting for their repositioning in Figure 6.66. Although each of these blocks had been recorded during excavation, they had fallen in a haphazard fashion. The puzzle is to find which blocks belong to each of the "Well" niche walls prior to their reinstallation. This project is ongoing.

With the 2006, recovery of the apsed *laconicum* in Trench 126 we realized we were dealing with extremely delicate remains having a set of fragile properties that would be damaged by being exposed to the elements. There were differences in the strategies we discussed, and, unfortunately, we elected to place zinc cover over the wrapped consolidated remains and postpone restoration. Were funding to become available, we are optimistic that these remains will retain enough structural integrity in the interim to be properly cared for and protected from deterioration.

The West Cistern-Reservoir (Figures 4.27, 4.91) also had to have its perimeter walls pointed. As excavated, these walls were a pastiche of blocks. After the walls were reconstructed in antiquity, they had suffered multiple fire damages, and many of the blocks had slumped out of position. This conservation was also undertaken in 2005–2006.

Fig. 6.65
Upper Temenos Roman-Byzantine Baths during excavation, showing apsidal niches of the "Well" Room that require consolidation and the reinsertion of the curved facing blocks that had fallen from the walls.

Fig. 6.66
Upper Temenos Roman-Byzantine Baths, "Well" Room curved facing blocks fallen from the walls awaiting restoration in the lapidary.

Fig. 6.67
Great Temple southeast double-engaged column base as excavated, to south.
Its upper shaft blocks had been slumped out of position. Each component
was measured, photographed and numbered before restoration could begin.

Temple

Beginning with the original *distyle in antis*
structure, conservation efforts in the temple
proper in 1997 and 2000 focused on the repair
and rebuilding of a number of column bases
and drums from the peripteral colonnades. In
the south in 1999, 11 courses of the southeast
heart-shaped double-engaged column were
re-erected. Figure 6.67 shows the state of this
column after the 1997 excavation. Figure 6.68
details the top of its composite heart-shaped
elements during reconstruction, and Figure 6.69
shows the column restored with its original
elements. The mirroring column in the southwest was also restored to a height of seven
meters using original components excavated and
recorded in 1998. In the temple west, fragments
of white cable-fluted plaster were re-adhered to
an exposed column shaft following their *in situ*
discovery in 1999.

When recovered, the crumbling architectural fabric of the heavily eroded (or absent)
Porch column drums (see Figure 6.7) was
removed. The central west column had been
knocked off the stylobate in the Great Temple
collapse and needed to be completely replaced.
Because its Attic base was missing, we replaced it
and the columns with restacked porch drums
without mortar. *In situ* plaster fragments found
on the columns themselves or on the walls were
treated with sealant to bond the decoration and
forestall further deterioration. As can be seen in
Figure 6.70, in a few cases, capital components
were restored only to the corridor columns,
because no capital elements with certainty could
be identified as belonging to the Porch columns.

In the temple interior, work focused on
the conservation of the corridor and walkway
walls. During 1996 and 1997, consolidation
was undertaken in the temple West Corridor
with the reconstitution of fallen ashlars into the
masonry of the northwest wall. The northwest
section of the West Corridor with its arch was
then dismantled, reconstructed and pointed
both to reinforce the wall and to close large gaps
between its ashlars. Figure 6.71 dramatically
portrays the result of the blocks pulling away
from each other. Figure 6.72 pictures the scaffolding in place to support the arch ashlars, and
Figure 6.73 shows the removal of the *voussoirs*
so they could be cleaned before their restora-

tion. Figure 6.74 shows the West Corridor Wall west face before pointing in 1997. In 1999, the east face of the West Corridor Wall was stabilized following the exposure of delicate *in situ* fresco elements consolidated in 1998. In 2000, the consolidation of the West Corridor Wall was all but completed, as shown in Figure 6.75. In 2004, however, it was found that some of the frescoes shown in Figure 6.76 had suffered from water damage, so in 2005 we constructed an unobtrusive sloping roof on the top of the West Corridor West Walkway wall to deflect the winter rains. This roof can also be seen in Figure 6.75. Restoration was continued throughout the fall and winter of 2005–2006, and continues at this writing.

Additional conservation efforts in the West Corridor included the re-erection of the north entryway. Figure 6.77 shows the com-

Fig. 6.69
Great Temple southeast double-engaged (heart-shaped) column, restored.

Fig. 6.68
Top of the Great Temple southeast double-engaged (heart-shaped) column during restoration.

Fig. 6.70
Moving the lower order of the Nabataean capital into place on one of the Great Temple corridor columns.

Fig. 6.72
Great Temple West Corridor
Arch. The underside is
supported with wood planks
for restoration.

Fig. 6.71
Great Temple West
Corridor Arch jostled out
of its original position.
The underside is supported
with wood planks until
restoration can begin.

Fig. 6.73
Great Temple West Corridor Arch with *anastylosis* in preparation for
its reassembly and restoration.

Fig. 6.74
Great Temple West Corridor
Wall before pointing and
anastylosis.

Fig. 6.75
Great Temple West Corridor Wall in mid-conservation
of ashlars and paintings.

Fig. 6.76
Great Temple West Corridor Wall fresco in a state of
deterioration after minimal consolidation.

Fig. 6.77
Great Temple West
Corridor Wall and arch
after consolidation.

Fig. 6.78
Great Temple West Corridor during consolidation, to south.

pleted arched doorway, and Figure 6.78 is a view showing the rebuilding of the adjacent West Corridor Wall to a uniform elevation following its reinforcement and pointing in 1995 using re-chiseled ashlars bonded with mud mortar.

In the south, conservation efforts focused on the consolidation of the South Corridor intercolumnar Wall, which was in part dismantled in 1997 and reconstructed to allow for the adjacent re-erection of the southeast double-engaged heart shaped column shown in Figures 6.67–6.69. The ashlars were numbered, removed from the fill and returned to their original places in the wall. To divert potentially destructive water accumulation following this restoration, a protective drainage ditch was dug south of the column niche. In 2000, the upper courses of the north face of the South Corridor Wall were consolidated and pointed following the preliminary investigation of the area. In 2001, consolidation of the South Corridor Wall was completed and the *in situ* plaster discovered on the wall's north face flanking the central doorway was reinforced to preserve its structural integrity. These frescoes had to wait until 2005–2006 for further support and restoration.

Turning to those architectural elements of the temple contemporary with the construction of the central Theater, consolidation efforts in the north included the restoration of the upper wall of the *cavea* in 1999. Also at this time, the Theater staircases, aisles, and seats were assessed and rebuilt from original and recycled materials. Figure 6.79 shows the restored west side of the Theater and Figure 6.80 shows the restored Theater front staircase. After the Special Project 200 Theater sondage was completed in 2005 we elected to keep the sondage open for public viewing. An iron frame was constructed around the excavated area with a grill so the public could view the excavations. This covering can be seen in the aerial view of the temple at the beginning of Chapter 5.

Flanking the Theater *cavea*, preliminary restoration work began in 1999 with the East Interior Staircase (Figure 5.69), consolidating the first two courses of the vaulted ceiling in preparation for the consolidation of the lower section of the surrounding walls. In 1997, efforts in the east continued and the West Interior

Fig. 6.79
Great Temple Theater after
consolidation.

Fig. 6.80
Great Temple Theater
scalaria after consolidation.

Fig. 6.81
West (north-south) interior Theater Stairs restored, to south.

Staircase was partially restored to undo erosion damage caused by winter rains (Figure 6.81). The foundations of the staircase were repaired using mud mortar and small fieldstones and original and new limestone treads were fit into place. Full restoration of the staircase was completed in 2000.[11]

In 2006 we had excavated Trench 123 in the Theater seating. After a number of possible alternatives were proposed, including back filling, we elected to construct metal support frames underneath the seats which would bear the weight of the two rows of ashlar seats that had been removed. Then the seats would be replaced and mortared in place. The logic behind this endeavor was that any researcher in the future who wanted to analyze this sondage's stratigraphy would be able to remove the mortar and the seats and take a ladder down to view the stratigraphy.

Also in 1997, a central portion of the West Corridor's intercolumnar wall, which had undergone significant earthquake damage, was taken down and rebuilt. Later work in 1998 included the full restoration of the East and West Interior Staircases and the complete *anastylosis* of the West Corridor intercolumnar Wall and its arches and windows, which can be seen in Figure 6.82.

In the West Interior Chamber, gaps between the wall stones were filled with mud mortar mixed with small fieldstones. A niche discovered in the south wall was reinforced using flat fieldstones and mortar to shore up the surrounding wall. *Anastylosis* was undertaken in the east side of the room through the removal and replacement of vault stones bonded with local mud mortar. Figure 6.83 pictures the West Chamber east wall with its arch springers. In 1999, the arch stones of the doorway into the East Interior Chamber were consolidated.

At the temple rear, preliminary consolidation began in 1995 with the investigation of the Central Arch leading to reconstruction efforts in 1996 and 1997 to insure stability for upcoming excavation. During the 1998 season, once excavation had begun, the Central Arch exhibited complex structural needs, requiring the erection of a 55-ashlar support wall to stabilize the arch. Figure 6.84 depicts this Central Arch wall. Following the excavation of the adjacent South Corridor in 2001, the lintel above the doorway to the Central Arch (shown in Figure 5.47 in a state of collapse) cut into the South Corridor's intercolumnar wall was reinforced (shown in Figure 6.85).

Above the Central Arch, the 1998 season also saw the replacement of some 18 or 19 steps at the top of the rear East and West (east-west) Staircases, which had been robbed out in antiquity. In 1999, the full extents of the East and West Rear Staircases were rebuilt to permit visitor access to the second story of the building. Figure 6.86 is the restored east staircase and Figure 6.87 shows the corresponding west staircase.

To preserve the archaeological integrity of the site, bold lines were painted in prominent areas of conservation within the temple interior. the lines differentiate *in situ* remains from the present level of consolidation as is shown in Figure 6.88.

Fig. 6.82
West (north-south) interior Theater Stairs arched window during restoration.

Fig. 6.83
West Chamber interior wall restored.

Fig. 6.84
Central Arch interior restored.

Fig. 6.85
Central Arch doorway from the South Corridor restored.

Fig. 6.86
East rear east-
west Theater
Stairs restored,
to east.

Fig. 6.87
West rear east-west
Theater Stairs restored,
to west.

Fig. 6.88
Restored portions of walls
indicated by painted lines to
point out where restoration
has taken place.

Conclusion

Overall, conservation efforts at the Petra Great Temple have been relentless, insuring the annual renewal of the site's structural stability and the preservation of its unique architectural and decorative features. One of the high points of our day-to-day excavation and conservation efforts, and what keeps our sanity, is a glass of sweet Bedouin tea cooked over a wood fire, shown in Figure 6.89. During the years of excavation, conservation has permitted a deeper understanding of architectural developments nearly 2000 years old. We have restored or protected every wall and most of the sculpture enable us to examine the structure of the Great Temple in a form close to its original incarnation and to draw substantiated conclusions about its construction and the lives of its inhabitants. At its heart, conservation is a means of cultural and physical preservation—an unspoken tribute to the ancient Nabataean creators of this commanding edifice and a promise for the continued study and enjoyment of its splendor today. If we can protect the site and promote the sustainability of archaeological ecosystems at Petra, and at the same time conserve and preserve the site for use and for the benefit of future generations, we have achieved our goal. Petra will remain with us as long as we succeed in protecting her legacy.

Fig. 6.89
Tea Time!

Notes

1
This chapter addresses the challenges of preserving the unique architecture of the Petra Great Temple. In respecting its appearance as we found it, our interventions intentionally have been subtle. Our aim is to preserve the precinct and the Great Temple as a partial ruin so that the visitor can interpret it for himself or herself. Unfortunately there has been seismic damage combined with the perilous infiltration of water, air and salts that has led to the deterioration of much of the standing architecture. Always there will be consolidation and preservation work to be done, and we view our achievements as beginning interventions for the site's preservation. We are proud of our efforts over the years.

With regard to the artifacts, we have undertaken on-site repair of individual ceramics, and have spent months looking for joins for the restoration of the inscriptions, specifically those of the Small Temple. We have worked on the stabilization of our metals, particularly the coins, and we also have restored many of our glass fragments. Once preserved, our spectacular artifact repertoire has been turned over to the Jordanian Department of Antiquities for future conservation efforts.

2.
This fencing that surrounded the site has now been removed.

3.
For their protection, five of the pilaster blocks were moved into the niches of the East Exedra in 2006.

4.
In 2006 every Great Temple architectural fragment was removed from the East Cryptoporticus lapidary, examined for number and trench designation, sorted, placed in an appropriate pile, and reburied. For the study of fragments that were found in the Theater excavations, the fragments with the designations of Trenches 40, 47, 62 and 92 were separated from the rest, and a list was made of those fragments. The lapidary was first refilled with fragments that did not bear the Theater trench numbers. A white plastic mesh was placed over the corpus of fragments. On top of the white plastic mesh are placed those fragments from the Theater trenches, and they are easily accessible. Finally zinc sheets were positioned over the storage area. A separate list was drawn up in Excel indicating specific fragments that had been located, and the Petra Great Temple Architectural Fragment database will allow the researcher to examine the dimensions and characteristics of each piece. This burdensome exercise took five working days to complete, but in the end we know where these specific architectural fragments are located.

5.
However, the museum storage capacity has been exhausted.

6.
In some senses the Nabataeans were among the earliest water conservationists.

7.
May Shaer and Stefan Simon published their results "The Plasters, Renders and Mortars of the Petra Great Temple," for *The 6th International Symposium on the Conservation of Monuments in the Mediterranean Basin* (in press). Brown University student Emily Catherine Egan also undertook a study of the plaster decoration and published the results of her research, "Stucco Decoration from the South Corridor of the Petra Great Temple: Discussion and Interpretation." in *ADAJ*, the Jum'a Kareem Memorial Volume, Vol. 46: 347–361.

8.
Ulrich Bellwald, experienced in the conservation of plaster in Petra, notably at Ez Zantur, undertook these varied and complicated and deteriorated individual projects. Emily Catherine Egan offers her analysis of the plaster in Volume III.

9.
If preservation efforts fail, the site is endangered and extinction will occur.

10.
In 2006 large sculpted architectural fragments like capitals and volutes were moved into this vault for their protection from the elements. This vault now serves as an informal "site museum."

11.
Rune Frederiksen presents his analysis of the theater-in-the-temple in Volume III.

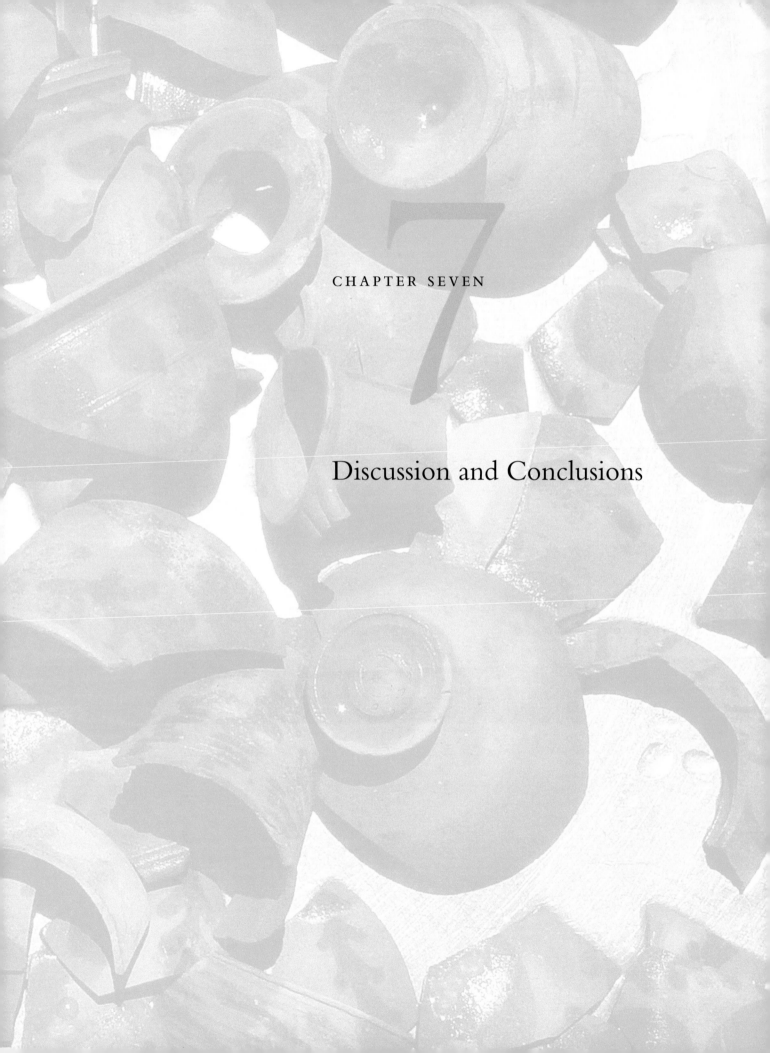

CHAPTER SEVEN

Discussion and Conclusions

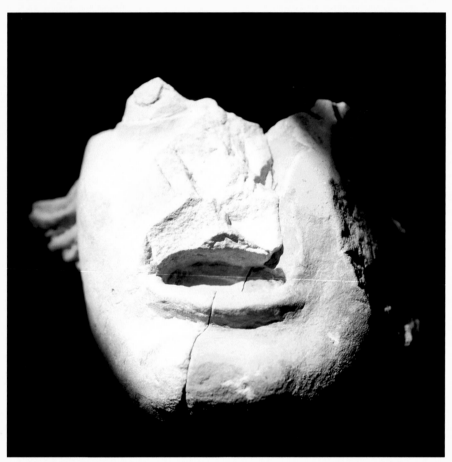
Evocative facial fragments from the Great Temple.

Discussion and Conclusions

C. Kanellopoulos (2001, 11) states:

> The slope south of Wadi Musa was originally (third-first centuries B.C.E.) occupied with dwellings (Parr 1970). Later, this area acquired a public character with the piazzas that accommodated the Great Temple complex and the so-called markets.

Over the years, the excavations conducted to the south of the Roman Street give us a fascinating picture of the Petraean capital of the Nabataeans. Figure 7.1 attests to several sites of great interest. The Great Temple is sited between the Petra Pool Complex[1] to its east, the "Baths-Palatial Complex" to its immediate west and the Temenos Gate[2] to its immediate northwest. Further to the west stands the small Imperial Cult Building.[3]

It is clear that the Petra Great Temple, the Garden-Pool Complex and the Baths-Palatial Complex serve as the religious, administrative, and cultural center of the Nabataeans throughout the Nabataean period. This Nabataean urbanization process takes place from the late first century BCE to the early second century CE, and from 106 CE, the Roman additions to the site were completed. The Roman Road, the Temenos Gate, the Roman-Byzantine Baths, and the Roman Imperial Cult Building (the Small Temple), embellish the urban fabric as Roman additions to the site.

The Nabataeans constructed these complexes on the city's southern slope above the sacred path, the *via sacra* (the precursor to the Roman Road),[4] which was the central

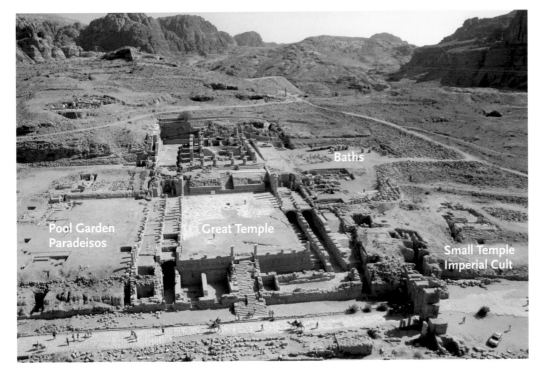

Fig. 7.1
Great Temple with the Pool Complex to the left and the Imperial Cult Building to the right.

0 ▬▬▬▬▬ 5 cm

Fig. 7.2
Nabataean bowl, Cat. No. 98-P-9, Seq. No. 53036. Upper
Temenos Trench 53, Locus 2. With painted triangular
division and typically painted with palm fronds, chevrons,
dots and zigzags, of 2.5YR5/6 red ware. Inverted rim
diameter 17.0 cm, thickness 0.44 cm. Dated to Phase 3c
or to 100 CE.

thoroughfare of this city sector. The Nabataean sacred way and the Roman Road served as the principal artery for an impressive network of four bridges[5] crossing the Wadi Musa to link the south and north sectors of the urban layout. Unearthed to date are various other Nabataean period buildings including the Qasr al-Bint to the far west, the Temple of the Winged Lions across the wadi on a slope to the north, and the Ez Zantur domestic buildings just above the Great Temple to the southeast. With additional Roman constructions of the paved road, the Temenos Gate[6] and the Imperial Cult Building, the site retained its urban character throughout the Roman period. The architectural plan of the city is as impressive as is the artifact record including the spectacular sculpture. These data present invaluable information about the Nabataean city's impressive appearance.

One of our quests has been to define Nabataean and Roman culture through the archaeological record, with an emphasis on the Nabataean aspects of the site. We have used the Petra Great Temple as a text and have undertaken a multidisciplinary archaeological journey to provide the primary data for reconstructing Nabataean culture. We have not taken our interpretation to the larger Nabataean context—to the discussion of other Nabataean cities and temples—but what we have found are the socioeconomic and cultural aspects in their development at the Great Temple site. As the preceding chapters have made clear, many facets about this record now are ready to be addressed by further research.

What makes Nabataean culture unusual and distinct? Petra[7] is a multi-faceted city infused with architectural marvels: both the freestanding architecture and the astonishing vast rock-cut tombs and Djinn blocks. Their architects interweave Hellenistic, Egyptian, Indian, and Nabataean symbols and motifs that unify their own cultural identity. They are also known for their decorative sculpture, both aniconic and representational, and for their brilliant stonemasons

Fig. 7.3
Nabataean bowl, Cat. No. 01-P-31, Seq. No. 84187. Upper Temenos Trench 84, Locus 22. Of 2.5YR5/8 red ware. Diameter 21.5 cm, height 5.4 cm. Both interior and exterior slipped with exterior wheel burnishing below the rim and 2.5YR5/5 red painted motifs on the interior. Dated to Phase 3b or 70–80 CE.

Fig. 7.4
Nabataean coin, Cat. No.
04-C-03. Propylaeum, SP87,
Locus 10. Obverse of King
Aretas IV and Queen Shaq-
ilat, dating to 18–40 CE.

Fig 7.5
Nabataean silver coin,
of King Rabbel II. 99-C-33,
Seq. No. 65412, Temple
1999, Trench 65, Locus 21.
Diameter 1.26 cm, thickness
0.30 cm, weight 2.90 g.
Obv. bust, pearled facing
right with inscription, dating
from 70–106 CE. Rev. Bust,
facing right with inscription.

Fig. 7.6
Bronze plaque with a partial Nabataean inscription.
Cat. No. 98-M-2, Seq. 53286. Upper Temenos Trench 53,
Locus 24. Length 13.55 cm, width 6.27 cm, thickness
0.48 cm. A small hook and another piece of bronze,
which may be a coin, were found together with this piece.
This is an example of an older Nabataean script that
reads as M L K T, Malakat or Queen. Christian Augé has
suggested that the queen referred to could be Huldu,
the first wife of Aretas IV, as there may be a Hu on the
plaque (personal communication). This would date the
plaque to the first quarter of the first century CE.

who carved the city out of the living rock or built their free standing buildings. The extraordinary sculptors who embellished their monuments had full command of snub-nosed and toothed chisels, the wedge and the awl. Celebrated are their eggshell thin ceramic wares (Figures 7.2 and 7.3) typically painted with geometric or foliate designs or rouletted, the coins[8] (Figures 7.4 and 7.5)[9] depicting Nabataean kings with their queens often pictured as partners of the king.[10, 11] The coins also reveal their language and script derived from Aramaic (Figure 7.6), their widespread trade routes, revenues from commerce, and trade in aromatics like frankincense (incense) and myrrh, and spices, bitumen from the Dead Sea, the sacred associations of their religion with Dushara[12] as their principal deity and al-'Uzza the goddess, their hydrologic engineering skills, agriculture, and their arts, including dancers, music, and musicians.[13] To quote from Strabo (*Geog* XVI.4.26), "…they eat their meals in companies consisting of thirteen persons. Each party is attended by two musicians."

Obviously, the Great Temple has been our central point of focus. From the vast collection of information we have gathered, we can now begin to articulate the Nabataean culture. The architecture and religious symbolism that defined the Nabataeans, and that they defined, has been clarified. We now want to bring their world to life and illustrate the complexities and intricacies of their culture. Although the specifics of some of these aspects will be covered by specialists in Volume III, we want to conclude this volume with some of our ideas as Volume III is in preparation.[14]

This concluding chapter presents some of the main issues that have emerged from the Great Temple excavations. These ideas spring from the debate as to whether the Great Temple, in fact, can be identified as a temple. We will begin with Nabataea and Petra, and then turn to the "Great Debate" about the function of the building. Following scholarly comments, we will look at the Great Temple site in its setting —its context, and its character and architecture, focusing on the Great Temple itself and its sculpture, and then consider comparable Nabataean temple landmarks. We then turn to the written record, the philological evidence. After a brief resumé of cult objects, altars and niches, ceramics and other artifacts, we will conclude the discussion in "The Great Debate." We will also offer a word about the Roman impact on the Great Temple site followed by a brief conclusion. We begin with general commentary about Nabataea.

Nabataea and Petra

Although Nabataea was a melding of tribal groups at certain times during its history, it was a centrally strong cohesive kingdom with prolonged periods of security, stability and prosperity. Its rise initially was the outcome of trade in a marginal region, but it boldly developed and controlled land trade routes on the west through the Negev leading to the Mediterranean, to the Wadi Arabah, to the Red Sea and Arabia and Egypt[15] to the south, and Aurantis (present day Hauran) in Syria to the north.[16] Active trade relations also moved through the Persian Gulf to the Tigris-Euphrates Valley and Mesopotamia, and over the Indian Ocean to India and perhaps as far afield as China.[17] Nabataea was a territorially defined polity comprised of a mosaic of farmsteads, camel breeding tribes, hamlets, villages and towns.

Petra lies in the great polychromatic semi-arid rift valley where there is presently a 150 mm (20 in) of average annual rainfall (Nehmé 2003, 162). The Great Temple lies on a natural rise in the city center to the south of the Wadi Musa. Its basic elevation is approximately 900 m above sea level.

The Nabataeans may have lived in Petra from before the third century BCE.[18] Although Nabataean rule technically begins in 168 BCE, it takes the Nabataeans more than 150 years before they begin to construct their capital city—Petra.

The grand scale building of Petra places most of the 3,197 monuments (Nehmé 2003, 156) including 1179 rock cut tombs (ibid.157) and freestanding structures firmly in the first century BCE. Thus Petra bears witness to the transformation of the Nabataean people from nomadism to monarchy. As their power increases with the resources provided from the trade routes,[19] Petra becomes their crystallization of a dense urban concept and the chief city of this geo-Nabataean political entity. The Nabataean awakening that takes place with the influx of wealth feeds their ambitions to quickly catch up with other great cities, and moves the Nabataeans into a new era away from their ancient nomadic roots. Thus Petra carries a unique past with a marked sensibility that inspires its own peculiar developing culture. Not content to fit into the frameworks of the cultures they borrowed from, Nabataean planners create their own rich aesthetic legacy. Because Petra and Nabataea are rather distant from other major cultures, and the Nabataeans give every indication of a unique individualism, there is a stylistic flexibility rather than conformity to a foreign ideal. This encourages a special aesthetic for the Nabataeans. They borrow architectural and sculptural concepts from their world at large—the Greeks, the Egyptians and those peoples to the east—but they are creative in their expression of them.

The Great Debate

Within Nabataean archaeology, there are uncertainties about various issues. One of the great debates is over the functional reconstruction of the Great Temple precinct. Most scholars have used our architectural evidence to argue there is no religious evidence. This is a debate that must be considered. Here we tackle this debate to understand what it reveals about concepts of royal building, religious iconography and attendant artifacts of the Petra Great Temple. In the following paragraphs, we cover scholarly comments beginning in 1998 (Volume I, 125–128), when I posed the question that sparked the Great Debate:

> The Great Temple stands alone above a large colonnaded Lower Temenos among thousands of architectural fragments, including elephant-headed capitals. The Temple itself is embellished with floral Nabataean capitals, and it cannot be forgotten that this well-preserved building is also decorated with masks, recovered from the West Walkway in 1995. The whole precinct is built with an emphasis on axiality and frontality.
>
> Interpreting this large public edifice is at the heart of the archaeological process—there has been a great deal of debate regarding the identity of this building. If our structure is, in fact, a Great Temple, the hypaethral (open-air) theater is certainly its dominant architectural element. On one hand, this structure is built like a temple, and on the other, it has a theater-like structure in place of the cella. It cannot have served as a sacred space, a religious building that was decommissioned and desacralized. In other words, it could not have been built as a temple

and then have become transformed into a civic structure; I have to assume that a shift in function would go against Nabataean religious tradition. Therefore, it must have served either as a religious or as a secular structure. And if it is a religious structure, why could it not have served as an instrument of religio-political propaganda? The kings of Nabataea certainly utilized religion to further their political ambitions.

For some time I have been puzzled about this monumental structure. Although the conventions of classical architecture proscribe this building to be the Great Temple, it is clear that Nabataean creativity, their lack of preconceived ideas and their unusual architectural borrowings from the classical world could have led them to utilize the Great Temple either for ritual or administrative purposes. The purpose of this structure has yet to be determined—it remains a riddle. We know that this theater-like structure must have served as the central focus for the Great Temple after it was rebuilt. Since the interpretation of this building is somewhat enigmatic, future excavation will hopefully clarify its function.

In future seasons we will test several hypotheses to explain and understand this building.
1) It was a temple or a theater-temple, or
2) It served as the civic center for Petra in the Nabataean and Nabataean-Roman periods as,
   a) a *bouleuterion* where the *boule* (city council) met or as a *comitium* or *curia*, a Roman political meeting place;
   b) an odeum or small concert hall, or
   c) a law court, council chamber, meeting hall.

Now it is possible that this is a civic structure — perhaps it is where the Nabataean "popular assembly" held their meetings. It is worth requoting Strabo (16.4) who states:

> Petra is always ruled by some king from the royal family; and the king has as Administrator one of his companions, who is called "brother." It is exceedingly well-governed; at any rate, Athenodorus, a philosopher and companion of mine, who had been in the city of the Petraeans, used to describe their government with admiration, for he said that he found both many and many other foreigners sojourning there, and that he saw that the foreigners often engaged in lawsuits, both with one another and with the natives, but that none of the natives prosecuted one another, and that they in

every way kept peace with one another... The king is so democratic that, in addition to serving himself, he sometimes even serves the rest himself in his turn. He often renders an account of his kingship in the popular assembly; and sometimes his mode of life is examined.

We must be mindful of the Latin Imperial inscription studied by Stephen V. Tracy and dated between 112 and 114 CE, found in the rear west vaulted room on the floor. Further investigations of the parallel room to the east... may determine the actual purpose of these interior chambers in the rear of the Temple. [Unfortunately, it was not helpful.][20] There is but a single entry into this west chamber, measuring 3.5 m in width x 5.5 m in depth with walls 4 m in height. It did serve for storage in the late Nabataean-Roman period (for stacks of roof tiles were found here lying in an earth deposit above the Latin inscription), but originally it may have served as a secure space for keeping records, a room for the storage of arms, a holding pen for prisoners or, although dark, a changing room for actors. Or its purpose may have been solely for the support of the cavea extending above it.

But perhaps the Great Temple was rebuilt as a *bouleuterion*? We should not forget the multiple references to the *boule* at Petra in the Babatha Archives discovered by Yigael Yadin from the Cave of the Letters.

The Great Temple precinct's location adjacent to the Temenos Gate and the most sacred Qasr al-Bint is not accidental. A Great Temple or a *bouleuterion-odeum* should be accessible to the citizens of Petra and provide a gathering place where the decisions of the day could be announced and discussed. So, was the Great Temple a center of worship where performances of a ritual nature were performed, or was it the location of the highest court? Or did this structure serve other or perhaps even multiple civic functions? We seek scholarly discussion of this issue.

Even if we restrict the interpretation of the function of the building, we are still left in the dark with a number of compelling questions. If it is a temple, what deity is worshipped here? And if it served as a civic center, what was its intended use—*bouleuterion, odeum, bouleuterion* and *odeum*; it is conceivable that it could have been used for both purposes. How does this precinct relate to the urban fabric of the city itself? It must be considered in relation to the city plan of central Petra. While the function of this structure remains obscure, it surely presents a significant architectural component of Petra.

Although we have shed new light on urban Petra, the implications of these finds have certainly opened new questions about the site and the city. The reappraisal of the Great Temple architecture, chronologically and stratigraphically, will greatly enhance our understanding of the socio-political and religious culture of Petra. More discussion will be given to the interpretation of these interesting architectural and functional questions...although we, as archaeologists, have the same general frame of reference, there may be differences in our interpretations...many questions may be answered by further excavation, but additionally, we are hopeful that our readers will reassess the evidence and provide us with the answers.

Following the 1998 publication several scholars questioned and took issue with my preliminary observations. I asked for scholarly input, and I received it. Writing her dissertation five years after we initiated the excavations of the Great Temple, my then graduate student, Erika Schluntz (1999) stated in her dissertation, *From Royal to Public Assembly Space: The Transformation of the "Great Temple" Complex at Petra, Jordan*:

> Although the Great Temple Complex at Petra has been referred to as a religious sanctuary ...[the] evidence uncovered...now casts serious doubt upon this interpretation. Recent excavation within the "temple" structure itself revealed an extensive, theater-like structure, secondarily constructed within the original first century BCE building. Analysis of this later structure shows that this second phase structure served as an *odeion*, a small (possibly covered) theater, complete with ample seating, orchestra....In the Roman East, such odeion buildings often served as city council halls (*bouleuteria*)....Due to very strong religious sensitivities, desacralization of religious precincts was virtually unheard of in antiquity....Specifically, the Great Temple building bears a striking resemblance to audience/banquet hall structures which were frequently incorporated within palace complexes of the first century BCE.

Wenning (2001, 87–88, note 17) refers to the Great Temple as:

> the so-called Great Temple.

Jane Taylor writes (2001, 109–111):

> ...the excavations have revealed [that the Great Temple] seems to have more in common... with Vitruvius' designs for a basilica—a style of building that in the Graeco-Roman world was not associated with temples but used for a wide range of secular and civic activities...From being a royal audience hall...it became a large meeting hall for both royal and non-royal functions, and was usually situated beside the agora; it could also house business transactions, a money or stock exchange, or shops. Its most usual function, however, was as a law court....This building could have been a temple; but given the existence of other temples in Petra, and the absence of any known building for civic or royal use, an alternative function has been mooted as a possibility....The only thing that seems clear is that the building remained in its unspecified use throughout the Roman period....

Fiema (2002, 65) writes:

> The Brown University excavations of the monumental structure known as the "Great" or "Southern Temple" revealed that a substantial rebuilding of the structure took place sometime in the late 1st or the early 2nd century A.D., probably changing its function and character.... The principal addition was a *theatron*...inserted inside the main building. Whether the entire structure then became a "sacred theater," *bouleuterion*...or an Odeon...cannot be ascertained. However this conversion makes it possible to suggest that the structure was not sacral prior to the rebuilding, and instead could have been related to the Nabataean royal, residential and ceremonial complex. It would make sense that the structure changed its appearance and function with the end of the Nabataean monarchy.

Stephan G. Schmid (2002a, 49–50) states:

> Recent investigations have focused on a major building called "Great" or "Southern Temple," located on the southern side of the Wadi Musa depression. The original rectangular structure built on the podium and supported by rows of columns appears to date from the late 1st century B.C. Later, in the late Nabataean or early Roman provincial period, the structure underwent some radical changes, and additions were made including a monumental temenos with triple colonnades. But it is still uncertain what was the original function of this monumental structure: a temple or a large audience hall? As a paradeisos (a luxurious recreation area)

has been found beside it, it is possible that the "Great Temple" actually belonged to a multifunctional complex related to the governing of the city (state) by a king in Nabataean times, or the governor and city council after the annexation of Nabataea by Rome in A.D. 106.

Jacques Seigne (2002, 507–516) also is skeptical of the religious function;

> Actually no structure, installation or document recovered can indisputably attribute this structure to be a sanctuary...this hypothesis of a "temple-theater" is not acceptable...it was not transformed into a theater for many years (tens of years) after its construction, and...there is nothing to suggest a religious function...the pseudo "cella" of the "Great Temple" was nothing less than the monumental throne room used for audiences. This building was the royal palace until 106, and thereafter it became the seat of municipal power when the Nabataeans were annexed by Rome...The importance of the revealed remains demonstrates the exceptional character of those buildings brought to light.... The possible existence in the Nabataean city of a true bouleuterion recasts the much discussed question about Roman Petra and the importance of its rebuilding—political, administrative, urban and material culture which occurred in the ancient capital after the annexation of the Nabataean kingdom. It is certain the American team will gain a point of honor in rapidly realizing that Volume II should be devoted to the "Petra Great Monument" or to the "Petra Royal Palace"—this is valuable and already waited for with impatience.[21]

One debate surrounds the dating of the temple. Some ascribe it to the Roman period or believe it to have been constructed after the Romans acquired Petra. Beyond all doubt, based on our findings, it is a Nabataean building constructed in the late first century BCE.

With regard to the Theater, we argue that this feature was constructed in Site Phase V or in the first century CE; it is not as late as 106 CE.

Leigh-Ann Bedal (2003, 183) in writing *The Petra Pool-Complex: A Hellenistic Paradeisos in the Nabataean Capital* supports the view of E. L. Schluntz that in its early period (Site Phases II–IV) the Great Temple served as a royal audience/banquet hall. She posits that the

addition of the theater should be placed in the context of ca. 106 CE or thereafter. She states:

> The former royal audience/banquet hall (the Great Temple) was converted into a theatron that probably functioned as a council hall, *bouleuterion*, or *odeion* (or a combination of these, fronted by a large public plaza. The current archaeological record indicates that this transformation may have begun as early as the late 1st century CE, during the reign of Rabb'el II, although it was not completed until after the Roman annexation in 106 CE. Because of its central location and close association with the Great Temple, the Pool-Complex must also have been converted into a public space at this point in time....The association of the Petra Garden with the Great Temple theatron... is reminiscent of Pompey's Portico Garden in Rome....

G.W. Bowersock (2003, 23–24) writes:

> ...It might have been at this time that some dramatic changes were made along the south side of the main street of Petra in the enigmatic complex....What had long seemed to be a temple with a large forecourt suddenly turns into a theater for some six hundred people or so....It has now become difficult to interpret the whole complex as a temple, since it would be implausible to postulate an abrupt secularization of a sacred space. In any case, the Great Temple looks more and more like a secular building, perhaps even the site of the litigation for which Babatha's documents provide such moving testimony.

Since 1998, I have proposed that the Great Temple served in both a sacral and administrative function. Does the evidence gathered from the Great Temple these past nine years further elucidate the Nabataean building as either a religious or administrative structure?

In 2003 Ehud Netzer published an important survey on Nabataean temples. In *Nabatäische Architektur insbesondere Gräber und Tempel*, Netzer agrees with my interpretation as a temple structure (72–81). The evidence adduced by Netzer is compelling. He goes on to suggest an idea about the placement of an altar in the temple itself—an idea which I rule out. However, the possibility exists, and his ideas suggest my re-analysis.

Temples in Petra to compare with the Great Temple are the Qasr al-Bint (Wright 1961, 1985; Paar 1967–1968; Zayadine 1981, 1982, 1985; Zayadine, Larché, and Dentzer-Feydy 2003), and the Temple of the Winged

Lions (Hammond 1993, 1994, 1996), both of which are dated to the Nabataean period. These structures differ with each other in architectural plan, and they do not resemble the Great Temple. If we look at other Nabataean temples—at Sur, Sahr, Seeia Temple of Baal Shamin, the Temple of Dushara at Seeia (Dentzer 1979, 1985; Dentzer and Dentzer 1981), or the South Temple at Seeia, Suweida, Wadi Ramm (Horsfield and Savignac 1935; Savignac and Horsfield 1935; Dudley, and Reeves 1997; Tolbecq 1998), Khirbet et-Tannur (Glueck 1937a, 1937b, Robert, Cazelles and Feuillet 1968; McKenzie 2002; McKenzie, Gibson and Reyes 2002), Khirbet edh-Dharieh (Villeneuvre 1984–1991; Dentzer-Feydy 1990; al-Muheisen and Villeneuvre 1994a–2003; Villeneuve 2000), Qasrawet (Oren 1982; Oren and Netzer 1977, 1982), Dibon (Tushingham 1954; Wright 1961), and Qasr Rabba (Calzini-Gysens 1996; Calzini-Gysens and Marino 1997)—we see such a panoply of forms it is impossible to categorize them into a single Nabataean temple canon. Comparative Nabataean temple plans can be viewed in Netzer (2003, Abb. 84) and they provide an interesting basis on which to build an interpretation.

There are then the aniconic *betyls*, the *nefesh*, horned altars, and offering benches all of which are Nabataean realities. What do these icons connote about the spirituality of the precinct? These symbols represent the god(s) and their dwelling places. The temple also, traditionally, is the dwelling of the god. Could a temple not have been an administrative center as well? Could people not express their dedication to their god as well as conduct the business of the day in the temple? Recalling the biblical story of Christ—in Matthew 21:12, Mark 11:15; and Luke 19:45, we find not only that Christ taught in the temple, but he also cleansed it of moneylenders. Scribes are also mentioned in every biblical temple reference. Therefore the temple as such served the scribes, teachers, money lenders and business people as well as representing the house of Yahweh. Could the once nomadic Nabataeans have differing visions of religion? Could they not have had differ-

ent religious relationships between themselves and their principal deity, Dushara? Our studies should focus on Nabataean ideals and not our modern conception of a temple.

In reflecting on the architecture and significance of the Great Temple and its place in Nabataean Petra my thoughts focus on the first century BCE and what a temple might be. I direct my ideas to the temple of Jerusalem and to the great Herodian temples as well. We know the Nabataeans are iconoclasts, who are well traveled and enjoy contacts with cultures and thoughts of other people. We might argue that two centuries of contacts with the Seleucid and Ptolemaic worlds, and with the great cities of the time, like Antioch, Jerusalem and Alexandria is a sort of pre-condition for what in our minds can be called a temple. I find no difficulty in sustaining the thesis that the Great Temple served as a temple and an administrative center for Petra. This, in fact, is where I would like to redirect the discussion, away from our modern Western concepts of religious versus secular buildings.

As an archaeologist I interpret the building and its architectural and sculptural concepts as a structure where both socio-religious and political ideas are represented. I believe that the Great Temple begins primarily as a religious structure that over time becomes an administrative center as well. The physical evidence and the building's architectural vocabulary manipulate the landscape of central Petra creating a monumental complex that dominates the city. Its design is purposefully over-scaled and does not follow any classical paradigm, especially with the addition of the theater. Classical architectural ideals, religious or otherwise, are completely discarded, and as we mentioned previously, this indicates that temple ritual has changed and may indicate the building is now used for meetings as well as sacred ritual and/or festive uses, or as a Nabataean *bouleuterion*. In summary, all architectural rules for theaters as well as temples appear now to be abandoned.

It is reasonable, then, or at least so I believe, to see that the Nabataeans united disparate architectural ideals—ideals closely related to those developed in Alexandria and introduced into Egypt via Alexander and have Greek sources; however, as we all know, such ideals are Syro-Palestinian in origin. Since I am neither an art historian nor a Nabataean architectural specialist, let alone an epigraphist, I know there will be continuing discussion of these issues in coming years from those with differing expertise and points of view.

As we have seen, many scholars totally reject identification of the Great Temple as a religious building; others think it functioned as a palace-audience hall or solely for administration. The field seems to be equally divided: There are those proponents who maintain that it functioned only as an administrative structure. Throughout the religious world, they say, there is no evidence of deliberate religious design, because the theater transforms the temple into a secular building. The main dispute in scholarly circles relates to the addition of the theater in place of the *naos* or *cella* (the inner part of a temple) that has given rise to much, often contradictory speculation. I continue to support the hypothesis that the Great Temple served as both a religious and to some degree, an administrative center. (We should note that the Roman Senate often met in the temple). The debate is welcome, but as yet it is far from being resolved. This debate and speculation about the "temple character" revolves around the questions: Is it a sacred building (Joukowsky and Wenning 2002, Netzer 2003)? Is it an administrative quarter (Schluntz 1999, Seigne 2002, Bowersock 2003)? Is it a palace? Can it be one, two, or all three? Without real textual evidence it is difficult to confirm exactly how it functioned.

Other questions that call for answers are: What are the beginnings of Nabataean religious ideas and worship? What are Nabataean ideals for a religious center? The controversy revolves around the possibility that a structure, a temple, in antiquity can serve multi-purposes. Does it have to serve only a single purpose, either secular or religious, and are these conflicting, mutually exclusive features of our architectural vocabulary?

The uphill sweep from the Wadi Musa points to a monument of special significance, but that does not prove that it is a temple. The Site Phase IV structure towers over the Petra central city, but that too does not prove it is a temple. But the Great Temple looks like a temple, and I argue that there is an earlier Nabataean temple (Site Phase II) constructed on the site, followed by a later Nabataean temple (Site Phase IV), which later enclosed the Site Phase V building of a theater or *bouleuterion*. We will explore this together. The Theater in the temple is a later Nabataean period incarnation; it is a Nabataean period, recycled renovation, and most of our critics tend to view the theater as administrative in nature.

One question to be asked is, "Who is the designer?" And that leads us back to, "Who are the Nabataeans?" The goals of our designers up to this point in time are completely mysterious. Presumably any pattern of data is consistent with our own views about religious buildings. But if we cannot infer anything about the design from the designer, maybe we can rephrase the question: what can we tell about the designer from the design? The use of the same archaeological evidence suggests the artifact record should be looked at more carefully.

We now turn to the context and character of the Great Temple Precinct.

The Great Temple Precinct

J. Patrich (1990, 165) states:

> Although the Nabataeans were always in contact with the world around them and were continuously exposed to the surrounding Hellenistic-Roman culture, there were two periods in which foreign influence was at its height: during the time of Obodas III (30–9 B.C.E.) and Aretas IV (9 B.C.E.– 40 C.E.), and after the Roman annexation and the formation of Provincia Arabia in 106.

The Petra Great Temple precinct is planned and built along the existing limits of the Wadi Musa and the Roman Street, as well as close to a steep slope in the south during an explosion of building activity at the end of the first century BCE. In the Great Temple Site Phase IV, an existing *distyle* temple structure is remodeled and enlarged to create a *tetrastyle* structure (see the Site Phasing, Chapter 1, and the detailed phasing in *Open Context*). By this time Petra becomes a leading commercial center, and in celebration of this new era, the precinct is constructed.

We have archaeologically discovered the physical evidence for the spatial arrangement of the Petra Great Temple as well as its decorative program. Let us revisit the visible elements of the temple; the architectural vocabulary of the building beginning with a Site Phase II small *distyle in antis* (with two columns) in the front that is constructed by the first century BCE. Originally it is a tripartite plan with a two-columned pronaos, cella, and corridors. Remembering that the physical reality of the Wadi Musa largely dictated its location and orientation, the eastern flank of the site was the ideal place to construct the temple because of the bedrock terrain.

The emergence of monumental buildings in Petra must have created dramatically new relationships between the Petraeans and their city. These architectural and artistic developments must have provided the catalyst for different interpersonal developments and a greater bond between the Petraeans and their city. The social, cultural and political relationships that once existed were permanently altered.

We look to Vitruvius, the Roman author who wrote the book on architectural conventions and rules about architecture to better understand the proportions of the Great Temple, especially the height. We reference Vitruvius, Book IV chapter VI 1:

> The top of the cornice which is put above the upper architrave, is made level with the tops of the capitals which are in the pronaos. The opening of the doorway is to be so determined that the height of the temple from the pavement to the panels of the ceiling is to be divided into 3½ parts, and of these 2½ in height are to be fixed for the opening of the folding doors. Let this in turn be divided into 12 parts and of these let 5½ be the breadth of the opening at the bottom. Let it be diminished at the top a third of the width of the architrave, if the opening be not more than 16 feet high…

The height of the Great Temple columns and the ceiling cannot be ascertained. The most complete column is the third from the west in the South Corridor colonnade of the temple rear. This column has an opening elevation of 914.1 m asl and a closing elevation 905.5 m. Comprised of 16 *in situ* column drums, it stands 8.60 m in height. Its base is 0.60 m in height and its plinth is 0.20 m in height, which makes the extant shaft 7.80 m high. The original height module, using Vitruvius as a guide, might have been modules of 8 > or 9 > in diameter. The diameter of this column is approximately 1.30 m, so in using the module 8 >, it would have originally stood in height to 10.40 m, and using the module 9 >, it would have stood 11.7 m in height. The capitals are 1.47 m in height, so adding the capital at module 8 > the column would have stood at 11.87 m and at module 9 >, 13.17 m.

The architrave and cornice thickness still remain a matter of conjecture, but they would have raised the wall heights by 0.50–0.60 m. Thus the ceiling height would have been somewhere between 12.37 and 13.77 m.

For the Ionic doorway, we also look to Vitruvius, Book IV chapter VI 3:

> …the opening must be of a height determined as in the Doric style. Let the breadth be determined so that the height is divided into 2½ parts, and let the breadth of the opening at the bottom be one part.

The central doorway in the South Corridor wall is composed of 12 ashlar courses; it stands 4.35 m in height and is 1.88 m wide. If we follow Vitruvius, one part would equal 1.74 m, which should be the width of the doorway at its bottom. In fact the width of the South Corridor doorway is 0.14 m wider than the Roman architect-engineer prescribed. If the height of the interior can be divided into 2.5 parts, the ceiling would have been at least 6.10 m in height, which is considerably lower than the height of the third column from the west in the south colonnade, the difference being at module 8 > 4.30 m and at module 9 > 5.60 m. Even with a slanting roof, as we project existed as roofing over the corridors—the difference of 4.00–5.00 m seems a bit excessive. In conclusion, we concur with other scholars that Vitruvian formulae cannot be applied as a rule to the buildings at Petra, at least not to the Great Temple.

So it would seem that the Nabataeans ignored Vitruvian principles and created their own rules, which as far as we know are unwritten, but are clear from the buildings they constructed. P. Hammond (1996, 22–23) states that he also has difficulty in following Vitruvian principles for the architecture of the Temple of the Winged Lions. The reflection of the Petraeans to imitate the great cities of the day by building an elegant showplace is catalyzed in the development of the Petra Great Temple, and the edifice that appears is designed at the discretion of the king, possibly the elite, and the city planners and architects. The Great Temple along with other Nabataean structures, becomes one of the single most important contributions of the Nabataeans to the history of architecture.

Temple walls are constructed using plain well-dressed ashlars set directly on the sculpted bedrock with no builders' trench foundations; however, in places there are striated incisions in the bedrock indicating a template for the positioning of the walls. To the west of the site where the bedrock has fallen away the architects construct walls and import fill to compensate, and create a solidly made platform as a building support. The platform is built up to the same height as the bedrock to create a level bedding for the foundation. The walls are Nabataean casemate walls with two parallel walls constructed of finely hewn and dressed ashlars filled in with wet ashlar rubble. Almost none of these ashlars has marginal drafts. Often masons' marks are found *in situ* on the walls[22] (Figures 7.7[23] and 7.8),[24] and at intervals wood was used as an anti-

Fig. 7.7
Mason's mark on a limestone ashlar with a Nabataean "w." This block was found covering the canalization system in the Great Temple Forecourt.

Fig. 7.8
Mason's mark in the shape of a Nabataean "h" carved at the corner of this sandstone ashlar.

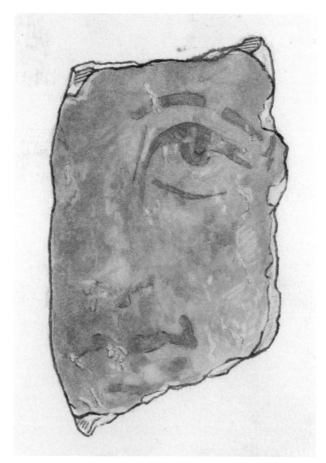

Fig. 7.9
Plaster painting of a face.
Cat. No. 98-CO-65, Seq.
No. 53086. Upper Temenos
Trench 53, Locus 2. Length
7.32 cm, width 4.85 cm,
thickness 3.26 cm. Painting
of an eye/nose/mouth
on a stucco fragment. The
iris of the eye is pale blue
with a dark pupil and eye
line suggesting eyelashes.
The eyebrow is dark. The
nose and mouth are natu-
rally depicted, reminiscent
of the Romano-Egyptian
mummy faces.

Fig. 7.10
Watercolor drawings of
stucco fragments.

earthquake measure. Masons' marks are also distinctive, particularly on the West Corridor Wall (Figure 5.67). They appear to have been executed by a single group of stonemasons.

In the interior of the structure is a decorative program of frescos (Figures 7.9–7.11), all of which exhibit extraordinary motifs from the spectacular facial fragment (Figure 7.9) to the fragments of simple painted designs (Figure 7.10) to the evolved swirling waves of Figure 7.11. The ashlar stone walls largely are not visible but are masked by extravagant plastering and frescoing in the East, the West, and the South Corridors. As one walks through the corridors, there is a visual movement in passing the decorative Second Style Pompeian architectural motifs (Figures 7.12–7.14).[25] This is an iconic representation of social structure and identity created by an elite society—demonstrating status and power. In antiquity the artisans of the Great Temple decorate the 28 temple columns with thick coats of white plaster, the layering measuring between four and five centimeters. They also apply the plaster against the raw stonewalls between the columns. Measuring 3.1 m above the column bases, the artisans sculpt a collar above which the plaster is carefully applied

Fig. 7.11
Decorative swirls drawn with watercolor.

Fig. 7.12
West Corridor fresco depicting the façade of a temple (in green) with Ionic columns.

Fig. 7.13
South Corridor fresco
decoration over the South
Corridor Wall Central
Doorway, north face.

to form cable fluting (Figure 7.15) that extends upwards to join the capitals placed some 15 m above the floor. Subsequently, each column is colorfully decorated with red and yellow natural pigments. The aforementioned capitals include the lower order of bushy acanthus and the upper order of fruits and flowers bursting forth from interlaced vines. Such embellishments set the interior world apart. The corridors are roofed with tiles that slightly slope to the exterior.

At the end of the first century BCE, a transformation takes place. Four columns are constructed in front of the *distyle* structure and the temple is lengthened from 36.00 m to 42.5 m. A new stylobate is positioned to accommodate the four porch columns and the temple becomes *tetrastyle in antis*. The former *distyle* façade is left in place to provide the strength required to support the expanded weight of the roof extending between the front *tetrastyle* and *distyle* columns. This transformation renders the temple structure the largest freestanding structure in Petra. The temple interior is not widened but remains 28 m in width. However with the additions of the walkways, the exterior now measures 35.5 m from the East Walkway to the West Walkway. The extension now measures 42.5 m in length and creates a more imposing building. Shown in a model created for virtual reality, a model can be seen in Figure 7.16. The tetrastyle porch on the front seems to be an add-on to the *distyle* temple; it has a distinctness, as if it is a separately constructed domain with a higher front and more imposing design.

There are also three elements in this extended Great Temple: the Porch and Portico-Pronaos, the East and West Walkways with three threshold accesses into the South, and the East and West corridors. The three South, East and West Corridor thresholds access the main chamber. All of these elements are structurally connected to the building. Their doorways divide the space into specific spatial components, planned so that movement through each is a key element. Their thresholds help the patron move closer to the deity or the ritual taking place in the interior.

There is a dramatic change in the later Nabataean period or in the second century CE (Site Phase V), when a small Theater is inserted into the central building, as can be seen in the virtual reality model in Figures 7.17 and 7.18. Why? Had temple ritual changed? Attendant with the construction for the architectural support of the Theater, intercolumnar walls are put in place between the columns, the Central Arch is constructed to support the upper Theater seats, and four massive stairways with arched walls are built to provide access at the rear of the Theater structure. In Site Phases II and IV it may be assumed that the temple elite went up the stairs, into the Pronaos and then into the main room or *cella/naos* where they stood (facing south). But it is with the Phase V theater addition that the patrons, again the elite, seated in the Theater faced north. What is curious is that the ritual focal point completely changed. Certainly future researchers will discuss this reorientation.

This change must have succeeded in translating the religious aesthetics and sociopolitical tastes of the Nabataeans into a language that was accepted by the Nabataean rulers. The Nabataean architects reworked the design of the earlier Greek-inspired temple but abandoned the earlier Greek architectural plan. In this process, the architects who inserted the Theater defined the architectural mainstream of the Nabataeans. The Great Temple became a more dynamic monument, with seating for some 600 in the Theater. The arrangement of the spatial units of the structure were arranged and ordered perhaps for a festive use? Or perhaps it served as a *bouleuterion* (council chamber), or an *odeion* (*oideion*), as speculated by a number of scholar/observers quoted above.

In Great Temple Site Phase IV, the Upper Temenos becomes an important courtyard for the temple. Off the South Passageway, standing apart from the Great Temple, a complex is constructed comprised of three rooms (plus a settling tank). Known as the Baroque Room

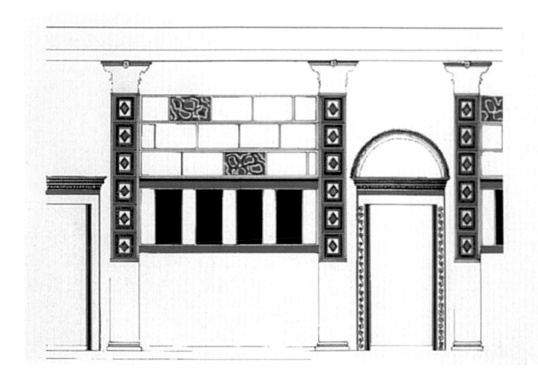

Fig. 7.14
Fresco wall decoration over the South Corridor Wall north face.

Fig. 7.15
Remains of cable
fluting found on a temple
column drum.

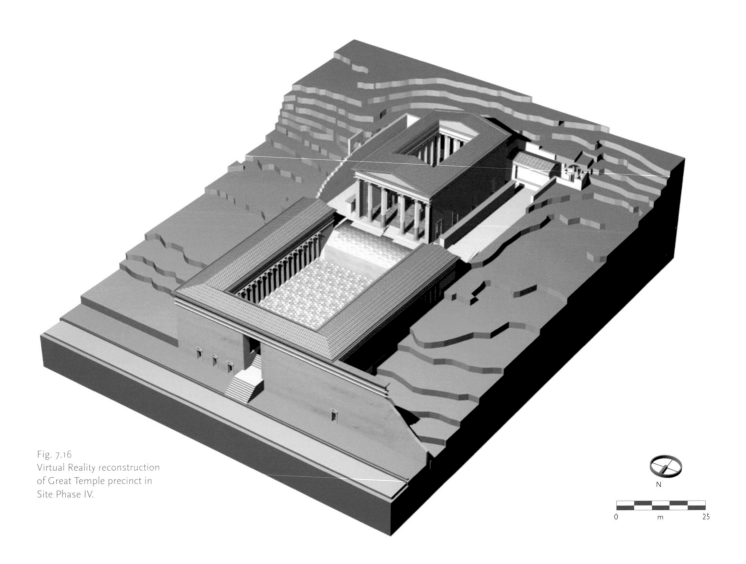

Fig. 7.16
Virtual Reality reconstruction
of Great Temple precinct in
Site Phase IV.

N

0   m   25

Complex, shown in Figure 4.14, here we have an anteroom connecting to a Shrine Room, which in turn accesses the Baroque Room, with its spectacular stucco ceiling (Figures 1.28 and 4.76–4.83).[26] Presumably no layman would have seen the inside of this complex. This part of the precinct has a boundary that limits access; it is divided into domains within which a special social group would have moved.

The temple is the result of a colossal, monumental, royal building complex. Only the monarchy could have financed such a project, quarried the enormous amounts of stone, and found the architects and manpower to carry out this ambitious building program. It serves as a conspicuous symbol that reflects the city's considerable prosperity, power, and prestige. The building delivers a political and theological message of a "national" and cultural identity with distinctive national characteristics. Its function is an ancient and important center of ritual, which also played a key political and perhaps economic function. Undoubtedly the Petra Great Temple was a potent symbol. It was relevant to all Petraean people's lives, and its monumentality symbolizes the awakening of a new order.

With its Site Phase V Theater shown in Figure 7.17, this Petra Great Temple precinct is now a grand statement; it mirrors status and power, as well as being a stunning focal point in the Petra cityscape. What is sure is that the precinct's position on the south side of the Wadi Musa was part of the Nabataean design. Therefore, working within the historical context of the Nabataeans and the geography of Petra, the architectural mainstream was dominated by Nabataean architects who grasped that it was possible to be respectful of history and mimicked it to a certain extent. We can wonder why Nabataean designers might not have followed a classical model more rigorously. Admittedly Nabataean design elements are over-emphasized and the site is scattered with Nabataean-specific styles referencing the classical paradigm.

Much of what we have found in the Great Temple stratigraphy is probably intrusive—the result of earthquakes and fallen debris. From an archaeological perspective, consequently, one of the most frustrating things about our question —the determination of its functional purpose

—is that without definitive evidence (such as an inscription), it is virtually impossible to test. However, the design of the structure encourages us to explore different explanations.

Now, briefly, let us seek comparative data in Nabataean buildings. There are a number of freestanding Nabataean landmarks besides the extravagant tombs found at Petra and Medain Saleh. If we take a close look at the temples to compare in Petra itself (Netzer 2003, 66, Abb. 84), there are two that are definitely identified as being temples: the Qasr al-Bint, and the Temple of the Winged Lions. However, neither of these structures has plans that compare with the Great Temple, and the orientation of all three buildings is different. Further afield there are also Nabataean temples at Sur, Sahr, Seeia, Suweida, Wadi Ramm, Khirbet et-Tannur, Khirbet edh-Dharieh, Qasrawet, Dibon, and Qasr Rabba. These structures (Netzer 2003, 84, Abb.84) and their arrangements function iconographically as Nabataean temples and are dated to the Nabataean period, based upon the ceramic evidence and the stratigraphy of the sites. With such a wide variety of architectural designs, it is nearly impossible to categorize them as originating from one Alexandrian or another classical paradigm. These temples are dissimilar in plan not only to the Great Temple, but to each other as well. Obviously there is fluidity in the Nabataean conception of the temple.

Fig. 7.17
Virtual Reality reconstruction of the Great Temple in Site
Phase V with the Theater.

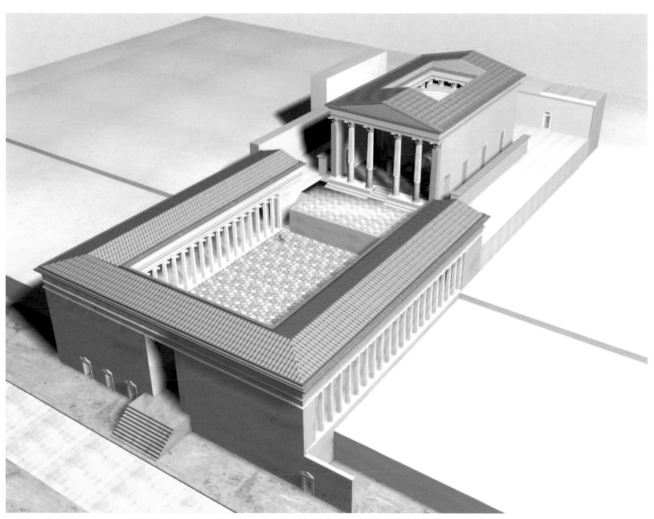

Fig. 7.18
Virtual Reality reconstruction of the Great Temple precinct
in Site Phase V with the Theater.

Sculpture

One of the languages of material culture is sculpture; that of the Great Temple must reflect the commonly held beliefs and desires of the elite that had it commissioned. Perhaps the biggest surprise from the Propylaeum and Lower Temenos excavations is the discovery of the elephant-headed capitals[27] (Figures 7.19a–c, 7.20a–c, 7.21a–d and Figure 3.24).

Elephant-headed capitals

In their earliest recovery, it was somewhat startling to identify these features (Joukowsky 2002a). They had been known from the site of Nabataean Tell Brak (Parr 1960a, 4–5, 134–136) and have been recovered by Patricia M. Bikai in the Beidha excavations. Stray unstratified examples had been placed on the Roman Street by the Temenos Gate in front of the Petra Great Temple. Still, no one knew to which structure those on the street belonged. To find them *in situ* was quite unexpected, and to date there are more than 1,050 elephant elements in our catalog and architectural fragment database.[28] This discovery added another dimension to the degree of Nabataean eclectic sculptural decoration.

What iconographic sources did the sculptors of the elephant-headed capitals use? Where did they find their inspiration? This unfamiliar motif expresses the imagination of the elite and the sculptor(s) based on unknown sources. We can only assume that this is a local Nabataean motif and is indicative of a different tradition. To date the elephant-headed capital is unprecedented in Hellenistic art.

The Indian elephant head had been represented on Hellenistic coins since the third century BCE. As India must have been the producer of spices trafficked by the Nabataeans, the Nabataeans could have discovered the motif in Hellenistic art or in India itself. Using the elephant head instead of the scroll on the ionic-type capital volutes of the Lower Temenos Triple Colonnades seems to have been an idea original to the Nabataeans. What we have found is a Nabataean artistic tradition with a mingling of Nabataean and Hellenistic symbols. They have the abilities to synthesize, modify, adapt, and perhaps invent various layers of ideas.

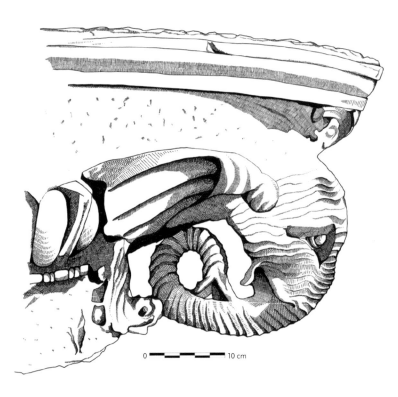

Fig. 7.19a
Elephant half capital
left head, right profile.

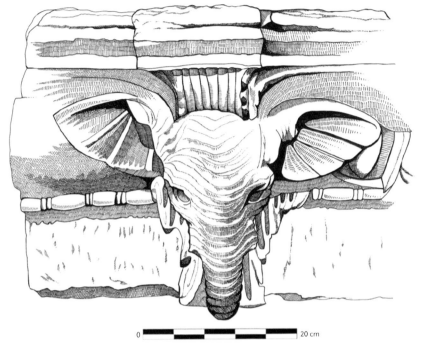

Fig. 7.19b
Half elephant-headed
capital, right head
front view.

0   20 cm

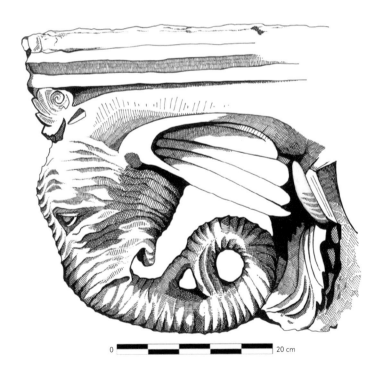

Fig. 7.19c
Elephant half capital right
head, left profile.

0   20 cm

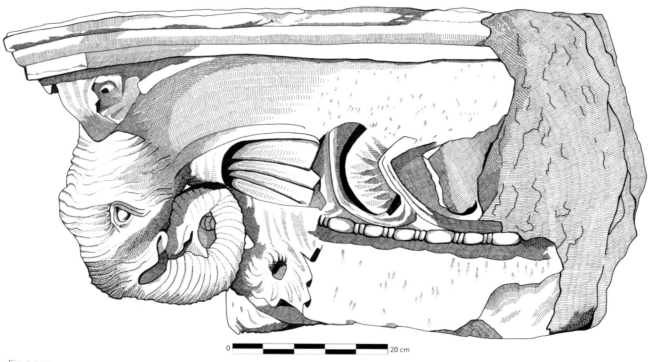

Fig. 7.20a
Elephant-headed capital
left profile.

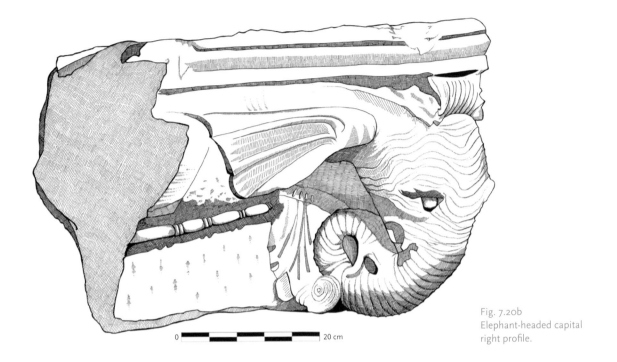

Fig. 7.20b
Elephant-headed capital
right profile.

0 ▰▰▰▰▰ 20 cm

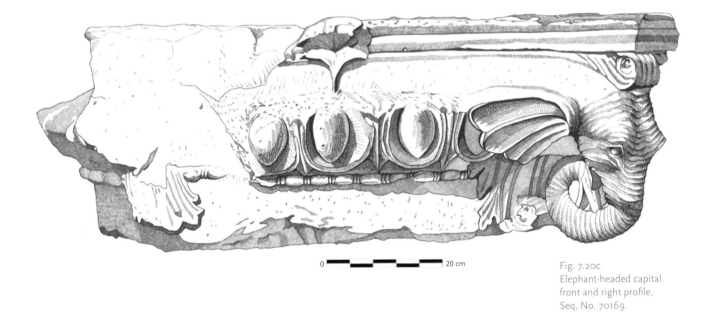

Fig. 7.20c
Elephant-headed capital
front and right profile,
Seq. No. 70169.

0 ▰▰▰▰▰ 20 cm

Fig. 7.21
Upper order of a Great Temple capital with poppies emerging from
hibiscus flowers and a pinecone in the corner.

Great Temple Capitals

Let us now examine the Great Temple capitals (Figures 7.21–7.23) of the temple proper as opposed to the elephant-headed capitals of the Lower Temenos. The temple capitals are especially decorative.[29] The upper order of these capitals is ornamented with carvings of poppy bulbs (Figure 7.21) and blooming hibiscus, surrounded by vine scrolls and repeated patterns of acanthus leaf helices. The pinecone boss (Figure 7.22) unites the four-part upper order. The two-part lower order depicts overflowing acanthus leaves. Together these exhibit the redundant use of the same imagery. The use of mixed plant forms allows for the incorporation and juxtaposition of different species within one entity. The Great Temple capitals, therefore, are part of a given sequence of Hellenistic motifs used by the Nabataeans, who employed master stone carvers and sculptors with technical virtuosity to embellish metropolitan Petra in the first century BCE.

Fig. 7.22
Pinecone boss set into an acanthus leaf. Limestone. Seq. No. 85046, Temple Trench 85, Locus 1. Height 16 cm, length 19 cm.

A preference is shown to the poppy that is most often represented dynamically bursting forth from an open hibiscus petal, or the pine-cone emerging from a network of vines or acanthus leaves, created by chiseling, gouging and channeling the leaf stems, flowers and fruits like grapes and pomegranates, and volutes (Figure 7.23). Although the juxtaposition of the various vegetal elements is contrived, each component is carved with pure lines. The plants and fruits physically explode from the back-ground, and there is skill in the combination of motifs that are hardly a mimicry of nature. The physical strength of the sculptural pattern is in the innovative ornamental patterns themselves, clearly demonstrating the Nabataean decorative fascination with three-dimensional high relief.

This sculpture demonstrates that the temple is a privileged space, since the repeated occur-rence of vine scrolls and fruits is typically used in ritual or sacred space associated with deities and kings. (We find this as well in Assyrian palaces.) We know that the inner chamber of the Temple of Jerusalem is described as having carvings of cones (pinecones) and blooms of flowers. Gold overlaid stucco and gilded chisel dressed masonry of the temple capitals would also mark this as a sacred place.

Did the sculptors design and create the complex details of the temple capitals? The iconographic tradition of the Corinthian type of temple capital already existed and was rede-signed by the Nabataean sculptor.

The Nabataean Corinthian capital devel-oped its own accepted, well-known tradition that is also represented at Al-Khazna (Figure 7.24). Thus we may surmise that the al-Khazna and Great Temple capitals are based on the same source. The Great Temple capitals, enhanced by their lively fruits, are carved more deeply with the depiction of a slightly different design pro-gram used to fill the space than the al-Khazna capitals. The subject matter is the same, but the compositions are different. Although there are manufacturing differences, their iconography and stylistic peculiarities lead us to assume they stem from the same tradition.

Fig. 7.23
Volute in the corner of the upper order of the Great Temple capitals.

Fig. 7.24
A capital from the front of Al-Khazna.

Fig. 7.25
Face of Tyche with her
turreted crown, in sand-
stone. Cat. No. 95-S-14,
Surface find. Of 7.5YR7.6
reddish yellow stone.
Length 38.3 cm, width
31.5 cm. Facial features
and crown partially eroded
away, nose missing.

Pilaster Reliefs

The pilaster reliefs are assumed to be part of the architectural façade of the Great Temple and perhaps were part of the decorative façade of the Propylaeum. Classical gods are represented as well as mortals, such as the man wearing the Roman toga from the Lower Temenos (Figure 3.29) or the soldier's helmet from the Propylaeum shown in Figure 2.37. However, most of the pilaster figures we have recovered are divine religious figures; others are noted for their appearance and a distinct style, which is formal, devoid of vitality, and rigid. Figures of gods and goddesses are carved in the frontal position. The figures look flat, and generally these figures are poor in detail and have parts of their bodies distorted (see the anatomical detail of the Fortuna in Figure 3.26). Even the garments are schematic. It is indeed unfortunate we do not have the faces that presumably showed more skill in carving. Generally there is little visual movement and energy in these sculptures, as can be noted in the representation of Tyche with her turreted crown shown in Figure 7.25. However there are rare exceptions as can be seen in the detail of Figure 7.26 with a female emerging from an acanthus helix and the

Fig. 7.26
Lively female figure emerging from a helix from the Propylaeum East. Limestone. This figure was probably part of a pilaster block or a frieze.

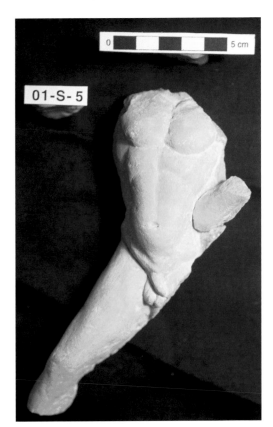

Fig. 7.27a
Male athlete in motion.
(See details below)

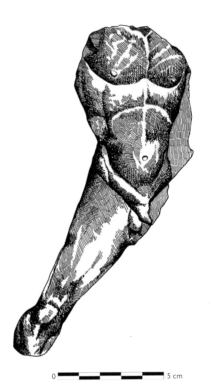

0 ▬▬▬▬▬ 5 cm

Fig. 7.27b
Male athlete in motion.
Cat. No. 01-S-5, Seq. No.
80267. Propylaeum Trench
80, Locus 11. Limestone of
2.5Y8/2 pale yellow color.
Length 15.84 cm, width
5.26 cm, thickness 3.38 cm.
Three fragments of a nude
male figure. The figure
is that of a young, physically
fit male. He has only a right
leg and a very small fragment of his left forearm.
The rear of the figure is
flat and unfinished, which
suggests that the piece was
placed against a surface.

wet-draped female which has a more naturalistic modeling shown in Figures 3.27 and 3.28.
The figure of a male athlete (Figures 7.27a and
7.27b,) which probably broke away from one
of the pilaster blocks, shows an active figure.
The differences indicate that these pieces are
carved by the more talented sculptors while
their apprentices executed poorer quality works.
These decorated pilasters are being studied by
Joseph J. Basile and will be presented in the
Great Temple Volume III.

The representations of divinities on the
pilasters may have been mounted on either side
of the temple front anta walls. What do these
icons connote about the deities represented?
From those found it is difficult to identify
one theme for these pilasters, except for a city
overflowing with bountiful fruits (blossoming
fruit denotes renewal), which at this point is the
only overall interpretation that can be found
in the pilaster reliefs. If there was a programmatic layout, it symbolizes and emphasizes
abstract concepts such as the fruits of summer
or the bountiful harvest that carry meanings for
the glory and power of the city. The underlying significance of the motifs was simply artists
depicting known themes, as there seems to be
no connective link between various themes.
The Greco-Roman-Nabataean correspondences
of these deities are Aphrodite–al-'Uzza–Isis,[30]
Athena[31]–the Nabataean warring goddess–Allat
(Figure 2.38),[32] Demeter–a divine attendant,
and Tyche–the celebration of the city.[33]

Does the frequent artistic representations of the cornucopia and other fruits on
the antae pilasters and on the capitals suggest
that al-'Uzza-Aphrodite might be the deity for
worshipped at the Petra Great Temple? Clearly
the poppy is an aspect of the Great Temple's
decorative attributes. The poppy was used exu-
berantly "…to induce a state of ecstasy essential
for the performance of the sacred rites."[34]

Let us now examine other features and
associated artifacts—perhaps they will offer
some solutions to the functional analysis of our
building? We will begin with the epigraphic
record and then turn to cult objects.

Epigraphic Records

Students quickly learn that in studies of the ancient world, textual references, to some scholars, can be the single most significant evidence. Unfortunately at Petra there are few contemporary historical accounts of the demographic and geopolitical status of the city. From later Roman accounts we have learned that Cleopatra petitioned Antony to give her Petra—one of the few requests Antony turned down. The Roman emperor Tiberius may have visited Petra between 112 and 114 CE, for his inscriptions imply that he did, and the emperor Hadrian toured Petra in 131 CE (and renamed the site for himself, "Hadriane Petra").

But what do we know from Nabataean references?[35] There are few to help us. No *in situ* inscriptions are recovered from the Petra Great Temple that give us any indication as to which deity is worshipped at the Great Temple or how the Nabataeans identified the structure. The fragment of a royal inscription ascribed to King Aretas IV recovered from the American Center of Oriental Research Petra Church excavations[36] and published by R. N. Jones and G.W. Bowersock (2001)[37] is shown in Figure 7.28. Although it was not found at the Great Temple, we do have one Petra royal Nabataean textual reference evidenced in Jones and Bowersock's translation:

> This is the…which Halpala, [son of…] made, and these are the theatron and shrine, colonnades, and porticoes to Dushara..in the month Tebet in the year eleven of Haretat (Aretas), king of the Nabataeans, who loved his people.

Presumably this text, which is dated to 2–3 CE, refers to an architectural entity of sacral character, and the combination of theatron, shrine, colonnades and porticoes might indicate that its reference is to the Great Temple.[38] This is an open acknowledgement of King Aretas IV's building program. Whether the king is referring specifically to the theater in the Petra Great Temple, to the temenos of the Great Temple or Qasr al-Bint, to some other structure like the Temple of the Winged Lions, or to some other as yet unexcavated building cannot be authenti-

cated. What is clear is that he is claiming credit for a significant building program. To date, only the Great Temple exhibits a combination of all of these features, although it would be some time later that the Theater would be built.

Other Nabataean inscriptions uncovered by Brown archaeologists at the Great Temple are a previously published bronze plaque (Joukowsky 2003, Figure 239, p. 220) shown in Figure 7.6 that provisionally reads: "Malicum," meaning queen. A faint inscription on a plaster molding (Figures 7.29a and 7.29b), provisionally reads "…good health,"[39] and Nabataean graffiti were found carved into the plaster of the north gallery wall of the West Propylaeum, shown in Figure 7.30.

There are several partial Greek inscriptions (Figures 4.104 and 4.105) found associated with the Great Temple Roman-Byzantine baths, which we commented on in Chapter 4,[40] and a series of small ostraca and as yet identified partial inscriptions, including a stamped jar handles shown in Figure 7.31c. Three Roman Imperial inscriptions (Figure 5.72) found in the west chamber of the Temple have been studied, dated and published by Steven V. Tracy (Joukowsky, 1998, 371–374) and dated to 112–114 CE,

Fig. 7.28
Inscription fragments of King Aretas IV from the Petra Church. This larger part of the inscription is set in a frame ca. 38.5 cm in width. The preserved height of the fragment is 27 cm; see Jones in Fiema et al. 2001, 346.

Fig. 7.29a
Faint painted inscription of plaster found in the East "Cistern," Cat. No. 98-S-64, Seq. No. 53204. Upper Temenos Trench 53, Locus 12. Length 14.91 cm, width 12.38 cm, thickness 2.34 cm. Nabataean inscription executed over a background of pale green paint.

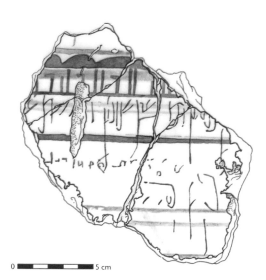

Fig. 7.29b
East "Cistern" Nabataean inscription, Cat. No. 89-S-64.

Fig. 7.30
Nabataean graffiti incised in the wall plaster from Wall K, the south wall of the North Gallery of the Propylaeum West. Trench 87, Locus 28. Opening elevation: 894.25 m. Closing elevation: 894.01 m. Size: 0.12 m east-west x no discernable width north-south. Width of the plaster overall is about 1 cm north-south. Its location is on the north face of Wall K. This is a three-line Nabataean inscription on plaster that covers portions of the north face of Wall K. The particular patch of plaster on which the inscription is written extends below the top of the bench and therefore likely predates it. The writing appears to be three words, one of which is repeated as the first and last line. It is most likely graffiti.

Fig. 7.31a
Painted potsherd, Cat. No. 00-P-14, Seq. No. SP70163.
Propylaeum Trench 70, Locus 8. Length 7.93 cm, thickness
0.74 cm. Of 5YR8/3 pink with buff slip. Coarse ware fragment
with handwritten characters in black ink.

Fig. 7.31b
Incised lamp base fragment, Cat. No. 00-P-13, Seq. No.
73109. Temple, Trench 73, Locus 15. Of 5YR7/4 pink ware.
Length 2.44 cm, width 1.73 cm, thickness 0.83 cm.
Small fragment with four characters. Could be lamp
base but the ceramic is rather thick? Red slip. See Khairy
1990:#83. #11, RAYT "I saw". Recognized as lamp base
fragment.

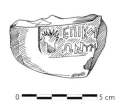

Fig. 7.31c
Amphora handle stamped with a Rhodian Rose, Cat. No. 01-P-10, Seq, No.
83140. Upper Temenos Trench 83, Locus 9. Of 2.5YR6/6 light red ware.
Length 5.72 cm, width 4.01 cm, weight 57.5 grams. Fragmented amphora
handle with very legible stamp, which looks like a snowman with a radiant
halo, perhaps a lighthouse (?) and the two lines of Greek, E, Pi, Iota, (..).
Maybe similar to Khairy 1990:51, which reads: "In the year of Pratophanes
month Dalios (December)" dating it to the second half of the third
or early second century BCE.

Fig. 7.31d
Ostracon? Cat. No. 01-P-5 Seq. No. 79056. Lower Temenos,
Trench 79, Locus 1. Length 6.71 cm, width 3.54 cm, thickness
0.95 cm, of 2.5YR6/8 light red ware. Possible jar fragment
with the script (?) written on slipped side.

Fig. 7.31e
Letters impressed into plaster/stucco in a vessel base, Cat. No. 01-CO-10,
Seq. No. 85202 Temple Trench 85, Locus 1. Length 8.72 cm, width 5.83 cm,
thickness 2.37 cm. possibly being the dried residue of plaster left in a
basket. On the underside of the mold appear to be some characters/
symbols, e.g., "V."

Fig. 7.32
PROVIN inscription. Front view Seq. No. 71256.

Fig 7.33a
Sandstone inscription fragment, Cat. No. 00-S-90 Seq. No. 71275. Lower Temenos, Trench 71, Locus 18. Length 22 cm, width 13 cm, height 11 cm. Height of letters: 3.18 cm, width: 2.68 cm. Notch height: 5.96 cm, width: 2.12 cm. Two characters, possibly "V" and "A" on one line with edges of other indecipherable letters to the left of "V" and beneath "A." There is a notch cut into the back of the stone, presumably for attaching to a surface.

Note that 7.33b–7.33d are found in the Lower Temenos Trench 98, 2004, and they are all marble fragments

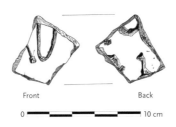

Fig 7.33b
Partial marble inscription, Cat. No. 04-S-8, Seq. No. 98256. Lower Temenos, Trench 98, Locus 3. Width 5.47 cm, thickness 1.92 cm, height 4.41 cm, weight 62.4 grams.

Fig. 7.33c
Partial marble inscription with two cut characters, possibly a "T" and an "A." Cat. No. 04-S-4 Seq. No. 98228. Lower Temenos, Trench 98, Locus 3. Width 7.11 cm, thickness 2.08 cm, height 9.15 cm; it exceeds 150 grams in weight.

Fig. 7.33d
Partial marble inscription with incised characters on both flattened sides. Cat. No. 04-S-5, Seq. No. 98260. Lower Temenos, Trench 98, Locus 3. Length 5.02 cm, width 4.24 cm, thickness 1.87 cm, and weight 78.4 grams.

Fig.7.33e
Partial marble inscription, Cat. No. 00-S-89 Seq. No. 71352. Lower Temenos, Trench 71, Locus 20. Length 13.14 cm, width 4.22 cm, thickness 2.31 cm. Partial inscription, could be the left side of "M." It has been cut professionally with a chisel, and there are veins of mica running through the block. Letter is at least 7.07 cm long.

although there remains some question about the accuracy of this dating. One partial unfinished Roman inscription on a sandstone slab reading, PROVI (Figure 7.32), was found in an unstratified fill in the West Cryptoporticus of the West Propylaeum. This inscription is a reminder that Petra was now a celebrated part of the *Provincia Arabia*, or the new Roman province of Arabia. It is obviously inscribed sometime after the Roman annexation in 106 CE and probably commemorates the Roman Emperor Trajan who transformed the Nabataean kingdom into a province. (Other partial Roman inscriptions are found in Figure 7.33a–e). Figure 7.34 shows a stamped jar handle that reads FELICI ?A, perhaps commemorating The Roman epithet for "Arabia Felix,"[41] or "blessed Arabia."

Unfortunately these meager philological hints give us no clues that will definitively answer the question as to the identity of the temple, so we will turn our attention to cult objects.

Fig. 7.34
Stamped double-strand amphora handle with FELICI?A/S impressed on it. Cat. No. 01-P-4, Seq. No. 77398. Upper Temenos, Trench 77, fill. Length 7.49 cm, width 5.53 cm, of 5YR7/3 pink ware.

Nabataean Retaining Wall

Blocked Passageway

West Entry Stairway Platform

Betyl

Nefesh and *Betyl*

Platform

Fig. 7.35
Lower Temenos platform with *nefesh* and *betyl in situ*.

Cult Objects

Writing in the second half of the first century BCE, Strabo (Geogr. XVI, 4, 26) reports of the Nabataeans: "Embossed works, paintings and moulded works are not produced in their country."

We know that statement may represent the true picture before the Great Temple and Al-Khazna were built, but there follows a Nabataean interdependence upon the nonfigurative and figurative art in the Nabataean sculptural canon. Patrich (1990, 39–40) states:

> The key to resolving the contradictions that arose in the attempts by scholars to understand the origins and essence of "Nabataean" art can be found in the demographic structure of the Nabataean kingdom. Its mixed ethnic composition led to a variety of trends within Nabataean art...the desert born Nabataeans also had distinctive art forms that were of long duration, and they were nonfigurative.

Betyls and Nefesh

Religious artifacts or cult objects of stone at the Great Temple include the *nefesh*, *betyls*, and horned altars. What do these artifacts mean? It is not only the objects themselves but their sacral context that is the deciding factor. Their *in situ* context is associated with the Propylaeum and Lower Temenos. Certainly the double *betyls* in the Propylaeum West (Figures 2.19 and 2.20) and the large horned altar (Figures 2.44 and 2.45) were sacred and served as places for offerings. Certainly a portable *betyl* (like the one shown in Figure 5.57) could have been placed in the Shrine Room niche (Figure 4.75) of the Baroque Room Complex. (The Shrine Room is such a modest sized room that it may have served as a private chapel.)

Commonly appearing together at Petra are anthropomorphic representations as we have seen on the Great Temple pilasters and the aniconic representations of deities. R.A. Stucky (1994, 278) states:

> The identification of the deity represented as an extremely abstract idol is difficult because there are several female deities represented in the same manner. Apart from the Nabataean-Arabian goddesses al-'Uzza and Allat, the North Syrian goddess Atargatis is mentioned in the inscription on one of these stelai as well. What seems to be

of some importance for explaining the difference between the anthropomorphic and the stylized idols is that the latter form was chosen exclusively for local or closely related Oriental deities, whereas the anthropomorphic type was used for foreign deities—although they were partially integrated into the Nabataean pantheon. The fear of "naturalistic" representation seems to be more or less restricted to the local deities; a broader spectrum of representation was obviously allowed or possible in the sphere of foreign gods.

The rich remains of the Great Temple sculpture are now contrasted with the preserved finds of standing idols—the *nefesh* and the *betyls*.

Both the *betyl* and the *nefesh* (Figures 3.6, 3.57 and 3.58) are thought to be the symbol and embodiment of the god himself.[42] These images (Figure 7.35) must have been a powerful part of the Nabataean ethnos. Their iconography is part of the Nabataean visual lexicon. The use of the *nefesh* and *betyl* must have been a reminder of the long-standing nomadic tradition, and their iconography and spiritual meaning became part of Nabataean cultural identity. In particular, the *betyl* demonstrates a visual continuity of ideas— the metaphysical presence of the divine, an icon with sacred power. *Betyls* range from plain rectangular to conically shaped blocks representing the deity; some of them have inscriptions indicating the deity represented. Some of them have eyes and noses and are known as "eye-idols." Wenning (2001:85, note 13) states:

> The Nabataeans burned incense and poured blood on the sacred stone....Only the blood of animals was offered to the deity (cf. Mettinger 1995, 191–192).

In her calculations, Laïla Nehmé (2003, 158) states that at Petra there are 15 independent *betyls*, and eight are independent groups of two to six *betyls*. Wenning (2001, 79–95) in his article, "The Betyls of Petra," classifies them into a typology, and (2001, 87) posits:

> Each group of betyls must be interpreted in its own context. Niches with two betyls are often attributed to Dushara and Al-'Uzza, the most venerated male and female deities at Petra.

Whether these *betyls* represent Dushara (the main deity of Petra) and the tutelary deity of the Nabataean tribe and its royal dynasty (Wenning 2001, 81) and Al-'Uzza is hypothetical and cannot be proved, but what is clear is that this was a sacred place.

As for the *nefesh*, by Laïla Nehme's count (2003, 157) there are 34 *nefesh*, groups of *nefesh*, or niches including a *nefesh* at Petra. Patrich (1990, 122) reminds us that the Nabataeans did not use the image of the deceased in their burial monuments, but used an architectonic shape to portray their dead. We can imagine that these images were worshipped in the same manner in the city as they had been in their nomadic lifestyle. Wenning (2001:87):

> The Nabataean *nephesh* is shaped like an obe-liskoid pilaster or a pointed cone, often with a blossom/pinecone or a stylized crown at the top. Most of the *nepheshes* are set upon a base, where the name of the dead person is given... Freestanding *nepheshes*...are rare.

By their *in situ* position on the West Entry stairway platform the *nefesh* and *betyl* are in a high place to view the city surround. Unfortunately we do not know to whom this *nefesh* was dedicated. Both symbolize the presence of the deity, and their location in a public, high, open-air space lends them a theological legitimacy. The prominently located stairway platform serves as a watch place, with steps to place offerings—a place that sees pedestrian traffic, and yet it serves a public cult. Their presence suggests a conspicuous cultic function for this platform.

To a great degree, these are silent sentinels that witnessed a fascinating but enigmatic past. But being placed where they are, they are far from silent about who witnessed their presence. As they are subject to interpretation, perhaps we can speculate that the *nefesh* marked a place to remember the honored dead? Unquestionably there is an cult of the dead associated with significant religious ritual in Petra; obviously death also plays a prominent role in life. Is the erection of these religious icons spontaneous and private, or do they serve as part of an official act? Did some elite Petraean commission a mason to execute these *steles*? These are intriguing questions that deserve more attention.

We cannot forget the *in situ* double *betyl*s in the West Propylaeum (Figures 2.19 and 2.20). A portable *betyl* found in the East Corridor excavations is shown in Figure 5.57. There may be additional *betyl*s set into the wall below the West Propylaeum *betyl*s. We seek expert opinion on this matter.

ALTARS

Shouldn't a temple have an altar?

Previously, I have argued there is an altar on the lowest steps built against the Portico Wall in the Propylaeum Central Staircase. In these excavations much burning, ash residue, charred bones and broken pottery were found. In the Lower Temenos a large cut out area in the Hexagonal Pavement (Figure 3.52) may have held a massive altar, which was dismantled in antiquity or in modern times before the area could serve as a farmer's field. E. Netzer (2003, 78) has proposed the placement of the temple altar on the upper platform in the rear of the temple behind the theater. Clearly the fact that no altar exists today is not proof that one did not exist at the Great Temple.

J. Patrich (1990, 92) states:

> Among the objects carved in relief on the cliffs of Petra, Dalman observed two types of incense altars. (These altars were not used in Nabataean ritual, they are simply cultic objects.) ...The first type is elongated; its height approximately double its width, with four "horns" at the corner....Dalman counted eighteen....In these votive representation, the altar is apparently perceived as a symbol of the worshipped deity.

As for horned altars, we have the large horned altar from the Propylaeum (Figures 2.44 and 2.45), which is associated with the double *betyl*s. Probably used for the burning of incense, the horned altars were found in different parts of the site and few are in closed contexts. Some are portable and small (we have a very small one, the size of a pea, that could be hand-held) and a carved hexagonally shaped altar shown in Figure 7.36. With low relief stylized horns on the top extending to the cavity for incense, it was also found in the Lower Temenos West Cryptoporticus debris contexts. A miniature altar is shown in Figure 7.37.

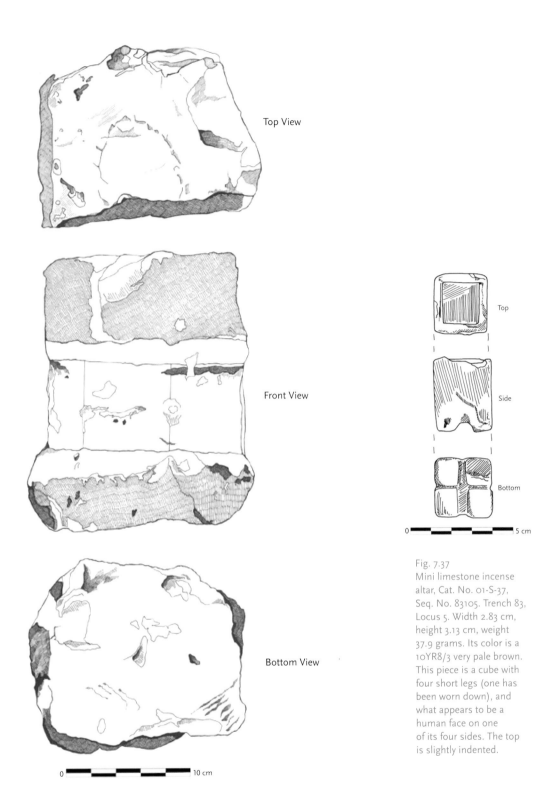

Top View

Front View

Bottom View

Top

Side

Bottom

0 ▬▬▬▬▬ 5 cm

Fig. 7.37
Mini limestone incense
altar, Cat. No. 01-S-37,
Seq. No. 83105. Trench 83,
Locus 5. Width 2.83 cm,
height 3.13 cm, weight
37.9 grams. Its color is a
10YR8/3 very pale brown.
This piece is a cube with
four short legs (one has
been worn down), and
what appears to be a
human face on one
of its four sides. The top
is slightly indented.

0 ▬▬▬▬▬ 10 cm

Fig. 7.36
Small limestone horned altar
Seq. No. 79039.

Benches and Offering Stands

Benches are conspicuous in the Propylaeum West South Gallery, in the West Cryptoporticus, and in the Upper Temenos set against the South Passageway Wall. These benches are too high to serve for sitting, so we propose they were used for offerings.[43] Probably cereal grain offerings including wheat and barley, milk, oil and honey, vegetables, fruits, flowers, wine, and incense were offered to the gods on the benches associated with these features as part of a religious ritual.[44] In praying for life, the prosperity of the fields and their herds, it is assumed that worshippers placed offerings that also included offerings of animals.

Votive Niches

Votive niches at Petra number in the hundreds (Wenning 2001, 88):

> Niches are cut into the rock as simple or framed recesses and are characterized by an upright rectangular outline…In some cases, the recess itself represents the betyl as a negative space.

Laïla Nehmé (2003, 158) counts 412 religious niches in Petra, which she sub-divides into whether or not they are empty, containing a *betyl* or sculpted figure, or an altar. The niche in the Shrine Room has a hollow at the bottom indicating that a *betyl*, offerings or perhaps incense was burned here. This niche resembles the one on the path to Jabal al-Khubtha shown by Wenning (2001, Figure 1). There was a prepared niche (Figures 2.19 and 2.21) created for the double *betyl*s in the West Propylaeum as well.

Ceramics

The number of ceramic fragments at the site (over 300,000) is noteworthy, but it is difficult to pinpoint which of these may have served a ceremonial function.[45] Schmid (2002, 56) generalizes:

> The pottery of the first half of the 1st century B.C., as found at Petra and at other Nabataean sites features the same forms as these of the contemporary late Hellenistic ceramics from neighboring Syria, Judaea and Mesopotamia, the only difference being the simple red painting sometimes applied on the interior of Nabataean bowls and cups.…From ca. 50 B.C. onwards… the pottery becomes finer and thinner, and it develops a very characteristic design painted in red, featuring vegetal elements such as leaves, and exclusively applied on the interior parts of drinking bowls.

And there are a few unusual pieces such as the ceramic cup (Figure 7.38), and the lentoid pilgrim flask (Figures 4.58 and 7.39) found in Room A of the East Perimeter Wall. One side of the body bulges out more than the other and the body is decorated with rouletting (one side of it is poorly preserved).

Figure 7.40 is a collection of painted plates from the Residential Quarter (Trench 94) and in Figure 7.41 are the fragments recovered from the Great Cistern in the East Plaza (SP85 Locus 23). As can be seen from the accompanying descriptions, most of this pottery finds correspondences with Schmid's Phases 3b and 3c dated from ca. 100 CE, the *terminus post quem*, to ca. 120 CE or the *terminus ante quem*. Obviously this is a mixture of earlier Nabataean wares of the first century CE with later forms. Based on the parallels the *terminus post quem* would be 50 CE and the *terminus ante quem* to the late second century CE when the Great Cistern was no longer in use.

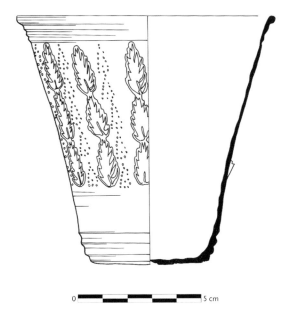

Fig. 7.38
Nabataean goblet with stamped leaf impressions Cat. No. 01-P-28, Seq. No. 84187. Upper Temenos, Trench 84, Locus 22. Height 10 cm, diameter 10.7 cm. dated to Phase 3 from 20 to 100 CE. Impressed design of palm leaves and dotted triangles. It also has linear horizontal incisions on the base and linear horizontal incisions just beneath its flaring rim with a rounded lip. It has a flat base with incised concentric circles.

0 |▬▬|▬▬|▬▬| 5 cm

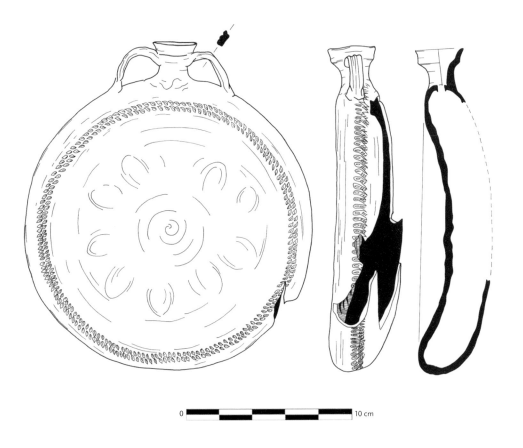

Fig. 7.39
Pilgrim Bottle with rouletted impressions Cat. No. 01-P-42, Seq. No. 84147, dated to Phase 3 from 20 to 100 CE. Upper Temenos Trench 84; of 5YR7/6 reddish yellow ware. Exterior slip 2.5YR6/8 light red. Interior slip 2.5YR4/2 dusky red. Maximum diameter: 16.3 cm, rim diameter 2.5 cm. Rouletting around both sides. Everted rim. Two incised vertical loop handles.

0 |▬▬|▬▬|▬▬| 10 cm

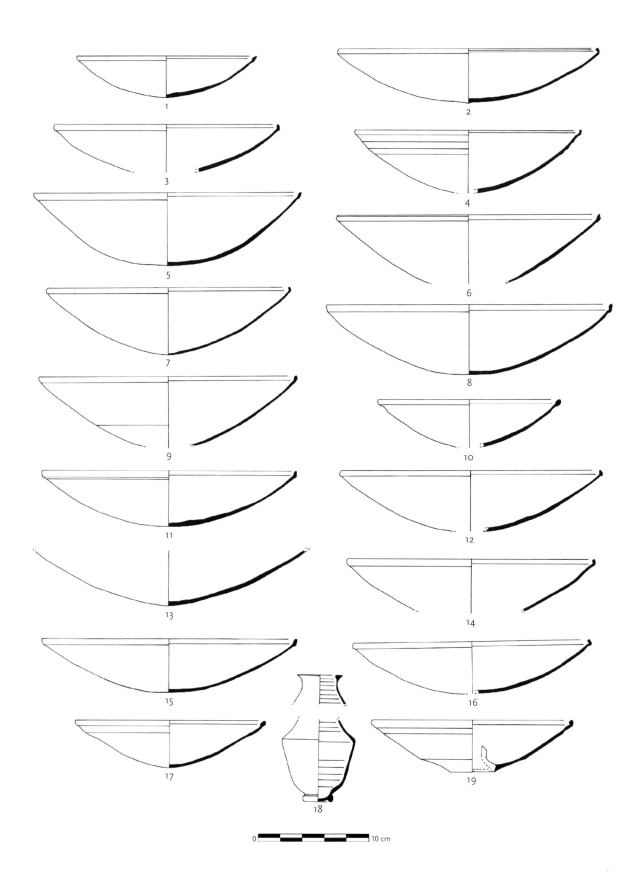

Fig. 7.40
Assorted painted fine Nabataean wares from the Residential Quarter, 2002, Trench 94.

Figure 7.40.
Assorted Nabataean Painted Fine Wares from the Residential Quarter, 2002 Trench 94

1. Cat. No. 02-P-65.
Shallow Bowl of 2.5YR 7.8 light red ware with a slightly inverted, thickened rim and rounded base. Interior decoration composed of a 2.5YR 4 dark gray palmette wreath surrounding a central palmette design with three pyramids and dotted chevrons. The rim is flattened on one side and decorated with a white slip on its exterior. A rough, 7.5YR 5/2 brown dot appears on the bottom of the vessel, possibly due to firing.

2. Cat. No. 02-P-66.
Shallow Bowl of 2.5YR 6/6 light red ware with an inverted rim and slight button base. The clay fabric has inclusions of lime. The interior decoration is composed of 2.5YR 5/4 reddish brown painted twin birds, dotted chevrons, a finely combed background, triangles with scalloped edges and a central medallion surrounded by a palmette wreath. The rim exterior retains vestiges of a red slip. See Schmid 1994, Phase 3b.

3. Cat. No. 02-P-68.
Upper body of a shallow Bowl of 10R 6/8 light red ware with an incurving rim with a slight exterior flange and a missing base. The clay fabric has inclusions of lime, straw and white and black grit. Interior decorations include a 2.5YR 5/6 red "parsnip," "orange," "hot pepper," two palmettes and a circle dotted with chevrons and triangles. The background is combed lines. Vestiges of white slip on rim exterior.

4. Cat. No. 02-P-70.
Upper body of a Deep Bowl of 10R 6/6 light red ware with an inverted, vertical rim and missing base. The upper third of the vessel's body is lined with shallow ridges that are accentuated by burnishing. The clay fabric has inclusions of white and black grit and very little lime. On the interior are 5YR 5/4 reddish brown twin sets of

pyramids, two palmettes stretching from the rim to the center, two dotted chevrons and combed lines across the background. Vestiges of white slip are visible on the rim's exterior. See Bikai and Perry 2001, 7:9, Tomb 2, Phase 3c with the addition of a combed background.

5. Deep Bowl of 2.5YR 7/6 ware with a slightly inverted rim and rounded base. The clay fabric has inclusions of lime and white and black sand. The interior decoration includes a 2.5YR 5/2 weak red painted palmette wreath across the tondo with angled lines stretching to the rim. The background shows a lattice pattern and lines with dots to either side. The exterior rim is painted with a white slip.

6. Cat. No. 02-P-74.
Upper body of a Deep Bowl of 2.5YR 6/8 light red ware with an everted, thickened rim and missing base. The clay fabric has inclusions of fine lime and white sand. The interior decoration is composed of a black and 2.5YR 4/2 weak red painted palmette wreath with sprigs and a palmette branch extending through the vessel's center. The background is covered with a lattice pattern divided by rows of dots on either side of a single line. On the exterior, the lower half of the vessel surface is smooth and the upper half is rough. The rim retains vestiges of a white slip.

7. Cat. No. 02-P-76.
Deep Bowl of 2.5YR 5/8 red ware with an inverted rim and rounded base. The interior decoration is a 10R 4/3 weak red palmette wreath with sprig lines from some branches extending through the center of the vessel. Lines with dots appear to either side and a lattice pattern overlies the palmette and dots. On the base is a pale black coloration probably resulting from firing and the rim exterior displays a worn white slip.

8. Cat. No. 02-P-67.
Deep Bowl of 2.5YR 7/8 light red ware with an inverted rim and rounded base. The clay fabric has inclusions of lime and gray and black grit. The interior decoration is a 2.5YR 5/6 red painted palmette wreath around the rim with sprigs, dotted chevrons, a plump bird, scalloped edge extending to an elongated blob and combed lines in the background. Vestiges of a 5YR 8/4 pinkish-white slip appear on the partially ridged, slightly warped rim exterior. See Schmid 1994, Phase 3b.

9. Cat. No. 02-P-69.
Upper body of a Deep Bowl of 2.5YR 6/8 light red ware with a slightly incurving rim and missing base. The clay fabric has minimal inclusions of lime and gray and white grit. The interior decoration is composed of a 2.5YR 4/3 reddish brown painted lattice background with a single line with dots to either side, one palmette wreath with sprigs around the outside and another across the diameter of the bowl. On the exterior are shallow ridges and the rim retains vestiges of 2.5YR 7/4 white slip overtop the red background.

10. Cat. No. 02-P-77.
Upper body of a shallow Bowl of 2.5YR 6/8 light red ware with a yellowish core, inverted, thickened rim and missing base. The clay fabric has inclusions of black and white grit and large and small particles of lime. The interior decoration is composed of 5YR 3/1 very dark gray outer tondo of concentric wavy lines, a plump bird, a dotted chevron, a second bird with a fan tail and a spherical object. The rim exterior is painted with a white slip.

11. Cat. No. 02-P-75.
Shallow Bowl of 2.5YR 6/8 light red ware with an inverted, vertical rim and a thick black core. Painted decoration on the vessel's interior is in the form of a 2.5YR 4/4 reddish brown palmette wreath around the vessel's edge with sprigs extending to the rim, compressed leaves and a lattice background. Two single lines flanked by dots are painted on either side of a central palmette and vestiges of white slip on rim exterior.

12. Cat. No. 02-P-71.
Upper body of a Shallow Bowl of 10R 6/6 light red ware with an inverted rim, black core and missing base. The clay fabric has inclusions of lime, black grit and white sand. Painted decoration appears on the vessel's interior in the form of a 7.5YR 4/2 brown palmette wreath with single "feather" lines every few leaves. A long palmette extends across the center of the vessel as do lattice fences separated by single lines and large and small dots. Vestiges of white slip appear on the rim exterior and a heavy, thin line appears beneath the rim. The upper half of the vessel exterior is rough and whitish, while the lower half is smooth.

13. Cat. No. 02-P-73.
Lower body of a Shallow Bowl of 2.5YR 6/8 light red ware with a rounded base and missing rim. The clay fabric has inclusions of lime and very fine white and gray sand. The interior decoration is divided into seven zones and includes an outside border with two painted "feather" bands on either sides of a single line, a central tondo with myrtle leaves surrounded by dots and lattices to either side of a myrtle branch bounded by multiple lines of dots with a solid line down the center. Several concentric lines are incised on the vessel's smooth exterior.

14. Upper body of a Shallow Bowl of 2.5YR 7/8 ware with an inverted rim, thick black core and missing base. Painted decoration appears on the vessel's interior in the form of a 2.5YR 5/3 brown palmette wreath around the outside with "feather" lines extending to the rim edge. A lattice pattern appears in the background and vestiges of white paint appear on the rim exterior.

15. Shallow Bowl of 10YR 6/8 brownish yellow ware with a thickened, plain vertical rim and rounded base. Black painted decoration appears on the vessel's interior in the form of a palmette wreath around the outside with wisps of single lines and a palmette frond through the bowl's center. In the central field are lattice fences separated by singles lines with large dots. A light white wash appears on the vessel's interior and exterior.

16. Upper body of a Shallow Bowl of 2.5YR 7/8 ware with an inverted rim and missing base. The clay fabric has inclusions of lime, black grit and straw. Painted decoration on the bowl's interior appears in the form of a 10R 5/6 red palmette wreath, dotted chevron, three triangles and combed lines with single lines crossing. The rim exterior is painted with a white slip.

17. Cat. No. 02-P-64.
Shallow Bowl of 10R 5/8 red ware with a slightly inverted, thickened rim and a rounded base. The clay fabric has inclusions of lime, straw and small white grit. Interior decoration includes a 10YR 4/1 black palmette wreath, triple triangles, a central palmette tondo and two dotted chevrons. Exterior decoration is a 7YR 8/4 pinkish-white slip appearing on the vessel's rim. See Bikai and Perry 2001, Fig. 7:10, Tomb 2, Phase 3c/3b.

18. Small Vase or Cup of gritty, 5YR 6/4 light reddish brown ware with a flared, thickened rim and ring base. The clay fabric of the vessel has a gritty texture and the two parts of the vessel shown here do not attach with surety. The vessel's interior is ridged and its exterior decorations include 10YR 3/1 very dark gray palmette wreaths both above and below the vessel's carination. Small painted "wisps" appear below the carination and black stripes decorate the top of the rim. The background field is painted a 2.5YR 5/6 red.

19. Cat. No. 02-P-72. Shallow Bowl of 2.5YR 6/6 light red ware with a thickened, incurving rim and string cut base with a "spout." The clay fabric has inclusions of lime and black and white grit. Painted decoration on the vessel's interior appears in the form of a 2.5YR 4 dark reddish gray bird with two tails, one of them long, a stylized palmette wreath and painted lines up and down the "spout". 10R 6/8 light red paint is used to heighten the effect of the painted decoration against the background of the bowl's interior.

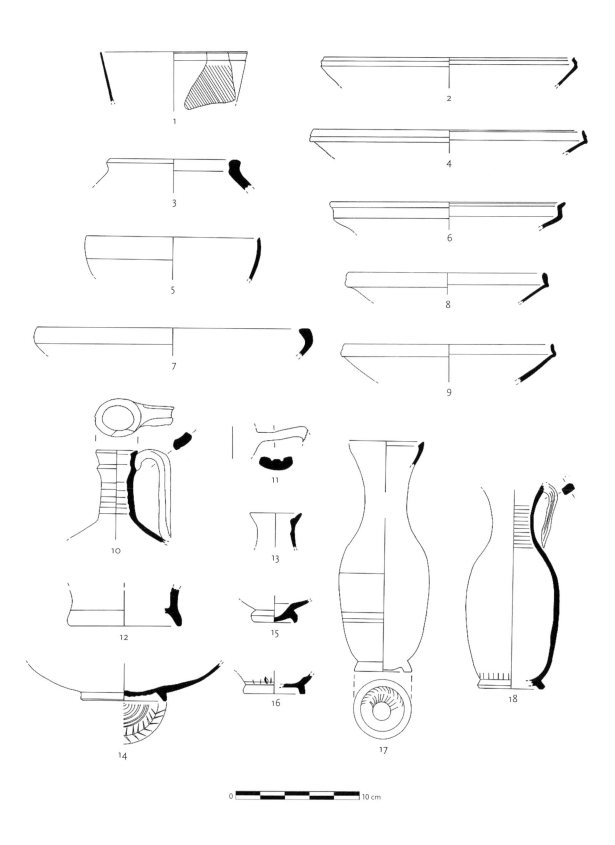

Fig. 7.41
Assorted wares from the Upper Temenos Great Cistern, Special Project 85.

Figure 7.41.
Assorted Wares from Special Project 85, Locus 23.

1. Seq. No. SP85172.
Upper part of a chalice or deep bowl of 2.5YR 7/8 ware with a flaring rim and sides and missing base. The clay fabric has a fine texture and has a few mica inclusions. Diagonal rouletting appears on the exterior of the vessel, spaced 2 mm apart. See Schmid 1996b, 646.

2. Seq. No. SP85172.
Upper part of a shallow bowl of 2.5YR 7/8 fine ware with an inverted, double ridged rim and a missing body and base. The clay fabric has fine, white inclusions and a 5YR 8/3 white slip appears on the vessel exterior below the carination.

3. Seq. No. SP85172.
Upper part of a closed-mouth vessel of 5Y8/2 white ware with a thickened, plain vertical rim and missing body and base. The clay fabric has inclusions of large white quartz, grog, and black grit. The exterior has a slight 5Y8/2 pale yellow hue.

4. Seq. No. SP85172.
Upper part of a large bowl of 2.6YR 6/8 light red ware with an inverted rim with a double ridge and missing body and base. The clay fabric has inclusions of bone and a 2.5YR 7/8 light red slip appears on the vessel's interior. On the exterior, the rim is painted with a white slip. See Schmid 1996b, Group 7:657, Phase 3 later than CE 50 and Bikai and Perry 2001, Fig. 9:4-6.

5. Seq. No. SP85172.
Upper part of a deep bowl of 2.5YR 7/8 fine ware with an incurving rim and missing body and base. The clay fabric has inclusions of white and black grit, straw and lime. A 2 cm band of white slip appears on the vessel's exterior.

6. Seq. No. SP85172.
Upper part of a shallow bowl of 2.5YR 7/8 light red ware with an everted rim, straight neck and missing body and base. The clay fabric has inclusions of bone and mica. A 5YR 8/2 white slip appears on the vessel's exterior, above the carination at the base of the neck. See Schmid 1996b Group 10:669, circa CE 50.

7. Seq. No. SP85172.
Upper part of a shallow bowl of 5YR 7/6 reddish yellow with incurving rim yellowish core, missing body and base. The fabric has inclusions of white and black grit and lime; a painted band 10YR 8/2 white slip appears on the rim exterior.

8. Seq. No. SP85172.
Upper part of a shallow bowl of 2.5YR 6/1 ware with a thickened, inverted rim, dark gray core along the exterior edge and missing body and base. The clay fabric is fine grained with a bumpy exterior. A 2.5YR 8/1 burnt white slip appears on the rim exterior. See Schmid 1996b, Group 6:651 and Bikai and Perry 2001, Fig. 9:2, Tomb 2.

9. Seq. No. SP85172.
Upper part of a shallow bowl of 5YR 7/6 reddish yellow ware with an inverted rim and missing body and base. The clay fabric has a gritty texture and contains white inclusions. The interior and exterior of the vessel's rim is painted with a 2.5YR 8/3 white slip.

10. Seq. No. SP85172.
Neck of a jug of 2.5YR 7/8 light red ware with an inverted rim and one plain vertical handle with inward-folded sides extending from the vessel's rim to its shoulder. The clay fabric has inclusions of shell and grit. The neck is painted with a white slip and shows evidence of interior and exterior ribbing.

11. Seq. No. SP85172.
Jug handle of 2.5YR 6/8 light red ware with two deep grooves cut into the upper surface. Exterior is finely textured and painted with a 10YR 8/2 white slip.

12. Seq. No. SP 85172.
Raised ring base of a 2.5Y7/4 pale yellow ware with missing body and rim. The vessel's interior is yellowish orange and the clay fabric has inclusions of lime, black grit, quartz and grog.

13. Seq. No. SP85172.
Upper part of a small jar of 2.5YR 6/8 light red ware with flaring rim and narrow neck. The clay fabric has inclusions of straw, grit and shell. The vessel's interior and exterior are painted with white slip. See Bikai and Perry 2001, Fig. 5:19, Phase 2c/3a).

14. Seq. No. SP85172.
Lower part of a shallow bowl of 2.5YR 6/8 light red ware with a ring base decorated with rouletting and an inscribed spiral design. The vessel's interior is marked by "slurpy" wash lines and two drips of pink slip are visible on the exterior wall.

15. Seq. No. SP85172.
Base of a cup or small bowl of 2.5YR 7/8 light reddish-orange ware with a thick black core, inclusions of straw, lime, long metallic bits and lots of gray and white grit.

16. Seq. No. SP85172.
Ring base of a Juglet (?) of dark orange ware with irregular rouletting on the vessel exterior. The fabric has inclusions of bone.

17. Seq. No. SP85172.
Juglet of 2.5YR 6/8 light red ware with a ring base, a neck with interior ridges and a missing rim. One plain vertical handle with fine combing on each side extends from the missing rim to the vessel's shoulder. Irregular rouletting appears on the juglet's exterior just above the base. Vestiges of a red slip are visible over the vessel's exterior and the clay fabric has inclusions of grit and small shells.

18. Seq. No. SP85172.
Juglet of 2.5YR 7/8 ware with an incurving rim and ring base with fine rouletting. The clay fabric has inclusions of white grit and four thin incised lines on the vessel's exterior. See Bikai and Perry 2001, 5:14.

Lamps

There is also a full repertoire of over 600 lamps.[46] Figure 7.42 is a Nabataean volute lamp dated to the first century CE, and Figure 7.43 is a later lamp of the late third century CE— an embodiment of the typical Roman lamp of the same period. By this time Nabataean lamp designs no longer assert themselves in the Great Temple record. These lamps lack imagination and are stylized and static. The lamps from the Great Temple excavations are currently being studied by Deirdre G. Barrett and will be published in Volume III.

Fig. 7.42
Nabataean volute lamp, Upper Temenos Trench 94, Locus 18. Seq. No. 89206. This lamp has a "chalice" on the nozzle and a ladder-like band surrounding a plain sunken discus. The shoulder rim is decorated with tight rays that are decorated with four rosettes, two of which are composed of four centered circles. The other two rosettes are smaller and are found at the rear of the lamp and just about the double volutes that top the nozzle. 7.5YR7/4 pink, splashes of red/brown slip over body. Length 8.66, w. 5.95, ht. 3.48, wt. 67.6g, filling hole diameter 1.40. Ref: Khairy 1990:10, Group II, fig. 5, No. 10. Dated to beginning of first century CE through 70 CE. No base inscription.

7.43
Nabataean round lamp, Cat. No. 98-L-2, Temple, Trench 57, Locus 12, Seq. No. 57408. A lamp of red ware 2.5YR6/6 with splashes of red slip on the upper half of the lamp. An ovolo decorated rim with two encircling ridges around a depressed discus with a small central filling hole, perforated handle, and rounded spout, and an impressed ring base. Height 2.63 cm, diameter 2.63 cm and the filling hole diameter is 0.79 cm. This lamp has a parallel dated to the late third century CE. (Broneer 1930, XXV, Rosenthal and Sivan 1978, 96.)

Figurines

Terracotta figurines[47] number 79–80 at the Great Temple and most of them are fragmentary. Figures include zoomorphic representations of camels, ibexes and horses, gods and goddesses, and women (Figure 7.44 a, b), including one which may be a representation of a deity[48] raising her right hand with, as Parr (1990, 79) states, the gesture of blessing or worship, which "… are well-known in ancient Near Eastern religious iconography." There are also hand-built coil figurines that mainly represent quadrupeds. They are found in all contexts of the site, and the majority is from mixed deposits. All such figurines belong to the Nabataean canon and can be considered cult objects or decorations that were intended to serve multiple functions including a domestic function involved with daily life, or they could be funerary or sacred objects.

Most of the figurines are manufactured with Petra clays in separate molds for the front and the back of the head and the front and back of the body, and some of the backs are left unmodeled. Each of these areas was joined by adhesive slip, and many fractured where they had originally been as separate parts by the potter during manufacture. Many of the molds are worn, and the features are blurred. Finding broken figurines in archaeological contexts is common; perhaps breakage was part of the ritual they served. Assorted figurines we have recovered are shown in Figures 7.45a–h and 7.46a–c.

Fig. 7.44a–b Nabataean figurine fragment Seq. No. 77141, Cat. No. 00-P-6. Upper Temenos, Trench 77, Locus 20. Length 4.56 cm, width 2.69 cm, thickness 0.47 cm. Of 2.5YR6/8 red ware. Nude female figurine probably representing the Nabataean goddess of fertility. She is raising her right hand with open palm symbolizing the bestowal of blessings, happiness, prosperity or success upon her worshippers and believers. She wears a bracelet on her right wrist. Her hair is arranged in plaits similar to the Hathor wig and reaches the shoulder. Her facial features and figure indicate that the goddess is young and physically attractive. See Khairy 1990:24#1; Schmitt-Korte 1976:43, Pl. 26; Glueck 1966:175. Pl 81.

Front  Right Profile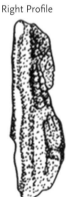

Front   Right Profile   Base View

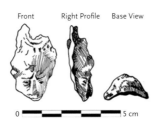

0 ▬▬▬▬▬▬ 5 cm

Fig. 7.45a
Figurine fragment, Seq.
No. 77142. Upper Teme-
nos, Trench 77, Locus
20 of 2.5YR6/8 red ware.
Length 3.5 cm, width 2.2,
thickness 0.7 cm. Frag-
ment of well delineated
half face with forehead,
hair, eyes and nose. Possibly some paint preserved.

Front   Right Profile   Bottom   Back

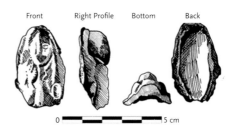

0 ▬▬▬▬▬▬ 5 cm

Fig. 7.45b
Figurine fragment, Seq.
No. 77139, Cat. No. 00-P-7.
Upper Temenos, Trench 77,
Locus 20, of 2.5YR6/8
red ware. Length 3.81 cm,
width 2.54 cm, thickness
0.55 cm. Hermaphroditic
figure. Male facial features
with short hair and visible
ears. He/she wears a necklace of small beads with a
crescent shaped pendant
in an inverted position.
The right hand is open

palmed in benediction and
the left arm carries a bas-
ket/container. The figure
is wearing a girdle around
the hips, displaying the
navel and rounded belly.
(Khairy 1990:24#2;
Schmitt-Korte 1976:43.
Pl.26.)

Fig. 7.45c
Nabataean figurine frag-
ment, Seq. No. 69198, Cat.
No. 00-P-11. Propylaeum,
Trench 69, Locus 6. Length
4.93 cm, width 3.19 cm,
thickness 0.58 cm. of
10R7/6 light red ware.
This piece is difficult to
interpret; It looks like drapery on a figure, banded
around the waist with two
thin girdles.

Front View   Profile   Top View

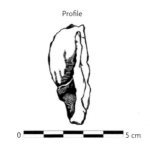

0 ▬▬▬▬▬▬ 5 cm

Fig. 7.45d
Figurine Seq. No. 76107, Cat. No. 00-P-10. Upper Temenos, Trench 76, Locus 9. Length 3.02 cm, width 1.90 cm, thickness 0.18 cm. Of 10R6/8 light red ware. Molded complete back and front of head, body missing, male with beard and diadem.

Front   Right Profile

Fig. 7.45e
Small plaque, Seq. No. 77097, Cat. No. 00-P-8. Upper Temenos, Trench 77, Locus 9. Of 2.5YR7/4 pale red ware. Length 2.35 cm, width 2.38 cm, thickness 0.63 cm. It may represent a head with an elaborate hairstyle/head-dress. Possibly an inverted crescent moon on top of the head. The whole is represented within a cartouche. The back of the plaque is smooth and shows traces of red slip.

Fig. 7.46a
Animal figurine Seq. No. 69008, Cat. No. 00-P-15. Propylaeum, Trench 69, Locus 1. Length 4.47 cm, width 2.66 cm, weight 37.7 grams. Crudely made animal figurine, possibly a lion, missing all four legs.

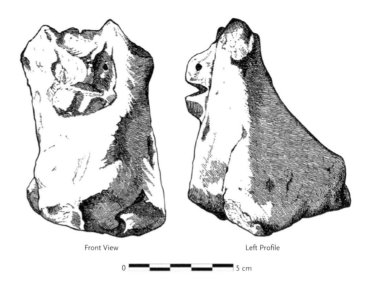

Front View   Left Profile

0 ▬▬▬▬▬▬ 5 cm

Fig. 7.46b
Horse figurine fragment, Seq. No. 77036, Cat. No. 00-P-3. Upper Temenos, Trench 77, Locus 10. Its length is 6.14 cm, height 5.00 cm, thickness 0.62 cm. It is of 2.5YR7/6 light red ware. Large fragment from the left side of a molded horse figurine, saddled and decorated with trappings. Head and foreleg are missing. (Khairy 1990:28#16.)

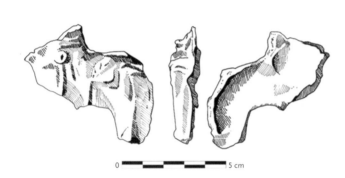

0 ▬▬▬▬▬▬ 5 cm

Right   Front   Left   Back

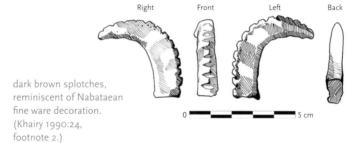

0 ▬▬▬▬▬▬ 5 cm

Fig. 7.46c
Ibex horn from a figurine. Seq. No. 77143, Cat. No. 00-P-9, Upper Temenos, Trench 77, Locus 20. Of 10R6/6 light red ware. Length 4.71 cm, width 1.22 cm, and thickness 0.78 cm. It has a scalloped edge on the exterior and the whole is painted with dark brown splotches, reminiscent of Nabataean fine ware decoration. (Khairy 1990:24, footnote 2.)

Metal Objects

The Petra Great Temple yielded a range of
artifacts including weapons such as arrow heads
(Figure 3.44) and helmet cheek pieces (Figure
3.45), and construction elements like nails.[49]
We also have found artifacts that may have
served as decorative horse trappings, such as bri-
dle fastenings, and animal figurines. There are
also long and short pins, bracelets, and jewelry
elements such as small disks. Two extraordinary
ornamental artifacts are bronze handles with the
finials shaped as flowers with twelve petals.[50]
Figure 7.47a illustrates the floral decoration
displaying the creativity and character of these
handles, which have an ornamental function,
and Figure 7.47b illustrates the rounded stem
used to form the handle.

Fig. 7.47a
Bronze flower handle,
top view. Cat. No. 97-M-2,
Seq. No. 42199/ Lower
Temenos, Trench 42, Locus 24.
Overall length 5.5 cm, width
4.0, length of flower 4.57 cm,
width of flower 3.81cm.
Attachment in the form of
a curved leaf, backed by a
scroll. The flower serves as
the actual handle.

Fig. 7.47b
Bronze flower handle, side view.

Glass Objects

Shown in Figure 7.48 is a delicately painted glass fragment found in association with the Great Cistern. It depicts the figure of a woman with flowing red hair. Besides a millefiore fragment published in Volume I, Figure 6.32, there is a wonderful head vase also shown in Volume I, Figure 6.127.[51] Glass fragments number 4,672. The glass is presently undergoing analysis by Margaret O'Hea and will be reported on in Volume III.

Bone Objects

Worked bone objects include spoons, spatulae, spindle whorls, needles, beads, pins, and a few other interesting artifacts.[52] The Great Temple database includes more than 26,000 animal bones. It is reasonable to assume that such remains include many sacrificial offerings, particularly during Nabataean times. Nabataean communal meals and royal cultic banquets also could have taken place within the Great Temple sanctuary. The bone collection is presently undergoing analysis and will be reported on in Volume III.

Does the foregoing artifact discussion distinguish the Great Temple as either sacred or secular space? Careful study of the architecture and artifacts within their contexts is of enormous value when we try to understand their unspoken meanings, and I would argue that they govern both the precinct's sacral and secular character. Religious implications, like the *nefesh* and *betyl*s are designed and placed in context to placate the gods, and the political propaganda responsible for the construction program supports both religious and secular interpretations.

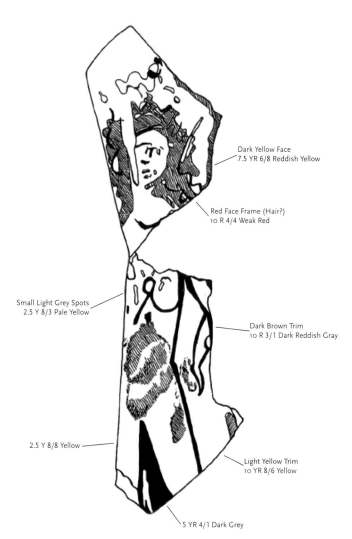

Dark Yellow Face
7.5 YR 6/8 Reddish Yellow

Red Face Frame (Hair?)
10 R 4/4 Weak Red

Small Light Grey Spots
2.5 Y 8/3 Pale Yellow

Dark Brown Trim
10 R 3/1 Dark Reddish Gray

2.5 Y 8/8 Yellow

Light Yellow Trim
10 YR 8/6 Yellow

5 YR 4/1 Dark Grey

Fig. 7.48
Painted glass, SP84099
2001. Found in eight fragments. Head: height 3.50 cm, width 3 cm, thickness 0.1 cm.

Great Debate Conclusions

William Mierse (1999, 158) states:

> The association of sanctuary with theater is not unknown in earlier Roman architecture. It was well established with the theater of Pompey in Rome.

The function of a building as both a temple and an administrative center is foreign to our way of thinking. In our modern world, such opposites are difficult for us to grasp and comprehend. The temple is established as a central place of assembly and perhaps a place of sacrifice. The congregation could come and celebrate religious ritual. Here one could pray, perform rituals and bring sacrifices. But in ancient times a temple could also serve as an administrative center where elite council meetings could be held, a place where the elite and the high priest could consult with the royal power. And who are these elite? They are the king's circle of officials, bureaucrats, priestly administrators, and wealthy aristocrats—an elite representing the centralization of power. These are the people who dominated the religious, political, and socio-cultural life in Petra.

It is not just the aspects of design that exhibit a relationship between the temple and the secular administrative center. If our excavations are correct in assigning the early Site Phases to a stand-alone temple, then the addition of the enlarged complex with its theater also has the potential for being a sacred and secular construction as well. The visible theater must serve the activities taking place in the Lower Temenos. This is not to say that there is no administration going on here. To be sure, there are elements of both sacred and secular activities as part of the composition of the Great Temple landscape, just as we proposed in 1998. The command of a theater overlooking a Lower Temenos, which is purposefully left free of major building, is by design. It is within sight of a number of possible activities, and the staircases permit movement between all the elements of the precinct.

If we consider the factors listed above, they certainly suggest that the Great Temple was a "sacred place." Each of them leads us to speculate that this is first a temple precinct that later took on administrative functions. We have examined a range of artistic ideas which are Nabataean architectural and sculptural concepts. We have briefly considered each in turn: location, inscriptions, architecture, standing stones—*betyl*s and *nefesh*, altars, including some horned altars, benches, votive niches, offering stands—ceramic vessels, sculpture, figurines, animal bones and remains. I would argue that this mass of evidence proves the sacral nature of the Great Temple and its precinct.

Great buildings like the Petra Great Temple happen by design. The architects and designers, project managers and craftspeople listened to the desires of the administrative council, the city planner, and of course, the king. Someone or some elite group in power wanted the Petra Great Temple "their way." Its architecture must have represented and aggrandized their personal values—religious, socioeconomic, political, aesthetic, public, and private. It must have involved delicate compromise, but just like the architectural schemes of the World Trade Center Memorial in New York or the World War II monument completed in Washington, it is the client's desires that take precedence.

The temple traditionally is the dwelling of the god. Could a temple not have been an administrative center as well? Could people not express their devotion to their god as well as conduct the business of the day in the temple? The temple in antiquity could have served the scribes, teachers, moneylenders and business people as well as representing the house of their god(s). Could the once nomadic Nabataeans have had differing visions of religion? Could they have celebrated a different religious relationship between themselves and their principal deities, Dushara and al-ʿUzza? Our studies should try to explore the minds of the Nabataean makers in an attempt to understand Nabataean ideals, not giving in to our modern conceptions of the temple solely as a house of worship.

On 22 March 106 CE Rome became the center of power for the Nabataeans. As part of the eastern empire, Nabataea succumbed to the sovereignty of Imperial Rome. The following brief comments are intended to view Petra's transition from its autonomous provincial kingdom to a Roman Imperial city.

Roman and Byzantine Periods

When trying to envision Petra in the Roman period, C. Kanellopoulos (2001, 13) gives us a coherent picture of the city center:

> This program of building and renovation can be adduced from the remains of the Temenos Gate (on top of the remains of a preexisting structure), the Colonnaded Street, the so-called Trajanic Arch,[53] the Nymphaeon, the odeion (and/or bouleuterion?) inside the Great Temple, and a renovation in the *paradeisos* ("Lower Market"). Such transformations suggest that Roman idealizations of civic life played an important role in defining the urban landscape of Petra. The development of the city plan involved the incorporation of pre-existing structures into a unified scheme. Most obvious is the addition of a new, paved, colonnaded street.

The Roman takeover[54] has been attributed to the political and military weakness of the Nabataeans and the new age and absolute power of the Roman Empire. By this time other kingdoms surrounding the Nabataeans had been absorbed into the Roman Empire—Judea, Egypt, and probably cities of the Decapolis. The idea that the Roman conquest was a peaceful one has become entrenched in the literature. For sure there is no great war of conquest, no wholesale catastrophic destruction that can be identified, but there are some signs of destruction. (See Phase VI Stratigraphy.) At least part of the destruction of Site Phase VI could have been caused during the Roman attack, otherwise as the result of local earthquakes and fires. The ballista ball assemblage (Figures 2.16, 2.17, and 2.41), the arrows (Figure 3.44) and the armored cheek piece (Figure 3.45) suggest such an attack, and there are more than a few signs of a violent destruction. Certainly the evidence suggests the Nabataeans were prepared for an attack. Cassius Dio reports that the governor of Syria, the legate Cornelius Palma, subdued the part of Arabia around Petra and made it subject to the Romans. There are no conclusive signs of a struggle that took place during the shift in power between the Nabataean and Roman period. In truth, the Nabataeans had lost their independent status to Rome under Pompey. They were defeated by Herod in 31 CE near Philadelphia, and appealed to him to become their *prostates*. Octavian agreed to the continu-ation of the two independent kingdoms, Nabataea and Judea, as Roman clients, so by this time Nabataean royalty had all but become obsolete.

The situation in Petra in 106 CE has also been the subject of lively debate and speculation. We may never know if Rabbel II[55] made an agreement with the Romans to leave Nabataea alone as a semi-autonomous kingdom until his death. Clearly Rabbel II's reign came to an end with his death in 106 CE when Trajan was emperor. But the Roman takeover is no longer as clear-cut as previously thought, because there is evidence of destruction and conflagrations at the Great Temple, at the Temple of the Winged Lions, and at Ez Zantur. These may have been isolated episodes or may have been part of a Roman offensive. We just do not know.

Roman issues now replaced the Nabataean autonomous coinage. The coinage seemed to present a straightforward situation. Roman coins struck five years after the annexation are inscribed with *Arabia adquista* (acquired), not *Arabia capta* (captured), meaning that the Nabataean kingdom had been acquired, not captured. The only reference we have about the annexation and the incorporation of the Nabataean kingdom as a major part of the new Roman province of Arabia is the report from Cassius Dio (LXVIII. 14.6). There are almost no references to the Roman takeover in contemporary accounts.

To wage an all out war in conquering Nabataea would have been contrary to Roman interests, because the Romans desired the expertise of the Nabataeans as the ongoing intelligence agency contacts for their new province. The Romans most certainly needed Petra and other Nabataean settlements for their knowledge of the trade routes, agricultural production, and taxes to provision whatever troops (Roman and Nabataean) were stationed in the country.

What was the fate of the temple and its status after the Roman takeover?

What the Romans knew even before they took over the city was that there were several grandiose architectural precincts that they easily could incorporate within their new possession. The Great Temple would serve them well, for it was located directly above the then major artery into the city center. The Great Temple continued to be occupied during the Roman period. Obviously it served as a center for the Roman city. The *Pax Romana* brought about certain Roman renovations to the precinct, including the construction of the Colonnaded Street, which, following the excavations of Z. Fiema (1998, 395–424) was constructed in the early second century CE. The Baths-Palatial Complex was in use, the Great Temple Roman-Byzantine Bath Complex was constructed, and there was a rearrangement of the East Propylaeum rooms and the additions to the Propylaeum Central Staircase. In many cases, such as with the Roman-Byzantine Baths, the Romans reused Nabataean building materials and largely built their buildings using architectural elements

of earlier structures. Not only can this be seen in the Great Temple Roman-Byzantine Baths, but in the East Propylaeum rooms as well.

The last Great Temple architectural narrative includes the large-scale closing of the entrances to the building itself. A few years after the Roman takeover, in Site Phase VII, dating to the mid-second century CE, the building may have been transformed into a fort. As can be seen in the virtual reality model shown in Figure 7.50, this is a curious transformation of the precinct. The architecture shows that the front Porch columns and all the doorways were blocked, as can be seen in Figure 5.54 showing the south face of the South Corridor Wall and Figure 5.68 showing the remnants of the

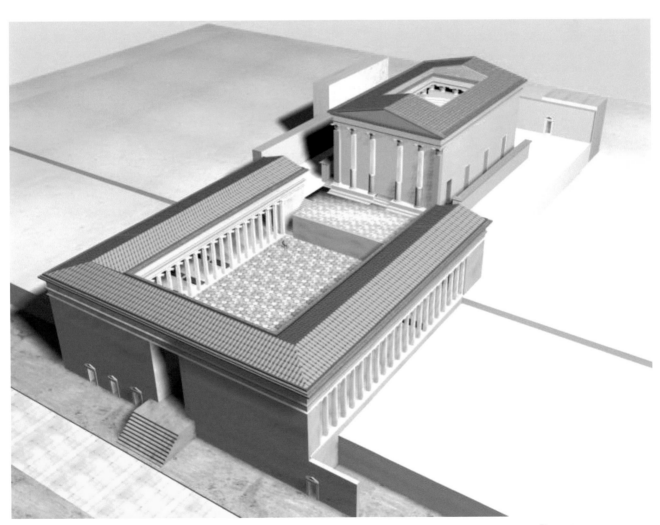

Fig. 7.49
Petra Great Temple virtual reality of Site Phase VII.

The Babatha Archive

Discovered at Nahal Hever near En-Gedi is the Babatha archive, which dates from 93 to 132 CE, ascribed to the Judaean Jewess Babatha. The archive spans the period when the area was under the control of the Nabataeans and its early days as a Roman province. These documents refer to the Judaean Babatha's ownership of property in Nabataea and her petition for legal retribution from the Nabataean-Roman judicial system. Repeatedly, Babatha is ordered to appear at court in Petra before the Roman authorities.

Babatha is a wealthy Jewess from a village located on the Dead Sea who inherits land in the then kingdom of Nabataea, consisting of houses and palm groves. After the annexation of Nabataea by the Romans in 106 CE, Babatha's family retains their land in the newly created Roman province of Arabia. Dating from 93/94–132 CE, Babatha's double documents (two copies of text on the same papyrus) contain deeds, money settlements and lawsuits. Before the revolt of Bar Kokhba against the Romans, Babatha took refuge in Judea, carrying this extraordinary collection of legal documents with her.

The 35 papyrus archives are found in a leather purse in 1961 at the Nahal Hever cave on the west shore of the Dead Sea. The languages in the documents are: Nabataean (6), Aramaic (3), and 26 in Greek. The latest document is written in the year the Bar Kokhba revolt began (132 CE), and it is possible that Babatha hid these documents in the cave, when she sought asylum. Nearly 2000 years later, these priceless documents, which were once merely family archives, have become a most valuable source of legal disputes in the province of Roman Arabia. (Joukowsky 1998, 128, note 42, 145–146).

north doorway in the West Corridor Wall.[56] It is for this reason that the Porch columns exhibit squared off niches cut into their Attic bases, as can be seen in Figure 5.26. The character of the building must have changed dramatically for some practical perceived danger. Could this have been due to the earthquake of 113–114 CE? Or are there some other forces at work? We suggest that the temple is transformed into a fort, for the entrance and all of the doorways are blocked off. The result is an altered vista being reshaped by the implementation of changes to ensure that its architecture does not buckle under whatever threats might impact its structural fabric.

The Nabataeans and Judaeans enjoyed shared interests. They had strong commercial ties, and intermarriage took place between those of high social and economic status. The Nabataeans had political ties with the Hasmonaeans and the Herodians as well, for they had common interests in their struggles against the Seleucids and the Ptolemies. No other political group resisted annexation by Rome as did the Nabataeans, and Nabataean influence continued to be a significant factor in the Roman period.

During the Roman period we can assume there was a marked opulence in the Petra Garden-Pool Complex (Bedal 2003) shown in the foreground of Figure 7.50, the Great Temple Roman-Byzantine Baths as well as at the Small Temple dedicated to Roman Imperial Cult (Reid 2006) illustrated in Figure 1.26.

Although we have been centered on the Great Temple, marvelous Nabataean, Roman and Byzantine monuments abound in Petra. Many of these are described briefly in "A Précis of Selected Major Structures at Petra," pages 427–431.

The Petraean people were able to carry on their previous lifestyle within the new administrative framework, and cultural continuity appears between 106 CE and thereafter, particularly in the mass-produced pottery and other artifact assemblages, resulting in the material record becoming mixed to some degree. Patrich (1990, 165) reminds us:

> Hellenization and Romanization did not destroy the Nabataean heritage. The traditional artistic modes of the desert people survived, but from that point on, the parallel manifestations of figurative art were much more obvious than before.

During the Roman period, the triumph of the Nabataean architectural vocabulary, which up to this point had been expressed in the precinct, is sadly compromised. In many cases there are signs of building maintenance being carelessly neglected, and this may indicate that to some degree the emphasis has shifted perhaps to other sectors of the city. The reasons for this shift are not altogether clear. Additionally there is a subtle shift in material culture as the Roman period continues[57] and the pottery[58] becomes coarser, as can be seen from the assemblage shown in Figure 7.51 and the Nabataean bowl with a bird painted on the interior in Figure 7.52. There is a general decline in decorative taste, but another artistic form is highlighted as glass objects become popular and emerge as an imaginative art craft with an elegant strength.

The Roman emperor Trajan constructed forts and completed the 400 km grand highway, the *Via Nova Traina*, which extended from Bostra in Syria to Petra, on to Aqaba on the Red Sea. Clearly, Nabataeans were used as labor for these projects, which helped the Romans achieve a network for the communication between Arabia and Roman Palestine. What is clear is that Petra did not experience a collapse, but continued to serve the Romans and the *Pax Romana*. Not surprisingly they continued to provide services for the Early Byzantines as well.

Fig. 7.51
A homogeneous collection of Nabataean 3-d wares, dating to after 106 CE.

The Romans oversaw urban development and expansion, and contained the commercial ties with Arabia and the Levant. However, with the rise of the Roman monoculture, the decline in trade revenues going into Nabataean hands was apparent,[59] and the Nabataean economic base was jeopardized. The political and economic realities of Roman control are difficult to analyze from the archaeological record. But there can be no doubt that the Nabataeans continued to prosper under the Romans, although it is probable that the elite fled or were exiled to other parts of their former kingdom. The Roman administration, consisting of a governor, some generals and a few senior Roman officials, controlled the city.

The first governor of the province of Arabia was Claudius Severus (107–115 CE) who organized the building of forts for the Roman legions who were brought in to keep peace and order. In 129 CE Sextius Florentinus, the Roman governor of Petra, chose to be buried at Petra in an elaborately carved tomb. And in 131 CE, Hadrian (117–138 CE), the Roman emperor, visited the site and named it after himself, *Hadriane Petra*. The city residents co-existed with the Romans, who took advantage of the local Nabataeans who remained. The Nabataeans were compelled to obey Roman law. We do know that the Roman army absorbed six "Petraean cohorts," the *Cohortes Ulpiae Petraeorum*—a total of 4500–6000 soldiers.[60] Petra is designated as a *metropolis* (mother city) and commemorated this in 114 CE. The city continued to flourish, at least up to this time in the Roman period, with a monumental Arch in the Bab as-Siq (which possibly carried an aqueduct) and tomb structures either carved out of the living rock or built free-standing. Under Roman rule, Roman classical monuments abounded; however, many continued to be embellished with Nabataean motifs. In the third century CE, Petra was elevated to a *colonia* under Severus Alexander (222–235 CE). With time, in the third and fourth centuries CE, the once flourishing caravan towns in the Negev lost their luster and began to wither away as their populations migrated to more important commercial centers. The Romans carried more of their goods by ship from Arabia to Egypt. As a

trading center, Petra was obscured by Palmyra in the Roman period, and this trend continued as the main trade routes slowly moved east to the Euphrates and the Persian Gulf, leaving Petra and her caravan cities "out of the loop." With this change in trade routes, Petra's commercial decline was inevitable. Just as Petra seems to have held on to some of its former glory, some of its former caravan towns in the Negev, once again, became independent centers of commerce. Pagan temples in the Negev were replaced with richly decorated Christian churches. They no longer had to be dependent on Nabataean routes, and the Nabataeans suffered from economic decline, Bedouin raids and piracy.

The inhabitants during the Byzantine period recycled many standing structures and rock-cut monuments, while they also constructed their own buildings, including churches, such as the now restored Petra Church and the Ridge Church, lying on the ridge above the Petra Church, excavated by Patricia M. Bikai. The shops along the Colonnaded Street were reconstructed. Among the rock-cut monuments the Byzantines reused is the Urn Tomb, which was modified into a church.

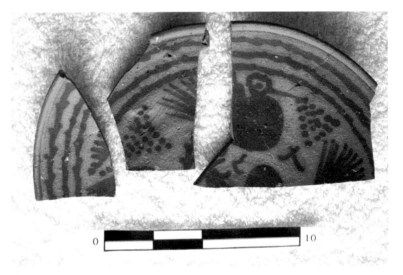

Fig. 7.52
Painted Nabataean bowl with the figure of a bird, dating to after 106 CE.

An even more devastating earthquake occurred in July in 551 CE, which some scholars believe brought the city, once again, to ruin. But, because the Petra Church papyri document land holdings for another decade or so, we now know that Byzantine Petra may have been a community more important and affluent than historians have assumed. Petra, serving as the seat of a Byzantine bishopric, retained its urban vitality into late antiquity. It appears that life continued, although Petra was absorbed by the Byzantine Empire.

The Islamic period, 636–1097 CE, begins with the foundation of this world religion by the Arabian apostle or prophet, Mohammad, in the seventh century. In 636 CE, the "Sword of Islam"—the Muslim Conquest—destroyed the Byzantine forces at the Battle of the Yarmuk River, and Petra, like most of Palestine, came under Muslim rule. All of the area comprising present-day Jordan fell to Muslim rule between 630 and 640 CE. The Muslim invasion probably left Petra as it was. We find little evidence of Islamic occupation. The Umayyads ruled from 660 to 750 CE, establishing their dynasty in Damascus in 661 CE. During this time (in

747–748 CE), Petra suffered yet another great earthquake, which was as devastating as its predecessor. The Abbasid Dynasty transferred its capital to Baghdad, and the center of power was focused farther to the east than ever before. At Petra, the Bedouin way of life returned. Thus, with the rise of Islam, Petra became a backwater community.

Last Days of the Great Temple

Until what time was the Great Temple in use? What caused its ultimate abandonment? The latest material finds from the Great Temple date from the Late Byzantine period, the second half of the fifth century CE and serves as our *terminus ante quem*; the latest pottery, lamps (Figure 7.53)[61] and coins come from the fifth to sixth centuries CE.[62] It is a possibility that the final blow was the earthquake that shook Petra on the 9th of July in 551 CE, for it is at around this time the site lacks a response to any use and only fragmented evidence exists.

Using the lamps and coins as dateable indicators, Deirdre G. Barrett in a personal communication (2 May 2006) states:

> …it would appear, from the Byzantine lamp presence, that the Temenoi and Temple were in longest use…. The majority of these lamps (some with Christian symbols, i.e., crosses and wheels) were concentrated in the West Exedra, and it is possible that this apsidal area served as a chapel during the Byzantine period, after the primary function of the Great Temple ceased. Any Christian gathering probably occurred after the 363 CE earthquake, taking into account the spread of Christianity within the Roman Empire. Constantine chose to worship the Christian god in 312 CE and the Council of Nicaea took place in 365 CE. Of twenty-eight coins found in the West Exedra, two are dated from 211 to 222 CE, and the remainder is dated from 350 to 395 CE.
>
> Only three Islamic lamp fragments were found at the Great Temple and they are definitely outliers by any statistical analysis. One was found in Locus 14 of Trench 14 in the East Colonnade (in which a coin dated from 335 to 337 CE was located), and the second was found in Locus 13 of Trench 16 in the West Exedra, both dating to the seventh to eighth century CE (five coins dating to the end of the fourth beginning of the fifth century CE were also found there). The third Islamic lamp fragment was

Fig. 7.53
Lamp, dating to the Islamic period from the Ridge Church.

found in Trench 76, Locus 6, in the Walkway of the Upper Temenos and dates from the sixth to eighth century CE. Being the only artifacts with such a late date, it is not likely that there was an active occupation during that period. Indeed, if an earthquake finally flattened the Great Temple, the Pompeii premise predicts that artifacts of this period should be abundant if there had been a thriving population, but there were no other accompanying artifacts of the same date. Therefore, I would suggest that the last occupation of the Great Temple was the second half of the fifth century CE.

To confirm this date a cache of 159 coins was found under the Central Arch in the Temple area, and 101 of these were dated to the late fourth century or early fifth century CE, and 20 were dated to the mid-fifth century CE: the remaining coins were illegible.

In central Petra Christianity now is centered on the north ridge overlooking the Wadi Musa where the Petra Church, the Blue Chapel and the Ridge Church are located. This brings about a new focal point for the city. Whatever communication may have existed between the Great Temple and these church complexes has not come to light with the exception of a partial elephant head and a floral capital fragment recovered from the Petra Church atrium cistern (Fiema et al. 2001, Fig. 51, p. 174). Other then these two fragments, there seems to be no conceptual relationship between the sites.

From the evidence, the conclusion that can be drawn is the fact that the Great Temple site is abandoned at some point in the late fifth or perhaps in the mid-sixth century CE. This is fairly certain. No other activities can be assigned to the remains. The archaeological evidence demonstrates that we have not overlooked more vestiges of continued use until Site Phase XIV, ascribed to the modern period.

Concluding Remarks

Architecture is used in support of theological and political ideologies. The Great Temple is the quintessential physical evidence of a royal building program with a Nabataean political and religious agenda. Its size and decoration inspires awe. In its building, we can imagine the Nabataeans beginning a new religious and socio-political day. I conclude that they aspired to a unique position among architects of the time. I am the first to admit that the design of the

Fig. 7.54
Lower face fragment, Cat. No. 05-P-14, Seq. No. 106357, Upper Temenos, Trench 105–106, Locus 28. Of 10R7/8 light red ware. Length 4.37 cm, thickness 0.40 cm, weight 0.40 grams.

Great Temple is a bizarre anomaly; however, the Nabataean elite demanded a grand, over scaled design executed with intelligence. It is clear that this architectural icon provides much physical evidence to be interpreted. With the meager textual record, and from what we know so far, I believe that we have to accelerate our discourse about Nabataean material culture and involve ourselves in its re-evaluation and reinterpretation. Anthropological, philological and art historic approaches can help us in analyzing the archaeological data. The challenge of archaeology is in the search for meaning of the ancients and their places. Fortunately the archaeologist has the intellectual freedom to change his/her mind!

The project goal to establish a chronology for the Petra Great Temple cultural sequence, as well as to attain an understanding of a thriving Nabataean culture through these excavations, has been attained. Through this synthesis we have identified a Nabataean center—a monumental institution—resulting in a better understanding of Nabataean religious, social, economic, and political traditions. Petra was a developed capital capable of ruling the desert highway. The kingship constituted the base of a new elite. The Great Temple is a remarkable story and has proven to be crucial to our understanding of the Nabataeans and their urban crystallization.

Notes

1

As Bedal (2001, 23) explains: With the goal of determining the function of the "Lower Market and the nature of its association with the Great Temple, a two-month season of survey and excavation in the "Lower Market" was undertaken in the summer of 1998, under the auspices of the Brown University excavations and under the direction of the author." Indications that the two sites were connected were clear, and it was essential that an investigation be undertaken under my Jordanian Department of Antiquities permit.

Bedal's "The Petra Pool Complex: A Hellenistic Paradeisos in the Nabataean Capital" (results of the Petra "Lower Market" Survey and Excavation, 1988), was her Ph.D. diss., University of Pennsylvania, 2000. It was published in 2003 as *The Petra Pool-Complex: A Hellenistic Paradeisos in the Nabataean Capital* in 2003.

2

Kanellopoulos (2001, 14) suggests that the oblique positioning of the Temenos Gate and the "Baths-Palace Complex" was aligned to the original flow of the Wadi Musa and should be dated to an earlier phase than the reconstructed Temenos Gate and the Roman Street.

3

Archaeological investigations of the Small Temple were initiated by Sara Karz Reid in 2000 and continued to 2002, under my direction and permit from the Jordanian Department of Antiquities. In 2004 Reid defended her Ph.D. dissertation, "The Small Temple: A Roman

Imperial Cult Building in Petra, Jordan," Brown University, Department of Anthropology and it was published in 2006.

4

In 1997, Z. Fiema (1998, 416) excavated the street and found two partially paved hard cobble-packed surfaces under the present street level. Segal (1997, 44–46) suggests the early street was a processional way intended for the Qasr al-Bint.

5

Kanellopoulos (2001, 14) states they are concentrated 65.60 m along the banks of the wadi. The west bridge measures 7.20 m in width, and is aligned with the Central Staircase of the Great Temple precinct.

6

It is suggested that there was an earthquake that destroyed an earlier gate structure here. Archaeologists (Stucky 1996, 14, 21; Hammond 1996, 13; and Fiema 1998, 419) wrestling with this question place this earthquake at the beginning of the second century CE after which the monumental Temenos Gate was rebuilt.

7

Petra's ancient name was *Rekem* or *Beqem*.

8

All of our coins have been read by numismatic expert Christian Augé of the Université de Paris I.

9

This silver coin of Rabbel II is a particularly fine specimen of his coinage; it is museum quality.

10

Cat. No. 04-C-03. SP87100. SP87, Locus 10. A bronze coin with jugate busts of King Aretas IV and Queen Shaqilat, dating between 18 and 40 CE, diameter 1.81 cm, thickness 0.35 cm.

11

Cat. No. 94-C-3, SP2 Locus 1. Jugate busts to the right of King Rabbel II and Queen Gamilat. On the reverse are crossed cornucopia and a legend in two lines *RB'L/GMLT*. Date ca. 75–102 CE. Diameter 1.69 cm, thickness 0.27 cm, weight 3.37 g. Meshorer, 163, 110–111, Pl. 8.

12

Dushara means "The One of Shara," probably referring to the mountains that overlook Petra, the Jebel esh-Shara.

13

In the Amman Archaeological Museum is a ceramic showing a group of musicians from Petra with a man and two women seated on a bench. In the middle a man plays a double flute, to his left a woman holds a stringed instrument, and to his right a woman plays a lyre. Height 8.7 cm. A good photograph is found in Bienkowski (1991, Figure 60, pg. 55). Strabo refers to Nabataean music.

14

Unfortunately there is a paucity of anthropological and palynological information. Peter Warnock (1998, 167–168) presented this analysis in Volume I.

15

From Eratosthenes we know of a site in the Wadi Tumilat in the east Egyptian Delta, which was connected through the territory of the Nabataeans to Babylon on the Euphrates and to the Persian Gulf.

16

It is difficult to determine the geographic boundaries of the Nabataean Kingdom, but by the later first century BCE, they were at the height of their control of a vast territory.

17

Perhaps there were silks from China, spices from India, and amethysts from Egypt. We do know that gold and silver were available in Nabataea.

18

Because we cannot fix the architectural events to absolute dates, our chronology is relative.

19

Strabo in his *Geography* 16.4, 2 [767] states that the Nabataeans took over the trade routes established by Minaeans after the collapse of the Minean kingdom.

20

Excavations in 1998 and 1999 in Trenches 55 and 55A yielded few clues to indicate its function.

21

Translation from the French by M.S. Joukowsky.

22

A plaster coating would have hidden these masons' marks.

23

This lapidary mark looks similar to a Nabataean "w", and the shape of the mark is similar to Macdonald's 1993 Row 6, from an inscription at Hegra, dated between the first century BCE and the first century CE.

24

This is a Nabataean "h" similar to the one found on the mid-first century CE Turkmaniyah inscription (Macdonald, 1993, chart p. 53, Row 5, although that letter shape has a stroke at the stem of the letter moving to the left).

25

Figures 7.14 and 7.15 are reconstructions of the South Corridor frescoed moldings and cassettes by Emily Catherine Egan (2002). Egan will present a full description of these designs in Volume III.

26

As envisioned by Ulrich Bellwald, the Baroque Room ceiling's restorer, Figure 1.28 illustrates the complete ceiling, whereas Figure 4.84 details its central medallion.

27

In her popular book on Petra, Taylor (2001: 109–110) states: "The appearance of this exotic animal in a major building is yet another indication of the wide-ranging imagination and eclectic tastes of this remarkable people. The Indian elephant, known in the Greek world since Alexander the Great first confronted them in battle against the Persians in 331 BC, had been represented in Hellenistic sculpture and coins since at least the early third century BC. They are known in Indian art from about the same time, and India was also the origin of many Nabataean trading goods, in particular, spices. The Nabataeans could have found the motif in Hellenistic sources, but it is also possible that India can be added to the list of countries from which they adopted design ideas, and adapted them to their own vision. Where the Nabataeans appear to have been original is to have used elephant heads as volutes on column capitals."

28

We can only assume many of these heads were carried away like the one found inside the cistern of the Petra Church (Kanellopoulos 2001, 174, Figure 51) and those found on the Roman Street.

29

We have found two plain well chiseled blocked out Nabataean capitals, (Figure 4.50) which would have been masked by plaster and paint.

30
We should be mindful of Parr's (1990, 79) statement: "Nabataean art was an eclectic art existing in an eclectic world, and the adoption by the Nabataeans of, for example, an iconographic detail of ultimately Egyptian origin, such as the symbol of Isis, need not imply a direct borrowing from Egypt. Nor does the borrowing of an iconography necessarily mean the adoption of the belief or cult to which that iconography originally pertained."

31
She is shown with her *Aegis* (her shield) and *Gorgoneion* (the Gorgon in Greek mythology). For a parallel to our bust with a slightly different angle, see Zayadine (1990, 40, 45, Plate 1.2)

32
Zayadine (1990, 127) in his discussion about Allat says, "There are four Nabataean dedications to al-'Uzza at Petra...but no single mention of Allat...."

33
Joukowsky 1998, Cat. No. 98-S-14, Figures. 6.79a–6.79b and the drawing in Figure 6.80. For the description see p. 294–295.

34
Is it not possible, then, that opium may have been used in a similar manner in Petra, tying Aphrodite ever more closely to the carved representations of the poppy in the Great Temple's architecture? But this is only a suggestion. See my article in a "Common Name: Poppy; Habitat: Nabataean Sculpture at the Petra Great Temple," Festschrift for Leonard H. Lesko, submitted April 27, 2004.

35
M. C. A. Macdonald in *Petra Rediscovered*, 2003, 41, states, "...whereas at Petra just under 1,100 inscriptions in Nabataean, Greek and Latin have been discovered, of which 82 percent are simple signatures."

36
This inscription is PCP Reg. No. 0187a Drawn and drafted by John Philip Hagen.

37
R. N. Jones and G. W. Bowersock, 2001, "Nabataean Inscriptions," in Fiema et al. *The Petra Church*, ACOR Publications 3, Amman, 346–349. We also published this inscription with comment in *BASOR* 324 p. 56, Fig.12.

38
This inscription was found on a column drum that has a diameter common to the Great Temple Lower Temenos column drums. The drum was not *in situ*. Other elements of the Great Temple have been discovered at the Petra Church such as an upper capital element and part of an elephant-headed capital, both of which were found in the atrium cistern.

39
This inscription has not been given an expert reading. Additional partial inscriptions are illustrated in Volume I (1998 p. 297 Figure 6.83).

40
These have been published in 2006 *ADAJ* Volume 50, Joukowsky, "Challenges in the Field," Figure 10.

41
To the south of Nabataea lay the kingdom of Saba or Sheba (Yemen and probably Aden) in southern Arabia, the region known as "Arabia Felix" to the Romans.

42
M. Gawlikowski 1972, "La notion de tombeau en Syrie romaine," *Berytus* 21: 5–16. "The concept of the *nefesh* thus seems a phenomenon introduced into Syria by the Arabs from the Hellenistic period. It does not belong to the religious foundation common to the Semites, if such a foundation ever existed, but rather is attached to a type of monument that, itself, is very ancient—the standing *stele* around the tomb that takes very diverse forms, architectural or anthropomorphic.... Under the [implosion?] of the Arab beliefs, one observes, everywhere where these nomads are established, the appearance of the *nefesh*."

In 1982 F. Zayadine considered the *nefesh* in his article, "The sacred space in ancient Arab religions," in *SHAJ* 1: 301–303. On p. 302, "The notion of *haram* ['set apart', 'sacred] was, in the Arabic traditions, attached to both the sanctuaries and burials. In both cases, these places could serve as an asylum and were considered sacred; the same name was also used to describe their character. The *stelae* called *nefesh*, representing deceased individuals placed usually but not necessarily on their tombs, have been identified, as is commonly accepted, with the souls of the dead who inhabited them, in the same way as a divinity inhabited a baetyl." F. Zayadine suggests that the origin of the architectural form is to be looked for in Alexandria, which is indeed very possible. "The underlying concepts and beliefs, however, need not be a tributary of the Egyptian practice. They seem, on the contrary, well in line with what is known about the customs of Arabia. The *nefesh* monuments are not mentioned in the Bible or other contempo-

rary sources, and appear only in the Hellenistic period. Older populations have sometimes adopted the term *nefesh*, but not the notion of the soul incorporated in it; instances can be quoted of family tombs thus called in Palestine, Palmyra, and elsewhere." Also see, Dalman 1908, Healey 2001, and Starcky 1965. See also M. C. A. Macdonald 2003, in *Petra Rediscovered*, 40. (I am grateful to Christopher A. Tuttle for these notes.)

43
There are also benches in the Theater against the south side of the *Parados* wall; these benches, however, are for sitting and may have served for the theater performers.

44
There is also the custom of sprinkling an altar or a *betyl* with blood presumably and animal sacrifices. See F. Zayadine 1993, in *Petra Rediscovered*, 59. Significantly, the bench under the *betyl* altar has a trough that extends the length of the wall.

45
Fortunately Stephan G. Schmid's (Stucky, et al. 1994, 281–285) painted fine wares typology derived from the Ez Zantur excavations has been exceedingly helpful for the correspondence and dating of similar Great Temple forms. Phase I–Date: second half of the second century BCE to mid-first century BCE. These shapes are developed from Hellenistic prototypes: shallow plates and bowls with incurving rims; plates with outturned rims. Most are covered with a reddish or brownish slip. Painted pottery is represented by deep bowls and S-shaped bowls with careless painting and thinly applied pale red slip consisting of straight and wavy lines cutting across each other at the bottom of

the vessel. Rims may show a tear-like decoration.

Phase 2 is characterized by shallow bowls with incurving rims and hemispherical bowls common unpainted forms. The ware is brighter, of a light red to orange color, often with a white slip on the exterior of the rim. Phase 2 has three sub-phases, Phase 2a, Date: 50 BCE to 30–20 BCE with shallow bowls having incurving rims (usually without a base), painted with branches of pulpous palmettes in red, radiating from the vessel's bottom to the rim, which is decorated with tear-like motives; Phase 2b: Date: 30–20 BCE to turn of the century. Walls become thinner and have an additional step. The twigs of palmettes are now finer, and they run in two lines concentrically around the body of the vessel. Phase 2c: Date: Turn of the century to 20 CE. Finally in Phase 2c the shape of the bowls is straighter, without steps and with inverted rims. In the vessel's upper zone the same palmettes occur as in Phase 2b, although they are even finer and are of a darker red to violet color. The lower zone is now painted with different motives such as clusters of palmettes and peacock eyes in various combinations.

Phase 3 has four subphases: Phase 3a: Date: 20 CE to 79 CE, The shape of the bowls is straighter, without steps and with inverted rims concentrically around the body of the vessel. Phase 3b: Date: 70 CE to beginning of the second century CE. This phase is dominated by shallow bowls with a diminished rim. The painting consists of stylized palmettes and geometric shapes and pomegranates. Characteristic for this sub-phase is the grid that covers the background and the dark color that ranges from brown to black. Phase 3c—Date: 100 CE. Shape of the bowl is almost the same but the rim becomes even more diminutive and merges more and more with the body. The decorative motives are the same as in 3b but they are cruder and more carelessly applied and the grid that interconnected the motives in the preceding sub-phase has disappeared. Phase 3d. Very coarse and carelessly painted shallow bowls.

During each transition the earlier and the later phase occurred together for a short time. A figurative painted Nabataean bowl with human beings, donkeys and a bird is dated to the early second century or to 100 CE. But such wares, Schmid mentions (1994, 285), could also be from the third or fourth centuries CE. The tradition of painted pottery in a specifically Nabataean style did not end with the Roman annexation in 106 CE.

46
Many of these are lamp fragments that have been dated, but have not been given Special Finds/Catalog numbers (Personal communication from Deirdre G. Barrett, April 30, 2006.)

47
The figurines from the Great Temple are being studied by Christopher A. Tuttle and will be part of his Brown University Institute of Archaeology and the Ancient World's dissertation entitled, "Life in Miniature: Figurines as Indicators for the Socio-Religious Culture of Petra and the Nabataean Kingdom." They will also be a part of the Great Temple Volume III.

48
This upper half of nude female figurine wearing a Hathor wig is Cat. No. 02-P-25, Seq. No. 89841, from the Upper Temenos, Trench 94, Locus 41, of 10R5/8 red ware. Her raised right hand is held with the palm facing out, her left hand is held close to her navel, but it has been broken off. Her small breasts and rounded belly suggest youth and fecundity. Her face is young and attractive and she is wearing a bracelet on her right wrist and a girdle under her belly. Width 2.24 cm, height 4.15 cm, weight 16.3 g. See Khairy 1990, 24 No. 1 for comparison.

49
Some 462 nails and nail fragments have been collected during our excavations.

50
These artifacts along with their drawings can be found in Joukowsky 1998 Volume I Figure 6.108. Other metal artifacts can also be seen there on pages 305–310.

51
Sara G. Karz discusses the glass finds in Joukowsky 1998, Volume I, 325–343.

52
Other artifacts of worked bone are described by Deirdre G. Barrett in Joukowsky 1998, Volume I, 310–313.

53
So named by Kanellopoulos for the great arch associated with Shop 28 when it was rebuilt in the Roman period. (2001, Note 3, page 9.)

54
Bowersock (1983, 85) discusses the disintegration of Nabataean royal rule under the Roman regime.

55
Rabbel II may have moved the Nabataean government from Petra to Bostra in Syria, but there is vigorous debate over this issue.

56
During the excavations we removed the recycled ashlar fill of the doorways purposefully leaving in place only the temple South Corridor central doorway and the West Corridor Wall doorway, which can be seen in Figure 5.22.

57
Nabataean kings had been replaced by Roman legates or deputies—members of the senatorial rank serving as governors. Although the Nabataean geopolitical fortunes had changed, at least in the beginning of the Roman takeover, the Roman control of the area seems to have had little effect on the flourishing Nabataean economy. With Roman domination, the Roman Legatus maintained order, which clearly manifested the dependence of the now allied city. The Nabataean language continued in use for administrative and legal purposes, although Greek and to a lesser extent Latin were in use as well.

58
The potters of Nabataean fine wares maintained their production, although the yield from this time demonstrates a decline in the painting, and the wares become coarser and sandier to the touch.

59
We have the *Periplus Marus Erythraei* of the mid-first century CE, which justifies sea faring traffic taking the place of the overland routes.

60
These soldiers would have been accorded Roman citizenship after they were discharged.

61
No complete lamps like the one shown above have been found at the Great Temple. This example is from the Ridge Church Excavations, Courtesy of Patricia M. Bikai and the American Center of Oriental Research in Amman.

62
Deirdre G. Barrett (personal communication of April 29, 2006) states: "There are three Late Byzantine lamp bodies Cat. Nos. 95-L-23, 96-L-47 and 96-L-50, which were sent for neutron activation analysis and were found to be from outside the Petra area. This lamp type is dated from the fifth to sixth century CE (Hadad 2002: 72–3, Type 31, No. 317). It is possible that these lamps were used by visitors to the Great Temple, after its abandonment, but they are the most recent of the dated ancient artifacts. The ten fragments found at the North Ridge site were most likely used by tomb robbers. Cat. No. 95-L-23 Trench 20, Locus 16 Lower Temenos, East Triple Colonnade; Cat. No. 96-L-47, Trench 24, Locus 4 Temple Pronaos East; and Cat. No. 96-L-50, Trench 34, Locus 7, Temple, East Corridor. Two more fragments from this type were found in Trench 97, one in Locus 2 (04-L-25) and the other (04-L-44) in Loci 1–4."

GLOSSARY

This glossary includes the terms used at the Great Temple. New terms we have used in our excavations are also included. General glossaries can be found on the web and in J. McKenzie, *The Architecture of Petra,* Oxford University Press 1990, 181–185; in D. S. Robertson, *Greek and Roman Architecture,* Cambridge 1945, 379–390 and in J. B. Ward-Perkins, *Roman Imperial Architecture,* Harmondsworth, 1981, 491–497.

^{14}C = Carbon-14: Radiocarbon is a geochronological method for determining the absolute date of an archaeological deposit.

A

Abacus: Flat stone slab underneath an entablature that forms the top of the capital of a classical column supporting a beam.

Absolute dating: Date given in specific years, in terms of chronometric dating, or the calendar, i.e., BP means before present or 1950, BCE means Before Christ, before the Common Era, and CE means the Common Era.

Abut: To touch or be adjacent to something along one side, as opposed to bond.

Acanthus: Any plant of the genus Acanthus having large spiny leaves and spikes or white or purplish flowers; native to Mediterranean region but widely cultivated. An ornament resembling the foliage or leaves of the acanthus (Acanthus spinosus); used in the capitals of the Corinthian and Composite orders.

Acculturation: Adoption of traits of one society by another.

Acroterion: Greek. A decorative element placed on the lower corners of a pediment, generally with a vase or eagle.

Aditus maximus: (Latin: most important or greatest entrance/access) Roman entrance to the orchestra between the *cavea* and the *scaenae*; one on either side of the orchestra; corresponds to the *parodos* in the Hellenistic theatre.

Adyton: A separately defined space inside a temple, usually behind or at the rear of the cella; the inner sanctuary.

Aegis: In Greek, meaning shield, usually referring to Athena's shield.

Aelius Gallus: A general of Caesar's who was the proconsul of Egypt. The Roman demand for incense and myrrh led the Romans to want to crush the Nabataean monopoly and control the trade route supply of these exotica. Using Nabataean guides, in 25–24 BCE, Aelius Gallus started an unsuccessful expedition from Nabataea down the Arabian side of the Red Sea to conquer Arabia Felix, the kingdom that lay to the south, Saba, present-day Yemen—the land of frankincense and myrrh. The Roman propaganda of the day made this expedition out to be a success.

Al-'Uzza: "The very strong." The principal Nabataean goddess who is the protector of Petra; the goddess of love and immortality. She is associated with the Egyptian goddess Isis and later with Aphrodite and Venus.

Alexander Jannaeus: Ruler who gained the Judean throne in 103 and held it until he died in 76 BCE. He ruled from Dan to Beersheba, calling himself king as well as high priest. Opposed to religious freedom and Hellenism, his mission was to Judaize the area. In this effort he became a warring, ruthless, military monarch who was successful in his goal and subjugated all of Palestine. Alexander Jannaeus provoked a conflict with the Nabataeans, who were in control of the trade routes and cities that he coveted.

Amphora (pl. amphorae): A jar, usually made of clay, with a narrow neck and two handles, used by ancient Greeks and Romans for holding oil or wine.

Anastylosis: The archeological reassembly of ruined monuments from fallen or decayed fragments (at the Great Temple, incorporating new materials when necessary).

Anathyrosis: A decorative smooth band or frame around an ashlar, created by chiseling.

Note:
I would like to thank Dr. Patricia Scola for suggesting the inclusion of this glossary.

Aniconic: Represented by a symbol, abstract (not anthropomorphic).

Anta (pl. antae): Pilaster or pier forming the ends of the lateral walls of a temple *cella*; it generally has a rectilinear shape and is a support which can either be free standing or engaged. When there is a corner pilaster pier, generally projecting just beyond or at the end of a row of columns. When the façade consists of columns set between two antae, the columns are referred to as *in antis*. *Tetrastyle in antis*, for example, implies there are four columns between the *antae*. The *anta* supports the entablature and may be decorated with pilasters.

Anthropomorphic: In human form.

Antony: Mark Antony In Latin, Marcus Antonius (83?–30 BC), Roman statesman and general, who defeated the assassins of Julius Caesar and, with Gaius Octavius and Marcus Aemilius Lepidus, formed the Second Triumvirate, which ultimately secured the end of the Roman Republic. He fell in love with Cleopatra and returned to Egypt with her in 41 BCE. Believing that Cleopatra was dead, he killed himself by falling on his sword.

Aphrodite: In Greek mythology, the goddess of love and beauty. She was the daughter of Zeus. She was also known as Cytherea; her Nabataean equivalent is al-'Uzza and her Roman equivalent is Venus.

Apodyterium: Room in an ancient bath where people would undress and leave their clothes while bathing.

Apsidal: Semicircular recess at the end of a sanctuary or temple.

Aramaic: Branch of the Semitic language used from the sixth century BCE as the lingua franca in the Near East. Later the Nabataean language was developed from Aramaic.

Arbitrary levels: Excavation units that are excavated metrically as opposed to natural levels excavated as they were formed.

Arch: Any part of a curved line in architecture, usually a curved member made up of wedge-shaped blocks.

Architectural Fragments: The Petra Great Temple database (FileMaker Pro 6) used to capture information about architectural fragments with the dimensions and description of each fragment. (For a full description, see Joukowsky 1998, 259.)

Architrave: Lintel at the top of a column, extending from one column to another. It is the lowest element below the frieze and the cornice in the entablature.

Arcosolia: Arched cell in a catacomb designed for a sarcophagus.

Aretas I: First king of the Nabataeans. The Nabataean King Aretas I (ca. 168 BCE) is referred to as the 'tyrant of the Arabs' and the 'King of the Nabatu,' or King of the Nabataeans. Aretas I is cited as the protector of the High Priest Jason, who asked for asylum in Petra, and ruled when cordial hospitality was offered to the Maccabean leaders Judas and Jonathan. If we look at the extant biblical record of the Roman period, we find that the Nabataean King Aretas I appears in 2 Maccabees 5:8 as the first known Nabataean king-ruler. There is scholarly debate (Bowersock 1983:71–73) as to whether Aretas I was or was not succeeded by a king known as Rabbel I.

Aretas II: Third king of the Nabataeans, 120/10–96 BCE, preceded by ? Rabbel I and succeeded by Obodas I. The city of Gaza requested his help to fight against the Hasmonaean King Alexander Jannaeus. He is mentioned as the victor in the siege of Gaza, opposing Alexander Jannaeus who attempted to capture the port city from the Nabataeans.

Aretas III: 85–62 BCE, Known as *Philhellenos*, fifth king of the Nabataeans, preceded by Obodas I and succeeded by Obodas II. (He is also known on his coins as "Philhellene," "Philhellenos" or "Philhellen," meaning "lover of 'Hellenism'"). Aretas III expanded Nabataean territory up to and including Damascus in southern Syria. During his reign the earliest Roman governor of Syria, Marcus Aemilius Scaurus, unsuccessfully carried out a military campaign against Petra. In 63 BCE, the Roman general Pompey captured Jerusalem. Thereafter, Nabataea became a client state of Rome. It appears that Nabataean control over Damascus was not secure, and the troops of Aretas III had to evacuate the city when the Armenian King Tigranes attacked central Syria.

Aretas IV: Known as the "Lover of His People," 9 BCE to 40 CE. At the death of King Obodas III, he took over the Nabataean throne without the Emperor Augustus' permission. Originally called "Arenas," he changed his name to Aretas, became the ninth king of the Nabataeans, preceded by Obodas III and succeeded by Malichus II. The rule of Aretas IV (9 BCE–40 CE) marks a 48-year golden age for the Nabataeans. To his people he was known as *hrtt mlk rhm amh*, "Haretat [Aretas] the King who loves His People." On his prolific coinage his queens, Huldu (until 16 CE) and Shaqilat (from 18 CE), are shown in profile. They are identified as "Huldu, the Queen of the Nabataeans" or *sqylt mlkt nbtw*, "Shaqilat, the Queen of the Nabataeans" (Glueck 1965:10). The representation of the queen on the Nabataean coin issue implies that royal women at least enjoyed a high status and perhaps even a position of some power in the Nabataean court, such as regent. He proudly mentions his sons and daughters on an inscription from Petra. Once again, Damascus came under Nabataean control.

The monuments at Petra reflect a flourishing economy and unsurpassed wealth from international trade. Aretas IV reigned over a cosmopolitan Petra, which Strabo states in his *Geography* 16.4.21 was where Romans and other foreigners frequently could be seen. He built splendid temples and tombs not only in the capital of Petra, but at Hegra (Egra) in the Hejaz (Medain Saleh, in present-day northwestern Saudi Arabia) and along the route to Gaza in the Israeli Negev. In 1964, Peter J. Parr found an inscription of Aretas IV on a bench in the Forecourt of the Temenos area of the Qasr al-Bint, in which Aretas IV credits himself with the Temenos' construction.

Artifact: Human made object, or one that has been modified by a human.

Ashlar brick (rock-faced brick): Brick whose face has been hacked to resemble roughly hacked stone.

Ashlar masonry: Smooth square or rectangular stones laid with mortar in horizontal courses. Coursed ashlar masonry is built of stones having the same height within each course, but each course varies in height. In random ashlar masonry, stones appear to be laid without a drawn pattern, although the pattern may be repeated. Most of the walls of the Great Temple show the interlacing of headers and stretchers, and the joints of one row are generally not set directly above the other.

Ashlar: Well-hewn, squared-off blocks of stone used in building, permitting very thin mortar joints. Found in almost all western styles of architecture. The Nabataeans most often dressed their ashlars at a 45-degree angle to provide support for a plaster or stucco surface.

Assemblage: Group of objects found in association. A full assemblage can be described as a culture.

Astragal: Narrow convex molding often in a bead shape or half a round profile. Used below an ovolo (generally decorated with the egg and tongue at the Great Temple). It is also used around the top of the column shaft below the capital attached to the column shaft.

Athena: In Greek mythology, the goddess of wisdom and warfare, and the patron goddess of Athens, (Roman equivalent Minerva). Medusa's hair was admired by her lover Poseidon; the jealous Athena turned her hair into snakes.

Attic base: Term given to the base of an Ionic architectural order consisting of an upper and lower *torus* (a convex molding at the base of a column) separated by a *cavetto* or *scotia* (a deep concave molding with the curve of a quarter circle) and fillets.

B

Baldric: Silk sash or leather band slung over one shoulder and round the opposite hip.

Balk (English spelling, baulk): Earth partition left standing between trenches and the edges of an excavation that provide vertical control of the site for the study of the stratigraphy.

Ballista: Projectile weapon; a stone missile.

Balneum (pl. *balnae*): Place for bathing; smaller than the public grand *thermae*.

Baroque Room Complex: The complex measuring 5.77 m north-south × 17.26 m east-west, located to the south of the Great Temple's South Passageway. The complex is composed of four rooms including an Anteroom, Shrine Room, Baroque Room, and a Settling Tank.

Barrel vault: Simple semi-cylindrical vault.

Bead and reel: Alternating long and short beads carved in an *astragal,* below the egg and tongue molding.

Bedrock-cut: Tool-etched bedrock in linear and grooved patterns is located in the Upper Temenos West Plaza of the Great Temple. These may be quarrying marks to level out the bedrock for the temple precinct. Such cut marks can be seen in Figures 4.18 and 4.19.

Betyl: Standing stone shaped as a cone; a rectangular or pyramidal shaped libation stone signifying the god's home and/or presence. It is usually freestanding and can be undecorated or bear schematic facial features. The Nabataeans represented their gods as *betyl*s. The base of the *betyl* is the *motab* and has a sanctity of its own.

Bitumen: Tar-like substance naturally derived from petroleum; a pitch used in ancient times to seal hulls of boats and used today as asphalt for roads.

Bond: Link in which one surface adheres to another; an overlapping pattern in which bricks or tiles can be laid. In archaeology it generally means that the walls are constructed at the same time.

Boss: In masonry construction, a projecting ornament, often located at the intersection of two components. The boss in the upper order of the Great Temple capitals is carved as a pinecone. The boss on the elephant-headed capitals is shaped like a flower.

Boule: Council or assembly; a governing body.

Bouleuterion: This Council House generally consists of a semicircular auditorium fronted by a shallow stage structure; it is where the council or city assembly meets.

Broken pediment: Two half pediments. At Petra the broken pediment can be seen at the al-Khazna where the cornices slope to the rear of the building.

Bronze: An alloy of copper and tin (9:1) which is cast in one- or a two-piece mold, or lost wax process (*ciré perdue*), and hammering, or plates which are then riveted together.

Burckhardt, Johann Ludwig: Swiss explorer who revealed Petra to the western world in 1812, for the first time since the Crusades.

Burial: The laying of the deceased in the ground, a chamber, or an urn. A collective burial is when more than one corpse is entered into the same repository. A secondary burial is the term used for the reburial of the same corpse, such as the collection of the bones after the flesh has been removed (See Inhumation).

Burnish: Technique used to close the pores and to shine a ceramic surface. Usually applied by a pebble, bone, or piece of wood; may also be applied by wheel.

Byzantine: Period during the Eastern Roman or Greek empire from 364 CE or 395 CE until the capture of Constantinople by the Turks in 1453 CE.

C

Cable fluted design: Square vertical overmold used at 3.16 m above the plain colored plaster on the upper column shaft of the Petra Great Temple, giving a semblance that the columns are molded in relief.

Caldarium (pl. *caldaria*): Hot room in an ancient bath.

Capital: Top element of a vertical support; typical shapes may include Doric, Ionic, Corinthian, and Nabataean orders.

Casemate wall: Nabataean casemate wall consists of parallel walls sometimes with perpendicular walls for support, but more often having a central core of mud rubble for support.

Cassette: Elaborate molding. In the case of the Great Temple, cassettes are fashioned in plaster, and appear on the temple corridor walls.

Cassius Dio: Roman historian of the early CE third century who writes about the end of the Nabataean kingdom.

Castellum aquae: Holding tank for water, part of the hydraulic installations for the Roman-Byzantine Baths.

Castellum: Holding tank for water.

Cauliculus (pl. *cauliculi*): Latin for the fluted sheath or stalk from which the helix and corner volute come together on a Corinthian capital.

Cavea (pl. *caveae*): Seating area for spectators in a Roman circus, theater, or amphitheater.

Cella: Latin (pl. *cellae*): Principal chamber and inner structure of a Greek or Roman temple in which the image of the divinity is kept. In a Roman temple the *cella* usually consists of a single room with only one opening, in front.

Chalcolithic: Of or relating to the period of human culture preliminary to the Bronze Age, characterized by the use of copper and stone tools.

Chiton: Piece of clothing in the Greek world usually worn by Aphrodite. It consists of two sheets of drapery with a belt. The *chiton* can be worn either by women or men.

Chlamys: Short mantle or cape fastened at the shoulder; worn by men in ancient Greece.

Christianity: The predominant religion of Petra during the fifth century CE.

Clast: An individual constituent, grain or fragment of a sediment or rock, produced by the weathering of a larger rock mass. Synonyms include "particle" and "fragment."

Cleopatra: (69–30 BCE), The ill-fated queen of Egypt (51–30 BCE), celebrated for her love affairs with Julius Caesar and Mark Antony. Cleopatra, or more precisely, Cleopatra VII, was the daughter of Ptolemy XII Auletes, king of Egypt. She was the last Pharaoh of Ancient Egypt.

Cohort: Roman military unit—one tenth of a legion.

Colonnade: Row of columns.

Column: Upright support generally shaped like a cylinder, but in the case of the Great Temple rear columns they can also be heart-shaped. Columns generally have three parts: the base, the shaft and the capital. Columns support a roof or entablature.

Column drum: Cylindrical stone that is one of the components of a column.

Consolidation: (Latin consolidare + solidare, to make firm, from solidus, firm) the concept of applying measures to protect the archaeological entity against further structural losses due to its exposure to the elements or to excavation. Consolidation at the Great Temple supports literally hundreds of structural elements on an as-needed basis to ensure the element is stabilized. The life cycle of the object, to increase its structural infrastructure, is monitored, analyzed, designed and implemented. The treatments must meet the standards for ensuring the stabilization of the structure.

Conservation: The protection of cultural property be it architectural or artifactual. It is the process of preserving, protecting and guarding the site and its artifacts for their preservation.

Coprolite: Fossilized or dried dung.

Corinthian: A type of capital decorated with acanthus leaves, volutes and in the case of the Great Temple with fruits and flowers bursting forth from vines with small tendrils like spirals known as helixes.

Cornelius Palma: A lieutenant and general of Trajan who fought in the Dacian Wars and who annexed and absorbed Nabataea in 106 CE. Petra became part of *Provincia Arabia* in 114 CE.

Cornice: Horizontal architectural molding that projects from the top of a wall or section of a wall.

Cornucopia: Vase or basket shaped like a horn and filled with fruits, flowers; a symbol of fertility and a plentiful harvest.

Couloir: Deep gorge; a gully.

Crepidoma: The base on which a classical temple is built.

Cryptoporticus (pl. cryptoportici): An underground gallery that may be a passageway. The word *crypta* means an underground cave or subterranean vault. Usually a slightly sunken arcade or barrel vault creating a long walkway or storage area. Architecturally, it often also functions as buttressing for larger, adjacent structures. It is often lit by openings piercing the upper part of the vault, as they are in the Petra Great Temple Lower Temenos West Cryptoporticus. In the Great Temple Cryptoportici were underground galleries covered over by the Lower Temenos Triple Colonnades with openings for both air and light.

Cultural level: Stratum or combination of strata that through its physical remains represents the way of life of a particular social group, such as the Classical Greeks. The data collected in such a level have a known and recognizable set of ideas that are represented as cultural products of that society, i.e., a regularly occurring assemblage of artifacts.

Culture: Shared behavior of a group of people.

Cuneus (pl. *cunei*): Wedge-shaped section of seats in a theater auditorium, usually bounded by the *scalaria* (stairway). It corresponds to the Greek *kerkis*.

Cyma reversa: An ogee molding that (in section) has the shape of an S with the convex part above and the concave part below.

D

Decadrachm: Greek silver coin worth 10 drachmas.

Decapolis: League of ten cities located east of the Jordan River. Pliny lists Damascus, Philadephia (Amman), Raphana, Scythopolis (Beth Shean), Gadara (Umm Qeis), Hippos (Susita/Tellel-Husn), Dium, Pella, Gerasa (Jerash) and Canatha. Other cities like Abila and Capitolias are also listed by other authors,

so it appears to have been a loose confederation. It may have Hellenistic origins but other scholars assume it was formed by Pompey ca. 63 BCE. After Trajan's conquest of Nabataea these cities found themselves in different provinces.

Demeter: In Greek mythology, the goddess of corn and the harvest, daughter of Cronus and Rhea and mother of Persephone. Her Roman equivalent is Ceres.

Diagonal dressing: Diagonal chisel marks to score an ashlar or a column drum. Used as a technique to hold plaster decoration on the stone. It provides a footing for the plaster. The diagonal dressing at the Great Temple is angled between 15 degrees and 45 degrees from the vertical.

Diazoma: Horizontal passageway or aisle, used most often for a theater.

Distyle: Widely spaced columns set at intervals equal to three or sometime four times the diameter of the column. The temple of Site Phase II is *distyle in antis* meaning that it is two columned in the front standing between anta sidewalls.

Djinn: Characters from Arabian folklore. The Bedouin believe they can be identified with malicious evil spirits and that certain blocks of stone are inhabited by such spirits.

Dressed masonry: A stone masonry block that has been squared and shaped for a precise fit with other blocks. Stone masonry utilizing dressed stones is known as ashlar masonry.

Dushara: The principal god of the Nabataeans. He is referred to as 'he who separates night and day,' and 'lord of the world.' In the Roman period he is associated with Dionysus.

E

Echinus: Lower curved element of a Doric capital.

Ecofact: Non-artifactual materials including inorganic and organic materials, such as seeds and animal bones. These may have cultural relevance when studying a site.

Egg and tongue: Molding consisting of a egg-shaped element alternating with a downward pointing tongue. (Easily confused with egg and dart.) At the Great Temple these are found decorating the elephant-headed capitals of the Lower Temenos.

Engaged column: A round semi-detached column or half or three quarter column attached to a wall. Only half the column projects from the wall.

Entablature: Architectural feature that consists of three parts; the architrave, the frieze, and the cornice, which rest on columns.

Entasis: In classical architecture, the slight swelling or bulge in the center of a column, which corrects the illusion of concave tapering produced by parallel straight lines.

Epigraphy: The study of inscriptions, the deciphering and interpretation of ancient inscriptions.

Exedra (pl. exedrae): A small room, one side of which opens up to a larger hall or court, a semi-circular recess with an arched or domed roof, generally with stone seats. At the Petra Great Temple the East and West Exedrae open onto the Lower Temenos Triple Colonnades.

F

Fabric: Color and texture of a stratigraphic deposit, or of a fired vessel.

Feature: Artifact that is non-portable, like a hearth. Generally it cannot be removed from its *in situ* position without its destruction.

Find spot: The actual place an object is found. In determining the accurate find spot, many archaeologists incorporate hand-held GPS device to determine global positioning systems (GPS) and geographic information systems (GIS) in the field.

Fluvial: Deposit created by water action, such as a flood deposit.

Frankincense: Lumps of a gum resin from the Arabian tree known as *Boswella sacra* found in the Dhofar region of southern Oman. The most prized frankincense originates in this region.

Fresco: Method of painting in which the watercolor pigment is applied to the plaster on a wall or a ceiling while the plaster is still wet. Fresco secco is applied after the plaster has dried.

Frieze: Long painted or carved architectural decoration.

Frigidarium: Latin term (from *frigidus*, cold) for a cold plunge in a bath.

Functional analysis: Determination of the operating function of a building or a tool.

G

Geochronology: Determination of age by association with geological processes.

Geography: Descriptive study of the earth's surface.

Geology: Study of the development of the earth.

Geomorphology: Analysis of the form and development of the landscape.

Gilded: Overlaid with gold.

Glaze: Shiny, smooth, generally transparent or glassy colored surface used as a coating on a ceramic. The shiny surface of the vessel is produced by firing the object in a kiln.

Gorgon: Mythical woman with snakes for hair who turned those who looked at her into stone.

Graben: Down-dropped block of the earth's crust resulting from extension, or pulling, of the crust.

Grid: Excavation technique using trenches of regular squares with balks set between them. The balks serve as sections to hold the stratigraphy in place. The size of the squares and the width of the balks are determined by the depth of the deposit to be excavated.

Groin vault: Vault formed by the intersection of two barrel vaults, producing a vault composed of four compartments.

GIS: Collection of computer hardware, software, and geographic data for capturing, managing, analyzing, storing and displaying all forms of geographically referenced information that is data identified according to location. A GIS is a set of intelligent maps and other views that show features and feature relationships on the earth's surface. Maps of the underlying geographic information can be constructed and used as "windows into the database" to support queries, analysis, and editing of the information.

GPS: The Global Positioning System is the only fully functional satellite navigation system. A constellation of more than two dozen GPS satellites broadcasts precise timing signals by radio, allowing any GPS receiver to accurately determine its location (longitude, latitude, and altitude) anywhere on the earth. GPS has become a vital archaeological utility, indispensable for excavation, as well as an important tool for map-making and land surveying. Archaeologists in urban or rural environments can use GPS to determine their position, with or without reference to separate maps.

Grosso Modo: Name given to the Great Temple recording procedure and database (FileMaker Pro 6) to chart the full range of material culture found at the site. (For a full description, see Joukowsky 1998, 239.)

H

Hadrian: Latin, Publius Aelius Hadrianus (76–138 CE), emperor of Rome (117–138 CE), who declared an end to the expansion of the empire. In 130 CE Hadrian named Petra after himself, *Hadriane Petra*.

Half-life: Period of time required for the activity of a radioactive sample to decrease to half of its original value—half of the nuclei originally present having changed spontaneously into a different nuclear type by emission of particles and energy. After two half-lives the radioactivity will be a quarter of its original value. A stable element is then formed which is expressed as a statistical constant. In radiocarbon analysis, the half-life of any living organism undergoes this change every 5730 years.

Header: Beam placed perpendicular to wall studs above doors, windows or other openings, to carry the weight of structural loads.

Hectare: Metric area unit often used by Old World archaeologists meaning 100 acres or 10,000 square meters.

Hegra: *See* Meda'in Saleh.

Helix (p. helices): Greek. Spirals that spring from acanthus leaves between the corner volutes of a capital.

Hellenism: The period in history between the death of Alexander the Great in 323 BCE and the Roman conquest of the Middle East (Judea in 63 BCE, Egypt in 31 BCE, Petra in 106 CE). This is a period in which Greek art was influenced by the Orient and adopted more effective representation.

Hermeneutic: Interpretive or explanatory. A branch of philosophy concerned with human understanding and the interpretation of texts. Recently the concept of texts has been extended beyond written documents to include, for example, speech, performance, works of art, and even events.

Herod the Great: The Roman vassal king, who invaded Nabataean territory when the Nabataeans neglected to pay tribute to Rome. In 37 BCE, Jerusalem fell to Herod. Of Nabataean descent, Herod the Great was the son of Herod Antipater, the advisor of John Hyrcanus; his mother, Cypros/Kypros, was a noblewoman from Petra, and he spent part of his boyhood in Petra. In 38 BCE, the Roman Senate appointed him King of Judaea, and with the help of the Roman legions, he captured Jerusalem in 37 BCE and Nabataea in 31 BCE, thereby gaining control over a large area of Nabataean territory and ending its independent status. In 63 CE Pompei captures Jerusalem and Judea becomes a Roman dependant. Nabataea becomes a client state of Rome, but Nabataean Kings continue to rule.

Hippalus: *See* Monsoons.

Horned altar: Structure upon which a religious sacrifice is offered with horns at the corners. Usually such altars served for the burning of incense.

Horst: Upthrown block lying between two steep-angled fault blocks.

Hypaethral: Term is generally used to describe sacred structures that are unroofed or placed in the open, thus having unrestricted access to the heavens.

Hypocaust tile: Pillars on which the floor in the hot room, the *caldarium,* of a Roman bath was supported. Hot air circulated between the pillars (composed of stacks of these square or round ceramic or stone tiles) in the space under the floor, warming the floor and the room.

Hypocaust: Chamber under the floors of a Roman bath in which the hot air from the furnace passed. A system for heating rooms, particularly the *caldarium* of a Roman bath; the heat from a furnace was accumulated to heat a room or a bath.

I–J–K

Ibex: Wild goat, *Capra Ibex-Nubiana,* found in southern Jordan and the Negev. This animal is often depicted in figurines.

Iconography: Study of artistic shapes or symbols.

Ima cavea: Latin, the lowest tier of *cavea* seating; the most desirable seats in the theater.

In antis: Used for a temple façade with two (*distyle in antis*) or more columns (four columns are called *tetrastyle in antis*) and two pillars (antae) at the ends of the projecting walls.

In situ: An object's original resting position in the earth; its find spot or its primary location.

Indian elephant: An Indian-Asian species of elephant, *Elephas maximus* with the forehead slightly indented having twin domes and with fan like ears that are considerably smaller than the *Loxodonta Africana,* the African elephant.

Inhumation: Burial of the dead (no cremation or exposure). "Extended" means bones in a straight line, "Supine" means on the back; "prone" means on the face or side; "flexed" means leg bones bent less than 90 degrees; "crouched" means hip and knees bent more than 90 degrees.

Inter-axial distance: Measurement of the shortest distance between the center part of one column and its neighbor, from column to column, or from column to wall or from wall to wall. Generally measured from the center of one feature to the center of the other.

Intercolumnar wall: Wall that extends between columns.

Intercolumniation: System used to space columns in a colonnade, based on the use of their diameters as a measurement.

Ionic: Typical of a Greek architectural order characterized by fluted columns and capitals with scroll-shaped volutes. The Ionic order rests on a curving base, a column shaft (height is generally a ratio of 8:1), and two spiraling volutes resembling two unrolled scrolls.

Itinera versurarum: Outer two door openings of the five doors in a Roman *scaenae frons* (stage); doors in the Roman *versurae* (section of the *scaenae* that flanks the stage).

Jamb: Vertical support on either side of a doorway that supports the lintel.

Judea: Region of wilderness bordered on the east by the Dead Sea, on the south by Beersheba. Ein Gedi is the only oasis in the region. The Judean Desert Caves where the Dead Sea Scrolls were found are located in this region.

Juniper: Evergreen scrub or tree of the genus *Juniperus*. It has prickly leaves and dark purple berry-like cones. It is the only tree we have on the Great Temple site.

Kerkis (pl. *kerkides*): Greek word for the wedge-shaped seating section of a theater, the Latin *cuneus*.

Keying: A device, such as a wedge or pin, inserted to lock together mechanical or structural parts.

Kiln: An oven chamber constructed for the purposes of baking pottery.

Koilon: Area in the Greek theater similar to the Latin *cavea* or theatron.

L

Laconicum: The sweating room of an ancient bath, generally contiguous to the *caldarium*.

Layer: Stratum, or one thickness, of a soil or a course of stone. A layer can be suggestive of change.

Legion: Roman division of 3,000 to 6,000 soldiers including the cavalry.

Lens: Archaeological deposit with a lens-shaped cross-section, i.e., a deposit of ash or shell.

Level: Horizontal line unbroken by noticeable elevations or depressions uniform in soil composition, color, and homogeneous material remains.

Levigate: To make clay into a smooth, fine powder or paste, as by grinding when moist. To separate fine particles from coarse in water.

Loculus: Rectangular recess cut in tomb chambers for the placement of the body.

Loom weight: Lump of clay that may be spherical, oblong or pyramidal in shape used to weigh down the threads of a loom for weaving.

Loutron: Small cold plunge in an ancient bath.

Lunette: Semicircular opening or flat decorative space in a vault that may or may not be filled by a window.

M

Malichus I: The seventh ruler of the Nabataeans. He was preceded by Obodas II and succeeded by Obodas III. This was a time of political upheaval in Rome when fortunes changed. In 55 BCE, Malichus

I was attacked by Gabinius, the governor of Syria, who forced him to pay tribute. Meanwhile, Caesar had defeated Pompey at Pharsalus, and Pompey was murdered in Egypt in 48 BCE. Malichus I supplied military aid to Caesar at Alexandria in 47 BCE, but he shifted his alliance to support the Parthians in their invasion of Judaea. In 40 BCE, the Parthians invaded Syria and captured Jerusalem. (King Herod fled to Masada with his family.) The Parthian invasion incurred the bitter enmity of Mark Antony as well as Herod the Great, and in 41 BCE they became allies. With the assassination of Antipater, Herod became the governor of Judaea. After the Roman victory, Malichus I was forced to pay an indemnity to Rome.

Malichus II: The tenth ruler of the Nabataeans 40–70 CE. He was preceded by Aretas IV and succeeded by Rabbel II. Malichus II was referred to by the Nabataeans as *mlkw mlk, mlk nbtw*, "Malichus the King, King of the Nabataeans." His queen, Shaqilat II, was called *sqylt 'hth, mlkt nbtw*, "Shaqilat, his Sister, queen of the Nabataeans" (Meshorer 1975.107). With the rule of Malichus II, Nabataea is thought by some scholars to have witnessed a decline in its fortunes. This, however, may not have been the case, for it has now been confirmed by scholars that Malichus II was the king referred to in the *Periplus Maris Erythraei* 19.49. This citation describes a great commercial success resulting from a linking of the Red Sea port city of Leuke Kome to Petra. The Nabataeans also seem to have been commercially and militarily successful at Hegra (Meda'in Saleh), and they occupied the north Arabian oasis in Wadi Sirhan of Dumah (Jauf). In 67 CE, Josephus (*Jewish Wars* III.IV.2.68) states that Malichus II sent 5000 infantrymen, including archers, and 1000 cavalry, to suppress the First Jewish Revolt.

Marginal draft: Stone has a chiseled draft, border or frame around it. Such drafts are 5 cm to 10 cm (2 to 5 inches) wide and 1.5 cm to 2 cm (¼ to ⅜ inches) deep. Generally the face is left rough, but with Nabataean ashlars it may also be finely chiseled.

Masons' marks: These are incised or carved into the sandstone wall ashlars and column drums, most often by the mason who dressed the stone. At the Petra Great Temple these are usually in the shape of Nabataean letters.

Meda'in Saleh: Hegra, in northwest Hejaz area of Saudi Arabia served as a Nabataean station and military presence on the incense route. It flourished as a large settlement with opulent tombs (similar to many of the tombs in Petra) from the reign of Aretas IV until the first century CE. Meda'in Saleh is its modern name.

Medusa: In Greek mythology, a Gorgon (a frightening female monster) who could turn to stone anyone who looked at her. She was killed by Perseus.

Mental template: Term coined by anthropologist James Deetz to mean a commonly shared idea of what an object or archaeological feature should look like. The mental template is a concept that is passed between generations.

Metonymy: Referring to a concept by an attribute of it, for example, "the crown" referring to a monarch.

Midden: Dump of domestic food refuse.

Minaeans: People who controlled the desert trade routes in the early fourth century BCE from eastern Arabia southwest to the Hadhramaut through Shabwa and Madina to the north through the Hejaz and onto Wadi Rum and points north. In the late second century BCE the Minaean kingdom crumbled and the Nabataeans took over the control of the trade routes. Strabo called the Minaeans 'barbarians.'

Model: Theoretical construct used to understand a specific set of data. There are descriptive models emphasizing the form and structure of data, and there are explanatory models that look for understanding the causes for the phenomena. Models may be dia-chronic (chronological explanations of how data change over time), or synchronic, or pertaining to data at one point in time.

Monsoons: In 20 CE, a Greek merchant and seaman, Hippalus, made the very significant discovery that from May to October the winds in the Indian Ocean blow from the southwest and from November to March they originate from the northeast. This had a tremendous impact on Arabian and Nabataean traders for they became less dependent on the overland trade routes.

Motab: Aramaic word meaning "to sit." The *motab* is the seat of the deity, a divine throne. Many *betyls* are placed on some sort of throne or *motab*.

Munsell Soil Color Charts: A standard for the description of colors, developed by A. Munsell, used primarily in archaeology for the objective reading of soil and ceramic colors. Three factors are charted; *hue*—10 colors, each with 10 subdivisions; *value*—the darkness or lightness of the color which are ranged from 0 to 10; and *chroma*—the grayness or purity of the color, again rated 0–10.

Myrrh: Gum resin from the *Commiphora myrrha* tree used for perfume, incense and medicine.

N

Nabataeans: The Nabataeans (Greek, *Nabataioi*) are identified as people from the Arab kingdom of Nabataea. They referred to themselves as *Nabatu* on Aramaic inscriptions from the Semitic *nbtw*. The Nabataeans come into prominence in the late first century BCE through their lucrative success as traders of frankincense, myrrh, spices, gold, precious gems, silks and medicinal products. They also became prosperous from harvesting Dead Sea bitumen. Nabataea and its capital, Petra, is famous for its extraordinary architecture, exquisite eggshell thin pottery painted with geometric and foliate designs, their script (a variant of Aramaic), and ingenious hydraulic systems that allowed them mastery of the desert and a successful agricultural economy. The Nabataeans rose to great power and the span of their civilization lasted 300 years.

In the Persian period (550–330 BCE), the Naba-taeans, an Arab tribe, migrated and settled in Edom and taxed those who traveled the corridor from the Red Sea to Syria. Writing in the Augustan period, Diodorus Siculus (II: 48–49) states that the nomadic Nabataean merchants of exotics from Arabia, Africa and India, took refuge when attacked by King Anti-gonus I in 312 BCE, and are described as a people fond of freedom, with camels and cattle living under the open sky without springs or rivers. But Strabo's later account portrays them as traders living in luxuri-ous houses and practicing viticulture. These are a wealthy, cosmopolitan, settled people numbering 10,000 men, who are ruled by a monarch and boast a fleet in the Red Sea for merchandising spices, incense and myrrh. By the late second century they con-trolled an area from the Hejaz to the Hauran in the north and from the Nile Delta to the Syrian Desert, and were actively trading with the Persian Gulf.

In 190 BCE, Antiochus IV ruled the Seleucids. Having seized most of Palestine and Jordan, the Maccabees under Judas Maccabaeus with John Hyr-canus I, led a revolt against Antiochus IV. As Seleucid power declined, the Hasmonaeans, successors of the Maccabees, ruled an independent Judaea from 142 to 63 BCE. From 135 to 104 BCE, the governor-king John Hyrcanus I conquered the Negev and land north to the Galilee. His successor, Aristobulus, took the Galilee. Alexander Jannaeus gained the throne in 103 and ruled from Dan to Beersheba, until he died in 76 BCE. He provoked a conflict with the Nabataeans, who were in control of the trade routes he coveted. Threatened, the Nabataeans joined forces with the Seleucid King Demetrius III, and they temporarily defeated the Hasmonaeans, but Alexander Jannaeus regained control. He died leaving his widow and successor, Salome Alexandra, ruling from 76 to 67 BCE. Her sons, John Hyrcanus II and Aristobulus, began their own civil war, but with Idumean Antipater and the military support of the Nabataean King Aretas III, John Hyrcanus II took his brother captive. Infighting between the Seleucids and Ptolemies allowed the Nabataeans to maintain their control over the caravan routes between Arabia and Syria. Nabataean trade flourished, and Petra became a metropolis with an estimated population of 20,000 to 30,000.

The Roman conqueror Pompey arrived in Damascus in 63 BCE and forced Aretas III's troops to withdraw from Jerusalem. Pompey selected John Hyrcanus II to rule as high priest and annexed his territory into the Roman province of Syria. Aristobulus was exiled to Rome, where he attempted to start a rebellion; this insurrection was halted by Mark Antony, and after a second rebellion in 55 BCE, the Romans appointed Antipater governor. The Parthians invaded Palestine in 40 BCE and placed the Hasmonaean Antigonus on the throne in Jerusalem, taking John Hyrcanus II prisoner. The Nabataeans made a tactical blunder by siding with the Parthians, for Rome, backing the Roman vassal king, Herod the Great, defeated the Parthians and captured Jerusalem. After the defeat of the Parthians, the Nabataeans were forced to pay a heavy fine to Rome. Jerusalem fell to Herod in 37 BCE and Nabataea crumbled in 31 BCE; Rome now controlled a large area of Nabataean territory and ended its independent status. Although geopolitically the Nabataeans lost their "national identity," their culture continued to flourish. The forces of Malichus I were overpowered at Philadelphia (modern Amman), and Antony and Cleopatra by Octavian at Actium. The Roman Empire controlled the Near East and Octavian received the title Augustus Caesar, becoming the first Roman Emperor.

By the mid-second century BCE, the Nabataeans controlled the trade routes from the Hejaz through Jordan and the Negev to the Mediterranean. Although the early rulers are shrouded in mystery, the eleven Nabataean kings begin with King Aretas I (ca. 168 BCE) who is referred to as the 'tyrant of the Arabs' and the 'King of the Nabatu,' in the war against the Seleucid King Antigonus of Syria. There is scholarly debate as to whether Aretas I was succeeded by Rabbel I; however, by ca. 110 BCE Aretas II ruled. Aretas II is mentioned as the victor in the siege of Gaza, opposing the Hasmonaean King Alexander Jannaeus. In ca. 96 BCE, the son of Aretas II, Obodas I, ascended to the Nabataean throne and ruled until 85 BCE, inheriting the struggle against Alexander Jannaeus. Ambushed, Alexander Jannaeus was driven by camels into a deep ravine and barely escaped, and Obodas I took land in Moab and Galaaditis. In a crucial battle that took place at Cana in southern Syria in 87 BCE, Obodas I and his forces defeated the army of the Seleucid Antiochus XII. Obodas was so revered that the city of Oboda in the Negev was named for him and served as the seat of his royal cult. From 85 to 62 BCE Nabataea was ruled by Aretas III who expanded Nabataean territory to include Damascus. In 63 BCE the Roman general Pompey captured Jerusalem and Nabataea became a client state of Rome.

The rule of Aretas IV (9 BCE–40 CE) marks a 48-year golden age for the Nabataeans. To his people Aretas was known as "Haretat [Aretas] the King who loves His People." Once again Damascus came under Nabataean control. On his coinage his queens, Huldu (until 16 CE) and Shaqilat (from 18 CE) are shown in profile indicating that royal women enjoyed a position of power in the Nabataean court. The monuments at Petra reflect a flourishing economy and unsurpassed wealth from international trade.

The rule of Aretas IV marks the most creative era in Nabataean history. As Hellenistic culture was pervasive, the now wealthy but eclectic Nabataeans borrowed art and architectural ideas both for their buildings and their artifacts from Egypt, Assyria, Parthia, Arabia and Greece. Aretas IV reigned over a cosmopolitan Nabataea with splendid temples, colonnades, palaces, fountains and ornamental pools, gardens, a theater and 800 tombs with *triclinia* (a room with three rock-cut benches). Column capitals were adaptations of the Ionic and Corinthian styles. Whole façades were plastered and interiors were decorated with wall paintings and elaborate stucco moldings depicting animals, human faces and figures. Non-figurative decoration with rectangular blocks, god block *betyls* and *nefesh* coexisted with finely carved vases, rosettes, flowers, fruits, leaves, entwined fronds, and mythological gods and animals, including Asian elephants. These decorative ideas are found not only in Petra, but at Hegra (Egra) in the Hejaz (Medain Saleh, in Saudi Arabia) and along the route to Gaza in the Israeli Negev.

Relations between Nabataea and the Herodians were generally peaceful. One of the daughters of Aretas IV was the wife of Herod Antipas (Herod's son), who divorced her to remarry. The aftermath was a conflict between the armies of Aretas IV and the Herodians. With the rule of Malichus II (40–70 CE), Nabataea is thought by some scholars to have witnessed a decline in its fortunes. This may not, however, be the case, for it has now been confirmed that Malichus II was the king referred to in the *Periplus Maris Erythraei* (19.49), describing the great commercial success resulting from linking the Red Sea port city of Leuke Kome to Petra. The Nabataeans were commercially and militarily successful at Hegra and occupied the north Arabian oasis in Wadi Sirhan.

Rabbel II (70–106 CE) ascended the throne with his queen mother, Shaqilat II serving as regent until he came of age in 75 CE. At this time, the city of Bostra in the Hawran (Syria) became a prominent city of Nabataea. Rabbel's reign ended in 106 CE, and Rome absorbed Nabataea, which completely succumbed to Roman hegemony under the Emperor Trajan and became the Roman province known as *Provincia Arabia*. In 130 CE the Roman Emperor Hadrian named Petra after himself, giving it an imperial imprint.

With Roman seafaring trade circumventing Arabia (directly related to the discovery of the monsoons), Nabataea began its decline as a leading trade center. The Nabataean language continued in use for administrative and legal purposes, although Greek and to a lesser extent Latin were used as well. The potters of Nabataean fine wares maintained their production, although the yield from this time demonstrates deterioration in the painting. By 114 CE Trajan had granted Petra the title of metropolis, and it served the Romans as the principal center for their southern holdings, extending from the south shore of the Dead Sea to the Gulf of Aqaba. Nabataean kings were no more, having been replaced by Roman legates or deputies, and members of the senatorial rank serving as governors.

Nabataea's apogee was from the first century BCE to the second century CE. Its material culture reached its zenith in the second half of the first century BCE, before the Romans established control.

Natatio (pl. *Natationis*): Swimming pool, generally part of an ancient bath.

Natural level: Unit of excavation defined by stratigraphy, as opposed to arbitrary levels.

Necropolis: Burial place, a cemetery.

Nefesh: Semitic word meaning "spirit" or "breath/inspiration of-the-genius." The soul of a person, referring to a memorial *stele* that associates the essence of the deceased with the stone. A *nefesh* is a sacred Nabataean commemorative monument. It is carved to consecrate a person or a family, and to be the receptacle of the soul. Often there is no burial associated with it, as in the case at the Great Temple West Entry Stairway platform. It serves as a witness to a Nabataean shared belief, because the Nabataeans often represented the dead with a pyramidal or conical form (as can be seen in the Obelisk Tomb in Petra).

Nomad: A member of a tribe that wanders from place to place in search for pasture.

Nymphaeum (pl. *nymphaea*): Monument constructed around a fountain or any source of running water, often of elaborate design with an apse and niches and decorated with statues; a public fountain.

O

Oboda (Avdat): When Hasmonaean John Hyrcanus and his son Alexander Jannaeus annexed parts of Moab, it threatened the Nabataeans, for it usurped their trade routes to the Mediterranean and Damascus. The first-century BCE Nabataean ruler, Obodas I, with the Seleucids deployed camels as tank corps to ambush Alexander Jannaeus, who ceded Moab and Galaaditis to the Nabataeans. When Obodas died and was interred in Oboda, the town was renamed in his honor. Inscriptions refer to him as 'Obodas the god,' and he was deified.

Oboda was a staging post along the trade routes through the southern Negev. Basically non-residential, it became a military base serving for the protection of Nabataean caravans and center of worship for surrounding tribes. During the Roman period, it was bypassed by a Roman road and went into decline. There are scanty remains of a temple at Oboda, perhaps dedicated to Obodas. The Oboda inscription ca. 100 CE contains Arabic poetry in Nabataean script.

In the Byzantine period a large communal wine production center was constructed here with separate sections for the tramping-pressing; each wine producer unloaded his grapes into a designated sector. In modern times, Nabataean terraces and water channels have been restored as part of an experimental irrigation project.

Obodas I: The fourth king of the Nabataeans, preceded by Aretas II and succeeded by Aretas III *Philhellenos*. He is the son of Aretas II. In ca. 93 BCE he defeats the Judeans and Alexander Jannaeus. In ca. 96 BCE, the son of Aretas II, Obodas I, ascends the Nabataean throne and rules until 85 BCE, inheriting the struggle against Alexander Jannaeus. In ca. 90 BCE, Josephus writes in his *Antiquities* (13.375ff), "after subduing the Arabs of Moab and Gilaadites, whom he forced to pay tribute…[Alexander] engaged in battle with Obedas [Obodas], king of the Arabs. Falling into an ambush in a rough and difficult region, Alexander Jannaeus was pushed by a multitude of camels into a deep ravine near Garada…and barely escaped with his own life, and fleeing from there came to Jerusalem." Obodas I, thereafter, took land in Moab and Galaaditis from the Hasmonaean. In a crucial battle that took place at Cana in southern Syria in 87 BCE, King Obodas I and his forces defeated the army of the Seleucid ruler, Antiochus XII, who was killed. As a result, Obodas was so revered that after his death the city of Oboda in the Negev was named for him and is said to have served as the seat of his royal cult.

Obodas II: The sixth king of the Nabataeans 62/61 to 59 BCE, preceded by Aretas III Philhellenos and succeeded by Malichus I.

Obodas III: The eighth king of the Nabataeans 30 to 9/8 BCE, preceded by Malichus I and succeeded by Aretas IV. Nabataean relations with Rome and Judaea were peaceful, and in 26 BCE Obodas III sent his minister-general, Syllaeus, with 1000 Nabataean troops to support the Roman march of Aelius Gallus into southern Arabia, known as *Arabia Felix*. Syllaeus wanted to marry Herod's sister Salome, but Josephus in his *Antiquities* (16.7.6) tells us that since the match would have been contingent on Syllaeus' conversion to Judaism, the attempt was aborted. With the death of Obodas III, the ambitious Syllaeus tried to take control of Nabataea. On his way to Rome to defend his claim and his reputation, his ship stopped in Miletus on the western shore of Anatolia (Turkey), where he dedicated a bilingual Nabataean-Greek inscription to Dushara. Syllaeus' attempt to exonerate himself was unsuccessful, and Strabo (16.4.24) states that by an order from Augustus, Syllaeus was decapitated or thrown off a cliff in Rome in 6 BCE.

Obsidian: Volcanic glass; a natural occurrence used for stone tool manufacture.

Odeion, odium (Greek, *oideion*): Building for musical performances.

Opus sectile: Stone parquetry that is generally luxurious; stone inlay using pieces of colored stone cut to follow a geometric design or pattern. This served as the most common type of flooring in the Roman-Byzantine Baths of the Petra Great Temple.

Orchestra: In Roman theaters, this was the semi-circular floor in front of the stage. It was surrounded by the semi-circular seating area, the *cavea*.

Orthostat: Large stone set upright. Menhirs and other standing stones are technically orthostats although the term is only used by archaeologists to describe individual prehistoric stones that constitute part of larger structures. Common examples include the walls of chamber tombs and other megalithic monuments and the vertical elements of the trilithons at Stonehenge, and the massebot in Palestine.

Ossuary: Container for the burial of human bones.

P–Q

Palaestra: An outdoor gymnasium.

Palestina Tertia: Diocletian (284–305 CE) reorganized the tax system of the Roman Empire and issued a price list for goods and services. In his desire to reduce the powers of the provincial governors, he divided the rule between four tetrarchs. The south of Arabia became *Syria Palestina*, which in the fourth century became *Palestina Tertia*. Its capital was Petra.

Palynology (archaeological palynology): is the science that sudies the influence of vegetation and climate change on human behavior and demographic patterns, in addition to the effect that humans have on the environment.

Pantile: A roofing tile, traditionally clay, with a pronounced s-shaped section, in which the downturn of one hooks over the upturn of its neighbor. Because there is no overlap, a pantiled roof is lighter than a tiled roof.

Parados (pl. *paradoi*): Passageway; a side entrance into the orchestra of a Greek theater. The space between the audience seating and the stage. The *parados* is the primary entrance for the chorus and is also used by the audience for entrance and exit from the theater. In Latin this is the *aditus maximus*.

Pax Romana: The long period of peace and stability that existed under the Roman Empire, especially in the second century CE.

Pediment: Triangular element with sloping sides used to crown building, doors, niches and windows.

Pedology: Science that deals with the study of soils.

Peripteral colonnade: Used to describe a classical building that has a single row of columns on all sides. The design of a temple in which the *cella* is surrounded by a peristyle.

Peristyle: Covered colonnade that surrounds a peripteral building or court. The Petra Great Temple is peripteral.

Petra: Greek name for "rock." The name given to the Nabataean capital by the Emperor Hadrian.

PETRA (Petra, "rock")
Located in the Wadi Musa valley in southern Jordan, Petra, 30°19′N, 35°25′E, is the capital of the Nabataean kingdom. The city stood on the flourishing overland trade route that linked Arabia and the Mediterranean Sea. The valley, surrounded by 300 m high precipitous mountains of Nubian sandstone, is approximately 1.5 km long × 1 km wide. In the last quarter of the first century BCE most of the city was constructed and remained independent until 106 CE when it was annexed by Rome. The principal rock-cut monuments of Petra are the Siq, the narrow gorge-entry into the city, the al-Khazna (the Treasury), theater, and the more than 800 tomb façades have been divided into four types, depending upon their decoration. The largest monument is the vast rock-cut Ed-Deir (the Monastery), 46.77 m in width × 48.30 m in height. Characteristic of both the Deir and the Khazna is that their façades have upper orders with a tholos framed by a broken pediment.

The most important of the free-standing structures are the Temple of the Winged Lions, the Qasr al-Bint Far'un, the Great Temple, the Colonnaded Street, and the Qasr al-Bint Far'un and its tripartite Monumental Gateway. The architecture of Petra has Egyptian, Assyrian, Persian, Parthian and Greek Hellenistic elements, but it also displays an eclecticism that is Nabataean.

Numbers of churches were constructed in the Byzantine period, including the Petra and Ridge Churches and the Blue Chapel. The site contains Islamic and Crusader remains.

Petroglyph: Rock painting or engraving.

Photogrammetry: Controlled measured aerial photograph.

Pilaster: Rectangular column or narrow block with a capital and base, projecting only slightly from a wall as an ornamental motif. In the case of the Great Temple, some pilasters blocks are carved in relief.

Pithos: Large storage jar, often plump in shape, that can be handleless or may have many handles. They are most commonly used for the storage of food or liquids but sometimes served for inhumation burials.

Plan: Horizontal map of a site (or any portion of it) that is plotted in relation to a fixed point or reference datum.

Pointing: The placement of mortar between the ashlar blocks. At the Great Temple the process involves scraping away the loose mortar and earth that over time has collected between the ashlars. Followed by rigorous cleaning between the ashlar blocks, finally new mortar is introduced and pointed flush with the surface of the ashlars.

Pompeian Second Style: Pompeian mural painting has been divided into four styles based on stylistic variations. The Second Style appeared in ca. 90–70 BCE and is characterized by three-dimensional architectural representations. The Petra Great Temple West Corridor murals are compared with this style.

Portico: Covered ambulatory consisting of a roof supported by columns placed at regular intervals, usually attached as a porch to a building.

Post hole: Hole that has been dug in the ground to hold a post.

Praefurnium: The furnace room, which provided the heating for the *caldarium* (hot room). Hot air flowed from the *praefurnium* and circulated under the floor through the hypocaust tiles.

Pronaos (pl. Pronaoi): The inner area of the portico of a Greek or Roman temple leading to the *cella*. This is the roofed room in front of the *naos* sanctuary of a temple. The location of this room varies with the design of the temple.

Propylaeum (pl. propylaea): Entrance to a sacred precinct. Often emphasized through elaborate architectural details and/or by projecting out from the precinct wall.

Propylon: Outer gateway; either an independent entrance building or an element in a wall, usually with a double door and columns supporting a porch on both fronts.

Proscenium: That part of the stage between the curtain and the orchestra pit. The architectural arch which encloses the curtain is called the proscenium arch.

Provenance: In archaeology, the area where an object was recovered.

Provenience: *Exact* spot where an object is found and recorded by the archaeologist.

Provincia Arabia: The Roman Province created out of the annexed territory of Nabataea in 106 CE.

Pulpitum: Actual stage or platform of a Roman theater.

Quern: Grinding stone for grain; a mortar.

R

Rabbel I: Uncertain dates. His was the second rule of the Nabataeans. The first Nabataean coins were minted during his reign.

Rabbel II: The eleventh ruler of the Nabataeans; his reign was preceded by Malichus II. Rabbel II (70–106 CE) ascended the throne with his queen-mother, Shaqilat II, serving as regent until he came of age in 75 CE. Rabbel II married two of Malichus II's daughters, who are also referred to as his "sisters"— Queen Gamilat (reigned 76–102 CE) and Queen Hagru (reigned 102–106).

This was a time of trouble for Nabataea and particularly for the royal house ruling from Petra, its capital. The royals at Hegra revolted, led by one known as Damasi, who was supported by northern Nabataean tribes as well as his fellow Hejaz people. David Graf (1992.IV.971) suggests that the phrase ascribed to Rabbel II as one "who brought life and deliverance to his people" is a reference to the king's successful in stamping out this rebellion.

It is thought that Rabbel II came to an agreement with Rome that, if they did not attack during his life-time, the Romans could take control after his death. Rabbel II's reign ended in 106 CE with his death, and in the same year Rome annexed Nabataea. Nabataea completely succumbed to Roman hege-mony when the Roman legate of Syria, A. Cornelius Palma, on behalf of Trajan took control. Whether or not this action was a peaceful or hostile takeover is not known, but it probably was an administrative for-mality carrying out the agreement between Rabbel II and Rome. Trajanic coinage carries the legend *Arabia adquista* instead of *Arabia capta*, which would seem to confirm the routine nature of the annexation. As would be expected, Roman coinage came with the creation of the province, and Nabataean coinage was often over struck by the Romans.

Rabotage: Careful horizontal scraping of the surface to find either discolorations or disturbances.

Radiocarbon dating: (See ^{14}C, page 413, and "Half-life").

Rekem: Nabataean, early Semitic name for Petra.

Relative dating: Date based on the chronological sequence of objects (see Seriation).

Revetment: Decorative facing of marble or other material applied to a wall.

Rhodian rose: Storage jar manufactured in Rhodes with the impression of a rose stamped on its handle.

Rillenkarren: Fine, parallel runnels or grooves with rounded troughs and sharp ridges. They are usually ½ to one inch deep, and are best developed near the crest of the outcrop where rainwater is more highly charged with CO_2. They occur mostly on limestone, rarely on dolomite, lacking any soil or plant cover.

Roman style: The Architecture of Ancient Rome adopted that external language of classical Greek architecture for their own purposes, which were so different from Greek buildings as to create a new architectural style. The ancient Greeks invented the architectural orders: Doric, Ionic and Corinthian. the Greek and Roman styles are often considered one body of classical architecture.

Rouletting: Decorative technique used on Nabataean pottery in which an instrument is used while the vessel is on the wheel to create designs on the leather hard pottery before it is fired.

S

Scaenae frons: Back wall of the stage in a Roman theater, usually two or three stories high and elaborately decorated with columns and statues.

Scalaria: Staircase of a theater.

Section: Vertical profile or a slice of archaeological deposits. The section drawing is the representation of the face of an excavated area.

Sela: Ancient Semitic word for "rock." In the Bible, Petra is referred to as "Sela."

Sequence Number: (abbreviated, Seq. No.) is allocated as a distinct, unique serial number to each field process we use and every feature and artifact recovered. Groups of artifacts, such as pottery sherds are allocated a single sequence number. The Sequence Number is always a part of the feature or artifact's identity, and it also serves for the chronology of excavation events in each trench and special project. (For a full description, see Joukowsky 1998, 239.)

Seriation: Method of relative dating by the ordering of specific artifact type over an earlier to later time sequence (see *typology*). Bar charts are most often used to count units of an artifact against time on horizontal and vertical scales, respectively.

Sextius Florentinus: The Roman governor of Petra who was buried in 129 CE at Petra in his elaborately carved tomb.

Shaqilat: Second wife of Aretas IV.

Shaqilat: Wife of Malichus II.

Sherd: Fragment of pottery or glass. (The British use the term "shard.")

Si'a: Sanctuary in the Hauran.

Sima reversa (also *cyma reversa*): In classical architecture the crowning molding on a cornice, *Cymatium,* when the convex part protrudes it is a *cyma* or *sima reversa;* the reverse of an ogee molding.

Site: Any place where human activity has taken place.

Slag: Vitrified waste by-product of glass manufacture, smelting and sometimes pottery manufacture.

Slip: Coat of liquid clay applied to ceramic usually by dipping. A slip is applied before the ceramic is fired.

Snecking stones: Small pieces of stone that are used to level a larger stone. Such stones are commonly found used in Nabataean buildings, especially to level stairway and wall ashlars.

Sobata (Shivta in Hebrew): Located in the west central Negev, 40 km southwest of Beersheba, this large site was situated on a route linking the Nabataean towns of Oboda, Sobata and Nessana. Founded in the Nabataean period during the reign of the Nabataean kings Obodas III (30 to 9–8 BCE) or Aretas IV (9–8 BCE to 40 CE), Sobata flourished under the last Nabataean king, Rabbel II (70–106 CE) with desert agriculture and horse breeding. Until the Byzantine period, the town was eclipsed, but by the mid-fourth century it became a monastic center, a site for Christian pilgrimages and an agricultural settlement. The splendid South Church with its cruciform baptismal font and North Church were constructed. After the Arab Conquest the site continued for another 200 years until the eighth to ninth centuries and perhaps later.

Sobata is important because of its Byzantine town plan covering 430 m north-south × 330 m east-west. It is situated on a gradual slope to the town center with three city squares. Emerging from the city squares are nine wide meandering streets with gates enclosing large plots of courtyard houses and cisterns. Water was carried down streets and Nabataean channels to two large Nabataean reservoirs in the town center.

First described by E. H. Palmer in 1870, its plan was drawn in 1901 by A. Musil. Surveys and excavations have continued at Sobata for many years: a dedicatory inscription to Dushara dated to Aretas IV was found in 1906, in 1958–1960 the town plan was defined, and A. Negev, A. Segal, S. Margalit, and J. Shershevski, representing various institutions have continued to work in different sectors. In the 1960s, the ancient terraces and water channels were restored as part of an environmental campaign under the direction of Michael Even-Ari.

Socle: Feature that projects from the bottom of a wall or other architectural structure.

Soffit: Under-surface of an arch or other architectural feature.

Sondage: A French word for a test excavation, probe or test pit excavated at an archaeological site to determine the content and/or the distribution of materials.

Spall: Fragment, usually of flaky shape, detached from a larger mass by pressure, expansion from within the larger mass, a blow, or by the action of weather.

Springer: First voussoir resting on the impost of an arch.

Stele (pl. *stelae*): An upright stone slab sometimes with incisions or reliefs.

Stratification: Many strata whose order of deposit is based on the law of superposition, i.e., the uppermost stratum was deposited last, and the lowest first. Thus, stratification involves the study of the layer-by-layer arrangement of archaeological deposits. It includes three factors:

    1) Superposition—of progressive accumulated layers implies that lower strata are generally older than the layers above them;

    2) Association—two or more artifacts found in the same closed archaeological context are contemporary and are therefore presumed to be culturally associated; and

    3) Correlation—once associations have been determined artifacts can be cross-culturally correlated.

Stratigraphy: Geological term meaning the study and analysis of stratification and artifacts so that the temporal and contextual sequence of a site can be reconstructed.

Stray find: An object that is not found in its original archaeological context.

Stretcher: The long side of a brick. A masonry unit laid flat with its longest dimension parallel to the face of the wall. Often laid by the mason with headers in between.

Stylobate: Platform on which colonnades of columns are placed (it is the "floor" of the temple). The stylobate was typically composed of an odd number of steps (most often three) above a leveling course that flattened out the area immediately beneath the temple. In some methodologies, (the Petra Great Temple included), the word *stylobate* is used to describe only the topmost step of the temple's base, while *stereobate* is used to describe the remaining steps of the platform beneath the *stylobate* and just above the leveling course.

Sudatorium: In an ancient bath, the hot dry room or sweat bath with moist steam.

Syllaeus: Ambitious, perfidious chief minister of Obodas III, referred to as 'brother' by Obodas (also see, Obodas III). He led the Roman troops with Aelius Gallus on an ill-fated journey to conquer Arabia Felix. He may have poisoned Obodas in 9 BCE. He was accused by Gallus of treachery and was killed either by being beheaded or thrown off a cliff in 6 BCE.

Synecdoche: A part of something substituted for the whole. Meaning is inferred by the specific part used. Ex: "A nice set of wheels."

T

Tabun: Arabic word for oven.

Tafoni: Formation of sandstone made when CO_2 and rain water forms a weak acid which gradually dissolves the calcium carbonate "cement" that holds the grains of sand together.

Tang: The projection on an arrowhead by which the arrow is held firm in the shaft.

Tell Brak: Site on the southeastern slope of Petra where elephant-headed capitals are also found.

Temenos (pl. Temenoi): Enclosed sacred space that is usually open aired where ceremonies in honor of deities were held.

Tepidarium: The warm room in an ancient bath.

Terminus ante quem: (From the Latin meaning time before which) and *terminus post quem* (time after which): These are relative archaeological terms used for dating archaeological deposits. Material that is found on a floor gives an *ante quem* for the floor construction, i.e., the floor cannot have been built after the material collected on it. It denotes the latest possible date for the floor, or an event or an object.

    The material under the floor gives a *terminus post quem* for the floor, since it could not have been deposited after the floor was laid. The earliest possible date of an event, object or stratum.

Terra Sigillata: Slip comprised of the smallest particles of clay that consequently resembles a burnished surface. The technique was used to impressive effect in the Greeco-Roman period.

Tesserae (pl. a): Small generally square stone, tile, ceramic or glass cubes used to make mosaics.

Tetrastyle in antis: Building fronted by four columns contained within two flanking antae.

Thermae: Term the Romans used for their public baths. Generally used to describe a large facility like the Baths of Caracalla in Rome.

Tholos: Circular temple element with a conical roof.

Time: An arbitrary period during which something— action, process, condition—exists and is measured. This period lacks spatial dimensions, but is a continuum of which events succeed one another from past through present to the future. Time is usually measured by a number representing the duration of a process or condition, or the interval elapsing between two events. This number is obtained arbitrarily to take place during the interval to be measured.

Trajan: (Latin, Marcus Ulpius Trajanus) (53?–117 CE), Roman emperor (98–117 CE), conqueror of Dacia and Mesopotamia.

Triclinium: (From the Latin, meaning 'three benches'). A chamber for ritual meals, feasting and meetings, generally with three rock-cut benches surrounding the room. The term is also used for the dining room in Roman house.

Triglyph: A decorative motif in a Doric entablature consisting of a vertical member with two central grooves, generally alternating with metopes.

Tyche: The city goddess of fortune, the protector of the city usually represented by wearing a turreted crown and carrying a cornucopia. An ear of corn can also be associated with her.

Tympanum: An area over a door between the lintel and the arch. This is a triangular area between the pediment and the architrave. It may be without decoration or carry a relief or a group of sculptures.

Types: A defined cluster of attributes in a class of objects. For example in the bowl types of Nabataean pottery, the type is a closely related form, e.g., the Nabataean bowl, in many cases, is homogeneous in its similarity and fabric, but variations can be found, it can be plain vertical, flaring, everted, everted with a flange, or, in a few cases, inverted.

Typology: Artifacts have formal attributes or standards that can be measured—raw material, length, width, thickness, color, weight, and so on—and these can be described. These attributes are thought to be a nonrandom standard followed by the maker. A typology is composed of types.

U–V

Unguentaria: Small glass or ceramic vials for make-up, perfumes or oils.

Ushabti: Literally translated it means "to answer." It is a small mummy figural form placed in tombs to perform duties in the afterlife on behalf of the deceased.

UTM: The Universal Transverse Mercator Grid is the most convenient way to identify points on the curved surface of the earth is with a system of reference lines called parallels of latitude and meridians of longitude. On some maps, the meridians and parallels appear as straight lines. On most modern maps, however, the meridians and parallels appear as curved lines. These differences are due to the mathematical treatment required to portray a curved surface on a flat surface so that important properties of the map (such as distance and areal accuracy) are shown with minimum distortion. The system used to portray a part of the round earth on a flat surface is called a map projection. This grid is designed so that any point on the map can be designated by its latitude and longitude or by its grid coordinates, and a reference in one system can be converted into a reference for another system. For additional information, visit the *ask.usgs.gov* Web site or the USGS home page at *www.usgs.gov*.

Vault: An arched structure of masonry resembling a dome forming a ceiling roof specifically engineered to support the weight above it. It can be a passage with a semicircular roof engineered to support the weight of the earth.

Veneered: A thin layer as a surface. A material bonded to the surface of another material. The cable-fluted design of plaster on the Great Temple columns is a veneer bonded to the sandstone column. At the Great Temple it begins at 3.16 m above the base of the column, above the deep red or yellow plain lower plastered surface.

Via Nova Traiana: The Emperor Trajan's New Road constructed between 111 and 114 CE between Bostra (Syria), Petra and Aela (Aqaba).

Virtual reality: The computer software generation of an image or environment that appears real to the senses.

Vitruvius: Marcus Vitruvius Pollio (born ca. 80–70 BCE?: died ca. 25 BCE). Roman writer, architect and engineer in the 1st century BCE. Vitruvius was born a free Roman citizen, and may have been a Roman army engineer, constructing war machines or sieges. Under his sponsor, the emperor Augustus, he authored *De architectura,* known as *The Ten Books of Architecture*—the only surviving major book on architecture from classical antiquity. Vitruvius is the first Roman architect to have written on his field, and is most famous for asserting that a structure must exhibit three qualities, it must be strong or durable, useful, and beautiful.

Volute: Spiral or scroll-like ornament on a column capital. Those of the Great Temple itself are spiral scrolls set at an angle to the capital and mark its corners. The volutes of the Lower Temenos capitals are elephant heads instead of spirals.

Voussoir: One of the wedge-shaped masonry blocks out of which an arch or vault is composed. The central voussoir is the keystone.

W–Z

Wadi: (Arabic) A valley or river, generally dry except when it rains.

Wash: A thin slip applied to a ceramic after it has been fired.

Zenon Papyri (*Papyri greci e latini*): Writings dated 259 BCE that identify the Nabataeans with the Hauran and northern Jordan, which they may have controlled as they expanded their territory and influence to the north.

A PRÉCIS OF SELECTED MAJOR STRUCTURES AT PETRA

Many of the traditional names given to Petra's monuments were inspired by local folklore and bear no meaning to the function of the monument. The names of sites and monuments in Petra and Jordan as presented in this report are based on the official transliteration system used by the Royal Jordanian Geographic Center (RJGC) 11/26/96. They follow the system used by the United Nations, the Board on Geographic Names (a division of the United States Defense Department) and the British Permanent Committee on Geographic Names. The aim is to use a consistent method of writing Arabic names in English based on formal Arabic.

The following list is a synopsis of the major monuments of Petra. It is not intended to be exhaustive.

Ad-Dayr: Also known as the "Monastery." An astounding tomb isolated from the rest of Petra with its ca. first century BCE façade cut into rock with a tholos (circular dome) and broken pediment. One of the largest of Petra's carved tomb façades, located on the Jabal ad-Deir. Carved in deep relief out of the parent rock-mountain, and crowned by an urn, the colossal grand façade is 42 m (127 feet) high-by-53 m (160 feet) in width. This tomb has only one chamber, 12 m (36 feet) square. The doorway is 8.6 m (26 feet) high, and the central urn is 10 m (30 feet) high. The façade is divided into two stories. The bottom storey has six high half columns with plain Nabataean capitals. A high broken entablature supports the second storey, which has half columns with plain blocked out Nabataean capitals on either side of three rectangular niches. On top is the large central tholos above a conical roof in the center of the broken pediment. There are crosses found on the walls that were carved in the Christian era.

Also to be seen is the vast circuit of ground in front of the structure, which forms a giant amphitheater. There is a pilastered niche in a cave near Ad-Dayr as well as cisterns, the Triclinium, and interesting petroglyphs.

In order to get to Ad-Dayr there is a spectacular but rugged climb of approximately 800 steps through a chasm filled with unexpected monuments and glorious scenic surprises. This is the sacred processional way to the largest monument in Petra.

'Ain Musa: (Moses' spring): Most abundant water source of Petra. Located in the upper part of the village of Wadi Musa, this is where folklore has it that Moses struck the rock with his staff and brought forth water to his people on their way to the Promised Land. This spring supplies the Wadi Musa after which the village is named.

Al-Bayda' (also Beidha): In Arabic, the "white one" because of the pale color of its sandstone. Located 3 km north of Petra, in the first century BCE and CE, it was developed into one of Petra's commercial suburbs.

Al-Budul: (Bedoul or Bidoul, In Arabic, meaning, "change") The Bedouin tribe that controlled Petra and the oldest known inhabitants of the Petra area who lived in the caves of the site until they were relocated in 1971 to the town of Umm Sayhum.

Al-Habis: (The Dungeon) Great rocky outcrop-massif at the western limit of the paved temenos of the Qasr al-Bint. Here there are the remains of a Crusader castle dating back to the beginning of the twelfth century CE. The Crusaders probably abandoned the Al-Habis castle after their defeat in 1187 CE.

Al-Khazna (Al Khazna Fir'awn: Pharaoh's treasury, in Arabic "The Treasury"), so named for its urn and façade cut into rock). Al-Khazna gained its reputation from a legend that a pharaoh's treasury was placed in the urn at the top. The most famous and spectacular monument at Petra. Perhaps constructed by Aretas III (84-62 BCE) or Aretas IV, and is probably connected with the Nabataean cult of the dead. Standing over 40 m in height, it has a tholos, topped by a large urn, and a broken pediment. It is decorated with Nabataean and Greek deities, including Castor and Pollux (the *Dioscuri*), Amazons, winged Victories, Tyche carrying the cornucopia, Medusa heads, eagles and griffins. Isis, the supreme goddess of the Egyptian pantheon, is also represented, as are beautifully carved flowers and fruits.

Al-Khubtha: One of the most important high places in Petra with courtyards, altars, a feast area, water basin and a large vaulted cistern.

Al-Layathina: The Bedouin tribe of the Wadi Musa town.

Al-Madhbah (In Arabic, for "High Place"): The High Place of Sacrifice the main high place of Petra, in an oval shape, measuring 14.5 m in length by 6.5 m in width. In its center is a sanctuary. It is reached by processional stairways, and a fort or tower guards its summit. It is appointed with a *motab*, or throne of the god, a sacrificial altar, a basin, and *triclinium* benches on the north, east and south sides facing the altar platform, probably used for feasting. Approached by three steps, the altar platform is oriented to the west, and is equipped with water channeling, basins, and drainage.

Al-Madras (in Arabic, 'rugged prominence,' or 'school' or 'oil press'): To the left of the Siq, this exotic spot is approached by a long flight of steps. It was suburb of Petra and is a showcase for a number of monuments. As Browning says, (1973, 111), it is a microcosm of Petra, and there is an inscription here which mentions that Dushara is the god of Madras.

Al-Mudhlim: A branch of the Wadi Musa where there is a tunnel to carry water from the Siq.

Al-Wu'ayra: A Crusader castle-fortress near Petra constructed by King Baldwin I of Jerusalem in 1115 CE. It was built to defend the eastern border against Saracen raids. The Muslims conquered the fortress in 1144 CE by massacring the Frankish garrison stationed there. It was abandoned following Crusader defeat in 1187 CE. Italian archaeologists from the Universities of Florence and Urbino have excavated this site.

Al-Turkmaniyya: Mid-first-century tomb dated to the mid-first century CE with the most elegant calligraphy and longest Nabataean inscription in Petra. The inscription details that Dushara will protect the regulations, 'the documents of consecration' as to whom is to be buried there and the funerary appointments of the tomb. It is planned with large and small burial chambers, niches, porticoes, rooms, gardens, a cistern, and walls.

Attuf: (Arabic for "merciful"; Zibb Atuf is a modern Bedouin name): This manmade plateau is cut on a ridge where a high place of sacrifice is located. The platform is divided into two parts with the one facing south where there are two remarkable giant obelisks, 7 m in height, which were created by leveling and cutting away the surrounding rock. They may represent the Nabataean gods, Dushara and al-'Uzza. The north side of the Attuf ridge across a ravine is the High Place of Sacrifice. *See* Al-Madhbah.

Bab as-Siq (In Arabic, 'the gateway to the gorge'): the east outer valley and pathway leading into the most dramatic entrance into Petra, the Siq. Here there are three Djinn blocks.

Byzantine Church (The Petra Church): A spacious church built in the later CE fifth or early CE sixth centuries north of the Colonnaded Street. It has a single apse to the east and an atrium and entry on the west. After its renovation in the CE sixth century and *opus sectile* pavement was laid in the central nave, a finely carved chancel screen was added as well as altars. Its floor is decorated with splendid sixth century CE mosaics portraying animals, birds, and figures in enclosed in vine roundels. Also there are a baptistery and cruciform baptismal font. In 1993 a cache of over 140 carbonized papyrus scrolls were recovered from one of the church rooms that were burned in a seventh-century CE fire. Excavated by the American Schools of Oriental Research, this work has been published by Z. Fiema et al. in 2001.

Columbarium: Located on the hill just to the west of the Buckhardt Center for archaeologists just below El Habis. This unfinished monument was given its name because of the tiers of shallow niches on its façade. In Latin a *columbarium* is a pigeon house or dove cote having similar niches; hence the monument's name. The purpose of this monument is unknown.

Corinthian Tomb: One of the Royal Tombs carved into the rock face of Jebel Khubtha. This tomb is a mixture of traditions—Nabataean and Hellenistic. This tomb was so named by Léon de Laborde a nineteenth century traveler who thought its capitals were of the Corinthian order.

Djinn Blocks. *See* Saharij al-Jinn.

Ez Zantur: Located on the southern slope of Petra, above the Great Temple to the southeast, this residential area is embellished with astonishing frescos (in the Pompeian Second Style), dated to the early first century CE.

High Place of Sacrifice: (See Al-Madhbah).

Jabal Harun (Mount Aaron, Aaron's Tomb): The area's highest peak. A large monastic complex, dedicated to Saint Aaron (the brother of Moses) is built on this site, which has been excavated by a Finnish expedition.

Lion Tomb: Located just off the climb to Ad-Dayr, this monument is a triclinium, not a tomb. It has corner pilasters, an elaborately carved frieze with an alternation of triglyphs and metopes and plain Nabataean capitals. Above is a low-pitched pediment. Above the door is a keyhole-shaped opening which at one time would have been a window. This tomb is named for the lions facing each other on either side of the door. The lion is thought to have been sacred to the goddess Al-'Uzza.

Mughur an Nasara (In Arabic, Nasara means 'Nazareth'): Located near the Wadi al-Nasara, this is a complex of tombs that may have been Nabataean in origin, but were used by the Christian population of Petra. Several crosses are carved into the walls and on the entrances to the tombs.

Nymphaeum: A fountain house decorated with statues of nymphs. In antiquity, in the Greco-Roman world, the volume of water in the nymphaeum was measured the status of a city. At one time it must have been elegant, but at the present only the foundations remain. The nymphaeum at Petra rests to the north of the Colonnaded Street, and it was well watered by the confluence of the Wadi Mataha and the Wadi Musa.

Obelisk Tomb: The tomb with four pyramidal obelisks on its façade, representing *nefesh*es or memorials to those buried inside. Five graves were found inside the tomb. It is located high in a cliff in the valley leading into the Siq.

Outer Siq: This name is a misnomer, because the area is a hollow gorge inside the city. This area is a wide clearing created by the Wadi Musa that descends after leaving the Al-Khazna and between this descent and the Main Theater. The Outer Siq is filled with rows of tombs high up on both its rock-cut terraced walls (known as the "Streets of Façades"). A channeling for water flow, an aqueduct that brings water into the city, can be seen cut away high up in the rock face. Many of the tombs in this area have been compromised by erosive action.

Palace Tomb: Largest of the Royal Tombs of Petra carved into the rock face of Jebel Khubtha. It is said to resemble a Roman palace. It is an unusual construction because it is three stories in height. The imposing width of its façade and its massive ground floor with large-scale doorways and two smaller stories above lend it a theatrical air. The middle storey has 18 half columns. In the interior are four enormous chambers, with the middle two interconnected.

Petra Church. *See* Byzantine Church.

Quarry: There are several quarries at Petra that are reasoned to be Nabataean. Many of them have footholds (as can be seen on the façade of the Al-Khazna) and masons marks. The Wadi as-Siyyagh quarry served for the building of many of Petra's freestanding monuments like the Great Temple.

Qasr al-Bint/Qasr Bint Fir'awn: (From the Arabic, "Palace/Castle of the Pharaoh's daughter.") This freestanding temple is a massive rectangular building probably constructed between 30 and 40 BCE. It measures 23 m in height and is probably the main Nabataean place of worship. The façade was adorned with a pediment (now gone) with geometric reliefs resting on columns. The building is divided into three parts, and it was probably dedicated to the god, Dushara.

Qattar ad Dayr: This is a rock balcony beside a huge cistern that can be visited on one of the paths leading to Qattar ad Dayr. Supplied by underground springs, the cistern remains full throughout the year.

Ridge Church: Late fourth-century CE church built on the north ridge of Petra, excavated by Patricia M. Bikai.

Roman Soldier Tomb: Located in Wadi Farasa is the Roman Soldier Tomb dated with its exterior first century CE. Despite its name this is a late Nabataean tomb with its exterior decorated with aniconic (non-representational) motifs. Of the two interior chambers, one is embellished with arched recesses. Across from the tomb is a large elaborately decorated *triclinium* (a three-sided chamber for ritual meals and meetings with three benches) with squared off niches between engaged half-columns. Guests attending the funeral feast in the *triclinium* would sit facing the center of the room to partake in the festivities.

Roman Street/Road: Sometimes referred to as the Colonnaded Street, but the columns bordering the street come to an end before the Great Temple precinct. Originally a gravel and sand road set parallel to the course of the Wadi Musa. This is the main thoroughfare into the central city. It is 17–18 m in width at its widest point but only 6 m in width in front of the Great Temple. It becomes a ceremonial street or *via sacra* extending from the Wadi Mataha to the Temenos Gate of the Qasr al-Bint/Qasr Bint Fir'awn. In the Roman period the road was paved with a limestone pavement that remains in place today and extends in front of the Central Stairway and West Entry Stairway of the Great Temple.

Royal Tombs: These are carved into the façade of the Al-Khubtha and include the enormous Palace Tomb (so-called because its façade looks like a Roman Palace), the Corinthian Tomb, the Urn Tomb, and the Silk Tomb.

Saharij al-Jinn (Djinn blocks): Bedrock-cut square towers, believed to be tombs by some. There are 20 such blocks in Petra. From Arabic folklore, the Bedouin believe them to house malevolent spirits or objects that protect them against such spirits.

Sextius Florentinus Tomb: Located on the western face of Jebel Khubtha. This tomb is for one of the early Roman governors of Petra under the Emperor Hadrian who died in 129 CE. He was buried at his own request at Petra, and his tomb is highly ornamented with a Medusa head and an arched pediment with an eagle above it. It has plain Nabataean capitals and a dedication to Sextius Florentinus in Latin on its entablature.

Silk Tomb: So named for its striking multicolored façade. This tomb has four worn engaged columns supporting a double cornice. The Silk Tomb stands on the east of Jebel Khubtha with the Royal tombs that overlook Petra to the west.

Siq: Approximately 1.5 km long natural cleft in the rock leading into Petra. The Nabataeans used it to channel water into Petra with rock-cut conduits and ceramic piping. The *Siq* passage is filled with wayside niches, many of which hold *betyl*s. The *Siq* entrance originally was embellished with an ornamental arch constructed in the Nabataean period. In the passage are the reliefs of two pairs of camels and cameleers carved into the cliff face. In 1963 a flash flood created havoc; a dam burst and 28 tourists caught by the floodwaters in the Siq were killed. With the Petra National Trust, the Jordanian Department of Antiquities has excavated the Siq and using the Nabataean dams as models they have created a safe passageway.

Siq al-Barid: In Arabic, the "cold gorge," which is located at the entrance to *al-Bayda*, (or Beidha)' the caravanserai north of Petra, serving the Negev, Gaza and the Mediterranean.

Snake Monument (Al Hayye): Located in the southwest of Petra, this heavily eroded monument is carved in the shape of the coils of a gigantic snake with its head pointing southwest. It is located on the summit of a high rocky outcrop with a Djinn block nearby. For the Nabataeans the snake symbolized continuity and eternity.

Temenos Gate: The majestic entrance to the Qasr al-Bint temple sacred temenos with flower-shaped and animal-shaped decorative details on north and south towers. On the east, free-standing columns were placed between each of the three openings of this triumphal arch, indicating that this was the principal façade of the structure. When the gates were open there would have been an impressive view of the Temenos plaza of the Qasr al-Bint. This gate is located only 6 m to the west of the West Entry Stairway of the Great Temple.

Temple of the Winged Lions: Situated on the north of the Roman Street opposite the Great Temple, this structure has an entrance that leads into a *cella* with a raised altar platform. The *cella* is appointed with numbers of columns, and those nearest the altar had winged lions instead of volutes, thus giving the temple its name. The precinct also has workshops, crypts, annexes and living quarters associated with it. One of the finest *betyl*s was found in a niche in the cella with an inscription, "the goddess of Hayyan,

son of Nybat." This temple has been excavated since 1974 by an American team under the direction of Philip Hammond. Some scholars believe this temple was dedicated to the goddess Al-'Uzza.

Theater (Main theater): This structure with 33 rows of seats is carved out of the living rock in the time of Aretas IV (9 BCE–40 CE) and had the capacity to seat over 5000 more people.

The Nabataeans cut many caves and tombs in the process of building the Theater. Under the stage floor are storerooms, constructed in the Roman period. Excavated by Philip Hammond, this structure underwent alterations under Malichus II and in the Roman period.

Tomb 825: A Hegra-style tomb that has been extensively studied at Petra by the German Technological Institute. They are interested in its preservation, and confirmed that the masons at Petra carved monuments from top to bottom, and that the whole façade of the tomb was colorfully plastered in antiquity.

Umm Sayhum: The modern Bedouin village above Petra, the home of the Al-Budul (Bedoul) tribe.

Umm al-Biyara: (in Arabic, the "mother of cisterns.") Located on a high rock 330 m above the central Petra, just to the west of the Great Temple and the Qasr al-Bint. Carved into the eastern outcrop are numerous tomb façades and on the summit there probably was a Nabataean sanctuary, which has not as yet been excavated. Here there is an important Edomite settlement with eight deep bell-shaped cisterns carved into the rock. Crystal-M Bennett who published the results excavated the Edomite site.

'Unayshu Tomb: This tomb was given its name by an inscribed loculus slab which bore the epitaph of 'Unayshu, (minister of the queen Shaqilat—the wife of Aretas IV and mother of Rabbel II.) Therefore this tomb can be dated to between 70– 76 CE. The tomb is located in the Outer Siq; it is slightly set back from the edge of the parent rock. It has a double cornice façade, and the doorway between the pilasters is crowned with an elegant pediment. The tomb originally had a graceful colonnaded courtyard in front of it onto which opened a triclinium.

Urn Tomb: This tomb, one of the Royal Tombs carved into the rock face of Jebel Khubtha, was carved in the first century CE for the burial of a king perhaps Malichus II. It has an open terrace constructed over two stories of double vaults. The interior room measures 20 × 18 m. In July 446 CE it was consecrated for Christian worship, and there is a Christian inscription on its wall as well as apses and a chancel area. The tomb takes its name from the urn placed at the top.

Wadi al-Farasa: Site of Roman Soldier Tomb. Its decoration is non figural. Steps lead from Wadi Farasa to the High Place of Sacrifice of Al-Madhbah. In Wadi Farasa there is a simple *betyl* and the carving of a human head above it inside a circular medallion. The soft sand in Wadi Farasa is used in the present day in the composition of mortar for the Great Temple preservation.

Wadi Mataha: Stream created by diverted Siq waters that were channeled to bypass the Siq around the Al-Khubtha peak; it is where this wadi joins the Wadi Musa. The Petra *nymphaeum* was built at the junction of the two water flows on the Roman Road/Colonnaded Street.

Wadi Musa: The name means "the Valley of Moses." Known as Elji until the 1850's, the ancient Gaia is the large town to the east of Petra, which is filled with modern hotels and tourist facilities. It is named for the wadi or Moses' River/Stream which issues from the 'Ain Musa.

Wadi Sabra and Sabra: A commercial Nabataean suburb south of Petra. In Nabataean times it must have been a sizeable town with a small theater, and its barracks it may have housed an army unit posted there to protect Petra. The site has many copper mining and smelting furnaces so it may have been an industrial suburb, and the barracks may have served to house those involved with mining and processing metals.

Wadi al-Khararib: The stream that runs northwest from the Petra Museum along which the traveler walks to reach the Lion Triclinium and Ed Deir.

Wadi as-Siyyagh: From the base of El Habis, this wadi flows to the west out of Petra where there are lush verdant springs including one of the main springs of Petra. Along the side of the wadi (stream), sacred niches are carved into the rock face. Inside a rock-cut chamber here is a painted room with columned architectural panels.

ILLUSTRATION CREDITS

PHOTOGRAPH CREDITS

All photographs are the work of Artemis W. Joukowsky unless otherwise noted.

Other credits are to Emily Catherine Egan: Figure 4.4; Sara Karz Reid: Figure 2.16.

J. Wilson Myers and Eleanor Emlen Myers: Figures 1.3, 1.6. 1.12; Christopher A. Tuttle: Figures 2.25, 3.12, 6.4, 6.6, 6.8–6.9, 6.28–6.31, 6.45–6.47, and 6.89.

PLAN CREDITS

Overall credits for Great Temple Plans: Figure 1.1. Map of the Petra city center, Courtesy of Chrysanthos Kanellopoulos and Talal S. Akasheh. Figure 1.2. Reconstruction of the Petra City Center 1999, © Chrysanthos Kanellopoulos. Marshall C. Agnew, Figures 1.7, 1.8, 1.11, 2.1, 3.20, 5.24. Marshall C. Agnew and Eleanor A. Power, Figures 4.29, 4.95. Paul C. Zimmerman, Brian A. Brown, Christian F. Cloke, Marshall C. Agnew, and Eleanor A. Power, Figures 1.9, 3.1, 4.1, 4.14, 4.24, 5.1, 5.10, 5.15, 5.21; Emma S. Libonati, Figure 4.85.

DRAWING AND DRAFTING CREDITS

Ueli Bellwald: Figures 1.28, 4.84; Brian A. Brown: Figure 2.46; Christian F. Cloke: Figures 5.51, 7.31c, 7.37, 7.48; Emily Catherine Egan: Map Chapter 1 Front, Figures 2.20, 2,46, 4.9, 5.12, 5.37, 5.50, 5.51, 7.13–7.14, 7.19a–7.19c, 7.20a–7.20c, 7.27b, 7.30, 7.31a–7.31e, 7.33a–7.33e, 7.36, 7.37, 7.38–7.39, 7.48; Catherine Escher: Figure 4.37; John Philip Hagen: Figures 2.44, 3.9, 3.31, 5.57, 7.19a–7.19c, 7.20a–7.20c, 7.28, 7.32, 7.33a; Amanda Henry: Figure 7.30; Jane Silviera Joukowsky: Figure 7.36; Artemis W. Joukowsky: Figures 2.35, 4.21, 4.91, 5.35, 5.46, 5.54, 5.56, 5.59; Martha Sharp Joukowsky: Figures 2.21, 2.35, 4.21, 4.37, 4.85, 4.91, 4.92, 5.12, 5.35, 5.46, 5.54, 5.56, 5.59, 7.40–7.41; Shari S. Saunders: Figures 7.40–7.41; Simon M. Sullivan: Figures 7.29a–7.29b; Susan B. Tillack: Figure 5.5; Qeis Twessi: Figures 7.3, 7.38–7.39; Christopher A. Tuttle: Figure 4.92; and Eileen L. Vote: Figures 1.21, 5.52, 7.17–7.18, 7.49.

INDEX

A

Abbasid Dynasty 406
Ad-Dayr 427
aditus maximus parados(oi) 228, 229
Aelius Gallus 31
Agnew, Marshall C. *12*
'Ain Brak 212n
'Ain Musa 212n, 427
Al-Budul xliii, 427
Alexandrian style 363
Al-Katute ridge xlvn, *5*, 12
Al-Khazna xlvn, 26, 372, *373*, 383, 427
Allat 376, 383
Altar 70, 122, 354
   horned 81, *82*, 354, 383, *385*
   incense 384, *385*
Altes Museum, Berlin 212n
Al-'Uzza (Aphrodite, Isis, Athena) 349, 376, 383
American Center of Oriental Research xxvii,
   xli–xlii, 4, 6, 283, 284, 377
American Express Award 285
Ammianus 31, 79
Anastylosis 297, 328, 334
Animal figures 396
Anta, East Porch 231
Anta, West *219, 220, 223,* 231, 246
Anteroom 146, 157, 190, 205, 210
Antony, Mark 376
Aphrodite 409n *See also* al-'Uzza
Apodyterium 205, 206
Aqaba 403
Arabia 79, 81, 209
Arabia Felix 31, 381
Aramaic 349
ARCAVE (or ARCHAVE) xl, 19, 250
Arch 110, 172, 289, *318, 319, 330–331,* 332, 405
   See also Central Arch
Arch springers 110, 171, 297, 334
Architectural fragments 70, 83, 101, 116, 194,
   253, 264, 270, *289,* 291, 341n
Aretas I and II 19, 412
Aretas IV (Haretat) 27, 348, 356, 377, 412–413
Arrowheads *119*
Ashlars 70, 78, 93, 101, 150, 170, 231, 289, 332
   arch 289, 326
   dressed 110, 145, 198, 249, 253, 266, 357
   limestone 95, 270, 294
   sandstone 58, 60, 81, 111, 142, 144, 166, 194,
      225, 227, 238, 292
   stone 121
Asian elephant-headed capital *95*
Atargatis 383
Athena 74

Athenodorus 351
Attic base(s) 96, 221, 231, *235,* 267, 289, 326, 402
Augé, Christian 348
Automated Pottery Reconstruction xl

B

Bab as-Siq 405
Babatha Archives 351, 353
Bachmann, W. 26
Baghdad 406
Ballista attack 67
Ballista balls 31, *32, 62–63,* 70, 72, 75, *79,*
   116, 400
Baroque Room xxxiii, 146, 157, *185–186, 187,*
   188–189, 190, 192, 194, 244, 288, 296, 361
   Anteroom 24, 30
   Complex 12, 14, 24, 26, 30, 137, 145, 147,
      153, 211, 383
   Settling Tank 24
   Shrine Room 24, 30, 145, 157, 363, 383
Barrett, Deirdre G. 205, 392, 406
Basile, Joseph J. 110, 270, 376
Basin
   limestone *155,* 201
   plastered 174
   rockcut 172, 176, 200
Bathroom (toilet) 154, *156, 202,* 205
Baths 27, 35, 209–210, *211 See also* Roman-
   Byzantine Bath Complex
Baths-Palatial Complex 65, 85, 93, 126, 129,
   131, 345, 401
Battle of the Yarmuk River 406
Beam holes *254, 255*
Bedal, Leigh-Ann 26, 353
Bedouin xxix, xliii, 35, 101, 122, 286, 295, 296,
   340, 405, 406
Beidha 192, 366
Bellwald, Ulrich 212n, 284
Bench(es)(offering) 83, 110, 111, 116, 297,
   354, 386
Betyl(s) 63, 64, 67, 83, 93, 126, 146, 185, *291,*
   297, 354, 383, 384
   portable 253, *255*
Biblical scriptures 354
Bikai, Patricia M. xxviii, 366, 405
Bikai, Pierre M. xxviii, xxix
Bisheh, Ghazi 283
Blackburn, Jean *122*
Blue Chapel xxvii, 407
Bodel, J. 34
Bones 24, 176, *177,* 192, 398
Boss(es) 161, 240, *371*
Bostra, Syria 209, 403

Bouleuterion 351, 353, 354, 355, 361
Bowersock, G.W. 353, 377
Bronze 96, 170, 348, 377
Brown University xxviii, xxxiii, xxxiv, xl, 3,
   18, 21, 36, 211, 297, 341n, 352, 377
   Petra Excavation Fund 285
   team *xxxiv–xxxviii, 303*
Brunnow, R.E. 3
Burial 174, 176
Byzantine period 19, 103, 158, 190, 230,
   231, 406
Byzantines 100, 260

C

CADD (computer-aided design and drafting)
   4, 5
Caldarium 200, 202, *203, 204,* 205, 209
Canalization system 12, 23, 96, 101, 103, 118,
   129, 157, 170, 245
   aboveground 158, 179, 185
   subterranean 126, 157, 166, *167, 168,* 228,
      236, 238, 250, 263–264, *271–272*
   Upper Temenos *143,* 191, 194, 199, 271,
      273, 320
Capital fragments 161, 168, 240 *See also*
   architectural fragments
Capital, Nabataean 170
Capstones 263, 270, 273
Carving 240
Casemate wall 142, 171, 172, 194, 357
CAVE (Cave Automatic Virtual Environment)
   xxxix, *xl,* 19
Cavea 227, 261, 263, 270, 271, *274*
Cave of the Letters 351
Caves xxxii, 150, 157, 193, 194
Caves 1 and 2 153, *195, 197–198,* 199

Cella/naos 361
Cement, hydraulic 171, 185, 199, 263, 293
Center for Old World Archaeology and Art
   (Brown University) xxxiv
Central Arch 17, 27, 217, 229, 249, 261,
   263–264, *265,* 267, 271, 334–335, 337,
   361, 407
Central Staircase 31, 72, *141,* 161, 166, *168, 169,*
   217, *226–227,* 273, 298, 306, 320, 321–322
Central Water Passage System 320
Ceramic pipe 158, 178, 320
Ceramic roof tiles 95
Ceramics 24, 157, 172, 176, 193, 200, 238, 386
   Nabataean 194, 238, 275, 349
Chamber 3 vault 297
Channel, limestone 129, 178

Channel, sandstone 100
Channels, subterranean 98, 169, 176, 292
Channels, water 185, 199
Christ 354
Christianity 405, 406–407
Cistern-Reservoir 14, 15, 31, 33, 145, 154, 157, 158, 195, 199–200, 205
Clay pipes 171
Cleopatra 376
Cloke, Christian F. 126, 144, *182*
Coins 126, 170, 188, 190, 200, 208, 264, 341n, *348,* 349, 406–407
   Hellenistic 366
Colonnaded Corridor 205, 206, 209
Colonnaded Street 400, 401, 405
Column drums 72, 78, 95, 101, 110, 120, 161, 231, 289, 304, 326, 356
Committee for the Preservation of Monuments of the German-Turkish Army 3
COMPASS 6
Conduit, tunneled 205
Conduit, water 203–204
Conservation 340
Conservation and Restoration Center (CARCIP) 294
Consolidation Ch. 6, esp. 286, 297, 305, 335
Control Points 5
Corinthian-Nabataean style capital 220, 229, 372
Cornell University 241
Cornice fragments 161 *See also* Architectural fragments
Corridor, East, West and South *219,* 221
   East *224, 222,* 225, 231, 238, *239,* 240, *241–243,* 245, 254, 266, 267, 298, 359, 360
   South 158, 182, 230, *246, 247, 249,* 250, *252–253,* 293, 294, 335
   West 30, 33, 240, *241,* 244–245, *246, 247, 260,* 288, 296, 326–327, *328–331,* 334, 401
Cryptoporticus(i) 33, 67, 96, 98
   East 21, 31, 100, 101, 103, 341n
   West 12, 20, 22, 62, 93, 96, 100, 111, 118, 120, 154, 288, 298, 304, 305, 381, 386, 396
Cult objects 383
Curb *58,* 96
Cyma reversa molding 106, 110

D

Dacians 31, 34
Databases 19
Demeter 376
Dendrochronology 20
Department of Antiquities (Jordanian) 6, 34, 283, 285
Diazoma 228
Dio, Cassius 31, 400
Distyle in antis temple 15, 20, 23, 24, 26, 98, 161, 217, 220–222, *223,* 228, 231, 238, 273, 275, 326, 360
Djinn blocks *347, 429*
Domaszewski, A. 3
Domestic architecture *See* Residential Quarter
Drain(s) 96, 98, 103
Drain cover 96, *99*
Drainage systems 158
Dushara 145, 277, 349, 354, 429

E

Earthquake(s) 20, 35, 245, 267, 275, 402
   312 BCE 47n
   113–114 CE 402
   363 CE xxvii, 34, 35, 58, 67, 70, 100, 120, 158, 182, 190, 191, 209, 230, 255, 264
   512 CE 101, 131
   551 CE 35, 158, 210, 406
East Boundary/East Stylobate Wall 118
East "Cistern" 21, 27, *169,* 170
East Colonnade 103, 303, 406
East Corridor 30, 225, 231, 238, 240, 244, 254, 266, 267, 298, 359, 360
East Exedra 30, 100, 110, *112–113, 114–115,* 121, 131, 169, 304
East Interior Staircase 30, 230, 238, 264, 332
East Perimeter Wall 14, 15, 24, 27, 31, 33, 100, 142, 170, 172, *173,* 178, 179, 210, *319, 386*
East Plaza 14, 35, 142, 143, 157, 171, 178, 179, 182, 186, 210, 254
   See also Upper Temenos
East Porch 35, 36, 231
East Propylaeum rooms 401
East Rear Staircase 141, 161, 266, 267
East Reservoir 171
East Staircase *161,* 169, 225, 304, 335
East Triple Colonnade 21, 35, *94,* 100, 103, 105, 110, 123, 126, 131, 303
East Vault(ed Chamber) 33, 171, 172, 225, *261, 262, 263,* 264, 267, 271
East Walkway 33, 35, 178, 217, *223,* 229, 250, *253–254,* 255, *256,* 360
East-West Retaining Wall 168, 306
East-West Support wall 24, 150, 157, 192, 194, 259
Ed-Deir 193
Egan, Emily Catherine 19, 188, 250, 341n
Electronic distance measurement (EDM) 4
Elephant head fragments 70, 111, 126, 161, 231, 298, 407
Elephant-headed capital(s) xxvii –xxviii, xxxi, xxxii, 72, 81, 83, 95, 96, 106, 110, 116, 120, 121, 123, 131,286, 288–289, 291, 296, 297, *300, 303, 366–369*
Entablature 110
Entasis 79, 95
Epigraphic records 377–381
Escher, Anne-Catherine 212n
Excavation xxviii, *10,* 70–83, 288
   chronological chart *37–46*
   history of at Petra xlv–xlvin, ch. 1, 284–286
   map *11, 12*
   Upper Temenos 141–162, 164, 168–179, 182, 185–186, 188
   See also stratigraphy
Ez Zantur 20, 199, 293, 341n, 347, 400, 409n

F

Faience 192, 208
Farajat, Suleiman 283, 206
Fieldstone 275, 317
Fiema, Z. 352, 401
Figurines 393, *394–396*
Fischer, Helge H. 294
Flagstone 126, 178, 220, *224,* 245, 289, 298
Flood channels 286
Flooding 293
Florentinus, Sextius 405

F (continued — Forecourt column)
Forecourt 168, 217, 250, 320, *321–322*
ForeSight 6
Fortuna 288, 375
Frederiksen, Rune 275, 341n
Frescos 259, 327, 332, 359, *360, 361*
   painted 95, 146
Fuste, Jose I. 212n

G

Gagos, Traianos 209
Garden Pool Complex/*Paradesios* xxviii, 101, 170, 345, 352, 353, 400, 402
   See also Pool Complex
German Technical Assistance (GTZ) 294
Glass 170, 192, *398,* 403
   Roman head vase 205
Global Information System (GIS) xxix, xl, 3, 19, 416
Global positioning system (GPS) xxix, 4, 5
Grain mill 198, *199*
Great Cistern 12, 21, 142, 144, 157, 174, 176, 179, 182, 210, 288, 386, 398
Great Temple xxvii, xxxiii, 3–4, 18, 31, 35, 81
   aerial photo *6, 8, 14, 16–17, 18, 216*
   dimensions 217–219
   Forecourt 33, 141
   Grand Design 26, 67, 98, 120, 131, 190, 191, 199, 209, 217, 222, 264, 320
   Precinct 355–365
   Site grid *10*
   Site plan *9*
   Topographic map *11*
Great Wall *292, 293,* 317
Greek influence 361
   See also Hellenistic influence
Grinders 291
Grosso Modo database 19
Ground penetrating radar (GPR) 12, 126, 341n

H

Hadrian 376, 405
Hadriane Petra 377, 405
Hammond, P. 357
Hague Convention 283
Halpala 377
Hashemite University xlii, 4, 6
Hasmonaeans 401
Hearth 174
Hellenistic influence 355
   ceramics 23
   motifs 371
   presence 231, 270
   style *201*
Hellenistic-Roman urban tradition 210, 211
Herod 400
Herodian Baths 210
Herodians 401
Hexagonal flagstones (pavers) 24, 72, 96, 101, 146, 157, 166, 185, 190, 217, 250, 317
Hexagonal Pavement (Lower Temenos) 30, 33, 67, 89, 96, 98, 100, 103, 120, 121, 123–125, 131, 141, 142, 250, 317, 384
Hibiscus flowers 289, *370*
Horned altar *See* Altar
Al-Humayma 212n
Hydraulic systems xxxi
Hypocaust chamber 202

I

Imperial Cult Building xxxi, xxxiii, 345, 347
Infant feeder/lamp filler 200, *201*
Infant jar burial 174
Inscriptions 34, 110, 111, 209, 341, 377, *379, 380*
    Greek 170, 208, 213n, 230, 377
    Nabataean 170, 241, 259–260, *348, 357, 377, 378*
    Roman (Latin) *209,* 351, 377, *380*
    Trajanic 262, *263*
Institute of Archaeology and the Ancient World (Brown University) xxxiv
Intercolumnar walls 27
International Committee on Archaeological Heritage Management 283
International Council on Monuments and Sites 283
Ionic style 96, 356, 366
Iron 60, *61, 119,* 170
Islamic period 158, 406

J–K

Jabal al-Khubtha 386
Jerash 270
Jericho 210
Jerusalem 354, 372
Jones, R. N. 377
Jordan (Hashemite Kingdom of Jordan) xxviii, 283, 202, 406
Jordanian Department of Antiquities xxix, xxxviii, xli, xlii, 296, 341n
Joukowsky, Artemis (Artie) W. xxvii, 432
Joukowsky, Martha Sharp xxvii, xxviii, *xliii*
Joukowsky Family Foundation xl, 285
Judea 400
Juniper 20, *241, 293*
Kanellopoulos, C. 345, 400
Kiln 158, 213n
Kitchen 174
Al-Kraysheh, Fawwaz 283

L

Laconicum 205, 325
Lamps 194, 208, 240, *392*
Lapidaries 289, 291, 294, 241n
Lead pipe (line) 31, 96, 100, 110, *115,* 129, 147, 191, 264
Lime manufacture 101
Limekiln 103, 111, 120
Limestone 281
    basin *155*
    capitals 96
    pavement 70, 110, 141, 182, 185, 199, 220, 245, 253, 256
Lion sculpture 249–250, *251 See also* 428
"Lower Market" 26
Lower Temenos xxix, xxx, 3, 12, 20, 24, 26, 30, 31, 33, 34, 35, 58, 64, 72, 83, *88,* ch.3, 291, 303, 371, 375, 383, 399
    aerial view *88*
    chart of trenches *102, 104, 106*
    Colonnades 83
    cryptoporticus (i) 33, 62, 63, 64, 74, 83, 384
    dimensions 89–91
    plan *89*
    Retaining Wall 21, 31, 98, 131, 140, 157, 161, 162, 306
    Triple Colonnade(s) 285, 366
Luther I. Replogle Foundation xli

M

Maioumas 26
Malcolm and Carolyn Wiener Laboratory for Aegean and Near Eastern Dendrochronology 20, 241
Malichus I 26, 27
Malichus II 208
Marble 27, 141, 143, 154, 170, 205, 208, 263, *380*
Marcus Aurelius Antoninus (Elagabalus) 34
Mask(s) 106, 256, 350
Masons' marks 166, 241, 259, *357, 359*
Masons' tools *294*
Medain Saleh 363
Medallion 146, 188, *189*
Medusa 74
Metal artifacts 116, *397 See also* ballista, bronze, iron, lead
Middle Pier Wall 118
Mierse, William 399
Millstones 291
Mortar, Nabataean 222
Museum of Applied Science (U. of Penn.) 3, 5
Myers, Eleanor E. xxvii, xxix, 4
Myers, J. Wilson xxvii, xxix, 4

N

Nabataean(s) 3, 19, 21, 23, 26, 27, 31, 79, 131, 190
    aesthetic 350, 383, 399
    bowl 83, *346, 347*
    capitals xxxi
    culture xxvii, 347
    history 421–423
    painted wares 70, *388, 389*
    period xxx, 20, 116, 270, 347
    pottery wares *390, 391*
    religion 349, 351 *See also* Cult objects, *betyl, nefesh*
    rulers 19 (chronology), 26, 348, 349, 351, 352, 361, 363
    sculpture 254, 347, 372
    small finds 192
    stairs 298
    stonemasons 126, 281
    style 270, 347
    technology 281, 288
    temples/architects 3, 21, 24, 67, 93, 131, 247, 275, 354
Nabataean-Roman period 30, 351
Nabataean-Roman transition 27
    See also Roman annexation
Nails 410n
Nalle, P. 168
Natatio 208
National Park Service (U.S.) 4
Nazzal 35
Nefesh (or *Nephesh*) 91, 126, 128, *129,* 133n, *291,*354, 383, 384
Negev 405
Nehmé, Laïla 383, 384, 386
Netzer, Ehud 353, 354, 384
Neutron Activation INAA analysis 19
Niche 110, 121, 142, 150, 172, 174, *184,*185, 197, 203, 297, 325, 334, 383, 384, 401
North Cave 194

O

Obodas I 421
Obodas II 26, 421
Obodas III 356, 421
Octavian 400
Odeum (odeion) 351, 361, 400
O'Hea, Margaret 398
Open Context xxxi, xxxviii, xxxix, 21, 36
Opium 409n
Orchestra 271
Ornamental Pool 205
Ostracon *379*
Oven 142, 174, 176

P–Q

Palaestra 157
Palma, A. Cornelius 31, 67, 79, 81, 229, 400
Palmyra 405
Parados See Aditus maximus
Paradeisos See Garden Pool Complex/*Paradesios*
Parr, Peter J. 275, 393
Patrich, J. 356, 383, 384, 402
Pavements, flagstone 126
Perimeter Wall, East 144
Perimeter Wall, South 144, 157, 179, 182, 192
Perry, Megan A. 176, 212n
Petra, chronology of 407
Petra Church xxvii, xxix, 405, 407
Petra, city of 350
Petra Excavation Fund 285
Petra Mapping Project (PMP) 6
Petra Museum xxxviii, xxxix, 212n, 291, 296, 297
Petra National Park 283, 292, 296
Petra Park xxvii
Petra Pool Complex 26, 345
"Petra Rediscovered: Lost City of the Nabataeans" xxxiii
Phases *See* Site phase overview, and by number
Pilaster block 288
Pilaster reliefs xxxi, 74, 106, 375–376
Pilgrim bottle (Nabataean) 172, *173, 387,*
Pinecone *371*
Pipe, ceramic 194
Pipes 169, 325 *See also* Lead pipe
Planning 131
Plaster 24, 95, 103, 110, 129, 142, 144, 146, 169, 185, 186, 188, 230, 240, 277, 325, 326, 332, 377
    bonding 247
    hydraulic 147, 179
    painted 95, 220, 222, 244, 245, 256, *358*
Plaster-enclosed pipe 194
Podium 110
Pompeian wall painting 188
Pompeii premise 407
Pompey 31, 400
Pompey's Portico Garden 353
Pool Complex 26, *27, 33,* 353 *See also* Garden Pool Complex/*Paradesios*
Poppy 289, *370,* 372, 376
Porch 162, 326, 360, 401 *See also* Pronaos
Porch Column 286
Porch stylobate 15, 162, 166
Porter, Barbara A. 284
Portico-Pronaos 360
Portico wall 15, 31, 58–59, 297
Postholes 150, 176, 190, *253*

Pottery 20, 21, 93, 98, 116, 121, 126, 157, 199, 264, 402
  Nabataean 110, 168, 174, 188, 192, 250, 402–403
  Roman 168, 250, 264
Power, Eleanor A. 213
Praefurnium 200, 202, *203*
Precinct 8
Pre-Site Phase I 22, 23, 67, 96, 116, 120, 157, 194, 264, 273
Pronaos (porch) 12, 21, 23, 26, 166, 217, 220, 230, 236, 238, 239, 271, 275, 361
Propylaeum xxix, xxx, xxxii, 3, 12, 14, 15, 20, 22, 26, 30, 33, 34, 35, *52*, 53–85, 154, 291, 375
  aerial view *52*, *56–57*
  Central Staircase 53, 58, *59*, 62, 64, 70, 72, 75, 78, 83, 98, 100, 122, 126, 297, 298, 401
  colonnade 21
  dimensions 53, 55
  East 21, 64, 72, 74, 126, 297
  East-west Portico Wall 24, 53, 58, 62, 67, 70, 75, 85
  plan *54*
  Retaining Wall 24, 33, 53, 59, 62, 67, 72, 75, 78, 83, 298
  Rooms 1–11 153
  Rooms 1–3 31, 58, 59–60, *61*, 62, 63, 67, 70, 74, 78, 288, 297
  Room 2 (East Propylaeum) 67, 75
  Room 3 *62*, *298*, *299*
  Rooms 4 and 5 62, 199
  Rooms 7 and 8 198
  Room 8 197
  small finds 62
  Trench 20
  West 27, 63, 75, 81, 116, 297, 383, 384
  West Entry Stairway 64, 65
  West Stairs 83
Provincia Arabia 356, 381
Ptolemies 402
Pulpitum 230, 273
Qasr al-Bint xxx, 34, 53, 199, 347, 351, 353, 363, 377, 429
Queen "Malicum" 377
Quarry cuts *150*
Quarrying 157, 192, 429

R
Rabbel I 19, 423
Rabbel II 27, 348, 353, 400, 423
Radiocarbon dating 20
Rast, Walter, chronology 47n
Reid, Sara Karz 18, 34
Reliefs 70, 74, 110, 188, 201
Religion 350, 351, 352, 353, 361, 398
Replogle Foundation *See* Luther I. Replogle Foundation
Reservoir 142
Residential Quarter *See* Upper Temenos
Restoration 283–284, 288, *338*, *339*
Rhodian rose *379*
Rhodian style 23, 231
Ridge Church xxvii, 405, 407
Robbed out 100, 101, 122, 158, 185, 190, 230, 231, 262, 284, 320, 335
Roman annexation (acquisition) xxx–xxxi, 19, 20, 30, 34, 67, 74, 79, 81, 96, 110, 211, 353, 356, 381, 399, 400–402
Roman architecture 399

Roman Imperial Cult (Building) 12, 34, 345, 402
Roman influence 355, 375, 401–402
Roman period 101, 103, 120, 210, 352
Roman remodeling 170
Roman Senate 355
Roman Street/Road 3, 12, 31, 53, 58, 59, 62, 85, 89, 93, 103, 131, 205, 298, 306, 345, 347, 356, 366, 429
Roman-Byzantine period xxx, xxxiii, 194
  aerial photograph *155*
  Bath Complex 12, 15, 101, 121, 154, 158, 199, 200, 210n, 401, 402
Roman-Byzantine Baths xxix, xxxi, xxxiii, 157, 158, 191, 195, 210, 306, 320, 345, 377
Roman-Byzantine Baths (Upper Temenos) 14, 31, 34, 35, 85, 91, 128, 145
Roof *299*
Roof tiles 103
Rooms A and B *See* Upper Temenos
Rooms 1–11 *See* Propylaeum
Royal Jordanian Air Force xli

S
Samuel H. Kress Foundation 284
Sandstone 281, *374*, *380*
  pavers 174
  stele 208, *209*
Schluntz, Erika L. 352, 353
Schmid, Stephan G. xi, 83, 352, 386
Scribes 354
Sculpture 72–*73*, *106*, 110, 201, 249–250, 256, 347, 366–376,
"Sculpture garden" 291
Second Style Pompeian wall painting 359
Seigne, Jacques 353
Seleucids 402
Serenus, Marcus Aelius Aurelius Theon 209
Settling Tank 147, 153, 185, 190, 200, 205, 210
Severus Alexander 34, 405
Severus, Claudius 405
S.H.A.P.E. (Shape, Archaeology, Photogrammetry, Entropy) xxxix
Shaer, May 284, 296, 341n
Shaqilat, Queen 348
Shrine Room *See* Baroque Room, Upper Temenos
Siculus, Diodorus 19
Sidewalk and curbing 14, 15, 70, 96, 298
Simon, Stefan 341n
Site grid 10
Site phase chart *22*
Site phase overview 20–24, 26–27, 30–31, 33–36, 67, 98
Site Phase I 126, 157, 209, 228, 275
Site Phase II 120, 129, 157, 185, 217, 228, 275, 353, 356, 361
Site Phase III 229, 263, 353
Site Phase IV 28–29, 72, 75, 78, 116, 122, 129, 131, 141, 157, 185, 190, 194, 209, 217, 229, 260, 320, 353, 356, 361
Site Phase V 28–29, 157, 190, 194, 217, 223, 229, 260, 264, 267, 270, 353, 355, 361, 363
Site Phase VI 121, 157, 158, 209, 229, 400
Site Phase VII 78, 100, 120, 174, 190–191, 230, 264, 270, 401
Site Phase VIII 100, 158, 191, 230
Site Phase IX 34, 75, 100, 158, 194–195, 199, 230, 264
Site Phase X 34–35, 100, 158, 191, 195, 209, 230

Site Phase XI 158, 191, 231
Site Phase XII 101, 131
Site Phase XIII 101, 131, 158
Site Phase XIV 158, 407
Site plan 2007 *11*
Slag deposits 101
Small finds 110, 121, 240, 262
Small Temple xxviii, 12, 18, 341n, 345, 402
  aerial view *34*
Small Upper Cave 153, 199
Sondages 12, 21, 67, 75, 96, 118, 332
South colonnade 356
South Corridor *See* Corridor
South Passageway 145, 146, 157, 182, 185, 190, 210, 259, 361, 386
Southwest Settling Tank 190
Special Finds 194
Special Projects 1, 2 and 3 256
Special Project 4 126, 161
Special Project 5 12, 70, 75, 79
Special Projects 22, 24, and 29 103
Special Project 25 103
Special Projects 26 and 31 121
Special Project 30 250
Special Project 38 101
Special Project 39 105
Special Projects 40, 42, and 43 266
Special Project 54 106
Special Project 72 247
Special Project 73 105
Special Project 84 174
Special Project 89 190
Special Project 92 126
Special Project 96 192, 194
Special Project 104 116, 118, 120, 298
Special Project 105 118, 120
Special Project 107 236, 238
Special Project 108 150, 191, 192–193, 194
Special Project 109 259
Special Project 110 191, 199, *200*, 213n
Special Project 111 198
Special Project 120 271
Special Project 121 185
Special Project 123 185
Special Project 124 126, 141, 161
Special Project 200 270–271, 332
"Splash Pool" 205
Stele 208, *209*
Stonemasons 295, 347, 349, 371
Strabo 349, 351, 383
Stratigraphy xxix, 20, 21, 36, 67, 96, 98, 100, 110, 116, 118, 157, 158, 172, 178, 186, 190, 198, 228–231, 255, 273, 334, 363
Stucco 140, 174, 186, 188, 194, 236, 238, 247, 266, *296*, 363, 372
  painted 169–170, 186, 249
Stucky, R. A. 383
Stylobate(s) 101, 103, 105, 166, 236, 326, 360
Surveys 6, 8
Sword Deity *144*, 145, 157, 210
Syria 31, 79
Syro-Palestinian architectural influence 355

T
Tabun Cave Room 142, 157, 172, 174, 176
Taylor, Jane 352
Tell Brak 366
Temenos (temene) 377
  Gate 3, 34, 53, 70, 345, 347, 351, 366, 430
  West Baths 67
  See also Lower Temenos, Upper Temenos

Temple xxx
  Forecourt 21, 24, 142, 162
  Pronaos 22
Temple of the Winged Lions 34, 353–354, 357, 363, 377, 400, 430
Temples 354, 363
Tent habitation 116
Terracing 118, 119, 129, 293
Terracotta figurines 393–396
Terracotta tiling 70
Terra Sigillata (TSA) 49n
Tetrastyle in antis 15, 20, 26, 157, 161, 217, 222, 231, 236, 275, 317, 356, 360
Theater/Theatron 27, 28–29, 35, 223, 225, 227–228, 229, 245, 260–261, 267, 270–271, 272, 275, 277, 332, 333, 350, 351, 352, 353, 355, 360–361, 363, 377
  Roman (Pompey's) 399
  Stairs 338, 339
  See also cavea, pulpitum
Tiberius 377
Tiles 79, 157
Toilet *See* Bathroom
Tomb of the Eleven Graces 294
Tombs 347
Topcon 5
Tracy, Stephen V. 351, 377
Trade and trade goods ix, 349, 350, 405
Trajan (Emperor) 31, 34, 381, 400, 403
Trench chart 13, 38–48, 71, 102, 104, 106, 159–150
Trench plan 72, 103
Trench 4 161, 162, 166
Trenches 5, 16 and 21 121
Trenches 8, 10 and 11 256
Trench 9 266
Trench 13 126
Trench 14 103, 122, 406
Trench 16 406
Trench 17 103, 105, 222, 285,
Trench 19 18, 32, 46, 161, 168
Trench 20 103
Trench 22 262, 266, 267
Trench 24 231
Trench 25 101
Trenches 26 and 27 263
Trenches 29 and 45 244
Trenches 30 and 33 101
Trenches 34 and 35 266
Trench 36 103
Trench 37 110
Trenches 41 and 53 169
Trench 42 126
Trenches 43 and 49 161
Trench 47 267
Trenches 50 and 51 75
Trench 52 108
Trench 54 171
Trenches 55 and 55A 260
Trenches 56 and 59 244, 245
Trench 58 238
Trench 59 267
Trenches 60 and 61 105
Trench 62 267, 270
Trench 63 256
Trench 64 250
Trench 65 240, 244
Trench 67 79, 171
Trench 68 171

Trench 71 111
Trenches 72, 74, 75 and 77 178
Trench 73 250, 255, 256
Trench 76 191
Trench 77 176
Trench 79 111
Trench 80 83
Trench 82 72
Trench 83 182
Trench 84 172
Trench 85 247
Trench 86 81
Trench 88 87
Trench 89 185
Trench 91 172
Trench 92 267
Trench 93 72
Trench 94 198, 388
Trenches 95 and 96 72, 75
Trench 97 79
Trenches 97 and 98 116
Trench 100 74
Trench 101 191
Trench 104 126
Trenches 105 and 106 200
Trench 120 200, 205
Trench 121 200, 202
Trench 123 273, 274, 276, 334
Trench 125 202, 203
Trench 126 200, 202, 203, 325
Trench 127 200, 202–203
Tullis, Terry 341n
Tuttle, Christopher A. 410n
Tyche 374, 375, 376

U
Umayyads 406
UNESCO Convention 283
Upper Cave 197
"Upper Market" xxvii
Upper Temenos xxx, xxxii, 3, 14, 22, 24, 26, 27, 33, 35, 89, 139, ch.4, 255, 288, 361, 386
  Baroque Room Complex 317
  canalization *See* Canalization
  dimensions 137–140
  East Arch 317
  "East Cistern" 169, 170, 317,
  East Perimeter Wall 174, 317
  East Plaza Great Cistern 317
  Forecourt 317, 321–322
  overview 140
  plan 138
  Residential Quarter xxxii, 14, 15, 24, 26, 27, 30, 33, 139, 145, 152 (plan), 157, 158, 191, 192, 193, 195, 196, 197–199, 210–211, 288, 317, 386
  restoration and conservation 317
  Room A 27, 31, 142, 157, 158, 172, 173, 174
  Room B 33, 142, 174, 175
  Shrine Room 184, 317
  South Passageway 317
  Temple Forecourt 140
Urn Tomb 405
UTM 8

V
Vaulted Chambers (East and West) 33, 35, 74, 227, 229, 230, 260–263, 351
Vaulted cryptoporticus 64, 75

Vaults 118, 173, 202, 298, 304–305, 332, 334, 341n
Vegetal ornament 372, 397
Venice Charter 283
Vestibule-*Frigidarium* 200, 203, 205
Via Nova Traina 403
Vitruvius 352, 356, 357
Volume III, Petra xxix, 110, 126, 144, 188, 213, 250, 275, 341n, 349, 376, 392, 398
Volute(s) 166, 192, 208, 291
Volute lamp 392
Vote, Eileen L. xl
Voussoir 72, 75, 79, 96, 103, 107, 111, 117, 285, 291, 298, 326

W
Wadi Farasa 295, 431
Wadi Musa xliii, 67, 79, 345, 347, 355, 356, 407
Walkways *See* East Walkway, West Walkway
Wall K 31, 58, 62, 67, 70, 72, 74, 75, 78, 81, 83, 85, 378
Water conservation xxviii, 341n
Water system 203, 205, 236, 273
Watzinger, C. 3
Weapons 397 *See also* Arrowheads, Ballista balls
"Well Room" 200, 203, 208, 325
Wenning, Robert 277, 352, 383, 384, 386
West Cistern-Reservoir 325
West Colonnade 33, 100, 303
West Corridor *See* Corridor, West
West Cryptoporticus *See* Cryptoporticus, West
West Entry Stairs (Stairway) 8, 12, 15, 35, 91–93, 98, 126, 128–129, 131, 205, 298, 305, 306
West Interior Chamber 334
West Interior Staircase 262, 266, 291, 332, 334
West Exedra 5, 30, 96, 110, 121, 129, 131, 154, 162, 303, 304, 406
West Plaza 14, 140, 150, 157, 191, 194
West Perimeter Wall 210
West Plaza 317
  Bedrock Installations 194
West Precinct Wall 24, 33, 140, 147, 150, 154, 157, 158, 191, 194, 199, 200, 209, 325
West Propylaeum 31, 89, 291, 386
  South Gallery 21
West Rear Staircase 267
West Staircase 162, 225, 227, 304, 305
West Triple Colonnade 98, 111, 116, 120, 123, 131, 305
West Vaulted Chamber 264, 266, 270
West Walkway 33, 35, 106, 140, 217, 223, 229, 252, 253, 257–260, 360
West Walkway Wall 147, 157, 158, 191, 192, 195, 317
Wiegand, T. 3
Wood 20 *See also* Juniper
World Heritage Convention 283
World Monuments Fund xli, 285
World Monuments Watch 285

Y–Z
Yadin, Yigael 351
Yahweh 354
Yemen 31
Zimmerman, Paul C. 6

PETRA
GREAT TEMPLE
Volume II

was designed and set in Bembo
by Gilbert Design Associates,
Providence, Rhode Island.

It was printed in an edition
of 750 copies
by Reynolds DeWalt
on Hannoart Silk paper
and bound by
Acme Bookbinding.

MAY MMVIII

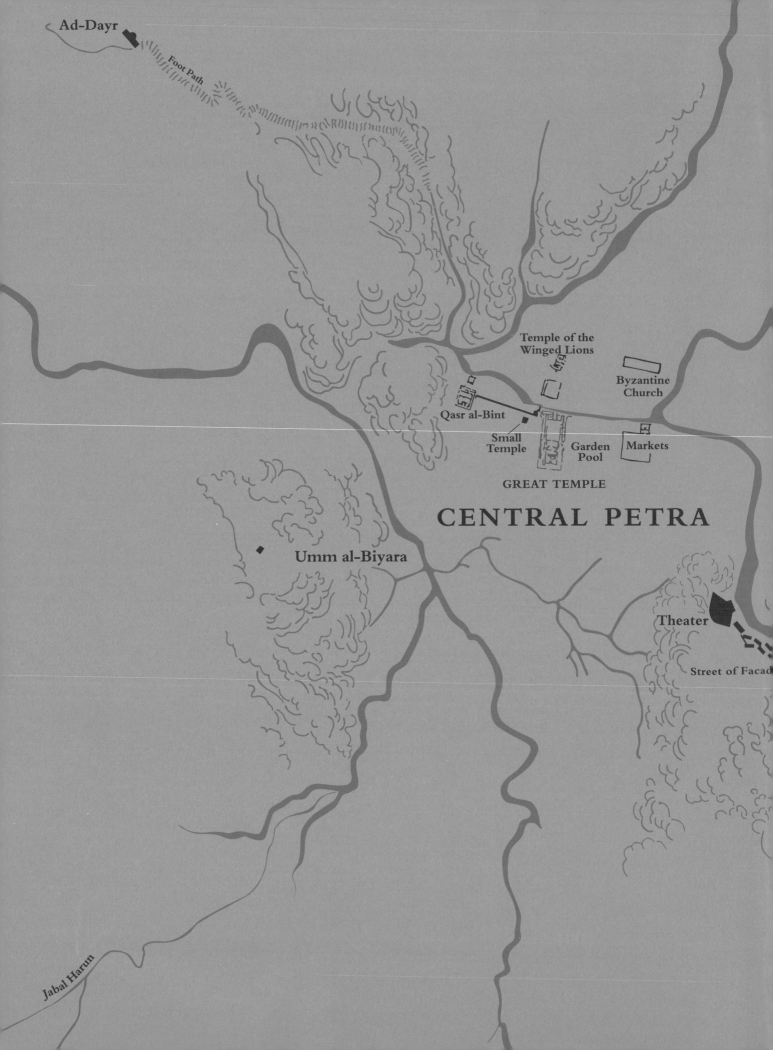

Ad-Dayr

Foot Path

Temple of the
Winged Lions

Byzantine
Church

Qasr al-Bint

Small
Temple

Garden
Pool

Markets

GREAT TEMPLE

CENTRAL PETRA

Umm al-Biyara

Theater

Street of Facad

Jabal Harun